THE TRUTH ABOUT WHERE YOU LIVE

For Reference

Not to be taken from this room

62318

THE TRUTH ABOUT WHERE YOU LIVE

AN ATLAS FOR ACTION ON TOXINS AND MORTALITY

BENJAMIN A. GOLDMAN

TIMES BOOKS

RANDOM HOUSE

Copyright © 1991 by Benjamin A. Goldman

All rights reserved under International and Pan-American Copyright Conventions. Published in the United States by Times Books, a division of Random House, Inc., New York, and simultaneously in Canada by Random House of Canada Limited, Toronto.

Library of Congress Cataloging-in-Publication Data

Goldman, Benjamin A.
  The truth about where you live: an atlas for action on toxins and mortality/by Benjamin A. Goldman.—1st ed.
    p.   cm.
  ISBN 0-8129-1898-3 (pbk.)
  1. Environmental health—United States.   2. Diseases—United States—Statistics.
I. Title.
RA566.3.G65   1991
363.17′91′0973—dc20   90-50676

Design by Robert Bull Design

Manufactured in the United States of America

9 8 7 6 5 4 3 2

First Edition

To my parents and in memory of my grandmother Lucy B. Lemann

ACKNOWLEDGMENTS

This atlas represents the culmination of five years of work at Public Data Access, Inc. (PDA). PDA was founded in 1986 to make government information more easily available to the general public, using the Freedom of Information Act and state-of-the-art computer processing techniques to appraise local environmental and health conditions, and other issues of vital concern. Our goal is to transform such information into usable forms, and to get it into the hands of people who need it the most.

Many people have lent their unique talents to ensuring that PDA has fulfilled its mission over the years. It is impossible to express adequately in these few paragraphs how thankful I am to everyone. First and foremost, Jay M. Gould and Michael Tanzer were the guiding forces in bringing PDA into existence and nurturing its development. Others who have made invaluable contributions to the creation of PDA and this atlas, include: William McDonnell, for holding down the fort throughout the years, Warren Barnett, Mike Chappelle, Reverend Benjamin F. Chavis, Jr., Ellen Davidson, Marty DeKadt, Fae Duchin, Michel Eckerseley, Samuel S. Epstein, Peter Fleischer, Phil Friedman, Mary Goldman, Michael Greenberg, Mary Hawker, Peter Hunt, Carla Jenkins, Si Kahn, Tom Kavet, Alice and John Tepper Marlin, Alison McGuire, Peter Montague, Kenneth Mountcastle, Jr., Robert Pollin, Idrian Resnick, Wilson Riggan, Steve Ross, Carlos Santiago, Phil Stern, Ernest Sternglass, Alexander C. Stewart, Jr., John Tanzer, Ken E. Tanzer, Tamsin Taylor, David Vladek, George Wallerstein, and Sybil Wong.

The atlas's database development work was funded in part by the generous contributions of the Deer Creek Foundation, Environmental Research Foundation, Grassroots Leadership, and a number of individual supporters of Public Data Access, Inc. (PDA) to whom we are extremely grateful. Various aspects of the database were developed as a result of work we did for the Association on American Indian Affairs, Inc., Clean Water Action Project, Commission for Racial Justice of the United Church of Christ, Council on Economic Priorities, Greenpeace USA, National Toxics Campaign, Public Interest Research Group in Michigan, and the Radiation and Public Health Project.

Heroic computer programming and systems development work was performed by PDA's staff and technical consultants, including: J. Jacob Wind, Chinnah Mithrasekaran, Ayse Can, David and Ken J. Tanzer, Richard Stone, Wendy Chiang, and Cornelia Dellenbough. Alvin Pellom of Integrated Laboratory Systems (Research Triangle Park, North Carolina) created the mapping system and produced the maps—and put up with endless tinkering with their design. Tracey Dewart, Karen Levine, Jorge Gonzalez Perez, and Eben Weitzman conducted untold hours of research. We are also indebted to the many people at the EPA and other government agencies who provided us with the gigantic quantities of information needed to produce the maps.

Charles Lee and my father, Dr. Allen S. Goldman, provided invaluable comments on the final draft of the manuscript. The editing of Charlotte Mayerson and Ruth Fecych at Random House and Times Books improved the writing considerably. I am very grateful to Della Smith, Naomi Osnos, and the rest of Times Books' production staff for their tireless efforts to ensure the quality of the final publication. Thanks also to Janice Mandel for her persistence in trying to find a publisher, and especially to Joe Spieler for succeeding.

Special thanks to Lois Geller for her patience and support.

Benjamin A. Goldman
New York, January 1991

CONTENTS

Chapter 1: OVERVIEW   3

Reading the Maps; The Lay of the Land

Chapter 2: AN ATLAS FOR ACTION   10

Untangling the Web; Patterned Clues; Stacking the Odds; Chasing Cures; Information Everywhere; Organizing Prevention

Chapter 3: MORTALITY   31

All Diseases; Heart Diseases; Infant Diseases; Birth Defects; All Cancers; Lung Cancers; Breast Cancers; Child Cancers; Acutely Hazardous Exposures; Young-Adult Infectious Diseases

Chapter 4: INDUSTRIAL TOXINS   169

Industrial Air Emissions; Industrial Water Discharges; Hazardous Wastes; Workplace Toxins

Chapter 5: NONINDUSTRIAL POLLUTION   229

Pesticides; Water Quality; Air Quality

Chapter 6: ENVIRONMENTAL JUSTICE   281

Demographics; Socioeconomics; Education; Health Services

LIST OF MAPS

INDUSTRIAL TOXINS

NONINDUSTRIAL POLLUTION

Water Quality:

Air Quality:

SOCIAL STRUCTURE

Demographics:

Socioeconomics:

Education:

Health Services:

LIST OF FIGURES
AND TABLES

THE TRUTH ABOUT WHERE YOU LIVE

CHAPTER 1

OVERVIEW

Three months after the December 1984 chemical disaster in Bhopal, India, the U.S. Senate held a hearing in Newark, New Jersey, to find out more about our ability to respond to such emergencies in this country. The testimony revealed a shocking lack of public knowledge about toxic hazards in our communities, as illustrated by the following exchange:

Mrs. Mary Keating: I was in the kitchen when I started smelling odors that smelled like bad sauerkraut. It kept on getting worse and worse. It seemed like it was coming from my drainpipes. It was in the basement of my house. It was upstairs in my children's room. I remember running to them thinking my husband had just installed a microwave, maybe something is wrong with the microwave, and I was gathering my children to go next door to my neighbor to see if there was something wrong in my kitchen when I opened the door and the fumes out there were outrageous.

Senator Frank Lautenberg, Democrat from New Jersey (to Mrs. Merty Mae Glamb, another local resident): You had no knowledge, no awareness, no direction in terms of anything you heard about, where to call, where to go, what to do?

Mrs. Glamb: No, none whatsoever. We didn't know how to go about it to even find out what it was. And I think a lot of the residents from the area didn't know how to proceed either.

Senator Lautenberg: You wouldn't know whether it was a backed-up sewer or something really to worry about.

Mrs. Glamb: Right.[1]

Mrs. Keating and Mrs. Glamb live downwind from an American Cyanamid factory in Linden, New Jersey. On Saturday morning, October 6, 1984, a chemical reaction caused a storage tank to overheat and the pesticide malathion leaked into the air. The toxic gases traveled over twenty miles across New Jersey to Staten Island, New York. More than a hundred people were rushed to the hospital. This was the first of fifteen toxic gas leaks from New Jersey chemical plants that winter—just as thousands were dying in Bhopal.

Across the United States, an average of four industrial accidents a day spill toxic chemicals into the environment. Factory mishaps release 370 thousand tons of toxins into the air each year. Industrial plants routinely discharge another 7 million tons of toxic chemicals into the air and water, and dump another 500 million tons of hazardous wastes into the ground—in full compliance with existing government regulations. To complete the picture, add another 4 billion tons of wastes that farms and cities discharge annually into the nation's air, waterways, and land.

If every American household kept a lifetime's share of hazardous wastes in their backyard, each would have a stack of 55-gallon drums 400 feet square, rising four stories high. The reality, of course, is that these wastes are not always so obvious, nor so evenly distributed. On occasion, their presence is immediately apparent, as it was to Mrs. Glamb and Mrs. Keating. But typically families find out years later, when tests reveal contaminated water, or when unusual illnesses appear. The toxins of modern society can be deadly even if invisible.

An average of 4 people a day are killed by acute exposure to hazardous substances in the United States. Birth defects kill 35 babies daily. Cancer kills 1,300 Americans each day. That comes to nearly half a million cancer deaths a year. Scientists remain uncertain as to what percentage of such death is due to environmental contamination, just as Mrs. Glamb and Mrs. Keating may still wonder if those odors will ever harm their families.

The Truth About Where You Live provides a comprehensive picture of communities across the country that are suffering from disproportionate shares of environmental contamination and death. New right-to-know and sunshine laws have made available to the public tremendous quantities of government information, collected at a cost of tens of billions of dollars to taxpayers and businesses. Yet this mass of data is of little value without sophisticated computer programming that transforms the raw numbers into understandable presentations. Using computer mapping techniques, this book synthesizes over a hundred million pieces of data culled from government files. Each map displays over 21,000 numbers (including geographic as well as pollution and mortality data), enabling any reader to see at a glance where people are dying at rates significantly above national norms, and where toxins may pose particular problems for the environment and human health.

Mrs. Glamb and Mrs. Keating could find out that in their home county of Middlesex, New Jersey, women suffer from among the worst white female mortality rates in the country: higher than 75 percent of

U.S. counties for all diseases, higher than 90 percent for lung cancer, and higher than 99 percent for breast cancer. What could be causing these significantly elevated death rates? Do Middlesex women smoke more than women elsewhere? When smoking is combined with exposures to certain toxins, cancer is even more likely to result. Could such synergistic effects be at work here? Could behavioral and socioeconomic factors such as poor diets and inadequate access to medical care be further aggravating death rates in Middlesex County? What role do toxic hazards play?

The maps yield many interesting leads. They show that Middlesex ranks among the nation's top counties for:

- people working in petrochemical plants
- industrial facilities releasing toxins to the air, water, and land
- facilities treating, storing, and disposing of hazardous wastes
- facilities violating air pollution regulations
- tons of hazardous wastes being generated
- tons of suspected cancer-causing chemicals being emitted into the air by industrial and nonindustrial sources

Middlesex County ranks 38th in the nation for its industrial toxic air emissions. On the other hand, its residents enjoy well-above-average socioeconomic conditions—higher home values, household incomes, and numbers of physicians per person—and a below-average percentage of families in poverty. Thus the maps suggest that environmental contamination may be contributing to excess cancer deaths among white females in Middlesex County.

Such suggestive evidence highlights areas of significant concern. Which facilities or nonindustrial sources emit the bulk of Middlesex County's suspected carcinogens? What action can be taken to reduce exposures? Other data that merit follow-up study, such as county smoking rates, are not publicly available. But what about the health impact from the industrial air emissions of suspected carcinogens in over 100 counties that ranked even higher than Middlesex for this measure—counties in Texas and West Virginia, Arizona and Wyoming, Illinois and Michigan, as well as in New Jersey? And why are babies in Issaquena County, Mississippi, dying from birth defects at a rate over three times the national average? The questions raised are innumerable; they reach all parts of the country, east and west, urban and rural, rich and poor. Our hope is that this book will stimulate further research, dissemination of critical data, and public discussion about some of the greatest dangers of our time.

New laws encourage the public to participate in environmental regulation, but we need adequate information to do so. When community leaders try to determine the extent of environmental contamination and potential health effects, they are all too often confronted with inappropriate, inconsistent, and highly technical data. Local efforts to prevent toxic hazards, to minimize health impacts, and to seek compensation are stymied as a result. The scant availability of appropriate data, and the sizable computing resources needed to make it meaningful, impede academic and public policy research as well. The maps and data in this book can be a starting place to overcome such problems, since they provide easily accessible and comprehensive data on toxins and mortality. The information will help readers assess whether their local environmental problem is, in the words of Senator Lautenberg, ''a backed-up sewer or something really to worry about.''

READING THE MAPS

The maps are designed to highlight the top counties for each factor. Counties are shaded from white to black with those among the top 2 percent shaded black. Counties among the lower 75 percent in the country are shaded white. The rest have three shades of gray. The five groups are defined as follows:

Shade	Percentile	Number of Counties in Group	Percent of Counties in Group
Black	98–99	61	Top 2%
Dark gray	95–97	92	3%
Medium gray	90–94	154	5%
Light gray	75–89	461	15%
White	0–74	2,305	Bottom 75%

Counties that are among the top and bottom 2 percent in the country are listed on the page facing each map. There are usually around 60 counties in each list, but this may vary in extreme cases when many counties share a common value, as, for example, when the amount of toxins for hundreds of counties is zero. In these circumstances the facing page reads: ''Note: too many counties to list had zero values for this measure.''

The legend beneath the map gives additional information, which you may or may not choose to use. For those interested in a detailed analysis, the left-hand scale shows the minimum and maximum values for each county group (or shade), which is the information a typical map legend provides. The distribution curve above the left-hand scale shows how often counties share each value. The right-hand scale shows the percentiles that define each county group. A percentile means the percentage of counties with lower data values. If a county's infant mortality rate is in the 99th percentile, for example, that means it is in the top percent (and shaded black); at least 99 percent of the counties have lower rates. The small black triangles indicate the national average (or mean). The small black vertical lines indicate the national median (or 50th percentile). For the mortality measures, counties must also pass a significance test to be shaded black or to be listed on the facing page. (The methods appendix describes the significance tests, as well as more advanced uses of the legend.)

THE LAY OF THE LAND

The atlas is divided into six major sections and two appendices, plus notes and an index of listed counties to help you find all of the maps where any one county is highlighted. The second chapter (following this overview) explains how to use the atlas for investigating the relationships between toxic pollution and public health, and discusses the intellectual and social roots of current efforts to do so. The next four chapters contain the maps. Each chapter and group of maps are introduced with local examples, summary information, and a discussion of the maps' most salient features. Chapter 3 examines mortality from ten causes, indicating where the highest rates and excess deaths occur. Chapters 4 and 5 look at various types of industrial and nonindustrial pollution that may be contributing to local mortality. Chapter 6 explores the issue of environmental justice, which considers how the geographic distributions of toxins, mortality, and social structure are related.

The first appendix provides detailed explanations of the methods and measures used to create the maps. The second appendix lists organizations and publications where you can get more information on how to fight for a clean and healthy community.

To help you get oriented, a map of the continental United States with the names of the major metropolitan areas (Fig. 1-1) and a map of county boundaries (Fig. 1-2) follow. The maps cover only the 48 continental states, due to the lack of data on Alaska and Hawaii for many measures.

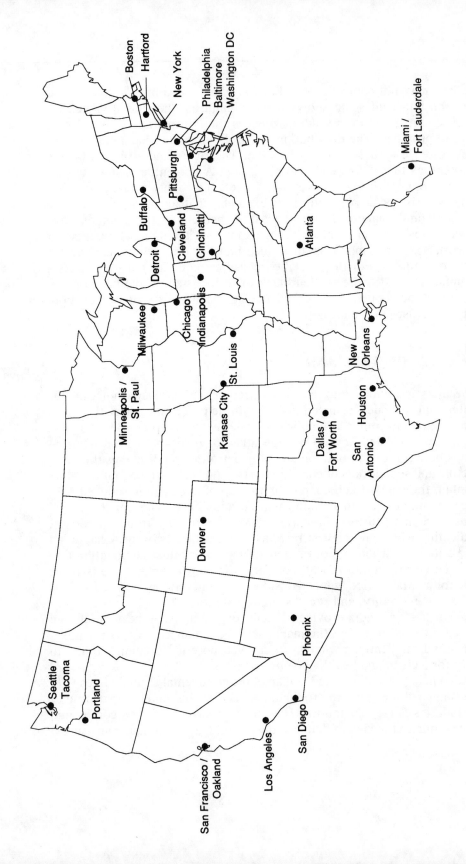

FIGURE 1-1. Major U.S. Metropolitan Areas

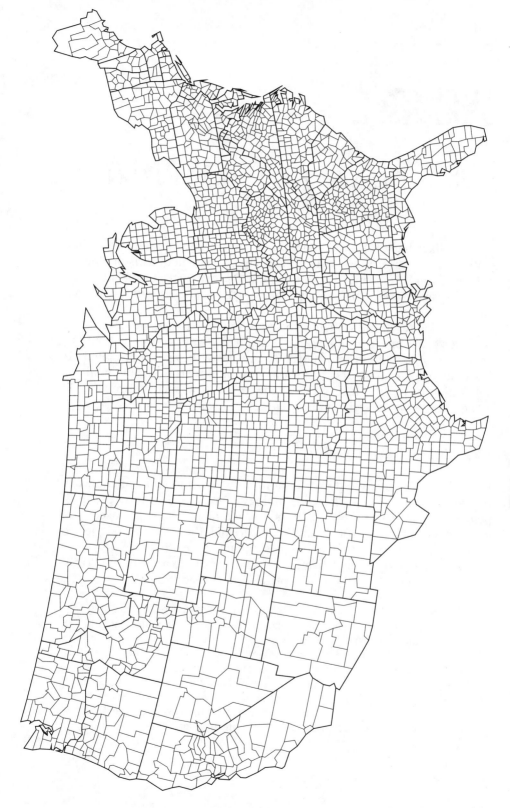

FIGURE 1-2. County Boundaries

CHAPTER 2

AN ATLAS FOR ACTION

Nobody likes high death rates, pollution, or poverty, and few people like statistics. Yet to use this atlas effectively for personal decisions or for public action, it is critical to understand the evidence it presents. The issues it raises are complex, the stakes high, and the politics often vicious.

This chapter discusses what you need to know to use the descriptive statistics that appear in this book. It highlights ways to think about the geography of pollution and mortality and how they are correlated. It examines which kinds of conclusions can be drawn from this material and which cannot. It also gives examples of how such information is being used in the emerging movement for environmental justice.

UNTANGLING THE WEB

Examining the causes and distribution of disease and injury is the work of epidemiologists. Usually epidemiology compares a healthy group of people to a group that either has a disease or has been exposed to a harmful substance. Through such comparisons the investigator tries to measure the impact of such exposures on human health.

Dr. John Snow's investigation of cholera in London during 1854, reported below in his own words, provides a classic example:

> The most terrible outbreak of cholera which ever occurred in this kingdom, is probably that which took place in Broad Street, Golden Square, and the adjoining streets, a few weeks ago. Within two hundred and fifty yards of the spot where Cambridge Street joins Broad Street there were upwards of five hundred fatal attacks of cholera in ten days. The mortality in this limited area probably equals any that was ever caused in this country, even by the plague; and it was much more sudden. . . . In less than six days from the commencement of the outbreak, the most afflicted streets were deserted by more than three-quarters of their inhabitants.

I suspected some contamination of the water of the much-frequented street-pump in Broad Street. . . . On proceeding to the spot, I found that nearly all the deaths had taken place within a short distance of the pump.

I had an interview with the Board of Guardians of St. James's Parish on the evening of Thursday, 7th September, and represented the above circumstances to them. In consequence of what I said, the handle of the pump was removed on the following day.[1]

Dr. Snow plotted the individual cholera deaths on a simple map, shown in Figure 2-1. The obvious clustering of deaths near the Broad Street pump led Dr. Snow to pursue his hunch with a detailed study of individual water-drinking habits. He traced the source of the cholera to sewage in the Thames River at a point where one of London's water supply companies drew its water. Cholera death rates in neighborhoods served by this company were eight to nine times higher than in those served by a rival water supply company that tapped the Thames at a less-polluted point upstream. Dr. Snow observed a "natural experiment" of sorts, with a large number of deaths occurring at a specific place, over a short period of time, and to a group of people whose individual behaviors differed from others in a single respect: each drank the contaminated water.

Dr. Snow's report not only persuaded the authorities to rip the handle off the Broad Street pump, to prevent people from drinking the contaminated water, but also led legislators to mandate the filtration of all of London's water supplies. The report's impact is all the more remarkable when one considers that the theory of infectious disease was not widely accepted at the time, nor was the cholera germ identified for almost thirty years.[2]

Unfortunately, identifying and eliminating the causes of most fatal diseases is usually far more complicated than removing a pump handle. Many factors contribute to ill health, including economic and environmental stresses.[3] Dr. Mostafa Tolba, director of the United Nations Environment Program, put it simply: "One of the single greatest threats to the environment is poverty."[4] The same is true for health.

The World Health Organization estimates that impure water and poor sanitation cause 80 percent of disease worldwide.[5] Without the huge sums needed to build sewage treatment plants, rivers become polluted and people become sick. Abuses of air and land yield equally vicious ecological processes that destroy human health and the environment.

What is the cause of the alarming worldwide death rate from infectious diseases? Is it due to people drinking contaminated water or to their lowered resistance to infection because of malnutrition? Is it the particles of pollution in the water or the failure of governments to protect water supplies? Is it the international economic pressures that inhibit necessary infrastructure investments?

Similar questions apply to the United States, where cancer has emerged as the most prevalent preventable disease, where some counties have rates of mortality as high as any in the Third World (see chapter 6), and where a generation of young adults has been devastated by the infectious disease AIDS.

Epidemiologists untangle such questions by classifying the causes of disease according to three factors:

- *Agents of disease* are specific factors that contribute to ill health—bacteria, viruses, toxic chemicals, ionizing radiation, cholesterol, and others.
- *Host factors* (or intrinsic factors) are personal characteristics that influence susceptibility or response—age, sex, social class, ethnicity, genes, behavior, nutritional state, heightened chemical sensitivity due to previous exposures, and the like.
- *Environmental factors* (or extrinsic factors) include any aspect of the physical, biological, or societal environment that influences the existence of an agent and exposure or susceptibility to it—food sources, occupation, economic conditions, government regulations, housing, climate, ambient pollution, and so forth.

This is a useful scheme for understanding causes of disease, but in reality these factors interact in a way that demands an appreciation of ecological interrelationships.[6]

This atlas derives its strength as well as its limitations from the complexity of ecological interactions. The maps and text identify places where any number of factors—mortality, industrial pollution, pesticides, poverty, and others—may be undesirably, and sometimes unexpectedly, high. They also suggest where certain factors are significantly correlated.

Epidemiologists coined the phrase "ecological fallacy" to identify the danger in confusing correlation with causation when interpreting a collection of statistics. A correlation is when two factors happen to rise and fall in tandem; causation, on the other hand, is when one factor *makes* the other rise or fall. Here's a well-known example of this kind of mix-up, demonstrating that the strength of the British Navy depends on the number of old maids in England:

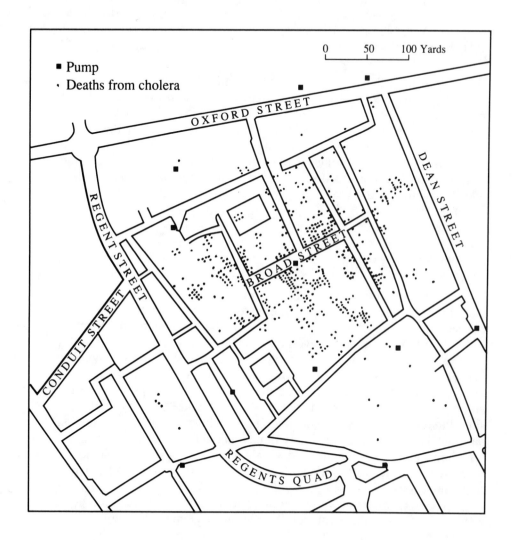

FIGURE 2-1.   Snow's Map of Cholera

SOURCE: Vignette Figure 1-1, in Melinda S. Meade, John W. Florin, and Wilbert M. Gesler, *Medical Geography* (New York, NY: The Guilford Press, 1988), p. 20.

Old English maids always keep cats to reduce the rat population. Since rats feed on the larvae of honey bees, fewer rats (the result of a large maid population) mean the production of honey will be high. As a consequence, there will be extensive cross-pollination of clover and other succulent cattle morsels. Of course the cows will grow fat, yielding a generous supply of canned beef, which is the main staple of the British Navy; a well-fed navy is a strong navy. *Quod erat Demonstrandum* (which was proved).[7]

Nature often does work in circuitous and unlikely ways, however, and at times with devastating consequences. The famous epidemiologist William Farr fell prey to the ecological fallacy in 1852. He observed that areas of London at higher altitudes had less cholera mortality than those at sea level, and inferred from the inverse correlation of elevation and death that a poisonous miasma (bad air) rising from the swamps and marshes was causing the disease. Two years later, as we have seen, John Snow found the real cause, not just a correlation, at the Broad Street pump.

PATTERNED CLUES

What Farr learned from Dr. Snow's proof was that "the death rate is a fact; anything beyond this is an inference."[8] Characteristics of a group can never prove the cause of an individual's death. This is an important distinction to bear in mind as you use this book.

Despite the wide variety of factors we considered in compiling the maps and statistics, we obviously could not include everything that determines why death rates may be higher in one geographic area than another. For one thing, even though the EPA and other agencies consider the following factors to be among the highest potential health risks, nationwide county data are simply not available for most of them: smoking, diet, alcohol use, radon, indoor air pollution, pesticide residues in food, acid rain, lead poisoning, electromagnetic radiation, ozone depletion, and others.[9]

Looking at what we know about national smoking habits is a good way to understand this problem. The Surgeon General has called cigarette smoking "the chief avoidable cause of death in the United States," accounting for as much as a third of deaths from heart disease and cancer, possibly 90 percent of those from chronic obstructive lung disease, and significant portions of infant mortality, birth defects, and child cancer.[10] The toll comes to more than 300,000 deaths per year, almost a fifth of all U.S. mortality from disease.[11] We do not have county data, but Fig. 2-2 shows state-level smoking data for men, women, and all adults, which the Census Bureau gathered for first time in 1985.[12] A fascinating aspect of these maps is the lack of correlation between male and female smoking patterns: states with the highest percentages of male smokers are clustered in the Deep South; whereas, high percentages of women smokers tend to be in the North and Midwest, with an overlap in Kentucky, West Virginia, and Nevada.[13] The mortality maps for all diseases, heart diseases, and especially for all cancers and lung cancers reveal similar regional divergences between the sexes.

Disturbing though the estimates of smoking's impact on American health may be, they also indicate that at least four-fifths of the variation in mortality is *not* attributable to smoking. Why, for example, does mortality from cancer and all diseases track the major U.S. river systems, such as the Mississippi and Ohio? It does not seem likely that riverside smoking habits account for this conspicuous geographic pattern. Two-thirds of Americans do not smoke (though passive smoking is also harmful). Occupational exposures to carcinogenic chemicals are estimated to produce at least 16,000 lung cancer deaths each year, and the combined effects of smoking and exposures to carcinogens in the workplace is often much greater than for either factor alone.[14] For example, the risk of dying from lung cancer for a smoker who is also exposed to asbestos is 2.5 to 7 times greater than for a smoker who has not been exposed, and 100 times greater than for a nonsmoker with no exposure to asbestos.[15]

Conservative estimates put the total cancer death toll from occupational and pollution hazards at 120,000 each year—more than double the Americans killed in ten years of the Vietnam War.[16] Others estimate that cancer deaths from environmental and occupational exposures are significantly higher, and emphasize that the rates are rising at an alarming pace.[17]

In the mid-1970s the National Cancer Institute (NCI) prepared maps that revealed cancer clusters in counties of the Northeast (causing quite a stir in New Jersey, which had the highest overall rate), the Southeast, and Gulf coasts.[18] A follow-up study found significantly higher rates of lung cancer mortality in counties with paper, petrochemical, and transportation industries.[19] The NCI scientists hypothesized that lung cancer in certain coastal counties (from Charleston, South Carolina, to northern Florida, and also in Louisiana, Maine, and Virginia) were due to ship building, and in particular, to asbestos.[20] Our lung cancer maps indicate that these disturbing trends continue to threaten health along the southern coast. Another NCI study reported a significant correlation of high cancer mortality with chemical industries, and in another study

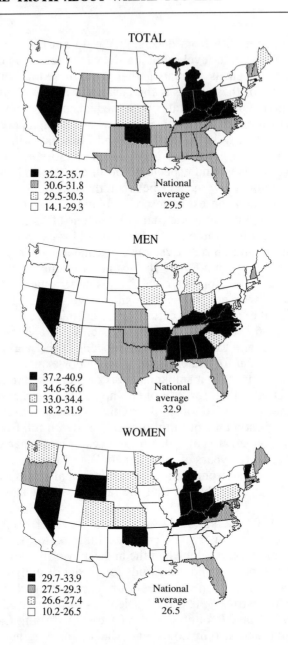

TOTAL

■ 32.2-35.7
▨ 30.6-31.8
⊡ 29.5-30.3
☐ 14.1-29.3

National
average
29.5

MEN

■ 37.2-40.9
▨ 34.6-36.6
⊡ 33.0-34.4
☐ 18.2-31.9

National
average
32.9

WOMEN

■ 29.7-33.9
▨ 27.5-29.3
⊡ 26.6-27.4
☐ 10.2-26.5

National
average
26.5

FIGURE 2-2. Smoking Adults (Percent of People 20 and Over)

Note: Percents are age adjusted
Source: U.S. Census Bureau, 1985 Current Population Survey

NCI found high rates of lung cancer mortality in communities where smelters emit arsenic into the air.[21]

The original NCI atlas proved so helpful in identifying areas for further research that three government atlases followed: cancer among racial minorities, mortality from selected diseases other than cancer, and an update of cancer mortality among whites through 1980.[22] In 1987 the U.S. Environmental Protection Agency (EPA) issued an atlas of cancer mortality rates and trends (1950–79), followed by an ecological study that found significant correlations of county cancer mortality with hazardous waste sites and groundwater pollution.[23]

In short, distinct geographic patterns of mortality suggest something environmental is contributing to death. Ecological studies help generate hypotheses, yielding clues about where to look and what to do next. The maps in this book will undoubtedly raise very different sets of questions for readers from varying backgrounds. This is their strength as an exploratory tool.

STACKING THE ODDS

Local residents often have the greatest insight into the health and environmental problems facing their communities. They also have the greatest need for reliable information. Many health departments, in contrast, have had the data all along—in fact, they are often the source. Community residents are frequently unable to document their suspicions in ways that health authorities consider significant.

An incident south of Philadelphia a few years ago illustrates the problem. A woman became alarmed about a large number of cancer deaths in her neighborhood where there was also considerable industrial activity. When she asked the health department to investigate, it confirmed that there was indeed a significant increase in cancer deaths in the area, but because the separate increases in deaths from cancer at each individual site (stomach, urinary tract, esophagus) were not "statistically significant," the department concluded there was no need for further action.

When health professionals say they are only concerned if mortality is statistically significant, they mean if more deaths occur than can reasonably be attributed to chance. Chance plays as large a role in death as it does in life. Mortality fluctuates randomly over time and from place to place. Health professionals determine statistical significance by looking at the difference between the number of deaths that are actually observed in a population and the number that would have been expected under normal conditions. Observed deaths are simply government tabulations of death certificates for a given county. Expected deaths are the number that would have occurred if the county had the same mortality rate as the United States as a whole. The bigger the gap between the observed and expected deaths, the less probable it is that the difference is due to chance. At a certain point, the probability that the fluctuation is random becomes so remote that the number of observed deaths is called statistically significant.

Statistical results are less reliable when dealing with a small sample. Just a few deaths can make mortality rates fluctuate wildly in a small county. For example, 8 deaths in a county with 1,000 residents would be expected at the national rate. We express this county mortality rate as 800 deaths per 100,000 people. If just 2 more people died in this county, however, its mortality rate would jump to 1,000 deaths per 100,000 people, moving the county from around the 50th percentile (shaded white) to the 98th percentile (shaded black)! In this case, the chance occurrence that 2 more people died would lead to an error statisticians call a false positive, that is, the appearance of a problem when in fact there is none.

A second type of error arising with small samples is called a false negative, that is, saying there is no problem when in fact there is one. The response of the local health department in Pennsylvania to the concerned woman illustrates precisely this mistake. By dividing up the local cancer rate into individual cancer body sites, the department made the sample sizes too small to get significant results. (Health and environmental officials often face tremendous political and professional pressure to downplay the impact polluters may have on health. If you try to make such a linkage in a public forum, you may receive a bevy of official responses that use statistics to derive negative results as an excuse for not taking action.[24])

In this book we have tried to reduce the chances of making such statistical errors. To avoid false positives and false negatives, there must be less than a 10 percent probability that a county's mortality rate is due to chance before it is shaded black, dark gray, or medium gray, or listed among the top and bottom counties on the page facing each map. (See the methods appendix for details about the cut off percentage and significance tests.) Also, we increased sample sizes for more reliable statistics by looking at broadly defined causes of death and 15-year time periods. All of the mortality data are adjusted for age, race, and sex, so such demographic factors do not affect which counties are highlighted in the mortality maps.

We provide maps of "excess" deaths to indicate the size of the population at risk from unusually high or low mortality rates. Excess deaths are the difference between the observed and expected deaths. These are the same measures used in testing statistical significance, so you can be fairly certain that mortality in counties that are darkened in the maps of excess death is highly significant (well under 1 percent probability of chance result).[25] Places with the largest numbers of excess deaths indicate where the most people are adversely affected by high mortality rates. Places with the smallest negative numbers of excess deaths show where the most people benefit from below-average mortality rates.

The maps of mortality rates by gender and racial group highlight where occupational, social, behavioral, and other disparities may be having impacts on health. Geographic divergences along gender lines, for example, may reflect different male and female smoking habits, or hazards peculiar to male- or female-dominated occupations, or to differences between work and home environments. Geographic disparities by racial group may indicate similar divergences in occupational and other environmental risks (chapter 6 discusses such questions in more detail). On the other hand, high rates for both sexes or racial groups might indicate shared environmental factors. (We do not separate male and female rates for children and infants under the assumption that they are generally exposed to the same external factors.)

Some errors of commission and omission may still be found in the maps despite our considerable efforts to avoid statistical and data-processing errors. The potential for such mistakes can never be completely eliminated when handling such a large quantity of government information. Their sources are diverse: for example, a company may submit an incorrect pollution report to a regulatory agency, or a clerk may enter a wrong number into a government computer system. Such random mistakes may change the ranking of an individual county, but they are unlikely to affect the overall picture presented in the maps.

A good example is Nantucket Island, Massachusetts, which ranks first in the nation for mortality from all diseases because two hundred excess deaths occurred there—a highly significant number. A local newspaper reporter investigated this surprising statistic, with follow-up calls to federal, state, and local officials. The National Center for Health Statistics confirmed our numbers, but state and local officials said their data suggested the two hundred excess deaths never occurred. After being informed of the discrepancy, NCHS told the reporter, "We don't have an explanation; it would appear that the data from the state would be the one for you to go by."[26]

As this case illustrates, our statistical techniques help identify counties where mortality is too high to be attributed reasonably to chance, but this still leaves open the question of whether the culprit is in fact a serious local health problem or merely a typographic error. Our nation spends billions of tax dollars collecting vital statistics to identify serious health problems when and where they occur. The best way to assure the reliability of these and other government data is through vigorous public scrutiny. This is one of the goals of this atlas.

CHASING CURES

The attraction of modern medicine is its promise of cures. If a problem can be disassembled, and the mechanics of its parts understood, then fixing them should be relatively easy. Along these lines, maybe we should be mapping morbidity (the incidence or prevalence of disease in a population), instead of mortality, to find out where ill people are in greatest need of treatment, rather than where death has already done its deed.

Differences between maps of morbidity would indicate places where rates of survival and recovery are the highest.[27] If medical treatment improves survival, one might expect more doctors where survival rates are higher. Yet counties with the best mortality rates from all diseases have *half* as many doctors per capita as the national average, and those with the worst mortality have 8 percent *more* doctors per capita than the country as a whole.[28] This does not necessarily mean doctors are bad for your health (the ecological fallacy applies here), but it does indicate that the factors affecting survival are as complex as those contributing to the incidence of disease.[29]

Environmental factors play large roles in morbidity and survival, as well as mortality. Pollution, for example, may not only increase an area's cancer incidence, it can also reduce chances of survival, as when a smog episode kills elderly people who are already infirmed by respiratory ailments. The greatest reductions in mortality during the past two centuries, for that matter, did not result from improved medical therapies at all. At the onset of the 20th century, infectious diseases were the leading killers in the United States. They were largely eradicated with environmental improvements: the introduction of sewage systems, purified public water supplies, improved housing, and better nutrition—long before the discovery of antibiotics and other medical cures.[30]

With the reemergence of infectious diseases such as AIDS as major causes of death in the United States and abroad, it is worth remembering that preventive measures have achieved far greater reductions in mortality during the 20th century than has any high-tech research into the microbiological agents of disease.

The "war on cancer," which Congress launched in 1971, provides the most disturbing evidence of the limitations of modern medicine's propensity for high-tech cures. After two decades and billions of dollars spent on research, the cancer epidemic still rages.[31] Remarkably little progress has been made to control cancer, and remarkably little is known about its exact causes and cures. Cancer is a collection of a hundred clinical diseases affecting various sites of the body in different ways. Some agents, such as chemicals, radiation, and viruses, can initiate cancer. Hormonal, immunological, environmental, nutritional, and genetic factors can also contribute to the formation of cancers. Still other factors, such as smoking and asbestos, are even more potent causes of cancer when combined.[32] Yet the International Agency for Research on Cancer lists only 30 chemicals for which there is "sufficient evidence of a causal relationship to human cancer."[33]

The paltry number of known human carcinogens is more an indication of the cost of thorough human tests and industry reluctance to conduct them than an accurate picture of chemical cancer risks.[34] Less than 2 percent of the 70,000 chemicals in commerce have been fully tested for human health effects, and there are no health data whatsoever for over 70 percent.[35] Cheaper laboratory animal tests have identified hundreds of chemical pollutants as suspected carcinogens, but these tests implicate just as many natural substances, some of which are found in common foods.[36] A number of prominent scientists claim diet causes 35 percent of all cancer, placing it above cigarettes as the number one cause of cancer.[37] Now there is evidence that the animal tests themselves cause the cancer, because massive doses of almost anything seem to make cells divide, increasing the risk of mutations associated with cancer.[38]

Man-made toxins have many adverse human and ecological effects other than cancer. They can cause birth defects, neurological, respiratory, immunological, and reproductive disorders. They can kill you outright through acute poisoning. When toxins damage immune systems, any number of individual diseases, including cancer, can lead to death. Little is known about the toxicological properties of most chemicals, and in most circumstances it is impossible to link specific diseases to specific chemical exposures. The amount of chemicals released in a certain county may not indicate the actual health risks they pose. Some chemicals are thousands of times more toxic than others. Just because a toxin is released does not necessarily mean anyone is exposed. A toxin released in one county may lead to exposures in another if the chemical is carried by the wind or by water or even by the distribution of contaminated food. An exposed person may migrate to another place well before symptoms emerge, let alone before death occurs. For all of these reasons, the maps of industrial toxins merely estimate where potential hazards are greatest; they do not show actual exposures or individual risks.[39]

Despite the increasingly complex interplay of environmental factors and disease, public health policy in the United States is dominated by the medical model, linking specific agents with specific diseases. AIDS is the latest focus, diverting a substantial portion of research funds and staffing previously directed to cancer, but so far with no greater success in finding a cure. Less well known is that AIDS is part of two ominous general trends: a deterioration in the health of young adults, and an increase in mortality from a wide variety of immune deficiency diseases (see "Young-Adult Infectious Diseases" section of chapter 3). Septicemia, a type of blood poisoning associated with immune deficiency, has experienced an astonishing 15-fold rise since the 1950s and today is the thirteenth leading cause of death in the country, accounting for $5 billion to $10 billion of health care expenditures each year.[40] Chronic fatigue syndrome, Lyme disease, candida albicans, herpes, multiple chemical sensitivity, and several other immune deficiency ailments are increasing rapidly as well, especially among young adults. Even pneumonia and influenza, the two infectious diseases that make up the sixth leading cause of death, are on the rise after years of decline.[41] And cancer itself has been linked to immune deficiencies as well.[42] A miracle cure for AIDS may be of no help in arresting the rise in these other diseases, all of which are significantly related to immune deficiencies, as well as assorted agents of disease.

These facts highlight the need for a national research, educational, and action agenda focused on disease prevention in the broadest sense, which acknowledges the multiple causes of disease and the necessity for multiple strategies for control. The enormous geographic disparities in mortality throughout the United States (and the world) suggest where attention is needed most urgently.

INFORMATION EVERYWHERE

Most government efforts to control the spread of toxic pollution are little more than a decade old.[43] Despite the passage of a number of laws that dramatically increased the Environmental Protection Agency's regulatory responsibilities throughout the 1980s, the agency's 1990 budget was scarcely higher than it was in 1975.[44] The government's track record for protecting the environment has received mixed reviews in the face of such crushing budgetary constraints.[45] Many of the goals set forth by environmental laws have not been met, and there are serious gaps in the laws themselves, especially with respect to toxic chemicals. Few of the more than 70,000 chemicals in commerce are controlled by environmental and occupational regulations: only 500 hazardous waste streams, 400 toxins in the workplace, 126 industrial water discharges, 100 drinking water contaminants, and only 7 hazardous air pollutants (though this number will increase with the new Clean Air Act).[46] And, we have only begun to appraise an alarming spectrum of global and regional repercussions, such as ozone depletion, climate change, and acid rain.

There is one concrete outcome from the 50 billion tax dollars spent by the EPA since it was established in 1970: the compilation of a mass of information unrivaled in scale regarding human activities and their impacts on health and the environment. One of the most important recent contributions to this information bank is the Toxic Chemical Release Inventory or TRI, which the EPA unveiled in the spring of 1989.[47]

TRI is the first congressionally mandated on-line public information system and is thus one of the most important advances in information policy since the Freedom of Information Act.[48] The EPA figures that 1.5 million factories and farms will spend about $4 billion over the next decade complying with right-to-know reporting requirements; manufacturers will devote more than 13 million hours to filling out forms; and more than 200,000 people across the country will base decisions on right-to-know data, including local emergency planning committees, fire fighters, corporate health and safety personnel, community activists, and others.[49] Anyone with a personal computer and a modem can dial the database and retrieve information on the amount of industrial toxins released in his or her community (the data are also available through other means). TRI is the EPA's most systematic attempt to date to collect information on industrial toxic releases to the environment.[50]

We began to assemble the data for this atlas three and a half years before TRI went on-line. At the time, the only data on toxic releases were in the massive computer files of the EPA's major regulatory programs, which dwarf TRI's resources. After considerable data processing work to derive consistent county estimates of industrial toxins, we merged these data with information from a variety of federal agencies on pesticides, workplace exposures, radioactive emissions, mortality, demographics, and other measures. Each set of data had its own set of peculiarities and problems.[51]

All told, it took five years and close to $2 million to acquire, standardize, unify, check, map, and analyze the hundreds of variables on thousands of counties from dozens of government sources. During this period, a revolution took place in computer technologies. A decade ago, the computer processing needed to prepare all the data and to generate the maps would have been almost unthinkable, even with the substantial resources that we invested.[52] Now most organizations in the country are computerized, and PCs have ever-increasing computational powers. While most of the data for the atlas were processed on gigantic mainframe computers, we were able to generate the maps on a personal computer!

The dramatic recent advances in information availability and computer technologies, combined with ever-rising public concern about the environment, are rapidly obliterating age-old barriers to investigating complex problems of pollution and health. Even so, it takes the government years to collect and process information for public release. The EPA takes two years to put each year of TRI data on-line, so data for 1991 will not be available until 1993. The 1990 census for counties is not expected to be available until 1992, and for ZIP codes not until 1993. The National Center for Health Statistics takes three years to publish the mortality statistics, and it has stopped releasing the computer file for years after 1985, since these years use county population estimates for which a private consulting firm has proprietary rights.[53] Similarly, a consortium of marketing firms paid the Census Bureau to produce the 1980 ZIP code data after budget cuts almost forced their cancellation, and in return, these firms received proprietary use of the data for a year and a half. Not until 1986 was the information made available to the public in printed form—and then by a nongovernmental organization affiliated with Public Data Access![54]

As a result of all of these complications, the data in the atlas are generally from the early to mid-1980s (see the methods appendix for specific dates). The complexity of the task and the recent availability of the data and computer processing technologies make this the first publication to present such a comprehensive view of toxins, mortality, and populations. In the future, the time and expense necessary to undertake such an atlas will diminish significantly, reflecting the swift pace of developments in computers, public information, and environmental awareness.

ORGANIZING PREVENTION

The 1980s have witnessed the emergence of an increasingly widespread and sophisticated grass-roots effort to prevent toxic hazards in the community and workplace. As green parties have spread throughout Europe, a distinctly American movement for environmental justice has arisen at home, with roots in local voluntary organizations, challenging the traditional separation of work and community in political activism.[55] Passage of the federal right-to-know law is testimony to the power of this new movement, and reverberates back through American history to Thomas Jefferson's remark: "If we think [the people] not enlightened enough to exercise their control with a wholesome discretion, the remedy is not to take it from them, but to inform their discretion."[56]

Local action has led to big politics. Success has been founded in broad-based coalitions that have overcome animosities between labor and environmental groups, stirred up in the 1970s by antiregulatory bumper-sticker rhetoric, such as "environmentalists are polluting our economy!"[57] A turning point came in 1973 when the Sierra Club agreed to support the Oil, Chemical and Atomic Workers (OCAW) in a boycott against Shell Oil Company over health and safety issues.[58] It became increasingly clear that "a hazard is a hazard, whether for workers or the community," and that the best way to get protection was to unite.[59] State worker right-to-know laws were first passed in California, New York, Maine, and Michigan in 1980. Community residents won right-to-know victories soon afterward, first in Philadelphia in 1981, followed by other cities and eventually the state of New Jersey in 1983. There was an explosion of two dozen state community and worker right-to-know laws in the wake of the 1984 chemical disaster in Bhopal, India, where over 2,500 people were killed from exposure to methyl isocyanate. More than 30 states and at least 65 cities and counties passed worker or community right-to-know laws prior to enactment of the Federal Emergency Planning and Community Right-to-Know Act of 1986.[60]

The Philadelphia Area Project on Occupational Safety and Health (PHILAPOSH) began its campaign for the first community right-to-know law in 1976. A fledgling Delaware Valley Toxics Coalition (DVTC) garnered the support of more than 40 organizations as diverse as the United Auto Workers, the League of Women Voters, Friends of the Earth, the Philadelphia Council of Neighborhood Organizations, and the Americans for Democratic Action. One organizer noted, "DVTC's opponents were unable to dismiss the right-to-know as simply a labor question or another item on a list of community concerns."[61] A city official viewed the opposition similarly, claiming, "Industry hasn't argued with the right-to-know. They think it's workable."[62] Even the Philadelphia Chamber of Commerce president conceded, "This is a very difficult thing to oppose, it sounds like you are standing up for cancer."[63]

The success of these local coalitions varied across the country, depending on their organizational strength relative to the business community's opposition. In New Jersey, a well-organized and highly mobilized grass-roots coalition overcame the intense lobbying and legal assaults of the chemical industry, which outspent door-to-door canvassers by tenfold and argued that federal statutes preempted the law even after the bill passed. In Texas, environmentalists and the Texas Chemical Council hammered out a less stringent compromise, which allowed access to fire fighters only.[64] In Massachusetts, citizens who obtained right-to-know data could not disclose the information to anyone else. In Louisiana, the chemical industry's influence on the state legislature was so strong that local advocates dubbed theirs the first "right-to-conceal" law.[65]

After a devastating *Cincinnati Post* series called "Cincinnati—Cancer Capital," a city council member introduced right-to-know as a public health amendment to the fire code, linking together the safety of schoolchildren and fire fighters with the conditions of sewers and cancer. A diverse coalition supported the measure: fire fighters, city employees, professionals, and representatives of environmental, neighborhood, women's, minority, and religious interests. Mobilized citizen groups testified at hearings, released reports, and agitated after every local toxins incident. Despite intensive lobbying from the business community to defeat the bill, the coalition prevailed: the city council passed the measure by a six-to-two margin in 1982.[66] Shortly afterward, residents found out that the Standard Oil Company of Ohio planned to ship benzene on the Ohio River from a terminal located where floods could sweep away a barge or tank. Benzene is suspected of causing cancer and birth defects. As community resistance mounted, Sohio agreed to use a more protected storage area and other safety measures. But the first shipment leaked. "After all the safety assurance we got, this thing goes kaput the first crack out of the box," complained a city council member. The city revoked permission for the project, and Sohio was forced to close a new $180 million benzene plant in Lima for more than a month. A company spokesperson acknowledged, "It's obvious we've suffered a considerable setback."[67]

These local events signal the public's growing impatience with the failure of large government bureaucracies to protect community health and environment. People are beginning to recognize the futility of "end-of-the-pipe'' regulatory controls: what is scrubbed from a flue ends up discharged into a river, what is buried in a specially lined landfill ends up leaking into the ground, what runs off a pesticide-drenched farm drains into a wetland habitat, what billows from a tall stack in Ohio comes down in the acid rain of Vermont.[68] A new science of risk assessment has developed to appraise the health and environmental hazards of modern technologies, such as nuclear power stations and chemical plants. But as the complexity of the assessment models matches that of the technologies, decision makers are left on shaky ground. Costs and benefits are weighed with a presumption of objectivity, but in all such calculations, an arbitrary value must be placed on human life, and a large margin of uncertainty is inherent in the multitude of unknowns (How often will an accident occur? What chemicals and isotopes will be released? How carcinogenic are the emissions? Through what pathways will exposures occur? How many people will be exposed? What are their susceptibilities to the risk? How much are their lives worth?).[69]

The field of ''risk communication'' has burgeoned within industry and government as the limits of risk assessment have become more widely known, teaching decision makers how not to alarm citizens when asking them to accept the uncertain hazards from proposed or existing technologies.[70] Citizens are offered more procedures to participate in environmental regulation than in any other policy area, yet those who do get involved often conclude the process is ''nothing more than a charade, the outcome of which is for all intents and purposes predetermined.''[71] Feeling manipulated by government and poisoned by polluters, many have turned to the courts, seeking remediation and compensation through toxic tort litigation. But the lack of data on exposures and chemical toxicity frequently makes overcoming the burden of proof untenable. More and more, people are demanding not merely liberty from unfair processes within government and industry, but sovereignty in preventing the hazards to which they are exposed.[72]

Unlike the environmental movement of the 1970s which was spearheaded by Washington, D.C.-based lawyers and scientists who advocated regulatory controls, the environmental justice movement of the 1980s began at the local level, where people are demanding not only the right to know but also the right to act on their own behalf.[73] The national environmental organizations that were founded in the 1970s are largely white, urban, middle class, and run by men.[74] In contrast, of the more than 7,000 local organizations in the emerging environmental justice movement, some 40 percent are nonwhite, working class, or rural, and many are run by women whose lives have been transformed by the threat of toxins in the home.[75] These local groups are joining together in national networks like the Citizens Clearinghouse for Hazardous Waste (CCHW), which has field offices in six states, the National Toxics Campaign (NTC), with a dozen regional offices, Citizen Action, with local affiliates in 26 cities, and Public Interest Research Groups (PIRGs) in 28 states. National activist organizations such as Greenpeace USA and Clean Water Action Project also emphasize their grass-roots focus, as Greenpeace's Ben Gordon puts it: "We now have so many allies in the environmental justice movement, we no longer need to draw on our own bookkeeper to go plug polluters' pipes—the local people are ready and willing to do it; the trend is to less commando-type action, and more people power." [76]

Industry labels them NIMBY (not in my backyard); they say NIABY (not in anyone's backyard). But no matter how you spell it, local groups are taking action with national and global consequences. More and more, grass-roots organizations are wielding technical information in the fight against toxins, using on-line information sources such as the EPA's Toxic Release Inventory, as well as desktop publishing, computer graphics, and electronic bulletin boards to spread the word. [77] They produced dozens of reports using right-to-know data during the first years TRI was up and running. [78] In San Diego, TRI data helped to develop legislation that protected a minority community plagued by emergency evacuations from toxic air emissions. In Houston, citizen groups found unregulated toxic hotspots in a major shipping channel. TRI data swayed the vote in Asheville, North Carolina, for a water treatment plant funding initiative. And in Akron, Ohio, TRI was used to pressure BF Goodrich to set a 70 percent reduction goal for toxic air emissions. [79]

In Suffolk County, New York, legislators banned plastic packaging such as Styrofoam. They were motivated not by the promise of immediate improvements in local health or economic conditions, but because the chlorofluorocarbons (CFCs) used in its manufacture are linked to stratospheric ozone depletion. McDonald's announced a $16 million Styrofoam recycling program and then decided to stop using Styrofoam altogether, after hundreds of citizen and church groups joined CCHW's "McToxics" campaign and dumped mounds of hamburger containers at the company's Illinois headquarters. [80] IBM decided to switch from CFC solvents to soap and water by 1993, because of bad publicity at its Santa Clara, California, plant, where the Silicon Valley Toxics Coalition staged an Earth Day rally after discovering the plant spewed over a million pounds of CFCs into the air. [81] With signs of similar local initiatives elsewhere, E. I. du Pont de Nemours Corporation, which accounts for about 25 percent of the world's CFC production, announced plans to cut production of CFCs by 95 percent—not to comply with federal regulation, but in fear of future citizen compensation suits for cancer and other diseases caused by ozone depletion.[82]

With advice from experts across the country, leading environmentalists in California drafted a referendum that goes a long way toward shifting the burden of proof from potential victims to polluters. California's Proposition 65 changes the threshold for regulatory action from hard-to-document evidence of exposures and adverse health impacts to the mere demonstration of a chemical release, laying aside the technical difficulties of conducting health assessments that have plagued citizen suits. The law bans discharges of chemicals suspected of causing cancer and birth defects into drinking water sources, makes companies post warnings before exposing workers and consumers to such chemicals, makes it a criminal offense for government officials to fail to disclose information in a timely manner, and is expected to create a new breed of toxic bounty hunters from among the ranks of community activists.[83] Though industry outspent Proposition 65's backers by four to one, the issue activated a coalition of environmental, labor, and consumer groups —as well as Hollywood stars and California's attorney general—which got 63 percent of California voters to approve the measure.[84]

In Massachusetts and Oregon, National Toxics Campaign and PIRG activists successfully lobbied for toxic use reduction laws, arguing that "industries must reduce their use of chemicals as the primary method of protecting the public health and environment."[85] These laws have far more extensive reporting provisions than under EPCRA, and establish oversight committees with citizen and worker members as well as industry and government representatives.[86] In New Jersey, organizations instrumental in the passage of New Jersey's Worker and Community Right-to-Know Act (a model for EPCRA) are developing legislation to move from the right to know to the power to act, by establishing workplace committees that enable workers to exercise rights to health-and-safety training, to inspect for hazards, to refuse unsafe work, and even to shut down temporarily processes that pose undue risks.[87] The United Auto Workers and others are developing a similar right-to-act initiative in Michigan.[88]

These initiatives indicate how varied local activism for pollution prevention can be, and reflect the potential for information provision to have tremendous repercussions on economic activity. Through engaged coalitions, local and statewide standard setting, citizen negotiations, community cost-benefit judgments, bans, and controlled consumption patterns, local residents can significantly alter the production technologies and toxic hazards in their community—decisions traditionally left to the private sector or federal directives.[89]

This atlas is an information tool to help people in their fight against toxic hazards. It tries to play a role similar to the Broad Street pump: it flags potential problems areas and helps generate hypotheses about possible causal factors. The atlas does not provide conclusive evidence about cause and effect, so common sense is required when interpreting the maps.

Health officials take pride in John Snow's epidemiological achievement, which led government authorities to clean up London's drinking water in the mid-19th century—some 30 years prior to the discovery of cholera's exact bacterial agent. But this is not the whole story.[90] Snow's evidence was presented within the context of a widespread Sanitary Reform Movement to improve the dreadful living and working conditions of English laborers. Led by Edwin Chadwick and helped by Charles Dickens's powerful words, the public health reformers believed it made good economic sense to prevent rather than cure diseases.[91] Backing them up was the growing unease within government chambers of "a very ugly spirit among the mass of the people."[92]

Across America today, people are organizing broad-based coalitions to prevent toxic pollution in their backyards. Government and industry are starting to listen.

CHAPTER 3

MORTALITY

Health is often measured by its opposite—mortality—because death records are the most comprehensive source of information on the quality of life nationwide. Public health experts have long examined geographic variations in death as "one of few ways to assess social inequalities in the risk of dying."[1] Though no one lives forever, there are important disparities in death rates. Not only do many other industrialized countries have better mortality rates than the United States, but there are also tremendous differences in mortality rates among communities across the country—some as great as between rich and poor nations.

Geographic disparities in mortality are associated with a wide range of community conditions that contribute to ill health: stressful and alienating living and working environments, poverty, exposure to toxins on the job or at home, lack of access to medical care, and others. This chapter examines the nationwide geographic variations in ten causes of death during a 15-year period from 1968 to 1983.[2] Before discussing the maps, we begin with two bar charts that summarize the statistics for these causes of death.

Figure 3-1 shows the average annual number of deaths from ten causes during 1979 to 1983 (the last 5 years of the 15-year period in the maps). It also shows the average annual changes since that time (negative changes indicate a decline, positive changes mean an increase).[3] Of the 2 million Americans who die each year, over 90 percent die from diseases. The rest die from "external" causes such as accidents, suicides, homicides, and legal intervention. Heart disease (including heart attacks, strokes, etc.) is the leading cause of death, accounting for close to a million deaths each year (half of the total).

Cancer is the second leading cause of death, killing almost half a million people annually. Cancer deaths are on the rise (unlike heart disease, which is declining), with the greatest increase seen in lung cancer. Deaths from breast cancer increased at about the same rate as deaths from all cancers. In contrast, childhood cancer deaths, which are

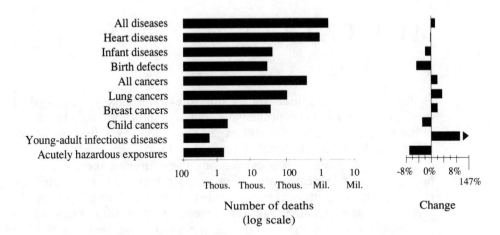

FIGURE 3-1. U.S. Deaths and Average Annual Changes
Since the Early 1980s

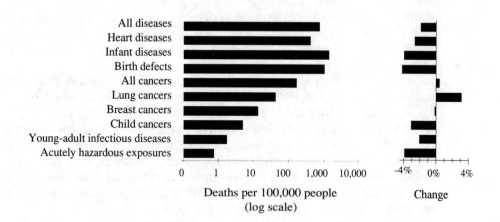

FIGURE 3-2. Age-Race-Sex-Adjusted Mortality Rates and Annual Changes

relatively rare to begin with, have declined—due largely to the effectiveness of improved therapies.[4]

Infant diseases and birth defects (including congenital anomalies and conditions arising during fetal development) represent the most devastating cause of death in terms of the years of potential life lost, even though they account for less than 2 percent of all mortality (about 40,000 deaths).

By far the greatest increase in deaths is in the category that includes AIDS: young-adult infectious diseases. On average, the number of such deaths more than doubled each year (147 percent annual increase). In contrast, the greatest decline in deaths was for acutely hazardous exposures, which includes a variety of external causes of death that are abruptly fatal, such as accidental poisoning outside the home, industrial explosions and fires, and large doses of radiation.

Figure 3-2 shows mortality rates per hundred-thousand people, adjusted for age, race, and sex, and their average annual changes during the 15-year period.[5] The change in mortality from all diseases highlights the importance of age adjustment: mortality is actually declining in the United States, even though the number of deaths is rising because the population is aging. Breast cancer mortality is also declining, though its rate of improvement is significantly slower than that for all diseases and its incidence is increasing. The change in young-adult infectious diseases also reversed itself from Fig. 3-1 to Fig. 3-2, representing the effect of the AIDS epidemic.[6]

Geographic disparities in mortality are declining for all causes of death except cancer (of which the greatest increase in disparities is for lung cancers) and especially young-adult infectious diseases.[7] Other researchers have found that young adults are experiencing the greatest increase in the geographic inequality of death of any age group for all causes of death (in addition to infectious diseases).[8] This ominous young-adult trend bodes increasing health disparities in the future as this population ages. Geographic inequalities for cancer mortality are also increasing, especially for lung cancers. Earlier research found cancer mortality in urban and rural areas was converging, due to the rapid spread of urban culture during the postwar period.[9] Yet the urban-rural convergence is apparently now counteracted by even stronger forces that are increasing geographic inequalities in cancer rates. In contrast, nationwide disparities in mortality from all diseases and from six other causes of death are declining; however, the disparities in heart disease and birth defects are diminishing more slowly than the others.

The inequities between gender and racial groups are even greater than geographic disparities for the entire population. Racial and ethnic minorities endure higher mortality rates from eight of the ten causes of death, and they are diverging even further for four of these (birth defects, all cancers, lung cancers, and acutely hazardous exposures). The two exceptions are breast cancers and child cancers, from which whites suffer a higher mortality than minorities. African Americans, Asian Americans, and native Americans are included among minorities in the mortality maps; Latino Americans are included among whites (see chapter 6 for more on how the government defines these groupings).

Males suffer from higher rates for nine of the ten causes, and they are diverging even further from females for five of these (all diseases, heart diseases, all cancers, child cancers, and young-adult infectious diseases). Women, of course, have a higher rate of breast cancer than men, and this divergence is increasing. The greatest disparities in mortality are between minority males and white females, which have the highest and lowest rates (respectively) for eight of the ten causes of death. The greatest difference between these groups is for mortality from acute toxic exposures, from which minority males die at a rate over six times higher than the rate for white females.

The following sections of chapter 3 display maps of the ten causes of death, and discuss important aspects of each in turn. The mortality maps portray two types of measures: age-adjusted rates and excess deaths. Age-adjusted rates indicate where the risks of dying from a particular cause are highest (irrespective of the average age of the population). Excess deaths indicate where the greatest numbers of people are affected. For more discussion on how to interpret these measures, see the "Stacking the Odds" section of chapter 2. In addition, the methods appendix provides more details about how these mortality measures are calculated, the disparities between population groups and counties, and the statistical results of how well the pollution and social structure factors correlate with each cause of death.

ALL DISEASES

Mortality rates are generally higher east of the Mississippi River. This has been common knowledge for decades.[10] But if images of crowded slums in the Northeast or churning factories in the Midwest first come to mind, you will be surprised by the map of mortality from all diseases.

For one thing, the Mighty Mississippi does not somehow separate poor health in the East from clean western living—it is in fact a locus for some of the worst mortality rates of the country. The river that *Harper's Magazine* called "the body of the nation" in 1863 is today showing signs of devastating illness.[11] In 1988, Greenpeace sailed the M.V. *Beluga* down the length of the Mississippi. The onboard laboratory detected such a soup of "toxic chemicals, pesticides, fertilizers, and misplaced nutrients" that Greenpeace scientists now call Old Man River "North America's largest waste conduit."[12]

Just as the *Beluga* found higher and higher levels of pollution as it traveled downstream, mortality rates rise as one travels farther south. Eighty percent of the counties bordering the Mississippi below the Ohio River confluence (where Kentucky, Illinois, and Missouri meet) have significant levels of excess death, as well as staggering levels of pollution, pesticides, and poverty.[13]

The map shows what one public health expert calls "the reality of the 1980s": the South has higher death rates than the urban Northeast.[14] Worsening mortality rates accompanied the Sunbelt's much-heralded economic growth during the 1970s—especially among young adults, suggesting continued divergence in the future.[15] Boom as well as bust can be harmful to health, as environmental degradation and job stress follow rapid economic growth.[16] In southern states, rising deaths from heart disease have been correlated with job growth, and rising deaths from lung cancer have been linked to increased cigarette consumption. Exposures to on-the-job hazards that can cause acute fatalities and long-term risks of cancer are no longer concentrated in the North. Arkansas, Kentucky, Mississippi, and West Virginia, for example, have larger proportions of their work force in manufacturing, construction, and mining than do Connecticut, New Jersey, New York, and Massachusetts.[17] Moreover, The Conservation Foundation and other environmental organizations have consistently given higher ratings to state environmental protection efforts in the North than in southern states.[18]

Particularly disturbing clusters of high mortality rates can be seen in the coastal plain states of the Southeast, including Georgia, South Carolina, and North Carolina, as well as in the Appalachian regions of Kentucky, Virginia, and West Virginia. In the Northeast, Pennsylvania also has a number of counties with high rates, but many of these are improving relative to the rest of the country. The same is true for the worst-ranked island of Nantucket, Massachusetts: its high rate of mortality from all diseases improved considerably throughout the period, due primarily to declines in mortality from heart disease. Nantucket's mortality from all cancers, in contrast, remained significant throughout the time period, and breast cancers were increasing significantly faster than the rest of the nation. It is difficult to say why Nantucket's mortality rates are so high. Most of the other measures in the atlas are not unusual there. Causes may be linked to the island's isolation from the mainland (leading to higher rates of alcoholism or smoking?) or to the lack of diversity in its occupational structure (hazards from fishing, boat repair, or working long hours in the sun?). The high rate may also simply be due to an error in the government data (as discussed in the "Stacking the Odds" section of chapter 2).

The urban Northeast—as well as major cities in other parts of the country—has the largest numbers of excess deaths, as might be expected because of their larger populations. In contrast, southwestern cities, especially in California, have the most residents benefiting from below-average mortality rates. Counties in the Great Plains and Mountain states have many of the lowest mortality rates, as has been true for decades.

When the rates are broken down by race and sex, we also see some disturbing mortality rates in Nevada, especially among women. The highest percentage of women smoke in Nevada, but the Nevadan counties with high female rates of lung cancer mortality are not the same as those with high rates of mortality from all diseases. Alcoholism has also been significantly higher among Nevadan women, but not the cancers associated with alcohol consumption.[19] Maybe the atmospheric nuclear weapons tests conducted in the 1950s at the Nevada Test Site are also partly to blame. The maps of mortality among minorities show especially high rates in Montana and the Dakotas, where native Americans constitute significant proportions of the minority population.

HEART DISEASES

Public health experts call the Southeast the "enigma area" when talking about heart disease. Nine of the ten states with the highest rates of heart disease mortality are in the South.[20] Yet why southerners have so much heart disease remains a matter of speculation. Risk factors such as smoking, cholesterol, lack of exercise, Type A personality, and blood sugar explain less than half of the geographic variation in heart disease.[21] Some have wondered whether southern cooking might be involved; others have examined water softness, trace elements from local soils, and altitude.[22] But most of this research is inconclusive.[23] One thing is certain: blood pressure is significantly higher in the South—among men and women, blacks and whites, and even children.[24] The results, too often, are fatal.

Heart conditions are the leading cause of death in the United States. Eighty percent of the deaths involve cardiovascular diseases such as heart attacks; much of the remainder are from cerebrovascular diseases such as strokes. Rates have been declining for decades, but at very different levels across the country. Metropolitan areas, particularly in the Northeast and Pacific states, started improving much earlier than nonmetropolitan areas, particularly in the South and the Midwest.[25] Areas with the highest levels of income, education, and white-collar employment began to decline first.[26] As the declines in heart disease mortality have varied throughout the country, the "stroke belt" along the southern coastal plain has become less concentrated, while clusters along the Mississippi and Ohio rivers have become more pronounced.[27] Excess deaths are particularly high in western Pennsylvania, as well as in population centers throughout the country.

The southeastern counties with the highest rates of heart disease are rural and among the poorest areas in the nation (see chapter 6 for more on this). Throughout the country, the average population density is 62 percent below the national average in counties with the highest heart disease mortality. Differences in heart disease mortality are as great between areas with markedly different socioeconomic conditions as between rural and metropolitan areas.[28] Within metropolitan areas, for example, heart disease is much higher in industrial inner cities than in suburbia.[29] Household incomes in counties with the highest rates of heart disease mortality are 13 percent below the national average. Poverty is 50 percent higher in these counties—more than for any of the ten other causes of death considered in the atlas. In general, people with low incomes have three times the heart conditions of the affluent.[30]

Community conditions provide the context for understanding a number of work and family related factors that contribute to elevated heart disease. More advantaged communities have greater resources for promoting healthy working and living conditions, as well as better medical care.[31] Unstable working and family environments often lead to heart disease. Men with more supportive co-workers and supervisors have less cardiovascular disease, and husbands have less coronary heart disease than unmarried and widowed men.[32] Whereas, suicides and homicides frequently increase when local economies falter, the rate of heart disease goes up with rapid economic expansion, as well.[33] Part of this may be due to increased risks of occupational exposures to the 1,466 chemicals that the national Institute of Occupational Safety and Health suspects of having cardiovascular effects—especially carbon monoxide among industrial laborers and craftsmen.[34] Better understood is the link between heart disease and job stress. Sources of occupational stress can be found in all sectors of the economy—the service sector, as well as

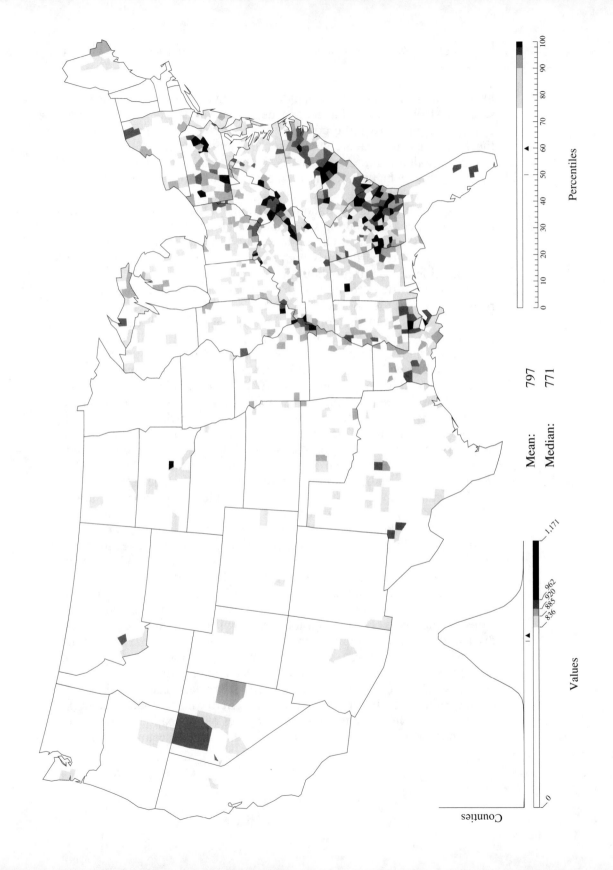

Mean: 797

Median: 771

Percentiles

Values

Counties

0   836 885 920 962   1,171

(DEATHS PER 100,000 PEOPLE)

TOP COUNTIES SHADED BLACK

RANK	COUNTY	STATE	VALUE
1	NANTUCKET	MA	1,171
2	NORTHUMBERLAND	PA	1,152
3	CALHOUN	GA	1,119
4	MINGO	WV	1,090
5	LONG	GA	1,073
6	SCHUYLKILL	PA	1,064
7	MC DOWELL	WV	1,059
8	BRANTLEY	GA	1,053
9	ATKINSON	GA	1,045
10	CARROLL	KY	1,038
11	FULTON	KY	1,037
12	WINSTON	AL	1,030
13	RUSSELL	AL	1,030
14	TALIAFERRO	GA	1,024
15	BELL	KY	1,022
16	WISE	VA	1,021
17	VENANGO	PA	1,020
18	BUFFALO	SD	1,020
19	TELFAIR	GA	1,019
20	LOGAN	WV	1,019
21	ALEXANDER	IL	1,009
22	JENKINS	GA	1,008
23	COCKE	TN	1,006
24	HARLAN	KY	1,006
25	EVANS	GA	991
26	GILES	VA	989
27	BALTIMORE CITY	MD	989
28	FAYETTE	WV	987
29	JASPER	SC	984
30	TAZEWELL	VA	983
31	SCOTLAND	NC	983
32	BACON	GA	982
33	BURKE	GA	982
34	SCHLEY	GA	982
35	SUMMERS	WV	982
36	MARLBORO	SC	982
37	WILSON	NC	981
38	ST LOUIS CITY	MO	981
39	MARION	GA	981
40	MARION	SC	980
41	DODGE	GA	979
42	KENTON	KY	979
43	BATH	VA	979
44	LIBERTY	GA	974
45	LUZERNE	PA	974
46	ORLEANS	LA	972
47	JEFF DAVIS	GA	972
48	SOMERSET	PA	971
49	CHESTERFIELD	SC	971
50	PEMISCOT	MO	969
51	WEBSTER	GA	969
52	SALINE	IL	968
53	STEWART	GA	966
54	DOOLY	GA	966
55	WASHINGTON	LA	966
56	BEN HILL	GA	965
57	CRISP	GA	964
58	WILKINSON	GA	964
59	PIERCE	GA	964
60	UNION	SC	963
61	FLORENCE	SC	963
62	DILLON	SC	962

BOTTOM COUNTIES SHADED WHITE

RANK	COUNTY	STATE	VALUE
1	YELLOWSTONE NAT. PARK	MT	403
2	KENEDY	TX	409
3	BANNER	NE	413
4	WHEELER	NE	454
5	SULLY	SD	480
6	MC PHERSON	NE	491
7	JUDITH BASIN	MT	498
8	TREASURE	MT	506
9	SAN JUAN	WA	506
10	BORDEN	TX	509
11	SMITH	KS	512
12	GOLDEN VALLEY	MT	515
13	GOSPER	NE	517
14	STARR	TX	517
15	WHEELER	OR	520
16	HANSON	SD	534
17	KEARNEY	NE	534
18	ROCK	MN	536
19	GLASSCOCK	TX	537
20	PITKIN	CO	539
21	LYON	IA	540
22	DECATUR	KS	541
23	FRONTIER	NE	541
24	BROOKINGS	SD	542
25	TORRANCE	NM	544
26	CUSTER	CO	544
27	CLARK	KS	545
28	MARION	KS	545
29	DAGGETT	UT	547
30	JACKSON	MN	548
31	ELBERT	CO	549
32	WAYNE	NE	551
33	SCOTT	KS	551
34	CACHE	UT	551
35	KIT CARSON	CO	552
36	IRION	TX	552
37	LINCOLN	KS	553
38	CARTER	MT	553
39	SIOUX	NE	553
40	GRUNDY	IA	553
41	MURRAY	MN	553
42	SHELBY	IA	555
43	HUMBOLDT	IA	556
44	DIXON	NE	557
45	LAKE	SD	557
46	CUMING	NE	558
47	EMMONS	ND	559
48	RAWLINS	KS	559
49	GARFIELD	WA	560
50	BUFFALO	WI	560
51	ADAIR	IA	561
52	JEFF DAVIS	TX	562
53	MC LEOD	MN	563
54	CARIBOU	ID	564
55	DODGE	MN	565
56	LIVE OAK	TX	565
57	PERKINS	NE	565
58	BILLINGS	ND	565
59	WICHITA	KS	565
60	COSTILLA	CO	566
61	STEARNS	MN	566

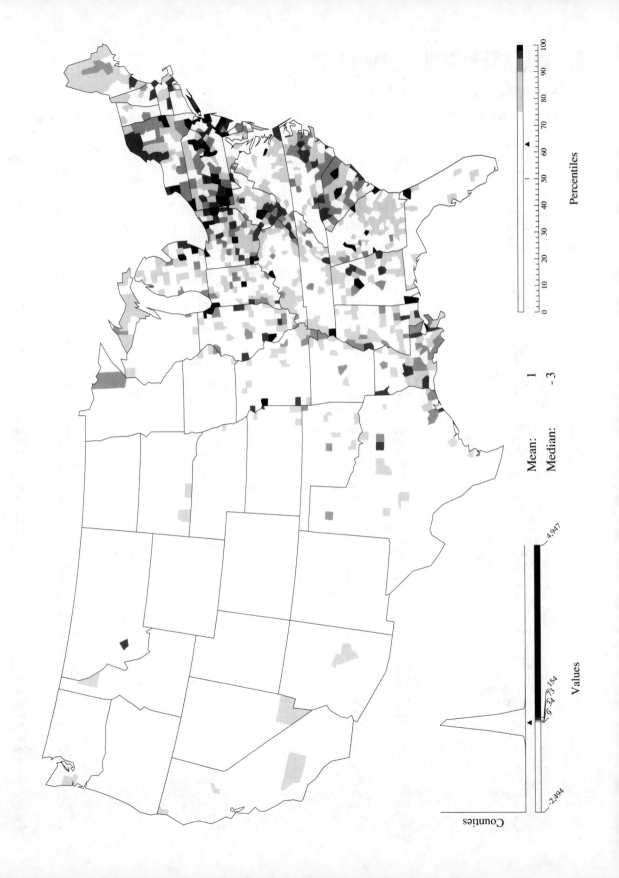

Percentiles

Mean: 1
Median: – 3

Values

Counties

TOP COUNTIES SHADED BLACK			
RANK	COUNTY	STATE	VALUE
1	COOK	IL	4,947
2	NEW YORK CITY	NY	4,304
3	PHILADELPHIA	PA	2,908
4	WAYNE	MI	1,913
5	ALLEGHENY	PA	1,599
6	BALTIMORE CITY	MD	1,584
7	ST LOUIS CITY	MO	1,055
8	ERIE	NY	1,045
9	ORLEANS	LA	990
10	HUDSON	NJ	982
11	CUYAHOGA	OH	938
12	SUFFOLK	MA	770
13	LUZERNE	PA	712
14	JEFFERSON	KY	631
15	DISTRICT OF COLUMBIA	DC	588
16	HAMILTON	OH	552
17	ESSEX	NJ	538
18	FRANKLIN	OH	532
19	FULTON	GA	520
20	LACKAWANNA	PA	479
21	LUCAS	OH	467
22	SCHUYLKILL	PA	434
23	MARION	IN	405
24	DUVAL	FL	402
25	SHELBY	TN	381
26	CAMDEN	NJ	368
27	LAKE	IN	357
28	DELAWARE	PA	310
29	HENRICO	VA	308
30	SUMMIT	OH	290
31	JEFFERSON	AL	285
32	FAYETTE	PA	283
33	ST CLAIR	IL	268
34	KANAWHA	WV	265
35	NASSAU	NY	259
36	ATLANTIC	NJ	259
37	ERIE	PA	251
38	MAHONING	OH	239
39	MIDDLESEX	NJ	225
40	CHATHAM	GA	220
41	KENTON	KY	215
42	NEW CASTLE	DE	213
43	CAMBRIA	PA	203
44	WASHINGTON	PA	202
45	BIBB	GA	197
46	BLAIR	PA	197
47	NORTHUMBERLAND	PA	194
48	JACKSON	MO	191
49	ALBANY	NY	188
50	MONMOUTH	NJ	185
51	MUSCOGEE	GA	183
52	DAUPHIN	PA	174
53	PASSAIC	NJ	171
54	GENESEE	MI	170
55	ORANGE	NY	169
56	RICHMOND	GA	166
57	RENSSELAER	NY	159
58	COLUMBIANA	OH	158
59	RICHLAND	SC	157
60	MOBILE	AL	156
61	FLORENCE	SC	154

BOTTOM COUNTIES SHADED WHITE			
RANK	COUNTY	STATE	VALUE
1	LOS ANGELES	CA	-2,494
2	DADE	FL	-1,908
3	BROWARD	FL	-1,814
4	PINELLAS	FL	-1,674
5	SAN DIEGO	CA	-1,508
6	ORANGE	CA	-1,485
7	PALM BEACH	FL	-1,078
8	MARICOPA	AZ	-1,056
9	SANTA CLARA	CA	-971
10	KING	WA	-655
11	SAN MATEO	CA	-612
12	HENNEPIN	MN	-599
13	ALAMEDA	CA	-596
14	SARASOTA	FL	-562
15	RIVERSIDE	CA	-561
16	MONTGOMERY	MD	-529
17	CONTRA COSTA	CA	-468
18	PASCO	FL	-449
19	MANATEE	FL	-432
20	FAIRFAX	VA	-408
21	HARTFORD	CT	-396
22	LEE	FL	-390
23	VENTURA	CA	-370
24	PIMA	AZ	-353
25	SALT LAKE	UT	-343
26	WESTCHESTER	NY	-337
27	FAIRFIELD	CT	-335
28	FRESNO	CA	-330
29	SAN BERNARDINO	CA	-327
30	ST LOUIS	MO	-320
31	SANTA BARBARA	CA	-309
32	OAKLAND	MI	-291
33	RAMSEY	MN	-271
34	HIDALGO	TX	-259
35	TRAVIS	TX	-257
36	JOHNSON	KS	-251
37	DANE	WI	-248
38	MONTEREY	CA	-243
39	LANE	OR	-240
40	NORFOLK	MA	-238
41	WASHINGTON	OR	-230
42	VOLUSIA	FL	-217
43	BERGEN	NJ	-216
44	MARIN	CA	-212
45	MONROE	NY	-209
46	BERNALILLO	NM	-207
47	SANTA CRUZ	CA	-206
48	SONOMA	CA	-203
49	CHARLOTTE	FL	-198
50	MORRIS	NJ	-197
51	ORANGE	FL	-197
52	NAPA	CA	-196
53	LAKE	FL	-194
54	DE KALB	GA	-194
55	DENVER	CO	-190
56	SAN FRANCISCO	CA	-186
57	JEFFERSON	CO	-185
58	DU PAGE	IL	-179
59	MARION	OR	-178
60	MONTGOMERY	PA	-177
61	LANCASTER	NE	-175
62	BREVARD	FL	-173

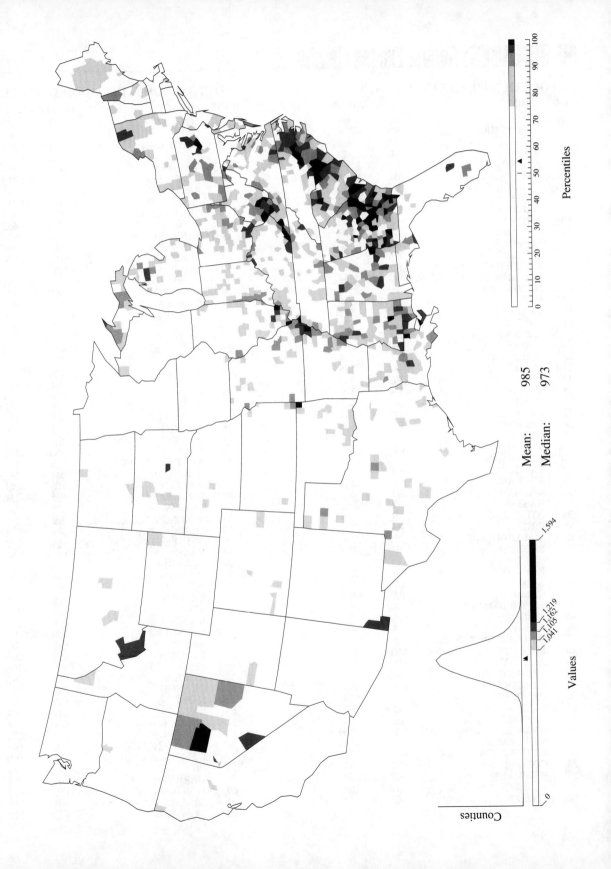

Mean: 985

Median: 973

Percentiles

Values

Counties

0   1.041 1.105 1.162 1.219   1.594

(DEATHS PER 100,000 PEOPLE)

TOP COUNTIES SHADED BLACK

RANK	COUNTY	STATE	VALUE
1	CALHOUN	GA	1,594
2	NANTUCKET	MA	1,520
3	BRANTLEY	GA	1,495
4	LONG	GA	1,448
5	TELFAIR	GA	1,398
6	ST HELENA	LA	1,384
7	TALIAFERRO	GA	1,367
8	ALLENDALE	SC	1,348
9	FULTON	KY	1,345
10	ATKINSON	GA	1,313
11	MINGO	WV	1,308
12	CRISP	GA	1,304
13	MC DOWELL	WV	1,298
14	JASPER	SC	1,292
15	RUSSELL	AL	1,287
16	HARLAN	KY	1,282
17	LOGAN	WV	1,280
18	BURKE	GA	1,278
19	WHEELER	GA	1,272
20	DODGE	GA	1,265
21	ALEXANDER	IL	1,264
22	CLAY	GA	1,263
23	WISE	VA	1,262
24	HAMPTON	SC	1,261
25	ST LOUIS CITY	MO	1,259
26	JEFF DAVIS	GA	1,258
27	BLECKLEY	GA	1,258
28	WEBSTER	GA	1,258
29	EMANUEL	GA	1,257
30	DOOLY	GA	1,256
31	PERSHING	NV	1,254
32	WILSON	NC	1,253
33	SCOTLAND	NC	1,250
34	ROBESON	NC	1,249
35	BALTIMORE CITY	MD	1,249
36	MARLBORO	SC	1,248
37	BELL	KY	1,246
38	SUMMERS	WV	1,246
39	CHARLTON	GA	1,246
40	PULASKI	GA	1,244
41	JOHNSTON	NC	1,243
42	MITCHELL	GA	1,243
43	MARION	SC	1,243
44	JENKINS	GA	1,236
45	CHESTERFIELD	SC	1,235
46	FAYETTE	WV	1,234
47	TOOMBS	GA	1,233
48	BEN HILL	GA	1,233
49	BACON	GA	1,232
50	OTTAWA	OK	1,232
51	SCHUYLKILL	PA	1,230
52	GREENE	NC	1,230
53	ORLEANS	LA	1,227
54	HARNETT	NC	1,227
55	PEMISCOT	MO	1,227
56	UNION	SC	1,226
57	LAMAR	GA	1,225
58	COVINGTON	MS	1,224
59	DILLON	SC	1,224
60	GALLATIN	IL	1,222
61	TREUTLEN	GA	1,221
62	WILKINSON	GA	1,219

BOTTOM COUNTIES SHADED WHITE

RANK	COUNTY	STATE	VALUE
1	KENEDY	TX	528
2	WHEELER	NE	572
3	BORDEN	TX	622
4	SUMMIT	CO	643
5	SAN JUAN	UT	647
6	TODD	SD	657
7	BANNER	NE	671
8	JAMES CITY	VA	672
9	JEFF DAVIS	TX	676
10	SAN JUAN	WA	681
11	MELLETTE	SD	692
12	JUDITH BASIN	MT	714
13	STARR	TX	714
14	GOSPER	NE	719
15	WASHINGTON	UT	723
16	TERRELL	TX	726
17	SULLY	SD	733
18	CACHE	UT	734
19	KEARNEY	NE	735
20	WHEELER	OR	737
21	NEWTON	TX	738
22	WABAUNSEE	KS	739
23	PITKIN	CO	740
24	NAPA	CA	746
25	HANSON	SD	748
26	MARION	KS	750
27	CARTER	MT	751
28	SMITH	KS	751
29	TRAVERSE	MN	752
30	FRONTIER	NE	754
31	GOLDEN VALLEY	MT	754
32	SHERIDAN	ND	757
33	CUSTER	CO	757
34	PIERCE	ND	757
35	HUDSPETH	TX	758
36	BALDWIN	GA	761
37	HARDING	NM	761
38	GARFIELD	WA	762
39	CLARK	ID	764
40	SIOUX	NE	765
41	SANDOVAL	NM	768
42	JACKSON	MN	768
43	WICHITA	KS	769
44	DECATUR	KS	775
45	CARIBOU	ID	775
46	DOUGLAS	WA	775
47	KIT CARSON	CO	776
48	OWYHEE	ID	776
49	EMMONS	ND	776
50	MURRAY	MN	777
51	TREASURE	MT	778
52	RICH	UT	778
53	CLARK	KS	779
54	WALKER	TX	779
55	SCOTT	KS	779
56	SHELBY	IA	780
57	MC LEAN	ND	780
58	STEARNS	MN	780
59	CATRON	NM	780
60	HARVEY	KS	781
61	COSTILLA	CO	781

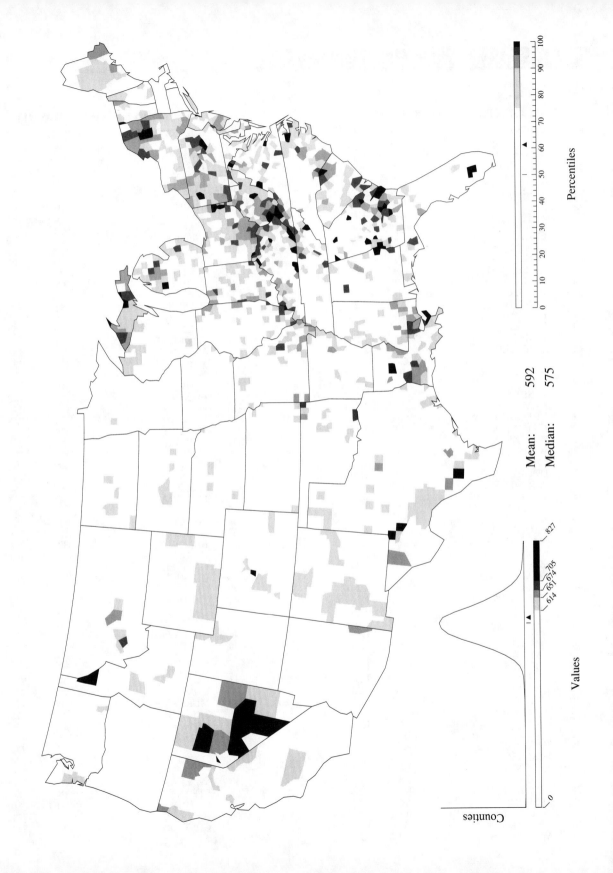

Mean: 592

Median: 575

Percentiles

Values

Counties

ALL DISEASES: White Female Mortality Rate

(DEATHS PER 100,000 PEOPLE)

TOP COUNTIES SHADED BLACK

RANK	COUNTY	STATE	VALUE
1	MINGO	WV	827
2	SCHLEY	GA	818
3	STOREY	NV	814
4	CHARLES CITY	VA	813
5	WINKLER	TX	808
6	KEWEENAW	MI	801
7	LA SALLE	TX	782
8	GALLATIN	KY	778
9	MC DOWELL	WV	777
10	QUITMAN	GA	775
11	NANTUCKET	MA	771
12	JENKINS	GA	770
13	EVANS	GA	769
14	COCKE	TN	767
15	LOGAN	WV	766
16	CARROLL	KY	766
17	ATKINSON	GA	761
18	LAKE	CO	757
19	LONG	GA	756
20	BUCHANAN	VA	754
21	RUSSELL	AL	752
22	MC INTOSH	GA	746
23	MC CREARY	KY	743
24	VENANGO	PA	740
25	CRANE	TX	736
26	HAMILTON	NY	733
27	SCHUYLKILL	PA	733
28	LIBERTY	GA	733
29	TALBOT	GA	731
30	MENIFEE	KY	729
31	LAKE	MI	728
32	HARDIN	IL	728
33	STEWART	GA	725
34	ALGER	MI	724
35	BELL	KY	722
36	JEFF DAVIS	GA	722
37	BACON	GA	721
38	NYE	NV	721
39	BATH	VA	716
40	CAMPBELL	KY	715
41	SHOSHONE	ID	712
42	PERSHING	NV	712
43	CUMBERLAND	KY	711
44	TALIAFERRO	GA	710
45	BERKELEY	WV	709
46	JEFFERSON	OH	709
47	MINERAL	NV	708
48	HENDRY	FL	708
49	DAWSON	GA	708
50	MARLBORO	SC	708
51	ST BERNARD	LA	708
52	GRAND ISLE	VT	708
53	COLUMBIANA	OH	707
54	WEBSTER	WV	707
55	BERTIE	NC	706
56	HARLAN	KY	706
57	WINN	LA	706
58	MONROE	KY	706
59	CHATTOOGA	GA	705
60	HUDSON	NJ	705

BOTTOM COUNTIES SHADED WHITE

RANK	COUNTY	STATE	VALUE
1	LOVING	TX	161
2	BANNER	NE	283
3	SHANNON	SD	298
4	MC PHERSON	NE	330
5	GARFIELD	MT	358
6	BLAINE	NE	373
7	SULLY	SD	374
8	TODD	SD	375
9	YELLOWSTONE NAT. PARK	MT	380
10	GOLDEN VALLEY	ND	382
11	TREASURE	MT	388
12	HYDE	SD	398
13	GADSDEN	FL	400
14	GLASSCOCK	TX	402
15	LOGAN	NE	411
16	KENEDY	TX	411
17	BALDWIN	GA	415
18	POWDER RIVER	MT	419
19	SIOUX	ND	425
20	ROCK	MN	426
21	SMITH	KS	428
22	GOLDEN VALLEY	MT	431
23	JUDITH BASIN	MT	431
24	HARVEY	KS	433
25	JEFFERSON	MS	435
26	KEITH	NE	435
27	JAMES CITY	VA	435
28	BROOKINGS	SD	437
29	GRUNDY	IA	438
30	KENT	TX	439
31	DODGE	MN	440
32	JONES	GA	440
33	HARTLEY	TX	440
34	PIERCE	ND	441
35	DEUEL	NE	442
36	MELLETTE	SD	443
37	WILKIN	MN	443
38	HARDEMAN	TN	444
39	PERRY	AL	445
40	ROBERTS	SD	448
41	OLMSTED	MN	449
42	LAKE	SD	450
43	GRANT	NE	451
44	WHITE	GA	451
45	ELBERT	CO	453
46	MINERAL	CO	454
47	MARION	KS	456
48	DOLORES	CO	456
49	WAYNE	NE	456
50	NOBLES	MN	457
51	NEWTON	TX	457
52	FREEBORN	MN	457
53	TRAILL	ND	458
54	REDWOOD	MN	458
55	LINCOLN	KS	458
56	LYON	IA	458
57	HOUSTON	MN	459
58	WHEELER	OR	459
59	AUDUBON	IA	459
60	EDMUNDS	SD	459
61	PARMER	TX	461
62	SAN JUAN	WA	463

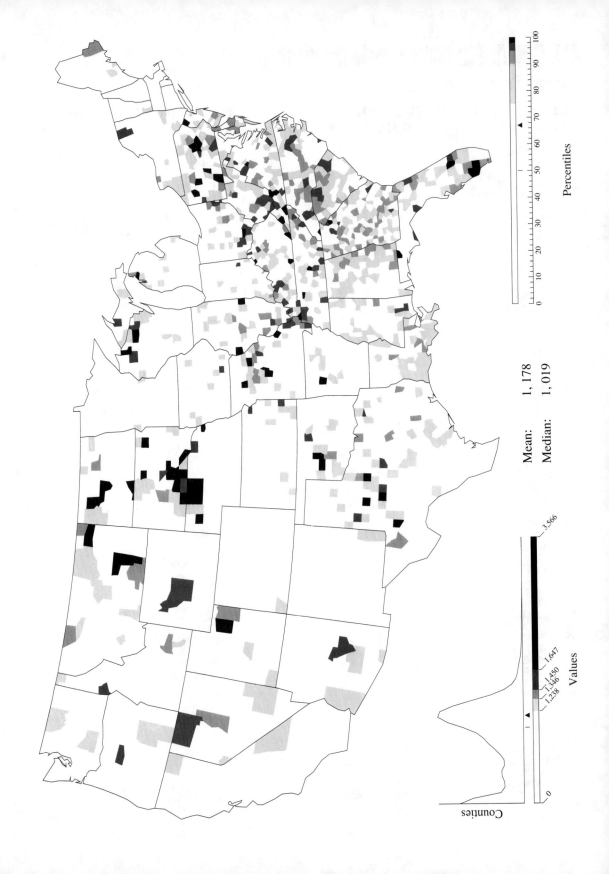

Mean: 1, 178
Median: 1, 019

(DEATHS PER 100,000 PEOPLE)

TOP COUNTIES SHADED BLACK

RANK	COUNTY	STATE	VALUE
1	NORTHUMBERLAND	PA	3,566
2	MONTOUR	PA	2,808
3	CHERRY	NE	2,550
4	STE GENEVIEVE	MO	2,491
5	MOUNTRAIL	ND	2,420
6	LYMAN	SD	2,391
7	SCHUYLKILL	PA	2,388
8	SOMERSET	PA	2,373
9	DUCHESNE	UT	2,267
10	BLAINE	OK	2,239
11	CANNON	TN	2,224
12	CHARLES MIX	SD	2,182
13	VENANGO	PA	2,179
14	SIOUX	ND	2,130
15	GARZA	TX	2,125
16	SUSSEX	NJ	2,102
17	BUFFALO	SD	2,079
18	JEFFERSON	PA	2,068
19	TRIPP	SD	2,054
20	MONROE	MO	2,007
21	LIVINGSTON	MO	2,000
22	MELLETTE	SD	1,983
23	MC LEAN	ND	1,955
24	COLLIER	FL	1,950
25	FRANKLIN	GA	1,941
26	ONEIDA	WI	1,933
27	DAY	SD	1,931
28	NANTUCKET	MA	1,885
29	MONITEAU	MO	1,878
30	WALWORTH	SD	1,872
31	GILES	VA	1,864
32	CRANE	TX	1,841
33	CHARLEVOIX	MI	1,827
34	JOHNSON	AR	1,825
35	WASHINGTON	VA	1,824
36	HOLMES	FL	1,805
37	PULASKI	VA	1,798
38	MITCHELL	TX	1,793
39	MORGAN	MO	1,785
40	THURSTON	NE	1,784
41	BLAIR	PA	1,774
42	CUSTER	OK	1,773
43	BENNETT	SD	1,761
44	ADAMS	IL	1,757
45	CARROLL	KY	1,749
46	ROOSEVELT	MT	1,734
47	BOX BUTTE	NE	1,731
48	OKEECHOBEE	FL	1,726
49	EDGAR	IL	1,719
50	GREENE	VA	1,718
51	CLAY	NC	1,705
52	ASHLAND	WI	1,703
53	BELL	KY	1,703
54	HASKELL	TX	1,697
55	PIKE	OH	1,691
56	COLUMBIA	PA	1,684
57	HOUSTON	TN	1,674
58	WISE	VA	1,670
59	ROSEBUD	MT	1,657
60	CUMBERLAND	KY	1,650
61	FULTON	KY	1,647

BOTTOM COUNTIES SHADED WHITE

NOTE: TOO MANY COUNTIES TO LIST
HAD ZERO VALUES FOR THIS MEASURE

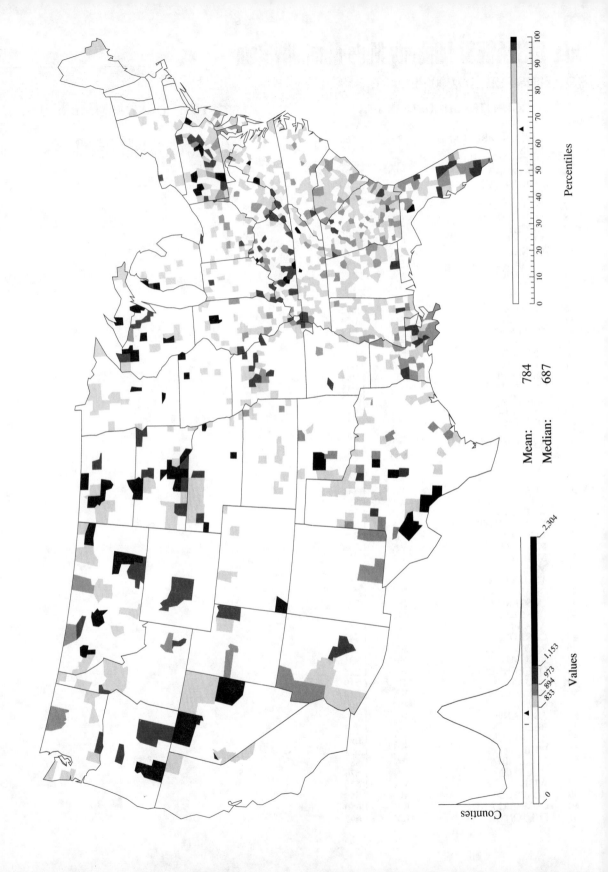

Mean: 784

Median: 687

Percentiles

0 10 20 30 40 50 60 70 80 90 100

Values

2,304

1,153

973

894

833

0

Counties

(DEATHS PER 100,000 PEOPLE)

TOP COUNTIES SHADED BLACK

RANK	COUNTY	STATE	VALUE
1	ELK	PA	2,304
2	NORTHUMBERLAND	PA	1,935
3	SNYDER	PA	1,807
4	MELLETTE	SD	1,737
5	JUNEAU	WI	1,700
6	SOMERSET	PA	1,669
7	MOUNTRAIL	ND	1,637
8	TRIPP	SD	1,625
9	ASHLAND	WI	1,600
10	SIOUX	ND	1,597
11	BLAINE	OK	1,595
12	CHARLES MIX	SD	1,569
13	MILLE LACS	MN	1,561
14	KINNEY	TX	1,560
15	LEELANAU	MI	1,517
16	DEWEY	OK	1,510
17	BOTTINEAU	ND	1,494
18	BUFFALO	SD	1,470
19	MANISTEE	MI	1,468
20	CASCADE	MT	1,458
21	FLOYD	IA	1,424
22	LINCOLN	WI	1,421
23	NICOLLET	MN	1,416
24	BARAGA	MI	1,414
25	SUSSEX	NJ	1,396
26	THURSTON	NE	1,375
27	VAL VERDE	TX	1,363
28	CORSON	SD	1,351
29	CARROLL	KY	1,348
30	CUSTER	OK	1,340
31	GRAINGER	TN	1,332
32	MENOMINEE	MI	1,326
33	BUTLER	KY	1,314
34	MC LEAN	ND	1,313
35	WHITE PINE	NV	1,307
36	LAFAYETTE	FL	1,305
37	GREENE	VA	1,280
38	ROSEBUD	MT	1,280
39	LA SALLE	IL	1,278
40	ALLAMAKEE	IA	1,269
41	COLEMAN	TX	1,234
42	ADAMS	NE	1,229
43	VENANGO	PA	1,227
44	STOREY	NV	1,218
45	PECOS	TX	1,214
46	MONTOUR	PA	1,200
47	LYMAN	SD	1,193
48	BATH	VA	1,190
49	SCOTTS BLUFF	NE	1,179
50	SAWYER	WI	1,177
51	CLARION	PA	1,176
52	STEPHENS	TX	1,174
53	TROUSDALE	TN	1,171
54	ROOSEVELT	MT	1,170
55	LAKE	MT	1,167
56	MONROE	KY	1,163
57	HUMBOLDT	NV	1,163
58	KLAMATH	OR	1,160
59	MONTEZUMA	CO	1,158
60	HUGHES	SD	1,153

BOTTOM COUNTIES SHADED WHITE

NOTE: TOO MANY COUNTIES TO LIST
HAD ZERO VALUES FOR THIS MEASURE

blue-collar jobs—including: automation, understaffing, overwork, and lack of control over job-related tasks.[35] In addition to stressful jobs, of course, unemployment and poverty are also major sources of stress.

Diet may also play a role in elevating heart disease in rural southern communities, but it is difficult to document this with available data. As a percent of individual food consumption, six high-fat and high-cholesterol food groups (red meat, eggs, fats and oils, cheese, ice cream, and butter) constitute a slightly higher portion of the southern diet than that of any other region, but the share in rural southern diets is lower than in the South as a whole. Moreover, people in the north central parts of the country actually eat more pounds per person of these foods than do southerners, especially in rural areas.[36]

While heart disease continues to fall rapidly among white males, the decline is slowing down among blacks and white females.[37] This divergence parallels trends in smoking, which is declining much more slowly among blacks than whites, and more slowly among women than men. Moreover, the declines in smoking are limited primarily to people with higher incomes and education.[38] Many more counties with high rates for women are found in the industrial Midwest than for men, paralleling differences in smoking rates (discussed in chapter 2). Smoking among blacks is also higher in the Midwest, where minority mortality from lung cancers is also highest, yet minority mortality from heart disease remains highest in the Southeast.[39] This discrepancy suggests that factors other than smoking are responsible for the high rates of heart disease mortality among minorities in the South.

African Americans have higher rates of heart disease than any other racial group in the country; Asian and native Americans, in contrast, have lower rates than whites.[40] Less well known is that prior to World War II, blacks had lower rates of heart disease than whites.[41] High rates of minority heart disease are much more concentrated in the Southeast than are minority rates of mortality from all diseases, because of the large proportion of blacks in the South. African Americans have higher levels of diabetes, cholesterol, and hypertension than whites, all of which are associated with increased risk of heart disease. Among black men with low socioeconomic status—those with the least stable working and living conditions—heart disease occurs at double the rate of that for black men who are better off.[42] Hypertension among black women is significantly higher in the Southeast than in any other region of the country, and more frequently goes uncontrolled. Black men and women with hypertension are also more likely to be obese in the Southeast than elsewhere. Only white males with hypertension in the Southeast, on the other hand, are more likely to smoke than their counterparts elsewhere in the United States.[43]

As wealthier people give up behaviors conducive to heart disease, tobacco companies and junk food producers target their advertising on poor and minority communities.[44] Significant increases in the geographic inequalities of heart disease among young adults mean future disparities will be even greater as these people age.[45] These trends lead one expert to conclude that heart disease "has become a disease of the poor within rich societies."[46]

INFANT DISEASES

From all appearances, Patricia Brown and her husband lived in an average suburban neighborhood when their daughter, Michelle, was born. Mrs. Brown had two miscarriages before carrying Michelle to term. By her first birthday, Michelle developed a tumor on her knee. As Michelle grew, so did the tumor. Exploratory surgery disclosed a rare mass of small tumors within the large one. Doctors sent the tumor to various hospitals in the United States and even in the Soviet Union, but none of the doctors could diagnose it.[47] Unbeknown to the Browns, 21,000 tons of toxic chemicals lay buried beneath the ground just behind their home.[48] They lived within the inner rings of Love Canal, New York.

More than a decade after the Browns were evacuated from Love Canal in 1978, along with a thousand other families, controversy still rages over the true health effects of the toxic dump. Both the New York Department of Health and independent scientists have found increased incidences of miscarriages and low-birthweight babies in the Love Canal area.[49] But the federal government now says it is safe to move back in, and many families are taking advantage of the low housing costs.[50] One permanent legacy of Love Canal is the Superfund law for cleaning up toxic dumps considered a risk to human health. At the top of the Superfund National Priorities List is the Lipari Landfill in Gloucester County, New Jersey, now that the state health department has also found significantly high rates of low-birthweight babies in communities surrounding the dump.[51] California's health department has even found significantly high rates of miscarriages and low-birthweight babies in Silicon Valley.[52] The solvents that clean computer chips have leaked into the water supplies of the surrounding communities and are suspected of endangering women workers of childbearing age, and increasing significantly the risk of low-birthweight babies.[53]

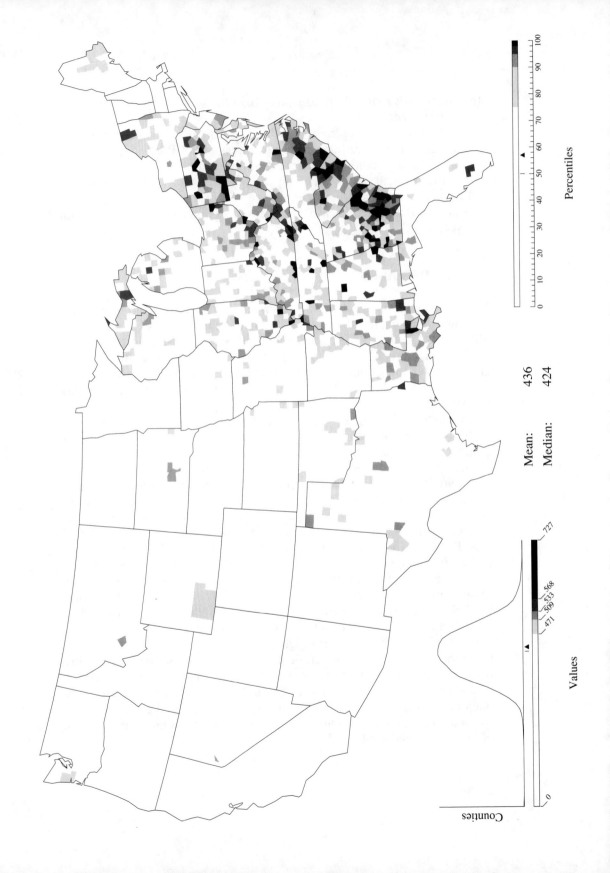

Mean: 436

Median: 424

Percentiles

Values

Counties

(DEATHS PER 100,000 PEOPLE)

TOP COUNTIES SHADED BLACK					BOTTOM COUNTIES SHADED WHITE			
RANK	COUNTY	STATE	VALUE		RANK	COUNTY	STATE	VALUE
1	CALHOUN	GA	727		1	YELLOWSTONE NAT. PARK	MT	199
2	ATKINSON	GA	666		2	SUMMIT	CO	213
3	WINSTON	AL	661		3	BORDEN	TX	228
4	CARROLL	KY	652		4	MORA	NM	237
5	BRANTLEY	GA	639		5	BANNER	NE	237
6	RUSSELL	AL	638		6	KENEDY	TX	239
7	JENKINS	GA	635		7	STARR	TX	246
8	LONG	GA	634		8	WHEELER	OR	250
9	CLAY	GA	634		9	TORRANCE	NM	253
10	TELFAIR	GA	633		10	COSTILLA	CO	257
11	FULTON	KY	626		11	GOLDEN VALLEY	MT	258
12	BURKE	GA	625		12	CATRON	NM	262
13	SCREVEN	GA	618		13	SCOTT	KS	262
14	NORTHUMBERLAND	PA	615		14	SANTA FE	NM	264
15	MINGO	WV	609		15	SAN JUAN	UT	264
16	UNION	SC	607		16	LOS ALAMOS	NM	267
17	BACON	GA	605		17	JUDITH BASIN	MT	271
18	SOMERSET	PA	604		18	SANDOVAL	NM	271
19	TURNER	GA	604		19	JEFF DAVIS	TX	272
20	GALLATIN	KY	603		20	SAN JUAN	WA	274
21	FLORENCE	SC	598		21	SAN MIGUEL	NM	274
22	EMANUEL	GA	598		22	UNION	NM	277
23	BEN HILL	GA	598		23	SULLY	SD	277
24	BELL	KY	596		24	COLFAX	NE	277
25	JEFF DAVIS	GA	595		25	GARFIELD	CO	278
26	SCOTLAND	NC	593		26	PRESIDIO	TX	279
27	MARION	GA	592		27	TAOS	NM	282
28	WHEELER	GA	592		28	GARFIELD	MT	282
29	CUMBERLAND	KY	589		29	MADISON	MT	283
30	MASON	KY	589		30	JACKSON	MN	283
31	CANNON	TN	587		31	GLASSCOCK	TX	283
32	MONROE	KY	585		32	WHEELER	NE	285
33	COCKE	TN	585		33	SEARCY	AR	286
34	SEMINOLE	GA	584		34	DECATUR	KS	287
35	NANTUCKET	MA	583		35	IRION	TX	287
36	TANGIPAHOA	LA	583		36	GRANT	NM	287
37	BRUNSWICK	VA	582		37	SAN MIGUEL	CO	287
38	MARLBORO	SC	582		38	JAMES CITY	VA	287
39	COFFEE	GA	581		39	KANDIYOHI	MN	288
40	LEE	VA	579		40	SAN JUAN	NM	289
41	GEORGETOWN	SC	579		41	OLMSTED	MN	289
42	JOHNSTON	NC	579		42	KEARNEY	NE	289
43	ALLEN	KY	578		43	ELBERT	CO	289
44	JASPER	SC	577		44	DEUEL	NE	289
45	WAYNE	GA	577		45	CARTER	MT	290
46	TAYLOR	GA	576		46	PITKIN	CO	291
47	MEIGS	OH	575		47	ROCK	MN	292
48	SALINE	IL	574		48	LAKE	SD	293
49	DARLINGTON	SC	574		49	GOSPER	NE	293
50	WEBSTER	GA	574		50	MARION	KS	293
51	FAYETTE	PA	574		51	NAPA	CA	295
52	COLUMBUS	NC	572		52	MINERAL	MT	296
53	DOOLY	GA	572		53	AUDUBON	IA	297
54	ALEXANDER	IL	572		54	CLARK	ID	297
55	COLUMBIANA	OH	570		55	EMMONS	ND	298
56	GREENE	PA	570		56	WEBB	TX	298
57	BENTON	TN	569		57	TRAVERSE	MN	298
58	VENANGO	PA	568		58	SAGUACHE	CO	298
59	CLINTON	PA	568		59	ZAPATA	TX	298
60	MARION	TN	568		60	THOMAS	KS	299
					61	NOBLES	MN	300

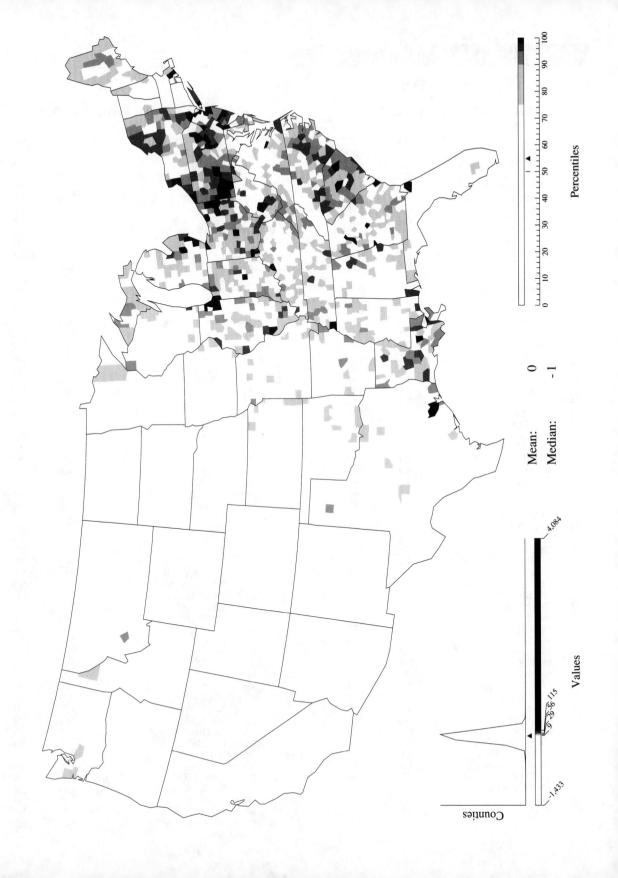

(DEATHS PER 100,000 PEOPLE)

	TOP COUNTIES SHADED BLACK					BOTTOM COUNTIES SHADED WHITE		
RANK	COUNTY	STATE	VALUE		RANK	COUNTY	STATE	VALUE
1	COOK	IL	4,084		1	DADE	FL	-1,433
2	NEW YORK CITY	NY	2,030		2	BROWARD	FL	-1,181
3	WAYNE	MI	1,106		3	PINELLAS	FL	-1,085
4	ALLEGHENY	PA	1,102		4	SAN DIEGO	CA	-1,075
5	ERIE	NY	696		5	MARICOPA	AZ	-968
6	HUDSON	NJ	650		6	ORANGE	CA	-839
7	BALTIMORE CITY	MD	580		7	PALM BEACH	FL	-659
8	ST LOUIS CITY	MO	572		8	SANTA CLARA	CA	-658
9	CUYAHOGA	OH	555		9	KING	WA	-591
10	ORLEANS	LA	495		10	HENNEPIN	MN	-556
11	LUZERNE	PA	377		11	SAN MATEO	CA	-447
12	ESSEX	NJ	353		12	MIDDLESEX	MA	-438
13	LACKAWANNA	PA	334		13	SAN FRANCISCO	CA	-422
14	LUCAS	OH	329		14	LOS ANGELES	CA	-418
15	SHELBY	TN	322		15	HARTFORD	CT	-412
16	JEFFERSON	KY	299		16	RIVERSIDE	CA	-386
17	LAKE	IN	291		17	PIMA	AZ	-373
18	CAMDEN	NJ	289		18	ALAMEDA	CA	-371
19	HAMILTON	OH	256		19	SARASOTA	FL	-370
20	FAYETTE	PA	256		20	CONTRA COSTA	CA	-351
21	ST CLAIR	IL	247		21	BERNALILLO	NM	-348
22	ATLANTIC	NJ	237		22	MANATEE	FL	-343
23	NASSAU	NY	237		23	DENVER	CO	-335
24	MAHONING	OH	221		24	MONTGOMERY	MD	-318
25	SCHUYLKILL	PA	205		25	NORFOLK	MA	-313
26	ERIE	PA	203		26	FAIRFIELD	CT	-300
27	WESTMORELAND	PA	202		27	SAN BERNARDINO	CA	-293
28	DELAWARE	PA	190		28	MONROE	NY	-288
29	FULTON	GA	187		29	SALT LAKE	UT	-280
30	MARION	IN	179		30	WESTCHESTER	NY	-274
31	KANAWHA	WV	175		31	LEE	FL	-270
32	FRANKLIN	OH	170		32	PASCO	FL	-259
33	WASHINGTON	PA	166		33	VENTURA	CA	-252
34	BIBB	GA	166		34	FAIRFAX	VA	-245
35	COLUMBIANA	OH	154		35	FRESNO	CA	-239
36	BLAIR	PA	152		36	BEXAR	TX	-236
37	MACOMB	MI	152		37	HILLSBOROUGH	FL	-228
38	GENESEE	MI	148		38	EL PASO	TX	-224
39	FLORENCE	SC	148		39	HIDALGO	TX	-213
40	CAMBRIA	PA	146		40	SANTA BARBARA	CA	-209
41	STARK	OH	144		41	SONOMA	CA	-204
42	PASSAIC	NJ	144		42	JACKSON	MO	-193
43	HENRICO	VA	143		43	RAMSEY	MN	-191
44	NORTHUMBERLAND	PA	141		44	ST LOUIS	MO	-191
45	CHATHAM	GA	139		45	MARIN	CA	-178
46	MIDDLESEX	NJ	138		46	ORANGE	FL	-173
47	TRUMBULL	OH	137		47	MONTEREY	CA	-169
48	BRISTOL	MA	136		48	TRAVIS	TX	-168
49	RICHLAND	SC	135		49	VOLUSIA	FL	-167
50	EAST BATON ROUGE	LA	134		50	JEFFERSON	AL	-162
51	MUSCOGEE	GA	130		51	CAMERON	TX	-156
52	DAUPHIN	PA	125		52	SANTA CRUZ	CA	-156
53	NORTHAMPTON	PA	124		53	SAN JOAQUIN	CA	-155
54	DUVAL	FL	124		54	NAPA	CA	-149
55	BEAVER	PA	123		55	JOHNSON	KS	-148
56	WILL	IL	122		56	LANE	OR	-144
57	ORANGE	NY	122		57	WASHINGTON	OR	-143
58	NEW CASTLE	DE	121		58	POLK	FL	-142
59	KENTON	KY	120		59	DANE	WI	-140
60	MONMOUTH	NJ	117		60	MULTNOMAH	OR	-138
61	HARRIS	TX	115		61	SACRAMENTO	CA	-134
					62	BARNSTABLE	MA	-133

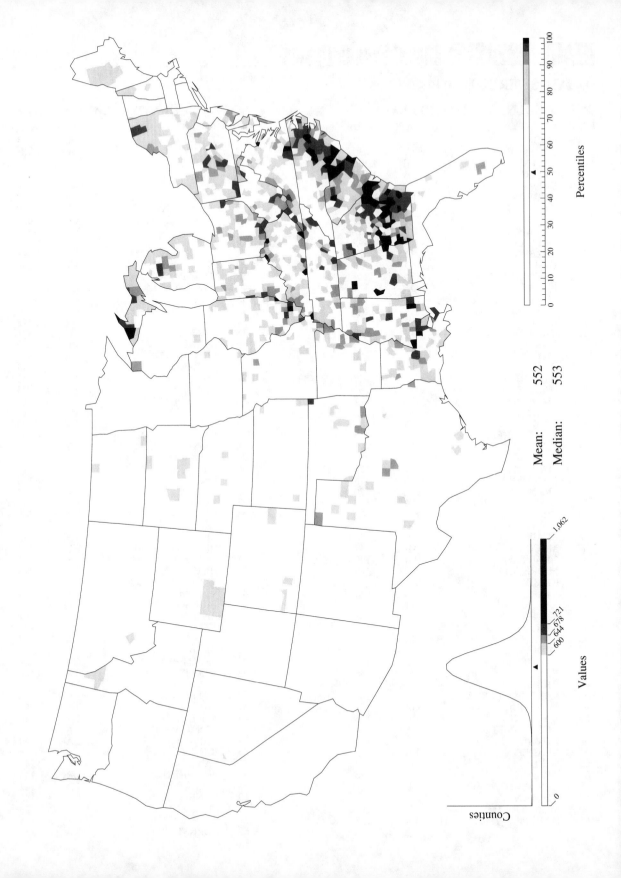

Mean: 552

Median: 553

Percentiles

Counties

Values

(DEATHS PER 100,000 PEOPLE)

TOP COUNTIES SHADED BLACK

RANK	COUNTY	STATE	VALUE
1	CALHOUN	GA	1,062
2	CHATTAHOOCHEE	GA	1,013
3	BRANTLEY	GA	948
4	TELFAIR	GA	878
5	ATKINSON	GA	858
6	CLAY	GA	857
7	FULTON	KY	843
8	LONG	GA	831
9	BURKE	GA	810
10	EMANUEL	GA	798
11	JASPER	SC	798
12	RUSSELL	AL	794
13	GEORGETOWN	SC	794
14	UNION	SC	789
15	NANTUCKET	MA	788
16	WEBSTER	GA	785
17	JEFF DAVIS	GA	779
18	JENKINS	GA	776
19	SCREVEN	GA	776
20	SEMINOLE	GA	774
21	SCOTLAND	NC	773
22	WABASH	IL	769
23	WHEELER	GA	767
24	CRISP	GA	767
25	GALLATIN	KY	766
26	ROBESON	NC	761
27	ST HELENA	LA	759
28	JOHNSTON	NC	757
29	MARLBORO	SC	757
30	BEN HILL	GA	757
31	GREENE	AL	754
32	CHESTERFIELD	SC	754
33	FLORENCE	SC	751
34	WINSTON	AL	751
35	DARLINGTON	SC	749
36	ALLENDALE	SC	746
37	BACON	GA	745
38	BELL	KY	742
39	ALLEN	KY	741
40	TOOMBS	GA	740
41	KING GEORGE	VA	738
42	KEWEENAW	MI	737
43	DODGE	GA	736
44	MASON	KY	735
45	PERRY	MS	735
46	HARNETT	NC	735
47	TAYLOR	GA	735
48	EARLY	GA	734
49	STEWART	GA	732
50	GREENE	NC	732
51	HAMPTON	SC	731
52	PITT	NC	730
53	DOOLY	GA	730
54	BRUNSWICK	VA	730
55	ONTONAGON	MI	729
56	WILKINSON	MS	727
57	COLUMBUS	NC	727
58	SALINE	IL	725
59	TURNER	GA	725
60	MARION	GA	724
61	APPLING	GA	721

BOTTOM COUNTIES SHADED WHITE

RANK	COUNTY	STATE	VALUE
1	BORDEN	TX	263
2	SUMMIT	CO	270
3	MORA	NM	317
4	SAN JUAN	UT	318
5	CATRON	NM	320
6	CROCKETT	TX	331
7	SANTA FE	NM	333
8	TERRELL	TX	335
9	SAN MIGUEL	NM	342
10	JEFF DAVIS	TX	344
11	STARR	TX	348
12	JAMES CITY	VA	352
13	WHEELER	OR	355
14	RIO ARRIBA	NM	358
15	SANDOVAL	NM	360
16	CUSTER	CO	364
17	TORRANCE	NM	366
18	TAOS	NM	368
19	WHEELER	NE	369
20	MELLETTE	SD	372
21	COLLIER	FL	374
22	NAPA	CA	374
23	GUADALUPE	NM	376
24	GRANT	NM	378
25	KENEDY	TX	379
26	SAN JUAN	WA	379
27	COSTILLA	CO	379
28	ARTHUR	NE	380
29	HARDING	NM	382
30	SAN JUAN	NM	382
31	BURNET	TX	384
32	COLFAX	NM	386
33	GLADES	FL	387
34	GARFIELD	CO	387
35	UNION	NM	388
36	PITKIN	CO	390
37	UVALDE	TX	390
38	SCOTT	KS	392
39	APACHE	AZ	392
40	SAN JACINTO	TX	393
41	BERNALILLO	NM	394
42	WABAUNSEE	KS	394
43	NEWTON	TX	396
44	CARTER	MT	397
45	HIDALGO	TX	398
46	LOS ALAMOS	NM	398
47	CLEARWATER	ID	398
48	LINCOLN	ID	401
49	PRESIDIO	TX	402
50	STONEWALL	TX	402
51	CLARK	ID	402
52	PONDERA	MT	402
53	MARION	KS	402
54	SAN MIGUEL	CO	403
55	GRAND	UT	403
56	OLMSTED	MN	403
57	GOLDEN VALLEY	MT	404
58	MERCER	ND	405
59	CAMERON	TX	406
60	WASHINGTON	UT	407
61	BENT	CO	407
62	DIMMIT	TX	408

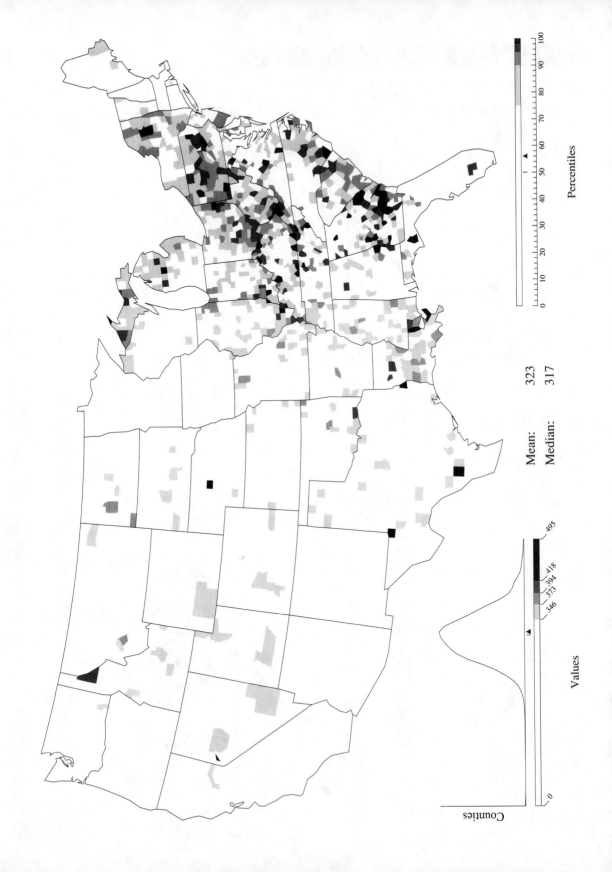

Mean: 323
Median: 317

Percentiles

Values

Counties

(DEATHS PER 100,000 PEOPLE)

TOP COUNTIES SHADED BLACK

RANK	COUNTY	STATE	VALUE
1	KEWEENAW	MI	495
2	ATKINSON	GA	485
3	JENKINS	GA	485
4	MARION	GA	484
5	MINGO	WV	477
6	GALLATIN	KY	474
7	RUSSELL	AL	471
8	LONG	GA	467
9	TALBOT	GA	466
10	HANCOCK	TN	463
11	BUCHANAN	VA	458
12	SCREVEN	GA	453
13	STOREY	NV	452
14	HARDIN	IL	452
15	LIBERTY	FL	452
16	THOMAS	NE	451
17	COCKE	TN	451
18	SCHLEY	GA	449
19	CALHOUN	GA	448
20	LA SALLE	TX	447
21	MONROE	KY	447
22	BACON	GA	446
23	BRACKEN	KY	446
24	WABASH	IL	445
25	JEFF DAVIS	GA	444
26	CARROLL	KY	444
27	SCHUYLKILL	PA	442
28	BURKE	GA	441
29	WAYNE	GA	438
30	WINKLER	TX	438
31	BRUNSWICK	VA	437
32	TURNER	GA	435
33	BUCKINGHAM	VA	431
34	QUITMAN	GA	430
35	HAMILTON	NY	430
36	LIBERTY	GA	430
37	COFFEE	GA	429
38	COLUMBIANA	OH	428
39	DAWSON	GA	426
40	SABINE	TX	426
41	APPLING	GA	425
42	WHEELER	GA	425
43	MASON	KY	425
44	MC CREARY	KY	425
45	FAYETTE	PA	424
46	TALIAFERRO	GA	423
47	BRECKINRIDGE	KY	423
48	COLUMBUS	NC	422
49	VENANGO	PA	422
50	SALINE	IL	422
51	CLARE	MI	422
52	JEFFERSON	WV	421
53	ALLEN	KY	421
54	JACKSON	TN	421
55	TANGIPAHOA	LA	420
56	ST BERNARD	LA	420
57	ROBERTSON	KY	420
58	LACKAWANNA	PA	419
59	MC DOWELL	WV	418
60	PIKE	IN	418
61	BELL	KY	418

BOTTOM COUNTIES SHADED WHITE

RANK	COUNTY	STATE	VALUE
1	BANNER	NE	108
2	TODD	SD	127
3	GARFIELD	MT	145
4	SULLY	SD	179
5	MC PHERSON	NE	185
6	SIOUX	ND	185
7	BLAINE	NE	189
8	GOLDEN VALLEY	MT	191
9	OLMSTED	MN	196
10	JAMES CITY	VA	197
11	KENT	TX	200
12	GADSDEN	FL	202
13	GLASSCOCK	TX	203
14	LOGAN	NE	209
15	SCOTT	KS	211
16	ROCK	MN	212
17	JUDITH BASIN	MT	213
18	COSTILLA	CO	213
19	NEWTON	TX	213
20	BALDWIN	GA	213
21	ELBERT	CO	214
22	KEITH	NE	216
23	SHERIDAN	NE	217
24	LOS ALAMOS	NM	217
25	DOLORES	CO	217
26	TORRANCE	NM	217
27	LAKE	SD	217
28	STARR	TX	217
29	FERRY	WA	218
30	SUMMIT	CO	218
31	SANDOVAL	NM	218
32	MEADE	KS	219
33	WHEELER	OR	220
34	COLLIER	FL	220
35	CORSON	SD	220
36	HARVEY	KS	221
37	HARTLEY	TX	222
38	PIERCE	ND	222
39	DECATUR	KS	222
40	SIBLEY	MN	222
41	MINERAL	CO	223
42	KANDIYOHI	MN	226
43	NORTON	KS	226
44	MORA	NM	227
45	ISSAQUENA	MS	227
46	GOLDEN VALLEY	ND	228
47	GRANITE	MT	228
48	ADAIR	IA	229
49	SAN JUAN	NM	229
50	MANATEE	FL	229
51	ROCKWALL	TX	229
52	COLFAX	NE	230
53	GUADALUPE	TX	230
54	AUDUBON	IA	231
55	NICOLLET	MN	232
56	DEUEL	NE	232
57	SANTA FE	NM	232
58	NOBLES	MN	233
59	DADE	MO	233
60	LEE	FL	234
61	TREASURE	MT	234
62	GRANT	NM	234

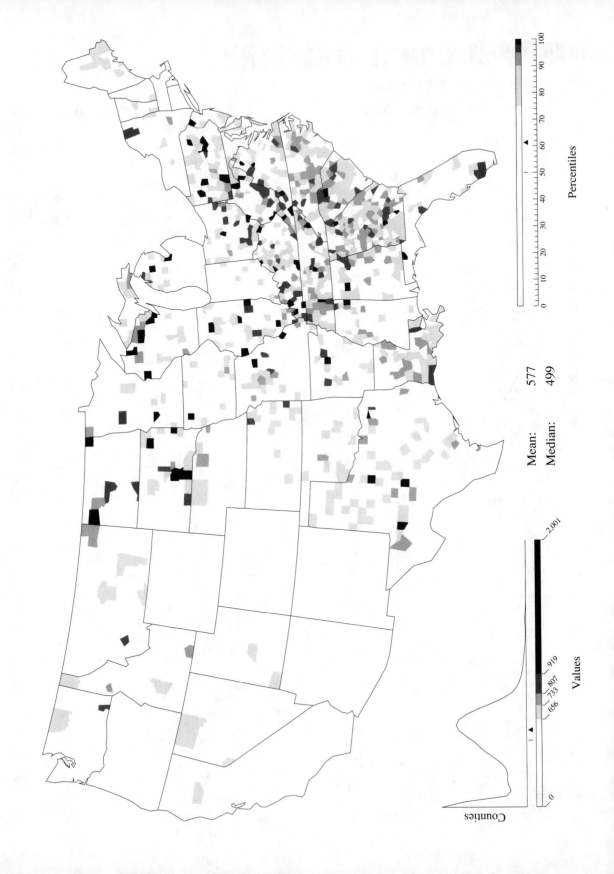

Mean: 577

Median: 499

Percentiles

Values

Counties

(DEATHS PER 100,000 PEOPLE)

TOP COUNTIES SHADED BLACK

RANK	COUNTY	STATE	VALUE
1	WINSTON	AL	2,001
2	CLEBURNE	AR	1,826
3	SOMERSET	PA	1,513
4	ONEIDA	WI	1,469
5	NORTHUMBERLAND	PA	1,435
6	JEFFERSON	PA	1,410
7	CARROLL	KY	1,372
8	POLK	WI	1,327
9	CANNON	TN	1,266
10	PRESTON	WV	1,264
11	OCONTO	WI	1,235
12	EDGAR	IL	1,229
13	MOODY	SD	1,204
14	FRANKLIN	GA	1,192
15	O BRIEN	IA	1,168
16	MORROW	OH	1,168
17	CHIPPEWA	MN	1,165
18	WYOMING	PA	1,151
19	TRIPP	SD	1,141
20	BAY	MI	1,125
21	PEMBINA	ND	1,119
22	LYMAN	SD	1,118
23	PULASKI	VA	1,116
24	CRITTENDEN	KY	1,105
25	VENANGO	PA	1,105
26	HOLMES	FL	1,092
27	GRANT	WV	1,081
28	CRANE	TX	1,077
29	SUSSEX	NJ	1,076
30	SCHUYLKILL	PA	1,076
31	GREENUP	KY	1,073
32	ASHLAND	WI	1,044
33	DICKENSON	VA	1,041
34	PERRY	IL	1,035
35	CUMBERLAND	KY	1,030
36	DAY	SD	1,023
37	BULLITT	KY	1,021
38	CONCHO	TX	1,017
39	MEIGS	OH	1,015
40	DE WITT	IL	1,013
41	CRAWFORD	MI	1,010
42	WARREN	VA	1,009
43	MONROE	MO	996
44	MONROE	KY	979
45	LEE	IL	976
46	TURNER	GA	973
47	LANIER	GA	965
48	WASHINGTON	VA	963
49	WILLIAMS	ND	958
50	HASKELL	TX	957
51	GREENE	VA	953
52	COCKE	TN	951
53	MC CRACKEN	KY	951
54	ADAMS	IL	950
55	STE GENEVIEVE	MO	943
56	MINGO	WV	938
57	DECATUR	TN	929
58	ITAWAMBA	MS	928
59	DELTA	TX	923
60	CHESTER	SC	920
61	CALLOWAY	KY	919

BOTTOM COUNTIES SHADED WHITE

NOTE: TOO MANY COUNTIES TO LIST
HAD ZERO VALUES FOR THIS MEASURE

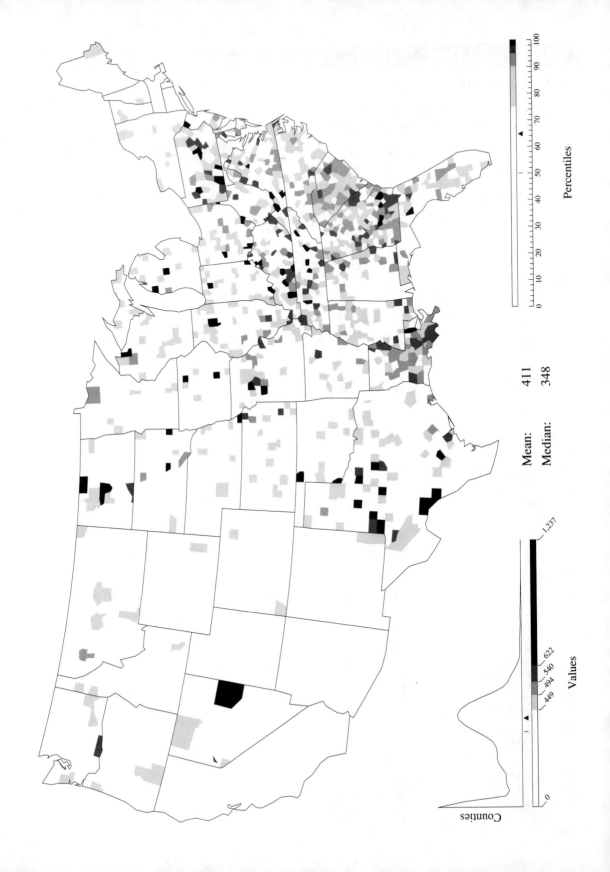

Mean: 411

Median: 348

Percentiles

0 10 20 30 40 50 60 70 80 90 100

Values

Counties

0   449 494 540 622   1,237

(DEATHS PER 100,000 PEOPLE)

TOP COUNTIES SHADED BLACK

RANK	COUNTY	STATE	VALUE
1	SOMERSET	PA	1,237
2	CARROLL	VA	1,096
3	BOTTINEAU	ND	1,026
4	CARROLL	KY	1,015
5	GRAINGER	TN	979
6	MANISTEE	MI	973
7	HARPER	OK	957
8	CLARION	PA	938
9	BENTON	TN	915
10	MAHASKA	IA	908
11	ASHLAND	WI	878
12	KINNEY	TX	861
13	LAFAYETTE	FL	851
14	RICHARDSON	NE	851
15	NORTHUMBERLAND	PA	827
16	FLOYD	IA	815
17	HARMON	OK	797
18	VAL VERDE	TX	791
19	MEIGS	OH	777
20	WHITE	TN	766
21	BUFFALO	SD	757
22	BUTLER	KY	755
23	FULTON	PA	754
24	SNYDER	PA	745
25	WILSON	TX	739
26	LA SALLE	IL	725
27	MONTOUR	PA	706
28	STEPHENS	TX	703
29	GREENE	VA	696
30	MC LEAN	ND	690
31	BROOKE	WV	683
32	ISABELLA	MI	674
33	TAZEWELL	VA	666
34	MONROE	KY	666
35	SPENCER	IN	662
36	GILES	VA	661
37	IRWIN	GA	658
38	CANNON	TN	658
39	MARSHALL	IN	658
40	CARROLL	MO	654
41	MOODY	SD	654
42	DEARBORN	IN	653
43	DAWSON	TX	651
44	SHELBY	OH	649
45	TANGIPAHOA	LA	647
46	BACON	GA	638
47	ANDREWS	TX	637
48	BROWN	OH	637
49	NOLAN	TX	637
50	KNOX	TX	637
51	HENRY	KY	633
52	CHRISTIAN	KY	632
53	SUSSEX	NJ	632
54	TURNER	GA	631
55	WAYNE	GA	629
56	WHITE PINE	NV	629
57	HART	KY	628
58	JOHNSON	MO	626
59	ROANE	TN	624
60	CROSBY	TX	622

BOTTOM COUNTIES SHADED WHITE

NOTE: TOO MANY COUNTIES TO LIST
HAD ZERO VALUES FOR THIS MEASURE

After a ten-year decline, the incidence of low-birthweight babies is rising in the United States.[54] Low birthweight is the second leading cause of infant death, following birth defects. Improvements in infant mortality slowed considerably in the 1980s. Birth defects cause an ever-increasing share of these deaths, and the gaps between black and white, and between rich and poor, are widening.[55] The White House Task Force on Infant Mortality has called for half a billion dollars a year to address the problem.[56]

"When we're talking about changing infant mortality rates, we're not talking about a simple intervention program. There is no one magic bullet," says Dr. Godfrey Oakley of the Centers for Disease Control (CDC) in Atlanta.[57] The CDC attributes much of the rise in low birthweight to fewer women receiving prenatal care, and to the use of crack cocaine.[58] We also found that the percent of families headed by single mothers, families in poverty, and low education levels are most significantly associated with variations in mortality from infant diseases. But causes are not well understood.

Detailed interview data on maternal and pregnancy factors cannot explain two-thirds of the variation in birthweight, and factors listed on birth certificates (such as mother's age and education, and infant's sex and birth order) fail to account for 95 to 99 percent of the geographic variation.[59] Many times babies with low birthweights also have fatal birth defects, and according to some experts, the causes of two-thirds of such congenital malformations are also unknown.[60] Sometimes environmental factors may cause increases that are too localized to be picked up by the county maps. For example, the significant clusters that state health departments found near Love Canal, the Lipari Landfill, and Silicon Valley are not large enough to show up on the maps of infant disease mortality (though the maps highlight excess deaths from birth defects in two of the three locations and all three for high cancer rates).

In marked contrast to mortality from all diseases, many of the counties with the highest rates of infant mortality are west of the Mississippi. Some of this may be due to small county sizes and less stable rates. In fact, a number of the western counties highlighted for infant diseases drop out when we look specifically at birth defects (as discussed along with the set of maps following those of infant diseases). Comparing white and minority mortality from infant diseases, we see an even starker western bias for whites, whereas minority infant disease rates are particularly high in the South, especially throughout Mississippi and Alabama. High rates for both whites and minorities overlap in Texas, notably in the panhandle as is discussed in the next section.

Other researchers have found that clusters of counties with high rates of low-birthweight babies in the Rocky Mountain region and certain northern and midwestern counties suggest the strong influence of environmental factors such as altitude, mining of heavy metals (lead, uranium, silver), heavy manufacturing (steel, automobile, chemical), or pesticides, whereas clusters in the Appalachian regions of Tennessee and West Virginia may be due to mothers at high risk because of socio-economic or other intrinsic factors recorded on birth certificates.[61]

As with mortality from all diseases, the highest rates of mortality from infant diseases are not primarily in urban counties in the Northeast. To some extent this may result from neighborhoods with better rates canceling out neighborhoods with poorer rates within the same urban county. In New York City, for example, central Harlem's infant mortality rate is more than double the rate for Washington Heights.[62] Yet even for minorities, who have the poorest infant mortality rates in northeastern urban counties, the highest rates of mortality from infant disease are not in the Northeast. This may be due to a variety of factors in rural southern communities with large minority populations, including poverty, environmental problems, and poor access to medical care and health education, among others.

BIRTH DEFECTS

Eight-year-old Jeret Moore is one of over 500 plaintiffs suing a chemical plant in Pampa, Texas, which, according to company documents obtained by attorneys and state officials, has contaminated air and water in the area with benzene and other pollutants.[63] Benzene is suspected of causing birth defects and cancer. Jeret has Down's syndrome, a genetic defect caused by an extra chromosome. Five other Down's syndrome babies were born in Pampa from 1980 to 1985, a number that the Texas Department of health and the federal Centers for Disease Control say is "significantly more than expected" in a city of 20,000 people. Dr. Gerald H. Holman, a former dean at Texas Tech Medical School who treated four of the babies, reported that "in all medical probability, the number of Down's syndrome cases is related to environmental pollution from the Celanese site." After a 1987 accident at the Hoechst Celanese plant killed 3 workers and injured 37 others, federal investigators cited the facility for violating occupational safety regulations, as well as air pollution laws, and were told by plant managers that the facility had contaminated the region's principal drinking water source with benzene concentrations eight times the level that the federal government considers safe.

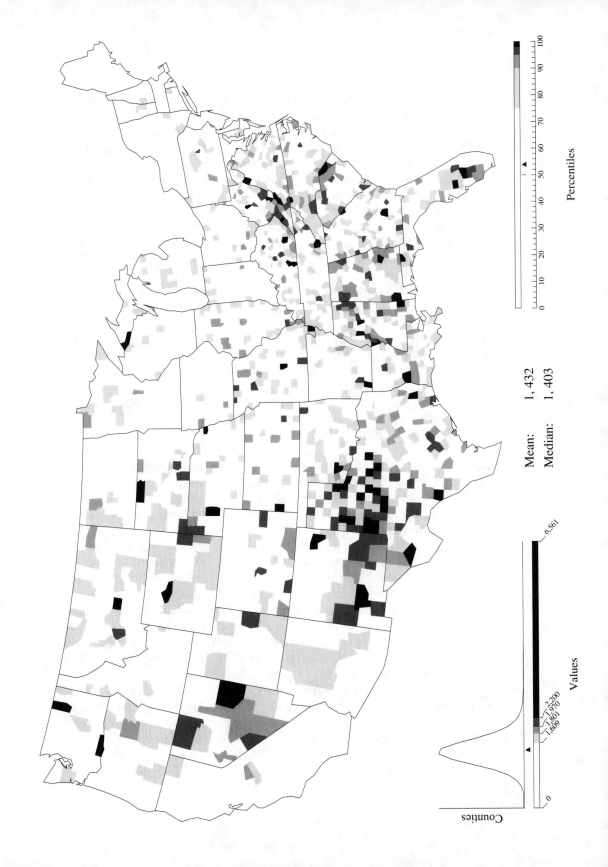

Mean: 1, 432
Median: 1, 403

Percentiles

Values

Counties

6,561

2,200
1,970
1,801
1,609

(DEATHS PER 100,000 LIVE BIRTHS)

TOP COUNTIES SHADED BLACK

RANK	COUNTY	STATE	VALUE
1	HARDING	NM	6,561
2	ISSAQUENA	MS	3,613
3	DICKENS	TX	3,361
4	STONEWALL	TX	3,334
5	FISHER	TX	3,175
6	MITCHELL	TX	3,058
7	CASTRO	TX	2,830
8	BLAND	VA	2,777
9	JEFF DAVIS	TX	2,756
10	VERNON	LA	2,746
11	GLADES	FL	2,726
12	LAMB	TX	2,662
13	HARDEE	FL	2,635
14	CUMBERLAND	KY	2,622
15	GAINES	TX	2,615
16	HAMILTON	KS	2,580
17	JACK	TX	2,577
18	SUMMERS	WV	2,539
19	CORSON	SD	2,528
20	GILES	VA	2,513
21	STEPHENS	TX	2,501
22	FERRY	WA	2,479
23	COLLINGSWORTH	TX	2,471
24	KINNEY	TX	2,457
25	LEFLORE	MS	2,449
26	LINCOLN	GA	2,379
27	HARDEMAN	TX	2,376
28	HOLMES	FL	2,364
29	COFFEE	GA	2,362
30	PULASKI	MO	2,353
31	WASHINGTON	AL	2,350
32	TYLER	TX	2,336
33	THROCKMORTON	TX	2,333
34	GOGEBIC	MI	2,323
35	CLAY	KY	2,316
36	PEMISCOT	MO	2,314
37	GARDEN	NE	2,298
38	HOWARD	TX	2,289
39	MARLBORO	SC	2,286
40	ALLEGHANY	NC	2,285
41	CALHOUN	WV	2,274
42	THURSTON	NE	2,272
43	KLICKITAT	WA	2,265
44	GREENE	MS	2,257
45	HOT SPRINGS	WY	2,257
46	DILLON	SC	2,257
47	WHITE PINE	NV	2,254
48	LAFAYETTE	AR	2,240
49	TERRY	TX	2,236
50	YOAKUM	TX	2,234
51	PENDLETON	WV	2,228
52	MONTGOMERY	MS	2,222
53	SIERRA	NM	2,217
54	DICKENSON	VA	2,216
55	WHEATLAND	MT	2,214
56	ADAIR	KY	2,214
57	KIOWA	OK	2,209
58	CHILDRESS	TX	2,208
59	BULLOCK	AL	2,201
60	MONROE	TN	2,200

BOTTOM COUNTIES SHADED WHITE

RANK	COUNTY	STATE	VALUE
1	KENT	TX	0
2	GREELEY	KS	124
3	JONES	SD	187
4	MOTLEY	TX	218
5	ELK	KS	287
6	CHASE	KS	335
7	HARDIN	IL	456
8	IZARD	AR	470
9	HANSON	SD	488
10	JOHNSON	NE	504
11	GOVE	KS	542
12	KIDDER	ND	560
13	FRANKLIN	NE	583
14	STEWART	TN	599
15	DOLORES	CO	601
16	PERKINS	SD	604
17	TRAILL	ND	619
18	MC HENRY	ND	634
19	JASPER	GA	656
20	CLAY	KS	658
21	CLARK	SD	661
22	SCHUYLER	MO	666
23	OSBORNE	KS	677
24	COTTON	OK	680
25	RUSH	KS	698
26	SALINE	NE	698
27	WAYNE	NE	698
28	HUMBOLDT	IA	698
29	DECATUR	KS	700
30	FILLMORE	NE	701
31	MERRICK	NE	701
32	CLEAR CREEK	CO	707
33	HARRISON	IA	715
34	RICHLAND	WI	719
35	WAYNE	UT	722
36	BALLARD	KY	731
37	ADAIR	IA	732
38	SEARCY	AR	736
39	PERQUIMANS	NC	761
40	GRANT	OK	764
41	FRANKLIN	ID	767
42	GARFIELD	WA	771
43	ELLSWORTH	KS	771
44	GOODING	ID	776
45	ANDREW	MO	776
46	WASHINGTON	IA	777
47	GUTHRIE	IA	784
48	WINNESHIEK	IA	786
49	WALWORTH	SD	787
50	FREMONT	ID	791
51	OWEN	IN	791
52	COLFAX	NE	792
53	NOBLE	OH	796
54	LYON	IA	796
55	KINGMAN	KS	797
56	POTTER	PA	798

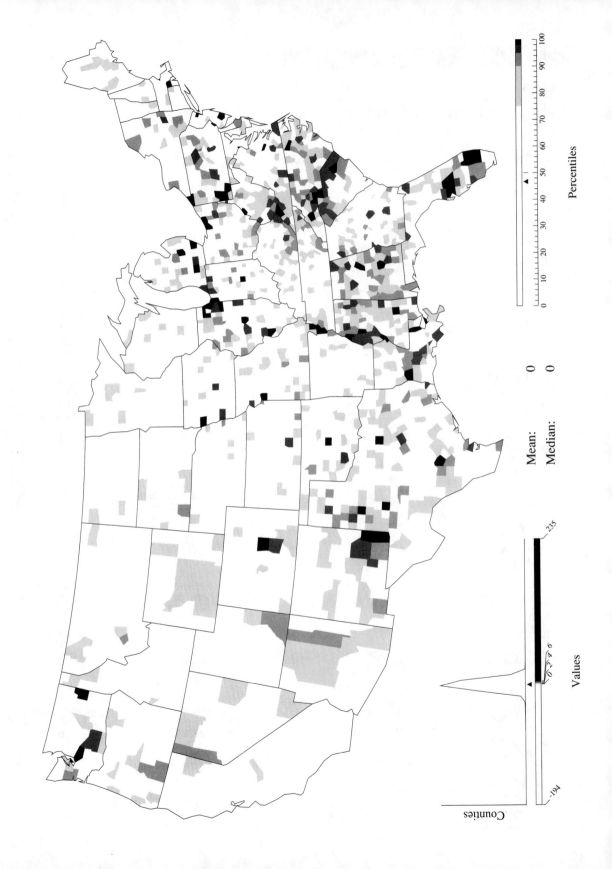

Mean: 0

Median: 0

Counties

−194   0 2 4 6   235

Values

Percentiles

0 10 20 30 40 50 60 70 80 90 100

TOP COUNTIES SHADED BLACK

RANK	COUNTY	STATE	VALUE
1	COOK	IL	235
2	PHILADELPHIA	PA	92
3	NEW YORK CITY	NY	76
4	WAYNE	MI	62
5	BALTIMORE CITY	MD	32
6	DISTRICT OF COLUMBIA	DC	29
7	ST LOUIS CITY	MO	28
8	ESSEX	NJ	22
9	LAKE	IN	21
10	TARRANT	TX	19
11	HUDSON	NJ	19
12	ERIE	PA	15
13	ALLEGHENY	PA	15
14	ORLEANS	LA	15
15	ST CLAIR	IL	14
16	HILLSBOROUGH	FL	13
17	BEXAR	TX	13
18	FLORENCE	SC	12
19	JACKSON	MO	11
20	POLK	FL	11
21	MARION	IN	11
22	CUYAHOGA	OH	11
23	LUBBOCK	TX	11
24	BROWARD	FL	11
25	LORAIN	OH	11
26	PROVIDENCE	RI	10
27	LEFLORE	MS	10
28	GENESEE	MI	10
29	CLEVELAND	NC	9
30	MONTGOMERY	AL	9
31	HENRICO	VA	9
32	PALM BEACH	FL	9
33	TANGIPAHOA	LA	9
34	COAHOMA	MS	9
35	OKLAHOMA	OK	8
36	FAYETTE	PA	8
37	MACON	IL	8
38	VERNON	LA	8
39	LEA	NM	8
40	WASHINGTON	PA	7
41	SPOKANE	WA	7
42	TALLADEGA	AL	7
43	WARREN	MS	7
44	ATLANTIC	NJ	7
45	YORK	SC	7
46	WOOD	WV	7
47	EL PASO	CO	7
48	KANE	IL	7
49	GASTON	NC	7
50	MC DOWELL	WV	6
51	JONES	MS	6
52	KANKAKEE	IL	6
53	HALIFAX	NC	6
54	BUCHANAN	VA	6
55	PIERCE	WA	6
56	MISSISSIPPI	AR	6
57	WOODBURY	IA	6
58	BUNCOMBE	NC	6
59	HOWARD	TX	6
60	SUFFOLK	MA	6
61	CALHOUN	MI	6

BOTTOM COUNTIES SHADED WHITE

RANK	COUNTY	STATE	VALUE
1	LOS ANGELES	CA	-194
2	SANTA CLARA	CA	-58
3	ORANGE	CA	-58
4	SAN DIEGO	CA	-55
5	ALAMEDA	CA	-52
6	SAN FRANCISCO	CA	-42
7	ST LOUIS	MO	-39
8	MIDDLESEX	MA	-38
9	SUFFOLK	NY	-36
10	SAN MATEO	CA	-35
11	MILWAUKEE	WI	-32
12	SACRAMENTO	CA	-30
13	SALT LAKE	UT	-29
14	CONTRA COSTA	CA	-28
15	BERGEN	NJ	-27
16	KING	WA	-26
17	HARRIS	TX	-25
18	FAIRFAX	VA	-23
19	HAMILTON	OH	-23
20	DADE	FL	-22
21	NASSAU	NY	-21
22	WESTCHESTER	NY	-21
23	TRAVIS	TX	-20
24	PIMA	AZ	-20
25	DU PAGE	IL	-19
26	BALTIMORE	MD	-19
27	DELAWARE	PA	-19
28	MONTGOMERY	MD	-19
29	DE KALB	GA	-18
30	BUCKS	PA	-15
31	VENTURA	CA	-15
32	FAIRFIELD	CT	-15
33	PRINCE GEORGES	MD	-13
34	UTAH	UT	-13
35	EAST BATON ROUGE	LA	-13
36	NORFOLK	MA	-13
37	SAN JOAQUIN	CA	-13
38	ANNE ARUNDEL	MD	-13
39	MONROE	NY	-12
40	JEFFERSON	CO	-12
41	MONTEREY	CA	-12
42	MORRIS	NJ	-12
43	PLYMOUTH	MA	-11
44	BURLINGTON	NJ	-11
45	DENVER	CO	-11
46	MONMOUTH	NJ	-10
47	UNION	NJ	-10
48	SANTA BARBARA	CA	-10
49	WAUKESHA	WI	-10
50	MIDDLESEX	NJ	-10
51	HENNEPIN	MN	-10
52	JEFFERSON	AL	-9
53	JEFFERSON	KY	-9
54	MARICOPA	AZ	-9
55	FRESNO	CA	-9
56	JOHNSON	KS	-9
57	RAMSEY	MN	-9
58	DANE	WI	-8
59	LANCASTER	NE	-8
60	SOLANO	CA	-8
61	SHELBY	TN	-8
62	KENT	MI	-8

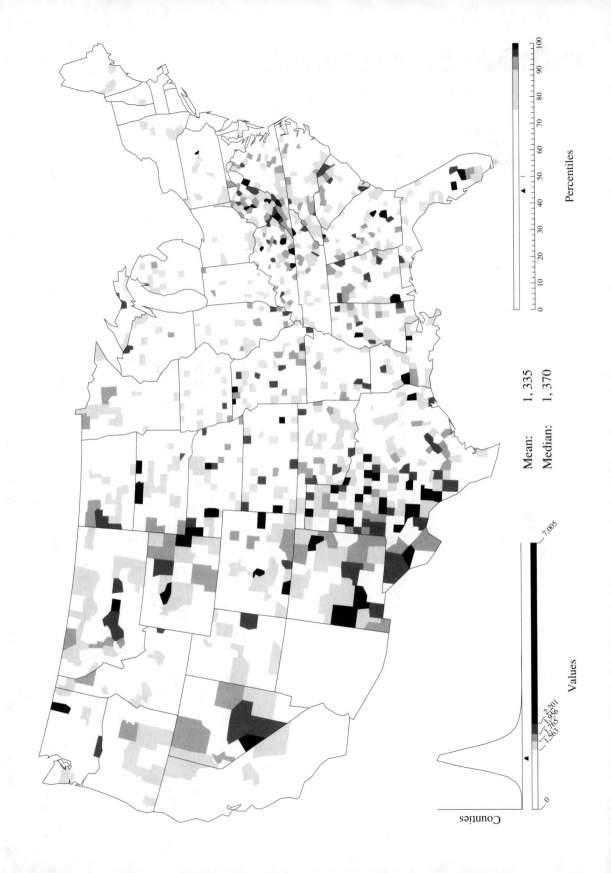

Mean: 1,335
Median: 1,370

Percentiles

Values

Counties

7,005

2,201
1,956
1,765
1,563

INFANT DISEASES: White Mortality Rate

(DEATHS PER 100,000 LIVE BIRTHS)

TOP COUNTIES SHADED BLACK

RANK	COUNTY	STATE	VALUE
1	HARDING	NM	7,005
2	STONEWALL	TX	3,812
3	JEFF DAVIS	TX	3,152
4	DICKENS	TX	2,962
5	HAMILTON	KS	2,950
6	CASTRO	TX	2,898
7	KINNEY	TX	2,810
8	BLAND	VA	2,717
9	THROCKMORTON	TX	2,669
10	VERNON	LA	2,637
11	GARDEN	NE	2,628
12	CALHOUN	WV	2,601
13	HARDEE	FL	2,561
14	GLADES	FL	2,559
15	CUMBERLAND	KY	2,540
16	SIERRA	NM	2,535
17	WHEATLAND	MT	2,532
18	CATRON	NM	2,503
19	SUMMERS	WV	2,482
20	MERCER	MO	2,479
21	HOT SPRINGS	WY	2,467
22	TOWNS	GA	2,454
23	FERRY	WA	2,428
24	CRANE	TX	2,425
25	PENDLETON	WV	2,423
26	SIOUX	NE	2,423
27	WORTH	MO	2,413
28	WHEELER	GA	2,413
29	TYLER	TX	2,412
30	NIOBRARA	WY	2,409
31	CHEYENNE	CO	2,408
32	ST HELENA	LA	2,407
33	CORSON	SD	2,389
34	LAMB	TX	2,382
35	COLLINGSWORTH	TX	2,379
36	SHACKELFORD	TX	2,368
37	MITCHELL	TX	2,367
38	CROCKETT	TX	2,362
39	SHERMAN	TX	2,359
40	NICHOLAS	KY	2,324
41	ESMERALDA	NV	2,315
42	LEFLORE	MS	2,308
43	ARCHULETA	CO	2,306
44	CHAFFEE	CO	2,305
45	WASHINGTON	AL	2,296
46	BUCHANAN	VA	2,284
47	MENARD	TX	2,282
48	WOODSON	KS	2,273
49	MONTOUR	PA	2,267
50	CLAY	WV	2,263
51	HARDEMAN	TX	2,259
52	HANCOCK	TN	2,255
53	COFFEE	GA	2,253
54	CLAY	KY	2,252
55	EDWARDS	TX	2,236
56	MC PHERSON	SD	2,233
57	JACK	TX	2,218
58	MC CREARY	KY	2,208
59	GARFIELD	NE	2,202
60	HOWARD	TX	2,201

BOTTOM COUNTIES SHADED WHITE

RANK	COUNTY	STATE	VALUE
1	KENT	TX	0
2	MOTLEY	TX	0
3	GREELEY	KS	141
4	SIOUX	ND	181
5	JONES	SD	213
6	WIBAUX	MT	244
7	ELK	KS	329
8	CHASE	KS	383
9	JASPER	GA	519
10	HARDIN	IL	521
11	WALWORTH	SD	533
12	IZARD	AR	537
13	LOWNDES	AL	540
14	JEFFERSON	MS	542
15	HANSON	SD	559
16	AMITE	MS	563
17	PERQUIMANS	NC	565
18	JOHNSON	NE	576
19	BACON	GA	597
20	GOVE	KS	620
21	KIDDER	ND	640
22	GRANT	OK	644
23	GREGORY	SD	662
24	FRANKLIN	NE	667
25	CUMBERLAND	VA	670
26	SEDGWICK	CO	672
27	STEWART	TN	685
28	TERRELL	GA	687
29	ROCKWALL	TX	689
30	PERKINS	SD	691
31	TRAILL	ND	708
32	PULASKI	GA	708
33	COTTON	OK	721
34	MC HENRY	ND	725
35	FAYETTE	GA	728
36	CLAY	KS	752
37	CLARK	SD	756
38	SCHUYLER	MO	762
39	LEE	GA	771
40	BALLARD	KY	773
41	WASHINGTON	IA	774
42	OSBORNE	KS	774
43	CHATTAHOOCHEE	GA	784
44	JEFFERSON	OR	793
45	JEFFERSON	GA	794
46	DICKINSON	IA	795
47	RUSH	KS	798
48	SALINE	NE	799
49	WAYNE	NE	799
50	HUMBOLDT	IA	799
51	DECATUR	KS	801
52	FILLMORE	NE	801
53	MERRICK	NE	801
54	CLEAR CREEK	CO	809
55	HARRISON	IA	817
56	SKAMANIA	WA	818

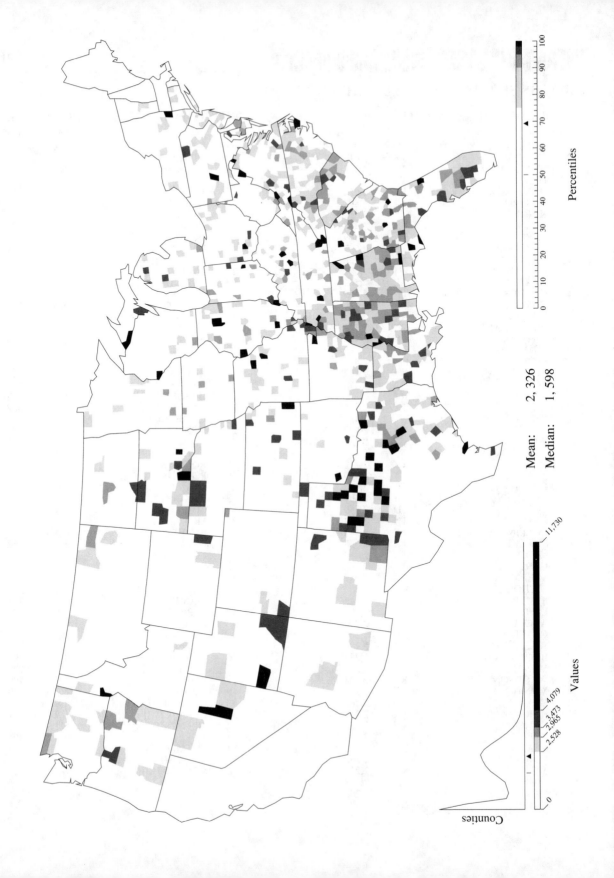

Mean: 2,326
Median: 1,598

Percentiles

Values

Counties

2,528
2,965
3,473
4,079
11,730

0

INFANT DISEASES: Minority Mortality Rate

(DEATHS PER 100,000 LIVE BIRTHS)

TOP COUNTIES SHADED BLACK

RANK	COUNTY	STATE	VALUE
1	FISHER	TX	11,730
2	MITCHELL	TX	7,872
3	GOGEBIC	MI	7,455
4	KNOX	TX	7,101
5	PIERCE	WI	6,807
6	TRIPP	SD	6,707
7	GREER	OK	6,485
8	DICKENS	TX	6,134
9	POSEY	IN	5,915
10	GRAYSON	VA	5,687
11	GILES	VA	5,556
12	COTTLE	TX	5,532
13	MONTGOMERY	MO	5,445
14	PERRY	TN	5,430
15	DONLEY	TX	5,322
16	LINCOLN	KY	5,295
17	HALL	TX	5,227
18	HARDY	WV	5,210
19	HYDE	NC	5,087
20	GREENE	AR	5,070
21	EUREKA	NV	5,070
22	JACK	TX	5,070
23	DAVISON	SD	5,028
24	FANNIN	TX	5,027
25	JONES	TX	4,990
26	PERRY	IL	4,971
27	LIMESTONE	TX	4,944
28	STEPHENS	TX	4,861
29	CROCKETT	TN	4,783
30	TURNER	GA	4,682
31	PIERCE	GA	4,676
32	LAMB	TX	4,612
33	CHEROKEE	NC	4,604
34	LA SALLE	IL	4,544
35	CRAWFORD	KS	4,542
36	MONROE	MO	4,521
37	MONROE	TN	4,509
38	LAKE	TN	4,465
39	CLINTON	OH	4,460
40	ISSAQUENA	MS	4,449
41	CALHOUN	FL	4,442
42	IRON	UT	4,427
43	DE KALB	AL	4,401
44	JEFFERSON	WV	4,396
45	ADAMS	IL	4,355
46	FRANKLIN	FL	4,327
47	SAN PATRICIO	TX	4,325
48	RANDOLPH	AL	4,317
49	HUMPHREYS	MS	4,295
50	CAMBRIA	PA	4,253
51	HOCKLEY	TX	4,215
52	ADAIR	KY	4,191
53	CHEROKEE	GA	4,184
54	BOSQUE	TX	4,154
55	FAYETTE	IN	4,149
56	JOHNSON	TX	4,124
57	GENEVA	AL	4,111
58	FLAGLER	FL	4,109
59	COLUMBIA	NY	4,108
60	BOURBON	KS	4,085
61	NEZ PERCE	ID	4,079

BOTTOM COUNTIES SHADED WHITE

NOTE: TOO MANY COUNTIES TO LIST
HAD ZERO VALUES FOR THIS MEASURE

"Jeret was conceived when I was seventeen," explains his mother, Kimberlee Moore. "I was told by my doctor Down's syndrome is very rare in a woman my age. I never drank, I never smoked, I took vitamins. I'm convinced this could not have been caused by anything else."[64]

Officials and hired specialists of Hoechst Celanese, on the other hand, dispute the OSHA violations and say the groundwater contamination is just under the site, exposing no one. They also say there is no evidence to support Dr. Holman's claims or Kimberlee Moore's fears.

Whatever the cause of Jeret's condition, many more babies have died from birth defects in Gray County, Texas, than would be expected by chance. The maps indicate that Gray is among the top 5 percent of counties for mortality and excess deaths from birth defects. Moreover, the maps reveal that the entire Texas panhandle is a national locus for mortality from birth defects.

Babies are the most vulnerable among us, especially when still in the mother's womb. During fetal development enormous rates of growth occur, with billions of cells multiplying and vital organs rapidly forming. The slightest environmental insult can lead to devastating health consequences after birth. Each year, 30,000 babies die from problems that arise during fetal development or within a month after birth, accounting for two-thirds of all infant mortality in the United States.

The fetus's special vulnerability makes mortality from birth defects one of the most sensitive indicators of environmental conditions that may be damaging human health. Birth defects, which occur in the first trimester and include congenital anomalies and malformations, cause about a third of these deaths. The rest stem from complications during the perinatal period, extending from the second trimester to a month after birth. About a quarter of perinatal complications are related to lack of oxygen (respiratory distress, intrauterine hypoxia, and birth asphyxia), the rest often involve premature birth and low birthweights, which can be debilitating and sometimes lethal for newborns. We use the words *birth defects* to indicate all mortality among infants arising from congenital anomalies and perinatal complications.

Many factors, or combinations of factors, can lead to geographic clustering of such deaths.[65] Residents of a county may be uninsured and have inadequate access to prenatal care. Expectant mothers may live in harsh poverty or have disrupted family and social support systems.[66] They may be exposed to teratogens, agents that cause birth defects and include toxic chemicals, radiation, medicines, and other agents.[67] Mothers may be exposed to such agents in their workplaces or homes, as a result of contaminated food or water supplies, and from routine or accidental industrial emissions. Toxic damage to the father's sperm may also be involved.[68] Some birth defects and perinatal complications may be due to inherited diseases, but in such cases, clusters would occur only in places with high rates of marriage among close relatives.

Topping the list of counties with the highest birth defect mortality is Issaquena, Mississippi, where the rate is more than three times the national average, followed by Harding, New Mexico; Stonewall, Texas; Hamilton, Kansas; and Billings, North Dakota. Other areas that stand out with clusters of high rates include: counties near the lower Mississippi River and western Louisiana, and counties in the Appalachian Mountains of North Carolina, Tennessee, and the Virginias. Counties with the lowest rates of birth defect mortality include: Grant, Nebraska; Motley, Texas; Webster, Georgia; and Greeley and Chase, Kansas.

Cook County, Illinois, which includes Chicago, has the most excess deaths from birth defects and perinatal complications of any county in the country. New York City is the second highest in excess deaths, and Niagara County, New York, home of Love Canal, is also among the top 10 percent. Seven other counties in Illinois rank among the top 2 percent of counties for excess deaths from birth defects. Seven Pennsylvania counties also rank among the top 2 percent, including Philadelphia and Allegheny (Pittsburgh). In contrast, 18 California counties dominate the list of places where the largest number of babies enjoyed better-than-average rates of infant mortality from birth defects.

Poverty is significantly higher in counties with high rates of birth defect mortality, but many of the other correlations with pollution and social structure factors are surprising. In counties with the worst birth defect mortality, the percent of families with single mothers is less than half the national average. There are 45 percent more hospital beds per person. And the average pesticide application rate is 24 percent below the norm. Also surprising is the fact that Latino Americans comprise almost double their national population percentage in counties with the highest birth defect rates. The majority of Latinos are Mexican Americans, among whom infant mortality and low birthweight rates compare relatively favorably with non-Latino whites.[69] Moreover, the highest percentages of Latino Americans and families in poverty are in the southwestern part of Texas, and not in the panhandle where birth defect mortality is highest. Even so, Latinos, especially in the Southwest, have less access to medical and prenatal care than any other racial and ethnic group in the United States, and this may be contributing to the unexpectedly high rates.[70]

The correlation between birth defect mortality and industrial releases of suspected teratogens is clearer: the top 10 counties for teratogenic pollution have significant above-average birth defect mortality, and

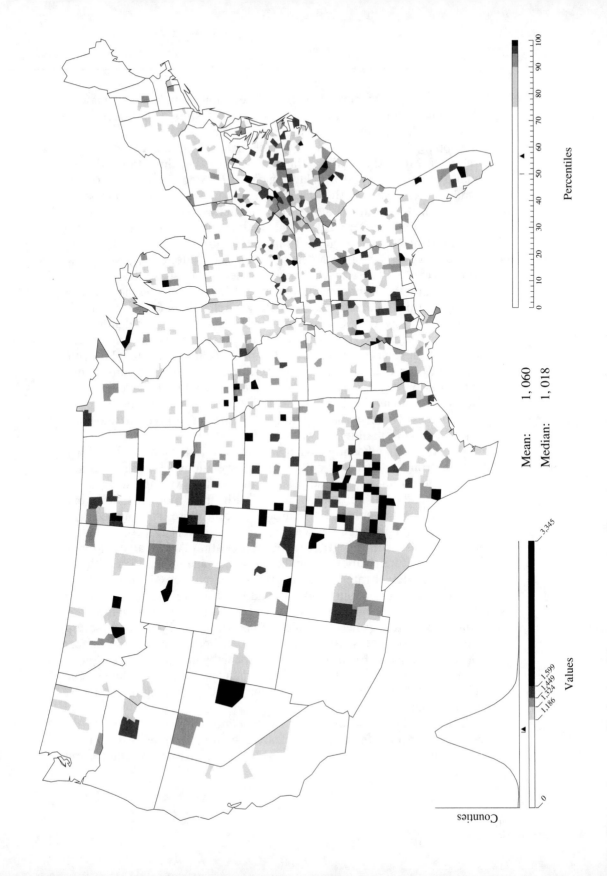

Mean: 1,060
Median: 1,018

Percentiles

100
90
80
70
60
50
40
30
20
10
0

Values

3,345

1,599
1,449
1,324
1,186

0

Counties

(DEATHS PER 100,000 LIVE BIRTHS)

TOP COUNTIES SHADED BLACK

RANK	COUNTY	STATE	VALUE
1	ISSAQUENA	MS	3,345
2	HARDING	NM	3,221
3	STONEWALL	TX	2,962
4	HAMILTON	KS	2,430
5	BILLINGS	ND	2,404
6	COLLINGSWORTH	TX	2,280
7	DICKENS	TX	2,271
8	GLADES	FL	2,252
9	MITCHELL	TX	2,187
10	SIOUX	NE	2,118
11	VERNON	LA	2,078
12	WHITE PINE	NV	2,045
13	PENDLETON	WV	2,033
14	SUMMERS	WV	2,020
15	WOODSON	KS	1,987
16	KINNEY	TX	1,971
17	GAINES	TX	1,970
18	WORTH	MO	1,953
19	LEFLORE	MS	1,899
20	GARDEN	NE	1,898
21	MERCER	MO	1,895
22	CASTRO	TX	1,885
23	CUMBERLAND	KY	1,883
24	CORSON	SD	1,874
25	FISHER	TX	1,864
26	SHERMAN	TX	1,847
27	THROCKMORTON	TX	1,834
28	CALHOUN	WV	1,834
29	HEARD	GA	1,807
30	LEE	SC	1,800
31	FALL RIVER	SD	1,794
32	WHEATLAND	MT	1,791
33	HOT SPRINGS	WY	1,788
34	MONTGOMERY	MS	1,785
35	CARROLL	MO	1,784
36	ARCHULETA	CO	1,784
37	MC PHERSON	SD	1,761
38	JACK	TX	1,757
39	CHILDRESS	TX	1,755
40	KIOWA	OK	1,752
41	GILES	VA	1,746
42	ADAMS	IA	1,721
43	HOLMES	FL	1,715
44	HARDEMAN	TX	1,707
45	GOGEBIC	MI	1,699
46	DICKENSON	VA	1,673
47	STERLING	TX	1,673
48	CHEYENNE	CO	1,671
49	LAKE	MI	1,667
50	HOWARD	TX	1,647
51	GREENE	NC	1,643
52	BRULE	SD	1,640
53	JEFFERSON	MT	1,639
54	FLAGLER	FL	1,637
55	MERCER	KY	1,626
56	DILLON	SC	1,624
57	TYLER	TX	1,615
58	WASHINGTON	KS	1,613
59	MARTIN	TX	1,606
60	PERRY	MS	1,605
61	MONTOUR	PA	1,604
62	STEPHENS	TX	1,599

BOTTOM COUNTIES SHADED WHITE

RANK	COUNTY	STATE	VALUE
1	GRANT	NE	0
2	MOTLEY	TX	0
3	WEBSTER	GA	18
4	GREELEY	KS	124
5	CHASE	KS	136
6	SHERMAN	OR	150
7	WHEELER	OR	166
8	JONES	SD	187
9	GOVE	KS	209
10	HANSON	SD	211
11	JOHNSON	NE	249
12	ELK	KS	287
13	KIDDER	ND	300
14	LANE	KS	332
15	LOWNDES	AL	335
16	TETON	MT	341
17	LINCOLN	KS	346
18	FRONTIER	NE	362
19	DOLORES	CO	373
20	HARDIN	IL	390
21	CUMBERLAND	VA	401
22	IZARD	AR	402
23	WAYNE	UT	414
24	BACON	GA	420
25	HARRISON	IA	422
26	COTTON	OK	424
27	GILCHRIST	FL	429
28	SEARCY	AR	436
29	STEWART	TN	438
30	SCHUYLER	MO	440
31	MERRICK	NE	446
32	BANKS	GA	447
33	CLEAR CREEK	CO	451
34	JEFFERSON	OR	451
35	FAYETTE	GA	452
36	RICHLAND	WI	462
37	GRANT	OK	462
38	LYON	IA	464
39	PAYETTE	ID	474
40	JASPER	GA	482
41	NOBLE	OH	484
42	WARREN	GA	488
43	RUSSELL	KY	488
44	ELLSWORTH	KS	491
45	FOREST	WI	499
46	MARSHALL	SD	505
47	ADAIR	IA	505
48	OSBORNE	KS	510
49	BALLARD	KY	511
50	WATONWAN	MN	512
51	MAGOFFIN	KY	513
52	MC HENRY	ND	514
53	JACKSON	TN	515
54	DICKEY	ND	516
55	WASHINGTON	IA	518

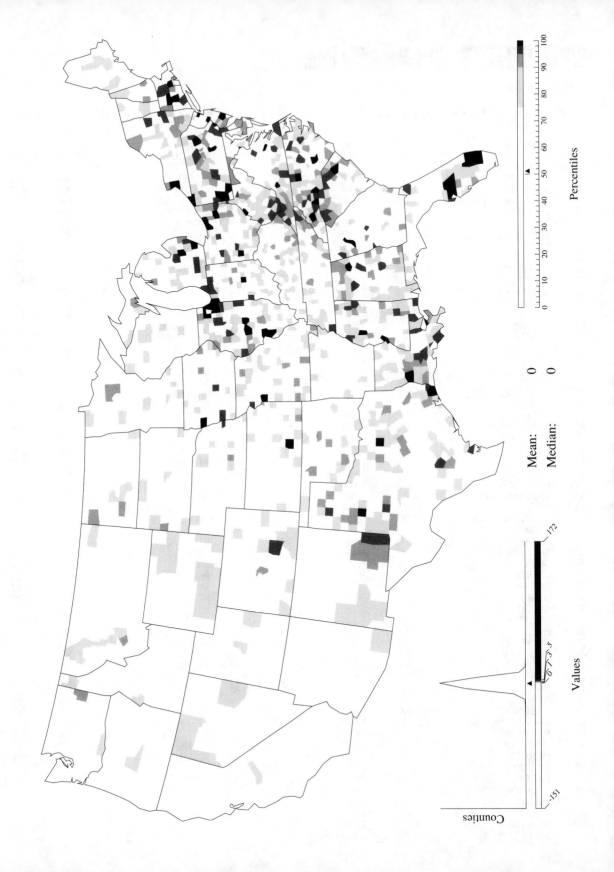

Mean: 0

Median: 0

Percentiles

Values

Counties

TOP COUNTIES SHADED BLACK				BOTTOM COUNTIES SHADED WHITE			
RANK	COUNTY	STATE	VALUE	RANK	COUNTY	STATE	VALUE
1	COOK	IL	172	1	LOS ANGELES	CA	-151
2	NEW YORK CITY	NY	90	2	SAN DIEGO	CA	-51
3	PHILADELPHIA	PA	85	3	SANTA CLARA	CA	-50
4	WAYNE	MI	68	4	ALAMEDA	CA	-43
5	DISTRICT OF COLUMBIA	DC	49	5	ORANGE	CA	-40
6	BALTIMORE CITY	MD	28	6	SAN FRANCISCO	CA	-34
7	ALLEGHENY	PA	27	7	KING	WA	-30
8	ST LOUIS CITY	MO	24	8	MILWAUKEE	WI	-30
9	ESSEX	NJ	22	9	SACRAMENTO	CA	-28
10	HUDSON	NJ	18	10	SUFFOLK	NY	-26
11	ORLEANS	LA	18	11	SAN MATEO	CA	-26
12	ERIE	NY	18	12	SALT LAKE	UT	-25
13	TARRANT	TX	17	13	MIDDLESEX	MA	-23
14	CUYAHOGA	OH	15	14	CONTRA COSTA	CA	-22
15	LAKE	IN	14	15	HARRIS	TX	-20
16	BROWARD	FL	14	16	ST LOUIS	MO	-20
17	ERIE	PA	13	17	PIMA	AZ	-16
18	HENRICO	VA	12	18	TRAVIS	TX	-15
19	GENESEE	MI	12	19	BERGEN	NJ	-13
20	ST CLAIR	IL	11	20	MONTEREY	CA	-13
21	JACKSON	MO	11	21	SAN JOAQUIN	CA	-13
22	PROVIDENCE	RI	11	22	HIDALGO	TX	-13
23	LORAIN	OH	11	23	FAIRFAX	VA	-12
24	SUFFOLK	MA	10	24	MARICOPA	AZ	-12
25	HILLSBOROUGH	FL	9	25	MULTNOMAH	OR	-11
26	PALM BEACH	FL	9	26	DENVER	CO	-11
27	FLORENCE	SC	9	27	JEFFERSON	CO	-11
28	POLK	FL	8	28	VENTURA	CA	-11
29	LUBBOCK	TX	8	29	BALTIMORE	MD	-10
30	SEDGWICK	KS	8	30	UTAH	UT	-10
31	WILL	IL	7	31	RAMSEY	MN	-10
32	LEFLORE	MS	7	32	HENNEPIN	MN	-9
33	DAUPHIN	PA	7	33	RIVERSIDE	CA	-9
34	STARK	OH	7	34	MONTGOMERY	MD	-9
35	MACON	IL	7	35	SNOHOMISH	WA	-9
36	FULTON	GA	7	36	BUCKS	PA	-8
37	HARTFORD	CT	7	37	DE KALB	GA	-8
38	WOOD	WV	7	38	APACHE	AZ	-8
39	MECKLENBURG	NC	6	39	BERNALILLO	NM	-8
40	VERNON	LA	6	40	WASHINGTON	OR	-8
41	WARREN	MS	6	41	EL PASO	TX	-8
42	MARION	IN	6	42	HAMILTON	OH	-8
43	CUMBERLAND	NC	6	43	SANTA BARBARA	CA	-8
44	MADISON	IL	6	44	SAN BERNARDINO	CA	-8
45	LUZERNE	PA	6	45	SONOMA	CA	-8
46	BUNCOMBE	NC	6	46	PLYMOUTH	MA	-8
47	MERCER	NJ	6	47	LANE	OR	-8
48	MONTGOMERY	OH	5	48	ANNE ARUNDEL	MD	-7
49	ATLANTIC	NJ	5	49	DU PAGE	IL	-7
50	ETOWAH	AL	5	50	DELAWARE	PA	-7
51	CLEVELAND	NC	5	51	WESTCHESTER	NY	-7
52	GUILFORD	NC	5	52	NORFOLK	MA	-6
53	FAYETTE	PA	5	53	NASSAU	NY	-6
54	WASHINGTON	PA	5	54	DANE	WI	-6
55	KANE	IL	5	55	CAMERON	TX	-6
56	HAMPDEN	MA	5	56	IMPERIAL	CA	-6
57	ROANOKE	VA	5	57	ARAPAHOE	CO	-6
58	JEFFERSON	TX	5	58	MARIN	CA	-6
59	SANGAMON	IL	5	59	CLARK	WA	-6
60	WOODBURY	IA	5	60	JOHNSON	KS	-6
61	LAFAYETTE	LA	5	61	WAUKESHA	WI	-6
				62	DADE	FL	-6

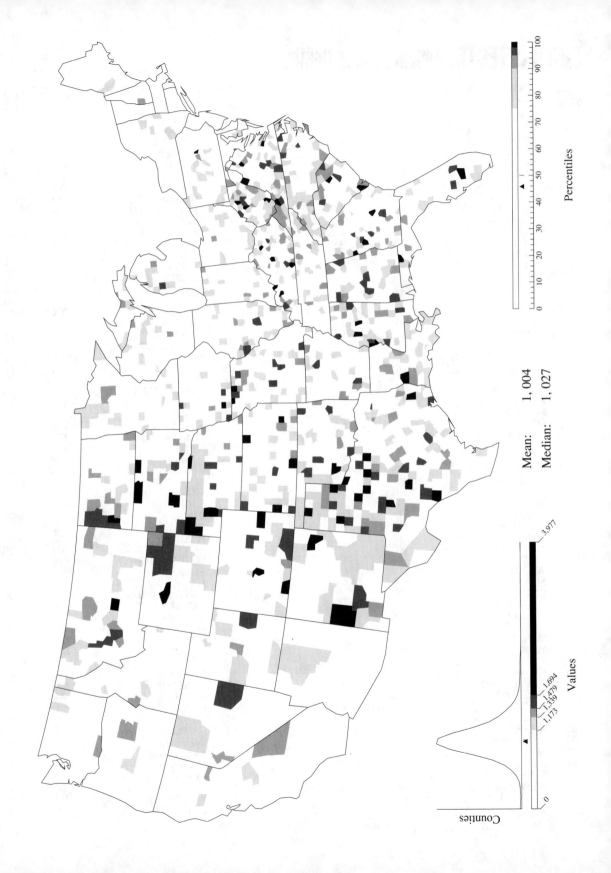

Mean: 1, 004

Median: 1, 027

Percentiles

Values

Counties

(DEATHS PER 100,000 LIVE BIRTHS)

RANK	COUNTY	STATE	VALUE
	TOP COUNTIES SHADED BLACK		
1	JACKSON	SD	3,977
2	ISSAQUENA	MS	3,493
3	STONEWALL	TX	3,388
4	HARDING	NM	3,185
5	CHARLES CITY	VA	3,150
6	HAMILTON	KS	2,780
7	BILLINGS	ND	2,749
8	SIOUX	NE	2,423
9	GLADES	FL	2,308
10	WOODSON	KS	2,273
11	KINNEY	TX	2,254
12	COLLINGSWORTH	TX	2,252
13	WORTH	MO	2,234
14	PENDLETON	WV	2,200
15	GARDEN	NE	2,171
16	MERCER	MO	2,167
17	SHERMAN	TX	2,112
18	THROCKMORTON	TX	2,098
19	CALHOUN	WV	2,097
20	WHEATLAND	MT	2,048
21	ARCHULETA	CO	2,040
22	VERNON	LA	2,017
23	MC PHERSON	SD	2,014
24	SUMMERS	WV	2,010
25	CASTRO	TX	1,996
26	ADAMS	IA	1,968
27	HOT SPRINGS	WY	1,930
28	TALBOT	GA	1,928
29	WHEELER	GA	1,925
30	CORSON	SD	1,918
31	STERLING	TX	1,913
32	CHEYENNE	CO	1,911
33	HEARD	GA	1,905
34	DICKENS	TX	1,869
35	WASHINGTON	KS	1,845
36	LEFLORE	MS	1,838
37	MONTOUR	PA	1,835
38	BARBER	KS	1,819
39	CHAFFEE	CO	1,819
40	CATRON	NM	1,808
41	DODDRIDGE	WV	1,793
42	MENARD	TX	1,791
43	MERCER	KY	1,783
44	JACK	TX	1,780
45	MONTGOMERY	MS	1,779
46	NICHOLAS	KY	1,778
47	MC LEAN	KY	1,768
48	RAPPAHANNOCK	VA	1,742
49	LEE	SC	1,734
50	DAWES	NE	1,730
51	KIOWA	OK	1,724
52	BOYD	NE	1,722
53	BLAND	VA	1,718
54	HARDEMAN	TX	1,702
55	HANCOCK	KY	1,700
56	CUMBERLAND	KY	1,695
57	TYLER	TX	1,695
58	JASPER	SC	1,694
59	HOLMES	FL	1,694

RANK	COUNTY	STATE	VALUE
	BOTTOM COUNTIES SHADED WHITE		
1	BAKER	GA	0
2	GRANT	NE	0
3	MOTLEY	TX	0
4	GREELEY	KS	141
5	CHASE	KS	155
6	SHERMAN	OR	171
7	LOWNDES	AL	180
8	SIOUX	ND	181
9	WHEELER	OR	190
10	CUMBERLAND	VA	207
11	JONES	SD	213
12	GOVE	KS	239
13	HANSON	SD	241
14	BACON	GA	275
15	JOHNSON	NE	285
16	GRANT	OK	299
17	JEFFERSON	OR	311
18	ELK	KS	329
19	WALWORTH	SD	338
20	KIDDER	ND	343
21	AMITE	MS	344
22	LANE	KS	380
23	TETON	MT	390
24	LINCOLN	KS	395
25	FAYETTE	GA	404
26	FRONTIER	NE	414
27	JASPER	GA	425
28	DOLORES	CO	427
29	COTTON	OK	428
30	HARDIN	IL	446
31	IZARD	AR	460
32	PERQUIMANS	NC	465
33	WAYNE	UT	473
34	HARRISON	IA	482
35	GILCHRIST	FL	491
36	FOREST	WI	497
37	SEARCY	AR	499
38	STEWART	TN	501
39	SCHUYLER	MO	503
40	MERRICK	NE	510
41	BANKS	GA	511
42	CLEAR CREEK	CO	515
43	JEFFERSON	GA	520
44	RICHLAND	WI	528
45	LYON	IA	530
46	JEFFERSON	MS	542
47	PAYETTE	ID	543
48	ROCKWALL	TX	543
49	NOBLE	OH	554
50	FALLS	TX	554
51	REFUGIO	TX	555
52	KENT	MD	557
53	RUSSELL	KY	558
54	ELLSWORTH	KS	561
55	BURKE	GA	568
56	LUMPKIN	GA	572

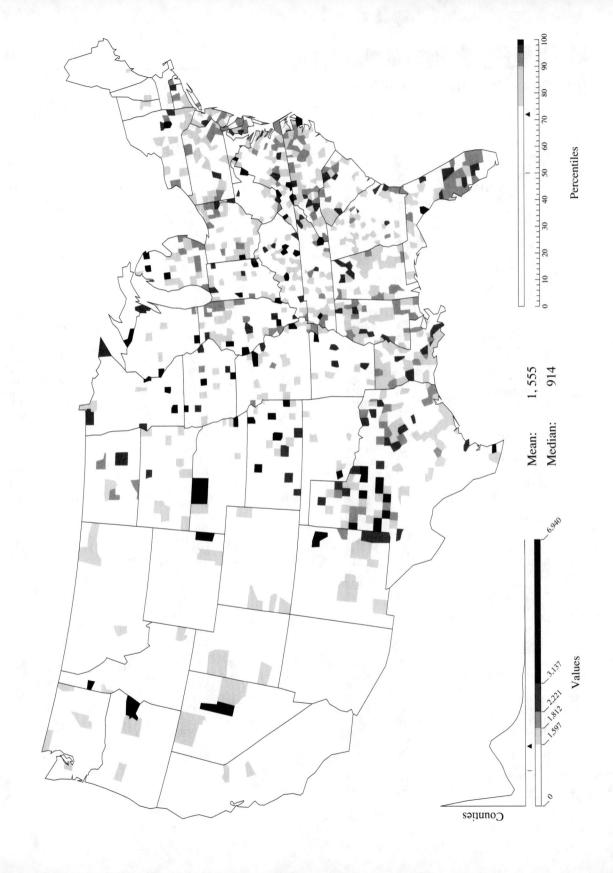

Percentiles

Mean: 1,555
Median: 914

Values

Counties

0   1,597 1,812 2,221 3,137   6,940

(DEATHS PER 100,000 LIVE BIRTHS)

TOP COUNTIES SHADED BLACK

RANK	COUNTY	STATE	VALUE
1	FISHER	TX	6,940
2	PIERCE	WI	6,807
3	WAYNE	KY	6,079
4	MITCHELL	TX	5,639
5	GAINES	TX	5,598
6	HARDY	WV	5,210
7	GREENE	AR	5,070
8	DICKENS	TX	5,070
9	BENEWAH	ID	4,561
10	MONROE	MO	4,521
11	GILES	VA	4,491
12	GOGEBIC	MI	4,351
13	GREER	OK	4,292
14	POSEY	IN	4,178
15	JEFFERSON	WV	4,166
16	PERRY	IL	4,103
17	GRAYSON	VA	4,090
18	BAYLOR	TX	3,889
19	JONES	TX	3,832
20	HYDE	NC	3,684
21	BOURBON	KS	3,629
22	PATRICK	VA	3,623
23	MARTIN	TX	3,553
24	BAILEY	TX	3,548
25	CROCKETT	TN	3,490
26	MARION	KS	3,473
27	NEMAHA	KS	3,473
28	ROOKS	KS	3,473
29	ALPENA	MI	3,473
30	OSCEOLA	MI	3,473
31	OTSEGO	MI	3,473
32	OTOE	NE	3,473
33	EUREKA	NV	3,473
34	HARDING	NM	3,473
35	SCHOHARIE	NY	3,473
36	PREBLE	OH	3,473
37	WILLACY	TX	3,473
38	GOSHEN	WY	3,473
39	LINCOLN	KY	3,459
40	CAPE GIRARDEAU	MO	3,356
41	HARDIN	IA	3,333
42	MONROE	TN	3,331
43	WARREN	IL	3,311
44	ADAMS	IL	3,293
45	DIXIE	FL	3,290
46	KNOX	TX	3,239
47	FOUNTAIN	IN	3,193
48	RIPLEY	IN	3,193
49	APPANOOSE	IA	3,193
50	DICKINSON	IA	3,193
51	OSAGE	KS	3,193
52	GRAYSON	KY	3,193
53	ROCKCASTLE	KY	3,193
54	CHISAGO	MN	3,193
55	COTTONWOOD	MN	3,193
56	LE SUEUR	MN	3,193
57	RALLS	MO	3,193
58	BAKER	OR	3,193
59	DICKENSON	VA	3,193
60	LAFAYETTE	WI	3,193
61	CHERRY	NE	3,137

BOTTOM COUNTIES SHADED WHITE

NOTE: TOO MANY COUNTIES TO LIST
HAD ZERO VALUES FOR THIS MEASURE

the rate is deteriorating compared with the United States as a whole.[71] The counties include, in order of the greatest releases of suspected teratogens: Warren, Virginia; Los Angeles, California; Cook, Illinois; Harris, Texas; Hamblen, Tennessee; McCleod, Minnesota; Wayne, Michigan; Jefferson, Louisiana; Middlesex, New Jersey; and Jefferson, Texas.[72]

ALL CANCERS

"Go get 'em," said Patty Frase's mother, as she lay dying at age 55 from a rare form of liver cancer. She was one of just five cases diagnosed in the state of Arkansas—all from Jacksonville, in Pulaski County.[73]

"Get 'em" is exactly what Patty Frase did.

Standing on the steps of the state capitol, she mobilized the National Toxics Campaign, Citizens Clearinghouse for Hazardous Waste, and Greenpeace to join her in making the accusation that "the state is in bed with the polluters." The EPA had awarded Jacksonville People with Pride (JPWP) $150,000 in grants intended for citizen groups concerned about toxic dumps in their neighborhood. Yet pamphlets from this group touted the town's "excellent quality of life." Frase helped expose the fact that JPWP was started with the financial support of Hercules, Inc., former owner of a Jacksonville plant that produced a quarter of the Agent Orange sprayed in Vietnam.[74] Now the plant lies abandoned and is listed as one of the most dangerous dumps in the nation, with dioxin contamination at higher levels than anywhere else in the country— higher even than in Times Beach, Missouri, which was evacuated in 1983 after dioxin-laced oils were sprayed on local roads. Dioxin is a by- product of Agent Orange and is one of the most potent promoters of cancer and birth defects in laboratory animals. Residents of Jacksonville now call their town "Dioxinville," and their cemetery "Babyland" due to the many infants buried there.[75]

"Back in the 1970s," recalls Mozelle Bergschneider, who lives just across from the old plant, "I started making a list of the illnesses within a four-block radius. Of fifty-two neighbors, twenty-six died of cancer— brain tumors, breast, and lung cancer. I have three grandchildren, but I should have five. My daughter lost a child to spina bifida. Then she miscarried another baby. You couldn't even tell the sex, it was so muti- lated . . . as if it had decayed in the womb."[76]

Despite such personal experiences, the Centers for Disease Control have not found significant cancer increases from dioxin in Jacksonville. Nor have they found conclusive evidence that Agent Orange caused cancer in exposed Vietnam veterans. In fact, the government believes dioxin's only proven human health effect is chloracne, a severe form of skin rash, even though the chemical is extremely carcinogenic to laboratory animals. Such negative findings are common in the more than 100 cancer cluster investigations the CDC has undertaken since the early 1960s. The CDC concludes from these studies that "no clear-cut etiologic relations [causes] were clearly and consistently defined."[77] Yet Pulaski County, Arkansas, shows up in the maps with higher cancer mortality rates than 90 percent of the counties in the country, and more excess cancer deaths than 95 percent of U.S. counties. What's worse, cancer mortality rates are increasing significantly faster in Pulaski than in the rest of the nation—for all cancers, lung cancer, breast cancer, and especially child cancers.

As a result of local protests, the EPA canceled their grant to JPWP, and the FBI began an investigation into possible fraud and bribery. But Jacksonville's problems are far from solved. Now the EPA proposes to burn close to 30,000 barrels of chemical pesticides at the site where Agent Orange was made—2,800 of which contain dioxin—24 hours a day, seven days a week, for as many months as it takes to destroy the wastes.[78] Jacksonville residents are up in arms.[79]

"There is a groundswell of people all over Arkansas who thought their government leaders were protecting them, then realized this just wasn't so," says Patty Frase, "but who are you going to believe—a bunch of housewives or the EPA and CDC?" One thing is certain. Patty, who now has a daughter of her own, "won't let her set foot in Jacksonville."[80]

As mortality from heart disease declined over the last quarter century, cancer mortality increased in importance. Cancer is now the second leading cause of death, killing half a million Americans each year. It is the number one killer of people ages 45 to 64.[81]

The trends for cancer mortality are markedly different than for the other causes of death mapped in the atlas. Cancer mortality rates are rising, whereas mortality rates are declining for all of the other causes of death. Geographic disparities are also increasing, despite the fact that cancer rates in rural areas have been catching up to those in urban areas. Only for young-adult infectious diseases, which includes AIDS, are geographic inequalities in mortality also rising. Disparities between races and sexes are increasing as well. (See the methods appendix for details on these trends.)

The geographic distribution of high cancer rates also differs markedly from the other causes of death: there is a clear concentration in the Northeast, especially in New Jersey, Connecticut, and parts of New

York. Excess deaths are even more highly concentrated in the New York City metropolitan area. Other researchers have found significant associations between chemical waste sites and cancer rates in New Jersey municipalities, and a convergence between suburban and inner-city rates throughout the metropolitan region.[82] Cancer differs from most of the other causes of death in another respect: higher rates are geographically associated with higher incomes.

Like mortality from all diseases, however, cancer mortality tracks the Ohio and Mississippi rivers, with a cluster of high-rate counties in the Louisiana delta. This pattern is especially true for white males, who also have high rates in counties along the southeastern coast. White female mortality, in contrast, is particularly high in upper New York State and Northern California. This north-south difference between the sexes parallels differences in smoking prevalences among men and women (as discussed in chapter 2). The geographic patterns for minorities are more dispersed than for whites, part of which may be due to less stable rates from smaller populations.

Scientists believe a large percentage of cancers are due to preventable causes—though just how large a percentage is a matter of considerable debate. Cancer is a collective name for more than a hundred clinical diseases that affect various sites of the body in different ways. Different malignant neoplasms may have similar or different causes. Diet, tobacco use, infection, reproductive and sexual behavior, occupation, alcohol, sunlight, pollution, and medicines are risk factors that have been associated with as much as 95 percent of all cancer deaths.[83]

Estimates of the contribution of exposures to carcinogenic substances in the workplace and environment run from around 5 percent to over 25 percent of cancer deaths, but no one knows for sure.[84] The National Toxicology Program lists 117 chemicals as potential human carcinogens.[85] The International Agency for Research in Cancer lists 30 chemicals, mixtures, or occupational exposures as carcinogenic to humans, 61 as probable human carcinogens, and 64 as carcinogenic to animals.[86] But for most chemicals, there simply is not enough information to appraise carcinogenicity reliably.

Even so, the measures of industrial toxins are more frequently associated with geographic variations in mortality from cancer than with any of the other causes of death mapped in the atlas. All but 1 of the 35 measures of industrial toxins are higher in the top-ranked cancer counties than in the rest of the country, and 12 of the measures are significantly correlated with cancer rates across the country, including industrial emissions of carcinogens, hazardous waste incinerators, air permit violators, facilities discharging toxins to surface water, toxic waste land disposal facilities, commercial hazardous waste management facilities, illegal occupational exposures, and others. Measures of non-industrial pollution, as well as a number of social structure measures, are also significantly correlated with cancer mortality.

LUNG CANCERS

Three-quarters of Louisiana's parishes (counties) have lung cancer mortality rates above the national average. More than a third of them are in the top 10 percent in the country. The Louisiana Chemical Association blames the high rates on smoking.[87] So does the National Cancer Institute (NCI), contradicting its own earlier findings that linked Louisiana's high lung cancer rates with chemicals and shipbuilding. Now NCI believes the only things in Louisiana other than smoking that are significantly increasing lung cancer risks are working in the lumber industry, living near lumber mills or petroleum refineries, and not eating enough fruits and vegetables.[88]

Amos Favorite thinks the petrochemical industry might also have something to do with the high lung cancer rates in Ascension Parish. Amos has seen hard times all his life: he cut sugarcane on the plantations as a boy, fought in the fierce Pacific battles of World War II, and protested the Ku Klux Klan, who burned crosses on his lawn during the 1960s civil rights movement.[89] His latest challenge is the 200 million pounds of toxic chemicals that 18 chemical plants emit into the air surrounding his hometown of Geismar each year—over 20 tons per resident.[90] According to EPA data, 2 of the chemical plants in Geismar (owned by the BASF and Arcadian corporations) rank among the top 50 chemical polluters nationwide.[91] EPA data indicate Ascension Parish is among the top two counties in the country for industrial releases of toxins to the air, and among the top four for releases of suspected carcinogens.[92]

"I've been in Geismar sixty-five years," says Mr. Favorite, "and never in my life seen it like it is today. Industries took over from agriculture, and ever since there's been a change in human health. They try to blame it on this and that, but all this mess is money mess. The old people used to smoke the strongest tobacco and lived to be eighty or ninety. An eleven-year-old boy who lived north of the BASF plant died recently of lung cancer. He never smoked. I don't think they should blame smoking —they put that out to neutralize their releases."[93]

Amos says the pollution falls down like snow on top of the houses, rusting the cars and eating through metal window screens. The river is

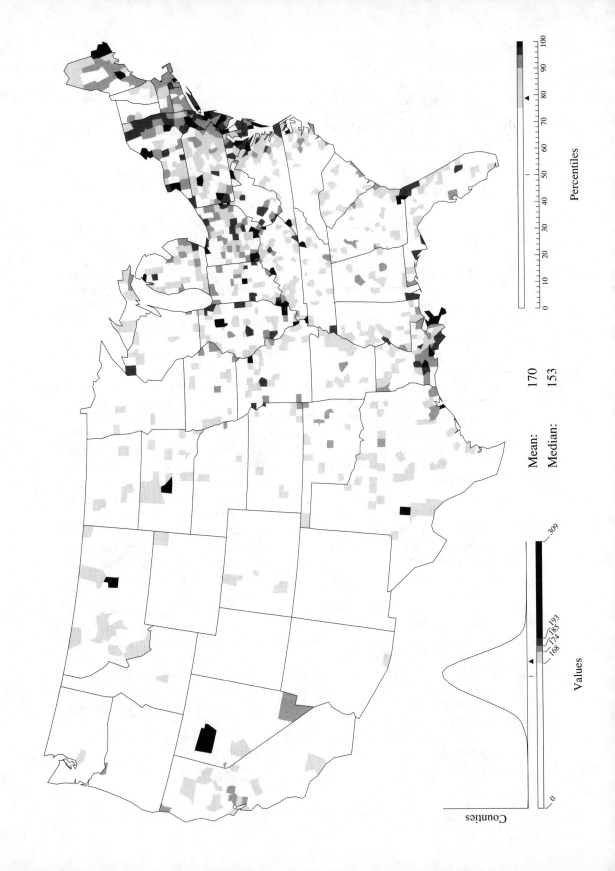

Mean: 170

Median: 153

Percentiles

Values

Counties

0   168 174 185 193   309

(DEATHS PER 100,000 PEOPLE)

TOP COUNTIES SHADED BLACK

RANK	COUNTY	STATE	VALUE
1	NANTUCKET	MA	309
2	ELK	PA	265
3	REAGAN	TX	233
4	PETROLEUM	MT	229
5	KENTON	KY	220
6	BALTIMORE CITY	MD	220
7	PERSHING	NV	218
8	STANLEY	SD	218
9	SUSSEX	NJ	212
10	CHARLTON	GA	212
11	ALEXANDER	IL	211
12	CHARLEVOIX	MI	210
13	ST LOUIS CITY	MO	208
14	NORTHAMPTON	VA	207
15	WASHINGTON	ME	207
16	HAMILTON	OH	204
17	ORLEANS	LA	204
18	PHILADELPHIA	PA	203
19	CAMPBELL	KY	202
20	OHIO	WV	202
21	POSEY	IN	202
22	SCIOTO	OH	201
23	SUFFOLK	MA	201
24	SCHOHARIE	NY	201
25	GALLATIN	IL	201
26	JACKSON	OH	200
27	JEFFERSON	KY	200
28	ANNE ARUNDEL	MD	200
29	SOMERSET	MD	199
30	MIDDLESEX	NJ	198
31	UNION	KY	198
32	SALINE	IL	198
33	ST BERNARD	LA	198
34	HUDSON	NJ	198
35	WISE	VA	197
36	ALLEGANY	MD	197
37	ACCOMACK	VA	197
38	BOYD	KY	197
39	MARION	MO	197
40	NEW CASTLE	DE	197
41	CHARLES	MD	196
42	HANCOCK	WV	196
43	MONMOUTH	NJ	196
44	ALLEGHENY	PA	196
45	IBERIA	LA	196
46	LA SALLE	IL	196
47	MARION	IN	195
48	CAMDEN	NJ	195
49	JEFFERSON	NY	195
50	GALVESTON	TX	194
51	LUCAS	OH	194
52	NEWPORT	RI	194
53	NASSAU	NY	194
54	ERIE	NY	194
55	ACADIA	LA	193
56	PLAQUEMINES	LA	193
57	CHOWAN	NC	193
58	KENNEBEC	ME	193
59	CAMPBELL	TN	193
60	ATLANTIC	NJ	193
61	FULTON	KY	193
62	ORANGE	NY	193

BOTTOM COUNTIES SHADED WHITE

RANK	COUNTY	STATE	VALUE
1	YELLOWSTONE NAT. PARK	MT	0
2	DAGGETT	UT	26
3	KENEDY	TX	36
4	RICH	UT	61
5	BANNER	NE	65
6	MC PHERSON	NE	75
7	BORDEN	TX	78
8	HARDING	NM	80
9	BOISE	ID	81
10	JUAB	UT	84
11	WAYNE	UT	87
12	CARTER	MT	88
13	MORGAN	UT	88
14	MADISON	ID	89
15	SIOUX	NE	89
16	BEAR LAKE	ID	89
17	SMITH	KS	90
18	JEFF DAVIS	TX	90
19	GOSPER	NE	91
20	OLIVER	ND	92
21	WASHINGTON	UT	92
22	CONEJOS	CO	93
23	OURAY	CO	93
24	HODGEMAN	KS	93
25	KANE	UT	93
26	JUDITH BASIN	MT	94
27	HARTLEY	TX	94
28	EUREKA	NV	94
29	GARFIELD	UT	94
30	WHEELER	NE	94
31	CHEYENNE	KS	95
32	TERRELL	TX	95
33	OWSLEY	KY	95
34	FRANKLIN	ID	95
35	WALLOWA	OR	97
36	SHANNON	SD	97
37	CARIBOU	ID	97
38	MAGOFFIN	KY	97
39	SULLY	SD	97
40	LANE	KS	98
41	MILLARD	UT	98
42	STARR	TX	98
43	MORA	NM	99
44	LIPSCOMB	TX	99
45	TREASURE	MT	99
46	YUMA	CO	99
47	GOVE	KS	100
48	FREMONT	ID	100
49	BLAINE	NE	100
50	WASATCH	UT	100
51	UINTA	WY	101
52	PIUTE	UT	101
53	GRIGGS	ND	101
54	SAN JUAN	UT	102
55	CACHE	UT	102
56	PRESIDIO	TX	103
57	CLEARWATER	ID	103
58	HAYES	NE	103
59	APACHE	AZ	104
60	ARCHULETA	CO	104
61	TORRANCE	NM	104

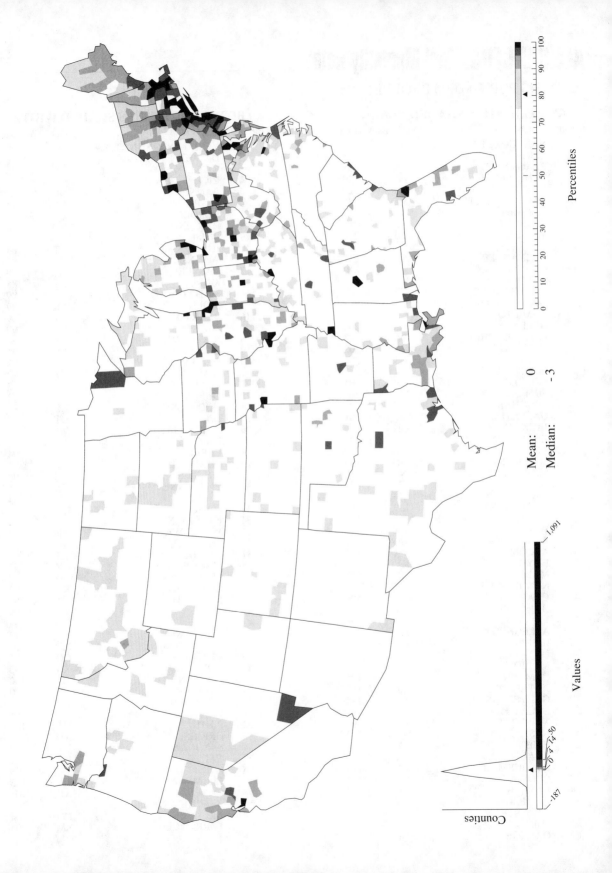

Mean: 0

Median: - 3

Percentiles

Values

Counties

-187   0 4 50   1,091

TOP COUNTIES SHADED BLACK

RANK	COUNTY	STATE	VALUE
1	NEW YORK CITY	NY	1,091
2	COOK	IL	919
3	PHILADELPHIA	PA	675
4	BALTIMORE CITY	MD	455
5	ALLEGHENY	PA	441
6	WAYNE	MI	384
7	CUYAHOGA	OH	375
8	HAMILTON	OH	317
9	NASSAU	NY	296
10	DISTRICT OF COLUMBIA	DC	267
11	ERIE	NY	249
12	ST LOUIS CITY	MO	226
13	SUFFOLK	MA	225
14	SUFFOLK	NY	219
15	MIDDLESEX	MA	219
16	ORLEANS	LA	214
17	JEFFERSON	KY	198
18	HUDSON	NJ	182
19	MARION	IN	179
20	ESSEX	NJ	174
21	WESTCHESTER	NY	159
22	BERGEN	NJ	158
23	PROVIDENCE	RI	151
24	SAN FRANCISCO	CA	141
25	MIDDLESEX	NJ	138
26	FRANKLIN	OH	134
27	MONMOUTH	NJ	125
28	SHELBY	TN	124
29	DELAWARE	PA	120
30	NEW HAVEN	CT	111
31	LUCAS	OH	110
32	MILWAUKEE	WI	109
33	BALTIMORE	MD	105
34	ESSEX	MA	103
35	CAMDEN	NJ	100
36	DUVAL	FL	97
37	UNION	NJ	93
38	JEFFERSON	AL	92
39	NEW CASTLE	DE	87
40	NORFOLK	MA	86
41	ONONDAGA	NY	85
42	OCEAN	NJ	85
43	FAIRFIELD	CT	84
44	HENRICO	VA	79
45	ST LOUIS	MO	73
46	HAMPDEN	MA	73
47	PASSAIC	NJ	73
48	BRISTOL	MA	69
49	HARTFORD	CT	67
50	MONROE	NY	64
51	ANNE ARUNDEL	MD	64
52	ORANGE	NY	63
53	KENTON	KY	57
54	ALBANY	NY	56
55	ATLANTIC	NJ	54
56	HILLSBOROUGH	NH	54
57	MACOMB	MI	53
58	LAKE	IN	52
59	ALAMEDA	CA	52
60	ST CLAIR	IL	51
61	JACKSON	MO	50

BOTTOM COUNTIES SHADED WHITE

RANK	COUNTY	STATE	VALUE
1	PINELLAS	FL	-187
2	MARICOPA	AZ	-186
3	SALT LAKE	UT	-150
4	BROWARD	FL	-149
5	DADE	FL	-129
6	HIDALGO	TX	-99
7	RIVERSIDE	CA	-98
8	PALM BEACH	FL	-91
9	SANTA CLARA	CA	-87
10	DENVER	CO	-84
11	PASCO	FL	-84
12	ORANGE	CA	-82
13	PIMA	AZ	-81
14	SAN DIEGO	CA	-75
15	CAMERON	TX	-68
16	FRESNO	CA	-65
17	SAN BERNARDINO	CA	-60
18	EL PASO	TX	-59
19	UTAH	UT	-58
20	MANATEE	FL	-58
21	WEBER	UT	-52
22	LEE	FL	-52
23	DE KALB	GA	-50
24	EL PASO	CO	-50
25	BERNALILLO	NM	-50
26	LOS ANGELES	CA	-46
27	VENTURA	CA	-46
28	LARIMER	CO	-46
29	SARASOTA	FL	-45
30	JEFFERSON	CO	-43
31	JOHNSON	KS	-41
32	WELD	CO	-41
33	PUEBLO	CO	-40
34	BOULDER	CO	-40
35	DANE	WI	-39
36	ARAPAHOE	CO	-38
37	DAVIS	UT	-37
38	WASHINGTON	OR	-36
39	LUBBOCK	TX	-35
40	TRAVIS	TX	-35
41	CHARLOTTE	FL	-34
42	MONTEREY	CA	-33
43	LANE	OR	-32
44	LAKE	FL	-31
45	ADAMS	CO	-30
46	BENTON	AR	-30
47	MARION	OR	-30
48	BELL	TX	-30
49	ROWAN	NC	-28
50	DAVIDSON	NC	-27
51	CLACKAMAS	OR	-27
52	TULARE	CA	-27
53	KING	WA	-26
54	STEARNS	MN	-26
55	POLK	FL	-26
56	LANCASTER	NE	-24
57	NAVAJO	AZ	-24
58	ROANOKE	VA	-24
59	SAN LUIS OBISPO	CA	-23
60	CACHE	UT	-23
61	RANDOLPH	NC	-23
62	CLEVELAND	OK	-23

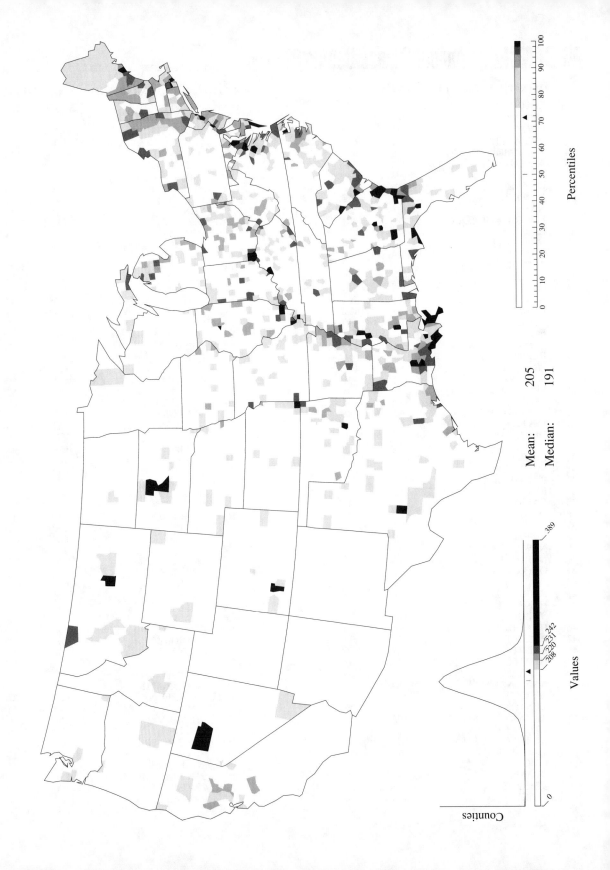

Percentiles

Mean: 205
Median: 191

Values

Counties

0   208 220 242   389
        231

(DEATHS PER 100,000 PEOPLE)

TOP COUNTIES SHADED BLACK

RANK	COUNTY	STATE	VALUE
1	HINSDALE	CO	389
2	PETROLEUM	MT	378
3	DEWEY	SD	321
4	NANTUCKET	MA	319
5	LONG	GA	302
6	CHARLTON	GA	294
7	MITCHELL	GA	279
8	BALTIMORE CITY	MD	277
9	BAKER	GA	277
10	REAGAN	TX	274
11	LIBERTY	GA	273
12	PULASKI	GA	272
13	PERSHING	NV	269
14	NORTHAMPTON	VA	268
15	ST LOUIS CITY	MO	267
16	STANLEY	SD	266
17	KENTON	KY	266
18	ST BERNARD	LA	264
19	BRYAN	GA	263
20	MC CORMICK	SC	261
21	PLAQUEMINES	LA	260
22	ALLENDALE	SC	259
23	CAMPBELL	KY	259
24	MC INTOSH	GA	258
25	ALEXANDER	IL	257
26	GILCHRIST	FL	257
27	FRANKLIN	FL	256
28	CRISP	GA	255
29	ORLEANS	LA	254
30	HUMPHREYS	MS	253
31	CAROLINE	VA	253
32	GALLATIN	IL	252
33	SUFFOLK	MA	252
34	ACCOMACK	VA	252
35	PUTNAM	IL	251
36	CAMDEN	GA	251
37	WAKULLA	FL	251
38	COAL	OK	251
39	CHARLES	MD	250
40	CHEROKEE	KS	249
41	PHILADELPHIA	PA	248
42	KENT	RI	248
43	NEWPORT	RI	247
44	LEFLORE	MS	246
45	ST JAMES	LA	246
46	TERREBONNE	LA	246
47	ANNE ARUNDEL	MD	246
48	CARLISLE	KY	246
49	EVANGELINE	LA	246
50	LINCOLN	ME	244
51	HUDSON	NJ	244
52	CHOWAN	NC	244
53	ST MARY	LA	244
54	LAWRENCE	MS	243
55	BOONE	KY	243
56	MIDDLESEX	NJ	243
57	SALINE	IL	243
58	HAMILTON	OH	243
59	JEFFERSON	KY	243
60	ACADIA	LA	242

BOTTOM COUNTIES SHADED WHITE

RANK	COUNTY	STATE	VALUE
1	DAGGETT	UT	0
2	KENEDY	TX	42
3	RICH	UT	54
4	SAN JUAN	CO	80
5	BANNER	NE	82
6	TODD	SD	90
7	HARDING	NM	95
8	BEAR LAKE	ID	95
9	PRESIDIO	TX	106
10	TERRELL	TX	107
11	OLIVER	ND	108
12	SHANNON	SD	110
13	SIOUX	NE	111
14	HODGEMAN	KS	111
15	WHEELER	NE	111
16	YUMA	CO	111
17	JACKSON	CO	111
18	MORA	NM	111
19	CARTER	MT	111
20	JEFF DAVIS	TX	112
21	MORGAN	UT	112
22	JUDITH BASIN	MT	113
23	MILLARD	UT	113
24	SEVIER	UT	113
25	JUAB	UT	114
26	BOISE	ID	114
27	BORDEN	TX	115
28	COSTILLA	CO	116
29	HUDSPETH	TX	116
30	OWSLEY	KY	117
31	CONEJOS	CO	117
32	WAYNE	UT	118
33	GOSPER	NE	119
34	MADISON	ID	121
35	HITCHCOCK	NE	121
36	MELLETTE	SD	121
37	SAGUACHE	CO	122
38	UINTAH	UT	122
39	ECHOLS	GA	122
40	SMITH	KS	122
41	JIM HOGG	TX	124
42	ELBERT	CO	124
43	EUREKA	NV	124
44	FRANKLIN	ID	124
45	WASHINGTON	UT	125
46	SULLY	SD	125
47	GARFIELD	UT	126
48	BENNETT	SD	126
49	VAN BUREN	TN	127
50	BOX ELDER	UT	128
51	GOVE	KS	128
52	STANTON	NE	129
53	BALDWIN	GA	129
54	SAN MIGUEL	NM	130
55	ARCHULETA	CO	130
56	SUMMIT	UT	131
57	POTTER	SD	131
58	WALLOWA	OR	131
59	CACHE	UT	132
60	CARIBOU	ID	132
61	DE BACA	NM	132
62	UTAH	UT	132

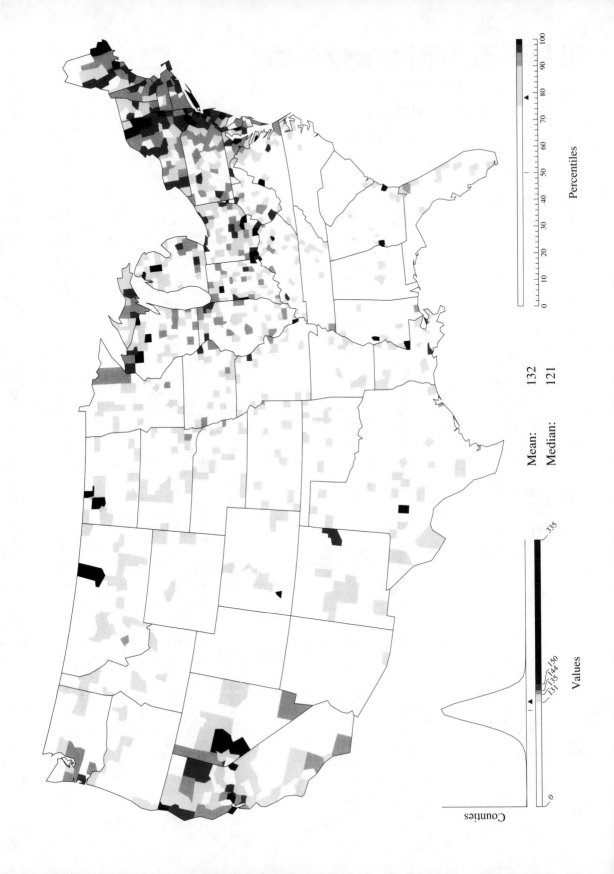

Mean: 132

Median: 121

Percentiles

0 10 20 30 40 50 60 70 80 90 100

Values

Counties

0   131 135 144 150   335

(DEATHS PER 100,000 PEOPLE)

TOP COUNTIES SHADED BLACK					BOTTOM COUNTIES SHADED WHITE			
RANK	COUNTY	STATE	VALUE		RANK	COUNTY	STATE	VALUE
1	ALPINE	CA	335		1	MC PHERSON	NE	24
2	SAN JUAN	CO	213		2	KENEDY	TX	40
3	NANTUCKET	MA	196		3	HARDING	SD	50
4	REAGAN	TX	194		4	GLASSCOCK	TX	61
5	MC INTOSH	GA	173		5	SLOPE	ND	61
6	MENIFEE	KY	170		6	LANE	KS	63
7	RICHMOND	VA	169		7	KANE	UT	64
8	STEWART	GA	168		8	SAN MIGUEL	CO	65
9	RENVILLE	ND	168		9	EUREKA	NV	66
10	FLORENCE	WI	163		10	MACON	GA	67
11	SAN FRANCISCO	CA	162		11	BANNER	NE	68
12	ALEXANDER	IL	161		12	PERRY	AL	70
13	ROSCOMMON	MI	161		13	OURAY	CO	70
14	FRANKLIN	NY	160		14	TREASURE	MT	72
15	NASSAU	NY	159		15	BOISE	ID	72
16	DEL NORTE	CA	159		16	APACHE	AZ	73
17	CAMPBELL	KY	159		17	WHITE	GA	73
18	SHARKEY	MS	159		18	WIBAUX	MT	74
19	MONMOUTH	NJ	158		19	HAYES	NE	74
20	KENTON	KY	157		20	CLAIBORNE	MS	75
21	WASHINGTON	ME	157		21	SAN JUAN	UT	75
22	BALTIMORE CITY	MD	157		22	OWYHEE	ID	75
23	BATH	VA	156		23	HARTLEY	TX	77
24	SAWYER	WI	156		24	MAGOFFIN	KY	77
25	GALLATIN	KY	156		25	BENNETT	SD	77
26	ORANGE	NY	155		26	GARFIELD	MT	77
27	SUSSEX	NJ	155		27	HYDE	SD	78
28	HAMILTON	OH	155		28	JACKSON	SD	78
29	ANNE ARUNDEL	MD	155		29	GILPIN	CO	78
30	SUFFOLK	NY	155		30	JUAB	UT	79
31	WALDO	ME	155		31	FAYETTE	TN	79
32	LINCOLN	WI	154		32	MITCHELL	GA	79
33	PHILLIPS	MT	154		33	BALDWIN	GA	81
34	CRAWFORD	MI	154		34	EFFINGHAM	GA	82
35	MOUNTRAIL	ND	154		35	CHEYENNE	KS	82
36	HOCKING	OH	154		36	WAYNE	UT	82
37	MIDDLESEX	NJ	154		37	MILLARD	UT	82
38	OHIO	WV	154		38	UNION	GA	82
39	PUTNAM	NY	153		39	ARCHULETA	CO	82
40	SUFFOLK	MA	153		40	JASPER	GA	82
41	ESSEX	NY	153		41	GOLDEN VALLEY	ND	82
42	PHILADELPHIA	PA	153		42	BULLOCK	AL	83
43	MINERAL	NV	153		43	MADISON	ID	83
44	PULASKI	IN	153		44	STEWART	TN	83
45	SOLANO	CA	152		45	BERRIEN	GA	83
46	CHARLEVOIX	MI	152		46	JEFFERSON	MS	83
47	MARIN	CA	152		47	GOSHEN	WY	84
48	RENSSELAER	NY	151		48	DE BACA	NM	84
49	SCIOTO	OH	151		49	GLASCOCK	GA	84
50	ATHENS	OH	151		50	LEE	SC	84
51	WILKINSON	MS	151		51	JOHNSON	GA	84
52	ESSEX	NJ	151		52	SCREVEN	GA	84
53	HUDSON	NJ	151		53	BEAVER	UT	84
54	VERMILLION	IN	151		54	MILLER	GA	84
55	CHURCHILL	NV	150		55	SMITH	KS	84
56	DEARBORN	IN	150		56	ST HELENA	LA	84
57	BERGEN	NJ	150		57	WASATCH	UT	85
58	CAROLINE	MD	150		58	CASTRO	TX	85
59	ATLANTIC	NJ	150		59	SEARCY	AR	85
60	WARREN	NY	150		60	MADISON	FL	85
					61	TWIGGS	GA	85

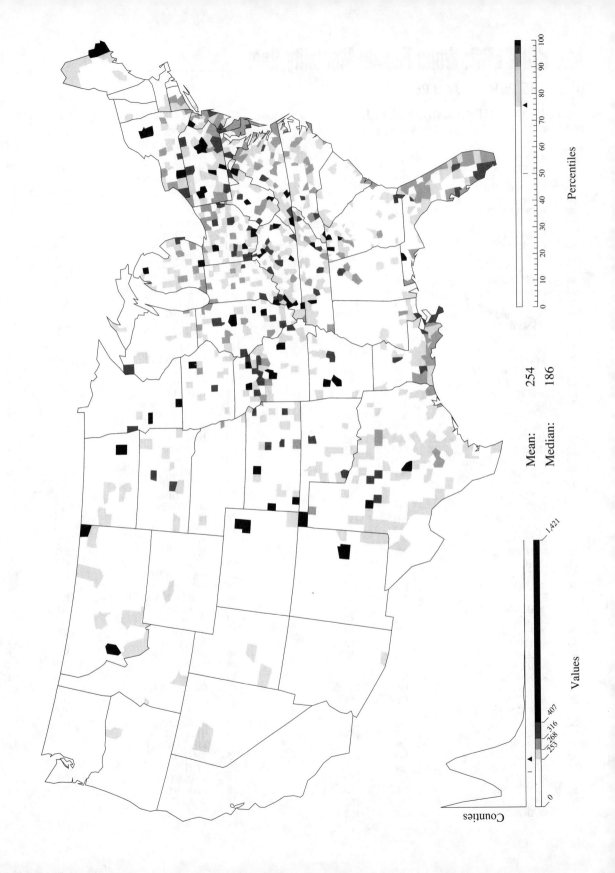

Mean: 254

Median: 186

Percentiles

Values

Counties

0   253 268 316 407   1,421

(DEATHS PER 100,000 PEOPLE)

TOP COUNTIES SHADED BLACK

RANK	COUNTY	STATE	VALUE
1	FULTON	PA	1,421
2	SAN SABA	TX	1,277
3	MONTOUR	PA	1,248
4	HAMPSHIRE	WV	1,222
5	ROOKS	KS	1,168
6	NORTHUMBERLAND	PA	1,073
7	GRANT	KY	1,017
8	NANTUCKET	MA	972
9	CARROLL	VA	829
10	MURRAY	GA	810
11	WASHINGTON	MO	761
12	SWIFT	MN	761
13	GRANITE	MT	761
14	BARNES	ND	761
15	SHELBY	MO	743
16	COLUMBIA	PA	681
17	FLOYD	KY	669
18	WASHINGTON	CO	609
19	FORSYTH	GA	609
20	UNION	GA	609
21	MARTIN	MN	609
22	CIMARRON	OK	609
23	GILMER	WV	609
24	BENTON	TN	608
25	CLAY	NC	608
26	MORGAN	MO	597
27	SUSSEX	NJ	591
28	RUSSELL	KY	577
29	ALLEGANY	NY	548
30	SCHUYLKILL	PA	545
31	JOHNSON	AR	514
32	LIVINGSTON	MO	504
33	GARZA	TX	497
34	FAYETTE	IA	492
35	POSEY	IN	474
36	CLINTON	OH	461
37	HANCOCK	OH	460
38	CLARION	PA	455
39	YELL	AR	452
40	SUMMERS	WV	450
41	MONITEAU	MO	438
42	WEBSTER	KY	429
43	VENANGO	PA	429
44	HILLSDALE	MI	424
45	SCOTT	VA	423
46	SHERIDAN	MT	423
47	CALLOWAY	KY	421
48	HOLMES	FL	421
49	LYON	KY	420
50	STEVENS	KS	419
51	WASHINGTON	ME	418
52	SCIOTO	OH	416
53	BLAIR	PA	413
54	MC LEAN	IL	412
55	CRITTENDEN	KY	412
56	HARRISON	KY	410
57	LOUDON	TN	409
58	CLAY	IL	407
59	CUMBERLAND	IL	407
60	GREELEY	KS	407
61	OTSEGO	MI	407
62	DE BACA	NM	407
63	HAMILTON	NY	407

BOTTOM COUNTIES SHADED WHITE

NOTE: TOO MANY COUNTIES TO LIST
HAD ZERO VALUES FOR THIS MEASURE

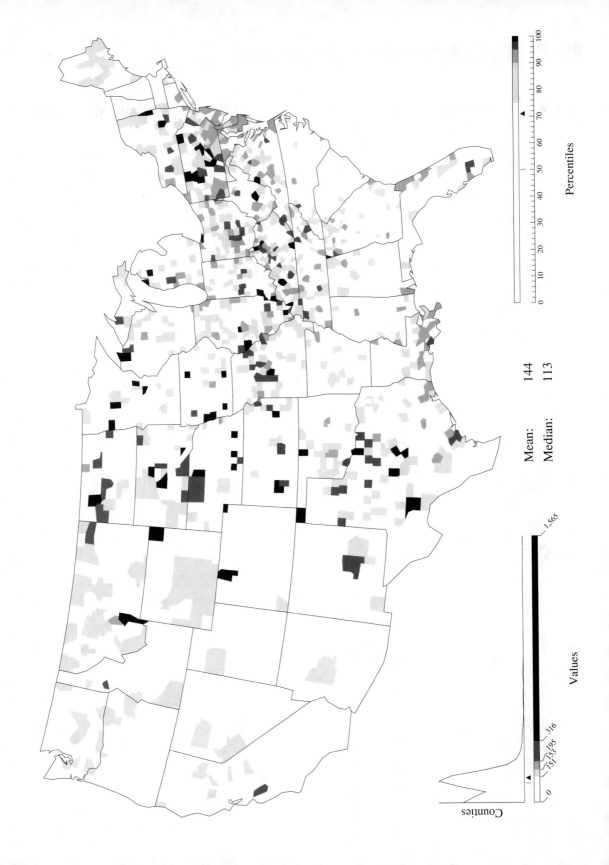

Mean: 144

Median: 113

Percentiles

Values

Counties

0   151   195   316   1,565
     153

(DEATHS PER 100,000 PEOPLE)

TOP COUNTIES SHADED BLACK

RANK	COUNTY	STATE	VALUE
1	ELK	PA	1,565
2	MENARD	IL	957
3	MONONA	IA	816
4	BROWN	NE	816
5	ALFALFA	OK	761
6	HAMILTON	TX	761
7	CROOK	WY	761
8	NORMAN	MN	756
9	DOUGLAS	SD	756
10	PERRY	PA	745
11	SNYDER	PA	649
12	NORTHUMBERLAND	PA	628
13	ROUTT	CO	609
14	FLOYD	IA	609
15	HARRISON	IA	609
16	COFFEY	KS	609
17	MC CREARY	KY	609
18	CIMARRON	OK	609
19	POTTER	SD	609
20	PIKE	IL	579
21	MONTOUR	PA	495
22	CLAY	TX	491
23	SUSQUEHANNA	PA	488
24	OTTAWA	OH	476
25	MC KEAN	PA	464
26	PENDLETON	KY	457
27	MOUNTRAIL	ND	450
28	WASHINGTON	NY	417
29	ADAMS	NE	415
30	SHERBURNE	MN	414
31	JEFFERSON	PA	411
32	OHIO	KY	410
33	PHELPS	NE	408
34	KANABEC	MN	407
35	NANTUCKET	MA	406
36	KALKASKA	MI	406
37	MONROE	IA	404
38	CROCKETT	TX	403
39	COLEMAN	TX	396
40	LEELANAU	MI	389
41	MORGAN	MO	388
42	LAMPASAS	TX	381
43	JOHNSON	IL	380
44	WABASH	IL	380
45	SALINE	NE	380
46	NICHOLAS	WV	380
47	HUBBARD	MN	378
48	NICHOLAS	KY	376
49	DADE	GA	366
50	SEDGWICK	CO	361
51	LIVINGSTON	KY	352
52	STANLEY	SD	350
53	HUNTINGDON	PA	345
54	FINNEY	KS	345
55	POSEY	IN	341
56	BATH	VA	329
57	MONTGOMERY	IA	327
58	KNOX	IN	325
59	GALLATIN	MT	324
60	BAYFIELD	WI	324
61	SCHOHARIE	NY	316

BOTTOM COUNTIES SHADED WHITE

NOTE: TOO MANY COUNTIES TO LIST
HAD ZERO VALUES FOR THIS MEASURE

so contaminated that people cannot eat fish out of it. He can reel off a list of cancer victims from the region: nine members of his own family; six brothers in another household died of cancer in a three-year span; even Amos's grandson is now riddled with cancer and has had to undergo chemotherapy and operations.

"It's another Hitler gas chamber out here," says Mr. Favorite."[94]

Lung cancer is the number-one cause of cancer deaths in the United States.[95] Lung cancer mortality has been increasing faster than any of the other causes of death mapped in the atlas, and the increase in its geographic disparities is second only to young adult infectious diseases (which includes AIDS). Lung cancer deaths have become more concentrated in the Southeast. The cluster in Louisiana has extended up the Mississippi River to Missouri, then up the Ohio River. This riverside trend is especially pronounced for white men, suggesting factors unique to this local population group, possibly relating to tobacco use and occupation.[96]

Most experts believe smoking accounts for an overwhelming share of lung cancer deaths in the United States, increasing an individual's risk of dying from lung cancer by tenfold compared with nonsmokers.[97] The state-by-state pattern of lung cancer mortality rates is very similar to the pattern for smoking rates (see chapter 2 for the state map of smoking). But there are some interesting exceptions, especially in the South. In the 1950s, seven of the eight states with the lowest cigarette consumption were in the South, and these southern states had below-average rates of lung cancer.[98] Today, the South claims seven of the eight states with the highest lung cancer mortality rates, but only three of the eight states with the largest percentages of their populations who smoke.[99]

Why the southern states show up more prominently for lung cancer mortality than for smoking may be due to a number of factors. The average southern smoker may smoke more heavily than the average northern smoker. In Louisiana, for example, NCI suggests the toll from smoking may be as high as 90 percent of all lung cancer cases because of the frequent use of hand-rolled cigarettes among the Cajun population.[100] There is considerable evidence that occupational exposures also contribute significantly to lung cancer mortality, especially when combined with smoking. The most widely quoted estimate is that as many as 16,000 lung cancer deaths per year may be due to occupational exposures in the United States (15 percent of total lung cancer deaths for men and 5 percent of the total for women).[101]

Asbestos is considered the second most important cause of lung cancer after tobacco, because it is such a potent carcinogen and because 8 to 10 million people have been exposed to the substance in the workplace.[102] Earlier NCI studies associated the high lung cancer rates along the coasts of Virginia, Georgia, Florida, and Louisiana with exposures to asbestos and other carcinogens in shipyards.[103] In addition to asbestos and shipbuilding, researchers have found elevated lung cancer risks for Georgia workers in the construction industry, for Florida workers in construction, fishing, and lumber, and for Louisiana workers in lumber, fishing, and sugarcane farming.[104] NCI has also found high rates of lung cancer in counties where many employees work in chemical plants producing industrial gases, medicines, detergents, paints, pigments, or synthetic rubber, and in counties with paper, petroleum, and transportation industries.[105] NCI's more recent negative results for many of these factors in relation to high lung cancer rates in Louisiana may be partly due to their study design. They compared lung cancer patients with other sick people in Louisiana hospitals. Many members of this control group may have had ailments that were also related to the factors causing the elevated lung cancer rates.[106]

In the Northeast, NCI has associated occupational exposures in a number of industries with increased lung cancer risks, after adjusting for smoking. In Eastern Pennsylvania (Lehigh, Northampton, and Carbon counties), for example, NCI found that employment in the steel industry carried a significantly increased risk of lung cancer mortality.[107] An NCI study of lung cancer deaths in these three counties found that in the mid-1970's residents living near a zinc smelter had twice the risk of lung cancer mortality compared with people living in parts of the counties where less metallic air pollution was found.[108] The NCI report, published in 1984, a few years after the smelter closed, said that there were too few people in the study and inadequate data to determine a causal connection, but that the findings warranted further investigation in other parts of the United States. The maps in this book indicate that lung cancer mortality for the entire population in these three counties is below the national average, although minority men there have rates that are above their national norm. In a 1975 study, NCI had found increased lung cancer mortality rates among both men and women living near copper, lead, and zinc smelters across the country.[109] In New Jersey, white male workers in over two dozen job categories have lung cancer risks that are more than 30 percent higher than for the rest of state residents, after adjusting for cigarette smoking.[110] The high lung cancer rates in upstate New York may be associated with the large paper industries there.[111]

In the West and other parts of the country, high lung cancer rates have been associated with exposures to radiation. Uranium miners in Arizona, Colorado, New Mexico, and Utah have had five times the expected rate of lung cancer.[112] In Colorado, the Rocky Flats nuclear weapons plant outside Denver has had significant problems controlling radioactive contamination.[113] Workers there have contracted an incurable lung disease called berylliosis, and increases in lung cancer have been correlated with levels of radioactive plutonium found in the soil for many miles around the site.[114] While the counties surrounding the facility do not show up in the maps, lung cancer mortality is in fact increasing significantly faster in Adams County and Boulder County than in the rest of the country. High lung cancer rates can be seen near Cincinnati, Ohio, where another nuclear weapons plant in Fernald spread radioactive uranium into the air and water.[115] And in counties surrounding the Savannah River nuclear weapons plant in South Carolina (Aiken and Barnwell counties), which experienced some of the worst nuclear reactor accidents ever reported in the United States, lung cancer mortality is significantly higher than the rest of the country—and is rising significantly faster.[116] In addition to occupational exposures to uranium, and exposures to man-made radiation from nuclear facilities, natural radon is also suspected of contributing significantly to lung cancer mortality by seeping into homes across the country, possibly causing as many as 24,000 cancer deaths per year.[117]

The geographic patterns of lung cancer mortality are markedly different for men and women. The tremendous southeastern concentration of lung cancer mortality is much more apparent for white men than for white women. Clusters of high rates of female lung cancer mortality can be seen throughout Florida and California, and hugging the southern Atlantic coast. From the 1950s to the 1970s, white women had the best improvements in cancer mortality relative to the other groups.[118] Now their increase in lung cancer mortality is greater than that for any other cause of death and population group in the atlas. The rapid rise in lung cancer among women, especially during the 1970s, may be due to their late start picking up the smoking habit relative to men, and to their relatively recent entrance to the industrial work force.

Minorities do not share the southeastern concentration of high lung cancer rates found among white men either. Their highest rates center in the Midwest, but can also be seen in counties throughout the Northwest and Northeast. Other researchers have found particularly high lung cancer rates among black men in Ohio who migrated there from the South.[119] Only small differences were found among whites and minorities born in Ohio. These findings suggest that the high midwestern lung cancer rates for minorities may be due to the migration experience itself and to occupational exposures in the heavily industrialized Midwest. Considerable evidence suggests that minorities have higher rates of occupational exposures than whites, and that recent immigrants in particular get the dirtiest jobs.[120] This hypothesis is supported by the absence of high minority lung cancer rates in the rural Southeast from where many of the immigrants came, and by the considerably higher rates among minority men than women.

Smoking is also very probably involved with the high lung cancer mortality rates among black men. In the 1950s, cancer mortality among black men was about 20 percent lower than for whites in the United States.[121] Now black men have the highest cancer mortality rates, especially for lung cancer. Their emergence as the highest risk group for lung cancer parallels the fact that African Americans picked up the smoking habit some 10 to 20 years after whites. Blacks began smoking largely after their mass migration from the rural South to the urban North, and their smoking rates did not match those of whites until the late 1950s.[122] Now a higher percentage of blacks than whites smoke, and it has been suggested that the toll can be found in higher rates of heart disease and lung cancer.[123] Yet black men smoke fewer cigarettes per capita than white men, which should reduce their relative risk to some extent.[124] Moreover, the geographic patterns for lung cancer among minority males differ markedly from those for heart disease, suggesting distinct causes for the clusters of high minority lung cancer rates in the Midwest, and the high rates of heart disease in the Southeast.

BREAST CANCERS

After five teachers at Ogden elementary school in North Woodmere, Long Island, were diagnosed with breast cancer from 1977 to 1982, the local Parent Teachers Association called for an investigation. The Nassau County Board of Health found that the air and water at the school were normal, and that the women fit the risk profile for breast cancer: they were older women of Jewish and Italian origins with family histories of the disease, relatively high socioeconomic status, and diets high in fat and alcohol.[125] Yet Bert Nelson, the school district superintendent still had questions, saying, "The matter is larger than the local board of health—the CDC in Atlanta, a national agency, should be looking into the picture."[126] In fact, breast cancer mortality in Nassau County is higher than 99 percent of the counties in the country—definitely something to worry about.

Groundwater contamination is the first thing Long Islanders think of with the mention of a cancer cluster. Almost all of Long Island's 2.5 million inhabitants get their drinking water from groundwater, much of

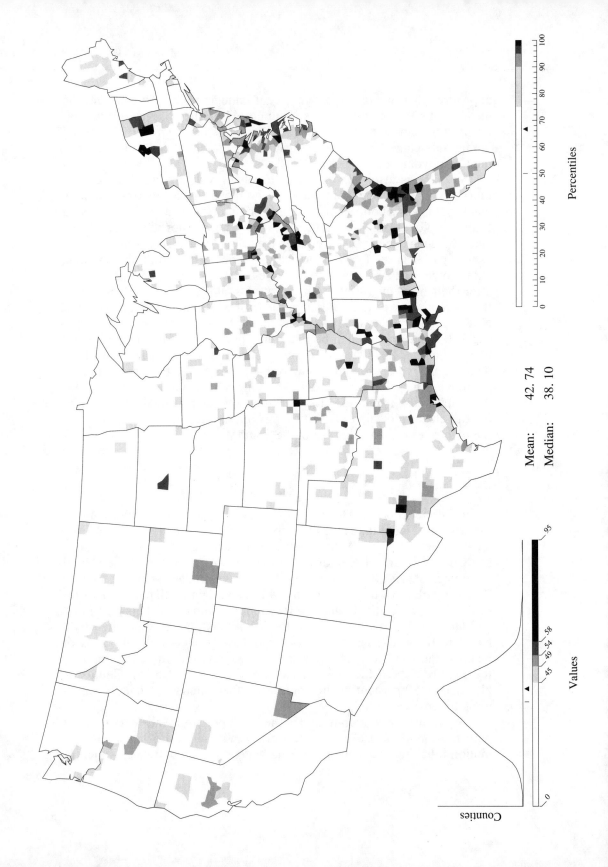

Mean: 42. 74

Median: 38. 10

Percentiles

Values

Counties

(DEATHS PER 100,000 PEOPLE)

TOP COUNTIES SHADED BLACK

RANK	COUNTY	STATE	VALUE
1	NANTUCKET	MA	95
2	MC CREARY	KY	95
3	REAGAN	TX	88
4	LONG	GA	75
5	ALLENDALE	SC	72
6	BAKER	GA	71
7	UNION	FL	71
8	CHARLTON	GA	70
9	HAMILTON	NY	67
10	BALLARD	KY	67
11	FRANKLIN	FL	66
12	SOMERSET	MD	66
13	FLOYD	KY	66
14	KENTON	KY	65
15	NORTHAMPTON	VA	65
16	LAWRENCE	MS	64
17	MITCHELL	GA	64
18	CRISP	GA	63
19	FULTON	KY	63
20	PERRY	MS	63
21	BRYAN	GA	63
22	MC INTOSH	GA	63
23	JEFFERSON	NY	63
24	BALTIMORE CITY	MD	63
25	CHEROKEE	KS	62
26	HUMPHREYS	MS	62
27	CAMPBELL	TN	62
28	ST LOUIS CITY	MO	61
29	LEFLORE	MS	61
30	DUVAL	FL	61
31	ALEXANDER	IL	61
32	ACCOMACK	VA	61
33	PERRY	KY	60
34	CABELL	WV	60
35	BRANTLEY	GA	60
36	LIBERTY	GA	60
37	EVANGELINE	LA	60
38	ST TAMMANY	LA	60
39	ST BERNARD	LA	60
40	GRANT	AR	60
41	CLAY	KY	60
42	MINGO	WV	59
43	JEFFERSON	KY	59
44	HOCKING	OH	59
45	CHARLES	MD	59
46	CLAIBORNE	TN	59
47	STONE	MS	59
48	IBERIA	LA	59
49	PULASKI	GA	59
50	GALVESTON	TX	59
51	CHAMBERS	TX	59
52	CAMDEN	GA	58
53	ACADIA	LA	58
54	WINKLER	TX	58
55	MARION	IN	58
56	PUTNAM	FL	58
57	RUSSELL	AL	58
58	CLARKE	VA	58
59	SOUTHAMPTON	VA	58
60	BATH	VA	58
61	MOBILE	AL	58

BOTTOM COUNTIES SHADED WHITE

RANK	COUNTY	STATE	VALUE
1	ALPINE	CA	0
2	KENEDY	TX	0
3	DAGGETT	UT	0
4	CARTER	MT	5
5	GOSPER	NE	6
6	FRANKLIN	ID	6
7	RICH	UT	7
8	HARDING	NM	7
9	MADISON	ID	7
10	OLIVER	ND	8
11	WAYNE	UT	8
12	CONEJOS	CO	8
13	KEARNEY	NE	9
14	GARFIELD	UT	9
15	THOMAS	NE	9
16	SEVIER	UT	9
17	CACHE	UT	10
18	BEAR LAKE	ID	10
19	LOS ALAMOS	NM	10
20	JUAB	UT	11
21	POWER	ID	11
22	SANPETE	UT	12
23	MORGAN	UT	12
24	HODGEMAN	KS	12
25	BILLINGS	ND	12
26	KIOWA	CO	12
27	CATRON	NM	12
28	WHEELER	NE	12
29	CUSTER	ID	13
30	PRESIDIO	TX	13
31	WASHINGTON	UT	13
32	SUMMIT	UT	13
33	CLARK	KS	13
34	DIVIDE	ND	13
35	ELBERT	CO	13
36	WIBAUX	MT	13
37	JEFFERSON	ID	13
38	MELLETTE	SD	13
39	GOVE	KS	13
40	MC PHERSON	NE	14
41	HITCHCOCK	NE	14
42	NESS	KS	14
43	OURAY	CO	14
44	BLAINE	NE	14
45	JUDITH BASIN	MT	14
46	NELSON	ND	14
47	WICHITA	KS	15
48	GRIGGS	ND	15
49	CARIBOU	ID	15
50	ZIEBACH	SD	15
51	LIPSCOMB	TX	15
52	TRAILL	ND	15
53	LINCOLN	KS	15
54	TETON	ID	15
55	IRON	UT	15
56	RANSOM	ND	15
57	YUMA	CO	15
58	MC CONE	MT	15
59	BOTTINEAU	ND	16
60	COSTILLA	CO	16
61	GUNNISON	CO	16

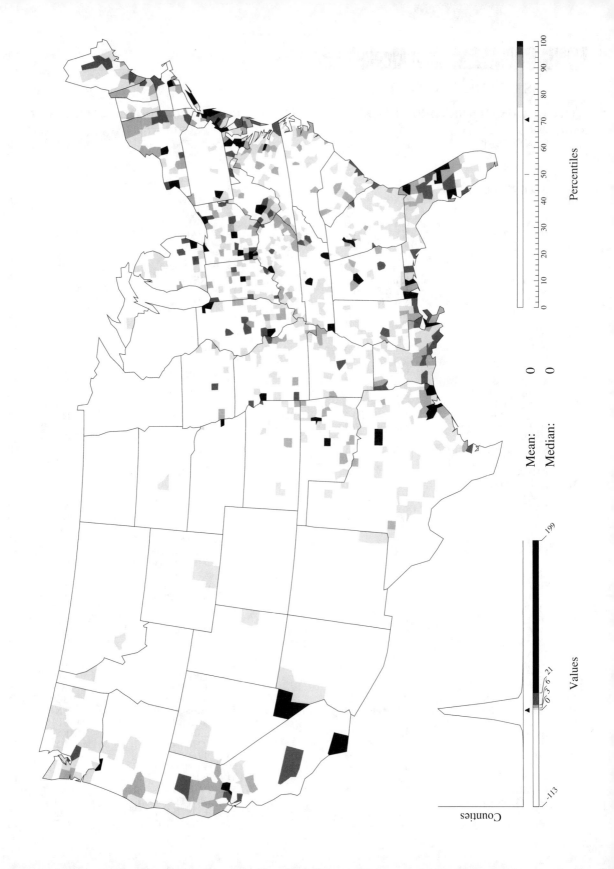

Values

Percentiles

Mean: 0

Median: 0

Counties

-113

0 3 6 21

199

TOP COUNTIES SHADED BLACK

RANK	COUNTY	STATE	VALUE
1	PHILADELPHIA	PA	199
2	BALTIMORE CITY	MD	171
3	WAYNE	MI	162
4	COOK	IL	149
5	HARRIS	TX	137
6	HAMILTON	OH	123
7	ALLEGHENY	PA	117
8	JEFFERSON	KY	112
9	MARION	IN	111
10	ST LOUIS CITY	MO	97
11	DUVAL	FL	82
12	CUYAHOGA	OH	82
13	ORLEANS	LA	80
14	DALLAS	TX	72
15	FRANKLIN	OH	70
16	HILLSBOROUGH	FL	68
17	JEFFERSON	AL	63
18	SUFFOLK	NY	58
19	ERIE	NY	56
20	SUFFOLK	MA	56
21	DISTRICT OF COLUMBIA	DC	53
22	SHELBY	TN	51
23	HENRICO	VA	47
24	LUCAS	OH	46
25	HUDSON	NJ	46
26	MONTGOMERY	OH	44
27	TARRANT	TX	43
28	BALTIMORE	MD	42
29	DAVIDSON	TN	38
30	MOBILE	AL	38
31	CAMDEN	NJ	38
32	JACKSON	MO	37
33	TULSA	OK	36
34	NEW CASTLE	DE	36
35	OKLAHOMA	OK	35
36	MULTNOMAH	OR	32
37	JEFFERSON	LA	32
38	OCEAN	NJ	31
39	MIDDLESEX	NJ	30
40	CLARK	NV	29
41	KANAWHA	WV	27
42	GALVESTON	TX	27
43	ST CLAIR	IL	27
44	KENTON	KY	26
45	SACRAMENTO	CA	26
46	ESCAMBIA	FL	26
47	MONMOUTH	NJ	25
48	PROVIDENCE	RI	25
49	PRINCE GEORGES	MD	25
50	DELAWARE	PA	25
51	SAN FRANCISCO	CA	24
52	ANNE ARUNDEL	MD	23
53	ONONDAGA	NY	23
54	JEFFERSON	TX	23
55	ORANGE	FL	23
56	DOUGLAS	NE	22
57	BREVARD	FL	21
58	FULTON	GA	21
59	SAN DIEGO	CA	21
60	HAMILTON	TN	21

BOTTOM COUNTIES SHADED WHITE

RANK	COUNTY	STATE	VALUE
1	NEW YORK CITY	NY	-113
2	SALT LAKE	UT	-75
3	DENVER	CO	-46
4	MARICOPA	AZ	-46
5	SANTA CLARA	CA	-43
6	LUZERNE	PA	-37
7	MONTGOMERY	MD	-36
8	LOS ANGELES	CA	-34
9	HENNEPIN	MN	-34
10	BERNALILLO	NM	-31
11	UTAH	UT	-29
12	HIDALGO	TX	-28
13	JEFFERSON	CO	-26
14	EL PASO	TX	-25
15	LANCASTER	PA	-25
16	WEBER	UT	-24
17	YORK	PA	-24
18	EL PASO	CO	-23
19	WORCESTER	MA	-23
20	MONTGOMERY	PA	-22
21	DANE	WI	-21
22	WAUKESHA	WI	-20
23	SCHUYLKILL	PA	-20
24	KENT	MI	-19
25	BERKS	PA	-19
26	CAMERON	TX	-18
27	LACKAWANNA	PA	-17
28	SHEBOYGAN	WI	-17
29	BOULDER	CO	-17
30	DAVIS	UT	-17
31	FAIRFIELD	CT	-17
32	DU PAGE	IL	-17
33	DADE	FL	-16
34	RAMSEY	MN	-16
35	LANCASTER	NE	-16
36	LEHIGH	PA	-16
37	LARIMER	CO	-16
38	ARAPAHOE	CO	-16
39	OTTAWA	MI	-16
40	MANITOWOC	WI	-16
41	MARATHON	WI	-16
42	HARTFORD	CT	-15
43	STEARNS	MN	-15
44	CAMBRIA	PA	-15
45	WESTMORELAND	PA	-15
46	BROWARD	FL	-15
47	WELD	CO	-14
48	SOMERSET	PA	-14
49	FRESNO	CA	-14
50	BROWN	WI	-14
51	OAKLAND	MI	-14
52	RIVERSIDE	CA	-14
53	OTTER TAIL	MN	-13
54	MILWAUKEE	WI	-13
55	ST LOUIS	MN	-13
56	INDIANA	PA	-13
57	JOHNSON	KS	-13
58	PALM BEACH	FL	-12
59	CHAUTAUQUA	NY	-12
60	PUEBLO	CO	-12
61	DAKOTA	MN	-12
62	PIMA	AZ	-12

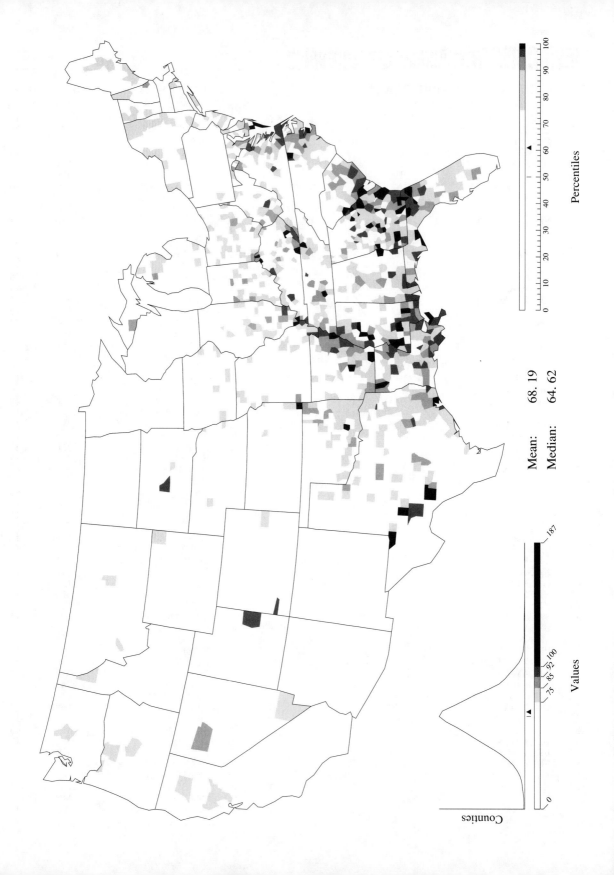

Mean: 68. 19

Median: 64. 62

Percentiles

Values

Counties

(DEATHS PER 100,000 PEOPLE)

TOP COUNTIES SHADED BLACK					**BOTTOM COUNTIES SHADED WHITE**			
RANK	**COUNTY**	**STATE**	**VALUE**		**RANK**	**COUNTY**	**STATE**	**VALUE**
1	CHATTAHOOCHEE	GA	187		1	ALPINE	CA	0
2	BAKER	GA	144		2	SHANNON	SD	0
3	LONG	GA	137		3	KENEDY	TX	0
4	ALLENDALE	SC	136		4	DAGGETT	UT	0
5	CHARLTON	GA	135		5	CATRON	NM	7
6	TALIAFERRO	GA	131		6	TREASURE	MT	8
7	LOVING	TX	130		7	RICH	UT	9
8	REAGAN	TX	129		8	HARDING	NM	10
9	UNION	FL	127		9	CARTER	MT	10
10	MITCHELL	GA	125		10	ZIEBACH	SD	11
11	CRISP	GA	122		11	THOMAS	NE	12
12	PULASKI	GA	120		12	CONEJOS	CO	13
13	LAWRENCE	MS	119		13	GOSPER	NE	13
14	BRYAN	GA	114		14	MADISON	ID	14
15	HUMPHREYS	MS	114		15	FRANKLIN	ID	14
16	MC CORMICK	SC	113		16	LOS ALAMOS	NM	14
17	NORTHAMPTON	VA	113		17	GARFIELD	UT	15
18	EDWARDS	TX	112		18	MORGAN	UT	15
19	CHAMBERS	TX	110		19	SEVIER	UT	15
20	GRANT	AR	110		20	HODGEMAN	KS	15
21	WAKULLA	FL	110		21	BILLINGS	ND	16
22	FRANKLIN	FL	110		22	DIVIDE	ND	17
23	WINKLER	TX	109		23	CARIBOU	ID	18
24	LIBERTY	GA	109		24	BEAR LAKE	ID	18
25	PERRY	MS	108		25	CACHE	UT	18
26	SOMERSET	MD	107		26	OLIVER	ND	18
27	CAMPBELL	TN	105		27	MAHNOMEN	MN	19
28	BURKE	GA	105		28	WAYNE	UT	19
29	LEFLORE	MS	105		29	TODD	SD	19
30	HAMPTON	SC	105		30	SIOUX	ND	19
31	ST BERNARD	LA	105		31	WASHINGTON	UT	19
32	ASHLEY	AR	104		32	KEARNEY	NE	20
33	ST LOUIS CITY	MO	104		33	JUDITH BASIN	MT	20
34	JEFFERSON	MS	103		34	ARCHULETA	CO	21
35	JEFFERSON DAVIS	MS	103		35	GOVE	KS	21
36	PERRY	KY	103		36	MELLETTE	SD	21
37	KENTON	KY	102		37	GUNNISON	CO	22
38	COAL	OK	102		38	WIBAUX	MT	23
39	BALLARD	KY	102		39	GRIGGS	ND	23
40	GALLATIN	KY	102		40	SUMMIT	UT	24
41	BALTIMORE CITY	MD	102		41	JUAB	UT	24
42	CLAIBORNE	MS	102		42	KIOWA	CO	24
43	CHEROKEE	KS	102		43	PRESIDIO	TX	24
44	CLINCH	GA	102		44	JACKSON	CO	24
45	FRANKLIN	MS	102		45	HITCHCOCK	NE	25
46	RUSSELL	AL	101		46	UINTA	WY	25
47	GRENADA	MS	101		47	POWER	ID	26
48	ALEXANDER	IL	101		48	SAGUACHE	CO	26
49	CRITTENDEN	AR	101		49	YUMA	CO	26
50	WARREN	NC	101		50	UTAH	UT	26
51	COLUMBIA	GA	101		51	CONCHO	TX	26
52	MC CREARY	KY	101		52	OURAY	CO	26
53	TWIGGS	GA	101		53	DUCHESNE	UT	26
54	MC INTOSH	GA	100		54	LINCOLN	KS	26
55	LEWIS	TN	100		55	ELBERT	CO	26
56	MONTGOMERY	GA	100		56	CUSTER	ID	26
57	PAMLICO	NC	100		57	SANPETE	UT	26
58	ACCOMACK	VA	100		58	MORA	NM	27
59	BOSSIER	LA	100		59	MC CONE	MT	27
60	GLASCOCK	GA	100		60	COSTILLA	CO	27
61	DUVAL	FL	100		61	BOUNDARY	ID	27
62	HAMILTON	FL	100		62	CLARK	KS	27

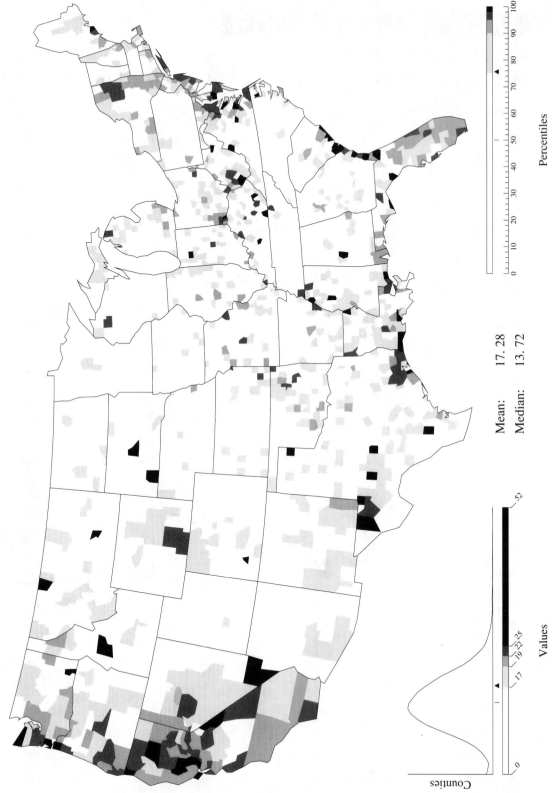

Mean: 17. 28

Median: 13. 72

Percentiles

Values

Counties

(DEATHS PER 100,000 PEOPLE)

TOP COUNTIES SHADED BLACK				BOTTOM COUNTIES SHADED WHITE			
RANK	COUNTY	STATE	VALUE	RANK	COUNTY	STATE	VALUE
1	MC MULLEN	TX	52	1	GLASCOCK	GA	0
2	CULBERSON	TX	46	2	TALIAFERRO	GA	0
3	MONO	CA	43	3	BOISE	ID	0
4	SAN JUAN	CO	42	4	BUTTE	ID	0
5	POWHATAN	VA	40	5	POWER	ID	0
6	SHANNON	SD	38	6	TETON	ID	0
7	CONCHO	TX	35	7	JEFFERSON	MS	0
8	CHARLES CITY	VA	35	8	GARFIELD	MT	0
9	MC INTOSH	GA	34	9	GOSPER	NE	0
10	VALLEY	ID	33	10	GOLDEN VALLEY	ND	0
11	RICHMOND	VA	33	11	OLIVER	ND	0
12	MINGO	WV	31	12	BENNETT	SD	0
13	TREASURE	MT	31	13	FAULK	SD	0
14	NANTUCKET	MA	30	14	HARDING	SD	0
15	DIXIE	FL	30	15	JERAULD	SD	0
16	PACIFIC	WA	30	16	LIPSCOMB	TX	0
17	NEW KENT	VA	29	17	OLDHAM	TX	0
18	STANLEY	SD	29	18	WAYNE	UT	0
19	FRANKLIN	FL	29	19	SUBLETTE	WY	0
20	CAMERON	LA	29	20	KEARNEY	NE	0
21	CAMDEN	GA	29	21	FRANKLIN	ID	1
22	REAGAN	TX	28	22	LYON	IA	2
23	DEL NORTE	CA	28	23	SANPETE	UT	2
24	CHOWAN	NC	27	24	JUAB	UT	2
25	HEMPHILL	TX	27	25	NELSON	ND	2
26	EDMONSON	KY	27	26	SAN JUAN	UT	2
27	LOGAN	WV	27	27	HETTINGER	ND	3
28	ARANSAS	TX	27	28	CLEARWATER	MN	3
29	CLARK	NV	27	29	WELLS	ND	3
30	CLATSOP	OR	27	30	BOWMAN	ND	3
31	MC CREARY	KY	27	31	JEFFERSON	MT	3
32	LAKE	CA	27	32	PIKE	GA	3
33	CAMPBELL	KY	27	33	MILLER	GA	3
34	BATH	VA	27	34	COLLINGSWORTH	TX	3
35	EAST CARROLL	LA	27	35	SHERIDAN	ND	3
36	COLUSA	CA	27	36	LYMAN	SD	3
37	COLUMBIA	WA	26	37	SURRY	VA	3
38	PULASKI	IN	26	38	CUSTER	ID	3
39	HARRISON	MS	26	39	HARTLEY	TX	3
40	WINKLER	TX	26	40	JEFFERSON	ID	3
41	CHARLESTON	SC	26	41	PRENTISS	MS	3
42	TUCKER	WV	26	42	MONTGOMERY	GA	3
43	GALVESTON	TX	26	43	CLARK	KS	3
44	PERRY	KY	26	44	ONEIDA	ID	3
45	CLALLAM	WA	26	45	MADISON	ID	3
46	SHASTA	CA	26	46	RANDOLPH	GA	4
47	JASPER	SC	26	47	LINCOLN	ID	4
48	WESTMORELAND	VA	26	48	WASHINGTON	KS	4
49	IBERIA	LA	26	49	PAWNEE	KS	4
50	HALE	AL	26	50	KNOX	MO	4
51	TOOLE	MT	25	51	FAYETTE	TN	4
52	YOLO	CA	25	52	HARPER	KS	4
53	DUVAL	FL	25	53	CAMPBELL	SD	4
54	KNOX	ME	25	54	DIXON	NE	4
55	BEAUFORT	SC	25	55	BENSON	ND	4
56	DORCHESTER	MD	25	56	CACHE	UT	4
57	SOLANO	CA	25	57	BUTLER	NE	4
58	LEFLORE	MS	25	58	MILLARD	UT	4
59	TUNICA	MS	25	59	BOYD	NE	4
60	MARIN	CA	25	60	WILKIN	MN	4
				61	HAAKON	SD	4
				62	MC LEOD	MN	4

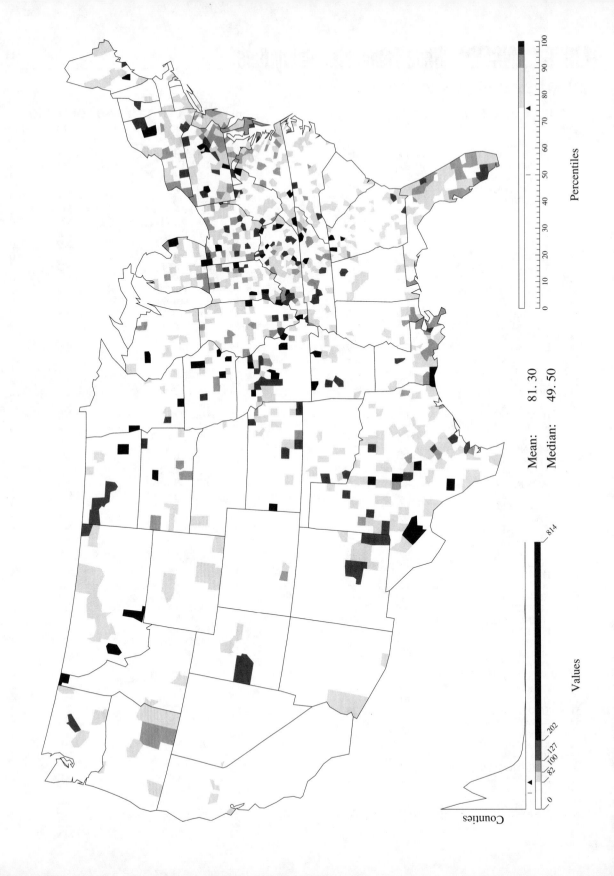

Mean: 81. 30
Median: 49. 50

Percentiles

Values

Counties

814

202
127
100
82

0

0 10 20 30 40 50 60 70 80 90 100

(DEATHS PER 100,000 PEOPLE)

TOP COUNTIES SHADED BLACK

RANK	COUNTY	STATE	VALUE
1	HAMPSHIRE	WV	814
2	FULTON	PA	812
3	STE GENEVIEVE	MO	761
4	GRANITE	MT	761
5	BARNES	ND	761
6	NORTHUMBERLAND	PA	641
7	SHARP	AR	609
8	FORSYTH	GA	609
9	UNION	GA	609
10	GRANT	KY	609
11	MARTIN	MN	609
12	PARK	MT	609
13	RUSK	WI	609
14	COLUMBIA	PA	574
15	NANTUCKET	MA	508
16	MAHASKA	IA	486
17	SHELBY	MO	480
18	OVERTON	TN	436
19	COLEMAN	TX	412
20	BUCHANAN	IA	407
21	GREELEY	KS	407
22	SANILAC	MI	407
23	HAMILTON	NY	407
24	WASHINGTON	MO	406
25	RUSSELL	KY	394
26	WILKIN	MN	380
27	POTTER	SD	380
28	FLOYD	KY	378
29	HENRY	IA	322
30	MURRAY	GA	305
31	MC LEAN	KY	305
32	WILLIAMS	OH	305
33	ZAVALA	TX	296
34	FAYETTE	IA	288
35	CLARION	PA	287
36	MUSCATINE	IA	285
37	CLAIBORNE	TN	284
38	MONITEAU	MO	278
39	RANDOLPH	IN	271
40	NICHOLAS	KY	261
41	LLANO	TX	254
42	POSEY	IN	252
43	GREENUP	KY	250
44	DAVIESS	IN	245
45	PECOS	TX	244
46	EDGAR	IL	238
47	ANDROSCOGGIN	ME	238
48	HANCOCK	OH	236
49	SCOTT	VA	221
50	BALLARD	KY	213
51	MORGAN	MO	210
52	CARROLL	VA	208
53	CAMERON	LA	207
54	CALDWELL	MO	204
55	HASKELL	TX	203
56	CARROLL	AR	203
57	BOUNDARY	ID	203
58	CARLISLE	KY	203
59	CLAY	IN	203
60	HILLSDALE	MI	202

BOTTOM COUNTIES SHADED WHITE

NOTE: TOO MANY COUNTIES TO LIST
HAD ZERO VALUES FOR THIS MEASURE

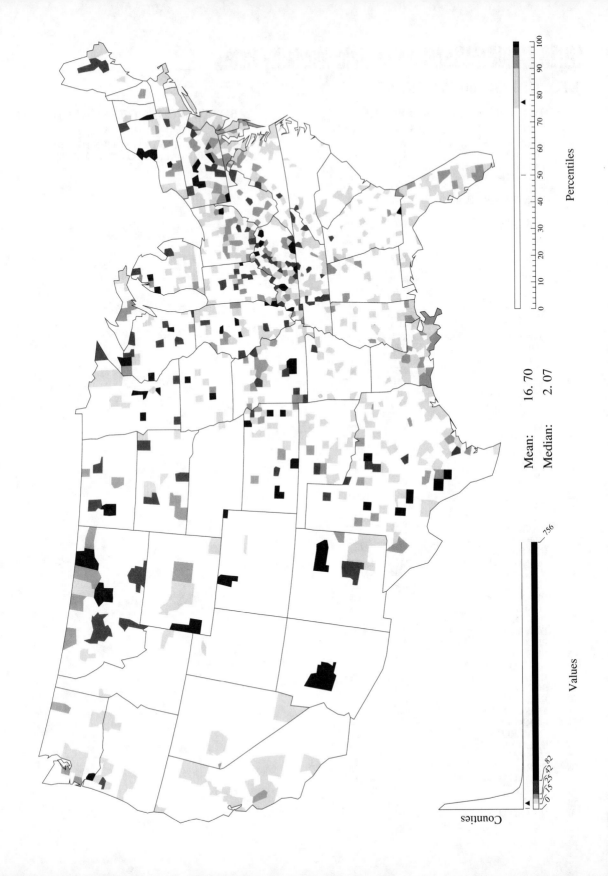

Mean: 16. 70
Median: 2. 07

Percentiles

Values

Counties

LUNG CANCERS: Minority Female Mortality Rate

(DEATHS PER 100,000 PEOPLE)

TOP COUNTIES SHADED BLACK

RANK	COUNTY	STATE	VALUE
1	MENARD	IL	756
2	ROUTT	CO	609
3	FLOYD	IA	609
4	MC CREARY	KY	609
5	PERRY	PA	609
6	WABASH	IL	380
7	TEXAS	MO	380
8	FRIO	TX	254
9	SEDGWICK	CO	253
10	ECHOLS	GA	241
11	GREEN LAKE	WI	204
12	ELK	PA	203
13	JEFFERSON	PA	203
14	FERGUS	MT	201
15	CARTER	KY	190
16	LINCOLN	WY	190
17	FLEMING	KY	165
18	UNION	IN	163
19	FINNEY	KS	160
20	NANTUCKET	MA	152
21	JACK	TX	152
22	REAGAN	TX	152
23	SCHLEICHER	TX	152
24	MARSHALL	IL	152
25	PENDLETON	KY	152
26	KALKASKA	MI	152
27	SHERBURNE	MN	152
28	WHITLEY	KY	142
29	DUNN	ND	136
30	WASHINGTON	NY	135
31	WRIGHT	MO	127
32	YATES	NY	127
33	SAN MIGUEL	NM	122
34	CLINTON	PA	122
35	UVALDE	TX	122
36	GREENE	PA	120
37	BAYFIELD	WI	119
38	COLUMBIA	OR	109
39	ST CROIX	WI	109
40	OSWEGO	NY	108
41	JEFFERSON	NY	108
42	BARBER	KS	102
43	LIVINGSTON	KY	102
44	SCOTT	MN	102
45	DALLAS	IA	102
46	MILLE LACS	MN	100
47	POPE	MN	100
48	FRANKLIN	KS	93
49	HARRISON	OH	92
50	POSEY	IN	92
51	GARZA	TX	91
52	VALLEY	MT	87
53	DE WITT	IL	87
54	NEMAHA	KS	87
55	MANISTEE	MI	87
56	YAVAPAI	AZ	85
57	ALLEN	KS	85
58	OHIO	KY	83
59	MONROE	KY	82

BOTTOM COUNTIES SHADED WHITE

NOTE: TOO MANY COUNTIES TO LIST
HAD ZERO VALUES FOR THIS MEASURE

which is threatened with chemical contamination. Dozens of public wells in Nassau County and thousands of private wells in Suffolk County have been closed since suspected carcinogens were detected in the water in 1980.[127] Yet when the New York State Department of Health recently looked into the relationship between breast cancer and groundwater pollution across Long Island, it found that breast cancer rates were lower in areas with contaminated wells and hazardous waste sites than elsewhere on the island. Instead, water districts with the highest incomes had the highest rates of breast cancer.[128] And, fortunately for women in Nassau County, the mortality rate from breast cancer there is improving considerably faster than in the country as a whole.

The picture is more complicated elsewhere: in New Jersey, researchers have found breast cancer mortality is significantly correlated with chemical waste disposal sites.[129] And in the three New Jersey counties with the highest rates (Essex, Monmouth, and Bergen), breast cancer mortality is increasing significantly. Moreover, we found high breast cancer rates are significantly correlated with a number of toxic waste measures nationwide. For example, breast cancer is the only cause of death of the ten examined in this book that is significantly associated with toxic waste Superfund sites, and there were almost four times as many facilities that treat and store toxic wastes in counties with the highest rates of breast cancer than in the nation as a whole. Despite this, the connection between environmental carcinogens and breast cancer is still an open question.

Breast cancer is the leading cause of cancer deaths among women, and the leading cause of death for women ages 35 to 55.[130] There is a striking concentration of the highest rates in the Northeast, especially in urban and suburban areas, and this has been the case for many years; however, the North-South differences are diminishing as southern rates increase, especially in Appalachia.[131] A number of personal characteristics have been associated with higher risks of breast cancer: family history of the disease, late childbearing, having no (or few) children, early menarche (first ovulation), late menopause, and obesity.[132] Women with higher socioeconomic status are more likely to get breast cancer (possibly because of delayed childbirth), but women with lower socioeconomic status are more likely to die from it (possibly because of poorer preventive care and treatment).[133] Early diagnosis is a major determinant of survival.

The predominance of breast cancer mortality in northern counties is primarily among postmenopausal women, whereas breast cancer mortality among premenopausal women is distributed almost uniformly across the country. The NCI has linked northeastern concentrations of breast cancer among older women to extrinsic risk factors they could not as yet identify, while the pattern for younger women would suggest reproductive and genetic determinants.[134] At all ages, breast cancer mortality is higher among urban residents in the Northeast than among rural residents in the South. There are also clusters of high rates in a number of midwestern and western states, especially among white women. Many counties with high breast cancer mortality rates among minority women are clustered in Ohio, Pennsylvania, West Virginia, and Tennessee.

Researchers have identified an unusual racial crossover for breast cancer: among women over 40, whites have higher rates than blacks, whereas among women under 40, whites have lower rates than blacks. Young black women with higher socioeconomic status have the highest rates of breast cancer before the age of 40, according to a study of San Francisco incidence rates. Researchers suggest this may be due to reproductive behavior (such as delayed childbearing and contraceptive use), but the risk factors are not certain.[135] Debate continues over the possible roles of abortion, oral contraceptive use, and diet.[136]

CHILD CANCERS

Children are the healthiest among us; they rarely die from natural causes. Since the early 1900s, most childhood deaths in the United States have been the result of injuries.[137] Fewer than 1 child in 10,000 dies from cancer, though it is the leading fatal disease among children.[138] The incidence of childhood cancer has increased slightly over the past decade, yet the rate of children dying from the disease is declining more than that for any other age group. Experts attribute much of the decline in mortality to improved therapies for childhood leukemia, the most common form of cancer among children.[139] For all of these reasons, clusters of child cancer mortality are remarkable.

Parents were understandably distressed when 8 children in the Denver suburb of Friendly Hills died of cancer between 1976 and 1984, and another 40 children suffered from cancer, birth defects, immunological disorders, and other serious diseases. They organized the Friendly Hills Action Group and uncovered state records dating back to 1957 that indicated toxic chemicals from a nearby Martin Marrietta weapons plant may have leaked into a water supply facility. Soon after the parents' group went public with their findings, the Denver water board shut the water plant down. Water board officials denied their action had anything

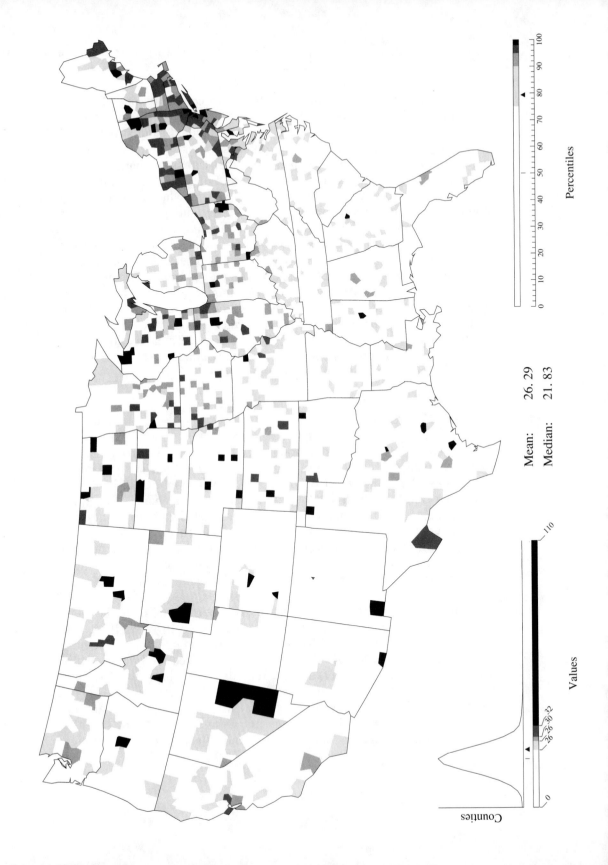

Mean: 26. 29

Median: 21. 83

Percentiles

Values

Counties

(DEATHS PER 100,000 WOMEN)

TOP COUNTIES SHADED BLACK

RANK	COUNTY	STATE	VALUE
1	CAMAS	ID	110
2	PETROLEUM	MT	84
3	SHERMAN	TX	80
4	ALLEGANY	NY	47
5	HITCHCOCK	NE	47
6	WHEELER	OR	46
7	THOMAS	NE	46
8	LA CROSSE	WI	45
9	SAN JUAN	CO	43
10	GOLIAD	TX	42
11	WASHINGTON	VT	42
12	CORSON	SD	42
13	WHITE PINE	NV	41
14	SCHOHARIE	NY	41
15	SUBLETTE	WY	40
16	NANTUCKET	MA	40
17	WELLS	ND	40
18	TALIAFERRO	GA	39
19	ADAMS	NE	39
20	DODGE	WI	39
21	LA SALLE	IL	38
22	BUTTE	ID	38
23	MARSHALL	IN	38
24	GOLDEN VALLEY	MT	37
25	HOWARD	NE	37
26	RENVILLE	ND	37
27	FULTON	NY	37
28	NOWATA	OK	36
29	SOMERVELL	TX	36
30	NASSAU	NY	35
31	LUNA	NM	35
32	SANTA CRUZ	AZ	35
33	WALSH	ND	35
34	ESSEX	NY	35
35	MARION	MO	34
36	ASHLAND	WI	34
37	PITKIN	CO	34
38	CAMERON	PA	34
39	BAYFIELD	WI	34
40	HAMILTON	OH	34
41	CHOCTAW	MS	34
42	ESSEX	NJ	34
43	MONMOUTH	NJ	34
44	QUEEN ANNES	MD	33
45	LAC QUI PARLE	MN	33
46	ALLEGANY	MD	33
47	WESTCHESTER	NY	33
48	DISTRICT OF COLUMBIA	DC	33
49	WASHINGTON	TX	33
50	SCOTT	KS	33
51	OHIO	WV	33
52	BERGEN	NJ	33
53	BELMONT	OH	33
54	JERAULD	SD	33
55	KENNEBEC	ME	33
56	LINCOLN	NV	33
57	LACKAWANNA	PA	32
58	HARRISON	OH	32
59	JEFFERSON	OH	32
60	UNION	NJ	32

BOTTOM COUNTIES SHADED WHITE

RANK	COUNTY	STATE	VALUE
1	ISSAQUENA	MS	0
2	SLOPE	ND	0
3	IRION	TX	0
4	STERLING	TX	0
5	PIUTE	UT	0
6	CHARLES CITY	VA	1
7	SHANNON	SD	2
8	OWYHEE	ID	2
9	POWELL	KY	4
10	JOHNSON	GA	4
11	UNION	FL	4
12	GREELEY	KS	5
13	WIBAUX	MT	5
14	SABINE	TX	5
15	HARDING	SD	5
16	JONES	SD	5
17	GOLDEN VALLEY	ND	6
18	WAYNE	KY	6
19	BROADWATER	MT	6
20	SAN MIGUEL	CO	6
21	MILLARD	UT	6
22	SHANNON	MO	6
23	BAILEY	TX	7
24	ARCHER	TX	7
25	FRANKLIN	AR	7
26	ECHOLS	GA	7
27	LA SALLE	TX	7
28	TWIGGS	GA	7
29	GUADALUPE	NM	7
30	HANCOCK	TN	7
31	SEQUATCHIE	TN	8
32	HIGHLAND	VA	8
33	TATTNALL	GA	8
34	SPENCER	KY	8
35	LINCOLN	AR	8
36	RUSSELL	KY	8
37	SAGUACHE	CO	8
38	UPTON	TX	8
39	MARTIN	KY	8
40	DELTA	TX	8
41	LIBERTY	FL	8
42	DECATUR	TN	9
43	ST HELENA	LA	9
44	WASHINGTON	FL	9
45	MONROE	GA	9
46	CLAY	WV	9
47	BAKER	GA	9
48	BOUNDARY	ID	9
49	OREGON	MO	9
50	WHEELER	TX	9
51	COLUMBIA	WA	9
52	HAYWOOD	TN	9
53	REEVES	TX	9
54	RED LAKE	MN	9
55	CATRON	NM	9
56	DUCHESNE	UT	10
57	CASTRO	TX	10
58	LIVE OAK	TX	10
59	LUCE	MI	10
60	BANDERA	TX	10
61	PAMLICO	NC	10
62	MONTMORENCY	MI	10

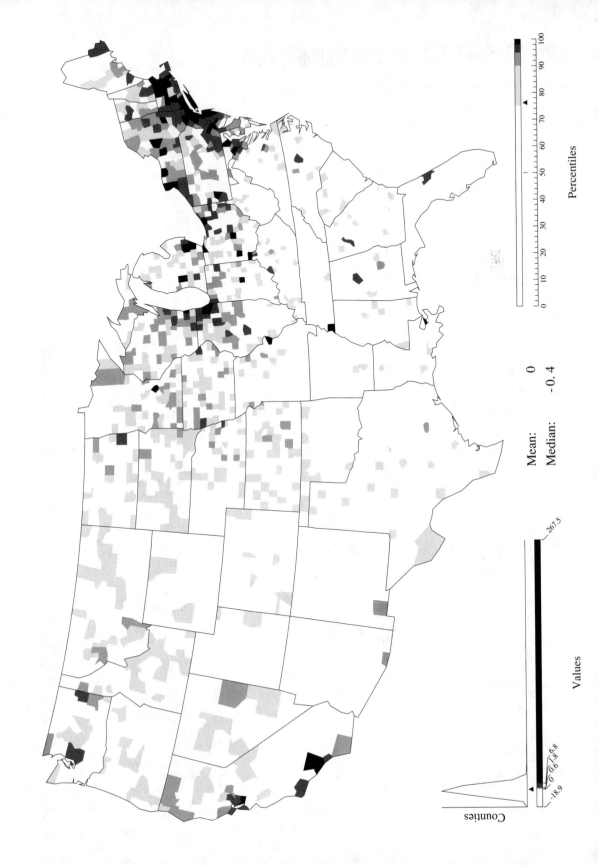

Percentiles

Mean: 0
Median: -0.4

Values

Counties

-18.9   0 6.8   267.5
     0.6.8

TOP COUNTIES SHADED BLACK

RANK	COUNTY	STATE	VALUE
1	NEW YORK CITY	NY	268
2	COOK	IL	132
3	NASSAU	NY	77
4	LOS ANGELES	CA	70
5	CUYAHOGA	OH	50
6	PHILADELPHIA	PA	50
7	HAMILTON	OH	42
8	BERGEN	NJ	41
9	ALLEGHENY	PA	41
10	WESTCHESTER	NY	40
11	SUFFOLK	NY	39
12	ESSEX	NJ	39
13	ERIE	NY	39
14	MIDDLESEX	MA	38
15	WAYNE	MI	34
16	MILWAUKEE	WI	34
17	DISTRICT OF COLUMBIA	DC	27
18	NORFOLK	MA	23
19	MONMOUTH	NJ	22
20	MONROE	NY	21
21	NEW HAVEN	CT	21
22	UNION	NJ	21
23	BALTIMORE CITY	MD	20
24	HARTFORD	CT	19
25	SAN FRANCISCO	CA	19
26	MIDDLESEX	NJ	19
27	SUFFOLK	MA	18
28	OAKLAND	MI	17
29	DELAWARE	PA	17
30	MONTGOMERY	MD	16
31	HUDSON	NJ	16
32	ESSEX	MA	16
33	PASSAIC	NJ	16
34	MONTGOMERY	PA	16
35	ALAMEDA	CA	15
36	ONONDAGA	NY	15
37	ST LOUIS	MO	15
38	PROVIDENCE	RI	14
39	HENNEPIN	MN	14
40	FAIRFIELD	CT	13
41	WORCESTER	MA	12
42	DU PAGE	IL	12
43	ORLEANS	LA	11
44	FRANKLIN	OH	11
45	CAMDEN	NJ	11
46	MARION	IN	11
47	BRISTOL	MA	11
48	ST LOUIS CITY	MO	10
49	MORRIS	NJ	10
50	HAMPDEN	MA	10
51	OCEAN	NJ	9
52	ALBANY	NY	9
53	BALTIMORE	MD	8
54	LUCAS	OH	7
55	ORANGE	NY	7
56	KENT	MI	7
57	NIAGARA	NY	7
58	MONTGOMERY	OH	7
59	ONEIDA	NY	7
60	SHELBY	TN	7
61	ROCKLAND	NY	7

BOTTOM COUNTIES SHADED WHITE

RANK	COUNTY	STATE	VALUE
1	MARICOPA	AZ	-19
2	PINELLAS	FL	-19
3	BROWARD	FL	-17
4	BEXAR	TX	-13
5	HIDALGO	TX	-13
6	PASCO	FL	-11
7	CAMERON	TX	-9
8	FRESNO	CA	-9
9	DADE	FL	-9
10	HILLSBOROUGH	FL	-9
11	OKLAHOMA	OK	-8
12	SAN BERNARDINO	CA	-8
13	EL PASO	TX	-8
14	RIVERSIDE	CA	-8
15	TARRANT	TX	-8
16	PALM BEACH	FL	-7
17	DAVIDSON	TN	-7
18	GASTON	NC	-7
19	PIMA	AZ	-7
20	HARRIS	TX	-7
21	LUBBOCK	TX	-6
22	MANATEE	FL	-6
23	ESCAMBIA	FL	-6
24	POLK	IA	-6
25	PUEBLO	CO	-6
26	POLK	FL	-6
27	NUECES	TX	-6
28	BIBB	GA	-6
29	PULASKI	AR	-6
30	STANISLAUS	CA	-6
31	MC LENNAN	TX	-6
32	TRAVIS	TX	-6
33	TULARE	CA	-5
34	KANAWHA	WV	-5
35	SARASOTA	FL	-5
36	LARIMER	CO	-5
37	FORSYTH	NC	-5
38	KNOX	TN	-5
39	LEE	FL	-5
40	DE KALB	GA	-5
41	MUSCOGEE	GA	-5
42	MONTGOMERY	TX	-5
43	DALLAS	TX	-4
44	LANE	OR	-4
45	ROANOKE	VA	-4
46	WELD	CO	-4
47	OUACHITA	LA	-4
48	SALT LAKE	UT	-4
49	MADISON	AL	-4
50	TUSCALOOSA	AL	-4
51	VENTURA	CA	-4
52	COBB	GA	-4
53	HAMILTON	TN	-4
54	BRAZORIA	TX	-4
55	SULLIVAN	TN	-4
56	BELL	TX	-4
57	HOUSTON	AL	-4
58	KERN	CA	-4
59	ROCK ISLAND	IL	-4
60	WILKES	NC	-4
61	WICHITA	TX	-4
62	WEBER	UT	-4

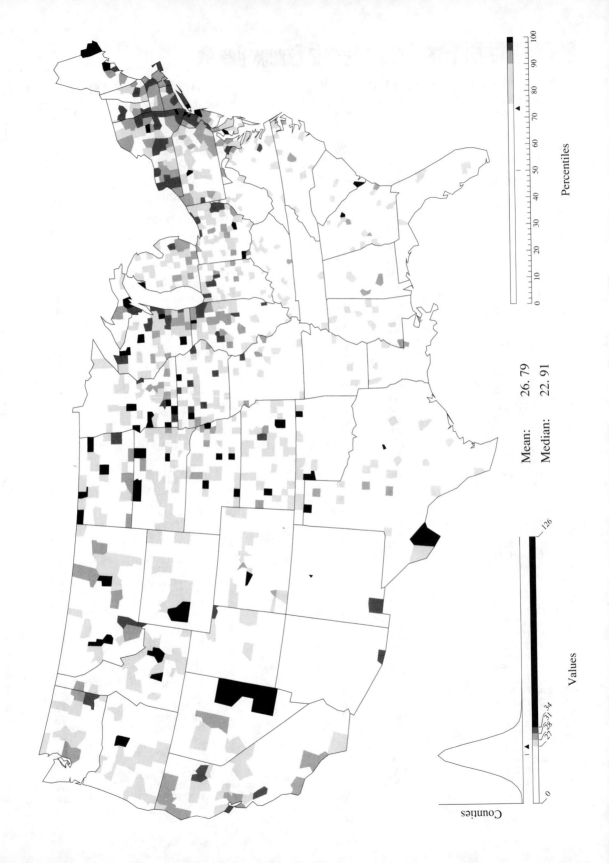

Mean: 26. 79

Median: 22. 91

Percentiles

Values

Counties

(DEATHS PER 100,000 WOMEN)

TOP COUNTIES SHADED BLACK

RANK	COUNTY	STATE	VALUE
1	CAMAS	ID	126
2	PETROLEUM	MT	97
3	SHERMAN	TX	91
4	HITCHCOCK	NE	54
5	WHEELER	OR	53
6	THOMAS	NE	52
7	SUBLETTE	WY	46
8	WELLS	ND	46
9	CORSON	SD	45
10	BUTTE	ID	44
11	HOWARD	NE	42
12	RENVILLE	ND	42
13	NANTUCKET	MA	41
14	SOMERVELL	TX	41
15	JASPER	SC	41
16	WALSH	ND	40
17	PITKIN	CO	39
18	CAMERON	PA	39
19	TALIAFERRO	GA	39
20	NOWATA	OK	39
21	LAC QUI PARLE	MN	38
22	SCOTT	KS	38
23	WHITE PINE	NV	38
24	JERAULD	SD	37
25	LINCOLN	NV	37
26	ADAMS	NE	37
27	TRAVERSE	MN	37
28	BREWSTER	TX	37
29	DIVIDE	ND	36
30	WATONWAN	MN	36
31	NASSAU	NY	36
32	JACKSON	MN	36
33	LEELANAU	MI	36
34	CALUMET	WI	36
35	GREENWOOD	KS	36
36	FULTON	NY	36
37	BROWN	SD	36
38	MITCHELL	IA	36
39	PIPESTONE	MN	35
40	POWELL	MT	35
41	HOCKING	OH	35
42	BURT	NE	35
43	TODD	MN	35
44	MONMOUTH	NJ	35
45	PUTNAM	NY	35
46	ASHLAND	WI	35
47	IOWA	WI	35
48	CHIPPEWA	MN	35
49	ESSEX	NJ	35
50	WALDO	ME	34
51	LOS ALAMOS	NM	34
52	BOONE	IL	34
53	ELLIS	OK	34
54	DELTA	MI	34
55	QUEEN ANNES	MD	34
56	WASHINGTON	ME	34
57	LINCOLN	WI	34
58	CHEROKEE	IA	34
59	HAMILTON	OH	34
60	BERGEN	NJ	34

BOTTOM COUNTIES SHADED WHITE

RANK	COUNTY	STATE	VALUE
1	ISSAQUENA	MS	0
2	TREASURE	MT	0
3	SLOPE	ND	0
4	IRION	TX	0
5	STERLING	TX	0
6	PIUTE	UT	0
7	CHARLES CITY	VA	0
8	OWYHEE	ID	3
9	UNION	FL	3
10	POWELL	KY	5
11	JOHNSON	GA	5
12	GREELEY	KS	5
13	SABINE	TX	6
14	GOLDEN VALLEY	ND	7
15	WAYNE	KY	7
16	LINCOLN	AR	7
17	BROADWATER	MT	7
18	MILLARD	UT	7
19	SHANNON	MO	7
20	BAKER	GA	7
21	REFUGIO	TX	8
22	BAILEY	TX	8
23	PAMLICO	NC	8
24	TATTNALL	GA	8
25	ARCHER	TX	8
26	ST HELENA	LA	8
27	FRANKLIN	AR	8
28	HAYWOOD	TN	8
29	LA SALLE	TX	8
30	TWIGGS	GA	8
31	GUADALUPE	NM	8
32	MONROE	GA	8
33	WASHINGTON	FL	8
34	HANCOCK	TN	8
35	TRINITY	TX	9
36	HOUSTON	TN	9
37	EFFINGHAM	GA	9
38	CLAIBORNE	MS	9
39	SEQUATCHIE	TN	9
40	HIGHLAND	VA	9
41	LANIER	GA	9
42	BULLOCK	AL	9
43	SPENCER	KY	9
44	COOK	GA	9
45	RUSSELL	KY	9
46	SURRY	VA	9
47	SAGUACHE	CO	9
48	UPTON	TX	9
49	MARTIN	KY	9
50	DELTA	TX	9
51	LIBERTY	FL	9
52	PERRY	AL	10
53	DECATUR	TN	10
54	BARBOUR	AL	10
55	TALBOT	GA	10
56	WYOMING	WV	10
57	GRADY	GA	10
58	CLAY	WV	10
59	FRANKLIN	TX	10
60	BOUNDARY	ID	10
61	OREGON	MO	10
62	WHEELER	TX	10

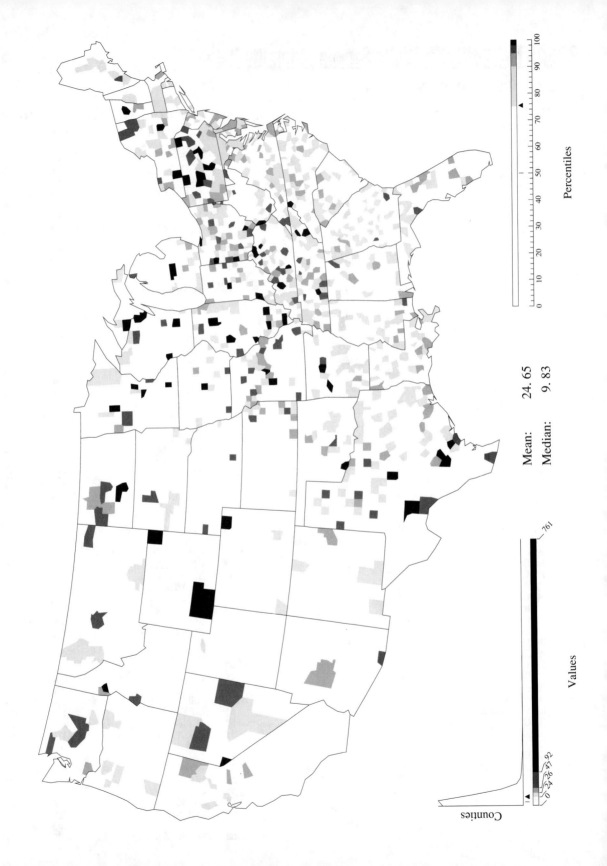

Mean: 24.65
Median: 9.83

Percentiles

Values

Counties

0 2 6 47 92

761

(DEATHS PER 100,000 WOMEN)

TOP COUNTIES SHADED BLACK

RANK	COUNTY	STATE	VALUE
1	CROOK	WY	761
2	WASHINGTON	IL	711
3	KANABEC	MN	407
4	JOHNSON	IL	380
5	PENDLETON	KY	305
6	DOUGLAS	NV	305
7	MORTON	ND	305
8	SNYDER	PA	305
9	IRON	MI	254
10	WAYNE	IL	214
11	BRACKEN	KY	201
12	GRATIOT	MI	201
13	JERSEY	IL	190
14	CLINTON	IN	190
15	MONTOUR	PA	190
16	WAYNE	WV	190
17	UNION	IL	189
18	ATASCOSA	TX	189
19	SUSQUEHANNA	PA	185
20	HUBBARD	MN	178
21	FULTON	IL	172
22	ALLEGANY	NY	160
23	LA CROSSE	WI	152
24	GOLIAD	TX	141
25	NORTHUMBERLAND	PA	141
26	STORY	IA	140
27	JACKSON	OH	137
28	VAN BUREN	AR	136
29	SEVIER	TN	130
30	LOGAN	CO	127
31	VAN WERT	OH	127
32	JEFFERSON	PA	127
33	SHERBURNE	MN	126
34	STEELE	MN	126
35	MONITEAU	MO	126
36	METCALFE	KY	125
37	BENTON	MO	122
38	WILSON	TX	122
39	MARINETTE	WI	122
40	ASHE	NC	122
41	COLEMAN	TX	118
42	TILLMAN	OK	109
43	NICHOLAS	KY	109
44	MC KEAN	PA	109
45	LEWIS	TN	108
46	MONTCALM	MI	107
47	OTTAWA	OH	106
48	SWEETWATER	WY	105
49	LOGAN	AR	104
50	HUNTINGDON	PA	104
51	GRANT	KY	102
52	GRAINGER	TN	102
53	PREBLE	OH	102
54	DODGE	WI	102
55	OHIO	KY	101
56	CROCKETT	TX	100
57	WASHINGTON	VT	100
58	KNOX	IN	99
59	CLEARFIELD	PA	98
60	LA SALLE	IL	96
61	LEWIS	ID	95
62	SCHOHARIE	NY	92

BOTTOM COUNTIES SHADED WHITE

NOTE: TOO MANY COUNTIES TO LIST
HAD ZERO VALUES FOR THIS MEASURE

to do with fears about toxic contamination; they said they closed the plant because it was old and the water was no longer needed. Twelve families from the action group filed suit, alleging the water board and the weapons plant conspired to cover up the water contamination, and in April 1990, the U.S. District Court ruled the plaintiffs had sufficient evidence to warrant a trial.[140]

In Morgan City, Louisiana, Helen Solar became alarmed when she found a lump in her one-and-a-half-year-old granddaughter Nicole's back —soon after a friend's baby was diagnosed with neuroblastoma, a rare cancer of the nervous system. Helen's worst fear came true: Nicole had the same disease. The tumor stretched throughout the toddler's body, toward her heart and lungs on one end, resting on her kidney at the other, and bursting out of her chest cavity into her spinal canal where her grandmother first detected it.[141] In all, five kids from the Morgan City area were diagnosed with neuroblastoma within an 18-month period. They all lived within 35 miles of Marine Shale Processors, the nation's largest hazardous waste incinerator. Parents formed South Louisiana Against Pollution (SLAP), threatened to sue Marine Shale, and lobbied legislators to close it down. Soon afterward, the state proposed to fine Marine Shale $4.5 million for numerous air and water violations, fines which the company is appealing. In a separate plea bargaining with the federal Justice Department, the company pleaded guilty to violation of federal hazardous waste and pollution laws and agreed to pay $1 million in penalties. Even so, the incinerator still operates, burning 100,000 tons of toxic chemicals each year.[142]

Despite these heartrending stories, childhood cancer remains so rare that often there are too few cases to document a significant event even if an environmental exposure has occurred. Childhood cancer mortality in Jefferson County, Colorado (including Friendly Hills), was significantly higher than the rest of the country during the late 1970s, but was not statistically significant by the early 1980s. Saint Mary Parish, Louisiana (including Morgan City), has more excess deaths from childhood cancers than 90 percent of the counties in the country, but even so, its mortality rate is statistically insignificant.

Though rare, the incidence of childhood cancer in North America is among the highest in the world for whites in particular, and is increasing slightly for both sexes.[143] Yet the causes and occurrence of childhood cancer clusters remain obscure. The 75 measures included in our analysis were least able to explain the geographic variations in mortality from child cancers of the ten causes of death examined (see the methods appendix discussion of Fig. A-6 for more on this). Certain populations may have genetic predispositions to childhood cancers; parental occupations can increase their risk; fetuses can be exposed to carcinogens and babies can be exposed when breast-feeding. A newly discovered retrovirus (HTLV-1) has been linked to certain forms of leukemia. And a number of widespread environmental factors have been implicated, including the benzene in gasoline and radiation.[144] Children are at greater risk from environmental pollutants because they are still growing, they have higher metabolic rates, and they inhale two to three times as much air (and hence pollution) as adults per unit of body weight.[145]

There is a striking pattern of counties with high child cancer mortality rates scattered through the middle of the country, from Texas to North Dakota, especially in the Great Plains states. The same geographic pattern has been found for adult leukemia, especially among white males who, like children, are also experiencing a slightly upward trend in the central part of the United States. The clusters of leukemia in the middle of the country remain significant even after adjusting for urbanization, socioeconomic factors, and the high concentrations of people of Scandinavian, German, and Russian descent.[146] This is an important adjustment. Leukemias are prevalent in Scandinavia, and the high rates in the New Jersey-New York-Philadelphia region have been linked to the significant population of Russian-born residents in the area.[147]

High childhood cancer rates for nonwhite minority populations in the central United States can be seen where many native Americans reside, as in the Dakotas and Oklahoma. There are also high minority child cancer rates throughout the southern United States, from Southern California to Virginia. Minority children historically have had lower rates of childhood cancer than white children, particularly leukemia. Improvements in chemotherapy have significantly reduced cancer mortality among white children, but minority rates have remained unchanged. Now there is little racial difference in childhood cancer mortality rates. Even so, underreporting may account for the lower incidence among minority children in the past, and survival rates among minority kids with cancer continue to fall behind those for whites, due to poorer access to health care, socioeconomic conditions, and possibly biological differences.[148]

Many of the counties in the center of the country with the highest childhood cancer mortality rates are in areas with intensive agricultural activities, especially cotton production, where heavy pesticide use is common.[149] Detailed studies of leukemia rates in Nebraska and Wisconsin have found associations with a range of agricultural activities.[150] Parental exposures to pesticides, not only from working on farms but also from household and garden use, have been consistently associated with increased risks of childhood leukemias in Los Angeles County and

Southern California.[151] Seven of the ten states in the central United States with the highest rates of acute leukemia also have the highest percentage of men employed in agriculture.[152] Pesticide exposures can occur in nonagricultural areas as well: the Marine Shale incinerator in Morgan City, Louisiana, for example, burned train cars full of soil contaminated with the pesticide dinoseb at a time when its emission controls were not working properly.[153] The soils came from a Southern California area where yet another mysterious cluster of child cancers occurred (see chapter 5).

Increased childhood cancer risks have also been associated with families where the parents suffered occupational exposures to chlorinated solvents, plastics, and lead, maternal exposure to paints, pigments, metal dusts, and sawdusts, or were employed in transportation equipment manufacturing.[154] According to a noted expert on occupational health, Dr. Irving J. Selikoff of the Mount Sinai School of Medicine, "The spread of occupational illness to families of workers is a general rule, not a curiosity."[155]

Radiation is also a well-known cause of childhood cancers, but there is considerable debate over how dangerous low levels may be. In England, researchers have associated as much as two-thirds of the geographic variation in childhood leukemia with background radiation.[156] British scientists have also found significantly higher rates of leukemia among children whose fathers worked in the nuclear facilities at Sellafield.[157] Children of practicing radiologists in the United States also are at increased risk of developing cancer.[158] Excess leukemia has been linked to proximity to the Pilgrim nuclear reactor in Plymouth, Massachusetts, and significant increases have been found in counties near the Three Mile Island reactors in Pennsylvania.[159] Nonionizing radiation from electric power lines has also been associated with childhood cancer in the Denver, Colorado, area, and with leukemia among men working near electric fields in Washington State and Los Angeles, and has raised concern about childhood cancers in Guilford, Connecticut.[160] High child cancer rates in Texas may be associated with farming and with recently discovered high levels of radiation in oil fields. The radioactive substances are pumped up from underground along with the crude oil.[161]

ACUTELY HAZARDOUS EXPOSURES

The May 4, 1988, blasts at Pacific Engineering and Production Company of Henderson, Nevada (PEPCON), registered as high as 3.5 on the Richter scale. (Measurements were taken 200 miles away in Pasadena,

California.) Just after the explosion, Rick Rieckmann was standing 20 feet outside the rocket fuel plant, dazed and missing his hard hat and unable to hear. As he and another 100 employees raced to the surrounding desert for protection, three more awesome explosions hurled the fleeing workers to the ground, and an orange mushroom cloud rose into the air.[162]

Eight million pounds of the highly reactive rocket fuel ingredient ammonium perchlorate ignited during the blasts.[163] Flames shot 100 feet into the air and smoke billowed for 40 miles over Las Vegas Valley. Local officials closed all roads for fear of toxic gases.[164] Twelve buildings at the rocket fuel plant were flattened, as was a neighboring marshmallow factory. The blasts caused $75 million in damages within a several-mile radius, ripping apart homes, upending cars, and disrupting electricity for 12,000 area residents.[165] Windows shattered for miles around the site, including one that "blew up in somebody's face" at a convalescent hospital six miles away.[166] In all, the explosions injured 350 people and killed 2 workers. Governor Richard Bryan appointed a blue-ribbon commission to investigate, and it developed 43 recommendations to improve existing regulations on fire, health and safety, zoning, insurance, community planning and response, and transportation. The state legislature introduced new chemical safety measures soon afterward.[167]

In marked contrast to disease-related mortality, fatal exposures to acutely hazardous substances usually leave a clear trail of evidence linking cause to effect. For this reason, acute exposures are the easiest cause of death for governments and industry to regulate and control. In fact, there are fewer deaths from such accidents than from any other cause in the atlas—fewer even than from child cancer—and the numbers of deaths are declining more quickly than for any of the other causes. Fatal accidents of all kinds cause more than 250 deaths a day nationwide—or nearly a 100,000 deaths a year. Only 1 percent of these deaths (about 1,000 per year) involve acutely hazardous exposures, two-thirds of which result from poisoning and the rest from industrial explosions and fires. Motor vehicle accidents, in comparison, cause fifty times more fatalities than acutely hazardous exposures, and the government counts seven times as many fatal poisonings due to narcotics than due to industrial chemicals.[168] So experts have a hard time understanding why people fear such rare exposures as much as they do.

Expert calculations often ignore the rich variety of social and psychological factors that influence public perceptions of risk. Most people think of more than theoretical probabilities when faced with technological hazards: Was the accident preventable or controllable? Was the risk taken voluntarily or was it forced upon the victim? Was the hazard

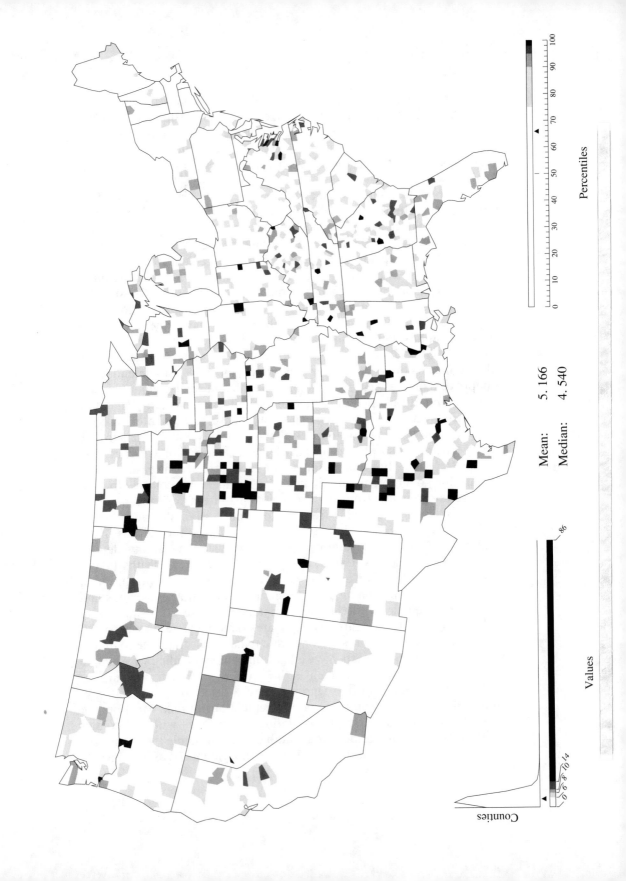

Mean: 5. 166

Median: 4. 540

Percentiles

Values

Counties

(DEATHS PER 100,000 CHILDREN)

TOP COUNTIES SHADED BLACK

RANK	COUNTY	STATE	VALUE
1	MONTGOMERY	IA	86
2	STOREY	NV	47
3	JAY	IN	44
4	CHARLES CITY	VA	42
5	TALIAFERRO	GA	39
6	ARMSTRONG	TX	38
7	KENT	TX	33
8	DEWEY	OK	30
9	GOLDEN VALLEY	ND	29
10	TALBOT	GA	27
11	GARFIELD	NE	26
12	BLAINE	NE	25
13	MC MULLEN	TX	24
14	AMELIA	VA	24
15	KINNEY	TX	23
16	MONTGOMERY	MS	23
17	PULASKI	IL	21
18	JUAB	UT	21
19	HAYES	NE	20
20	BILLINGS	ND	20
21	STANLEY	SD	20
22	COSTILLA	CO	20
23	BAYLOR	TX	20
24	CROCKETT	TN	20
25	LINCOLN	NE	20
26	WASHINGTON	TX	20
27	IROQUOIS	IL	20
28	SAN MIGUEL	CO	20
29	WAHKIAKUM	WA	19
30	CARSON	TX	19
31	JUNEAU	WI	19
32	GILLIAM	OR	19
33	HITCHCOCK	NE	19
34	FRONTIER	NE	19
35	JOHNSTON	OK	18
36	FISHER	TX	18
37	SCHUYLER	MO	18
38	LINN	KS	18
39	HOOKER	NE	18
40	MASON	TX	18
41	COLLINGSWORTH	TX	18
42	TRIGG	KY	18
43	ESSEX	VA	17
44	SHERMAN	NE	17
45	QUITMAN	MS	16
46	MATHEWS	VA	16
47	JONES	SD	16
48	THROCKMORTON	TX	16
49	MILLS	TX	16
50	BOYD	KY	16
51	WIBAUX	MT	16
52	WALLER	TX	16
53	COLEMAN	TX	15
54	CONCORDIA	LA	15
55	SIOUX	ND	15
56	MERCER	MO	15
57	HAND	SD	15
58	WEST FELICIANA	LA	15
59	SMITH	TN	15
60	RAINS	TX	14
61	CLAIBORNE	LA	14

BOTTOM COUNTIES SHADED WHITE

NOTE: TOO MANY COUNTIES TO LIST
HAD ZERO VALUES FOR THIS MEASURE

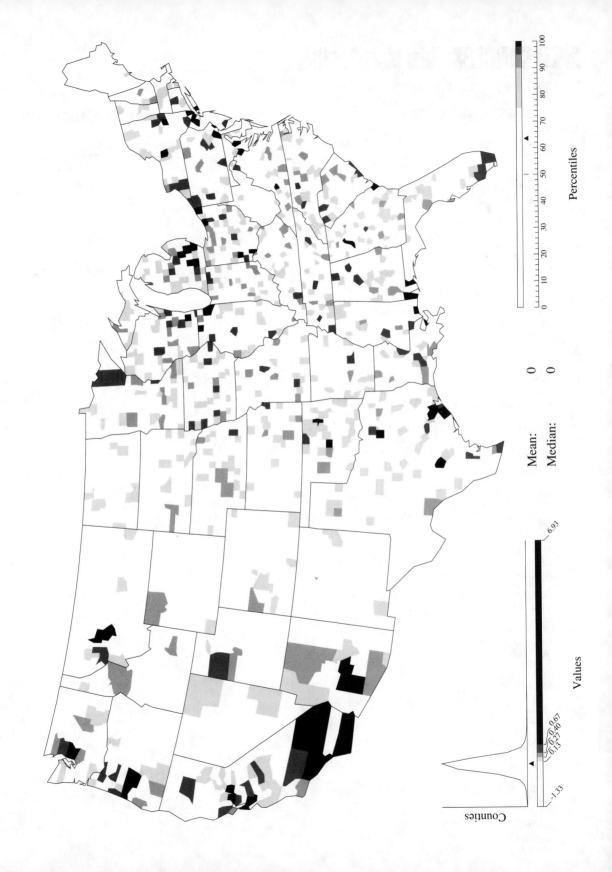

Mean: 0

Median: 0

Percentiles

Values

Counties

6.93

0.67
0.40
0.27
0.13

-1.33

TOP COUNTIES SHADED BLACK

RANK	COUNTY	STATE	VALUE
1	LOS ANGELES	CA	7
2	NEW YORK CITY	NY	6
3	HARRIS	TX	5
4	BEXAR	TX	4
5	CUYAHOGA	OH	3
6	SAN DIEGO	CA	3
7	PHILADELPHIA	PA	3
8	FULTON	GA	3
9	WAYNE	MI	2
10	OKLAHOMA	OK	2
11	SAN FRANCISCO	CA	2
12	FAIRFAX	VA	2
13	NASSAU	NY	2
14	KING	WA	2
15	GENESEE	MI	2
16	PASSAIC	NJ	2
17	DALLAS	TX	2
18	SAN BERNARDINO	CA	1
19	DISTRICT OF COLUMBIA	DC	1
20	BERGEN	NJ	1
21	MOBILE	AL	1
22	ANNE ARUNDEL	MD	1
23	MORRIS	NJ	1
24	ALBANY	NY	1
25	CHATHAM	GA	1
26	MONTGOMERY	OH	1
27	ONONDAGA	NY	1
28	LANE	OR	1
29	WAUKESHA	WI	1
30	ORANGE	CA	1
31	SOLANO	CA	1
32	INGHAM	MI	1
33	WESTCHESTER	NY	1
34	CHESTER	PA	1
35	MARICOPA	AZ	1
36	SACRAMENTO	CA	1
37	SAN MATEO	CA	1
38	SANTA CLARA	CA	1
39	ESCAMBIA	FL	1
40	WINNEBAGO	IL	1
41	ASHTABULA	OH	1
42	IMPERIAL	CA	1
43	VENTURA	CA	1
44	COOK	IL	1
45	DU PAGE	IL	1
46	ORLEANS	LA	1
47	JACKSON	MI	1
48	CLERMONT	OH	1
49	TULSA	OK	1
50	BRAZORIA	TX	1
51	ROANOKE	VA	1
52	OAKLAND	MI	1
53	HARRISON	MS	1
54	LEWIS AND CLARK	MT	1
55	CONTRA COSTA	CA	1
56	HARTFORD	CT	1
57	DADE	FL	1
58	WHITESIDE	IL	1
59	SAGINAW	MI	1
60	ST LOUIS	MN	1
61	BOONE	MO	1

BOTTOM COUNTIES SHADED WHITE

RANK	COUNTY	STATE	VALUE
1	PALM BEACH	FL	-1
2	DAVIDSON	TN	-1
3	BURLINGTON	NJ	-1
4	BUCKS	PA	-1
5	FAIRFIELD	CT	-1
6	JEFFERSON	LA	-1
7	BRISTOL	MA	-1
8	LAKE	IN	-1
9	ESSEX	MA	-1
10	ST LOUIS	MO	-1
11	CLARK	NV	-1
12	TRAVIS	TX	-1
13	BROWARD	FL	-1
14	MARION	IN	-1
15	ONEIDA	NY	-1
16	MONTGOMERY	PA	-1
17	SALT LAKE	UT	-1
18	DUVAL	FL	-1
19	MADISON	IN	-1
20	EAST BATON ROUGE	LA	-1
21	PLYMOUTH	MA	-1
22	OSWEGO	NY	-1
23	ALLEGHENY	PA	-1
24	EL PASO	CO	-1
25	LITCHFIELD	CT	-1
26	COBB	GA	-1
27	HENRICO	VA	-1
28	MILWAUKEE	WI	-1
29	MANATEE	FL	-1
30	PEORIA	IL	-1
31	ST LAWRENCE	NY	-1
32	CLARK	OH	-1
33	HAMILTON	OH	-1
34	ADAMS	CO	-1
35	OKALOOSA	FL	-1
36	ORANGE	FL	-1
37	GRANT	IN	-1
38	SCOTT	IA	-1
39	CLAY	MO	-1
40	MIDDLESEX	NJ	-1
41	CUMBERLAND	PA	-1
42	LANCASTER	PA	-1
43	MC LENNAN	TX	-1
44	RALEIGH	WV	-1
45	PULASKI	AR	-1
46	NEW CASTLE	DE	-1
47	KANE	IL	-1
48	VAN BUREN	MI	-1
49	SUFFOLK	NY	-1
50	ROBESON	NC	-1
51	LYCOMING	PA	-1
52	NORTHAMPTON	PA	-1
53	NORTHUMBERLAND	PA	-1
54	UTAH	UT	-1
55	WAYNE	NC	-1
56	ROSS	OH	-1
57	INDIANA	PA	-1
58	YORK	PA	-1
59	SUMTER	SC	-1
60	GRAYSON	TX	-1
61	KANAWHA	WV	-1
62	RACINE	WI	-1

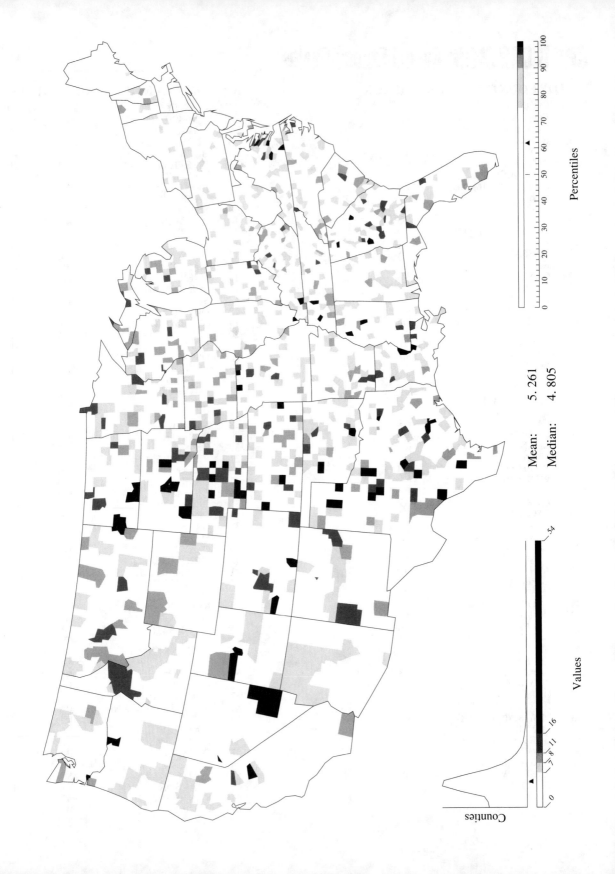

Mean: 5.261
Median: 4.805

Percentiles

Values

Counties

(DEATHS PER 100,000 CHILDREN)

TOP COUNTIES SHADED BLACK

RANK	COUNTY	STATE	VALUE
1	STOREY	NV	54
2	CHARLES CITY	VA	48
3	TALIAFERRO	GA	45
4	ARMSTRONG	TX	43
5	KENT	TX	38
6	DEWEY	OK	34
7	GOLDEN VALLEY	ND	33
8	TALBOT	GA	30
9	GARFIELD	NE	29
10	BLAINE	NE	28
11	MC MULLEN	TX	28
12	AMELIA	VA	27
13	KINNEY	TX	27
14	MONTGOMERY	MS	25
15	SHANNON	SD	24
16	JUAB	UT	23
17	HAYES	NE	23
18	BILLINGS	ND	23
19	STANLEY	SD	23
20	COSTILLA	CO	23
21	BAYLOR	TX	23
22	CROCKETT	TN	23
23	PULASKI	IL	23
24	SAN MIGUEL	CO	22
25	WAHKIAKUM	WA	22
26	CARSON	TX	22
27	GILLIAM	OR	21
28	HITCHCOCK	NE	21
29	FRONTIER	NE	21
30	WASHINGTON	TX	21
31	JOHNSTON	OK	21
32	FISHER	TX	21
33	SCHUYLER	MO	21
34	LINN	KS	21
35	HOOKER	NE	20
36	MASON	TX	20
37	COLLINGSWORTH	TX	20
38	SHERMAN	NE	19
39	ESSEX	VA	19
40	MATHEWS	VA	19
41	JONES	SD	19
42	THROCKMORTON	TX	19
43	MILLS	TX	18
44	WIBAUX	MT	18
45	QUITMAN	MS	18
46	GREENSVILLE	VA	18
47	WALLER	TX	17
48	MERCER	MO	17
49	CONCORDIA	LA	17
50	HAND	SD	17
51	WEST FELICIANA	LA	17
52	RAINS	TX	16
53	SIOUX	ND	16
54	HODGEMAN	KS	16
55	WALLACE	KS	16
56	PICKENS	GA	16
57	GRANT	ND	16
58	BENTON	TN	16
59	TRIGG	KY	16
60	MARIPOSA	CA	16
61	LINCOLN	NV	16

BOTTOM COUNTIES SHADED WHITE

NOTE: TOO MANY COUNTIES TO LIST
HAD ZERO VALUES FOR THIS MEASURE

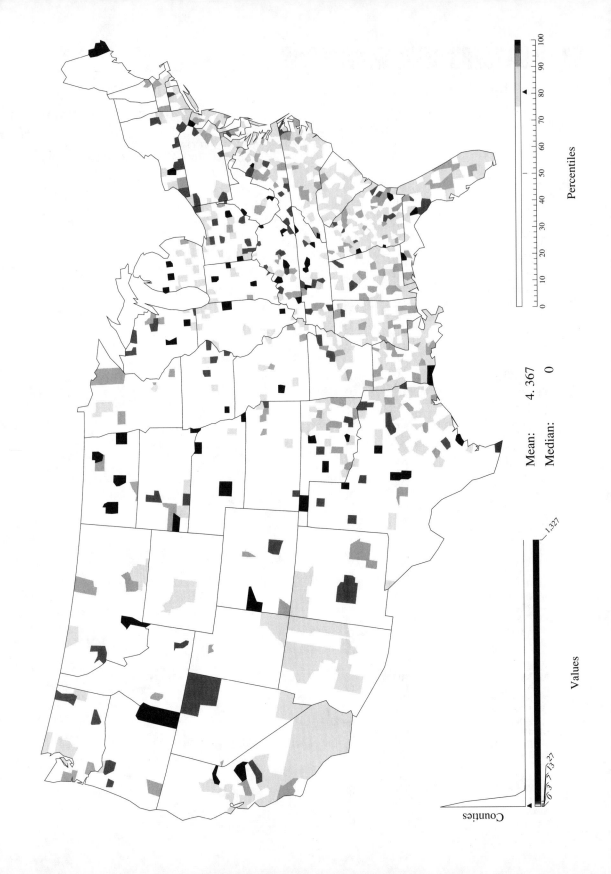

Mean: 4. 367

Median: 0

Percentiles

Values

Counties

0 3 7 13 27

1,327

(DEATHS PER 100,000 CHILDREN)

TOP COUNTIES SHADED BLACK

RANK	COUNTY	STATE	VALUE
1	UNION	SD	1,327
2	MONTGOMERY	IA	637
3	RICHARDSON	NE	401
4	HANCOCK	TN	390
5	JAY	IN	293
6	GALLATIN	MT	221
7	ST CLAIR	MO	195
8	PREBLE	OH	166
9	GRAHAM	NC	152
10	CUSTER	SD	145
11	TEXAS	OK	134
12	MESA	CO	121
13	RAMSEY	ND	106
14	IROQUOIS	IL	102
15	LINCOLN	NE	95
16	SUSSEX	NJ	86
17	JUNEAU	WI	84
18	GREEN	KY	81
19	MC CULLOCH	TX	80
20	BOYD	KY	79
21	MASON	MI	71
22	LAFAYETTE	FL	69
23	CHILDRESS	TX	67
24	HOLMES	FL	62
25	SUMMERS	WV	57
26	REFUGIO	TX	55
27	TAYLOR	KY	54
28	NEVADA	CA	53
29	SALINE	IL	51
30	PARKER	TX	51
31	JEFFERSON	WI	51
32	NOBLE	OK	50
33	SMITH	TN	49
34	COLEMAN	TX	47
35	LOUDON	TN	45
36	CUSTER	OK	42
37	CHEATHAM	TN	39
38	KOSCIUSKO	IN	38
39	CASS	ND	38
40	GREENE	VA	36
41	BURLEIGH	ND	36
42	MECOSTA	MI	36
43	CAMERON	LA	35
44	PUTNAM	TN	33
45	BRANTLEY	GA	33
46	DUNN	ND	33
47	QUITMAN	GA	32
48	WOOD	WV	32
49	GUERNSEY	OH	31
50	MONROE	IN	30
51	HEARD	GA	30
52	WASHINGTON	ME	29
53	LIVINGSTON	NY	29
54	PERRY	KY	29
55	KNOX	NE	29
56	TRIGG	KY	29
57	MALHEUR	OR	29
58	BRECKINRIDGE	KY	29
59	MURRAY	OK	28
60	MIDLAND	MI	27
61	TUOLUMNE	CA	27

BOTTOM COUNTIES SHADED WHITE

NOTE: TOO MANY COUNTIES TO LIST
HAD ZERO VALUES FOR THIS MEASURE

familiar or something new and exotic? Were the consequences unfair, hurting people who would not otherwise benefit from the technology?[169] When a chemical accident kills two people outright, flattens buildings, and shakes up communities for miles around, most people also wonder whether such powerful substances might have latent effects as well. In most cases and for most substances, the experts really do not know. Such uncertainty makes most of us feel very uncomfortable, even if catastrophes have a low probability of occurring.

In fact, regulations can be lax and controls do break down, as the rocket fuel explosion clearly illustrates. Such mishaps occur at widely unequal rates across the country. There is the greatest degree of geographic inequality for acutely hazardous exposures of the six less frequent causes of death in the atlas. The greatest disparity between race-sex groups for any cause of death is the sixfold difference between acute exposures among minority men and white women.[170] Fatality rates from acute exposures in the top ten counties are more than 20 times higher than the national average. Accidents result in more years of potential life lost than any other cause of death, and by contributing just 1 percent of this loss of productive life, acutely hazardous exposures rob society of $3.5 billion in lost personal income each year.[171] Though rare, such deaths are inherently shocking and unfair.

Surprisingly, the highest rates of acutely hazardous exposures are not highly correlated with industrial toxins. In fact, there is considerably less industrial pollution in the counties with the highest fatality rates from acute exposures than the average for the rest of the country. The highest rates are in rural areas of the West and Southwest. This geographic pattern closely parallels the distribution of mortality from all unintentional injuries and may be due in part to particularly hazardous occupations in those areas.[172] Fatal injuries are more than eight times more frequent in rural jobs such as mining and agriculture than in urban jobs such as manufacturing, trade, and services.[173] Heavy use of chemical pesticides and explosives would presumably account for the bulk of acute exposures in these rural industries. The rocket fuel accident was not an isolated incident either: the PEPCON plant is located in Clark County, Nevada, which ranks among the top 10 percent of counties for excess deaths from acutely hazardous exposures. In addition to Nevada, Montana, New Mexico, western Texas, and Wyoming stand out with particularly high mortality rates from acute exposures, and the San Joaquin Valley in California is also displayed prominently in the maps for large numbers of excess deaths.

Be it from risky occupations, risky behaviors, lax regulation, or some combination of the three, the American Southwest is more accident prone than the rest of the country.[174] Given this fact, it is quite ironic that the federal government has decided to store the nation's most dangerous radioactive wastes in precisely these areas. It hopes to keep all of the high-level radioactive wastes from commercial nuclear reactors safe for 10,000 years by burying them in Yucca Mountain, Nevada, which happens to be in a county that ranks among the top fifty in the country for fatal accidents involving acutely hazardous exposures (Nye County). And it plans to bury radioactive military wastes in Carlsbad, New Mexico, which is in a county that ranks among the top thirty for excess deaths from acute exposures (Eddy County). Government experts seem to have overlooked the simple fact that accidents involving acutely hazardous exposures occur more frequently in these counties than almost anywhere else in the nation. There is a certain wisdom in public apprehensions of technological risks that escapes even the most sophisticated theoretical models—human error is hard to predict. Accidents can happen.

YOUNG-ADULT INFECTIOUS DISEASES

The single most disturbing trend in U.S. mortality is the rise in deaths among young adults. While mortality for every other age group improved throughout the 1980s, death rates among young adults increased for the first time in the 20th century when America was not engaged in a major war. Acquired immunodeficiency syndrome (AIDS) is the primary reason for this ominous trend, but it may not be the only one.

The most notable aspect of the mortality rate maps for young-adult infectious diseases is their portrayal of geographic patterns that are nearly the opposite of what might be expected given the AIDS epidemic. The maps show the highest rates in southern and central parts of the country; the high rate counties are rural and significantly poor, with large percentages of Latino and native Americans, and significantly more violations of public water supply health standards than the rest of the country. In contrast to the mortality rate maps, the map of excess deaths from infectious diseases reflects the AIDS epidemic we hear about in the news. Urban areas have the greatest numbers of excess deaths, with New York City topping the list, followed by Chicago, some urban counties in New Jersey, the District of Columbia, and San Francisco, among other places. There are surprises in this map as well, such as the below-average young adult mortality from infectious disease in Los Angeles, St. Louis, and many Southern California counties at the start of the 1980s.

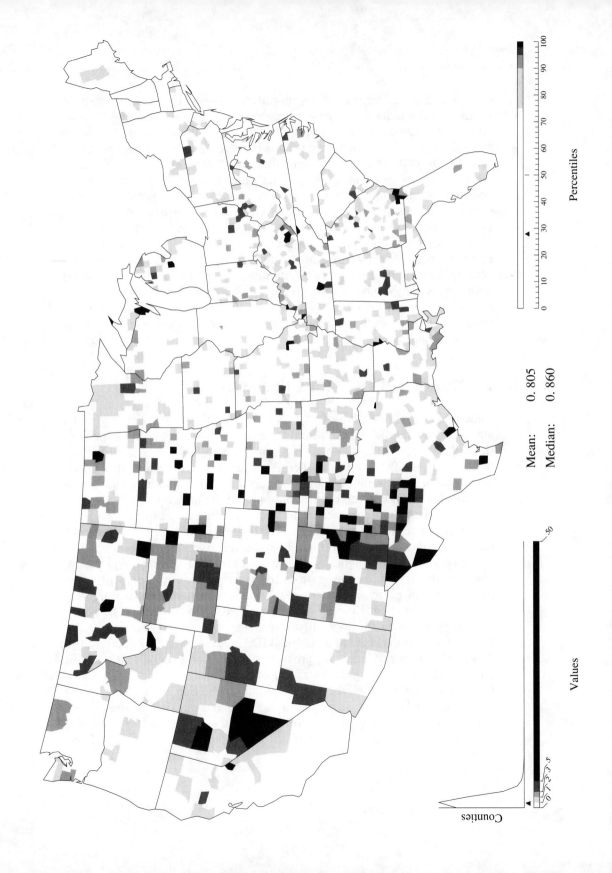

Percentiles

Values

Counties

Mean: 0. 805

Median: 0. 860

(DEATHS PER 100,000 PEOPLE)

TOP COUNTIES SHADED BLACK

RANK	COUNTY	STATE	VALUE
1	HANCOCK	TN	50
2	BRULE	SD	38
3	PRESIDIO	TX	27
4	RAMSEY	ND	15
5	MENOMINEE	MI	15
6	BROOKS	TX	14
7	ESMERALDA	NV	13
8	QUAY	NM	12
9	CLAY	KY	12
10	CAMDEN	GA	10
11	IRION	TX	9
12	HARDIN	IL	9
13	MOORE	TX	8
14	HICKMAN	KY	8
15	BLAINE	NE	8
16	WHEELER	TX	8
17	CHARLTON	GA	7
18	JUDITH BASIN	MT	7
19	THOMAS	NE	7
20	HAMILTON	KS	7
21	YOAKUM	TX	7
22	SIOUX	NE	7
23	DEWEY	OK	7
24	CASTRO	TX	6
25	REAGAN	TX	6
26	BORDEN	TX	6
27	HITCHCOCK	NE	6
28	DE BACA	NM	6
29	GREELEY	NE	6
30	CARSON	TX	6
31	ELLIS	KS	6
32	HARPER	OK	6
33	HUDSPETH	TX	6
34	LESLIE	KY	6
35	CLARK	ID	6
36	PERSHING	NV	6
37	COKE	TX	6
38	KIOWA	CO	6
39	IRON	MO	6
40	CRANE	TX	6
41	ALPINE	CA	5
42	CAMP	TX	5
43	MIDLAND	MI	5
44	WESTON	WY	5
45	SCHLEICHER	TX	5
46	POWDER RIVER	MT	5
47	ISSAQUENA	MS	5
48	NYE	NV	5
49	MENARD	TX	5
50	SANBORN	SD	5
51	KEWEENAW	MI	5
52	MAURY	TN	5
53	LAMB	TX	5
54	CONCHO	TX	5
55	ROOSEVELT	NM	5
56	GARZA	TX	5
57	TAOS	NM	5
58	BENNETT	SD	5
59	HARDEMAN	TX	5
60	JACKSON	TX	5

BOTTOM COUNTIES SHADED WHITE

NOTE: TOO MANY COUNTIES TO LIST
HAD ZERO VALUES FOR THIS MEASURE

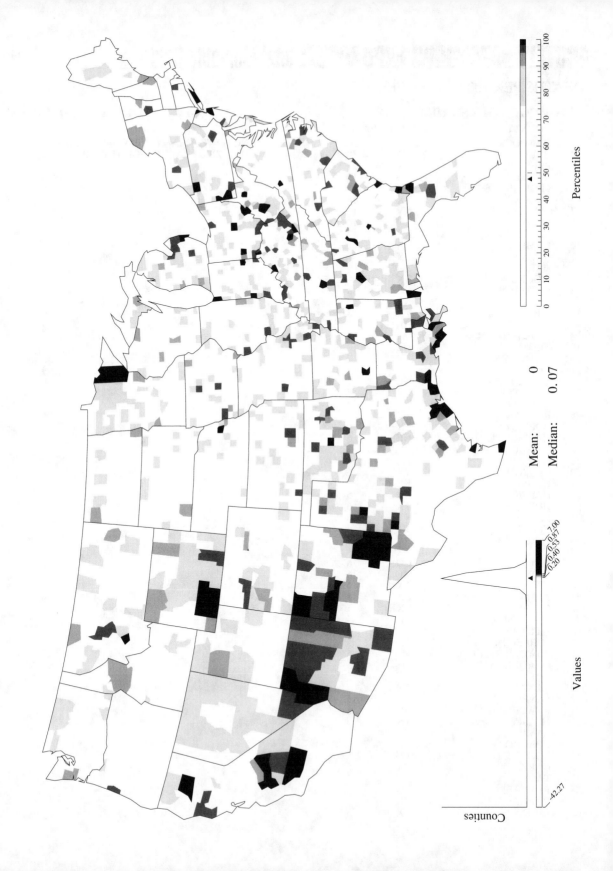

Mean: 0

Median: 0. 07

Percentiles

Values

Counties

TOP COUNTIES SHADED BLACK

RANK	COUNTY	STATE	VALUE
1	HARRIS	TX	7
2	OKLAHOMA	OK	3
3	GALVESTON	TX	3
4	JEFFERSON	LA	3
5	FULTON	GA	3
6	JEFFERSON	TX	2
7	WAYNE	IN	2
8	MAURY	TN	2
9	WASHINGTON	OH	2
10	MOBILE	AL	2
11	MONMOUTH	NJ	2
12	ECTOR	TX	2
13	CLAY	KY	2
14	CAMDEN	GA	2
15	CALCASIEU	LA	2
16	SAN JUAN	NM	2
17	JEFFERSON	KY	2
18	KERN	CA	2
19	KENTON	KY	2
20	BRAZORIA	TX	2
21	CAMERON	TX	1
22	KANAWHA	WV	1
23	LAKE	IN	1
24	TERREBONNE	LA	1
25	BEAVER	PA	1
26	CHATHAM	GA	1
27	EDDY	NM	1
28	WASHINGTON	PA	1
29	BIBB	GA	1
30	DODGE	NE	1
31	CHAVES	NM	1
32	MONTGOMERY	OH	1
33	LEA	NM	1
34	NUECES	TX	1
35	DUVAL	FL	1
36	ST CLAIR	MI	1
37	SUFFOLK	NY	1
38	ST MARY	LA	1
39	LICKING	OH	1
40	WOOD	WV	1
41	MOHAVE	AZ	1
42	VIGO	IN	1
43	HARLAN	KY	1
44	ST LOUIS	MN	1
45	SILVER BOW	MT	1
46	VALENCIA	NM	1
47	WARREN	PA	1
48	LUBBOCK	TX	1
49	JEFFERSON	AL	1
50	OUACHITA	AR	1
51	FRESNO	CA	1
52	SHASTA	CA	1
53	ST CHARLES	LA	1
54	LEE	MS	1
55	BERGEN	NJ	1
56	ORANGE	TX	1
57	ROANOKE	VA	1
58	HARRISON	WV	1
59	SWEETWATER	WY	1
60	COCHISE	AZ	1
61	TULARE	CA	1

BOTTOM COUNTIES SHADED WHITE

RANK	COUNTY	STATE	VALUE
1	NEW YORK CITY	NY	-42
2	LOS ANGELES	CA	-14
3	WAYNE	MI	-8
4	PHILADELPHIA	PA	-7
5	NASSAU	NY	-7
6	COOK	IL	-5
7	MIDDLESEX	MA	-5
8	SAN DIEGO	CA	-5
9	ORANGE	CA	-5
10	MILWAUKEE	WI	-5
11	ALAMEDA	CA	-4
12	SANTA CLARA	CA	-4
13	ST LOUIS	MO	-4
14	DADE	FL	-4
15	PRINCE GEORGES	MD	-4
16	FAIRFIELD	CT	-4
17	KING	WA	-4
18	MONTGOMERY	MD	-3
19	SACRAMENTO	CA	-3
20	SUMMIT	OH	-3
21	DALLAS	TX	-3
22	HARTFORD	CT	-3
23	WESTCHESTER	NY	-3
24	PINELLAS	FL	-3
25	BALTIMORE	MD	-3
26	BROWARD	FL	-3
27	SAN MATEO	CA	-2
28	DISTRICT OF COLUMBIA	DC	-2
29	FAIRFAX	VA	-2
30	FRANKLIN	OH	-2
31	OAKLAND	MI	-2
32	MONTGOMERY	PA	-2
33	NORFOLK	MA	-2
34	DU PAGE	IL	-2
35	PROVIDENCE	RI	-2
36	SAN FRANCISCO	CA	-2
37	MORRIS	NJ	-2
38	MONROE	NY	-2
39	CAMDEN	NJ	-2
40	BALTIMORE CITY	MD	-2
41	BRISTOL	MA	-2
42	MIDDLESEX	NJ	-1
43	MARION	IN	-1
44	MACOMB	MI	-1
45	HENNEPIN	MN	-1
46	JEFFERSON	CO	-1
47	ERIE	NY	-1
48	DAVIDSON	TN	-1
49	RIVERSIDE	CA	-1
50	KENT	MI	-1
51	PIERCE	WA	-1
52	DE KALB	GA	-1
53	KANE	IL	-1
54	ANNE ARUNDEL	MD	-1
55	ESSEX	NJ	-1
56	MERCER	NJ	-1
57	TRAVIS	TX	-1
58	WORCESTER	MA	-1
59	WASHTENAW	MI	-1
60	SNOHOMISH	WA	-1
61	LUCAS	OH	-1
62	STARK	OH	-1

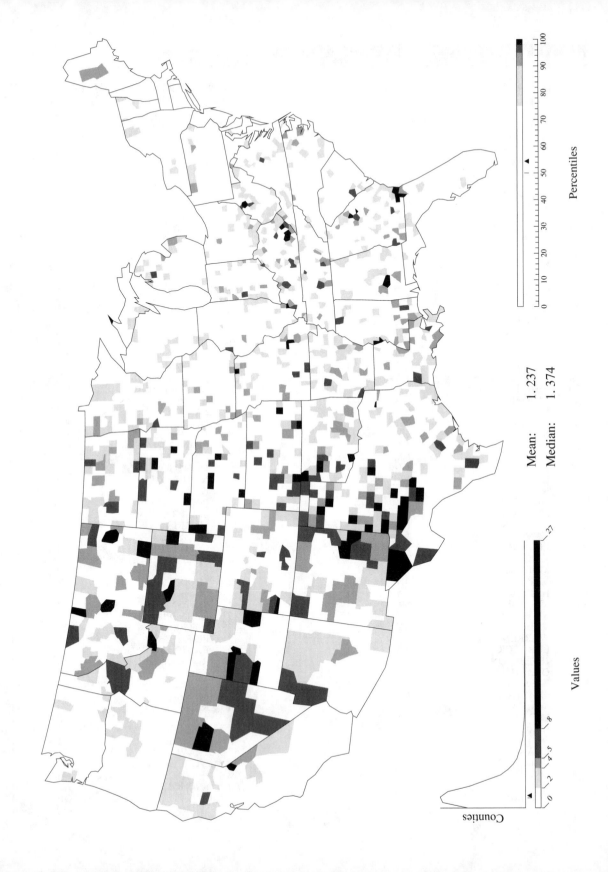

Mean: 1.237

Median: 1.374

Percentiles

Values

Counties

(DEATHS PER 100,000 PEOPLE)

	TOP COUNTIES SHADED BLACK				BOTTOM COUNTIES SHADED WHITE

RANK	COUNTY	STATE	VALUE
1	CLAY	KY	27
2	HARDIN	IL	21
3	BLAINE	NE	18
4	IRION	TX	17
5	THOMAS	NE	17
6	SIOUX	NE	15
7	REAGAN	TX	15
8	CHARLTON	GA	15
9	BORDEN	TX	15
10	GREELEY	NE	14
11	CARSON	TX	14
12	HARPER	OK	14
13	HUDSPETH	TX	14
14	LESLIE	KY	14
15	CLARK	ID	14
16	PERSHING	NV	14
17	COKE	TX	13
18	CRANE	TX	13
19	JUDITH BASIN	MT	13
20	ALPINE	CA	13
21	WESTON	WY	12
22	POWDER RIVER	MT	12
23	ISSAQUENA	MS	12
24	MENARD	TX	12
25	SANBORN	SD	12
26	KEWEENAW	MI	12
27	CAMP	TX	11
28	BENNETT	SD	11
29	TALIAFERRO	GA	11
30	GLASCOCK	GA	10
31	IRON	MO	10
32	FAULK	SD	10
33	LIBERTY	MT	10
34	HITCHCOCK	NE	10
35	ROOSEVELT	NM	10
36	DEWEY	OK	10
37	ANDERSON	KS	9
38	HOT SPRINGS	WY	9
39	ANDREWS	TX	9
40	MOORE	TX	9
41	UPTON	TX	9
42	CHAUTAUQUA	KS	9
43	THROCKMORTON	TX	9
44	CULBERSON	TX	9
45	WILCOX	AL	9
46	RITCHIE	WV	8
47	YOAKUM	TX	8
48	DE BACA	NM	8
49	SCHUYLER	MO	8
50	LAMB	TX	8
51	CLARK	KS	8
52	SUTTON	TX	8
53	JUAB	UT	8
54	COTTON	OK	8
55	DAWSON	MT	8
56	GRAND	UT	8
57	KNOTT	KY	8
58	DOLORES	CO	8
59	CAMDEN	GA	8
60	BEAVER	UT	8

NOTE: TOO MANY COUNTIES TO LIST
HAD ZERO VALUES FOR THIS MEASURE

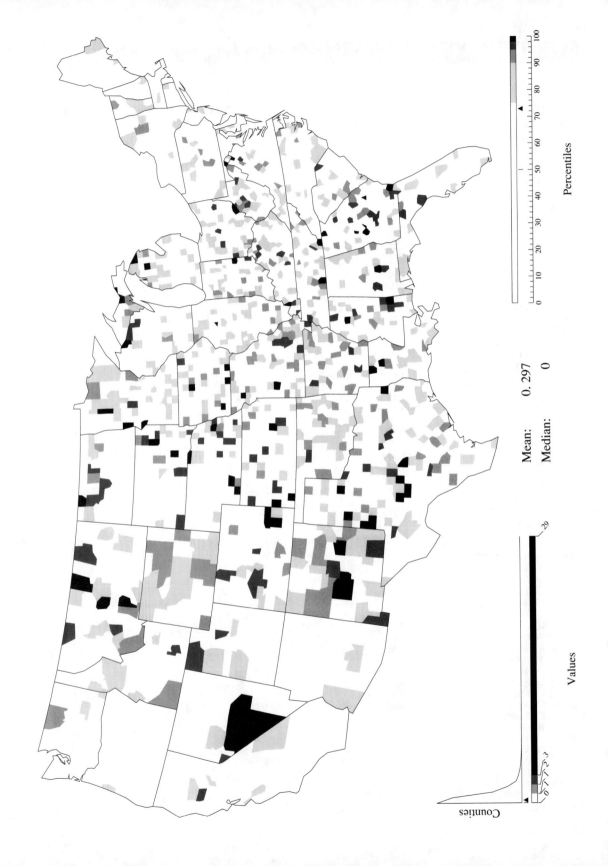

Mean: 0. 297

Median: 0

Percentiles

Values

Counties

(DEATHS PER 100,000 PEOPLE)

TOP COUNTIES SHADED BLACK

RANK	COUNTY	STATE	VALUE
1	ESMERALDA	NV	29
2	HAMILTON	KS	10
3	KIOWA	CO	9
4	CONCHO	TX	7
5	YOAKUM	TX	7
6	DE BACA	NM	6
7	SCHLEICHER	TX	6
8	YALOBUSHA	MS	6
9	IRION	TX	5
10	UNION	GA	5
11	BLAINE	MT	5
12	CHASE	KS	5
13	MORGAN	WV	5
14	DE KALB	MO	5
15	CRAWFORD	MI	5
16	POLK	TN	5
17	NYE	NV	5
18	BURKE	ND	5
19	WAYNE	MS	4
20	PUTNAM	IL	4
21	BOYD	NE	4
22	HITCHCOCK	NE	4
23	SOCORRO	NM	4
24	MINERAL	NV	4
25	FRONTIER	NE	4
26	LOWNDES	AL	4
27	WASHINGTON	OH	4
28	ST CLAIR	MO	4
29	PRESQUE ISLE	MI	4
30	BENT	CO	4
31	WAYNE	IN	4
32	TAYLOR	GA	4
33	CLEARWATER	MN	4
34	CLARK	SD	4
35	CANDLER	GA	4
36	WILKIN	MN	4
37	IRON	WI	4
38	CAMDEN	GA	4
39	CLARKE	VA	4
40	MONTGOMERY	IA	4
41	WRIGHT	IA	3
42	JUDITH BASIN	MT	3
43	SAN SABA	TX	3
44	GAINES	TX	3
45	JACKSON	LA	3
46	BIG STONE	MN	3
47	STEVENS	KS	3
48	LAMB	TX	3
49	LIVINGSTON	KY	3
50	GILES	TN	3
51	DAVIS	IA	3
52	HALL	TX	3
53	PANOLA	TX	3
54	AURORA	SD	3
55	LAMAR	GA	3
56	CLAIBORNE	LA	3
57	PEACH	GA	3
58	DODGE	NE	3
59	WAYNE	IA	3
60	SWEET GRASS	MT	3
61	ALGER	MI	3

BOTTOM COUNTIES SHADED WHITE

NOTE: TOO MANY COUNTIES TO LIST
HAD ZERO VALUES FOR THIS MEASURE

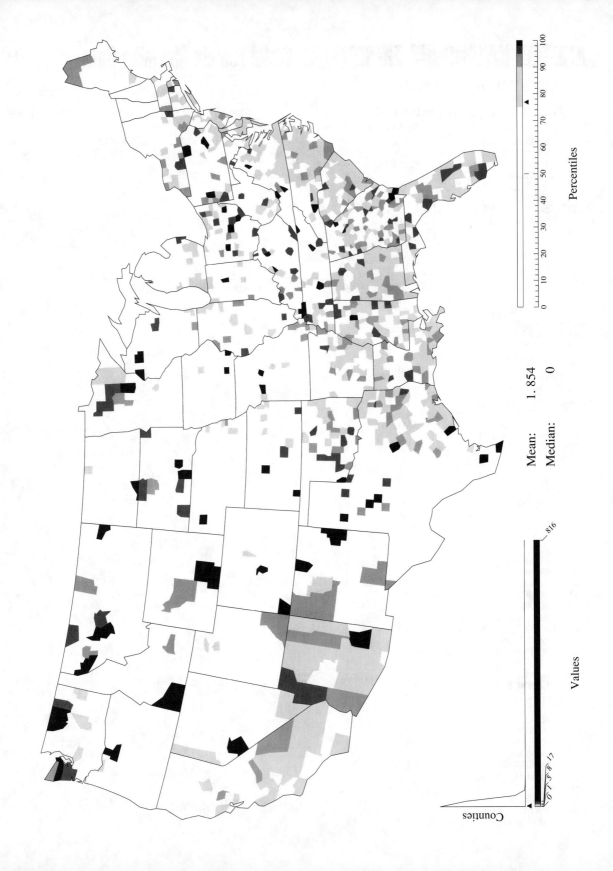

Mean: 1.854

Median: 0

Percentiles

Values

Counties

(DEATHS PER 100,000 PEOPLE)

TOP COUNTIES SHADED BLACK

RANK	COUNTY	STATE	VALUE
1	HANCOCK	TN	816
2	BRULE	SD	609
3	BROOKS	TX	203
4	RICHLAND	MT	189
5	BULLITT	KY	127
6	CASTRO	TX	96
7	ELLIS	KS	84
8	HICKMAN	KY	77
9	WASCO	OR	67
10	SCHUYLKILL	PA	67
11	BOSQUE	TX	59
12	QUAY	NM	58
13	BRADFORD	PA	54
14	JEFFERSON	WA	51
15	AITKIN	MN	50
16	FLOYD	VA	47
17	MIAMI	IN	47
18	MORGAN	OH	45
19	BOX BUTTE	NE	40
20	CARBON	WY	37
21	GARZA	TX	37
22	BURNETT	WI	37
23	HARRISON	OH	36
24	WAPELLO	IA	33
25	LEWIS AND CLARK	MT	30
26	CHAFFEE	CO	30
27	TAOS	NM	29
28	SAWYER	WI	29
29	GILES	VA	28
30	HARMON	OK	27
31	GRAVES	KY	26
32	OWYHEE	ID	25
33	MAURY	TN	24
34	SANDERS	MT	24
35	GRAHAM	AZ	22
36	MONTEZUMA	CO	21
37	BUTLER	PA	21
38	JACKSON	TX	21
39	FRANKLIN	GA	21
40	CAMERON	TX	20
41	TRIPP	SD	20
42	ROANE	TN	20
43	PAGE	VA	20
44	RUTHERFORD	NC	20
45	CAMDEN	GA	20
46	OKANOGAN	WA	19
47	SCURRY	TX	19
48	DES MOINES	IA	19
49	HOWARD	MO	19
50	BARROW	GA	19
51	CALLOWAY	KY	19
52	LAFAYETTE	MO	18
53	SEWARD	KS	18
54	MINERAL	NV	18
55	LOGAN	OH	18
56	SCOTT	KY	17
57	SIOUX	ND	17
58	CURRY	NM	17
59	BRANTLEY	GA	17
60	LICKING	OH	17
61	CALHOUN	MS	17

BOTTOM COUNTIES SHADED WHITE

NOTE: TOO MANY COUNTIES TO LIST
HAD ZERO VALUES FOR THIS MEASURE

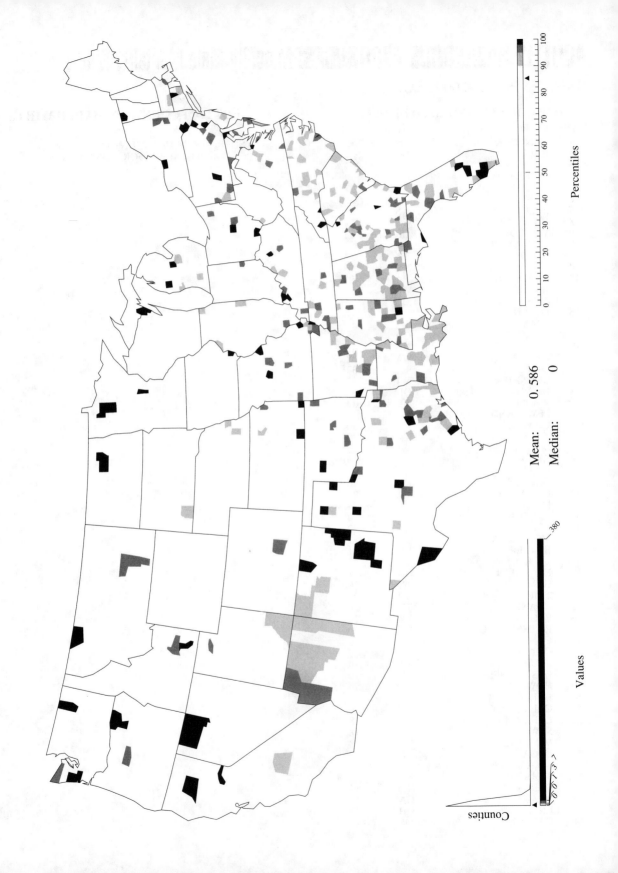

Mean: 0. 586

Median: 0

Percentiles

Values

Counties

(DEATHS PER 100,000 PEOPLE)

TOP COUNTIES SHADED BLACK

RANK	COUNTY	STATE	VALUE
1	PRESIDIO	TX	380
2	RAMSEY	ND	204
3	MENOMINEE	MI	201
4	FRANKLIN	VT	97
5	QUAY	NM	95
6	WHEELER	TX	81
7	MIDLAND	MI	68
8	MOORE	TX	65
9	CAMDEN	GA	63
10	RUNNELS	TX	58
11	NEVADA	CA	52
12	HARDEMAN	TX	37
13	DEWEY	OK	36
14	CHEROKEE	KS	31
15	OKEECHOBEE	FL	25
16	SUSSEX	NJ	23
17	HUNTERDON	NJ	21
18	MONTGOMERY	GA	21
19	LICKING	OH	20
20	POLK	NC	17
21	MILLE LACS	MN	17
22	HUMBOLDT	NV	17
23	DES MOINES	IA	17
24	BANNOCK	ID	16
25	HENDERSON	KY	16
26	PIKE	MO	16
27	JACKSON	TX	15
28	COWLEY	KS	14
29	SEVIER	AR	14
30	GRAYS HARBOR	WA	14
31	WEBSTER	KY	14
32	GLADES	FL	13
33	COOPER	MO	13
34	BENSON	ND	13
35	SHASTA	CA	12
36	SULLIVAN	NY	12
37	SCOTT	MO	12
38	CHAVES	NM	11
39	FERRY	WA	11
40	LAKE	MI	11
41	TAOS	NM	11
42	CURRY	NM	11
43	BELTRAMI	MN	10
44	FRANKLIN	FL	10
45	TOLLAND	CT	10
46	LEON	TX	10
47	HALE	TX	9
48	SCOTT	KY	9
49	LAKE	TN	9
50	CECIL	MD	9
51	COLLIER	FL	9
52	JONES	MS	8
53	MORRIS	TX	8
54	GLACIER	MT	8
55	FRANKLIN	GA	8
56	UMATILLA	OR	8
57	WAYNE	NY	8
58	JACKSON	NC	8
59	SCIOTO	OH	7
60	KING GEORGE	VA	7
61	CAMBRIA	PA	7

BOTTOM COUNTIES SHADED WHITE

NOTE: TOO MANY COUNTIES TO LIST
HAD ZERO VALUES FOR THIS MEASURE

The AIDS story is unfolding at such a rapid pace that any snapshot of nationwide variations is quickly replaced by another pattern. The maps are current through 1983, at which point young adult mortality had just begun its ascent, reversing the trend of the previous decade. What percentage AIDS constituted of the young adult mortality in the maps remains unclear, because the official classification for AIDS was not fully incorporated in the U.S. vital statistics until 1987 (at which point AIDS comprised nearly two-thirds of infectious disease mortality for young adults). Its share of all deaths among young adults has more than doubled since then, from 6 percent in 1987 to 12 percent in 1989. Diagnosed AIDS cases increased by 14 percent from 1988 to 1989, and in that year AIDS mortality increased by nearly 30 percent, jumping from the 15th to the 11th leading cause of death.[175] AIDS incidence is highest in large American cities, and rates are generally higher in the Northeast than in other regions of the country. New York City, Los Angeles, and San Francisco account for over a third of the reported cases, and the majority of cases nationwide as of 1990 are among relatively affluent gay white men.[176]

Yet the picture is still changing. Regionally, the greatest *increase* in reported cases is occurring in the South, and AIDS is being diagnosed more frequently in smaller communities. The overall increase in AIDS cases has slowed, reflecting increased preventive measures taken by the gay community, as well as a decline in AIDS among blood transfusion recipients. A comparable slowdown in AIDS mortality among white men should follow, but this is not yet evident due to the lag between the onset of symptoms and death. When we look at the statistics racially, minorities are experiencing the most frightful increase in AIDS. AIDS is nearly four times higher among African Americans than among whites, and is increasing twice as fast. In areas that previously had low rates among both whites and blacks, detection of the HIV virus is increasing more quickly among blacks. And in epidemic urban areas such as New York City, Miami, Houston, and San Francisco, it is increasing only among blacks.[177] AIDS among Latino Americans is nearly three times the white rate, and is increasing 40 percent more quickly. There is also a staggering increase in AIDS among heterosexual men and women who use intravenous drugs, as well as among their children.[178]

In short, the picture of young-adult infectious diseases in the United States appears to be returning to the image depicted in the maps, disproportionately affecting poorer urban and rural minority communities—though with considerably higher mortality rates than existed prior to the AIDS epidemic. Given the resurrection of the historical patterns, it is worth considering AIDS within the more general trends of infectious diseases and young adult mortality.

There is a wide variety of infectious diseases in addition to AIDS: tuberculosis, septicemia, measles, allergies, syphilis, and others. Some are caused by parasites or viruses; some are sexually transmitted or transmitted by contaminated water or air. These diseases were the leading cause of death in the United States at the start of the 20th century. As noted in the last chapter, most were largely eradicated by the introduction of sewage systems, purified public water supplies, improved housing, and better nutrition—long before the discovery of antibiotics and other cures.[179] Since then, epidemics of infectious diseases in U.S. history have tended to be intermittent with erratic geographic patterns, yet poor and minority communities consistently have had higher rates.[180] Despite the overall decline in infectious disease, pneumonia and influenza remain the sixth leading cause of death in the United States, killing 75,000 Americans in 1989—more than three times the number of AIDS deaths (though the CDC estimates AIDS mortality may reach a comparable level by 1993).[181]

The rise in young-adult mortality is clearly due to diseases (fatal accidents and other external causes of death are declining for this age group), yet anywhere from one-fifth to one-third of the increased deaths are not classified as AIDS.[182] Some of the rise in deaths from diseases other than AIDS may be due to misclassification. No one actually dies of the AIDS virus *per se;* rather, AIDS is a syndrome through which a variety of previously defined diseases and infections (such as non-Hodgkin's lymphoma, pneumocystis pneumonia, and Kaposi's sarcoma) can lead to the patient's death. The CDC has found that the greatest increases in non-AIDS deaths among young men are occurring where the AIDS incidence is also highest—the District of Columbia, New York, Florida, New Jersey, and California.[183] As a result, the CDC suggests all the other causes of the increase in young-adult mortality may be related to HIV infection as well. But no one is certain. The opposite may also be true: some factor or factors others than HIV may be contributing to the rise in young-adult mortality among people who test seropositive, as well as among those who do not.

Minority rates of young adult infectious diseases are nearly five times higher than white rates—the highest ratio of minorities to whites of all ten causes of death in the atlas. The disparities become even more severe when major outbreaks occur: for example, poor and minority children had 12 times the rate of diphtheria among affluent white children during an epidemic in San Antonio, Texas.[184] Pneumonia is nearly 50 percent higher among African Americans than among white Americans. Tuberculosis is almost nonexistent among the affluent, but continues to ravage urban poor and minority populations. Among native Americans, immunization has eliminated many of the diseases for which there are vaccines, yet mortality from infectious diseases is still twice the U.S. average, largely because of inadequate water supplies, sanitation, and housing.[185] The maps make the persistence of this native American health tragedy obvious: high minority mortality rates for young adult infectious diseases cluster stubbornly in the Four Corners region of the Southwest. In addition to poorer environmental conditions and health care access, social and psychological stresses are involved: tuberculosis mortality among young adults who are divorced or widowed, for example, is four to eleven times higher than rates among married young adults.[186]

The data used to produce the maps clearly indicate that a problem in young adult mortality from infectious diseases was brewing prior to the 1980s, even though the maps themselves do not reflect this development since they are snapshots of a single period in time. While young-adult infectious disease mortality declined throughout the period 1968 to 1983 (see Fig. 3-2), the unequal distribution of such deaths increased dramatically—more so than for any other cause of death in the atlas, and especially among white men (see the methods appendix discussion of Fig. A-1). Now other researchers are finding significant increases in geographic inequalities among all causes of young-adult mortality as well, including major heart diseases, just as we found for young-adult infectious diseases.[187] These trends indicate a menacing problem among young adults that is more widespread than AIDS or infectious diseases in general.

Non-AIDS deaths contribute an increasing share of the rise in young-adult mortality toward the end of the 1980s.[188] A host of diseases associated with immune deficiencies other than AIDS are now rising rapidly among young adults and others: chronic fatigue syndrome, multiple chemical sensitivity, Lyme disease, candida albicans, herpes, septicemia, and others.[189] Far more years of potential life are lost due to cancer than to AIDS.[190] Cancer has also been associated with immune deficiencies and is increasing among young adults.[191] Pneumonia and influenza are on the rise again after years of decline.[192] Allergies are increasing significantly in this country and in industrialized countries throughout the world.[193] Deaths from asthma are on the rise after years of decline, with the fastest increases among females, blacks, and economically disadvantaged children, and the highest rates in metropolitan New York City, Chicago, Detroit, Phoenix, and Riverside, California, and in rural areas of the central Midwest, the Appalachians, and the Hawaiian Islands.[194] Annual health care expenditures for asthma alone exceeded $4 billion by 1988.[195]

Diseases are rare given how many parasites we are subjected to. We succumb only when the stresses and strains of life overwhelm our natural resistances.[196] Germs are no longer considered the sole cause for most infectious diseases. An individual's susceptibility to tuberculosis, for example, depends upon his nutritional state, genetics, medical care, housing conditions, and other factors, as well as the presence of the tubercle bacteria.[197] Many of the very same activities that are considered a high risk for spreading the AIDS virus, such as drug use and blood transfusions, suppress immune system responses even without the presence of HIV.[198] Half of all patients receiving blood transfusions die within a year whether HIV is present in the blood or not.[199] Transfusions are often given to transplant patients in order to suppress the immune system's rejection of the new organ. The gay community engaged in heavy use of immune suppressant drugs such as amyl nitrite and antibiotics. Even semen contains immunosuppressive agents that enables sperm to fertilize eggs without triggering an immune system reaction, but which may have more deleterious effects when multiple partners engage in high risk sex. Drug addicts suppress their immune systems by the very act of injecting chemicals into their veins, and by their very high rates of malnutrition. In contrast, only one health care worker—of the thousands who have been accidentally stuck with HIV-contaminated needles and lack other identified risk factors—has developed AIDS.[200]

Certain activities clearly contribute to the spread of the AIDS virus, but there may also be combinations of immune suppression factors that provide HIV with the opportunity to wage a fatal attack. Few directly contest the role of HIV in the spread of AIDS, yet now even Luc Montaigner, the French co-discoverer of the AIDS virus, no longer believes HIV alone causes the disease.[201] Other viruses and bacteria are suspected as potential cofactors.[202] As summed up in a recent history of AIDS, the question remains: "Does the AIDS virus act alone . . . or does it require an accomplice? The answer is still not known."[203]

While organized medicine concentrates most of its research efforts on microbiology, 3 to 9 million workers are exposed to suspected carcinogens used in large amounts in the workplace; pesticide residues contaminate almost all of our food; 300,000 miles of high-voltage power lines and hundreds of military and civilian reactors routinely emit low levels of electromagnetic and ionizing radiation; and industry spews billions of pounds of toxins into the air, water, and land each year.[204] Add to this the billions of tons of toxic chemicals that industry has released into the

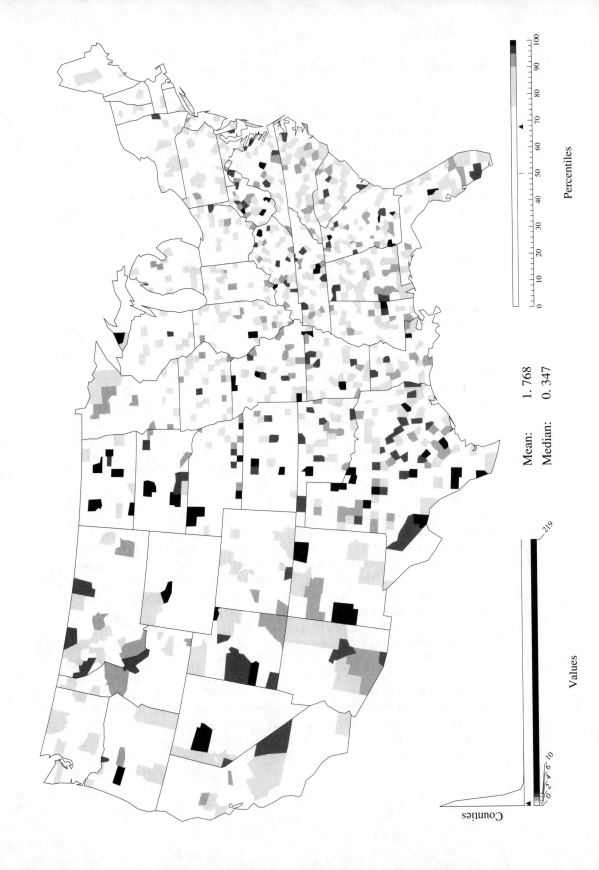

Mean: 1. 768

Median: 0. 347

Percentiles

Values

Counties

YOUNG-ADULT INFECTIOUS DISEASES: Total Mortality Rate

(DEATHS PER 100,000 YOUNG ADULTS)

TOP COUNTIES SHADED BLACK

RANK	COUNTY	STATE	VALUE
1	MACOUPIN	IL	219
2	CARTER	KY	218
3	BOONE	WV	80
4	DAGGETT	UT	57
5	HANCOCK	KY	49
6	FOARD	TX	40
7	COLLINGSWORTH	TX	39
8	LUMPKIN	GA	36
9	PAWNEE	NE	35
10	PERSHING	NV	34
11	EDWARDS	KS	29
12	TERRELL	TX	25
13	LA SALLE	TX	24
14	HOWARD	MO	21
15	BENSON	ND	21
16	DEWEY	SD	20
17	WOODWARD	OK	18
18	ADAMS	ND	17
19	OSBORNE	KS	17
20	SHERIDAN	NE	17
21	MERCER	MO	17
22	SUMTER	FL	16
23	JACKSON	SD	16
24	MASON	TX	16
25	KIDDER	ND	16
26	EARLY	GA	15
27	ST HELENA	LA	15
28	COLFAX	NM	14
29	ONTONAGON	MI	14
30	LINCOLN	OR	14
31	BEN HILL	GA	14
32	GRIGGS	ND	13
33	NEWTON	MO	13
34	WIRT	WV	13
35	WILBARGER	TX	13
36	MATHEWS	VA	13
37	LANIER	GA	13
38	WEBSTER	NE	12
39	ZAPATA	TX	12
40	HOT SPRINGS	WY	12
41	CATRON	NM	12
42	TRINITY	TX	12
43	CHILDRESS	TX	12
44	FISHER	TX	12
45	HITCHCOCK	NE	12
46	DIMMIT	TX	11
47	MOUNTRAIL	ND	11
48	DUNKLIN	MO	11
49	DAWES	NE	11
50	MONTGOMERY	AR	11
51	PUTNAM	MO	11
52	HAYS	TX	11
53	SUMMERS	WV	11
54	COFFEE	TN	11
55	BUCKINGHAM	VA	11
56	GARZA	TX	11
57	DE WITT	TX	11
58	GRUNDY	TN	10
59	CLARKE	MS	10
60	BEAVER	UT	10

BOTTOM COUNTIES SHADED WHITE

NOTE: TOO MANY COUNTIES TO LIST
HAD ZERO VALUES FOR THIS MEASURE

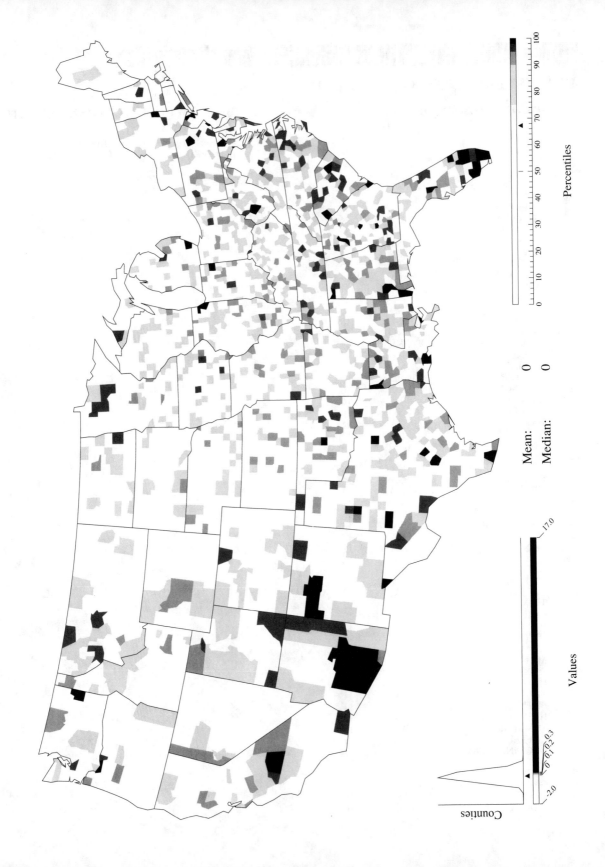

Mean: 0

Median: 0

Percentiles

Values

Counties

TOP COUNTIES SHADED BLACK

RANK	COUNTY	STATE	VALUE
1	NEW YORK CITY	NY	17
2	COOK	IL	3
3	ESSEX	NJ	3
4	HUDSON	NJ	2
5	MARICOPA	AZ	2
6	DADE	FL	2
7	PHILADELPHIA	PA	2
8	PASSAIC	NJ	2
9	PALM BEACH	FL	1
10	FLORENCE	SC	1
11	WAYNE	MI	1
12	DISTRICT OF COLUMBIA	DC	1
13	MOBILE	AL	1
14	PIMA	AZ	1
15	SAN FRANCISCO	CA	1
16	BALTIMORE	MD	1
17	UNION	NJ	1
18	MC KINLEY	NM	1
19	CHATHAM	GA	1
20	ORLEANS	LA	1
21	RENSSELAER	NY	1
22	FULTON	GA	1
23	EL PASO	TX	1
24	LUBBOCK	TX	1
25	ST LUCIE	FL	0.5
26	ALLEN	IN	0.5
27	CADDO	LA	0.5
28	LUZERNE	PA	0.5
29	PINAL	AZ	0.4
30	COLLIER	FL	0.4
31	BIBB	GA	0.4
32	OKLAHOMA	OK	0.4
33	MULTNOMAH	OR	0.4
34	BEXAR	TX	0.4
35	HIDALGO	TX	0.4
36	MIDLAND	TX	0.4
37	CLARKE	AL	0.3
38	COLBERT	AL	0.3
39	GILA	AZ	0.3
40	TULARE	CA	0.3
41	SUMTER	FL	0.3
42	CRISP	GA	0.3
43	VERMILION	LA	0.3
44	SANDOVAL	NM	0.3
45	ANDERSON	SC	0.3
46	ECTOR	TX	0.3
47	HAYS	TX	0.3
48	TARRANT	TX	0.3
49	SPOKANE	WA	0.3
50	KANAWHA	WV	0.3
51	LAWRENCE	AL	0.3
52	KINGS	CA	0.3
53	FAIRFIELD	CT	0.3
54	BROWARD	FL	0.3
55	CHARLOTTE	FL	0.3
56	SEMINOLE	FL	0.3
57	COFFEE	GA	0.3
58	COLUMBIA	GA	0.3
59	EARLY	GA	0.3
60	MARION	IL	0.3
61	BOONE	IN	0.3

BOTTOM COUNTIES SHADED WHITE

RANK	COUNTY	STATE	VALUE
1	LOS ANGELES	CA	-2
2	PRINCE GEORGES	MD	-2
3	SAN DIEGO	CA	-2
4	ORANGE	CA	-2
5	KING	WA	-1
6	MIDDLESEX	MA	-1
7	DALLAS	TX	-1
8	ALAMEDA	CA	-1
9	FAIRFAX	VA	-1
10	SANTA CLARA	CA	-1
11	HARTFORD	CT	-1
12	ST LOUIS	MO	-1
13	FRANKLIN	OH	-1
14	HILLSBOROUGH	FL	-1
15	PLYMOUTH	MA	-1
16	ERIE	NY	-1
17	PIERCE	WA	-1
18	MILWAUKEE	WI	-1
19	OAKLAND	MI	-1
20	SAGINAW	MI	-1
21	HENNEPIN	MN	-1
22	MONROE	NY	-1
23	SHELBY	TN	-1
24	LAKE	IN	-0.5
25	JEFFERSON	KY	-0.5
26	ESSEX	MA	-0.5
27	GENESEE	MI	-0.5
28	MONTGOMERY	OH	-0.5
29	MONTEREY	CA	-0.4
30	DE KALB	GA	-0.4
31	HINDS	MS	-0.4
32	BURLINGTON	NJ	-0.4
33	CLARK	OH	-0.4
34	CUYAHOGA	OH	-0.4
35	LANCASTER	PA	-0.4
36	RICHLAND	SC	-0.4
37	DAVIDSON	TN	-0.4
38	NUECES	TX	-0.4
39	SNOHOMISH	WA	-0.4
40	MARIN	CA	-0.3
41	JEFFERSON	CO	-0.3
42	NEW HAVEN	CT	-0.3
43	DU PAGE	IL	-0.3
44	WILL	IL	-0.3
45	JOHNSON	KS	-0.3
46	INGHAM	MI	-0.3
47	KENT	MI	-0.3
48	MIDDLESEX	NJ	-0.3
49	WESTCHESTER	NY	-0.3
50	WESTMORELAND	PA	-0.3
51	SALT LAKE	UT	-0.3
52	PRINCE WILLIAM	VA	-0.3
53	ROCKLAND	NY	-0.3
54	GREENE	OH	-0.3
55	BEAVER	PA	-0.3
56	DELAWARE	PA	-0.3
57	MONTGOMERY	PA	-0.3
58	PROVIDENCE	RI	-0.3
59	CHARLESTON	SC	-0.3
60	BELL	TX	-0.3
61	WICHITA	TX	-0.3
62	ROANOKE	VA	-0.3

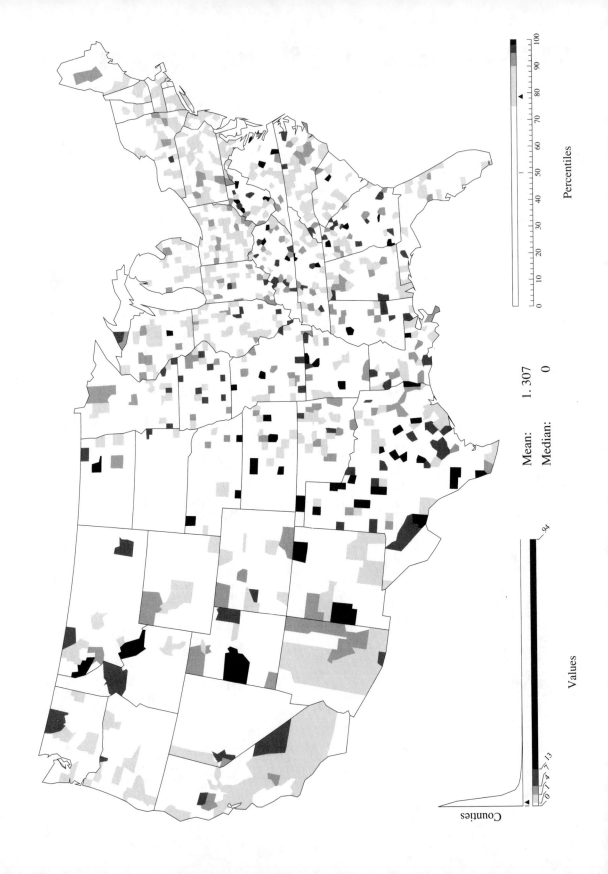

Values

Counties

94

0 7 7 13

Mean: 1. 307

Median: 0

Percentiles

0 10 20 30 40 50 60 70 80 90 100

(DEATHS PER 100,000 YOUNG ADULTS)

TOP COUNTIES SHADED BLACK

RANK	COUNTY	STATE	VALUE
1	FOARD	TX	94
2	TERRELL	TX	58
3	LA SALLE	TX	56
4	OSBORNE	KS	40
5	MERCER	MO	39
6	ST HELENA	LA	35
7	EDWARDS	KS	33
8	COLFAX	NM	33
9	BEN HILL	GA	32
10	WIRT	WV	31
11	MATHEWS	VA	29
12	ZAPATA	TX	29
13	CATRON	NM	29
14	CHILDRESS	TX	27
15	FISHER	TX	27
16	COLLINGSWORTH	TX	27
17	HITCHCOCK	NE	27
18	DIMMIT	TX	27
19	DAWES	NE	27
20	MONTGOMERY	AR	26
21	GARZA	TX	25
22	FULTON	AR	24
23	BLANCO	TX	24
24	MILLARD	UT	24
25	BENSON	ND	22
26	NEWTON	TX	22
27	JUAB	UT	22
28	HAMILTON	TX	21
29	PICKETT	TN	21
30	RUSSELL	KY	20
31	RICHMOND	VA	20
32	GRIMES	TX	20
33	BUCKINGHAM	VA	19
34	BRUNSWICK	VA	19
35	OSAGE	KS	18
36	HOOD	TX	18
37	LAMPASAS	TX	18
38	DODDRIDGE	WV	18
39	MARION	KS	17
40	STONE	AR	17
41	JOHNSON	KY	17
42	GRUNDY	TN	17
43	COOPER	MO	17
44	MARQUETTE	WI	16
45	TUCKER	WV	16
46	ROOKS	KS	16
47	LIMESTONE	TX	16
48	SUMMERS	WV	16
49	SANDERS	MT	15
50	NOLAN	TX	15
51	BEAVERHEAD	MT	15
52	TALLAHATCHIE	MS	15
53	MORGAN	GA	15
54	TEXAS	OK	15
55	MOORE	TX	14
56	JEFFERSON	NE	14
57	CROSBY	TX	14
58	GILMER	GA	14
59	EARLY	GA	13
60	BATH	KY	13
61	LEE	SC	13

BOTTOM COUNTIES SHADED WHITE

NOTE: TOO MANY COUNTIES TO LIST
HAD ZERO VALUES FOR THIS MEASURE

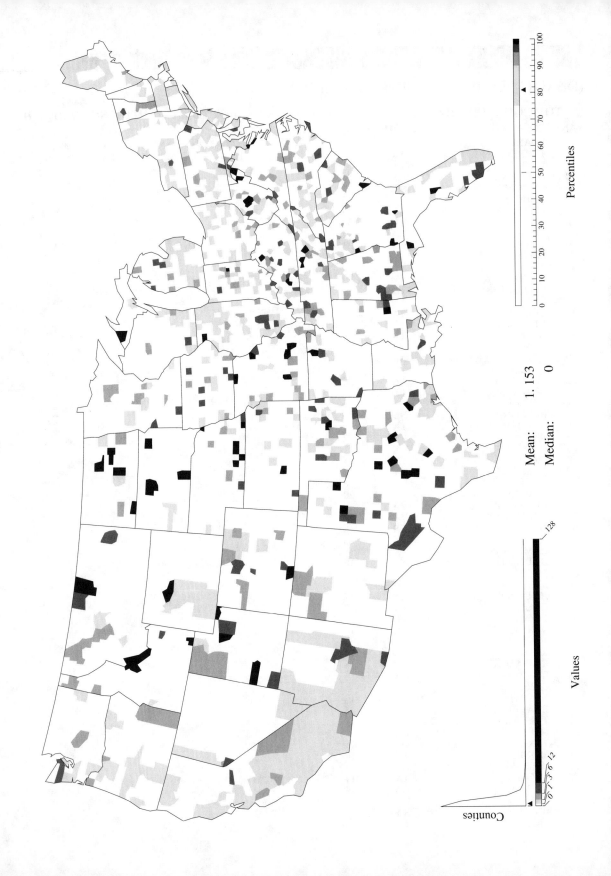

Mean: 1 . 153

Median: 0

Percentiles

Values

Counties

0 1 3 6 12

128

YOUNG-ADULT INFECTIOUS DISEASES: White Female Mortality Rate

(DEATHS PER 100,000 YOUNG ADULTS)

TOP COUNTIES SHADED BLACK

RANK	COUNTY	STATE	VALUE
1	DAGGETT	UT	128
2	PAWNEE	NE	79
3	DEWEY	SD	44
4	ADAMS	ND	38
5	MASON	TX	35
6	KIDDER	ND	35
7	EDWARDS	KS	33
8	GRIGGS	ND	30
9	COLLINGSWORTH	TX	29
10	LANIER	GA	28
11	WEBSTER	NE	28
12	HOT SPRINGS	WY	27
13	TRINITY	TX	27
14	PUTNAM	MO	25
15	BENSON	ND	24
16	SUMTER	FL	23
17	BEAVER	UT	23
18	KING GEORGE	VA	22
19	FOSTER	ND	21
20	ONTONAGON	MI	21
21	LEMHI	ID	21
22	CALHOUN	WV	19
23	STEPHENS	TX	18
24	TRIPP	SD	18
25	BLAINE	MT	18
26	SHARP	AR	17
27	HAMPSHIRE	WV	17
28	KEARNEY	NE	17
29	DAY	SD	17
30	CONEJOS	CO	17
31	HEARD	GA	16
32	CLAY	NE	16
33	DALLAS	MO	15
34	MC CULLOCH	TX	15
35	ESSEX	VA	15
36	WASATCH	UT	15
37	HILL	TX	15
38	RALLS	MO	15
39	JASPER	SC	15
40	GILMER	WV	15
41	EARLY	GA	14
42	OKFUSKEE	OK	14
43	DENT	MO	14
44	DAKOTA	NE	13
45	HAYS	TX	13
46	CALHOUN	FL	13
47	JACKSON	TN	13
48	FILLMORE	NE	13
49	CARROLL	IL	13
50	BUTLER	KY	13
51	BRAXTON	WV	13
52	OVERTON	TN	13
53	BLACKFORD	IN	13
54	OWEN	KY	13
55	REYNOLDS	MO	12
56	COMANCHE	TX	12
57	JASPER	MS	12
58	MORGAN	TN	12
59	SWISHER	TX	12
60	FRANKLIN	ID	12
61	GRANT	WV	12

BOTTOM COUNTIES SHADED WHITE

NOTE: TOO MANY COUNTIES TO LIST
HAD ZERO VALUES FOR THIS MEASURE

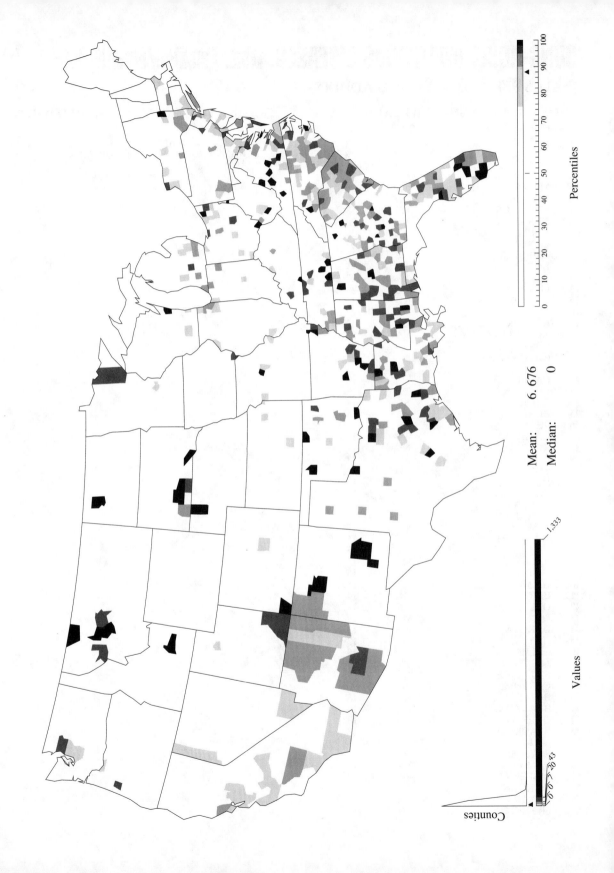

Mean: 6. 676

Median: 0

Percentiles

Values

Counties

(DEATHS PER 100,000 YOUNG ADULTS)

TOP COUNTIES SHADED BLACK

RANK	COUNTY	STATE	VALUE
1	BOONE	WV	1,333
2	LUMPKIN	GA	606
3	HOWARD	MO	351
4	WOODWARD	OK	303
5	SHERIDAN	NE	278
6	MANITOWOC	WI	256
7	GEAUGA	OH	238
8	MOUNTRAIL	ND	190
9	JACKSON	SD	185
10	LEWIS AND CLARK	MT	163
11	LEON	TX	142
12	CLEVELAND	AR	136
13	MELLETTE	SD	136
14	DUNKLIN	MO	133
15	WILBARGER	TX	131
16	BOTETOURT	VA	117
17	COFFEE	TN	104
18	MARION	TN	104
19	GLADES	FL	98
20	SCHLEY	GA	89
21	OKEECHOBEE	FL	87
22	HAYS	TX	87
23	MONTEZUMA	CO	82
24	CALHOUN	AR	81
25	CHARLES MIX	SD	81
26	TYLER	TX	78
27	RENSSELAER	NY	77
28	MIDDLESEX	VA	75
29	BATH	VA	74
30	CHILTON	AL	74
31	AUSTIN	TX	73
32	CHAVES	NM	71
33	CHOCTAW	OK	69
34	MC DOWELL	NC	63
35	OHIO	WV	62
36	WINN	LA	61
37	LAWRENCE	MS	60
38	PERRY	MS	60
39	HERNANDO	FL	60
40	LAWRENCE	AL	59
41	LUNENBERG	VA	59
42	TREUTLEN	GA	58
43	MADISON	GA	56
44	LAWRENCE	OH	55
45	AMHERST	VA	54
46	PULASKI	VA	54
47	NORTHAMPTON	VA	50
48	PAMLICO	NC	50
49	LINCOLN	TN	50
50	COLLIER	FL	48
51	KAY	OK	48
52	CRISP	GA	47
53	CLAIBORNE	LA	46
54	SIMPSON	KY	44
55	GLACIER	MT	44
56	BUCKINGHAM	VA	44
57	BINGHAM	ID	44
58	GARLAND	AR	44
59	DENTON	TX	43
60	SANDOVAL	NM	43

BOTTOM COUNTIES SHADED WHITE

NOTE: TOO MANY COUNTIES TO LIST
HAD ZERO VALUES FOR THIS MEASURE

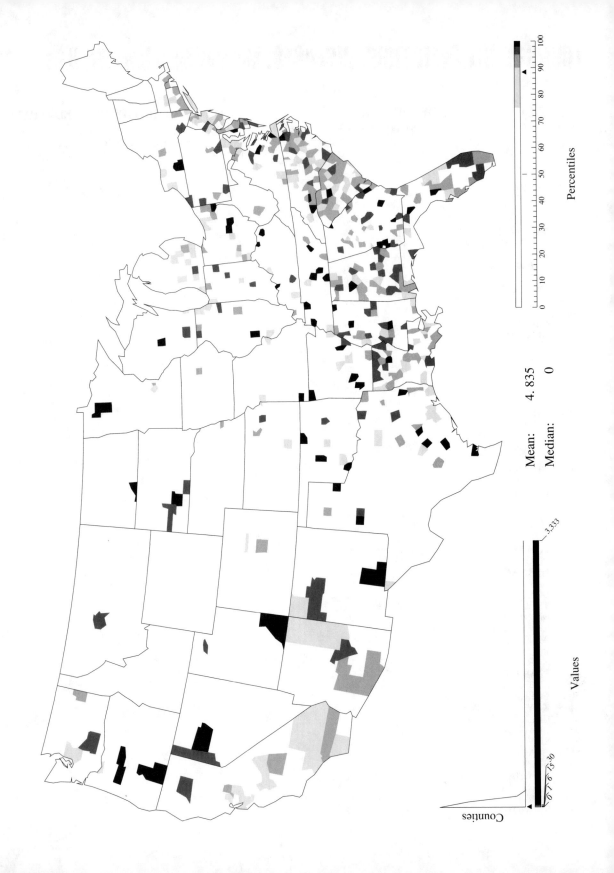

Mean: 4.835

Median: 0

Percentiles

Values

Counties

3.333

(DEATHS PER 100,000 YOUNG ADULTS)

TOP COUNTIES SHADED BLACK

RANK	COUNTY	STATE	VALUE
1	MACOUPIN	IL	3,333
2	CARTER	KY	3,333
3	HANCOCK	KY	667
4	PERSHING	NV	513
5	COLLINGSWORTH	TX	230
6	LINCOLN	OR	196
7	NEWTON	MO	167
8	STEUBEN	NY	128
9	HOCKLEY	TX	115
10	CALDWELL	LA	100
11	DE WITT	TX	97
12	WOOD	WI	93
13	COLUMBIANA	OH	87
14	KAY	OK	86
15	MASON	KY	78
16	JACKSON	SD	74
17	ROANE	TN	73
18	TILLMAN	OK	71
19	BLAINE	OK	69
20	SUMTER	FL	68
21	JEFFERSON	OR	60
22	BURLESON	TX	57
23	KLEBERG	TX	56
24	SAN AUGUSTINE	TX	55
25	CAROLINE	MD	54
26	COFFEE	TN	54
27	BENTON	AR	53
28	CLAY	GA	52
29	APPLING	GA	50
30	HENRY	TN	50
31	LICKING	OH	49
32	BELTRAMI	MN	49
33	KLAMATH	OR	47
34	EFFINGHAM	GA	46
35	STEPHENS	GA	46
36	WALKER	AL	45
37	LINCOLN	NC	44
38	SAN JUAN	UT	44
39	SIOUX	ND	44
40	HEMPSTEAD	AR	42
41	OTERO	NM	42
42	LINCOLN	TN	41
43	RANDOLPH	GA	39
44	BASTROP	TX	39
45	DYER	TN	39
46	SIMPSON	MS	38
47	MUSKINGUM	OH	37
48	SUWANNEE	FL	36
49	ISLE OF WIGHT	VA	36
50	FAIRFIELD	SC	34
51	CLARK	AR	34
52	HERTFORD	NC	33
53	ALCORN	MS	33
54	YALOBUSHA	MS	31
55	HANOVER	VA	30
56	RUTHERFORD	TN	30
57	RUTHERFORD	NC	30
58	STEWART	GA	30
59	MONROE	AR	30
60	COOK	GA	30

BOTTOM COUNTIES SHADED WHITE

NOTE: TOO MANY COUNTIES TO LIST
HAD ZERO VALUES FOR THIS MEASURE

environment since World War II. Consider also that the Americans and the Soviets exploded the equivalent of 40,000 Hiroshima bombs from 1945 to 1962, releasing long-lived radioactive isotopes such as strontium 90 into the atmosphere. Some of it ended up in the milk of the mothers and the bones of the very babies who—if they survived—are now young adults.[205] Is it any wonder that the generation of young adults born in the heyday of atmospheric tests, cigarettes, leaded gas, and petrochemical pollution is now plagued by immune deficiencies?

The overall rise in young-adult mortality would indicate a need for a broader research strategy that investigates the role of multiple risk factors in immune system vulnerability and protection, in addition to chasing down viral agents and vaccines.[206] Even if an AIDS vaccine could be developed—the odds for which may have improved since the AIDS virus was identified—immunization may be impossible because of the very disruption of immuno defenses that is the dreaded hallmark of the disease. AIDS has settled into our central cities, where multiple environmental stresses ruin the health of children and young adults: homelessness, drug addiction, poor housing, and education. Infectious diseases also are on the rise in rural areas, where poverty and pesticides are rampant. With the reemergence of infectious diseases as major causes of death, it is worth remembering where the greatest improvements in public health came during the past two centuries. Maybe it is time to give prevention the same priority that has been reserved solely for the elusive pursuit of cures.

CHAPTER 4

INDUSTRIAL TOXINS

Man-made toxins are ubiquitous in modern life. Nearly 70,000 chemical products have been introduced since World War II and 1,500 new ones are added each year.[1] Total U.S. production of chemicals amounts to over 300 million tons annually.[2] Each household uses an average of 25 gallons a year for cleaning, lawn and automobile care, home improvement, and other purposes.[3] Industry uses the rest, over 90 percent, for manufacturing the products we depend on—from cosmetics to clothing, machines to medicines, paper to plastics.

While thousands of industrial chemicals are potentially hazardous to human health and the environment, less than 2 percent of those produced have been fully assessed for their toxic effects.[4] Even without complete information on toxicity, we know many of these chemicals have other hazardous properties; they can explode, react, ignite, and corrode.[5] Industries waste enormous quantities of these chemicals in their production processes, eventually having to treat, store, and dispose of 550 million tons of hazardous wastes each year.[6] Factories annually spew another 3 million tons of toxic chemicals directly into the air, water, and land, almost a quarter of which are chemicals suspected of causing birth defects, and 8 percent are suspected of causing cancer.[7]

In this chapter we examine the dangers these materials present from their creation and industrial use, to their ultimate fate in the environment. These dangers include community contamination from direct releases of industrial toxins to the air and water, from the management of hazardous wastes on land, and occupational exposures within the workplace. There is tremendous variation in the amount of toxic chemicals industrial plants handle and release. Some states release hundreds of times more toxins than others. At the county level the variation is even greater, with certain counties releasing thousands of times more toxins than others, depending on the types and amounts of manufacturing that take place.

Louisiana, with its heavy dependence on the oil, gas, and chemical industries, leads the nation in industrial toxic releases, followed by

Texas, Ohio, Indiana, and Illinois.[8] The Institute for Southern Studies ranked Louisiana the worst according to the institute's Poisons Index and third from the bottom in its overall Green Index, which considers public and worker health and environmental policies, as well as poisons.[9] The nicknames "chemical corridor" and "cancer alley" are widely used to describe the massive concentration of petrochemical plants along the 80-mile stretch from Baton Rouge to New Orleans. Public concern over health and environmental hazards in the area led thousands to join together in the Great Louisiana Toxics March of 1988, where protesters walked the 80 miles, demonstrating for ten days. The following year, Louisiana passed its first air quality law.[10]

Mary McCastle lives at the threshold of the corridor, downwind of a toxic waste incinerator in Alsen, Louisiana.[11] Along with 4,000 other local residents, Mrs. McCastle waged a class-action suit against the owners of the incinerator, alleging its emissions caused major discomfort and illness, including headaches, burning eyes, and upset stomach.[12] Doctors cite chemical burns in the throat. Mrs. McCastle claims she has suffered from emphysema and other ailments ever since the plant began operating in the early 1970s. Her monthly medication fills a shopping bag and her drugstore bills are enormous. Alsen residents depended on their gardens for vegetables and fruit until the facility moved in. Now almost nothing grows, and people are afraid to eat what does. One man who lived behind the site owned two mules. Both died after a weekend of dumping. Mrs. McCastle once fainted from chemical fumes when she opened her door, so windows stay shut despite the hot Louisiana summers. "Occasionally," says Mrs. McCastle, "black fogs from the site would rust the top of cars."[13]

Alsen is in East Baton Rouge County, which ranks in the very top percentile for 9 of 24 measures of industrial toxins mapped in this section, and in the top 10 percentiles for all but three of the rest. Only two counties—Harris and Galveston in Texas—rank higher across all of the measures of industrial toxins. Niagara County, New York (home of Love Canal), comes in fourth place, followed by Tulsa County, Oklahoma; Cook County, Illinois; Lake County, Indiana; Allegheny County, Pennsylvania; Baltimore City County, Maryland; and Nueces County, Texas. As a group, these top ten counties have a startling array of industrial toxins: 104 times the national average for commercial hazardous waste landfill capacity; 100 times the number of hazardous waste underground injection wells; 86 times the average reported water discharges of potential carcinogens; 42 times the number of hazardous waste incinerators; 35 times the number of industrial air pollution sources; 29 times the industrial air emissions of potential carcinogens; and 20 times the average percentage of toxic occupational exposures found during workplace inspections. Most of the remaining measures of industrial toxins are also more than 10 times greater in these counties than in the rest of the country.

As a whole, these ten counties are relatively well off, though pockets of poverty probably cluster near their more polluted sections. (Compared to the average U.S. county, their mean income is 26 percent higher; there are 19 percent fewer families in poverty; 10 percent more high school graduates and 43 percent more college graduates. They also have three times as many physicians per person.) Yet these counties also have disturbingly high rates of mortality. Mortality from all diseases is significantly above average in nine of the ten counties. Eight rank among the top 10 percent for mortality from all cancers. Six rank in the top 10 percent for lung cancer mortality, with the rest significantly above average. Five are in the top 10 percent for breast cancer, and four have significantly high mortality from birth defects. Mortality from birth defects in these counties, moreover, is getting significantly worse relative to the United States as a whole. In East Baton Rouge, mortality from all diseases, heart diseases, infant diseases, birth defects, lung cancer, and acute exposures are deteriorating significantly compared with the United States as a whole.

In comparison, the ten counties that rank lowest across the measures of industrial toxins generally have average or below-average mortality rates. These counties include three in Georgia (Baker, Echols, and Quitman); five in Nebraska (Arthur, Grant, Hayes, Hooker, McPherson); Gilchrist, Florida; and Robertson, Kentucky. According to EPA data, the five states with the smallest quantity of industrial toxic releases are Hawaii, Nevada, North Dakota, South Dakota, and Vermont.[14]

INDUSTRIAL AIR EMISSIONS

In the past 40 years, the daily operation of two dozen petrochemical plants has transformed West Virginia's Kanawha River Valley. *Life* magazine once called this prosperous 25-mile stretch amid the tree-covered foothills of the Appalachian Range "magic valley."[15] Now it is known as "chemical valley." Soon after the massive chemical accident in Bhopal, India, on December 3, 1984, Union Carbide shut down its sister plant in Institute, W.Va., in the heart of the valley. Carbide officials declared there had been 61 leaks of methyl isocyanate at the plant since 1980, but that these minor accidents were "not abnormal."[16] True enough: more than 7,000 other chemical accidents occurred throughout the United States during the same period.[17] But company officials decided to invest $5 million on safety improvements there just in case.[18] All eyes were on the Institute plant when Carbide reopened it in May of 1985.[19]

Three months later, on a lazy Sunday morning in August, a toxic plume of aldicarb oxime and methylene chloride drifted over Institute, sending 135 people to the hospital. Due to the post-Bhopal spotlight on Institute, this incident helped push widespread community demands for new toxins legislation into the national policy arena. Congress passed the Emergency Planning and Community Right-to-Know Act in 1986.

Data collected under the Right-to-Know Act indicate that accidental, or fugitive, releases account for only a third of toxic releases into the air.[20] Two-thirds are spewed out smokestacks—close to 3,000 of which are in Kanawha County alone. Nationwide, 78 percent of these smokestack emissions have no end-of-the-pipe pollution controls whatsoever.[21] As of 1990, federal emission standards had been set for only seven toxic air pollutants, even though more than a million tons of toxins are released into the air each year.[22] The new Clean Air Act will require regulation of approximately 80 percent of these toxic emissions by the year 2000.[23]

Breathing polluted air poses one of the most direct risks for toxic exposures. The EPA ranks toxic air pollutants among the most serious public health risks, estimating that just 20 air toxins cause 2,000 extra cancer cases each year.[24] Sure enough, Kanawha County's mortality rates from all cancers and lung cancers are significantly above the U.S. average, and many of the mortality maps show a distinct pattern that tracks West Virginia's chemical valley (see, for example, the map of child cancers among minorities). Problems elsewhere may be even worse: half the states in the country release more air toxins than West Virginia, according to federal right-to-know data.

The following six maps indicate places where industrial air toxins may be most problematic. The first shows where 145,000 industrial smokestacks are located across the country. Each has a permit under the Clean Air Act to emit air pollutants. The next three maps show how much of the hazardous substances, suspected carcinogens, and acutely hazardous substances these smokestacks release. The amounts are estimated from the actual particulate and volatile organic compound emissions reported to the EPA under the Clean Air Act for each smokestack during 1985. The fifth map shows where the 219 operating toxic waste incinerators were located in 1987.

The sixth map shows where 52 million curies of radioactive emissions from commercial power reactors were released by the early 1980s (the amounts from other sources, such as military reactors, are not included). Ten million curies were released by the 1979 Three Mile Island accident alone. In the ten counties surrounding Three Mile Island (Adams, Cumberland, Dauphin, Franklin, Lancaster, Lebanon, Montour, Northumberland, Perry, and York), mortality from child cancers, birth defects, infant diseases, and breast cancers increased significantly relative to the country as a whole from the period prior to the plant's start-up to the five years after the accident. Radioactive emissions in these counties are 19,000 times greater than in the rest of Pennsylvania. None of the other measures of air toxins are significantly higher than in the rest of the country or Pennsylvania as a whole, though other measures are: the total, cancer, and extreme hazard potential of pesticide usage, and the number of Superfund toxic waste sites requiring cleanup (the number of physicians per person was also higher).[25]

INDUSTRIAL WATER DISCHARGES

The promise of cheap power from the Kentucky Dam has lured industrial producers to Calvert City, Kentucky, since the 1940s. By the 1980s, local industries were dumping so much toxic wastewater into the Tennessee River (a tributary of the Mississippi) that surrounding Marshall County now ranks among the country's top ten counties for governmentally permitted discharges of hazardous and acutely hazardous chemicals, and among the top fifty for discharges of suspected carcinogens. Chemical and metal pollutants have been found in fish and water supplies throughout the area.[26] Despite official warnings about the polluted waters, fishing, sailing, and swimming remain popular in Kentucky Lake, one of the world's largest engineered bodies of water, bordering Marshall County just above the dam.

Eight years ago Calvert City had no cancer treatment centers. Today there are two. Before Corinne Whitehead and other concerned citizens formed the Coalition for Health Concern in 1985, Mrs. Whitehead began to notice that "just too many friends were dying of cancer. At parties, anywhere you went, cancer was the topic of conversation."[27] She made a map of health problems in the community: red dots for cancer deaths, green dots for cancer patients who were still alive. "I saw small children, teenagers, people under thirty-five with leukemia and brain tumors; workers in the plants were coming down with throat cancer and brain tumors."[28] The region also has unusually high rates of lupus, a rare immunological disorder that some call "chemically induced AIDS."[29]

Corinne Whitehead and other activists at the Coalition believe Cal-

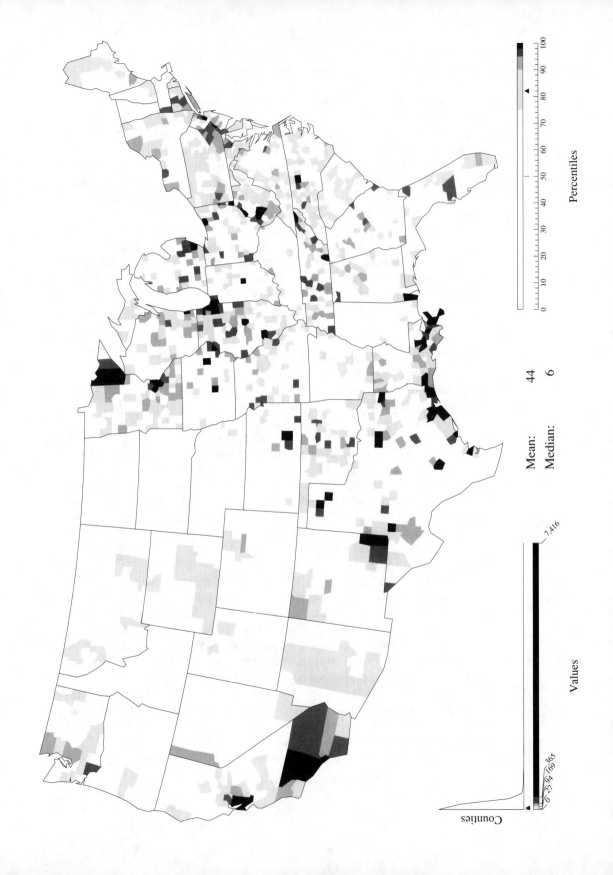

Percentiles

Mean: 44

Median: 6

Values

Counties

7,416

0 27 94 769 365

TOP COUNTIES SHADED BLACK

RANK	COUNTY	STATE	VALUE
1	HARRIS	TX	7,416
2	CONTRA COSTA	CA	3,188
3	JEFFERSON	TX	3,133
4	KANAWHA	WV	2,984
5	LOS ANGELES	CA	2,697
6	BRAZORIA	TX	2,378
7	COOK	IL	1,826
8	KERN	CA	1,749
9	NUECES	TX	1,724
10	GALVESTON	TX	1,575
11	ST CHARLES	LA	1,517
12	ST LOUIS	MN	1,079
13	LAKE	IN	1,006
14	WAYNE	MI	967
15	ALAMEDA	CA	963
16	RAMSEY	MN	936
17	MARSHALL	WV	903
18	TARRANT	TX	870
19	HARRISON	TX	867
20	SULLIVAN	TN	828
21	CALCASIEU	LA	813
22	ASCENSION	LA	806
23	IBERVILLE	LA	790
24	SANTA CLARA	CA	740
25	EAST BATON ROUGE	LA	728
26	MIDDLESEX	NJ	712
27	HENNEPIN	MN	705
28	HUTCHINSON	TX	680
29	DALLAS	TX	652
30	BALTIMORE CITY	MD	639
31	MACON	IL	629
32	PUTNAM	WV	595
33	PLAQUEMINES	LA	570
34	ORANGE	TX	564
35	PHILADELPHIA	PA	561
36	ST BERNARD	LA	558
37	SCOTT	IA	551
38	DAKOTA	MN	539
39	MADISON	IL	537
40	GRAY	TX	526
41	WASHINGTON	MN	517
42	PLEASANTS	WV	512
43	POLK	IA	481
44	BEXAR	TX	469
45	LINN	IA	459
46	CUYAHOGA	OH	458
47	WILL	IL	457
48	BUTLER	KS	452
49	MARION	IN	450
50	LEA	NM	435
51	MOBILE	AL	433
52	GUILFORD	NC	427
53	ECTOR	TX	408
54	WOOD	WV	401
55	ORANGE	CA	392
56	CALHOUN	TX	388
57	VENTURA	CA	372
58	HAMILTON	TN	369
59	SAN MATEO	CA	365
60	MILWAUKEE	WI	365

BOTTOM COUNTIES SHADED WHITE

NOTE: TOO MANY COUNTIES TO LIST
HAD ZERO VALUES FOR THIS MEASURE

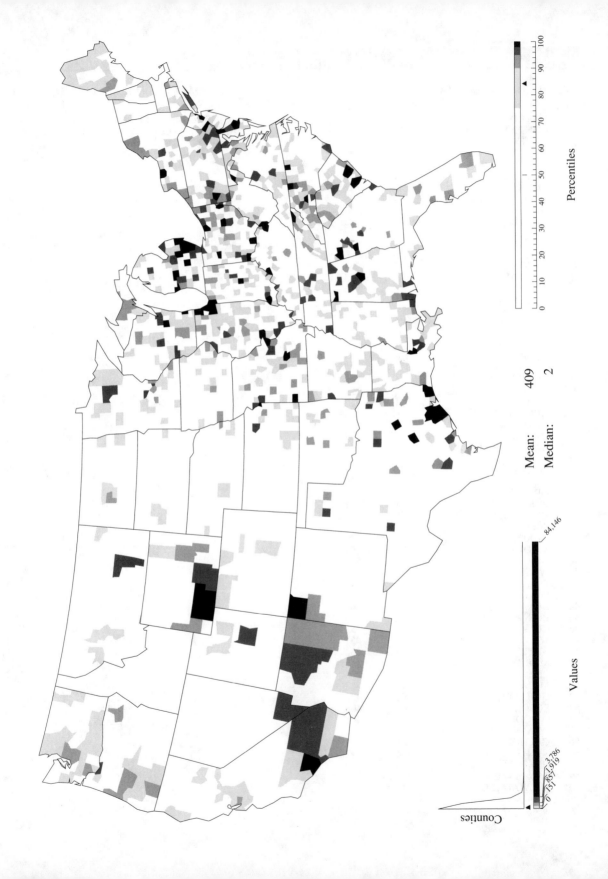

Values

Mean: 409

Median: 2

Percentiles

Counties

0 131 857 1,919 3,786   84,146

(TONS PER YEAR)

TOP COUNTIES SHADED BLACK

RANK	COUNTY	STATE	VALUE
1	WAYNE	MI	84,146
2	INGHAM	MI	48,844
3	BUCKS	PA	34,750
4	HARRIS	TX	26,277
5	COOK	IL	22,834
6	MINERAL	WV	22,405
7	JEFFERSON	TX	22,228
8	SUSSEX	DE	18,867
9	MACOMB	MI	16,064
10	ALLEN	OH	11,023
11	FREESTONE	TX	10,578
12	BARTOW	GA	10,438
13	SULLIVAN	TN	10,356
14	LOS ANGELES	CA	10,230
15	CATAWBA	NC	9,690
16	POINTE COUPEE	LA	8,295
17	COLBERT	AL	8,144
18	GENESEE	MI	7,954
19	MILAM	TX	7,658
20	HAMILTON	OH	7,302
21	LAKE	IN	7,058
22	GIBSON	IN	6,855
23	SHELBY	AL	6,711
24	PERSON	NC	6,502
25	FORT BEND	TX	6,451
26	MUSKEGON	MI	6,386
27	BERKELEY	SC	6,178
28	LAKE	IL	6,161
29	COSHOCTON	OH	5,989
30	ORANGE	TX	5,956
31	WAYNE	WV	5,927
32	MILWAUKEE	WI	5,844
33	MONROE	NY	5,322
34	ALLEGHENY	PA	5,210
35	HUDSON	NJ	5,197
36	MARION	IN	5,171
37	SAN JUAN	NM	5,063
38	MIDDLESEX	NJ	5,032
39	LAWRENCE	KY	4,933
40	JASPER	MO	4,841
41	ADAMS	OH	4,819
42	DENT	MO	4,798
43	GALVESTON	TX	4,739
44	MADISON	IL	4,673
45	COLLETON	SC	4,663
46	MONTCALM	MI	4,636
47	JEFFERSON	KY	4,550
48	BRAZORIA	TX	4,447
49	LORAIN	OH	4,441
50	OAKLAND	MI	4,435
51	SWEETWATER	WY	4,411
52	FLOYD	GA	4,329
53	WINNEBAGO	WI	4,307
54	WILL	IL	4,212
55	STOKES	NC	4,180
56	ST LOUIS	MO	4,174
57	NEW CASTLE	DE	4,171
58	COWETA	GA	4,144
59	ST CLAIR	MI	3,795
60	JEFFERSON	OH	3,794
61	WYANDOTTE	KS	3,786

BOTTOM COUNTIES SHADED WHITE

NOTE: TOO MANY COUNTIES TO LIST
HAD ZERO VALUES FOR THIS MEASURE

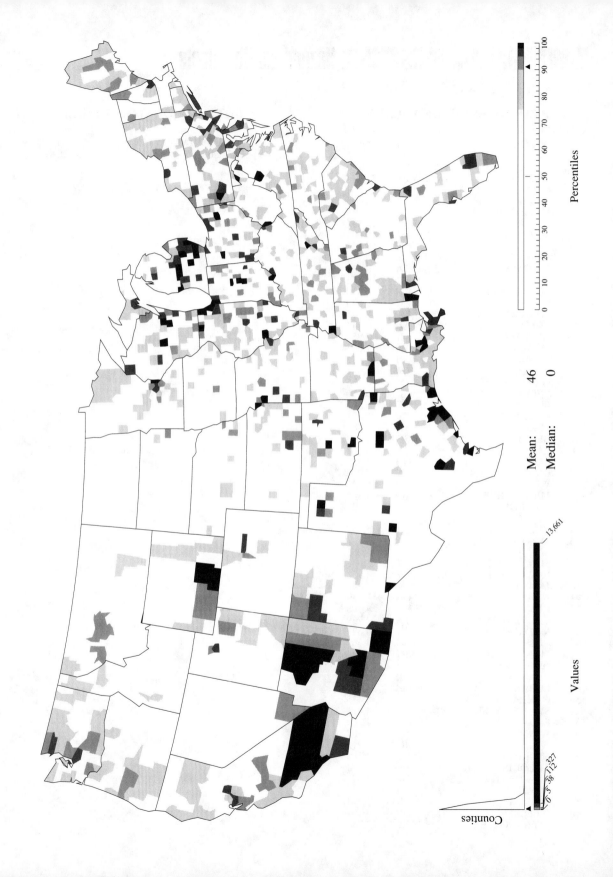

Percentiles

Mean: 46
Median: 0

Values

Counties

13,661

(TONS PER YEAR)

TOP COUNTIES SHADED BLACK

RANK	COUNTY	STATE	VALUE
1	WAYNE	MI	13,661
2	MINERAL	WV	12,147
3	JEFFERSON	TX	8,587
4	INGHAM	MI	8,324
5	ALLEN	OH	6,569
6	WAYNE	WV	5,769
7	HUDSON	NJ	4,998
8	HARRIS	TX	4,730
9	GALVESTON	TX	3,606
10	MACOMB	MI	2,340
11	BRAZORIA	TX	2,098
12	MADISON	IL	1,949
13	CARBON	WY	1,933
14	LOS ANGELES	CA	1,809
15	EAST BATON ROUGE	LA	1,582
16	AUGUSTA	VA	1,229
17	IBERVILLE	LA	982
18	MUSKEGON	MI	980
19	ASCENSION	LA	975
20	PLATTE	MO	930
21	ALLEGHENY	PA	915
22	MARION	IN	856
23	GENESEE	MI	853
24	LAKE	IN	846
25	PINAL	AZ	799
26	COOK	IL	790
27	WINNEBAGO	WI	778
28	LAKE	IL	673
29	CASS	TX	604
30	MONTCALM	MI	604
31	NUECES	TX	598
32	WASHTENAW	MI	595
33	ANDERSON	TN	529
34	HARRISON	IN	528
35	BEXAR	TX	527
36	HAMILTON	IN	515
37	COCHISE	AZ	486
38	WOOD	WI	462
39	JACKSON	MO	458
40	SAN BERNARDINO	CA	455
41	WINNEBAGO	IL	446
42	CARTER	OK	443
43	COCONINO	AZ	439
44	OKLAHOMA	OK	424
45	HOWARD	IN	407
46	MOBILE	AL	407
47	DALLAS	TX	406
48	SHELBY	TN	404
49	TARRANT	TX	400
50	KERN	CA	396
51	ECTOR	TX	383
52	WASHINGTON	MN	380
53	CALHOUN	TX	378
54	UNION	AR	367
55	EL PASO	TX	364
56	ORANGE	CA	362
57	GRATIOT	MI	360
58	STARK	OH	330
59	OUTAGAMIE	WI	330
60	YELLOWSTONE	MT	328
61	HUTCHINSON	TX	327

BOTTOM COUNTIES SHADED WHITE

NOTE: TOO MANY COUNTIES TO LIST
HAD ZERO VALUES FOR THIS MEASURE

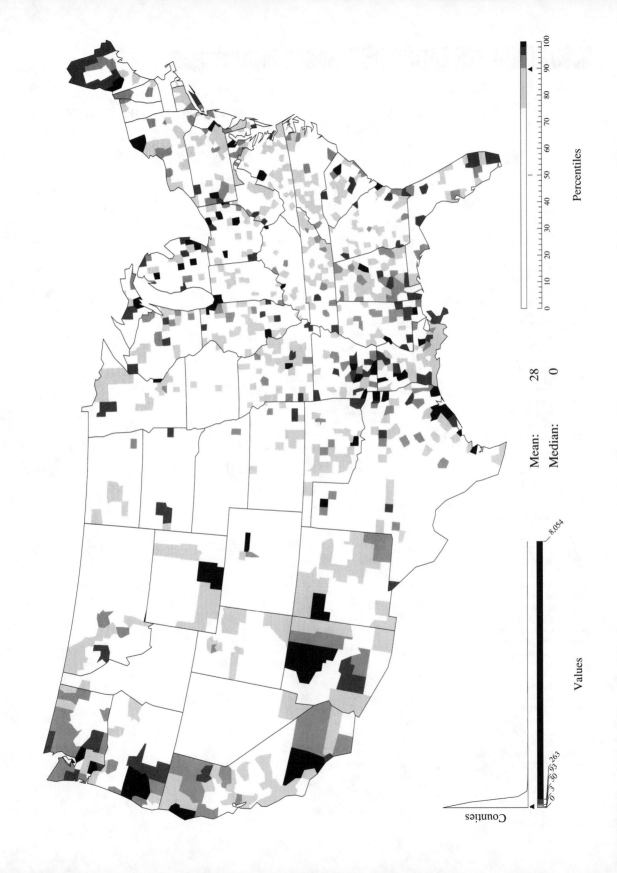

Mean: 28

Median: 0

Percentiles

Values

Counties

8,054

263

95

30

3

0

(TONS PER YEAR)

TOP COUNTIES SHADED BLACK

RANK	COUNTY	STATE	VALUE
1	JEFFERSON	TX	8,054
2	ALLEN	OH	6,570
3	HUDSON	NJ	4,972
4	WAYNE	MI	3,614
5	GALVESTON	TX	2,543
6	CARBON	WY	1,933
7	INGHAM	MI	1,929
8	MADISON	IL	1,803
9	HARRIS	TX	1,790
10	LAKE	IN	1,182
11	AUGUSTA	VA	1,111
12	HARRISON	TX	1,059
13	MUSKINGUM	OH	973
14	EAST BATON ROUGE	LA	954
15	COOK	IL	753
16	BALTIMORE	MD	733
17	CHATHAM	GA	732
18	FRANKLIN	ME	715
19	COCONINO	AZ	676
20	BRAZORIA	TX	592
21	BUCKS	PA	587
22	CUYAHOGA	OH	581
23	PORTER	IN	571
24	STONE	MS	564
25	MACOMB	MI	562
26	LANE	OR	551
27	CASS	TX	495
28	PIERCE	WA	485
29	DELTA	MI	482
30	PULASKI	MO	470
31	NUECES	TX	469
32	HANCOCK	KY	455
33	GRANT	AR	454
34	MC KINLEY	NM	450
35	CARTER	OK	441
36	UNION	AR	402
37	WEBSTER	LA	399
38	WARREN	MS	393
39	BUTLER	PA	390
40	NATCHITOCHES	LA	385
41	HANCOCK	WV	373
42	BOYD	KY	372
43	FLORENCE	SC	346
44	GRATIOT	MI	343
45	CALHOUN	TX	332
46	CLARK	AR	332
47	HUMBOLDT	CA	318
48	YORK	VA	311
49	WASHINGTON	MN	308
50	TALLADEGA	AL	307
51	STARK	OH	306
52	ADAMS	CO	304
53	DOUGLAS	OR	302
54	YELLOWSTONE	MT	299
55	ST LAWRENCE	NY	298
56	HUTCHINSON	TX	296
57	LITTLE RIVER	AR	277
58	KALKASKA	MI	276
59	LOS ANGELES	CA	272
60	COWLITZ	WA	267
61	KERN	CA	263

BOTTOM COUNTIES SHADED WHITE

NOTE: TOO MANY COUNTIES TO LIST
HAD ZERO VALUES FOR THIS MEASURE

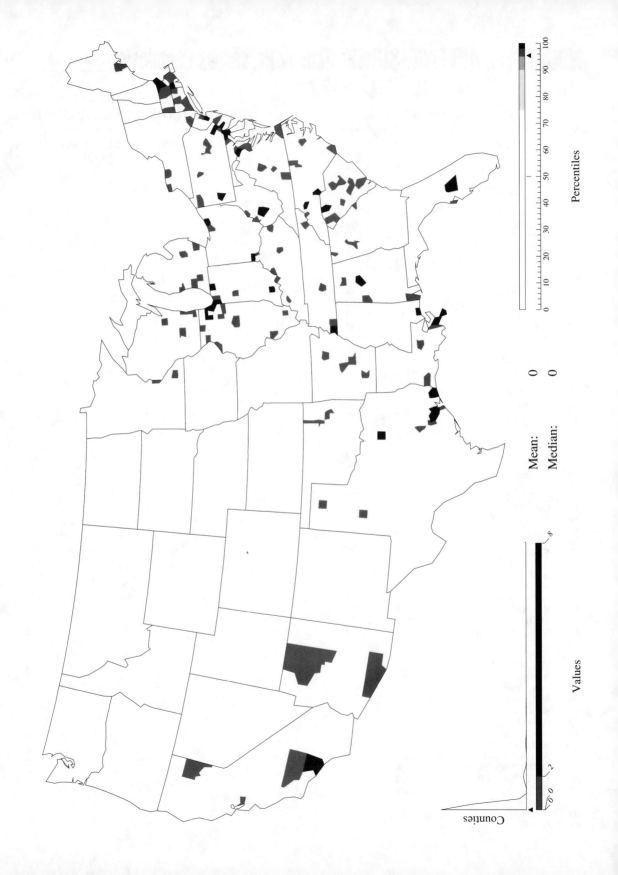

Percentiles

Mean: 0

Median: 0

Values

Counties

TOP COUNTIES SHADED BLACK

RANK	COUNTY	STATE	VALUE
1	HARRIS	TX	8
2	COOK	IL	5
3	MIDDLESEX	NJ	5
4	MONTGOMERY	PA	5
5	PLAQUEMINES	LA	4
6	DISTRICT OF COLUMBIA	DC	3
7	LAKE	IN	3
8	BALTIMORE CITY	MD	3
9	MIDDLESEX	MA	3
10	MECKLENBURG	NC	3
11	HAMILTON	OH	3
12	JEFFERSON	TX	3
13	KANAWHA	WV	3
14	JEFFERSON	AL	2
15	LOS ANGELES	CA	2
16	NEW CASTLE	DE	2
17	POLK	FL	2
18	KANE	IL	2
19	DUBOIS	IN	2
20	ST JOSEPH	IN	2
21	CECIL	MD	2
22	MONTGOMERY	MD	2
23	ESSEX	MA	2
24	HARRISON	MS	2
25	GLOUCESTER	NJ	2
26	CALDWELL	NC	2
27	CUYAHOGA	OH	2
28	ALLEGHENY	PA	2
29	PHILADELPHIA	PA	2
30	PROVIDENCE	RI	2
31	SPARTANBURG	SC	2
32	SHELBY	TN	2
33	DALLAS	TX	2

BOTTOM COUNTIES SHADED WHITE

NOTE: TOO MANY COUNTIES TO LIST
HAD ZERO VALUES FOR THIS MEASURE

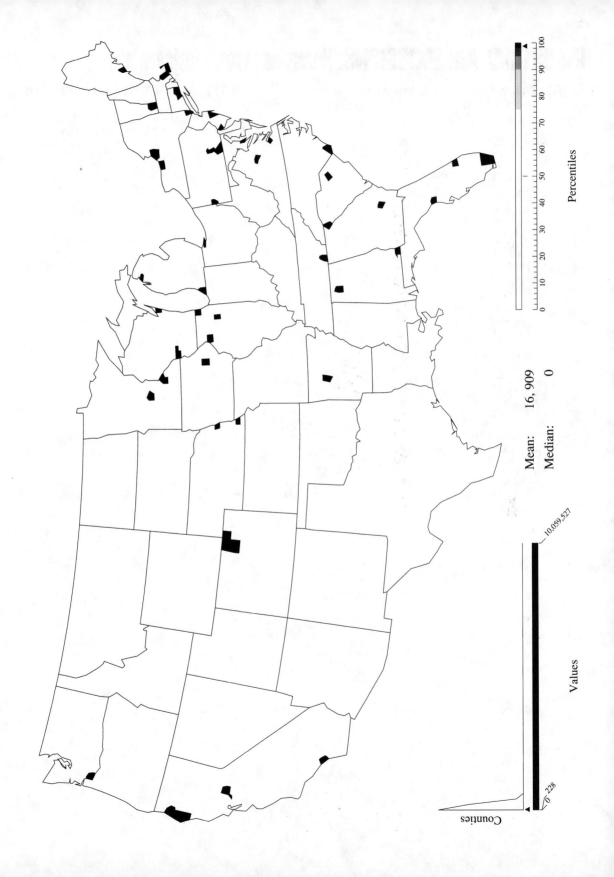

Mean: 16, 909

Median: 0

Values

Percentiles

Counties

10,059,527

0 228

INDUSTRIAL AIR EMISSIONS: Radiation From Commercial Power Reactors

(CURIES)

TOP COUNTIES SHADED BLACK

RANK	COUNTY	STATE	VALUE
1	DAUPHIN	PA	10,059,527
2	GRUNDY	IL	9,230,653
3	NEW LONDON	CT	6,711,343
4	OCEAN	NJ	5,223,000
5	OSWEGO	NY	4,052,327
6	WRIGHT	MN	3,458,290
7	HUMBOLDT	CA	2,796,000
8	WHITESIDE	IL	2,271,900
9	PLYMOUTH	MA	1,514,100
10	CHARLEVOIX	MI	1,385,970
11	BRUNSWICK	NC	1,063,890
12	LAWRENCE	AL	1,042,100
13	YORK	PA	553,701
14	VERNON	WI	425,190
15	WINDHAM	VT	327,280
16	LAKE	IL	312,484
17	OCONEE	SC	250,000
18	CITRUS	FL	158,910
19	ST LUCIE	FL	103,790
20	NEMAHA	NE	103,070
21	DADE	FL	100,160
22	POPE	AR	96,806
23	WESTCHESTER	NY	91,771
24	CALVERT	MD	82,360
25	SURRY	VA	80,277
26	KEWAUNEE	WI	75,659
27	APPLING	GA	74,701
28	BERRIEN	MI	73,358
29	LOUISA	VA	30,180
30	HOUSTON	AL	26,134
31	LINN	IA	24,167
32	WAYNE	NY	23,648
33	SACRAMENTO	CA	21,105
34	LINCOLN	ME	19,806
35	ORANGE	CA	18,402
36	MIDDLESEX	CT	16,276
37	HAMILTON	TN	12,040
38	DARLINGTON	SC	11,197
39	WASHINGTON	NE	10,132
40	OTTAWA	OH	9,410
41	GOODHUE	MN	7,217
42	COLUMBIA	OR	6,519
43	BEAVER	PA	3,081
44	SALEM	NJ	2,034
45	BARNSTABLE	MA	1,332
46	WELD	CO	228

BOTTOM COUNTIES SHADED WHITE

NOTE: TOO MANY COUNTIES TO LIST
HAD ZERO VALUES FOR THIS MEASURE

vert City's industrial pollution is responsible for the outbreak of disease, but they have had a hard time getting the word out. One newspaper would not run their paid advertisement for a public meeting about a local toxic incinerator. "The press here is pro-industry," says Mrs. White-head. "Local papers bend over backward to avoid environmental reporting." While some in the press say she is out "to assassinate the character of local business leaders," others call her the "grande dame of environmentalists." Government officials have also tried to block environmental criticism. In 1987 the town's mayor filed a defamation suit against a chemistry professor who dubbed the quality of local toxic waste disposal practices "a joke." The mayor also happened to be general manager of the toxic waste plant in question—Liquid Waste Disposal, Inc.[30] (The suit was later dropped, and the mayor voted out of office.)

Calvert City is not alone. Throughout the country (and the world), rivers have drawn industry to their banks with their ample supply of power, cooling water, and a seemingly automatic flush. The capacity of surface waters to assimilate effluents has led state and federal agencies to permit the dumping of over 150 million tons of toxic wastes into our nation's rivers, streams, and coastal waters each year.[31] Twice this amount of hazardous waste is managed by wastewater and sewage treatment plants annually.[32] Ironically, nearly half of the toxic discharges are large amounts of chlorine—the same element that 4,000 sewage plants use to treat wastewater. Chlorine kills harmful bacteria that cause infectious diseases, but in the same amounts it can also form compounds with organic materials that accumulate as they rise up the food chain. Such "chlorinated organics" can be highly toxic to aquatic life and humans. Public concern has focused on the dangers of chlorinated discharges from the bleaching processes used by the paper industry, yet sewage plants dump a thousand times more chlorine into surface waters with little attention.

Much is unknown about the environmental impacts of the vast array of chemicals being discharged into our surface waters. Public information on toxic discharges and toxins in surface water is less consistent and of poorer quality than any other data considered in the atlas, and estimates of the amounts of toxins released range widely. The EPA's Toxic Release Inventory, for example, states that manufacturing industries discharge 180 thousand tons of toxins into surface water, with the chemical, paper, and metals industries contributing the largest shares.[33] Yet this estimate excludes major nonmanufacturing sources such as utilities, mining, and military production, and is totally inconsistent with the amount reported in the government's database of permitted discharges.

In the latter database, plants reported discharging a thousand times more toxins than in the TRI estimate, and for just six of the hundreds of chemicals listed in TRI.

To correct these gaps in government information, activists around the country have taken matters into their own hands. Recent reports by Clean Water Action Project, Environmental Defense Fund, Natural Resources Defense Council, and others combine TRI data with independent information to identify dangerous concentrations of toxic chemicals in Virginia's South River, Georgia's Chattahoochee River, the Houston ship channel, Galveston Bay, and elsewhere.[34] The Council on Economic Priorities, Greenpeace, Inform, and the National Toxics Campaign used other data to uncover problems in the Chesapeake Bay, the Mississippi and Hudson rivers, and Boston Harbor.[35] In addition to routine discharges—both permitted and unregulated—there are also accidental spills. In 1988, a one-million-gallon, 40-foot wave of diesel fuel burst from a fuel tank along the Monongahela River, contaminating drinking water in the Pittsburgh area and for more than 800,000 people downstream. Many industries took advantage of the spill, dumping carcinogenic solvents into the Ohio River under the cover of the oily wake.[36] (Surface water pollution from farm and city runoff is considered in chapter 5.)

Because the problem is so vast and the data so poor, the following maps provide only a sample of some of the potential toxic hotspots in rivers and streams around the country. They show where the licensed wastewater discharges are located, as well as the amounts of toxic discharges they released into surface waters in the mid-1980s with government permission. The maps show the distribution of nearly 40,000 tons of toxic discharges (about a fifth of the amount reported in TRI) from nonmanufacturing industries, as well as the manufacturers included in TRI.[37] Unfortunately, discharge data for Maine, Massachusetts, Michigan, and Ohio are missing from the government database we used, though there are many facilities with water discharges in these states, as indicated in the first map.

Counties with large numbers of facilities and toxic discharges cluster in western Pennsylvania, West Virginia, upstate New York (especially along the Hudson and Niagara rivers), along the chemical crescent from Houston to New Orleans, in parts of Florida and Washington, and elsewhere. Discharges of carcinogens appear more concentrated than those of all hazardous substances, whereas discharges of acutely hazardous substances appear more diffuse. Otherwise, there is a strong similarity between the maps.

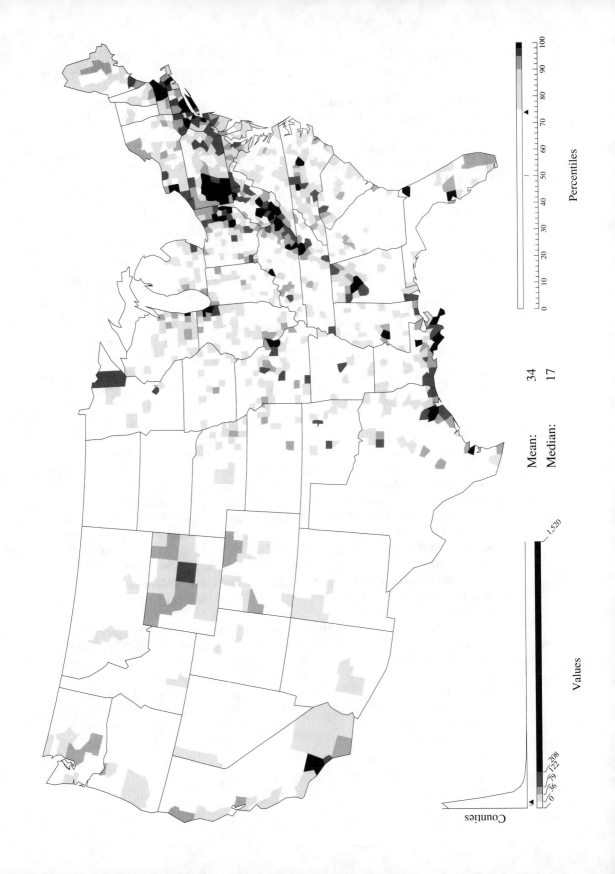

Mean: 34

Median: 17

Percentiles

Values

Counties

0 36 79 122 208   1,520

TOP COUNTIES SHADED BLACK

RANK	COUNTY	STATE	VALUE
1	HARRIS	TX	1,520
2	PIKE	KY	829
3	LOS ANGELES	CA	791
4	ERIE	NY	596
5	BELMONT	OH	464
6	CLEARFIELD	PA	452
7	KANAWHA	WV	430
8	JEFFERSON	MO	405
9	ALLEGHENY	PA	405
10	SUFFOLK	NY	395
11	CAMPBELL	TN	393
12	JEFFERSON	KY	378
13	TERREBONNE	LA	377
14	WESTMORELAND	PA	372
15	MIDDLESEX	MA	362
16	CLARION	PA	360
17	JEFFERSON	AL	352
18	DUVAL	FL	346
19	FORSYTH	NC	339
20	BRISTOL	MA	303
21	SCOTT	TN	302
22	FLOYD	KY	299
23	MC DOWELL	WV	296
24	INDIANA	PA	291
25	JEFFERSON	PA	281
26	JEFFERSON	OH	277
27	SOMERSET	PA	275
28	ARMSTRONG	PA	273
29	EAST BATON ROUGE	LA	264
30	PLAQUEMINES	LA	263
31	WAKE	NC	263
32	MONONGALIA	WV	263
33	WORCESTER	MA	254
34	COOK	IL	253
35	RALEIGH	WV	251
36	TUSCARAWAS	OH	250
37	WYOMING	WV	249
38	WHITLEY	KY	248
39	BERGEN	NJ	247
40	MILWAUKEE	WI	243
41	WASHINGTON	PA	242
42	LOGAN	WV	240
43	BUTLER	PA	233
44	HINDS	MS	232
45	WALKER	AL	231
46	NICHOLAS	WV	230
47	LAUREL	KY	229
48	NEW HAVEN	CT	227
49	FAYETTE	PA	226
50	MIDDLESEX	NJ	222
51	ORANGE	NY	220
52	NUECES	TX	220
53	HILLSBOROUGH	FL	219
54	STARK	OH	216
55	BALTIMORE CITY	MD	214
56	ST MARY	LA	212
57	ST LOUIS	MO	211
58	FAIRFIELD	CT	209
59	ESSEX	MA	209
60	MUSKINGUM	OH	208

BOTTOM COUNTIES SHADED WHITE

RANK	COUNTY	STATE	VALUE
1	HERNANDO	FL	0
2	BAKER	GA	0
3	ECHOLS	GA	0
4	WEBSTER	GA	0
5	BUTTE	ID	0
6	CLARK	ID	0
7	YELLOWSTONE NAT. PARK	MT	0
8	ARTHUR	NE	0
9	GRANT	NE	0
10	MC PHERSON	NE	0
11	EUREKA	NV	0
12	MINERAL	NV	0
13	HARDING	NM	0
14	HARNEY	OR	0
15	DICKENS	TX	0
16	EDWARDS	TX	0
17	GLASSCOCK	TX	0
18	KING	TX	0
19	LOVING	TX	0
20	TERRELL	TX	0
21	UPTON	TX	0
22	PIUTE	UT	0
23	RICH	UT	0
24	KING AND QUEEN	VA	0

NOTE: TOO MANY COUNTIES TO LIST
HAD THE VALUE OF 1 FOR THIS MEASURE

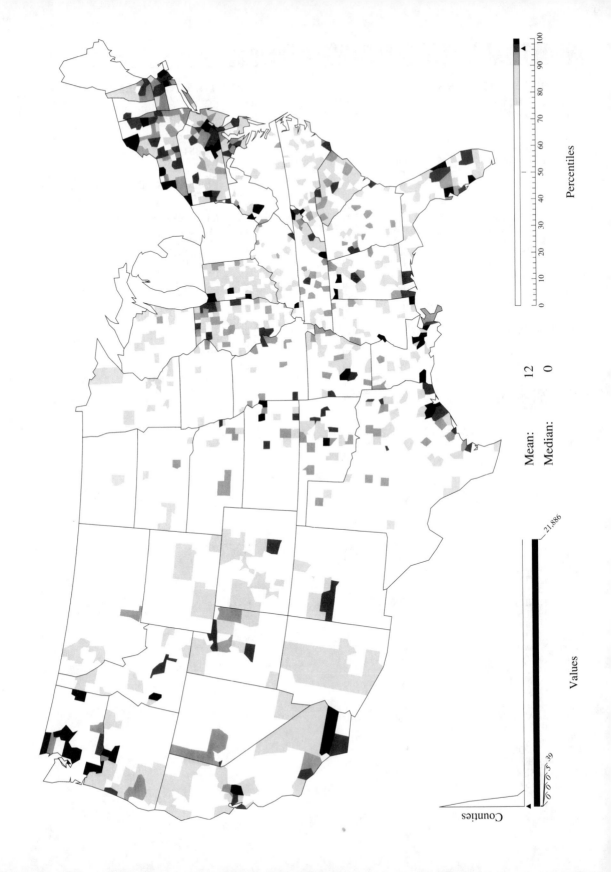

Percentiles

Mean: 12

Median: 0

Values

Counties

21,886

(TONS PER YEAR)

TOP COUNTIES SHADED BLACK

RANK	COUNTY	STATE	VALUE
1	ST JAMES	LA	21,886
2	RIVERSIDE	CA	3,252
3	ST CHARLES	LA	632
4	WYANDOTTE	KS	502
5	BALTIMORE CITY	MD	451
6	HILLSBOROUGH	FL	436
7	SULLIVAN	TN	412
8	JOHNSON	KS	375
9	MARSHALL	KY	367
10	COWLITZ	WA	310
11	HARRIS	TX	302
12	YORK	PA	301
13	TIPPECANOE	IN	264
14	ST LAWRENCE	NY	255
15	NIAGARA	NY	250
16	KANAWHA	WV	238
17	CALCASIEU	LA	192
18	PROVIDENCE	RI	190
19	ERIE	PA	183
20	SHAWNEE	KS	181
21	LAKE	IN	172
22	WARREN	MS	168
23	PLYMOUTH	MA	163
24	DISTRICT OF COLUMBIA	DC	152
25	SAN JOAQUIN	CA	152
26	OKLAHOMA	OK	137
27	MITCHELL	NC	134
28	MORGAN	AL	111
29	DELAWARE	PA	105
30	IBERVILLE	LA	101
31	KING	WA	98
32	COLBERT	AL	95
33	EAST BATON ROUGE	LA	91
34	ERIE	NY	90
35	WHATCOM	WA	88
36	BUTLER	PA	81
37	BUCKS	PA	80
38	PLEASANTS	WV	80
39	VIGO	IN	72
40	GALVESTON	TX	69
41	ADA	ID	66
42	DAUPHIN	PA	64
43	WARREN	NY	64
44	MULTNOMAH	OR	60
45	LEE	FL	60
46	MASON	WV	59
47	ASCENSION	LA	58
48	CHELAN	WA	58
49	CUMBERLAND	PA	57
50	PORTER	IN	53
51	CLARK	WA	52
52	HOT SPRING	AR	48
53	GARLAND	AR	48
54	JACKSON	MS	45
55	MONTGOMERY	PA	42
56	PIERCE	WA	42
57	SPOKANE	WA	41
58	BREVARD	FL	41
59	MONROE	NY	40
60	HAMILTON	TN	40
61	WASCO	OR	39

BOTTOM COUNTIES SHADED WHITE

NOTE: TOO MANY COUNTIES TO LIST
HAD ZERO VALUES FOR THIS MEASURE

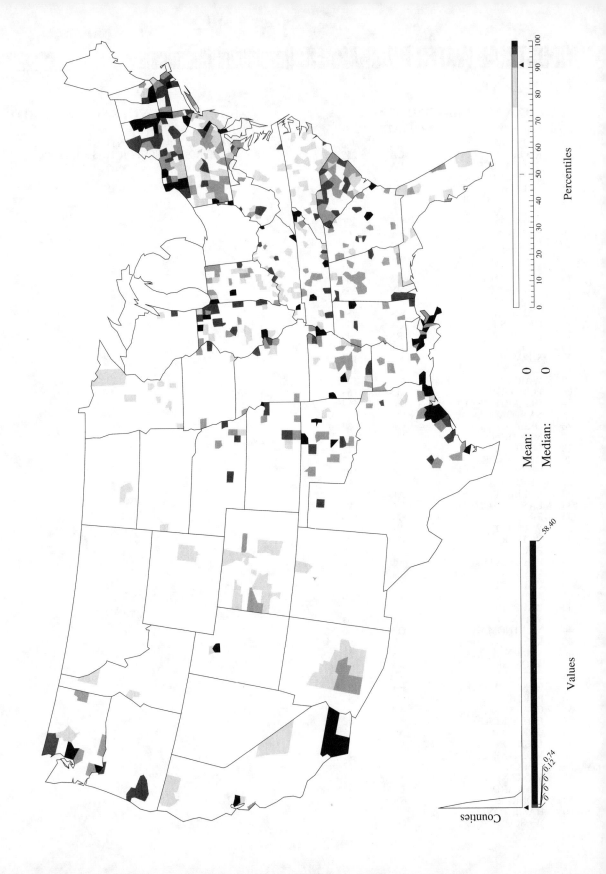

Percentiles

Mean: 0

Median: 0

Values

Counties

58.40

0.74
0.12

(TONS PER YEAR)

TOP COUNTIES SHADED BLACK

RANK	COUNTY	STATE	VALUE
1	HARRIS	TX	58.40
2	NIAGARA	NY	35.04
3	KING	WA	34.44
4	PROVIDENCE	RI	25.52
5	RENSSELAER	NY	21.82
6	ASCENSION	LA	15.85
7	JEFFERSON	TX	15.79
8	WYANDOTTE	KS	15.79
9	CONTRA COSTA	CA	15.18
10	SARATOGA	NY	15.14
11	CHATHAM	GA	14.77
12	BUCKS	PA	14.60
13	ERIE	NY	13.75
14	GALVESTON	TX	10.81
15	SAN DIEGO	CA	9.50
16	MONROE	NY	7.38
17	MARSHALL	WV	5.23
18	NEW CASTLE	DE	4.74
19	RIVERSIDE	CA	4.65
20	NUECES	TX	4.56
21	ESSEX	NY	4.21
22	LAKE	IN	4.08
23	BELL	KY	3.98
24	WINNEBAGO	IL	3.90
25	SEBASTIAN	AR	3.68
26	MADISON	IL	3.24
27	FULTON	NY	3.14
28	BRAZORIA	TX	2.52
29	IBERVILLE	LA	2.49
30	CALCASIEU	LA	2.36
31	PLAQUEMINES	LA	2.32
32	TULSA	OK	2.16
33	ORANGE	TX	2.13
34	BEAVER	PA	2.08
35	EAST BATON ROUGE	LA	2.02
36	HUMPHREYS	TN	1.96
37	WARREN	NY	1.90
38	CLEVELAND	OK	1.88
39	CLARK	WA	1.79
40	ST CHARLES	LA	1.76
41	CHESHIRE	NH	1.73
42	SALT LAKE	UT	1.73
43	MARION	TN	1.51
44	FORT BEND	TX	1.47
45	HILLSBOROUGH	NH	1.38
46	MARSHALL	KY	1.34
47	ORLEANS	LA	1.26
48	ST JAMES	LA	1.25
49	ORANGE	NY	1.24
50	LAURENS	GA	1.24
51	SULLIVAN	TN	1.00
52	COLUMBIA	NY	0.95
53	KAY	OK	0.95
54	CATTARAUGUS	NY	0.93
55	BOYD	KY	0.88
56	GARLAND	AR	0.79
57	MONROE	MS	0.77
58	KANE	IL	0.76
59	CARTER	TN	0.76
60	TIPPECANOE	IN	0.75
61	MISSISSIPPI	AR	0.74

BOTTOM COUNTIES SHADED WHITE

NOTE: TOO MANY COUNTIES TO LIST
HAD ZERO VALUES FOR THIS MEASURE

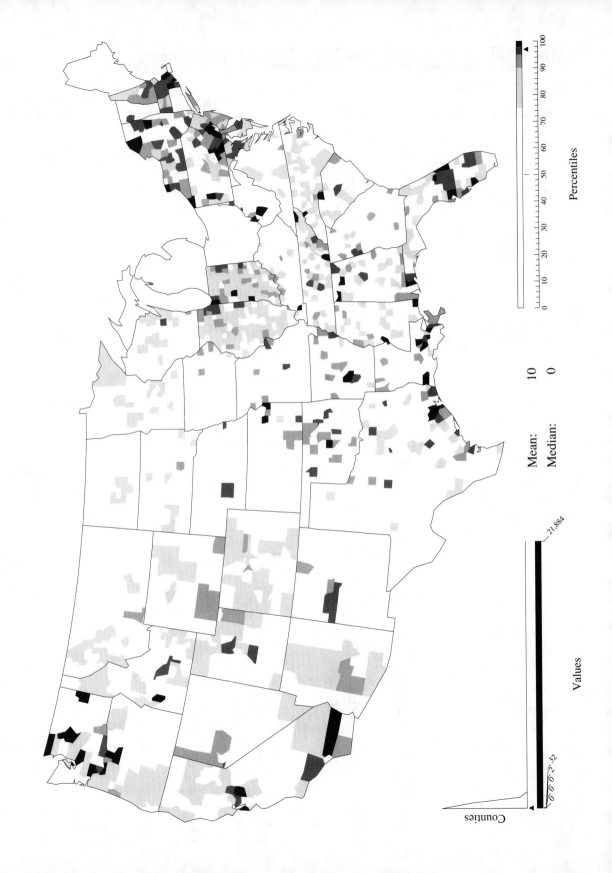

Percentiles

Mean: 10

Median: 0

Values

Counties

21,884

9,000
7,000
5,000
3,000
32

(TONS PER YEAR)

TOP COUNTIES SHADED BLACK

RANK	COUNTY	STATE	VALUE
1	ST JAMES	LA	21,884
2	ST CHARLES	LA	628
3	BALTIMORE CITY	MD	451
4	WYANDOTTE	KS	439
5	HILLSBOROUGH	FL	436
6	SULLIVAN	TN	394
7	JOHNSON	KS	375
8	MARSHALL	KY	360
9	COWLITZ	WA	309
10	YORK	PA	301
11	TIPPECANOE	IN	263
12	KANAWHA	WV	229
13	ST LAWRENCE	NY	220
14	CALCASIEU	LA	190
15	ERIE	PA	183
16	SHAWNEE	KS	180
17	WARREN	MS	168
18	PLYMOUTH	MA	163
19	LAKE	IN	153
20	DISTRICT OF COLUMBIA	DC	152
21	SAN JOAQUIN	CA	152
22	OKLAHOMA	OK	137
23	MITCHELL	NC	134
24	HARRIS	TX	130
25	MORGAN	AL	111
26	PROVIDENCE	RI	103
27	IBERVILLE	LA	97
28	COLBERT	AL	95
29	NIAGARA	NY	92
30	BUTLER	PA	81
31	WHATCOM	WA	74
32	EAST BATON ROUGE	LA	73
33	VIGO	IN	72
34	ADA	ID	66
35	DAUPHIN	PA	64
36	RIVERSIDE	CA	60
37	LEE	FL	60
38	MULTNOMAH	OR	59
39	MASON	WV	59
40	CUMBERLAND	PA	57
41	CHELAN	WA	57
42	GALVESTON	TX	57
43	BUCKS	PA	56
44	WARREN	NY	52
45	HOT SPRING	AR	48
46	JACKSON	MS	44
47	MONTGOMERY	PA	42
48	SPOKANE	WA	41
49	BREVARD	FL	41
50	HAMILTON	TN	39
51	WASCO	OR	39
52	GARLAND	AR	38
53	SEMINOLE	FL	35
54	CHESTER	PA	35
55	NEWPORT	RI	34
56	SUFFOLK	MA	34
57	ESCAMBIA	FL	34
58	YORK	SC	33
59	SAN MATEO	CA	33
60	KENT	RI	33
61	PIERCE	WA	32

BOTTOM COUNTIES SHADED WHITE

NOTE: TOO MANY COUNTIES TO LIST
HAD ZERO VALUES FOR THIS MEASURE

HAZARDOUS WASTES

Houses on the south side of Ponca City, Oklahoma, are surrounded by pits, ponds, and lagoons brimming with hazardous wastes, over 600 storage tanks—some damaged and leaking—three incinerators, and a toxic sludge farm where wastes are spread onto the ground for the soil to absorb. These facilities are all part of a giant Conoco–Du Pont oil refinery and chemical complex. Orange sludge has seeped into parks, yards, and basements, and tests reveal over 20 pollutants in the ooze, including arsenic and carcinogens such as trichloroethylene and benzene. Childhood cancer mortality in surrounding Kay County is significantly higher than in the rest of the country. A visit to Ponca City led National Toxics Campaign activist Adrienne Anderson to say, "This place makes Love Canal look like a health spa."[38]

Conoco claims the orange sludge is harmless. A company representative suggested the orange discoloration in one resident's basement "was due to juniper berries dropping from the tree in the backyard," and, as a neighborly gesture, offered the homeowner a sump pump to clean up the mess if he would sign a release from any and all claims against the company.[39]

Faced with company denials, the EPA's refusal to get involved (citing the petroleum exclusion in the Superfund cleanup law), and state intransigence, residents organized Ponca City Toxic Concerned Citizens in 1988 and filed a class-action suit against Conoco in federal court in 1989.[40] In July 1990, Conoco agreed to one of the largest toxic tort settlements ever made, offering $23 million to buy 400 local homes that were contaminated with poisonous groundwater. The company settled without admitting any fault or wrongdoing, and residents are barred from seeking punitive damages, though they may sue to recover actual medical expenses.[41] Similar buyouts are now occurring throughout the country where residents are threatened by hazardous wastes.[42]

Hazardous wastes are the perilous residues of decades of industrial production. They lie scattered in tens of thousands of abandoned sites across the country. Most are either buried in landfills, left to stand in open trenches, or injected deep below the earth's surface. Conclusive evidence of the effects on human health at specific sites rarely emerge, because so little is known about which chemicals are present, how they disperse underground, or their precise toxic properties.[43] Eventually, each and every deposit of such waste leaks out, threatening underground water sources, health, and the environment. Leakage is often difficult to detect and can take many years to occur, but no technology is yet available that can guarantee it will not happen. Current laws require owners to maintain the sites for 30 years after disposal operations cease, yet many waste products, such as heavy metals, remain deadly for centuries. They can cause cancer, genetic defects, congenital anomalies, reproductive disorders, neurological problems, and the destruction of immune defenses. Depending on the nature of the exposure and the individual involved, toxic wastes can destroy every aspect of human health.[49]

The EPA and others have found that counties with hazardous waste sites and groundwater contamination correlate significantly with excess deaths from a variety of cancers, especially gastrointestinal and breast cancer.[45] Our data show significant correlations between all cancers, lung cancers, breast cancers, and all diseases with onsite hazardous waste management facilities, commercial disposal facilities, abandoned waste sites, Superfund priority sites, and operating facilities that violate groundwater monitoring regulations.

Wherever there is industry, there are hazardous wastes. The maps show where ongoing industrial activities are generating new wastes, where these wastes are being managed, and where old and abandoned sites litter the countryside. The first two maps show that extensive amounts of waste are generated in every region of the country and in almost every state. Treatment, storage, and disposal activities are never far behind, as indicated by the next three maps of on-site management facilities. There are a number of confusing facts about hazardous waste management. Underground injection is concentrated in fewer parts of the country than most other types of hazardous waste disposal, but the largest share of wastes are disposed of with this technique.[46] The vast bulk of hazardous wastes are dealt with on site, but most generators send some materials away to commercial facilities that specialize in handling hazardous refuse.[47] These facilities are located in industrial areas, or in rural farmland, depending on the economics of the regional waste business.[48] In addition to the on-site and off-site facilities, there are also the closed sites that contain the wastes from years of past dumping. These closed sites total in the tens of thousands, about 2,000 of which the EPA requires priority cleanup under the Superfund law. The maps display each of these categories of hazardous waste sites.

Given the inevitable problems of leakage and groundwater contamination, government and industry have begun turning to incineration as a possible solution to the hazardous waste crisis. Unfortunately, this strategy merely shifts much of the problem from the land to the air. Citizens have banded together throughout the country—in places like Jacksonville, Arkansas, Moab County, Utah, Caldwell County, North Carolina,

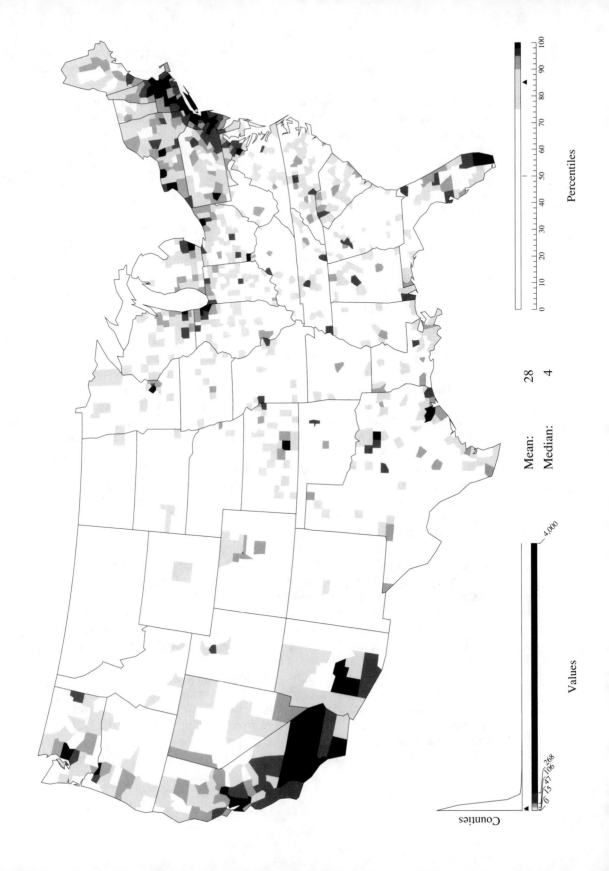

Mean: 28

Median: 4

Percentiles

Values

Counties

TOP COUNTIES SHADED BLACK

RANK	COUNTY	STATE	VALUE
1	LOS ANGELES	CA	4,000
2	NEW YORK CITY	NY	1,821
3	MIDDLESEX	MA	1,712
4	COOK	IL	1,542
5	ORANGE	CA	1,243
6	BERGEN	NJ	1,103
7	SANTA CLARA	CA	993
8	SAN DIEGO	CA	956
9	PROVIDENCE	RI	951
10	SUFFOLK	NY	932
11	NASSAU	NY	834
12	MIDDLESEX	NJ	833
13	ESSEX	NJ	797
14	WORCESTER	MA	775
15	KING	WA	753
16	UNION	NJ	699
17	ALAMEDA	CA	686
18	ESSEX	MA	612
19	FAIRFIELD	CT	602
20	HARTFORD	CT	593
21	HARRIS	TX	590
22	NEW HAVEN	CT	586
23	SEDGWICK	KS	533
24	MORRIS	NJ	521
25	NORFOLK	MA	507
26	ERIE	NY	491
27	DADE	FL	473
28	MILWAUKEE	WI	471
29	BALTIMORE CITY	MD	467
30	MONMOUTH	NJ	459
31	HENNEPIN	MN	455
32	CUYAHOGA	OH	455
33	PASSAIC	NJ	440
34	WAYNE	MI	437
35	MONROE	NY	436
36	HUDSON	NJ	435
37	SUFFOLK	MA	419
38	HAMPDEN	MA	408
39	MONTGOMERY	PA	408
40	DALLAS	TX	402
41	WESTCHESTER	NY	400
42	ALLEGHENY	PA	397
43	PHILADELPHIA	PA	396
44	SAN BERNARDINO	CA	380
45	BRISTOL	MA	375
46	CAMDEN	NJ	374
47	MARICOPA	AZ	359
48	KERN	CA	358
49	CONTRA COSTA	CA	356
50	HILLSBOROUGH	NH	355
51	BROWARD	FL	331
52	ONONDAGA	NY	324
53	SAN MATEO	CA	314
54	ST LOUIS CITY	MO	307
55	BURLINGTON	NJ	299
56	HAMILTON	OH	287
57	MERCER	NJ	286
58	MULTNOMAH	OR	284
59	FAIRFAX	VA	279
60	SACRAMENTO	CA	278
61	VENTURA	CA	268

BOTTOM COUNTIES SHADED WHITE

NOTE: TOO MANY COUNTIES TO LIST
HAD ZERO VALUES FOR THIS MEASURE

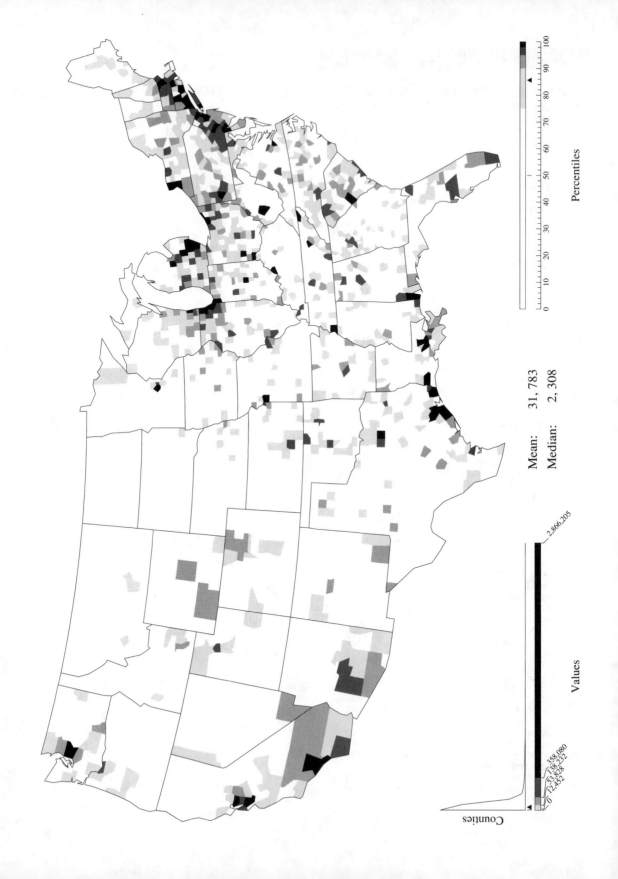

Mean: 31, 783

Median: 2, 308

Percentiles

Values

Counties

(TONS PER YEAR)

TOP COUNTIES SHADED BLACK

RANK	COUNTY	STATE	VALUE
1	COOK	IL	2,866,205
2	HARRIS	TX	2,857,042
3	LOS ANGELES	CA	2,832,905
4	WAYNE	MI	1,535,516
5	BRAZORIA	TX	1,290,159
6	ANDERSON	TN	1,271,924
7	HAMILTON	OH	1,236,179
8	JEFFERSON	TX	1,218,802
9	MIDDLESEX	NJ	1,088,092
10	NEW YORK CITY	NY	1,055,926
11	CUYAHOGA	OH	1,037,064
12	UNION	NJ	933,905
13	EAST BATON ROUGE	LA	886,330
14	NIAGARA	NY	873,881
15	MIDDLESEX	MA	777,093
16	ST LOUIS CITY	MO	748,581
17	ALLEGHENY	PA	727,641
18	AIKEN	SC	726,934
19	MIDLAND	MI	703,416
20	ESSEX	NJ	694,766
21	KANAWHA	WV	689,433
22	OAKLAND	MI	672,808
23	BERGEN	NJ	649,969
24	PHILADELPHIA	PA	638,586
25	MILWAUKEE	WI	636,310
26	MARION	IN	635,454
27	IBERVILLE	LA	634,360
28	ERIE	NY	616,271
29	MONTGOMERY	PA	612,133
30	LAKE	IN	593,119
31	PRINCE GEORGE	VA	591,171
32	BALTIMORE CITY	MD	576,752
33	NEW HAVEN	CT	572,520
34	PASSAIC	NJ	563,377
35	JEFFERSON	KY	553,524
36	SANTA CLARA	CA	544,099
37	JACKSON	MO	535,801
38	SULLIVAN	TN	534,570
39	DALLAS	TX	532,521
40	HARTFORD	CT	516,452
41	FAIRFIELD	CT	511,862
42	SALEM	NJ	497,499
43	CALCASIEU	LA	496,766
44	KING	WA	487,654
45	SOMERSET	NJ	484,906
46	CONTRA COSTA	CA	476,838
47	SHELBY	TN	470,429
48	LAKE	OH	461,512
49	NEW CASTLE	DE	444,024
50	PROVIDENCE	RI	437,904
51	ORANGE	CA	416,103
52	MACOMB	MI	415,952
53	HENNEPIN	MN	413,115
54	NASSAU	NY	412,126
55	LAKE	IL	401,426
56	ASCENSION	LA	383,682
57	NEW LONDON	CT	382,553
58	MOBILE	AL	373,428
59	MONTGOMERY	OH	370,962
60	GENESEE	MI	358,106
61	GALVESTON	TX	358,080

BOTTOM COUNTIES SHADED WHITE

NOTE: TOO MANY COUNTIES TO LIST
HAD ZERO VALUES FOR THIS MEASURE

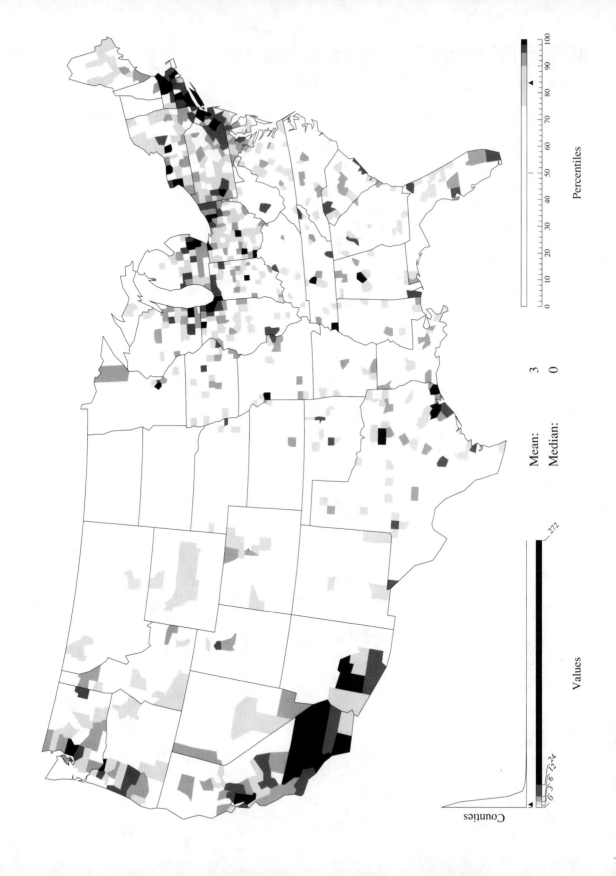

Mean: 3

Median: 0

Percentiles

Values

Counties

TOP COUNTIES SHADED BLACK

RANK	COUNTY	STATE	VALUE
1	LOS ANGELES	CA	272
2	COOK	IL	211
3	HARRIS	TX	119
4	CUYAHOGA	OH	99
5	WAYNE	MI	88
6	SANTA CLARA	CA	87
7	ORANGE	CA	79
8	KING	WA	74
9	HARTFORD	CT	70
10	FAIRFIELD	CT	68
11	NEW HAVEN	CT	68
12	MILWAUKEE	WI	67
13	MIDDLESEX	NJ	62
14	SAN DIEGO	CA	60
15	BALTIMORE CITY	MD	57
16	DALLAS	TX	55
17	HAMILTON	OH	52
18	ESSEX	NJ	51
19	ALAMEDA	CA	50
20	ERIE	NY	50
21	BERGEN	NJ	49
22	ALLEGHENY	PA	48
23	MIDDLESEX	MA	47
24	MONTGOMERY	PA	46
25	MULTNOMAH	OR	45
26	CONTRA COSTA	CA	44
27	MARICOPA	AZ	43
28	PHILADELPHIA	PA	41
29	NASSAU	NY	40
30	MARION	IN	38
31	LAKE	IN	37
32	FRANKLIN	OH	37
33	LUCAS	OH	37
34	OAKLAND	MI	36
35	SUFFOLK	NY	36
36	UNION	NJ	35
37	SAN BERNARDINO	CA	34
38	HENNEPIN	MN	34
39	NEW YORK CITY	NY	34
40	MONROE	NY	34
41	SUMMIT	OH	33
42	BUCKS	PA	33
43	DAVIDSON	TN	33
44	ST LOUIS CITY	MO	32
45	SHELBY	TN	32
46	HUDSON	NJ	31
47	TARRANT	TX	31
48	KERN	CA	30
49	ESSEX	MA	28
50	ONONDAGA	NY	28
51	WINNEBAGO	IL	27
52	JACKSON	MO	27
53	PASSAIC	NJ	27
54	JEFFERSON	AL	26
55	DU PAGE	IL	26
56	BRISTOL	MA	26
57	WORCESTER	MA	26
58	MORRIS	NJ	25
59	MONTGOMERY	OH	25
60	JEFFERSON	TX	24
61	WAUKESHA	WI	24

BOTTOM COUNTIES SHADED WHITE

NOTE: TOO MANY COUNTIES TO LIST
HAD ZERO VALUES FOR THIS MEASURE

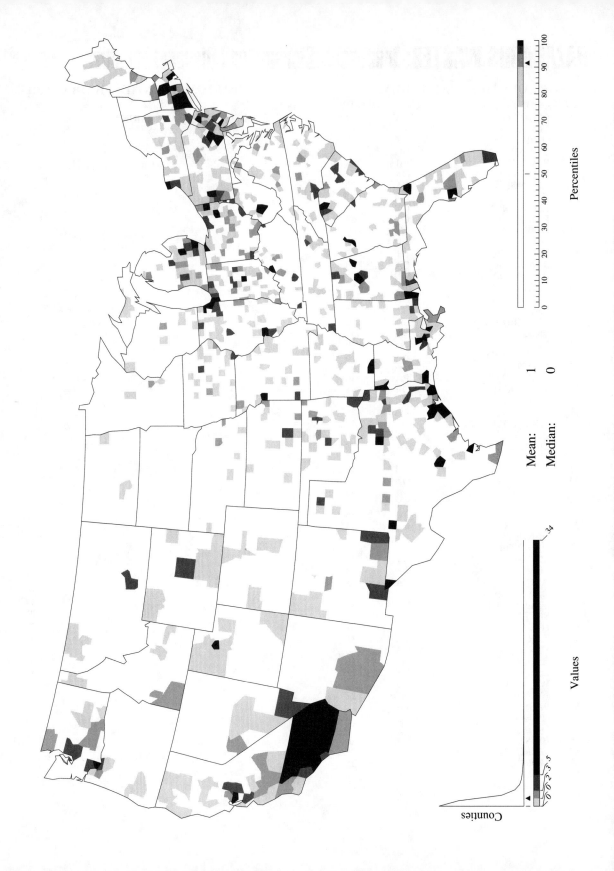

Values

Percentiles

Mean: 1
Median: 0

Counties

TOP COUNTIES SHADED BLACK

RANK	COUNTY	STATE	VALUE
1	HARRIS	TX	34
2	NEW HAVEN	CT	28
3	HARTFORD	CT	25
4	FAIRFIELD	CT	23
5	NUECES	TX	15
6	CONTRA COSTA	CA	14
7	COOK	IL	14
8	MARION	IN	13
9	MADISON	IL	12
10	JEFFERSON	TX	12
11	LOS ANGELES	CA	11
12	LITCHFIELD	CT	11
13	WAYNE	MI	11
14	LAKE	IN	10
15	JEFFERSON	AL	9
16	DUVAL	FL	9
17	BRISTOL	MA	9
18	KERN	CA	8
19	MIDDLESEX	CT	8
20	EAST BATON ROUGE	LA	8
21	BUTLER	PA	8
22	MOBILE	AL	7
23	WINDHAM	CT	7
24	FULTON	GA	7
25	CADDO	LA	7
26	CALCASIEU	LA	7
27	BALTIMORE CITY	MD	7
28	JACKSON	MO	7
29	MORRIS	NJ	7
30	NIAGARA	NY	7
31	GALVESTON	TX	7
32	CALHOUN	AL	6
33	HILLSBOROUGH	FL	6
34	GLOUCESTER	NJ	6
35	BERKS	PA	6
36	BEXAR	TX	6
37	ECTOR	TX	6
38	UNION	AR	5
39	RIVERSIDE	CA	5
40	SAN BERNARDINO	CA	5
41	JEFFERSON	KY	5
42	ASCENSION	LA	5
43	ST CHARLES	LA	5
44	WORCESTER	MA	5
45	GENESEE	MI	5
46	LUCAS	OH	5
47	STARK	OH	5
48	TRUMBULL	OH	5
49	LANCASTER	PA	5
50	SPARTANBURG	SC	5
51	BRAZORIA	TX	5
52	EL PASO	TX	5
53	TARRANT	TX	5
54	SALT LAKE	UT	5
55	CLARK	WA	5
56	KANAWHA	WV	5

BOTTOM COUNTIES SHADED WHITE

NOTE: TOO MANY COUNTIES TO LIST
HAD ZERO VALUES FOR THIS MEASURE

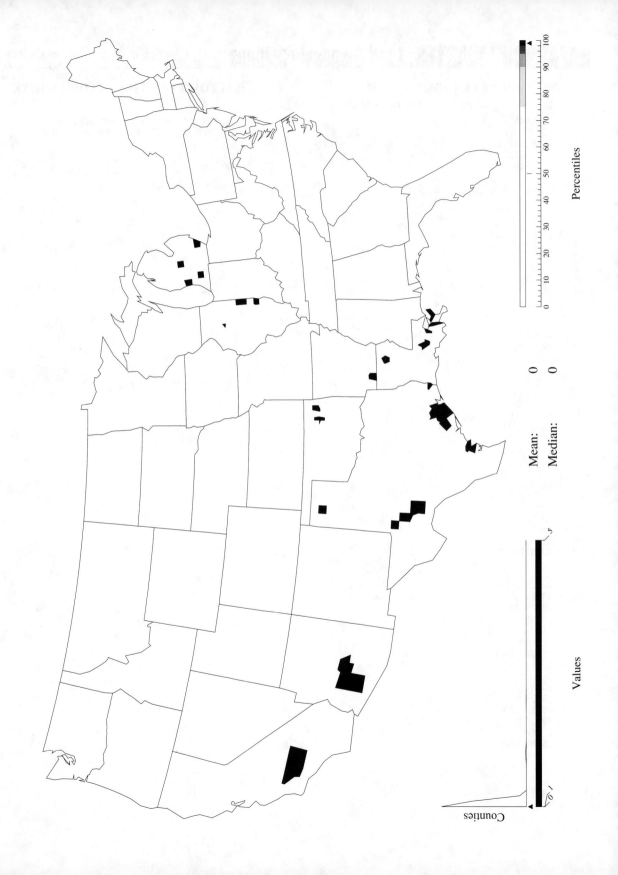

Percentiles

Mean: 0

Median: 0

Values

Counties

TOP COUNTIES SHADED BLACK

RANK	COUNTY	STATE	VALUE
1	HARRIS	TX	5
2	KERN	CA	2
3	IBERVILLE	LA	2
4	OTTAWA	MI	2
5	TULSA	OK	2
6	GALVESTON	TX	2
7	MARICOPA	AZ	1
8	COLUMBIA	AR	1
9	CLARK	IL	1
10	PUTNAM	IL	1
11	VERMILION	IL	1
12	JEFFERSON	LA	1
13	OUACHITA	LA	1
14	ST BERNARD	LA	1
15	ST JOHN THE BAPTIST	LA	1
16	WEST BATON ROUGE	LA	1
17	GRATIOT	MI	1
18	KALAMAZOO	MI	1
19	WAYNE	MI	1
20	MAYES	OK	1
21	BRAZORIA	TX	1
22	CROCKETT	TX	1
23	ECTOR	TX	1
24	FORT BEND	TX	1
25	MOORE	TX	1
26	NUECES	TX	1
27	ORANGE	TX	1
28	SAN PATRICIO	TX	1
29	UPTON	TX	1
30	WHARTON	TX	1

BOTTOM COUNTIES SHADED WHITE

NOTE: TOO MANY COUNTIES TO LIST
HAD ZERO VALUES FOR THIS MEASURE

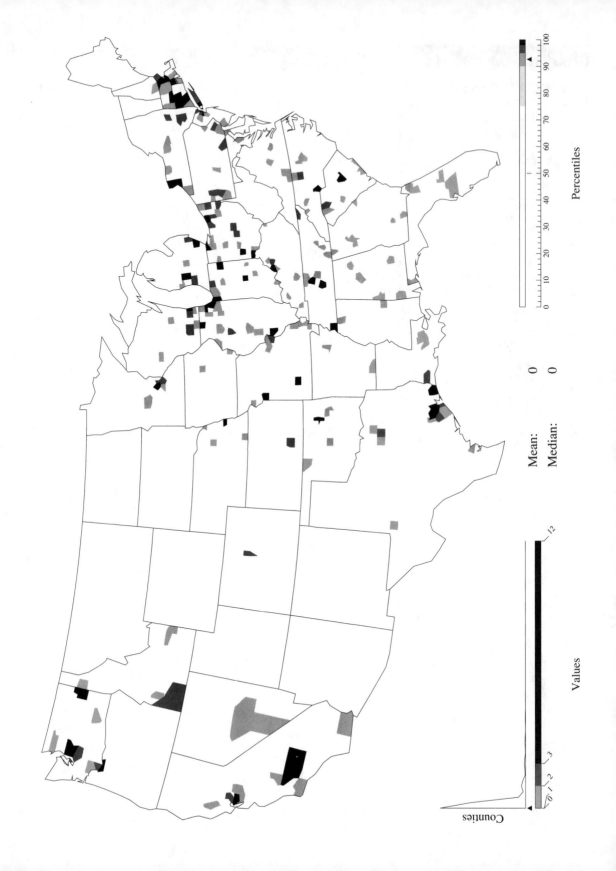

HAZARDOUS WASTES:
Commercial Treatment, Storage, and Disposal Facilities

(ACRE-FEET)

TOP COUNTIES SHADED BLACK

RANK	COUNTY	STATE	VALUE
1	COOK	IL	12
2	WAYNE	MI	12
3	CUYAHOGA	OH	10
4	KING	WA	9
5	NIAGARA	NY	8
6	JACKSON	MO	7
7	HARRIS	TX	7
8	MULTNOMAH	OR	6
9	SHELBY	TN	6
10	MARION	IN	5
11	MIDDLESEX	MA	5
12	NEW YORK CITY	NY	5
13	PROVIDENCE	RI	5
14	MILWAUKEE	WI	5
15	CONTRA COSTA	CA	4
16	KERN	CA	4
17	HARTFORD	CT	4
18	ST CLAIR	IL	4
19	LAKE	IN	4
20	KENT	MI	4
21	HENNEPIN	MN	4
22	HAMILTON	OH	4
23	MONTGOMERY	OH	4
24	TULSA	OK	4
25	MAURY	TN	4
26	LITCHFIELD	CT	3
27	NEW HAVEN	CT	3
28	WINNEBAGO	IL	3
29	ALLEN	IN	3
30	JEFFERSON	KY	3
31	HAMPDEN	MA	3
32	NORFOLK	MA	3
33	GREENE	MO	3
34	ST LOUIS CITY	MO	3
35	DOUGLAS	NE	3
36	HUDSON	NJ	3
37	UNION	NJ	3
38	ERIE	NY	3
39	NASSAU	NY	3
40	MECKLENBURG	NC	3
41	LUCAS	OH	3
42	SUMTER	SC	3
43	DAVIDSON	TN	3
44	JEFFERSON	TX	3
45	SPOKANE	WA	3

BOTTOM COUNTIES SHADED WHITE

NOTE: TOO MANY COUNTIES TO LIST
HAD ZERO VALUES FOR THIS MEASURE

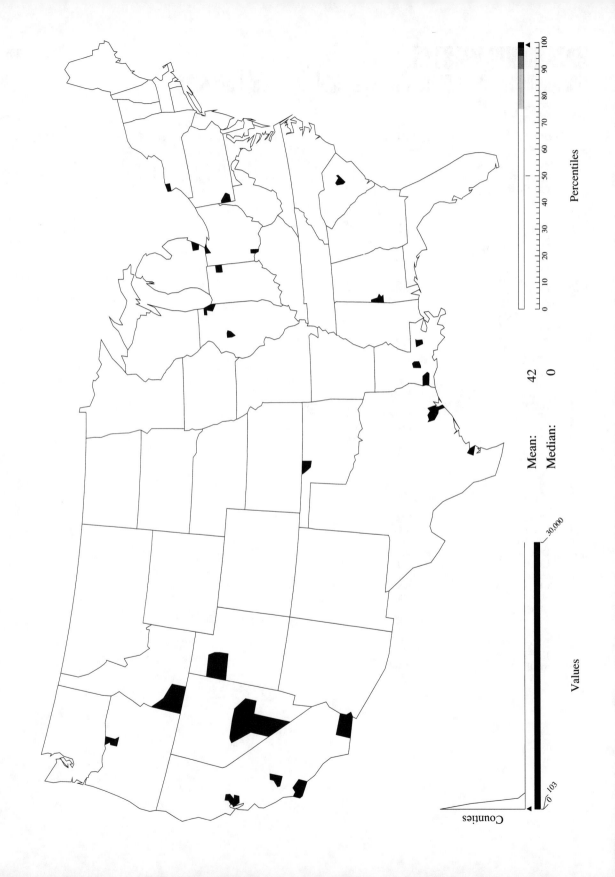

Mean: 42

Median: 0

Percentiles

Values

Counties

(ACRE-FEET)

TOP COUNTIES SHADED BLACK

RANK	COUNTY	STATE	VALUE
1	SUMTER	AL	30,000
2	COOK	IL	25,206
3	EVANGELINE	LA	22,400
4	EAST BATON ROUGE	LA	14,400
5	KINGS	CA	6,670
6	CALCASIEU	LA	5,656
7	LUCAS	OH	5,637
8	OWYHEE	ID	3,670
9	NUECES	TX	3,150
10	WAYNE	MI	3,000
11	CLERMONT	OH	2,293
12	PEORIA	IL	1,360
13	WASHINGTON	PA	1,250
14	NYE	NV	800
15	TOOELE	UT	632
16	GILLIAM	OR	535
17	SOLANO	CA	300
18	SUMTER	SC	289
19	ALLEN	IN	140
20	NIAGARA	NY	139
21	SANTA BARBARA	CA	131
22	WOODS	OK	118
23	GALVESTON	TX	110
24	CONTRA COSTA	CA	103
25	IMPERIAL	CA	103
26	HARRIS	TX	103

BOTTOM COUNTIES SHADED WHITE

NOTE: TOO MANY COUNTIES TO LIST
HAD ZERO VALUES FOR THIS MEASURE

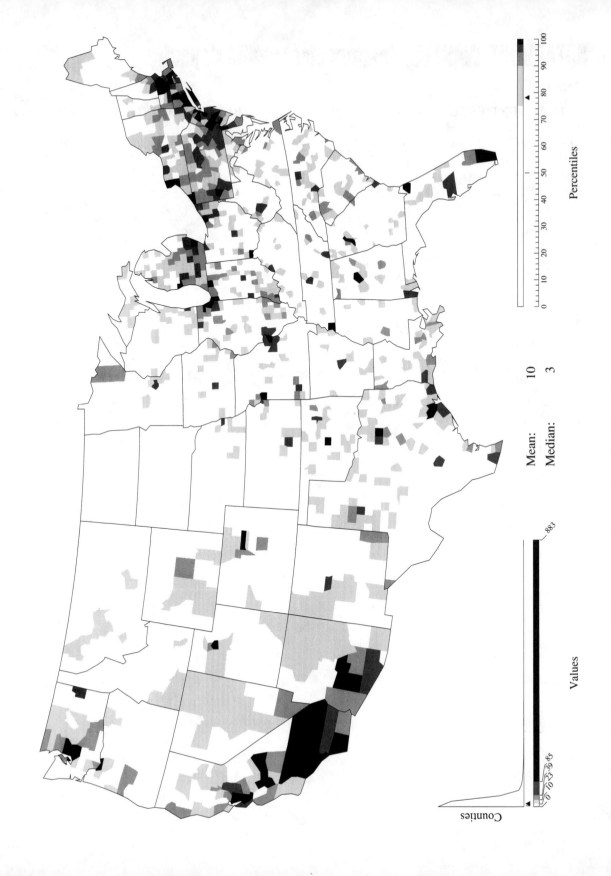

Percentiles

Values

Counties

Mean: 10
Median: 3

TOP COUNTIES SHADED BLACK

RANK	COUNTY	STATE	VALUE
1	LOS ANGELES	CA	883
2	COOK	IL	328
3	SANTA CLARA	CA	293
4	HARRIS	TX	284
5	MARICOPA	AZ	280
6	ST LOUIS CITY	MO	262
7	ST LOUIS	MO	219
8	SHELBY	TN	213
9	BROWARD	FL	207
10	KING	WA	197
11	MIDDLESEX	MA	191
12	MIDDLESEX	NJ	190
13	ORANGE	CA	179
14	MONTGOMERY	PA	175
15	NIAGARA	NY	166
16	ERIE	NY	163
17	ALAMEDA	CA	155
18	WAYNE	MI	146
19	CONTRA COSTA	CA	139
20	CUYAHOGA	OH	138
21	SAN DIEGO	CA	135
22	PIERCE	WA	134
23	DALLAS	TX	131
24	DUVAL	FL	130
25	ALLEGHENY	PA	129
26	LAKE	IN	127
27	NEW CASTLE	DE	122
28	FULTON	GA	122
29	BERGEN	NJ	122
30	HUDSON	NJ	122
31	ESSEX	NJ	121
32	MORRIS	NJ	119
33	JACKSON	MO	116
34	MULTNOMAH	OR	114
35	NEW HAVEN	CT	113
36	ERIE	PA	113
37	SUFFOLK	NY	112
38	BUCKS	PA	111
39	PROVIDENCE	RI	107
40	BURLINGTON	NJ	104
41	ADAMS	CO	98
42	HARTFORD	CT	98
43	DADE	FL	98
44	SAN BERNARDINO	CA	97
45	JEFFERSON	AL	96
46	BRISTOL	MA	95
47	GLOUCESTER	NJ	94
48	SALT LAKE	UT	94
49	NEW YORK CITY	NY	92
50	HAMILTON	OH	91
51	KERN	CA	90
52	ST JOSEPH	IN	89
53	MUSKEGON	MI	89
54	OKLAHOMA	OK	89
55	PHILADELPHIA	PA	88
56	VENTURA	CA	87
57	FAIRFIELD	CT	86
58	WORCESTER	MA	86
59	FRESNO	CA	85
60	DENVER	CO	85

BOTTOM COUNTIES SHADED WHITE

NOTE: TOO MANY COUNTIES TO LIST
HAD ZERO VALUES FOR THIS MEASURE

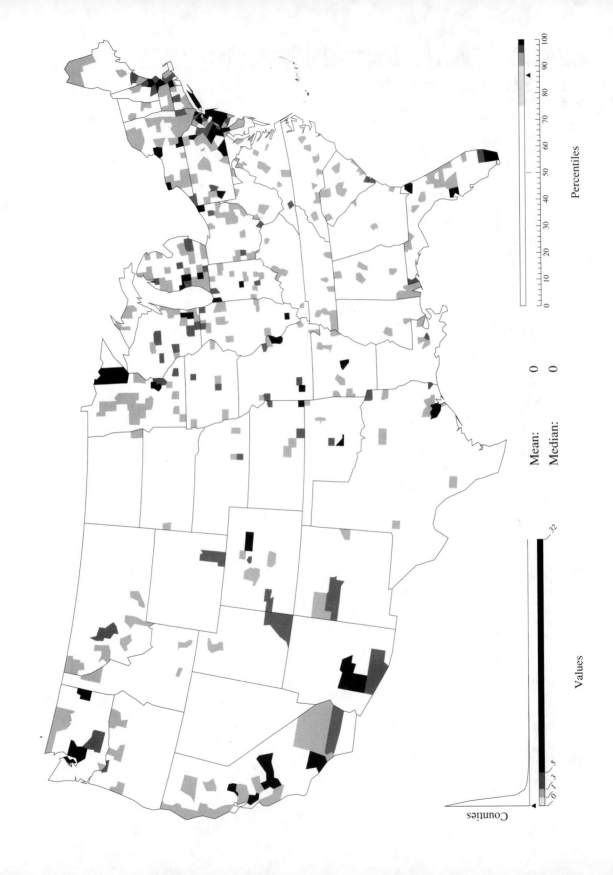

Mean: 0

Median: 0

Percentiles

Values

Counties

TOP COUNTIES SHADED BLACK

RANK	COUNTY	STATE	VALUE
1	DENVER	CO	32
2	BURLINGTON	NJ	20
3	ADAMS	CO	17
4	LOS ANGELES	CA	15
5	SANTA CLARA	CA	15
6	MIDDLESEX	NJ	15
7	OCEAN	NJ	15
8	PIERCE	WA	15
9	NEW CASTLE	DE	14
10	FRESNO	CA	12
11	BERGEN	NJ	12
12	HENNEPIN	MN	11
13	JEFFERSON	MO	11
14	LAWRENCE	MO	11
15	PROVIDENCE	RI	11
16	MIDDLESEX	MA	10
17	MORRIS	NJ	10
18	NASSAU	NY	10
19	ARAPAHOE	CO	9
20	ANOKA	MN	9
21	ST LOUIS	MO	9
22	ASHTABULA	OH	9
23	MONTGOMERY	PA	9
24	WILLIAMSON	IL	8
25	KENT	MI	8
26	ROCKINGHAM	NH	8
27	CHESTER	PA	8
28	MARICOPA	AZ	7
29	SACRAMENTO	CA	7
30	HILLSBOROUGH	FL	7
31	MUSKEGON	MI	7
32	ATLANTIC	NJ	7
33	MONMOUTH	NJ	7
34	BROOME	NY	7
35	SUFFOLK	NY	7
36	ADAMS	PA	7
37	BERKS	PA	7
38	HARRIS	TX	7
39	SPOKANE	WA	7
40	DADE	FL	6
41	ST LOUIS	MN	6
42	CAMDEN	NJ	6
43	GLOUCESTER	NJ	6
44	WAUKESHA	WI	6
45	PULASKI	AR	5
46	DUVAL	FL	5
47	BOONE	IN	5
48	LAKE	IN	5
49	CHEROKEE	KS	5
50	KALAMAZOO	MI	5
51	ESSEX	NJ	5
52	NIAGARA	NY	5
53	OSWEGO	NY	5
54	MC CLAIN	OK	5
55	ALLEGHENY	PA	5
56	LACKAWANNA	PA	5
57	YORK	PA	5
58	KING	WA	5
59	KITSAP	WA	5
60	WASHINGTON	WI	5

BOTTOM COUNTIES SHADED WHITE

NOTE: TOO MANY COUNTIES TO LIST
HAD ZERO VALUES FOR THIS MEASURE

and Danbury, Connecticut—to protest this new source of toxic contamination, setting back or canceling over 60 proposed facilities in 1989 alone.[49] Their counter-demand: reduce the generation of toxic wastes at the source through raw material and product substitutions, process modifications and internal reuse and recycling. A map in the industrial air emissions section shows where existing incinerators are turning the problem of hazardous wastes in the ground into a potential problem for the air as well.

WORKPLACE TOXINS

Frank Carsner had worked as a truck painter in Portland, Oregon, for over a decade. He was regularly exposed to commonly used toxic solvents, chromates, heavy metals, and isocyanates. In the late 1970s, he began waking up in the middle of the night coughing up blood. Frank's vision became blurred, and he suffered blackout spells and disorientation. Tumors developed on his eyelids and the back of his hands. The company doctor said he could not find the cause and speculated that Frank was allergic to a catalytic agent used in the shop. Frank was eventually fired for absenteeism after losing his voice for four months and being forced in and out of hospitals by his health problems. He now takes half a dozen pills twice a day for his ailments. Among other symptoms of immune deficiency, Frank's wounds would not heal, so doctors tested for AIDS. The results were negative, suggesting Frank's symptoms were chemically induced.[50]

Frank Carsner and other chemically disabled industrial painters incorporated the Toxic Victims Association (TVA) in 1985 to gather information on the causes of and treatments for their various afflictions. At first, TVA provided advice to painters and other workers using industrial chemicals on where to get medical, psychological, financial, and legal help, but soon they began reaching out to other groups in the community that were also concerned about toxic hazards. They joined Oregon Fair Share, a citizen activist group, and others to push for the passage of the state's right-to-know law in 1984. They testified before Congress on ways to improve the labeling of paints and other products containing hazardous materials. They shared information with the Pesticide Task Force, the Chronic Epstein-Barr Association, and other organizations on chemical exposures and chronic immune system disorders.[51] And in 1989 they joined forces with the Oregon Public Interest Research Group and others to help win the passage of one of the nation's first toxic-use reduction laws.

Across the country, workers are demanding more rights to prevent chemical exposure on the job, and are actively seeking community support.[52] Employees at General Motors' Lordstown, Ohio, factory, for example, organized Workers Against Toxic Hazards (WATCH) and tried to document their suspicions that many of their co-workers had been fatally disabled from occupational exposures. They identified 75 potentially work-related deaths in the obituary sections of local papers during an 18-month period in 1987 and 1988, a third of which involved people younger than 50. WATCH demanded that GM and the United Auto Workers initiate a study of excess deaths at the plant. Ten months of petitioning paid off: the union and auto company set up a joint committee to investigate. The inquiry revealed among the Lordstown workers, cases of stomach and pancreatic cancer were three to six times higher than expected, fatal car accidents were 80 percent higher, and cancer deaths were 37 to 48 percent above the norm. WATCH organizers attributed the car accident statistic to the everyday symptoms of Lordstown workers: headaches, dizziness, and numbness in the hands and feet, including when driving home from work.[53]

The UAW-GM joint committee conceded that the high cancer rates might be related to activities in the fabrication plant, because the rates among unexposed managerial and assembly-line employees were normal. Even so, the committee cautioned that the results did not prove cause and effect, and few procedures were changed after the findings. The Lordstown plant continues to release some 4 million pounds of toxins each year, and at the end of 1989, OSHA charged the plant with 750 safety violations and levied a $211,000 fine.[54] WATCH commemorated the annual AFL-CIO Workers' Memorial Day with a hearing about ongoing chemical exposures, and staged a mock funeral procession to drive the point home. Lordstown workers want the right to refuse work that endangers their lives, and are beginning to strengthen their alliances with community and environmental groups to achieve this demand.[55]

More and more, workers are overcoming fears of job blackmail and are speaking out in cooperation with community activists to reduce the hazards of industrial toxins. In southern New Jersey, the Coalition Against Toxics (CAT) negotiated a "good neighbor agreement" with a local industry, based on the National Toxics Campaign's three-rights organizing model: the right to know, the right to inspect, and the right to negotiate. CAT targeted facilities using state and federal right-to-know data, they secured union cooperation, and then wrote to arrange on-site inspections. The president of Dynasil Corporation of America, a glass manufacturer in Berlin, New Jersey, responded first, saying, "If neighbors are concerned about the operation of my plant, that is of concern to me.''[56] A variety of local activists, government officials, and safety experts attended an inspection in May 1988.[57] The inspection team developed a five-point plan to improve accident prevention at the site. The company agreed to implement the plan and to maintain an ongoing dialogue with the community group to ensure continued worker and community safety.[58]

Such negotiations are part of an emerging nationwide coalition to expand activities from lobbying for right-to-know laws about toxic hazards to taking local action to reduce toxic exposures in the workplace and the community. Activists in New Jersey and Michigan are trying to codify these efforts in state right-to-act laws, which would serve as models for federal legislation, just as state right-to-know laws were the forerunners of the federal statute. The right-to-act initiatives aim to grant community and worker representatives investigative powers to inspect and negotiate for improved conditions.[59] They would also compel employers to develop toxic-use reduction plans, a goal that labor-community coalitions in Oregon and Massachusetts have already achieved— thanks in part to the work of Frank Carsner and others at TVA.[60]

These struggles illustrate some basic facts about occupational exposures to toxic chemicals. First, whatever health effects neighbors of industrial polluters may experience, the problems faced by workers are usually more severe. Not only are workplace exposures more direct, continual, and concentrated, but employees are often more reluctant to protest because they depend on the industry for their livelihoods. The EPA has declared that worker exposure to chemicals poses greater cancer and noncancer health risks than any other cause.[61] Experts estimate that occupational exposures cause twice as many cancer deaths as does pollution.[62] Each year, as many as 50,000 to 70,000 American women and men die from occupational diseases, and new cases of work-related illness are estimated at 125,000 to 350,000.[63] Occupational injuries occur at twice the rate of those off the job, involving 10 million workers each year, disabling 2 to 3 million of them (70,000 permanently), and killing 10,000.[64]

Second, many health effects from occupational exposures are not officially recorded as such, despite these large estimates of occupational disease and death. Government statistics, for example, would generally fail to classify car accidents as occupational fatalities even when the cause was chemically induced dizziness from the workplace. They also underestimate the occurrence of occupational diseases that have long latency periods between exposure and the manifestation of symptoms.[65] The National Institute of Occupational Safety and Health (NIOSH) has found more than 8,000 different exposure agents in a sample of 5,000 workplaces. Yet OSHA regulates only about 500 substances—just 19 of which account for nearly three-quarters of all the samples the agency collects and analyzes for illegal exposures.[66] Health care professionals are often insufficiently educated about the chronic health effects of the workplace, which contributes to inadequate identification of causes when harmful working conditions lead to long-term illness.[67]

Third, a wide range of occupations are affected. Though the full extent of the problem is unknown, research to date has uncovered a seemingly endless list of occupationally related disease: 8 to 10 million workers have been or are currently exposed to asbestos and may develop asbestosis or mesothelioma; over half a million workers have been exposed to cotton dust, causing 35,000 cases of byssinosis with 83,600 more expected; nearly 5 percent of coal miners develop pneumoconiosis (black lung disease), which kills 4,000 of them each year; 1 million workers are exposed to silica in mines, foundries, blasting operations, and stone and glass industries, causing 60,000 cases of silicosis; there are high leukemia rates among shoemakers, rubber tire workers, glue workers, and others using benzene-based compounds; high bladder cancer rates among dye workers; encephalopathy and neurological damage among industrial painters and pesticide manufacturers; angiosarcoma of the liver among vinyl chloride workers; lung cancer among chloromethyl ether workers; multiple myeloma among workers in the petroleum industry; pancreatic and rectal cancer among thorium refinery workers; berylliosis among nuclear weapons manufacturers—and on, and on, and on.[68]

Nor are occupational diseases limited to blue-collar and industrial jobs. White-collar and service sector occupational diseases are also affecting women and men.[69] For example, carpal tunnel syndrome is now one of the leading occupational diseases, affecting video display terminal workers and other nonindustrial workers.[70] Modern office buildings with sealed windows result in internal environments with high levels of chemical irritants, including formaldehydes in carpets, any number of volatile organics, mutagens, and carcinogens in wall paints, glues, cleaners, Sheetrock, and insecticides (not to mention cigarette smoke). Workers can suffer unexpected adverse consequences, such as hypersensitivity to any chemical presence.[71] According to the EPA, indoor air pollution poses some of the highest risks of cancer and other diseases of any preventable cause.[72]

The following maps of workplace toxins indicate where some of these hazards are located. The first shows counties where petrochemical industries employ the most workers. NCI studies have reported significant correlations of cancer mortality among men in such counties that "could not be explained by confounding variables such as urbanization,

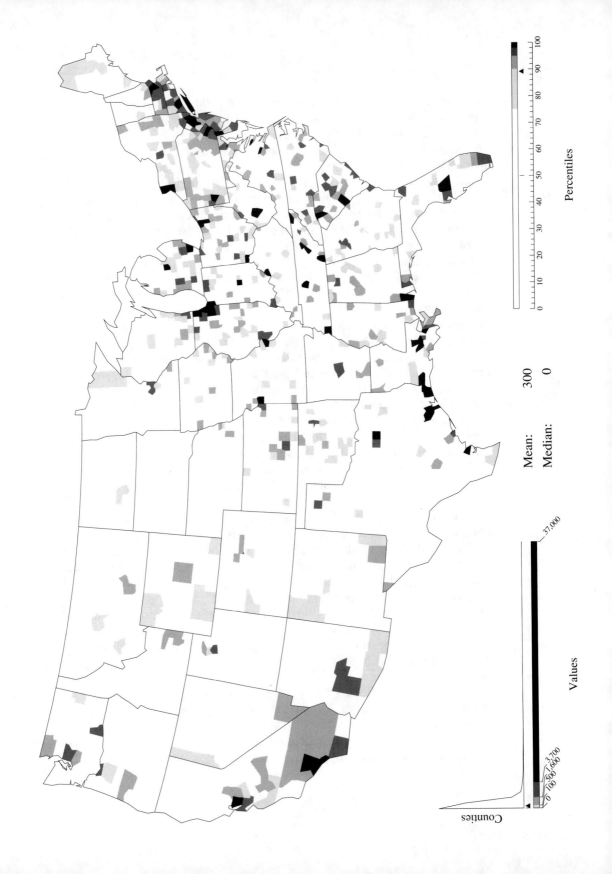

Percentiles

Mean: 300

Median: 0

Values

Counties

(PERSONS PER YEAR)

<table>
<tr><td colspan="4">TOP COUNTIES SHADED BLACK</td><td colspan="2">BOTTOM COUNTIES SHADED WHITE</td></tr>
</table>

RANK	COUNTY	STATE	VALUE
1	LOS ANGELES	CA	37,000
2	HARRIS	TX	28,600
3	COOK	IL	27,000
4	JEFFERSON	TX	19,300
5	SULLIVAN	TN	15,000
6	HAMILTON	OH	14,800
7	UNION	NJ	14,600
8	ESSEX	NJ	13,400
9	PHILADELPHIA	PA	11,100
10	EAST BATON ROUGE	LA	10,400
11	MARION	IN	10,100
12	NEW YORK CITY	NY	10,100
13	WAYNE	MI	9,800
14	CALCASIEU	LA	9,500
15	BERGEN	NJ	9,000
16	CUYAHOGA	OH	8,800
17	SOMERSET	NJ	8,400
18	ST LOUIS CITY	MO	8,300
19	CONTRA COSTA	CA	8,100
20	ORANGE	CA	8,000
21	KANAWHA	WV	7,800
22	GALVESTON	TX	7,300
23	MONTGOMERY	PA	7,200
24	JEFFERSON	KY	7,100
25	BALTIMORE CITY	MD	7,100
26	LAKE	IL	7,000
27	MIDLAND	MI	7,000
28	PASSAIC	NJ	7,000
29	AIKEN	SC	7,000
30	ANDERSON	TN	7,000
31	ROANE	TN	7,000
32	HENRICO	VA	7,000
33	RICHMOND	VA	7,000
34	SHELBY	TN	6,900
35	HUDSON	NJ	6,600
36	DALLAS	TX	6,000
37	HAMILTON	TN	5,500
38	NEW CASTLE	DE	5,400
39	MIDDLESEX	MA	5,300
40	WILL	IL	5,200
41	JACKSON	MO	5,100
42	ALLEGHENY	PA	5,100
43	ROCKLAND	NY	5,000
44	ALAMEDA	CA	4,900
45	ST LOUIS	MO	4,900
46	LAKE	IN	4,800
47	MORRIS	NJ	4,800
48	NIAGARA	NY	4,800
49	ST CHARLES	LA	4,700
50	MOBILE	AL	4,600
51	POLK	FL	4,500
52	ASCENSION	LA	4,500
53	ERIE	NY	4,500
54	ORANGE	TX	4,400
55	NUECES	TX	4,100
56	NASSAU	NY	4,000
57	SUFFOLK	NY	4,000
58	DAVIDSON	TN	3,900
59	IBERVILLE	LA	3,800
60	NEW HAVEN	CT	3,700
61	SUMMIT	OH	3,700
62	GREENVILLE	SC	3,700

BOTTOM COUNTIES SHADED WHITE

NOTE: TOO MANY COUNTIES TO LIST
HAD ZERO VALUES FOR THIS MEASURE

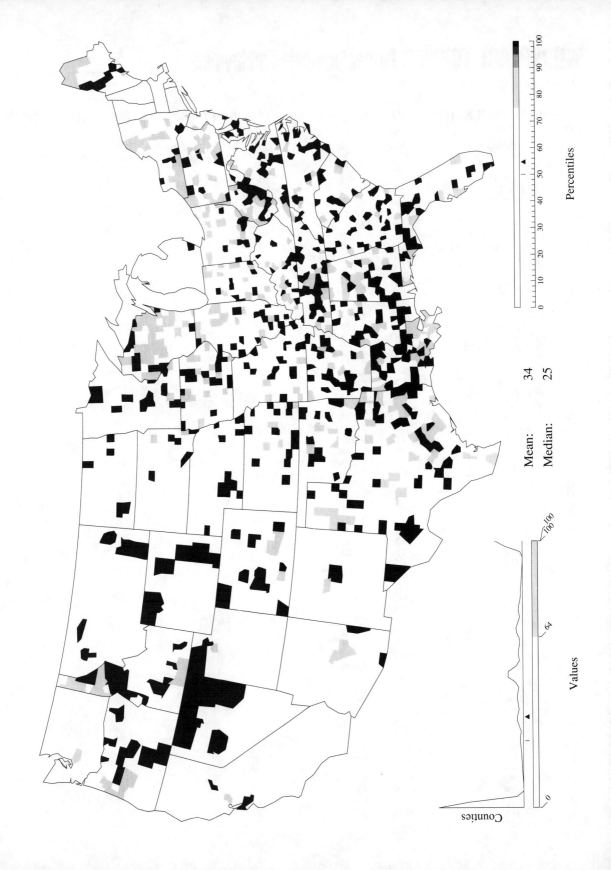

Mean: 34

Median: 25

Percentiles

Values

Counties

(PERCENT OF TOTAL)

TOP COUNTIES SHADED BLACK	BOTTOM COUNTIES SHADED WHITE
NOTE: TOO MANY COUNTIES TO LIST HAD MAXIMUM VALUES FOR THIS MEASURE	NOTE: TOO MANY COUNTIES TO LIST HAD ZERO VALUES FOR THIS MEASURE

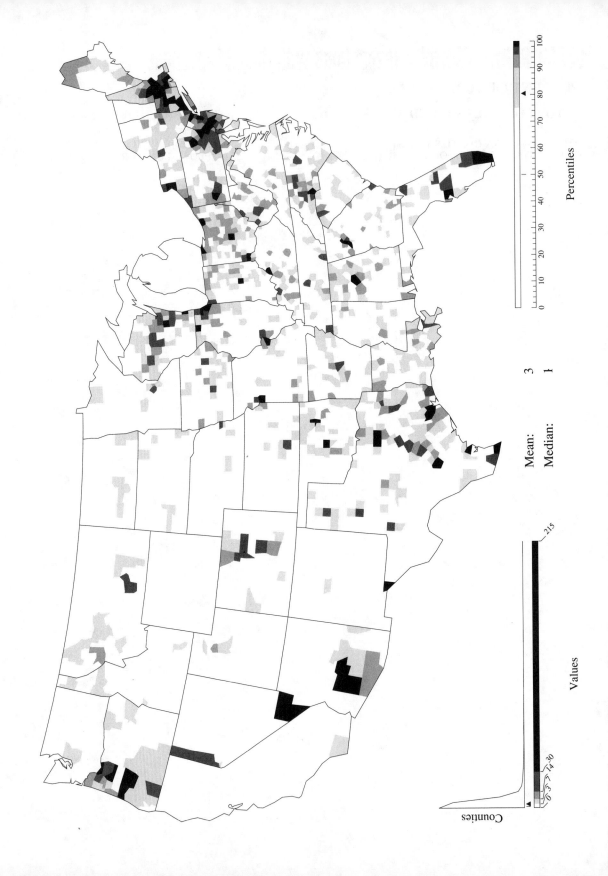

Mean: 3

Median: 1

Percentiles

Values

Counties

TOP COUNTIES SHADED BLACK

RANK	COUNTY	STATE	VALUE
1	COOK	IL	215
2	HARRIS	TX	211
3	WORCESTER	MA	139
4	JEFFERSON	KY	106
5	PROVIDENCE	RI	103
6	MULTNOMAH	OR	85
7	NEW YORK CITY	NY	82
8	FRANKLIN	OH	80
9	HAMPDEN	MA	78
10	BERGEN	NJ	70
11	PHILADELPHIA	PA	70
12	JEFFERSON	AL	64
13	DENVER	CO	64
14	PASSAIC	NJ	64
15	HARTFORD	CT	63
16	DALLAS	TX	63
17	TULSA	OK	62
18	NEW HAVEN	CT	60
19	EL PASO	TX	60
20	BEXAR	TX	59
21	CUYAHOGA	OH	53
22	MIDDLESEX	MA	51
23	MIDDLESEX	NJ	50
24	BUCKS	PA	49
25	DADE	FL	47
26	HAMILTON	OH	47
27	FAIRFIELD	CT	46
28	CAMDEN	NJ	46
29	JACKSON	MO	43
30	BURLINGTON	NJ	43
31	TARRANT	TX	42
32	CLARK	NV	41
33	UNION	NJ	41
34	HILLSBOROUGH	FL	40
35	ESSEX	MA	40
36	FULTON	GA	39
37	MONTGOMERY	PA	39
38	OKLAHOMA	OK	38
39	ALLEGHENY	PA	38
40	MARICOPA	AZ	36
41	MARION	IN	36
42	BRISTOL	MA	36
43	NUECES	TX	35
44	WINNEBAGO	WI	35
45	LEHIGH	PA	34
46	HILLSBOROUGH	NH	33
47	MARION	OR	33
48	LANE	OR	32
49	LUZERNE	PA	32
50	MILWAUKEE	WI	32
51	BROWARD	FL	31
52	WINNEBAGO	IL	31
53	MECKLENBURG	NC	31
54	NORTHAMPTON	PA	31
55	ST LOUIS	MO	30
56	ST LOUIS CITY	MO	30
57	ERIE	NY	30
58	LUCAS	OH	30
59	CAMERON	TX	30

BOTTOM COUNTIES SHADED WHITE

NOTE: TOO MANY COUNTIES TO LIST
HAD ZERO VALUES FOR THIS MEASURE

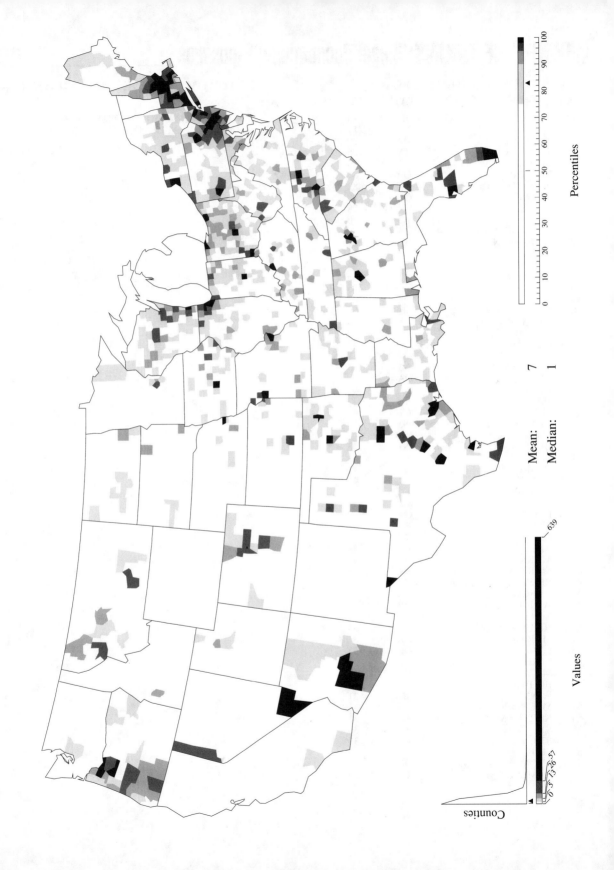

Mean: 7

Median: 1

Percentiles

Values

Counties

639

WORKPLACE TOXINS: Inspections

TOP COUNTIES SHADED BLACK

RANK	COUNTY	STATE	VALUE
1	COOK	IL	639
2	HARRIS	TX	502
3	NEW YORK CITY	NY	346
4	WORCESTER	MA	242
5	JEFFERSON	KY	226
6	MULTNOMAH	OR	211
7	BERGEN	NJ	202
8	FRANKLIN	OH	191
9	HAMPDEN	MA	184
10	PROVIDENCE	RI	182
11	DENVER	CO	157
12	MIDDLESEX	MA	157
13	JACKSON	MO	149
14	PHILADELPHIA	PA	148
15	TULSA	OK	143
16	PASSAIC	NJ	141
17	DALLAS	TX	134
18	HAMILTON	OH	130
19	BEXAR	TX	125
20	HARTFORD	CT	124
21	MILWAUKEE	WI	124
22	NEW HAVEN	CT	112
23	TARRANT	TX	109
24	CLARK	NV	105
25	OKLAHOMA	OK	105
26	MIDDLESEX	NJ	102
27	CUYAHOGA	OH	101
28	EL PASO	TX	101
29	JEFFERSON	AL	100
30	CAMDEN	NJ	99
31	MARION	IN	98
32	ESSEX	MA	98
33	ALLEGHENY	PA	97
34	LUCAS	OH	94
35	UNION	NJ	93
36	MARICOPA	AZ	91
37	NUECES	TX	91
38	FAIRFIELD	CT	89
39	HILLSBOROUGH	FL	85
40	FULTON	GA	84
41	DADE	FL	83
42	WASHINGTON	OR	83
43	ST LOUIS CITY	MO	80
44	BURLINGTON	NJ	79
45	SUFFOLK	MA	73
46	MECKLENBURG	NC	73
47	HILLSBOROUGH	NH	72
48	TRAVIS	TX	72
49	DE KALB	GA	71
50	POLK	IA	71
51	ST LOUIS	MO	71
52	BUCKS	PA	66
53	LUZERNE	PA	66
54	BRISTOL	MA	63
55	GUILFORD	NC	63
56	MONTGOMERY	PA	62
57	ERIE	NY	61
58	DOUGLAS	NE	60
59	NASSAU	NY	58
60	MARION	OR	58
61	LEHIGH	PA	57

BOTTOM COUNTIES SHADED WHITE

NOTE: TOO MANY COUNTIES TO LIST
HAD ZERO VALUES FOR THIS MEASURE

socioeconomic class, or employment in nonchemical industries," and suggested that "the actual risk of cancer among certain chemical workers must be very high."[73]

The remaining three maps show that toxic exposures occur not only among chemical manufacturers but also among the many industries that use such chemicals. Nearly every part of the country is affected. The second map shows the percentage of OSHA inspections that detected chemicals in the workplace that exceeded Permissible Exposure Limits (PELs). From 1980 to 1985, OSHA took chemical samples in facilities spread throughout two-thirds of the counties in the United States. A third of these inspections revealed illegal exposures. In 10 percent of the counties, every inspection yielded such a violation—far too many counties even to list. There is little correlation between petrochemical employment and the percentage of inspections with illegal exposures. However, counties with significant petrochemical employment are correlated 60 percent with those where OSHA took chemical samples and with counties where violations were found. These measures are shown in the last two maps.

These latter two maps are important, because OSHA did not inspect facilities in all counties or states. Counties with low rates of illegal exposures may simply be due to the lack of inspections. Some states conduct their own occupational safety and health programs, so they appear nearly blank in the maps (see, for example, California, Michigan, Vermont). OSHA suffered some of the severest budget cuts of any federal regulatory agency during the 1980s, undermining all of its standard-setting, inspection, and enforcement activities.[74] At the same time, occupational illness, injuries, and fatalities rose steadily in the United States throughout the decade.[75] The costs in lost wages, insurance premiums, medical care, and related expenses reached $140 billion per year.[76] An unknown fraction of this burden is caused by illegal exposures to workplace toxins, exposures that appear to be occurring almost everywhere OSHA looks.

The health and safety of working Americans are clearly at risk, with tragic repercussions, both in human and in financial terms. Around the country, workplace and community activists believe new laws establishing workplace health and safety committees are essential to reducing these costs.

CHAPTER 5

NONINDUSTRIAL POLLUTION

The maps that follow consider major nonindustrial sources of toxic pollution, that is, sources other than factories. Governments call them ''nonpoint'' and ''area'' sources of pollution because they are so diffuse. They include the 1.5 to 10 million underground storage tanks (many of which are owned by gas stations and other small businesses, and many of which may be leaking toxins into groundwater) and the nearly 1 million small-quantity generators of hazardous waste—such as car repair shops, dry cleaners, small metal shops, insect exterminators, and photolabs—discarding lead acid batteries, spent solvents, acids, and alkalies.[1] Much of this hazardous waste is simply flushed down the sewer, leading to treatment plants that often cannot handle it adequately. Another source of nonpoint pollution is the contaminated runoff from countless farms, lumber forests, construction sites, mines, and urban areas, which flows directly into rivers, streams, and estuaries.[2] And, there are the fumes from motor vehicles, solvent users, sewage plants, and commercial and residential fuel combustion, which contain a variety of toxins such as heavy metals, phenols, and trichloroethylene.[3]

In many places, these nonindustrial sources pose risks as great as any factory.[4] The residents of Brooklyn's Greenpoint-Williamsburg section, for example, must contend with the suffocating exhaust from heavy commercial traffic, the reeking stench of the Newtown Creek sewage plant, the overworked garbage incinerator deemed substandard by the federal government, the dozens of oil tanks and pipelines that crisscross the area and have leaked 14 million gallons of fuel onto the streets and underground, and the unknown number of former industrial sites that might be contaminated with toxic wastes. Barbara Fife, New York City deputy mayor for policy and development, describes this jumble of people and pollution as ''an egregious example of zoning policy.''[5]

Tired of seeing their neighborhood used as a dump, Greenpoint-Williamsburg residents are fighting back through organizations such as Greenpoint Against Smell and Pollution (GASP), the Williamsburg Around the Bridge Block Association, and the youth group called Toxic

Avengers. Their efforts have won a moratorium on new permits for garbage transfer stations, and have spurred state monitoring of air toxins, such as benzene, emitted by gas stations and industries.

Leaving the city does not necessarily improve matters. In the late 1970s, members of the Northwest Coalition for Alternatives to Pesticides (NCAP) tried to stop a paper company from spraying herbicides over timberland near homes in Rose Lodge, Oregon, only to be drenched in poisons by the helicopters flying overhead, in full view of journalists.[6] Despite NCAP's subsequent successes in reducing aerial pesticide spraying in Oregon forests, more and more pesticides are used each year in farm and timberland areas throughout the country, exposing farm workers, residents, and consumers.

On average, nearly 70 percent of the measures of nonindustrial pollution that we examined are significantly associated with the ten causes of death discussed in chapter 3 (see the methods appendix discussion of Fig. A-6). The federal government has a hard time regulating nonpoint sources. There are too many places to inspect, with the majority run by small businesses with far fewer resources for corrective action than are available to the corporate owners of large industrial point sources. In addition, highly organized and influential lobbies, such as that of the agricultural industry, have managed to fend off most regulatory efforts to curb pesticide usage while achieving unparalleled regulatory controls on foreign competition. Many sources of nonindustrial pollution have never been counted, let alone controlled. Here we examine some of the available data on pesticides, water quality, and urban air quality, for a view of how nonindustrial sources of pollution are affecting various parts of the country.

PESTICIDES

The San Joaquin is no ordinary valley. Half of the fruit, nuts, and vegetables consumed in the United States are grown in the valley's 30,000 square miles of central California.[7] It is one of the most intensely cultivated areas in the world . . . and among the most laden with pesticides. Seven percent of all pesticides used in this country are sprayed onto crops in the San Joaquin, even though the valley comprises just 1 percent of the nation's cropland.[8] The maps indicate that four of the top five counties posing the greatest potential pesticide hazards are in the valley. So are a disturbing number of counties with excess deaths from acutely hazardous exposures and child cancers.

Almost everywhere you look in the San Joaquin Valley, there is a cluster of child cancer or another disease that people suspect is due to agricultural chemicals. Paul Buxman owns a 40-acre farm southeast of Fresno. His son Wyeth developed leukemia at the age of 3. Since infancy, Wyeth drank water that in 1984 was found to be contaminated with ten times the allowable concentrations of DBCP (dibromochloropropane), a common worm-killing pesticide that was banned in 1977 as a suspected carcinogen and known sterilizer of men. Three other kids within five miles of the Buxman farm also had cancer—one of whom died.[9] DBCP has been found in 2,499 drinking water wells throughout the valley.[10]

In Earlimart, about 60 miles south of Fresno, another five children developed cancer in 1989. Four of their mothers worked in grape fields while pregnant. In response to growing evidence of adverse health effects, Cesar Chavez, the president of the United Farm Workers, has helped organize the fieldhands there, as well as a broad boycott of California grapes because they are sprayed with more pesticides than any other fresh food crop.[11]

About 20 miles south of Earlimart, the town of McFarland calls itself "the heartbeat of agriculture," but parents there think pesticides caused the deaths of at least 8 children. In addition to the 8 fatal cases, 22 local children have been diagnosed with several different forms of malignancy.[12] The first was Connie Rosales's son, who was diagnosed in 1984. The state has spent hundreds of thousands of dollars investigating the cause of McFarland's child cancer cluster, but to no avail.[13] The studies have failed to turn up any definitive answers, except that 80 percent of the children's fathers worked in the fields before the children were conceived.[14]

In a federal housing tract outside of McFarland, Marta Salinez's entire family has had a variety of health problems she thinks were caused by pesticides in the drinking water. Her three daughters suffered skin rashes, dizziness, diarrhea, and nausea. Marta herself had seizures and frequently lost all muscle control in her legs. She took a door-to-door survey and found the majority of her neighbors had tumors, blood disorders, birth defects, intestinal problems, gynecological difficulties, and other ailments.[15]

Parents are taking matters into their own hands in the face of interminable and inconclusive state investigations. Connie Rosales and others are suing various agencies, officials, and chemical manufacturers. "Our goal," she says, "is never to have this happen again."[16] Paul Buxman converted to organic farming and founded California Clean Growers, a network of farmers dedicated to protecting the environment and improving the quality of their produce. Watching his son Wyeth scream from spinal injections to treat the leukemia prompted these efforts. "After that," says Buxman, "you look at farm chemicals differently." Today Wyeth is 10 years old, healthy, and in remission.[17]

Many of the Salinez family's health problems have also improved since they stopped drinking their tap water. But Violet, Marta's middle daughter, still has a heart murmur, and Melissa, 8, the youngest daughter, weighs only 40 pounds and has had to drop out of school. Marta continues to raise hell to improve conditions in her community. She has written letters to politicians, organized rallies and demonstrations, and gotten national figures such as Jesse Jackson, Cesar Chavez, and Tony Anaya, the former governor of New Mexico, to march through town. McFarland is 90 percent Latino, so its residents have a particularly hard time getting a government response. "We are poor Mexicans," explains Salinez. "Most of us don't even speak English. Most of us can't even vote. We have no constituency. We have no clout." She hoped the presence of Chavez and others would help raise people's consciousness. "The plague we're suffering affects everyone in America who eats a fruit or vegetable or nut harvested in the San Joaquin Valley," says Marta Salinez. "There's a link here that joins everyone together, from the Mexican worker to the millionaire who eats grapes with his cereal."[18]

This link has yet to express itself in effective politics and public policy. California voters, for example, soundly defeated the 1990 ballot initiative dubbed Big Green, which was one of the most progressive and ambitious pieces of environmental legislation ever presented to voters. It would have banned pesticides known to cause cancer and reproductive harm. Organized agricultural and industrial groups outspent Big Green supporters by more than two to one, and were able to convince voters that the complex initiative simply tried to do too much. In part, the defeat reflects a general backlash against initiatives across the country, especially at a time when fears of recession made people less willing to spend money or raise taxes further. But it also reflects the many difficulties in getting farm owners, farm workers, environmentalists, and voters to organize around their common interests to reduce the pesticide dependency of agricultural production.[19]

Pesticides are a uniquely destructive product of the domestic and international economy.[20] Their manufacture creates toxic releases, toxic wastes, and workplace exposures. Their use exposes farm workers, and contaminates ground and surface waters. The EPA estimates that nearly 10,000 community water systems and 446,000 rural wells are contaminated with one of over 100 pesticides for which the agency tested.[21] Residents of those counties could end up paying nearly $1.5 billion a year to monitor for pesticides, and $12,000 to hook up each household to a public water system if their wells are contaminated.[22] Pesticide residuals remain in nearly all of the produce we eat, contributing to as many as 20,000 new cases of cancer each year, and over 400,000 cancer deaths over the lifetime of the U.S. population.[23] Pesticides in human breast milk expose infants to 6 to 14 times the government limits for adults—and babies, of course, are much more susceptible to the toxic effects of such chemicals.[24]

Many pesticides that have been banned in this country are still sold by U.S. firms to agricultural producers throughout the Third World, exposing farm workers there and often ending up back on our own plates in imported fruit, vegetables, meat, and other foodstuffs. Many have characterized the global pesticide problem as a "circle of poison."[25]

Total pesticide usage has reached 1.3 million tons a year, involving some 50,000 pesticide formulations.[26] This is three times the amount that was in use in 1962, when Rachel Carson alerted the nation to their dangers in *Silent Spring*.[27] Farmers annually spend nearly $6 billion on pesticides, amounting to almost half of their variable costs.[28] Much of this is wasted expense . . . and hazardous. Only 10 to 15 percent of most pesticide applications actually reach their intended site; the rest can drift as far as 20 miles away.[29] The number of insecticide-resistant bugs nearly doubled between 1970 and 1980, while crop loss due to pests has doubled since 1940.[30] Much agricultural chemical use is merely for cosmetic purposes anyway—making redder apples and unblemished peaches, for example. Forty to 60 percent of the pesticide applications on tomatoes, and 60 to 80 percent of the applications on oranges are solely to improve the fruits' appearance, according to a study by the California Public Interest Research Group.[31]

Farm workers pay the highest price for our addiction to agricultural chemicals. According to the National Safe Workplace Institute, farm work has displaced mining as America's deadliest job, due to the combination of occupational and environmental risks.[32] Up to 25 percent of farm workers killed on the job are 15 years old or less. Unlike any other group in the United States, farm workers have been excluded from most occupational safety and health regulations and other protective labor laws, including the federal Right-to-Know Act, the National Labor Relations Act, the Fair Labor Standards Act, workers' compensation, unemployment compensation, and social security, and only a few states recognize the right of farm workers to organize unions and bargain collectively.[33]

Farm workers suffer from significantly higher cancer rates than the rest of the population, including leukemias, and cancers of the prostate, brain, testicle, and blood.[34] The effects of pesticides on pregnant women and children are even more pronounced, including birth defects and spontaneous abortions, as well as cancer.[35] Recent studies indicate many farm chemicals can also cause neurological disorders such as Parkinson's, Alzheimer's, and Lou Gehrig's disease.[36] Fatal motor neuron disease has been geographically correlated with rural farming throughout the country.[37] Symptoms of neurological impairment can range from drowsiness, depression, dizziness, and confusion, to death.[38] Pesticides can also cause immune system malfunctions.[39] When acute poisoning is not involved, workers often do not even realize they are suffering from pesticide-related illness.

Under congressional auspices, Dr. Marion Moses of the University of California Medical School at San Francisco is heading up the most comprehensive studies ever undertaken of farm worker exposures to pesticides. Dr. Moses's team is tracking migrant farm workers from the summertime vegetable gathering in Ohio, to the fall fruit picking in Michigan, and to the winter and spring citrus harvests in Florida. "If you protect these workers in their workplace," Dr. Moses points out, "you'll do much more to protect the consumer in the marketplace.[40]

The pesticide maps show a number of potential problem areas from different perspectives. They use EPA county estimates of 25 common pesticides applied to over 70 crops, which amount to more than 200,000 tons nationally—16 percent of total pesticide use in the United States. (See the methods appendix for more details about these estimates.) Crops sprayed in one part of the country may be transported to others prior to consumption, so these data reflect human exposures through farm work and water contamination more closely than exposures through eating pesticide residues in food.

The first map indicates where the bulk of these chemicals is applied. In addition to the San Joaquin Valley in California, there are major concentrations of pesticide use throughout the Midwest, especially Iowa and Illinois, as well as along the Mississippi River, in a band across the Southeast coastal plain, and in the states of Florida and Washington. Iowa, Illinois, Minnesota, Indiana, and Ohio all account for larger shares of pesticide use than does California.[41]

Different pesticides can pose different hazards, and the next three maps approximate where various dangers may be the greatest. These maps weight the amount of pesticides used in each county by factors that approximate their potential overall health hazard, their potential cancer hazard, and their potential hazard for acute poisoning and other short-term effects. The resulting measures roughly indicate the potential hazards these selected pesticides pose in one county relative to another (the specific index values have no absolute meaning). The three potential hazard maps share certain features, such as high ratings for the San Joaquin Valley and for certain counties along the Mississippi and in the Southeast, but they differ markedly in other respects. The map of total potential hazards, for example, highlights a band of counties down the center of the country, which overlaps with the child cancer maps in chapter 3, but not with the other pesticide maps. Potential cancer hazards are concentrated in the Midwest, while areas of potential acute hazards are scattered across the country.

The final two pesticide maps look at the data in two other ways. The map of average application rates indicates the intensity of pesticide usage in the specific areas of each county where the pesticides are sprayed. This measure of pounds per treated acre highlights a cluster in Alabama and Georgia—where cotton fields are sometimes sprayed as often as fifteen times per growing season—and areas in the Midwest and Northeast.[42] This measure is significantly correlated with nine of the causes of death considered in this book—a more frequent association than any other environmental or toxins measure we examined. This association may be spurious, however. The application rates appear to cut off sharply at state lines, indicating that some of the geographic variation is an artifact of the EPA's estimating methods. The final map shows the percentage of cropland in each county that these pesticide applications affect. It indicates that most of the older farming areas of the Southeast have been covered, whereas a larger portion of farming acreage in the Midwest and West have not been sprayed with these pesticides. This measure also appears to be somewhat affected by estimation problems as indicated by the sharp breaks between states.

WATER QUALITY

In the industrial town of East Woburn, Massachusetts, in 1979, nearly 200 toxic waste drums were found along the Aberjona River near the town's principal drinking water wells. Nineteen children who had drunk the water prior to the drums' removal later contracted leukemia. Only two survived. Affected families sued the corporate giants W. R. Grace and Beatrice Foods for allegedly contaminating their drinking water with carcinogenic industrial solvents and so far have reached a settlement reportedly of $8 million with Grace (Beatrice was absolved).[43]

In Mountainview, New Mexico, a baby nearly died after drinking formula mixed with local well water in 1980. State regulators subsequently found agricultural chemicals in local wells that were five times above the federal drinking water standards. To their surprise, they also

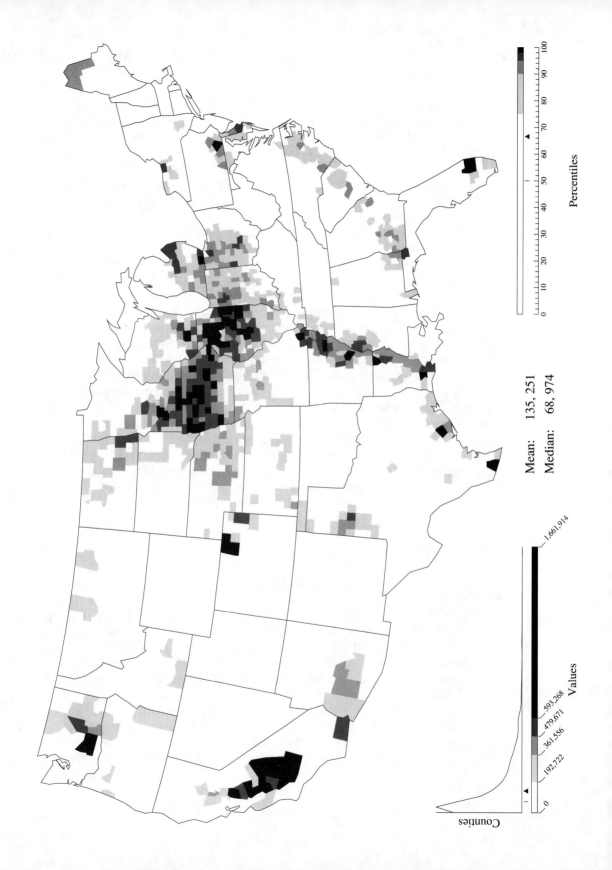

Mean: 135, 251

Median: 68, 974

Percentiles

(POUNDS PER YEAR)

TOP COUNTIES SHADED BLACK

RANK	COUNTY	STATE	VALUE
1	PALM BEACH	FL	1,661,914
2	MC LEAN	IL	1,332,440
3	FRESNO	CA	1,208,182
4	IROQUOIS	IL	1,156,894
5	LA SALLE	IL	1,110,867
6	LIVINGSTON	IL	1,068,545
7	HIDALGO	TX	1,065,578
8	CHAMPAIGN	IL	1,059,670
9	KOSSUTH	IA	1,054,704
10	KERN	CA	922,255
11	BUREAU	IL	911,384
12	HENRY	IL	855,768
13	POTTAWATTAMIE	IA	854,688
14	SIOUX	IA	837,364
15	VERMILION	IL	824,830
16	PLYMOUTH	IA	809,126
17	DANE	WI	782,492
18	LANCASTER	PA	777,502
19	LEE	IL	771,365
20	SANGAMON	IL	759,273
21	DE KALB	IL	755,257
22	OGLE	IL	753,105
23	TULARE	CA	752,778
24	POINSETT	AR	739,654
25	WOODBURY	IA	739,372
26	WHITESIDE	IL	736,858
27	LENAWEE	MI	728,639
28	WHARTON	TX	724,626
29	CLINTON	IA	721,476
30	WEBSTER	IA	709,563
31	ARKANSAS	AR	706,457
32	RENVILLE	MN	702,824
33	STODDARD	MO	691,171
34	BENTON	IA	685,490
35	CHRISTIAN	IL	668,475
36	REDWOOD	MN	668,023
37	KANKAKEE	IL	662,704
38	SAN JOAQUIN	CA	658,312
39	FAYETTE	IA	643,219
40	LOGAN	IL	639,282
41	FRANKLIN	IA	637,876
42	MARTIN	MN	629,518
43	WRIGHT	IA	629,396
44	JASPER	IA	627,846
45	HAMILTON	IA	625,735
46	CEDAR	IA	620,704
47	FARIBAULT	MN	619,455
48	HANCOCK	IA	618,992
49	BUENA VISTA	IA	617,537
50	POCAHONTAS	IA	617,170
51	MOREHOUSE	LA	615,571
52	WELD	CO	614,685
53	TAMA	IA	611,356
54	O BRIEN	IA	609,630
55	HARDIN	IA	607,766
56	MERCED	CA	606,545
57	FREEBORN	MN	601,787
58	JEFFERSON DAVIS	LA	596,464
59	CARROLL	IA	596,166
60	YAKIMA	WA	593,354
61	KNOX	IL	593,268

BOTTOM COUNTIES SHADED WHITE

RANK	COUNTY	STATE	VALUE
1	SAN FRANCISCO	CA	0
2	DISTRICT OF COLUMBIA	DC	0
3	FRANKLIN	FL	0
4	MONROE	FL	0
5	ORLEANS	LA	0
6	BALTIMORE CITY	MD	0
7	SUFFOLK	MA	0
8	KEWEENAW	MI	0
9	ST LOUIS CITY	MO	0
10	YELLOWSTONE NAT. PARK	MT	0
11	STOREY	NV	0
12	HUDSON	NJ	0
13	LOS ALAMOS	NM	0
14	HAMILTON	NY	0
15	DARE	NC	0
16	PHILADELPHIA	PA	0
17	ARLINGTON	VA	0
18	SHOSHONE	ID	1
19	ALPINE	CA	2
20	CARSON CITY	NV	10
21	GILPIN	CO	55
22	MARIPOSA	CA	73
23	NEW YORK CITY	NY	73
24	COOK	MN	82
25	HARLAN	KY	104
26	MINGO	WV	110
27	CLEAR CREEK	CO	133
28	BOONE	WV	133
29	DENVER	CO	138
30	PASSAIC	NJ	154
31	MINERAL	NV	164
32	MARTIN	KY	175
33	MC INTOSH	GA	176
34	CAMDEN	GA	193
35	UNION	NJ	214
36	GLYNN	GA	221
37	CRAWFORD	MI	221
38	NANTUCKET	MA	228
39	LOGAN	WV	242
40	DUKES	MA	255
41	ROSCOMMON	MI	264
42	CLARK	NV	266
43	PLUMAS	CA	270
44	RAMSEY	MN	304
45	DEL NORTE	CA	314
46	LAKE	MN	322
47	CHATTAHOOCHEE	GA	326
48	NEVADA	CA	333
49	LINCOLN	NV	345
50	LETCHER	KY	365
51	ESSEX	VT	367
52	ST BERNARD	LA	383
53	NYE	NV	402
54	CAMERON	PA	412
55	LESLIE	KY	427
56	HANCOCK	WV	462
57	ESMERALDA	NV	480
58	PERRY	KY	483
59	DOUGLAS	NV	492
60	BARAGA	MI	508
61	GOGEBIC	MI	517
62	LANDER	NV	537

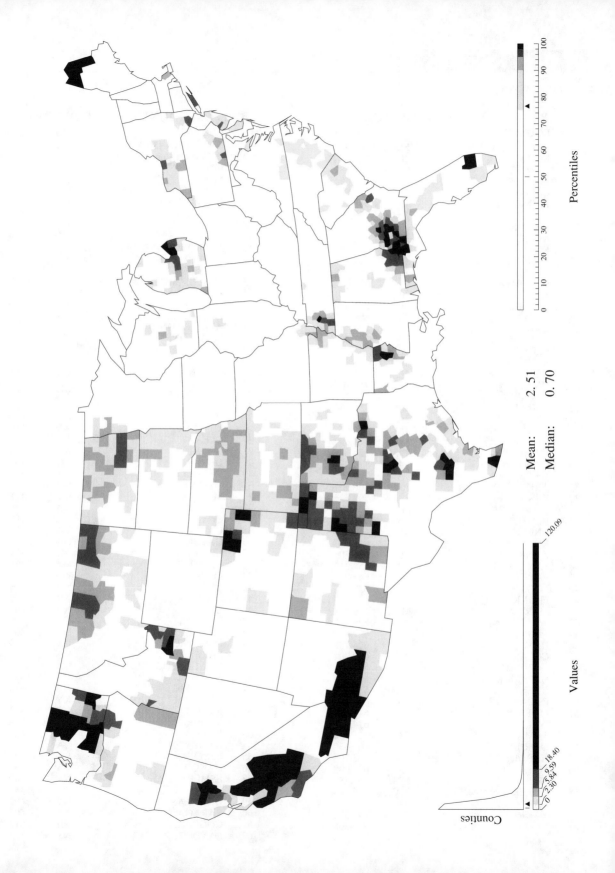

Mean: 2. 51

Median: 0. 70

Percentiles

Values

Counties

120.09

18.40
9.59
3.84
2.30
0

PESTICIDES: Potential Total Hazard Index

TOP COUNTIES SHADED BLACK

RANK	COUNTY	STATE	VALUE
1	KERN	CA	120.09
2	YAKIMA	WA	114.86
3	FRESNO	CA	109.06
4	STANISLAUS	CA	103.18
5	MERCED	CA	101.16
6	COMANCHE	TX	83.32
7	TULARE	CA	76.44
8	SAN JOAQUIN	CA	71.78
9	IMPERIAL	CA	63.61
10	BUTTE	CA	58.29
11	MADERA	CA	56.48
12	HIDALGO	TX	52.33
13	EASTLAND	TX	49.06
14	FRIO	TX	43.71
15	MONTEREY	CA	38.21
16	OKANOGAN	WA	38.04
17	SUTTER	CA	36.28
18	AROOSTOOK	ME	36.00
19	WILSON	TX	34.87
20	WHITMAN	WA	34.23
21	ATASCOSA	TX	30.45
22	CHELAN	WA	30.08
23	GRANT	WA	30.06
24	HURON	MI	29.89
25	MARICOPA	AZ	29.65
26	EARLY	GA	27.79
27	WELD	CO	26.36
28	KINGS	CA	25.09
29	WORTH	GA	24.39
30	GAINES	TX	24.02
31	CADDO	OK	23.91
32	PALM BEACH	FL	23.65
33	GLENN	CA	23.34
34	YUMA	CO	22.70
35	DOUGLAS	WA	22.69
36	YUMA	AZ	22.38
37	HENRY	AL	22.23
38	DEAF SMITH	TX	21.90
39	BENTON	WA	21.73
40	FANNIN	TX	21.52
41	YUBA	CA	21.30
42	TUSCOLA	MI	21.28
43	DOOLY	GA	21.09
44	CROCKETT	TN	20.61
45	RICHLAND	LA	20.53
46	TURNER	GA	20.42
47	PARMER	TX	20.33
48	TEXAS	OK	20.25
49	HOUSTON	AL	20.23
50	MITCHELL	GA	20.04
51	OCHILTREE	TX	19.80
52	BINGHAM	ID	19.65
53	PINAL	AZ	19.30
54	RIVERSIDE	CA	19.25
55	TERRELL	GA	18.84
56	JACKSON	FL	18.75
57	RANDOLPH	GA	18.67
58	LEE	GA	18.51
59	DECATUR	GA	18.49
60	MILLER	GA	18.46
61	FRANKLIN	LA	18.40

BOTTOM COUNTIES SHADED WHITE

RANK	COUNTY	STATE	VALUE
1	SAN FRANCISCO	CA	0.00
2	DISTRICT OF COLUMBIA	DC	0.00
3	FRANKLIN	FL	0.00
4	MONROE	FL	0.00
5	ORLEANS	LA	0.00
6	BALTIMORE CITY	MD	0.00
7	SUFFOLK	MA	0.00
8	KEWEENAW	MI	0.00
9	ST LOUIS CITY	MO	0.00
10	YELLOWSTONE NAT. PARK	MT	0.00
11	STOREY	NV	0.00
12	HUDSON	NJ	0.00
13	LOS ALAMOS	NM	0.00
14	HAMILTON	NY	0.00
15	DARE	NC	0.00
16	PHILADELPHIA	PA	0.00
17	ARLINGTON	VA	0.00
18	ALPINE	CA	0.00
19	SHOSHONE	ID	0.00
20	CARSON CITY	NV	0.00
21	PLUMAS	CA	0.00
22	GILPIN	CO	0.00
23	NEW YORK CITY	NY	0.00
24	COOK	MN	0.00
25	HARLAN	KY	0.00
26	MINGO	WV	0.00
27	CLEAR CREEK	CO	0.00
28	DENVER	CO	0.00
29	MARTIN	KY	0.00
30	BOONE	WV	0.00
31	GLYNN	GA	0.00
32	LOGAN	WV	0.00
33	RAMSEY	MN	0.00
34	SAGADAHOC	ME	0.00
35	LAKE	MN	0.00
36	CHATTAHOOCHEE	GA	0.00
37	LETCHER	KY	0.00
38	CAMDEN	GA	0.00
39	ESSEX	VT	0.00
40	MC INTOSH	GA	0.00
41	DUKES	MA	0.00
42	NANTUCKET	MA	0.00
43	PIKE	KY	0.00
44	MC DOWELL	WV	0.00
45	ST CHARLES	LA	0.00
46	LAKE	CO	0.00
47	MINERAL	MT	0.00
48	WYOMING	WV	0.00
49	CLAY	WV	0.00
50	SUMMIT	CO	0.00
51	MARION	TX	0.00
52	YORK	VA	0.00
53	SAN JUAN	CO	0.00
54	BELKNAP	NH	0.00
55	KNOTT	KY	0.00
56	SABINE	TX	0.00
57	TALIAFERRO	GA	0.01
58	PERRY	KY	0.01
59	PASSAIC	NJ	0.01
60	HANCOCK	WV	0.01
61	DE KALB	GA	0.01
62	WEBSTER	WV	0.01

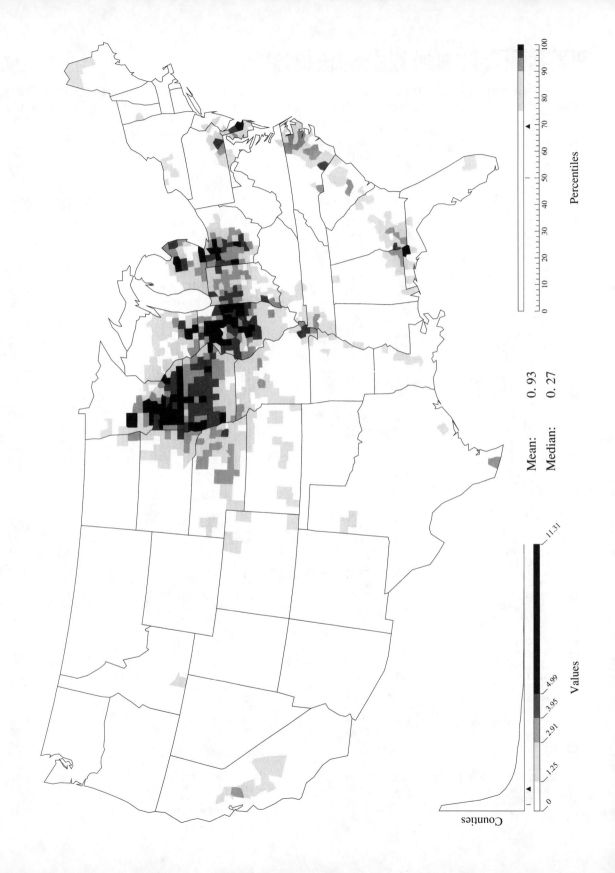

Mean: 0. 93

Median: 0. 27

Percentiles

Values

Counties

0   1.25   2.91 3.95 4.99   11.31

PESTICIDES: Potential Cancer Hazard Index

TOP COUNTIES SHADED BLACK

RANK	COUNTY	STATE	VALUE
1	MC LEAN	IL	11.31
2	IROQUOIS	IL	9.81
3	LA SALLE	IL	9.45
4	LIVINGSTON	IL	9.06
5	CHAMPAIGN	IL	8.98
6	RENVILLE	MN	8.79
7	REDWOOD	MN	8.62
8	LENAWEE	MI	8.42
9	MARTIN	MN	8.25
10	FARIBAULT	MN	8.00
11	KOSSUTH	IA	7.94
12	FREEBORN	MN	7.80
13	SAGINAW	MI	7.79
14	BUREAU	IL	7.74
15	NOBLES	MN	7.66
16	JACKSON	MN	7.62
17	STEARNS	MN	7.57
18	BLUE EARTH	MN	7.48
19	HENRY	IL	7.27
20	MOWER	MN	7.13
21	VERMILION	IL	6.99
22	SUSSEX	DE	6.94
23	MONROE	MI	6.79
24	COTTONWOOD	MN	6.59
25	LEE	IL	6.55
26	LYON	MN	6.54
27	YELLOW MEDICINE	MN	6.48
28	DE KALB	IL	6.43
29	SANGAMON	IL	6.42
30	OGLE	IL	6.41
31	POTTAWATTAMIE	IA	6.40
32	SIOUX	IA	6.33
33	WHITESIDE	IL	6.26
34	MURRAY	MN	6.23
35	FILLMORE	MN	6.20
36	DARKE	OH	6.11
37	JACKSON	FL	6.08
38	PLYMOUTH	IA	6.08
39	OTTER TAIL	MN	6.04
40	WOOD	OH	5.99
41	DANE	WI	5.79
42	BROWN	MN	5.67
43	KANDIYOHI	MN	5.67
44	SWIFT	MN	5.66
45	CHRISTIAN	IL	5.64
46	KANKAKEE	IL	5.58
47	WOODBURY	IA	5.56
48	GOODHUE	MN	5.48
49	CLINTON	IA	5.47
50	LOGAN	IL	5.42
51	WEBSTER	IA	5.33
52	MADISON	OH	5.30
53	HANCOCK	OH	5.28
54	GRATIOT	MI	5.23
55	SIBLEY	MN	5.17
56	BENTON	IA	5.16
57	SENECA	OH	5.15
58	PUTNAM	OH	5.15
59	ROCK	WI	5.09
60	KNOX	IL	5.02
61	MEEKER	MN	4.99

BOTTOM COUNTIES SHADED WHITE

NOTE: TOO MANY COUNTIES TO LIST
HAD ZERO VALUES FOR THIS MEASURE

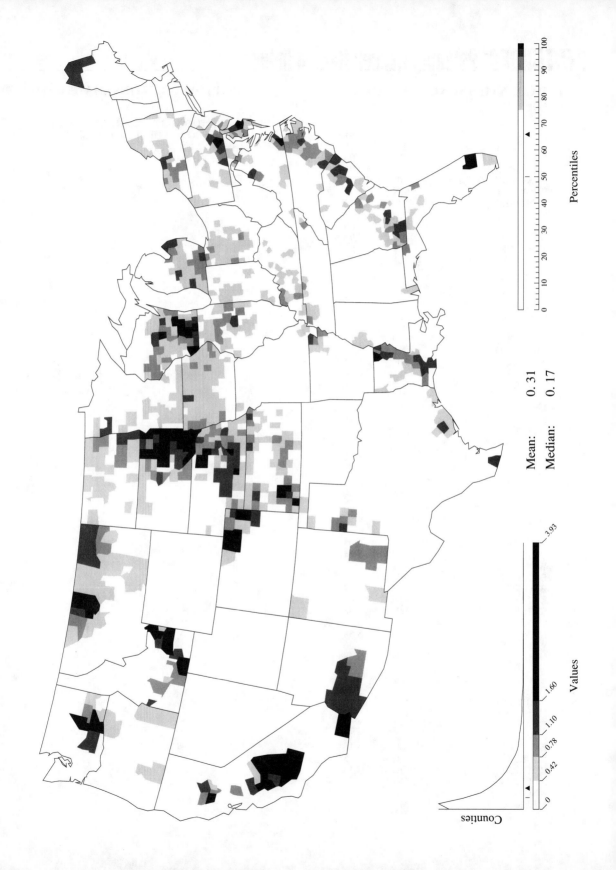

Mean: 0. 31

Median: 0. 17

Percentiles

Values

Counties

TOP COUNTIES SHADED BLACK

RANK	COUNTY	STATE	VALUE
1	WELD	CO	3.93
2	YUMA	CO	3.71
3	MINNEHAHA	SD	3.66
4	HUTCHINSON	SD	3.61
5	BINGHAM	ID	3.52
6	KERN	CA	3.48
7	FRESNO	CA	3.38
8	BROWN	SD	3.21
9	LINCOLN	SD	3.15
10	BROOKINGS	SD	3.14
11	SPINK	SD	3.14
12	TURNER	SD	3.06
13	LANCASTER	PA	2.86
14	DANE	WI	2.82
15	SOUTHAMPTON	VA	2.79
16	BEADLE	SD	2.74
17	GRANT	WA	2.58
18	UNION	SD	2.57
19	MC COOK	SD	2.51
20	CHARLES MIX	SD	2.48
21	LAKE	SD	2.45
22	MOODY	SD	2.40
23	BON HOMME	SD	2.35
24	KINGSBURY	SD	2.33
25	BONNEVILLE	ID	2.32
26	HILL	MT	2.25
27	CASSIA	ID	2.16
28	CHOUTEAU	MT	2.15
29	MADISON	ID	2.13
30	SUSSEX	DE	2.09
31	FRANKLIN	WA	2.08
32	PALM BEACH	FL	2.04
33	ROBERTS	SD	2.02
34	FREMONT	ID	1.96
35	DODGE	WI	1.95
36	CLAY	SD	1.92
37	ROCK	WI	1.92
38	TULARE	CA	1.91
39	GRANT	WI	1.84
40	YANKTON	SD	1.80
41	FINNEY	KS	1.77
42	CLARK	SD	1.74
43	PORTAGE	WI	1.73
44	DEUEL	SD	1.73
45	BENTON	WA	1.73
46	HAND	SD	1.70
47	COLUSA	CA	1.68
48	MOREHOUSE	LA	1.68
49	HAMLIN	SD	1.68
50	PHELPS	NE	1.67
51	IMPERIAL	CA	1.67
52	MORGAN	CO	1.66
53	COLUMBIA	WI	1.64
54	HANSON	SD	1.63
55	GRAY	KS	1.63
56	ANTELOPE	NE	1.63
57	STEVENS	KS	1.61
58	FOND DU LAC	WI	1.61
59	HOLT	NE	1.61
60	GRANT	SD	1.61
61	HAMILTON	NE	1.60

BOTTOM COUNTIES SHADED WHITE

NOTE: TOO MANY COUNTIES TO LIST
HAD ZERO VALUES FOR THIS MEASURE

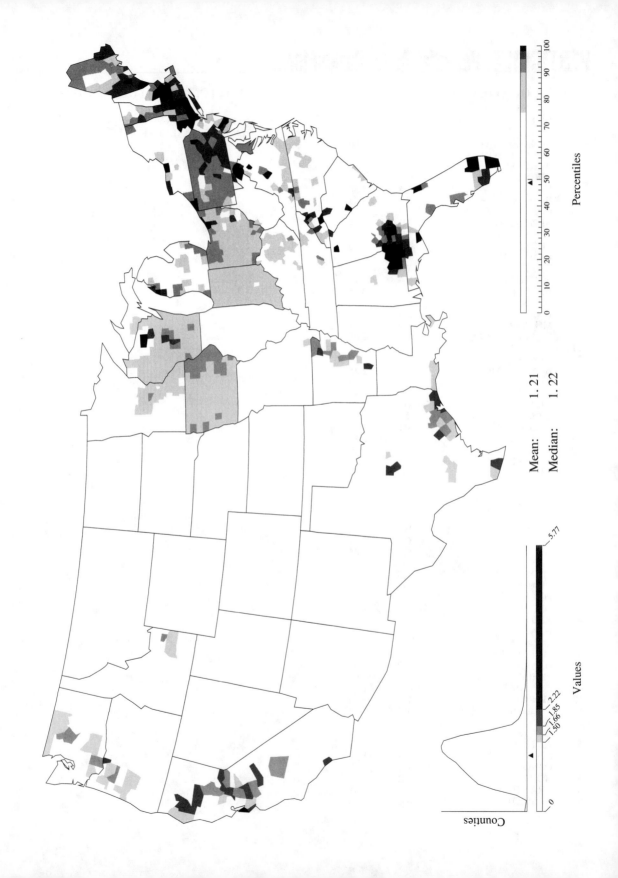

Mean: 1. 21
Median: 1. 22

Percentiles

Values

Counties

(POUNDS PER TREATED ACRE)

TOP COUNTIES SHADED BLACK

RANK	COUNTY	STATE	VALUE
1	SAN MATEO	CA	5.77
2	MORGAN	WV	4.46
3	ULSTER	NY	4.07
4	HENDERSON	NC	3.95
5	BERGEN	NJ	3.68
6	BERKELEY	WV	3.64
7	PUTNAM	NY	3.59
8	FREDERICK	VA	3.40
9	QUITMAN	GA	3.21
10	WESTCHESTER	NY	3.19
11	GILMER	GA	3.17
12	HAMPSHIRE	WV	3.04
13	HENRY	AL	2.93
14	WEBSTER	GA	2.93
15	DADE	FL	2.93
16	DALE	AL	2.92
17	YORK	ME	2.88
18	ROCKLAND	NY	2.88
19	POLK	NC	2.82
20	FAIRFIELD	CT	2.77
21	MIDDLESEX	MA	2.76
22	BARBOUR	AL	2.72
23	CUYAHOGA	OH	2.71
24	TURNER	GA	2.70
25	PIKE	AL	2.62
26	EDGEFIELD	SC	2.61
27	CLAY	GA	2.60
28	WAKULLA	FL	2.58
29	ATLANTIC	NJ	2.56
30	RANDOLPH	GA	2.55
31	MITCHELL	NC	2.55
32	MIDDLESEX	CT	2.54
33	ONEIDA	WI	2.54
34	WORCESTER	MA	2.52
35	NORFOLK	MA	2.52
36	NEW HAVEN	CT	2.51
37	WAYNE	NY	2.51
38	COFFEE	AL	2.50
39	LACKAWANNA	PA	2.50
40	PALM BEACH	FL	2.50
41	CAMDEN	NJ	2.49
42	HILLSBOROUGH	NH	2.46
43	ORANGE	NY	2.44
44	MILLER	GA	2.43
45	STEWART	GA	2.41
46	JEFFERSON	WV	2.41
47	EARLY	GA	2.41
48	HARTFORD	CT	2.39
49	ANDROSCOGGIN	ME	2.38
50	ST JOHNS	FL	2.38
51	TIFT	GA	2.34
52	NELSON	VA	2.33
53	BENZIE	MI	2.30
54	LAKE	OH	2.29
55	HOUSTON	AL	2.29
56	ERIE	PA	2.28
57	HAMPDEN	MA	2.27
58	WORTH	GA	2.27
59	LEE	GA	2.24
60	RAPPAHANNOCK	VA	2.23
61	CALHOUN	GA	2.22

BOTTOM COUNTIES SHADED WHITE

RANK	COUNTY	STATE	VALUE
1	SAN FRANCISCO	CA	0.00
2	DISTRICT OF COLUMBIA	DC	0.00
3	FRANKLIN	FL	0.00
4	MONROE	FL	0.00
5	ORLEANS	LA	0.00
6	BALTIMORE CITY	MD	0.00
7	SUFFOLK	MA	0.00
8	KEWEENAW	MI	0.00
9	ST LOUIS CITY	MO	0.00
10	YELLOWSTONE NAT. PARK	MT	0.00
11	STOREY	NV	0.00
12	HUDSON	NJ	0.00
13	LOS ALAMOS	NM	0.00
14	HAMILTON	NY	0.00
15	DARE	NC	0.00
16	PHILADELPHIA	PA	0.00
17	ARLINGTON	VA	0.00
18	NEVADA	CA	0.26
19	ESSEX	VT	0.33
20	TUOLUMNE	CA	0.40
21	WASHINGTON	VT	0.47
22	ARAPAHOE	CO	0.48
23	WILLIAMS	ND	0.49
24	MOFFAT	CO	0.49
25	MEAGHER	MT	0.49
26	PERSHING	NV	0.49
27	CAVALIER	ND	0.49
28	DIVIDE	ND	0.49
29	JUDITH BASIN	MT	0.49
30	POWELL	MT	0.50
31	MISSOULA	MT	0.50
32	SANDERS	MT	0.50
33	GRANITE	MT	0.50
34	GLACIER	MT	0.50
35	LINCOLN	CO	0.50
36	WHEATLAND	MT	0.50
37	RIO BLANCO	CO	0.50
38	MINERAL	MT	0.50
39	LEWIS AND CLARK	MT	0.50
40	SWEET GRASS	MT	0.50
41	LINCOLN	MT	0.50
42	ROUTT	CO	0.50
43	DEER LODGE	MT	0.50
44	BEAVERHEAD	MT	0.50
45	TETON	MT	0.50
46	SILVER BOW	MT	0.50
47	FERGUS	MT	0.50
48	PARK	MT	0.50
49	DOUGLAS	CO	0.50
50	PETROLEUM	MT	0.50
51	GILPIN	CO	0.50
52	SAN JUAN	CO	0.50
53	BREWSTER	TX	0.50
54	LOVING	TX	0.50
55	MC DOWELL	WV	0.50
56	MINGO	WV	0.50
57	MINERAL	CO	0.50
58	WINKLER	TX	0.50
59	CRANE	TX	0.50
60	CROCKETT	TX	0.50
61	EDWARDS	TX	0.50
62	HINSDALE	CO	0.50

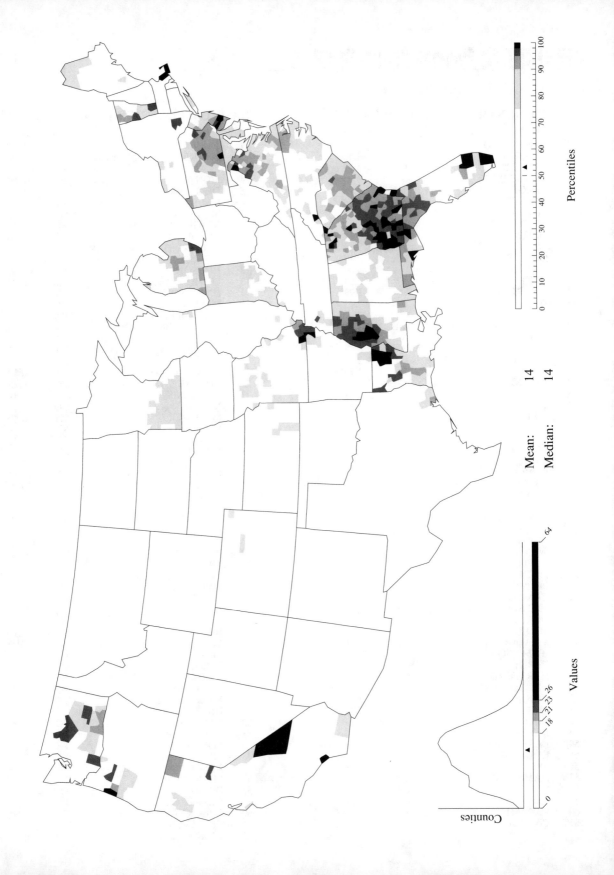

Percentiles

| | | | | | | | | | | |
|0|10|20|30|40|50|60|70|80|90|100|

▲ I

Mean: 14
Median: 14

Values

Counties

0   18 27 23 26   64

(PERCENT OF CROPLAND)

TOP COUNTIES SHADED BLACK

RANK	COUNTY	STATE	VALUE
1	CAMDEN	GA	64
2	INYO	CA	41
3	ATLANTIC	NJ	37
4	PALM BEACH	FL	35
5	MC INTOSH	GA	33
6	DAWSON	GA	33
7	RICHLAND	LA	31
8	DUNKLIN	MO	30
9	QUITMAN	GA	30
10	RABUN	GA	30
11	GILMER	GA	29
12	MOREHOUSE	LA	29
13	WEST CARROLL	LA	29
14	CLINCH	GA	29
15	ORANGE	CA	29
16	DADE	FL	29
17	RANDOLPH	GA	29
18	WEBSTER	GA	29
19	CLAY	GA	28
20	FRANKLIN	LA	28
21	DOOLY	GA	28
22	LIBERTY	GA	28
23	IRWIN	GA	28
24	BEN HILL	GA	28
25	SCHLEY	GA	27
26	TURNER	GA	27
27	TERRELL	GA	27
28	BAY	FL	27
29	CALHOUN	GA	27
30	PULASKI	GA	27
31	CALDWELL	LA	27
32	HENDERSON	NC	27
33	OUACHITA	LA	27
34	GRADY	GA	27
35	TIFT	GA	27
36	HOLMES	MS	27
37	SEMINOLE	GA	27
38	FREDERICK	VA	27
39	BARNSTABLE	MA	27
40	LEFLORE	MS	27
41	ADAMS	PA	27
42	GLOUCESTER	NJ	27
43	COLQUITT	GA	27
44	BROOKS	GA	27
45	BUTLER	MO	27
46	LEE	GA	26
47	SUNFLOWER	MS	26
48	LINN	OR	26
49	LEON	FL	26
50	TWIGGS	GA	26
51	WHITE	GA	26
52	PLYMOUTH	MA	26
53	SUMTER	GA	26
54	BAKER	GA	26
55	EARLY	GA	26
56	HUMPHREYS	MS	26
57	TOOMBS	GA	26
58	MILLER	GA	26
59	BLECKLEY	GA	26
60	MORGAN	GA	26
61	YAZOO	MS	26

BOTTOM COUNTIES SHADED WHITE

RANK	COUNTY	STATE	VALUE
1	SAN FRANCISCO	CA	0
2	DISTRICT OF COLUMBIA	DC	0
3	FRANKLIN	FL	0
4	MONROE	FL	0
5	ORLEANS	LA	0
6	BALTIMORE CITY	MD	0
7	SUFFOLK	MA	0
8	KEWEENAW	MI	0
9	ST LOUIS CITY	MO	0
10	YELLOWSTONE NAT. PARK	MT	0
11	STOREY	NV	0
12	HUDSON	NJ	0
13	LOS ALAMOS	NM	0
14	HAMILTON	NY	0
15	DARE	NC	0
16	PHILADELPHIA	PA	0
17	ARLINGTON	VA	0
18	CALAVERAS	CA	0
19	TUOLUMNE	CA	0
20	HUMBOLDT	CA	1
21	SHASTA	CA	1
22	DEL NORTE	CA	1
23	AMADOR	CA	1
24	NEVADA	CA	1
25	MENDOCINO	CA	1
26	CUSTER	SD	1
27	LAWRENCE	SD	1
28	SHANNON	SD	2
29	MEADE	SD	2
30	SHOSHONE	ID	2
31	ALPINE	CA	2
32	FALL RIVER	SD	2
33	HARDING	SD	2
34	LUCE	MI	2
35	GOGEBIC	MI	2
36	ROSCOMMON	MI	2
37	TODD	SD	2
38	BUTTE	SD	2
39	MARIN	CA	2
40	CRAWFORD	MI	3
41	ONTONAGON	MI	3
42	MELLETTE	SD	3
43	MINERAL	NV	3
44	ESMERALDA	NV	3
45	LINCOLN	NV	3
46	NYE	NV	3
47	ZIEBACH	SD	3
48	WASHOE	NV	3
49	LANDER	NV	3
50	SAN LUIS OBISPO	CA	3
51	BARAGA	MI	3
52	CARSON CITY	NV	3
53	PENNINGTON	SD	3
54	GUERNSEY	OH	3
55	ELKO	NV	3
56	BREWSTER	TX	3
57	CRANE	TX	3
58	LOVING	TX	3
59	WINKLER	TX	3
60	CROCKETT	TX	3
61	TERRELL	TX	3
62	JEFF DAVIS	TX	3

found traces of toxic explosives, incriminating the nearby Kirkland Air Force Base. Many residents of this low-income, minority community could not afford to hook up to the Albuquerque municipal water system. So with the help of the South West Organizing Project, they formed the Mountainview Advisory Council (MAC) and demanded a concrete role in planning the air force base cleanup. MAC members secured a congressional hearing on groundwater contamination in the area, and so ensured that the EPA and the air force would take their demands seriously. Free water testing, expanded city water and sewer lines, and affordable hookup rates soon followed.[44]

In the backwoods of Tennessee, residents of Hardeman County complained to the county health department in 1977 that their water smelled and tasted like chemicals. They suspected the 300,000-barrel pesticide waste dump owned by the Chicago-based Velsicol Chemical Corporation, but no one knew much about it. The department conducted routine bacteriological tests and deemed the water safe, telling local families to "go ahead and drink it." But many residents continued to suffer from headaches, nausea, fatigue, and skin rashes, so they petitioned the state for additional testing. Grim news came soon: a dozen chemicals, half of them carcinogens, were detected in the water. The state agency told the families not to drink the water. Many feared it was too late. One child was born with a serious birth defect, and after that none of the local couples were able to conceive a child for over four years. A medical study also found liver damage among those who drank the water. "Who knows," wonders Nell Graham, a licensed nurse who was one of those affected, "in twenty years my kids may have cancer. I may never have grandchildren. I may not even live to see my kids grown."[45]

The sources of toxic water contamination are myriad and can turn up in the most unexpected places. Abandoned dumps, military sites, municipal landfills, toxic waste pits, underground tanks and injection wells, pesticide applications, mining and oil exploration sites, transportation accidents, and even septic tanks and hazardous household wastes can leak into water supplies that tap rivers, streams, lakes, and underground water sources (called aquifers). Officials in Nassau County, New York, for example, estimate that 83,000 gallons of organic chemicals from hazardous household products end up in its sole-source groundwater supply each year.[46] And many water supplies can become polluted even if the original sources are clean. The EPA estimates that more than a quarter-million children are exposed to lead in drinking water at levels high enough to impair their mental and physical development. The source: lead in plumbing.[47]

No part of the country—urban or rural—is spared. This is partially due to the natural hydrologic cycle by which many air pollutants that are brought down with rain contaminate lakes and streams. Rain also causes pollutants left in or on the land to seep into water sources, as when pesticides are found in streams or when chemicals in landfills percolate into groundwater. Hazardous waste landfill technologies, in fact, must do as much to keep the rain out as they do to keep the wastes in! If there is no rainwater, leakage is rare. Contaminated groundwater often pollutes surface waters because many streams and aquifers are interconnected. A third of our nation's stream flow is from groundwater.[48] Eventually much of this contaminated water ends up in our nation's estuaries and wetlands—the most fertile sources of wildlife.

About half of the population gets its water from underground sources and the other half from surface waters. Some cities, such as New York, depend entirely on surface water sources such as reservoirs and rivers. Others, such as Memphis and Miami, depend almost entirely on groundwater supplies. Over 80 percent of the population in Nebraska, South Dakota, and Iowa depends on groundwater.[49] In rural areas, as many as 97 percent of Americans depend on underground water sources. Rural Americans with private wells are expected to carry the brunt of the costs of groundwater contamination.[50] Public supplies also are at risk: the EPA's latest survey found that community water systems were two and a half times more likely to register pesticides above minimum reporting limits than were private rural wells.[51]

Data on toxic contamination of ground and surface waters are particularly scanty (also noted in chapter 4 with respect to industrial water discharges).[52] We know that over 180,000 tons of toxic chemicals are discharged directly into surface waters and that 500 million tons of hazardous wastes are dumped into the ground, two-thirds by deep-well injection.[53] But we do not know exactly what happens to these wastes once they enter ground and surface waters. Moreover, nonpoint sources of water pollution, such as pesticides, are rapidly emerging as potentially even more severe water polluters than point sources such as landfills, and there is even less information on where these nonpoint pollutants have caused the most trouble.[54] The latest Department of Agriculture estimates indicate that areas with the greatest potential groundwater contamination from agricultural pesticides include the San Joaquin Valley in California, western Texas and Oklahoma, Kansas and eastern Nebraska, much of the Midwest, parts of Pennsylvania, and the entire southeastern coastal plain from Florida to southern New Jersey.[55]

The following five maps indicate various aspects of where people and the environment may be most vulnerable to water quality problems.

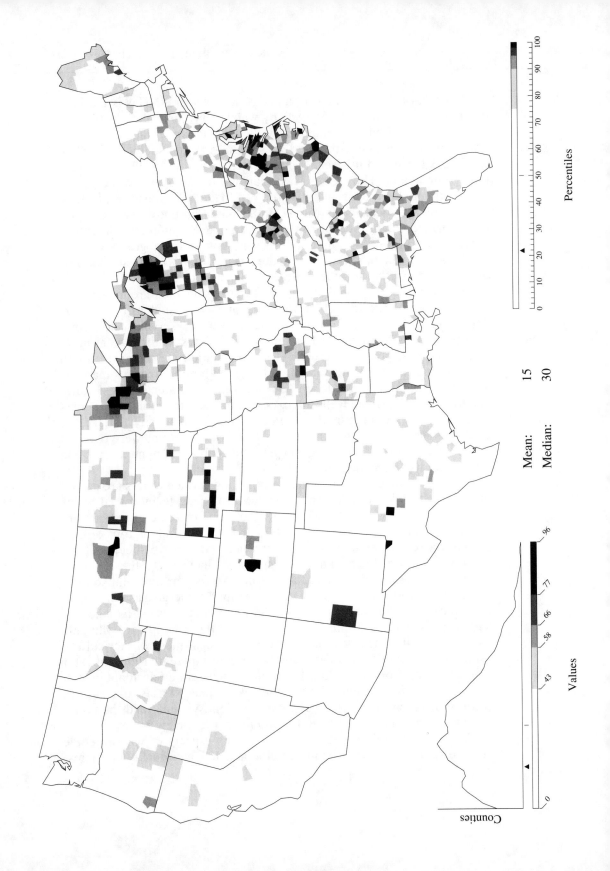

Percentiles

Mean: 15

Median: 30

Values

Counties

0 43 58 66 77 96

(PERCENT OF TOTAL)

TOP COUNTIES SHADED BLACK

RANK	COUNTY	STATE	VALUE
1	MATHEWS	VA	96
2	AMELIA	VA	95
3	MC PHERSON	NE	95
4	GLASSCOCK	TX	95
5	BANNER	NE	94
6	LOUP	NE	94
7	KING AND QUEEN	VA	93
8	ROSCOMMON	MI	93
9	LAKE	MI	92
10	MONTMORENCY	MI	92
11	OSCODA	MI	91
12	POWHATAN	VA	91
13	CHARLES CITY	VA	91
14	PRAIRIE	MT	89
15	OGEMAW	MI	88
16	ARTHUR	NE	87
17	CUMBERLAND	VA	86
18	KALKASKA	MI	86
19	ALCONA	MI	86
20	GLADWIN	MI	86
21	QUEEN ANNES	MD	85
22	LOVING	TX	84
23	MISSAUKEE	MI	84
24	MARQUETTE	WI	84
25	GLOUCESTER	VA	84
26	WAUSHARA	WI	84
27	LEELANAU	MI	83
28	BUCKINGHAM	VA	83
29	GOOCHLAND	VA	83
30	BUCHANAN	VA	82
31	CRAWFORD	MI	82
32	MAGOFFIN	KY	82
33	HEARD	GA	82
34	OZARK	MO	82
35	MIDDLESEX	VA	82
36	LOUISA	VA	81
37	CASWELL	NC	81
38	PENDER	NC	80
39	CASS	MN	80
40	BURNETT	WI	80
41	NEWAYGO	MI	79
42	KNOTT	KY	79
43	LAFAYETTE	FL	79
44	RICHMOND	VA	79
45	ADAMS	WI	79
46	GEAUGA	OH	79
47	PAMLICO	NC	78
48	AITKIN	MN	78
49	CLARE	MI	78
50	CURRITUCK	NC	78
51	FLUVANNA	VA	78
52	GILCHRIST	FL	78
53	ELLIOTT	KY	78
54	PARK	CO	78
55	HAYES	NE	77
56	LIVINGSTON	MI	77
57	LAGRANGE	IN	77
58	OTSEGO	MI	77
59	OGLETHORPE	GA	77
60	APPOMATTOX	VA	77
61	NORTHUMBERLAND	VA	77

BOTTOM COUNTIES SHADED WHITE

RANK	COUNTY	STATE	VALUE
1	YELLOWSTONE NAT. PARK	MT	0
2	LOS ALAMOS	NM	0
3	ST BERNARD	LA	0
4	SUFFOLK	MA	0
5	DISTRICT OF COLUMBIA	DC	0
6	ST LOUIS CITY	MO	0
7	BALTIMORE CITY	MD	0
8	SAN FRANCISCO	CA	0
9	ARLINGTON	VA	0
10	JEFFERSON	LA	0
11	NEW YORK CITY	NY	0
12	HUDSON	NJ	0
13	PHILADELPHIA	PA	0
14	LAFOURCHE	LA	0
15	DENVER	CO	0
16	TERREBONNE	LA	0
17	ORANGE	CA	0
18	EMERY	UT	0
19	CARBON	UT	0
20	ST CHARLES	LA	0
21	NASSAU	NY	0
22	LOS ANGELES	CA	0
23	UNION	NJ	0
24	DE KALB	GA	0
25	ORLEANS	LA	0
26	SAN MATEO	CA	0
27	JACKSON	MO	0
28	ROCKWALL	TX	0
29	SAN JUAN	CO	0
30	ESSEX	NJ	0
31	SHELBY	TN	0
32	PLAQUEMINES	LA	0
33	DALLAS	TX	0
34	FAYETTE	KY	0
35	ALAMEDA	CA	0
36	WYANDOTTE	KS	0
37	ST JAMES	LA	1
38	WAYNE	MI	1
39	WICHITA	TX	1
40	HAMILTON	OH	1
41	JOHNSON	KS	1
42	ST JOHN THE BAPTIST	LA	1
43	WASHINGTON	UT	1
44	KENTON	KY	1
45	ST LOUIS	MO	1
46	SALT LAKE	UT	1
47	CUYAHOGA	OH	1
48	WEBB	TX	1
49	MULTNOMAH	OR	1
50	VENTURA	CA	1
51	PINELLAS	FL	1
52	SAN DIEGO	CA	1
53	MARIN	CA	1
54	MARICOPA	AZ	1
55	CAMPBELL	KY	1
56	MUSCOGEE	GA	1
57	BROWARD	FL	1
58	JEFFERSON	KY	1
59	EAST BATON ROUGE	LA	1
60	COOK	IL	1
61	TULSA	OK	1
62	SANTA CLARA	CA	1

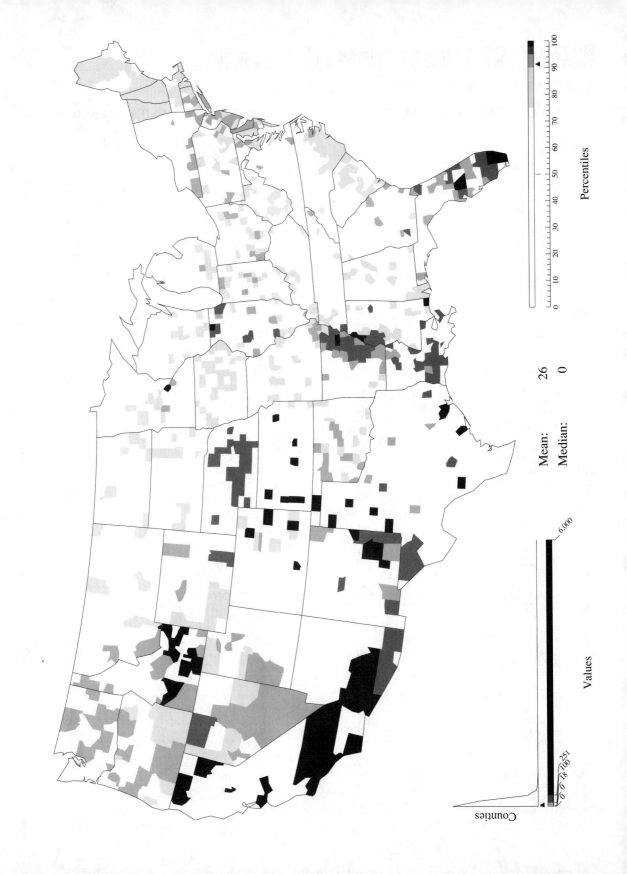

Percentiles

Mean: 26

Median: 0

Values

Counties

6,000

251
100
18
0   0

(MILLON GALLONS PER DAY)

TOP COUNTIES SHADED BLACK

RANK	COUNTY	STATE	VALUE
1	KERN	CA	6,000
2	MERCED	CA	3,750
3	GRANT	KS	3,501
4	KEARNY	KS	3,501
5	JEROME	ID	3,000
6	STAFFORD	KS	1,851
7	THOMAS	KS	1,851
8	WICHITA	KS	1,851
9	SUTTER	CA	1,750
10	MINIDOKA	ID	1,500
11	POWER	ID	1,500
12	LINCOLN	ID	1,350
13	MARICOPA	AZ	1,251
14	LOS ANGELES	CA	1,198
15	HENNEPIN	MN	1,175
16	MORGAN	CO	1,003
17	KIT CARSON	CO	1,000
18	SANTA CRUZ	CA	750
19	PINAL	AZ	651
20	ARMSTRONG	TX	600
21	GAINES	TX	600
22	HARTLEY	TX	600
23	LUBBOCK	TX	600
24	SANTA CLARA	CA	599
25	CASSIA	ID	599
26	COAHOMA	MS	550
27	JACKSON	MS	550
28	TUNICA	MS	550
29	HARRIS	TX	451
30	JACKSON	TX	451
31	ZAVALA	TX	451
32	HARVEY	KS	426
33	SHAWNEE	KS	426
34	BROWARD	FL	400
35	DADE	FL	400
36	POLK	FL	400
37	YUMA	AZ	375
38	ALAMOSA	CO	353
39	BENT	CO	350
40	WINNEBAGO	IL	350
41	ELMORE	ID	324
42	TEXAS	OK	300
43	LASSEN	CA	300
44	ORANGE	CA	300
45	SAN BERNARDINO	CA	300
46	SAN DIEGO	CA	300
47	SANTA BARBARA	CA	300
48	SISKIYOU	CA	300
49	VENTURA	CA	300
50	ADA	ID	300
51	BONNEVILLE	ID	300
52	BUTTE	ID	300
53	CANYON	ID	300
54	FREMONT	ID	300
55	JEFFERSON	ID	300
56	POINSETT	AR	253
57	CHAVES	NM	251
58	CURRY	NM	251

BOTTOM COUNTIES SHADED WHITE

NOTE: TOO MANY COUNTIES TO LIST
HAD ZERO VALUES FOR THIS MEASURE

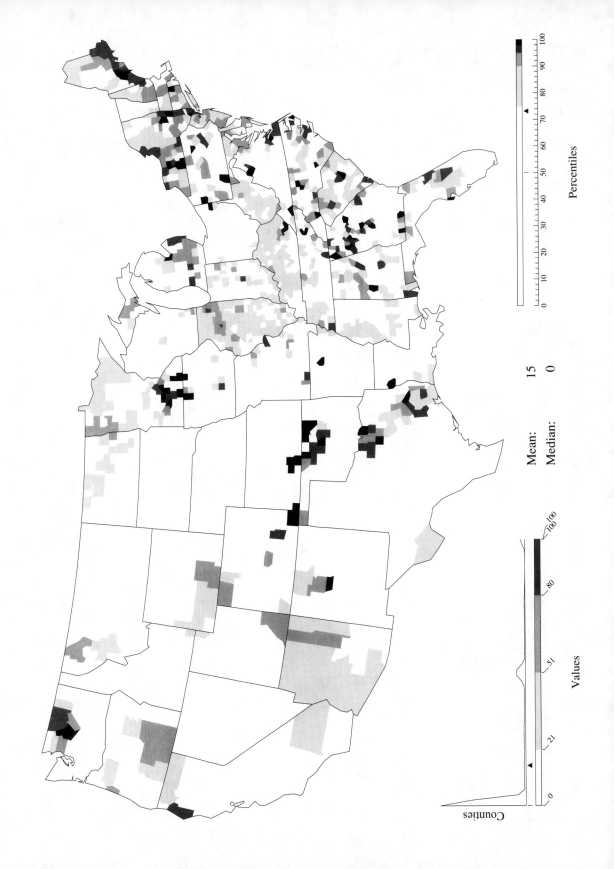

Percentiles

Mean: 15

Median: 0

Values

Counties

WATER QUALITY:
Miles of Impaired Rivers and Streams
(PERCENT OF TOTAL)

BOTTOM COUNTIES SHADED WHITE

NOTE: TOO MANY COUNTIES TO LIST
HAD ZERO VALUES FOR THIS MEASURE

TOP COUNTIES SHADED BLACK

RANK	COUNTY	STATE	VALUE
1	WINDHAM	CT	100
2	CHATTOOGA	GA	100
3	WALKER	GA	100
4	MITCHELL	IA	100
5	MORTON	KS	100
6	DE SOTO	LA	100
7	BALTIMORE CITY	MD	100
8	SIBLEY	MN	100
9	COLUMBIA	NY	100
10	ONTARIO	NY	100
11	SCHENECTADY	NY	100
12	STEUBEN	NY	100
13	DARE	NC	100
14	DAVIE	NC	100
15	FORSYTH	NC	100
16	HOKE	NC	100
17	MAHONING	OH	100
18	LOGAN	OK	100
19	MERCER	PA	100
20	SULLIVAN	PA	100
21	ANGELINA	TX	100
22	ROCKINGHAM	VA	100
23	HALE	AL	100
24	STONE	AR	100
25	BACA	CO	100
26	PINELLAS	FL	100
27	CLAYTON	GA	100
28	DE KALB	GA	100
29	DOUGLAS	GA	100
30	GRADY	GA	100
31	HOUSTON	GA	100
32	JONES	GA	100
33	LOWNDES	GA	100
34	OGLETHORPE	GA	100
35	PAULDING	GA	100
36	KOSSUTH	IA	100
37	BARBER	KS	100
38	KIOWA	KS	100
39	PRATT	KS	100
40	LETCHER	KY	100
41	PERRY	KY	100
42	ANDROSCOGGIN	ME	100
43	KENNEBEC	ME	100
44	SAGADAHOC	ME	100
45	BAY	MI	100
46	BROWN	MN	100
47	DODGE	MN	100
48	FARIBAULT	MN	100
49	LE SUEUR	MN	100
50	MOWER	MN	100
51	SCOTT	MN	100
52	HUDSON	NJ	100
53	BERNALILLO	NM	100
54	ALBANY	NY	100
55	ROCKLAND	NY	100
56	HENDERSON	NC	100
57	ALFALFA	OK	100
58	KAY	OK	100
59	OSAGE	OK	100
60	SOMERSET	PA	100
61	CLARENDON	SC	100
62	GRAINGER	TN	100
63	JEFFERSON	TN	100
64	GRAYSON	TX	100
65	TARRANT	TX	100
66	SURRY	VA	100
67	WASHINGTON	VA	100
68	CHELAN	WA	100

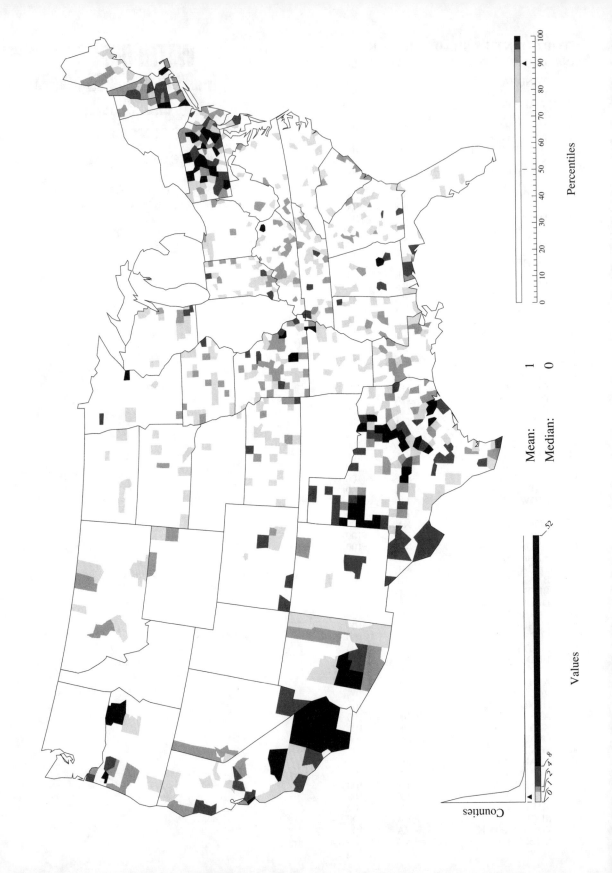

Mean: 1

Median: 0

Percentiles

Values

Counties

WATER QUALITY: Public Supply Violations

TOP COUNTIES SHADED BLACK

RANK	COUNTY	STATE	VALUE
1	HARRIS	TX	52
2	CAMBRIA	PA	42
3	LUZERNE	PA	36
4	MC LENNAN	TX	33
5	BERKSHIRE	MA	26
6	SAN BERNARDINO	CA	24
7	CLINTON	PA	19
8	ELLIS	TX	19
9	KINGS	CA	18
10	CENTRE	PA	17
11	LUBBOCK	TX	17
12	RIVERSIDE	CA	16
13	TULARE	CA	16
14	FAYETTE	PA	16
15	HAYS	TX	16
16	WILLIAMSON	TX	16
17	BLAIR	PA	14
18	NORTHUMBERLAND	PA	14
19	YAMHILL	OR	13
20	LEHIGH	PA	13
21	MC KEAN	PA	13
22	MARICOPA	AZ	12
23	FAIRFIELD	CT	12
24	CAMERON	PA	12
25	CUMBERLAND	PA	12
26	CORYELL	TX	12
27	DALLAS	TX	12
28	HALE	TX	12
29	LAMB	TX	12
30	PLYMOUTH	MA	11
31	BERKS	PA	11
32	LACKAWANNA	PA	11
33	HILL	TX	11
34	SAN DIEGO	CA	10
35	CARLTON	MN	10
36	UNION	OR	10
37	TIOGA	PA	10
38	MONTGOMERY	AL	9
39	CARTER	KY	9
40	PARMER	TX	9
41	SANTA CRUZ	CA	8
42	DUNKLIN	MO	8
43	ST FRANCOIS	MO	8
44	TEXAS	MO	8
45	UMATILLA	OR	8
46	JEFFERSON	PA	8
47	LANCASTER	PA	8
48	AUSTIN	TX	8
49	COCHRAN	TX	8
50	CONCHO	TX	8
51	CROSBY	TX	8
52	GAINES	TX	8
53	GRAYSON	TX	8
54	HOCKLEY	TX	8
55	HUNT	TX	8
56	JOHNSON	TX	8
57	MC CULLOCH	TX	8
58	YOAKUM	TX	8

BOTTOM COUNTIES SHADED WHITE

NOTE: TOO MANY COUNTIES TO LIST
HAD ZERO VALUES FOR THIS MEASURE

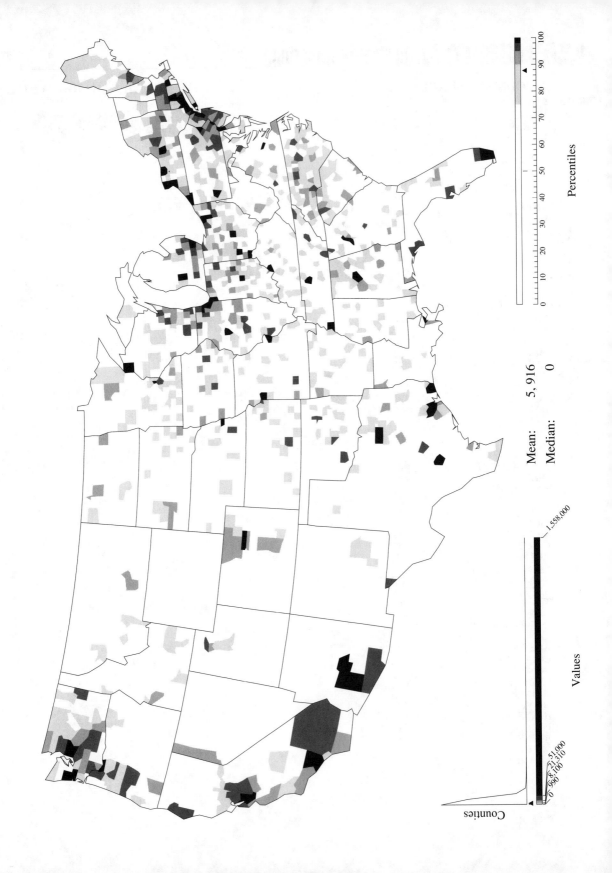

Mean: 5, 916

Median: 0

Percentiles

Values

Counties

1,558,000

51,000
21,310
8,100
990
0

(MILLON GALLONS PER DAY)

TOP COUNTIES SHADED BLACK

RANK	COUNTY	STATE	VALUE
1	NEW YORK CITY	NY	1,558,000
2	COOK	IL	1,335,400
3	LOS ANGELES	CA	773,920
4	WAYNE	MI	725,120
5	JEFFERSON	TX	352,230
6	ESSEX	NJ	267,691
7	KING	WA	256,300
8	ERIE	NY	232,080
9	MIDDLESEX	NJ	230,150
10	RAMSEY	MN	206,000
11	ALLEGHENY	PA	205,060
12	BALTIMORE CITY	MD	204,000
13	DALLAS	TX	203,920
14	PHILADELPHIA	PA	200,000
15	NORTHAMPTON	PA	186,400
16	ORLEANS	LA	165,100
17	BEXAR	TX	154,118
18	ST LOUIS CITY	MO	152,500
19	ST LOUIS	MO	149,075
20	FRANKLIN	OH	144,500
21	ALAMEDA	CA	142,140
22	UNION	NJ	141,750
23	ADAMS	CO	141,490
24	HAMILTON	OH	140,300
25	SHELBY	TN	140,000
26	SANTA CLARA	CA	125,200
27	FULTON	GA	124,960
28	CUYAHOGA	OH	117,870
29	MARICOPA	AZ	117,500
30	NEW CASTLE	DE	108,500
31	MARION	IN	106,500
32	HUDSON	NJ	106,210
33	LAKE	IN	105,000
34	FAIRFIELD	CT	104,300
35	NIAGARA	NY	103,600
36	PROVIDENCE	RI	103,440
37	SAN FRANCISCO	CA	101,000
38	JEFFERSON	KY	96,560
39	SUMMIT	OH	96,313
40	WESTCHESTER	NY	93,900
41	JACKSON	MO	92,700
42	MULTNOMAH	OR	91,750
43	ONONDAGA	NY	91,520
44	JEFFERSON	AL	86,250
45	HARRIS	TX	83,140
46	BERGEN	NJ	82,090
47	MONROE	NY	81,914
48	NEW HAVEN	CT	78,100
49	NASSAU	NY	73,570
50	TARRANT	TX	72,000
51	MONTGOMERY	OH	67,760
52	HARTFORD	CT	67,260
53	DOUGLAS	NE	61,200
54	DOUGLAS	WI	60,500
55	DAVIDSON	TN	59,650
56	KENT	MI	59,300
57	DADE	FL	59,100
58	HENRICO	VA	59,000
59	ERIE	PA	57,950
60	GRAYS HARBOR	WA	52,950
61	PEORIA	IL	51,000

BOTTOM COUNTIES SHADED WHITE

NOTE: TOO MANY COUNTIES TO LIST
HAD ZERO VALUES FOR THIS MEASURE

To get a fuller picture, you should also look at the maps of industrial water discharges, hazardous waste facilities, and pesticide usage. The first map shows where the largest percentage of houses are served by private wells. Northern Wisconsin and Michigan, as well as much of the Southeast stand out. The second indicates where the largest volumes of groundwater are actually used, highlighting many western counties, counties bordering the Mississippi River, and southern Florida.

The third map indicates where rivers and streams may be most severely impaired. It measures the percentage of river miles that cannot fully support their designated uses. This map must be interpreted carefully since it does not measure the actual degree of contamination. Designated uses can range from fishing and swimming to industrial. So if a stream is designated for industrial use, it might not be highlighted in the map even if it is severely polluted.[56]

The fourth map indicates the location of the most frequent violations of public water supply standards. Texas, Pennsylvania, Southern California, and western Massachusetts stand out in this map, although it appears that a number of states, such as Illinois, New York, Oklahoma, Washington, and possibly Idaho and Utah, may not have reported, since there are no shaded counties there. A recent EPA study found that during the early 1980s, contaminated water supplies accounted for more outbreaks of disease than in any other period since the Great Depression, and that the number of waterborne diseases may be 25 times reported incidence. The National Wildlife Federation is suing the EPA for negligence, alleging that the agency is exposing some 30 million Americans to potentially contaminated public water systems.[57] Sewage, of course, is a large part of the problem and is often contaminated with toxic chemicals. The last map indicates where sewage systems discharge the greatest quantities of human wastes, though the concentrations of toxins in these outflows remain largely unknown.

AIR QUALITY

Autopsies performed on over 100 Los Angeles youths who were killed by car accidents and homicides in 1988 revealed that 4 out of 5 had notable lung tissue abnormalities and nearly one-third had severe lesions in the lung. Dr. Russell Sherwin, the pathologist in charge, said they were simply "running out of lung."[58] Smoking and viral infections could be responsible for some of the lung damage, but Dr. Sherwin concluded that air pollution, and in particular the high level of ozone, was the principal culprit. The lesions were similar to those found in tests of ozone's effects on laboratory animals.[59]

Los Angeles residents are exposed to the worst air pollution in the nation. The county ranks in the top percentile in eight of the nine air quality maps, and tops the list for four. In addition to thousands of factories and other stationary sources, there are 10 million motor vehicles in the Los Angeles basin; 12.5 million people drive in the area, and population growth during the 1980s increased regional driving by 50 percent.[60] In response to choking smog in Los Angeles, the state's South Coast Air Quality Management District has promulgated the most severe air quality regulations in the nation, restricting everyday activities—from barbecuing to using gas-powered lawn mowers to parking—and requiring technological changes aimed at eliminating most of their emissions.[61] Yet many environmental activists think even these draconian measures are inadequate. Eric Mann, director of the Labor/Community Strategy Center, spells out why: "In virtually every public health report the conclusion is inescapable. The air in Los Angeles is slowly killing us."[62] Despite the 90 percent phaseout of leaded gasoline through the late 1980s, a quarter of the children in the Los Angeles area still have lead blood levels high enough to cause learning disabilities and behavioral problems.[63]

More than 120 million people across the country live in counties that fail to meet air quality standards.[64] The American Lung Association estimates that air pollution results in $40 billion of medical care, lost work days, and premature death each year.[65] Smog aggravates asthma and other respiratory diseases, inflames the air passages even of healthy children and adults, and has been increasingly linked to permanent lung damage through irreversible stiffening of lung tissue. And respiratory diseases are not the only toll: air pollution has been linked with heart disease, cancer, neurological disorders, and weakened immune systems. The strongest evidence of the health impact of ambient air pollution comes from the sudden surges in mortality rates during acute air pollution episodes, such as the famous incidents in Donora, Pennsylvania, during 1948 (killing 60 people), the London fog of 1952 (killing 4,000 people), and in New York in 1953 and 1962 (which helped lead to the passage of the U.S. Clean Air Act of 1963).[66]

Nonindustrial sources often emit as much—if not more—toxic pollution to the air as factories. The EPA data used in the following maps, for example, indicate that urban sources of air pollution such as road vehicles, fuel combustion, dry cleaners (and other solvent users), and emissions from sewage treatment plants may release more than twice as

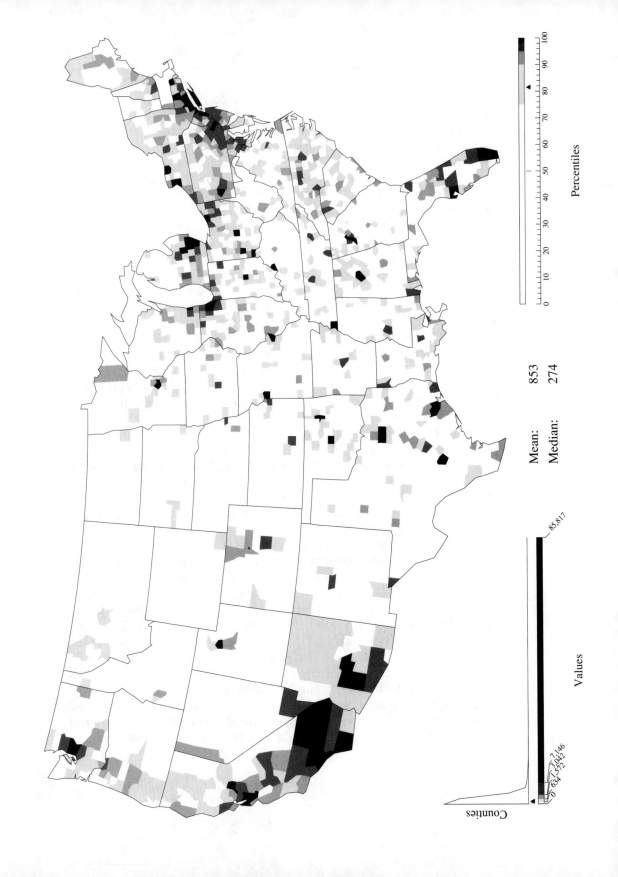

Percentiles

Mean: 853

Median: 274

Values

Counties

85,817

7,146
3,042
1,572
634

0

(TONS PER YEAR)

TOP COUNTIES SHADED BLACK

RANK	COUNTY	STATE	VALUE
1	LOS ANGELES	CA	85,817
2	COOK	IL	62,213
3	NEW YORK CITY	NY	51,902
4	HARRIS	TX	34,172
5	WAYNE	MI	26,693
6	DALLAS	TX	26,601
7	SANTA CLARA	CA	22,833
8	CUYAHOGA	OH	20,536
9	ORANGE	CA	20,449
10	SAN DIEGO	CA	18,789
11	DADE	FL	18,405
12	MARICOPA	AZ	17,898
13	ALLEGHENY	PA	14,799
14	ALAMEDA	CA	14,251
15	NASSAU	NY	13,911
16	HENNEPIN	MN	13,737
17	KING	WA	13,558
18	OAKLAND	MI	13,308
19	PHILADELPHIA	PA	13,184
20	TARRANT	TX	12,694
21	SUFFOLK	NY	12,335
22	BERGEN	NJ	11,761
23	BROWARD	FL	11,751
24	HAMILTON	OH	11,215
25	ERIE	NY	10,932
26	FAIRFIELD	CT	10,925
27	HARTFORD	CT	10,500
28	BALTIMORE CITY	MD	10,475
29	ST LOUIS CITY	MO	10,453
30	MARION	IN	10,171
31	BEXAR	TX	10,032
32	ESSEX	NJ	9,979
33	FRANKLIN	OH	9,944
34	ST LOUIS	MO	9,887
35	NEW HAVEN	CT	9,833
36	JACKSON	MO	9,550
37	FULTON	GA	9,417
38	MONTGOMERY	PA	9,331
39	SHELBY	TN	9,284
40	MILWAUKEE	WI	9,069
41	MACOMB	MI	9,062
42	OKLAHOMA	OK	8,598
43	UNION	NJ	8,589
44	MIDDLESEX	NJ	8,472
45	DU PAGE	IL	8,414
46	JEFFERSON	KY	8,367
47	WESTCHESTER	NY	8,351
48	SAN BERNARDINO	CA	8,349
49	MONTGOMERY	OH	8,260
50	TULSA	OK	8,194
51	MONROE	NY	8,048
52	PROVIDENCE	RI	8,044
53	JEFFERSON	AL	7,964
54	PINELLAS	FL	7,898
55	HILLSBOROUGH	FL	7,846
56	DENVER	CO	7,651
57	SALT LAKE	UT	7,531
58	GENESEE	MI	7,509
59	SAN MATEO	CA	7,354
60	SACRAMENTO	CA	7,290
61	RAMSEY	MN	7,146

BOTTOM COUNTIES SHADED WHITE

RANK	COUNTY	STATE	VALUE
1	NANTUCKET	MA	0
2	DUKES	MA	0
3	YELLOWSTONE NAT. PARK	MT	1
4	BARNSTABLE	MA	2
5	HINSDALE	CO	5
6	PETROLEUM	MT	6
7	MC PHERSON	NE	6
8	ARTHUR	NE	6
9	CAMAS	ID	8
10	SAN JUAN	CO	8
11	CLARK	ID	8
12	BRISTOL	MA	9
13	LOUP	NE	9
14	BUFFALO	SD	9
15	FRANKLIN	MA	10
16	MINERAL	CO	10
17	SUFFOLK	MA	10
18	BLAINE	NE	10
19	GOLDEN VALLEY	MT	11
20	HOOKER	NE	11
21	STOREY	NV	11
22	TREASURE	MT	12
23	GRANT	NE	12
24	LOGAN	NE	13
25	WHEELER	NE	13
26	HAYES	NE	13
27	JACKSON	SD	14
28	HARDING	SD	14
29	ZIEBACH	SD	14
30	THOMAS	NE	14
31	ECHOLS	GA	15
32	WIBAUX	MT	15
33	DAGGETT	UT	15
34	CARTER	MT	16
35	BANNER	NE	16
36	GARFIELD	MT	17
37	SLOPE	ND	17
38	JONES	SD	17
39	DOLORES	CO	18
40	ROBERTSON	KY	18
41	KENT	TX	18
42	NORFOLK	MA	18
43	SULLY	SD	18
44	HAMPSHIRE	MA	19
45	KING	TX	19
46	KEYA PAHA	NE	19
47	OURAY	CO	20
48	CUSTER	CO	20
49	KEWEENAW	MI	20
50	PLYMOUTH	MA	20
51	GILPIN	CO	20
52	HYDE	SD	21
53	PIUTE	UT	21
54	GILLIAM	OR	21
55	CAMPBELL	SD	21
56	OLIVER	ND	22
57	MELLETTE	SD	22
58	GREELEY	KS	22
59	ISSAQUENA	MS	22
60	STANLEY	SD	22
61	WAYNE	UT	22
62	TERRELL	TX	23

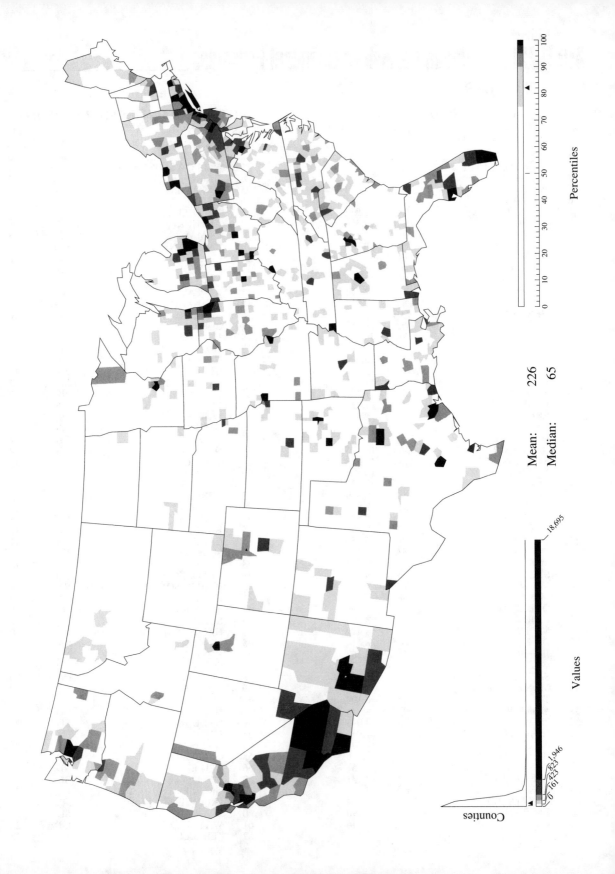

Percentiles

Mean: 226

Median: 65

Values

Counties

18,695

1,946
823
423
161
0

(TONS PER YEAR)

TOP COUNTIES SHADED BLACK

RANK	COUNTY	STATE	VALUE
1	LOS ANGELES	CA	18,695
2	COOK	IL	17,721
3	NEW YORK CITY	NY	13,290
4	HARRIS	TX	10,831
5	DALLAS	TX	8,048
6	WAYNE	MI	7,960
7	SANTA CLARA	CA	6,084
8	CUYAHOGA	OH	5,919
9	DADE	FL	5,116
10	MARICOPA	AZ	4,806
11	SAN DIEGO	CA	4,732
12	ORANGE	CA	4,519
13	ALLEGHENY	PA	4,350
14	NASSAU	NY	4,082
15	PHILADELPHIA	PA	4,076
16	HENNEPIN	MN	4,031
17	OAKLAND	MI	3,959
18	KING	WA	3,898
19	TARRANT	TX	3,857
20	ALAMEDA	CA	3,757
21	HAMILTON	OH	3,208
22	BROWARD	FL	3,187
23	FAIRFIELD	CT	3,161
24	ERIE	NY	3,147
25	BERGEN	NJ	3,102
26	ST LOUIS	MO	3,100
27	ST LOUIS CITY	MO	3,093
28	FULTON	GA	3,066
29	BALTIMORE CITY	MD	3,020
30	ESSEX	NJ	3,020
31	FRANKLIN	OH	3,007
32	SUFFOLK	NY	2,991
33	BEXAR	TX	2,972
34	HARTFORD	CT	2,913
35	MARION	IN	2,858
36	JACKSON	MO	2,795
37	SHELBY	TN	2,762
38	MONTGOMERY	OH	2,750
39	NEW HAVEN	CT	2,634
40	MONTGOMERY	PA	2,516
41	UNION	NJ	2,488
42	OKLAHOMA	OK	2,479
43	MILWAUKEE	WI	2,421
44	MIDDLESEX	NJ	2,411
45	DENVER	CO	2,372
46	RAMSEY	MN	2,358
47	WESTCHESTER	NY	2,355
48	MONROE	NY	2,327
49	JEFFERSON	AL	2,304
50	MACOMB	MI	2,304
51	TULSA	OK	2,231
52	GENESEE	MI	2,209
53	JEFFERSON	KY	2,190
54	DU PAGE	IL	2,184
55	SALT LAKE	UT	2,184
56	FAIRFAX	VA	2,148
57	PINELLAS	FL	2,071
58	PROVIDENCE	RI	2,044
59	SACRAMENTO	CA	1,966
60	HILLSBOROUGH	FL	1,965
61	SAN BERNARDINO	CA	1,946

BOTTOM COUNTIES SHADED WHITE

RANK	COUNTY	STATE	VALUE
1	NANTUCKET	MA	0
2	DUKES	MA	0
3	YELLOWSTONE NAT. PARK	MT	1
4	HINSDALE	CO	1
5	PETROLEUM	MT	1
6	MC PHERSON	NE	2
7	ARTHUR	NE	2
8	BUFFALO	SD	2
9	CAMAS	ID	2
10	CLARK	ID	2
11	SAN JUAN	CO	2
12	LOUP	NE	2
13	MINERAL	CO	2
14	BLAINE	NE	2
15	BARNSTABLE	MA	2
16	GOLDEN VALLEY	MT	3
17	STOREY	NV	3
18	HOOKER	NE	3
19	ECHOLS	GA	3
20	TREASURE	MT	3
21	GRANT	NE	3
22	HAYES	NE	3
23	ZIEBACH	SD	3
24	JACKSON	SD	3
25	HARDING	SD	3
26	WHEELER	NE	3
27	LOGAN	NE	3
28	KEWEENAW	MI	3
29	WIBAUX	MT	4
30	THOMAS	NE	4
31	SULLY	SD	4
32	ROBERTSON	KY	4
33	CARTER	MT	4
34	JONES	SD	4
35	DOLORES	CO	4
36	DAGGETT	UT	4
37	BANNER	NE	4
38	GILLIAM	OR	4
39	GARFIELD	MT	4
40	CAMPBELL	SD	4
41	HYDE	SD	5
42	OURAY	CO	5
43	ISSAQUENA	MS	5
44	SLOPE	ND	5
45	GREELEY	KS	5
46	KENT	TX	5
47	KEYA PAHA	NE	5
48	GILPIN	CO	5
49	SIOUX	ND	5
50	CUSTER	CO	5
51	MELLETTE	SD	5
52	STANLEY	SD	5
53	OLIVER	ND	5
54	FLORENCE	WI	5
55	WAYNE	UT	5
56	KIOWA	CO	5
57	PIUTE	UT	5
58	KING	TX	5
59	SHERMAN	OR	5
60	WALLACE	KS	5
61	MOTLEY	TX	5
62	LINCOLN	ID	5

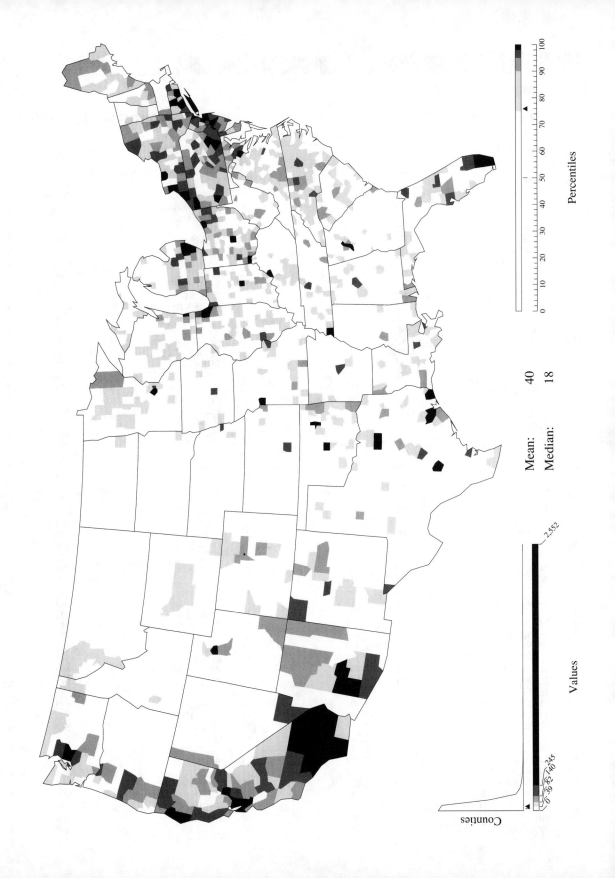

Mean: 40

Median: 18

Percentiles

Values

Counties

(TONS PER YEAR)

TOP COUNTIES SHADED BLACK

RANK	COUNTY	STATE	VALUE
1	LOS ANGELES	CA	2,552
2	COOK	IL	1,933
3	HARRIS	TX	1,296
4	NEW YORK CITY	NY	1,026
5	WAYNE	MI	886
6	DALLAS	TX	804
7	ORANGE	CA	646
8	SAN DIEGO	CA	625
9	CUYAHOGA	OH	579
10	ALLEGHENY	PA	577
11	MARICOPA	AZ	543
12	SANTA CLARA	CA	519
13	ALAMEDA	CA	490
14	NEW HAVEN	CT	457
15	ERIE	NY	446
16	DADE	FL	437
17	PHILADELPHIA	PA	437
18	KING	WA	431
19	TARRANT	TX	420
20	HAMILTON	OH	416
21	BEXAR	TX	391
22	HENNEPIN	MN	391
23	SAN BERNARDINO	CA	390
24	OAKLAND	MI	380
25	BALTIMORE CITY	MD	375
26	JEFFERSON	TX	374
27	NEW LONDON	CT	361
28	ST LOUIS CITY	MO	361
29	BERGEN	NJ	358
30	HARTFORD	CT	354
31	FRANKLIN	OH	346
32	OKLAHOMA	OK	343
33	NASSAU	NY	340
34	MILWAUKEE	WI	338
35	SUFFOLK	NY	336
36	FULTON	GA	318
37	HUMBOLDT	CA	317
38	MONMOUTH	NJ	315
39	BERKS	PA	314
40	BROWARD	FL	310
41	CHAUTAUQUA	NY	306
42	JACKSON	MO	306
43	MARION	IN	302
44	MIDDLESEX	NJ	294
45	DENVER	CO	291
46	SACRAMENTO	CA	287
47	RIVERSIDE	CA	286
48	SALT LAKE	UT	286
49	TULSA	OK	282
50	DU PAGE	IL	278
51	JEFFERSON	KY	277
52	MACOMB	MI	268
53	SAN MATEO	CA	267
54	HUDSON	NJ	264
55	MONROE	NY	263
56	BURLINGTON	NJ	260
57	CRAWFORD	PA	255
58	SHELBY	TN	253
59	FAIRFAX	VA	253
60	CONTRA COSTA	CA	246
61	LANCASTER	PA	245

BOTTOM COUNTIES SHADED WHITE

RANK	COUNTY	STATE	VALUE
1	YELLOWSTONE NAT. PARK	MT	0
2	NANTUCKET	MA	0
3	DUKES	MA	0
4	HINSDALE	CO	0
5	PETROLEUM	MT	0
6	ARTHUR	NE	0
7	MC PHERSON	NE	0
8	CLARK	ID	0
9	BUFFALO	SD	0
10	CAMAS	ID	0
11	SAN JUAN	CO	0
12	LOUP	NE	0
13	MINERAL	CO	1
14	BLAINE	NE	1
15	GOLDEN VALLEY	MT	1
16	GRANT	NE	1
17	STOREY	NV	1
18	HAYES	NE	1
19	HOOKER	NE	1
20	TREASURE	MT	1
21	HARDING	SD	1
22	JACKSON	SD	1
23	WHEELER	NE	1
24	KEWEENAW	MI	1
25	LOGAN	NE	1
26	JONES	SD	1
27	SULLY	SD	1
28	THOMAS	NE	1
29	DAGGETT	UT	1
30	SLOPE	ND	1
31	ROBERTSON	KY	1
32	GILLIAM	OR	1
33	BANNER	NE	1
34	CARTER	MT	1
35	WIBAUX	MT	1
36	KENT	TX	1
37	KING	TX	1
38	SIOUX	ND	1
39	LOGAN	ND	1
40	HYDE	SD	1
41	OLIVER	ND	1
42	CAMPBELL	SD	1
43	DOLORES	CO	1
44	OURAY	CO	1
45	PIUTE	UT	1
46	CUSTER	CO	1
47	STANLEY	SD	1
48	GARFIELD	MT	1
49	TERRELL	TX	1
50	PRAIRIE	MT	1
51	GILPIN	CO	1
52	WAYNE	UT	1
53	RICH	UT	1
54	GOSPER	NE	1
55	SHERIDAN	ND	1
56	WHEATLAND	MT	1
57	LINCOLN	ID	1
58	MOTLEY	TX	1
59	FLORENCE	WI	1
60	HANSON	SD	1
61	ONEIDA	ID	1
62	KIOWA	CO	1

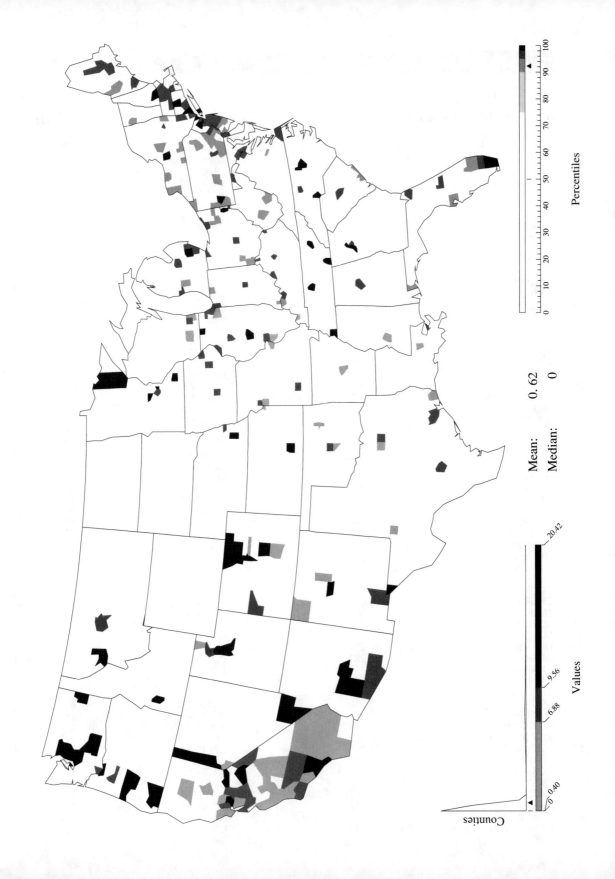

Mean: 0.62

Median: 0

Percentiles

Values

Counties

0 0.40   6.88   9.56   20.42

(PARTS PER MILLION)

TOP COUNTIES SHADED BLACK

RANK	COUNTY	STATE	VALUE
1	DENVER	CO	20.42
2	TUOLUMNE	CA	16.20
3	JACKSON	OR	15.49
4	LARIMER	CO	15.40
5	UTAH	UT	14.73
6	HILLSBOROUGH	NH	13.97
7	WELD	CO	13.89
8	PIERCE	WA	13.46
9	WASHOE	NV	13.37
10	JOSEPHINE	OR	13.36
11	SPOKANE	WA	13.06
12	MORRIS	NJ	12.92
13	YAKIMA	WA	12.78
14	LOS ANGELES	CA	12.71
15	JEFFERSON	CO	12.66
16	WAKE	NC	12.57
17	EL PASO	CO	12.31
18	RAMSEY	MN	12.16
19	BALTIMORE CITY	MD	12.02
20	EL PASO	TX	12.01
21	HAMILTON	TN	11.90
22	DURHAM	NC	11.77
23	ADA	ID	11.72
24	SALT LAKE	UT	11.68
25	DISTRICT OF COLUMBIA	DC	11.49
26	HARTFORD	CT	11.42
27	SHERBURNE	MN	11.36
28	NASSAU	NY	11.32
29	KNOX	TN	11.28
30	CLARK	NV	11.21
31	MULTNOMAH	OR	11.19
32	MISSOULA	MT	11.08
33	MARICOPA	AZ	11.06
34	UNION	NJ	10.80
35	BERGEN	NJ	10.78
36	KING	WA	10.73
37	BERNALILLO	NM	10.70
38	FAIRFIELD	CT	10.62
39	ALLEGHENY	PA	10.55
40	ORANGE	CA	10.53
41	ST LOUIS	MN	10.52
42	EL DORADO	CA	10.50
43	WINNEBAGO	IL	10.48
44	BOULDER	CO	10.42
45	DAVIDSON	TN	10.38
46	SOLANO	CA	10.32
47	OLMSTED	MN	10.24
48	ONONDAGA	NY	10.24
49	MECKLENBURG	NC	10.23
50	JEFFERSON	OH	10.20
51	FULTON	GA	10.20
52	SUFFOLK	MA	10.13
53	SHELBY	TN	10.07
54	NEW YORK CITY	NY	10.03
55	DADE	FL	9.95
56	LANCASTER	NE	9.87
57	SEDGWICK	KS	9.71
58	LANE	OR	9.70
59	OAKLAND	MI	9.66
60	SNOHOMISH	WA	9.65
61	SANGAMON	IL	9.56

BOTTOM COUNTIES SHADED WHITE

NOTE: TOO MANY COUNTIES TO LIST
HAD ZERO VALUES FOR THIS MEASURE

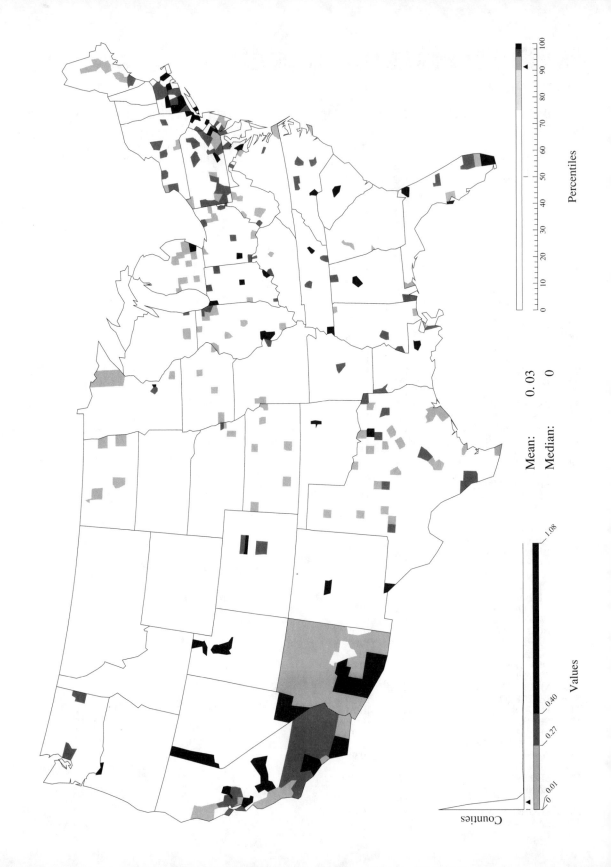

Mean: 0. 03
Median: 0

Percentiles

(MICROGRAMS PER CUBIC METER)

TOP COUNTIES SHADED BLACK

RANK	COUNTY	STATE	VALUE
1	COLLIN	TX	1.08
2	MULTNOMAH	OR	0.90
3	CLARK	NV	0.81
4	DENVER	CO	0.77
5	HAMPDEN	MA	0.76
6	MARICOPA	AZ	0.71
7	LOS ANGELES	CA	0.70
8	CACHE	UT	0.68
9	PASSAIC	NJ	0.65
10	SALT LAKE	UT	0.64
11	DUVAL	FL	0.63
12	SHELBY	TN	0.62
13	NASSAU	NY	0.61
14	EAST BATON ROUGE	LA	0.58
15	WEBER	UT	0.57
16	PLYMOUTH	MA	0.54
17	LAKE	IN	0.54
18	SANTA CLARA	CA	0.54
19	JEFFERSON	AL	0.54
20	ESSEX	NJ	0.53
21	UTAH	UT	0.53
22	WASHOE	NV	0.52
23	FLOYD	IN	0.52
24	DADE	FL	0.51
25	PROVIDENCE	RI	0.51
26	FRESNO	CA	0.50
27	BERNALILLO	NM	0.50
28	ST CLAIR	IL	0.50
29	WEST BATON ROUGE	LA	0.50
30	PRINCE GEORGES	MD	0.49
31	NEW HAVEN	CT	0.49
32	ARAPAHOE	CO	0.48
33	BERGEN	NJ	0.48
34	SANTA CRUZ	AZ	0.47
35	BALTIMORE CITY	MD	0.47
36	MARION	IN	0.47
37	ROANE	TN	0.47
38	NEW YORK CITY	NY	0.46
39	HUDSON	NJ	0.45
40	RICHLAND	SC	0.45
41	MECKLENBURG	NC	0.44
42	MADISON	IL	0.44
43	SACRAMENTO	CA	0.43
44	CLARK	IN	0.43
45	ST LOUIS CITY	MO	0.43
46	LITCHFIELD	CT	0.43
47	TULSA	OK	0.42
48	MONTGOMERY	OH	0.42
49	EL PASO	TX	0.42
50	DELAWARE	PA	0.42
51	MONTGOMERY	PA	0.42
52	MERCER	NJ	0.41
53	PINELLAS	FL	0.41
54	SAN DIEGO	CA	0.41
55	UNION	NJ	0.41
56	RAMSEY	MN	0.40
57	MIDDLESEX	CT	0.40
58	CUMBERLAND	PA	0.40
59	WAYNE	MI	0.40
60	WESTCHESTER	NY	0.40
61	PIMA	AZ	0.40

BOTTOM COUNTIES SHADED WHITE

NOTE: TOO MANY COUNTIES TO LIST
HAD ZERO VALUES FOR THIS MEASURE

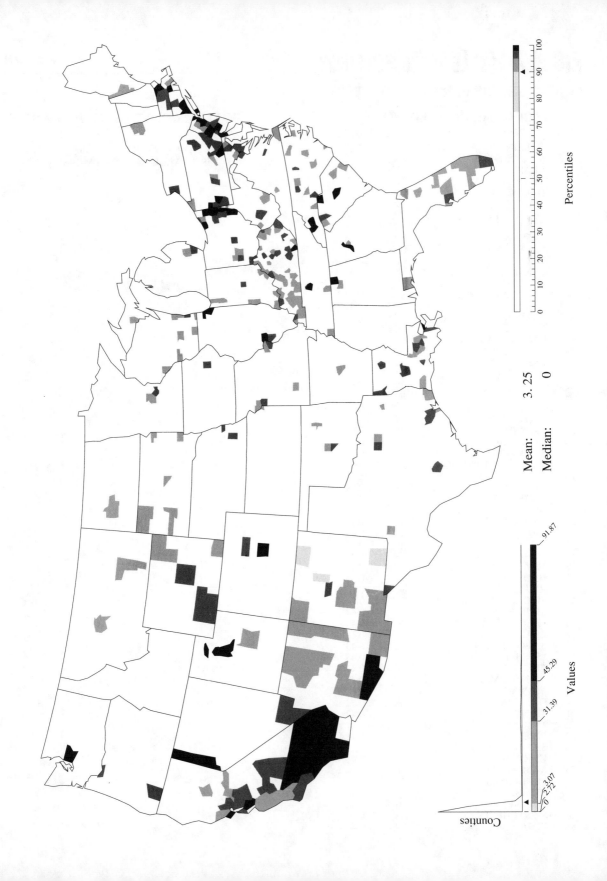

Mean: 3. 25

Median: 0

Percentiles

Values

Counties

91.87

45.29

31.39

3.07
2.72
0

(PARTS PER MILLION)

TOP COUNTIES SHADED BLACK

RANK	COUNTY	STATE	VALUE
1	DAVIDSON	TN	91.87
2	LOS ANGELES	CA	88.86
3	DENVER	CO	88.59
4	UNION	NJ	81.41
5	ORANGE	CA	76.85
6	PHILADELPHIA	PA	68.84
7	RIVERSIDE	CA	67.15
8	WASHOE	NV	66.14
9	ESSEX	NJ	65.83
10	COOK	IL	65.40
11	SAN BERNARDINO	CA	62.18
12	NASSAU	NY	61.51
13	NEW YORK CITY	NY	61.08
14	SALT LAKE	UT	61.08
15	SANTA CLARA	CA	60.68
16	BALTIMORE CITY	MD	60.17
17	BERGEN	NJ	59.73
18	BELMONT	OH	58.33
19	DISTRICT OF COLUMBIA	DC	57.64
20	ALLEGHENY	PA	57.40
21	HUDSON	NJ	57.24
22	NEW HAVEN	CT	57.22
23	JEFFERSON	OH	57.02
24	CAMDEN	NJ	56.60
25	COLUMBIANA	OH	54.64
26	GLOUCESTER	NJ	54.32
27	YORK	SC	53.18
28	BUNCOMBE	NC	53.05
29	ST LOUIS CITY	MO	52.77
30	FAIRFIELD	CT	51.62
31	EL PASO	CO	51.51
32	SAN FRANCISCO	CA	51.37
33	ORLEANS	LA	50.79
34	PIMA	AZ	50.73
35	MIDDLESEX	NJ	50.61
36	UTAH	UT	50.29
37	MAHONING	OH	50.22
38	BUCKS	PA	49.85
39	CUYAHOGA	OH	49.67
40	KING	WA	49.40
41	RICHLAND	SC	49.30
42	FULTON	GA	49.03
43	SOMERSET	NJ	48.89
44	MONROE	OH	48.77
45	SUFFOLK	MA	48.68
46	MIDDLESEX	MA	48.61
47	HAYWOOD	NC	48.55
48	KERN	CA	48.49
49	WEBER	UT	48.34
50	WHITLEY	KY	48.29
51	YORK	PA	47.97
52	SAN DIEGO	CA	47.71
53	MADISON	IL	47.47
54	PROVIDENCE	RI	47.31
55	ARLINGTON	VA	47.30
56	NEW CASTLE	DE	47.15
57	TRUMBULL	OH	47.03
58	MONTGOMERY	PA	46.14
59	MARIN	CA	45.63
60	MADISON	AL	45.42
61	LAWRENCE	PA	45.29

BOTTOM COUNTIES SHADED WHITE

NOTE: TOO MANY COUNTIES TO LIST
HAD ZERO VALUES FOR THIS MEASURE

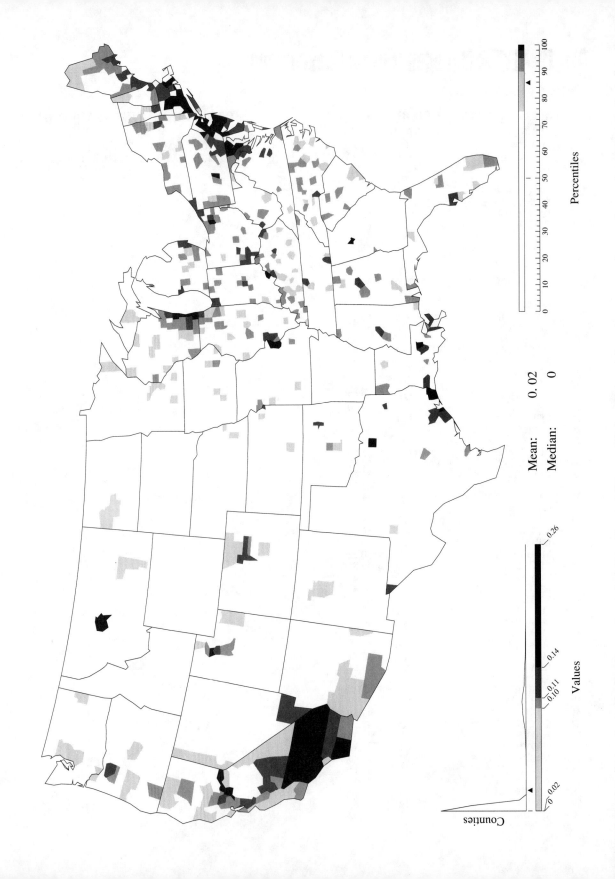

(PARTS PER MILLION)

TOP COUNTIES SHADED BLACK

RANK	COUNTY	STATE	VALUE
1	LOS ANGELES	CA	0.26
2	FAIRFIELD	CT	0.19
3	NEW HAVEN	CT	0.18
4	CASCADE	MT	0.18
5	MIDDLESEX	CT	0.18
6	NEW LONDON	CT	0.18
7	SAN DIEGO	CA	0.17
8	ATLANTIC	NJ	0.17
9	GALVESTON	TX	0.17
10	MIDDLESEX	NJ	0.17
11	BUCKS	PA	0.17
12	RACINE	WI	0.17
13	TOLLAND	CT	0.17
14	BLAIR	PA	0.16
15	KENT	RI	0.16
16	HARTFORD	CT	0.16
17	DENTON	TX	0.16
18	VENTURA	CA	0.16
19	HAMPDEN	MA	0.16
20	SAN BERNARDINO	CA	0.16
21	BURLINGTON	NJ	0.16
22	JEFFERSON	TX	0.16
23	GLOUCESTER	NJ	0.16
24	BERGEN	NJ	0.15
25	HUNTERDON	NJ	0.15
26	ESSEX	NJ	0.15
27	OCEAN	NJ	0.15
28	HARFORD	MD	0.15
29	KENOSHA	WI	0.15
30	EAST BATON ROUGE	LA	0.15
31	NEW YORK CITY	NY	0.15
32	CAMDEN	NJ	0.15
33	HUDSON	NJ	0.15
34	NORTHAMPTON	PA	0.15
35	NEW CASTLE	DE	0.15
36	ROCKDALE	GA	0.15
37	MORRIS	NJ	0.15
38	MONTGOMERY	PA	0.15
39	SHEBOYGAN	WI	0.14
40	PHILADELPHIA	PA	0.14
41	BALTIMORE	MD	0.14
42	DELAWARE	PA	0.14
43	ORANGE	TX	0.14
44	OZAUKEE	WI	0.14
45	MILWAUKEE	WI	0.14
46	PLACER	CA	0.14
47	NORFOLK	MA	0.14
48	SUMMIT	OH	0.14
49	ST LOUIS	MO	0.14
50	HAMPSHIRE	MA	0.14
51	DE KALB	GA	0.14
52	CLARK	IN	0.14
53	CARROLL	MD	0.14
54	JEFFERSON	MO	0.14
55	SOMERSET	NJ	0.14
56	DAVIS	UT	0.14
57	KERN	CA	0.14
58	SACRAMENTO	CA	0.14
59	HOWARD	MD	0.14
60	ANNE ARUNDEL	MD	0.14
61	BRISTOL	MA	0.14

BOTTOM COUNTIES SHADED WHITE

NOTE: TOO MANY COUNTIES TO LIST
HAD ZERO VALUES FOR THIS MEASURE

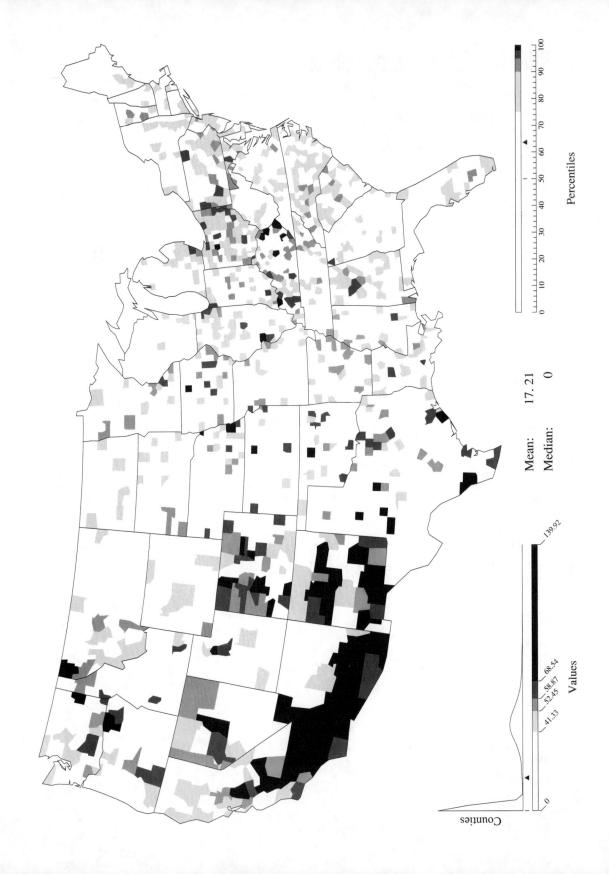

Mean: 17.21

Median: 0

Percentiles

Values

Counties

(MICROGRAMS PER CUBIC METER)

TOP COUNTIES SHADED BLACK

RANK	COUNTY	STATE	VALUE
1	IMPERIAL	CA	139.92
2	ARCHULETA	CO	110.89
3	MARICOPA	AZ	104.08
4	DENVER	CO	100.87
5	KINGS	CA	99.32
6	JONES	TX	97.62
7	SANTA CRUZ	AZ	96.63
8	GRAHAM	AZ	96.29
9	ROUTT	CO	94.03
10	SAN BERNARDINO	CA	90.07
11	YUMA	AZ	89.66
12	RIVERSIDE	CA	87.22
13	GRANT	NM	86.05
14	SPOKANE	WA	84.25
15	UMATILLA	OR	84.20
16	LOS ANGELES	CA	83.30
17	FRESNO	CA	83.14
18	COCHISE	AZ	82.98
19	DONA ANA	NM	82.89
20	KERN	CA	82.17
21	CERRO GORDO	IA	82.16
22	EL PASO	TX	82.02
23	ORANGE	CA	81.97
24	MADISON	IL	80.72
25	SAN MIGUEL	NM	80.44
26	CLARK	NV	79.66
27	SANDOVAL	NM	79.03
28	VALENCIA	NM	78.44
29	OTOE	NE	77.80
30	WEBB	TX	77.52
31	ADAMS	CO	77.47
32	GILA	AZ	77.22
33	SAN MIGUEL	CO	76.93
34	HOWARD	TX	76.53
35	BERNALILLO	NM	76.33
36	CASS	NE	75.14
37	PERRY	KY	74.38
38	PIKE	KY	74.04
39	TORRANCE	NM	73.48
40	DAKOTA	NE	73.34
41	OTERO	NM	73.25
42	LANDER	NV	72.97
43	DOUGLAS	CO	72.55
44	CHAVES	NM	71.92
45	CARTER	KY	71.67
46	STANISLAUS	CA	71.51
47	WYANDOT	OH	71.27
48	LINCOLN	MT	71.06
49	MADISON	KY	70.81
50	SAN JOAQUIN	CA	70.63
51	ECTOR	TX	70.44
52	PINAL	AZ	70.10
53	CLOUD	KS	70.02
54	LUBBOCK	TX	70.02
55	LAWRENCE	KY	69.89
56	BRAZORIA	TX	69.43
57	MIDLAND	TX	69.43
58	GARFIELD	OK	69.41
59	SALT LAKE	UT	68.72
60	HENDERSON	KY	68.66
61	GUNNISON	CO	68.54

BOTTOM COUNTIES SHADED WHITE

NOTE: TOO MANY COUNTIES TO LIST
HAD ZERO VALUES FOR THIS MEASURE

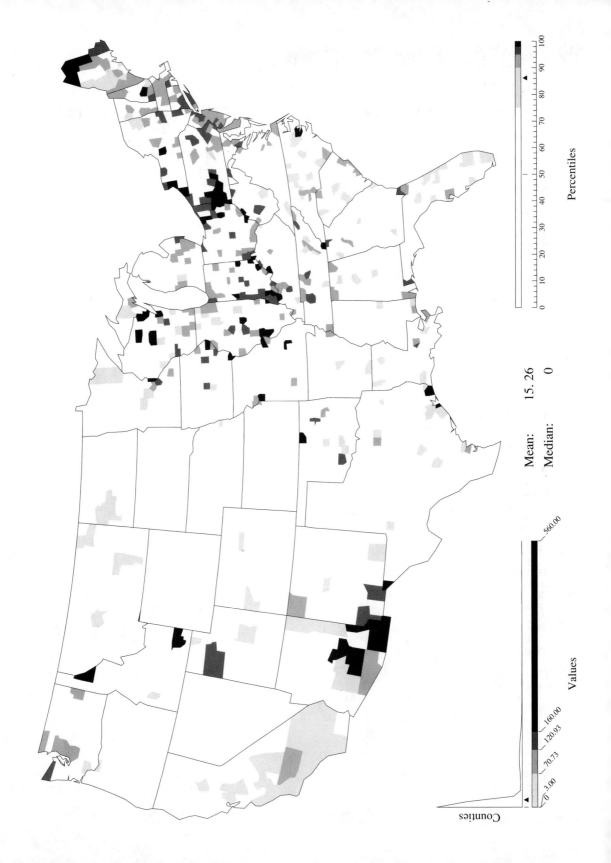

Mean: 15. 26

Median: 0

Percentiles

Values

Counties

AIR QUALITY: Sulfur Dioxide Concentrations

(PARTS PER MILLION)

TOP COUNTIES SHADED BLACK

RANK	COUNTY	STATE	VALUE
1	LEE	IA	560.00
2	CLINTON	IA	544.00
3	GREENLEE	AZ	487.00
4	JACKSON	MO	440.00
5	POLK	TN	373.50
6	ONEIDA	WI	349.20
7	BANNOCK	ID	327.93
8	GILA	AZ	312.78
9	MARINETTE	WI	305.22
10	TUSCARAWAS	OH	292.75
11	HANCOCK	WV	290.13
12	OHIO	WV	277.25
13	KAY	OK	276.00
14	WAYNE	IN	270.42
15	COCHISE	AZ	268.25
16	WARRICK	IN	264.27
17	CHAUTAUQUA	NY	260.00
18	ALLEGHENY	PA	256.66
19	BROOKE	WV	247.17
20	ST CHARLES	MO	246.98
21	PINAL	AZ	239.00
22	ONONDAGA	NY	236.69
23	CARIBOU	ID	235.44
24	BROWN	WI	234.99
25	MARSHALL	WV	225.67
26	EL PASO	TX	216.01
27	JEFFERSON	OH	214.00
28	MARATHON	WI	210.79
29	YELLOWSTONE	MT	210.13
30	GALVESTON	TX	208.50
31	SHOSHONE	ID	204.44
32	MACON	IL	204.17
33	WASHINGTON	MN	202.83
34	BOONE	KY	192.50
35	BEAVER	PA	190.65
36	SUMMIT	OH	184.62
37	FOUNTAIN	IN	183.33
38	ERIE	NY	182.75
39	BUTLER	PA	182.75
40	HENDERSON	KY	182.68
41	CAMBRIA	PA	182.40
42	MEIGS	OH	177.80
43	WOOD	WV	177.33
44	DEARBORN	IN	177.13
45	WABASH	IL	176.30
46	ST CLAIR	IL	174.60
47	COLUMBIANA	OH	174.00
48	MADISON	IL	172.89
49	WASHINGTON	PA	172.01
50	HIDALGO	NM	168.60
51	JEFFERSON	IN	167.60
52	MERRIMACK	NH	167.42
53	NEW YORK CITY	NY	167.39
54	IRON	MO	165.50
55	JEFFERSON	KY	165.01
56	PIKE	IN	164.83
57	JEFFERSON	TX	164.16
58	CUYAHOGA	OH	163.49
59	AROOSTOOK	ME	162.93
60	BEAUFORT	NC	162.38
61	WESTMORELAND	PA	160.00

BOTTOM COUNTIES SHADED WHITE

NOTE: TOO MANY COUNTIES TO LIST
HAD ZERO VALUES FOR THIS MEASURE

much toxic air pollution as industrial sources.[67] In a study of the Philadelphia metropolitan area, the EPA found that volatization of organic compounds from sewage treatment plants accounted for almost half of the estimated cancer risk to the population from breathing carcinogens in the air.[68] In other cases, the health impacts from the generally more diffuse urban sources of air emissions may be less severe than those from industrial point sources.

The first air quality map indicates where such nonindustrial urban sources emit the largest quantities of hazardous chemicals into the air, using EPA estimates of 76 chemicals (the methods appendix provides detailed lists of the specific chemical used in each map). These selected urban hazardous chemical emissions amount to nearly 3 million tons nationwide. The second map shows a similar geographic distribution for 22 suspected carcinogens, which comprise over a quarter of the urban hazardous chemical emissions depicted in the first map. The third map shows where 9 acutely hazardous chemicals are emitted in the greatest quantities, amounting to about 5 percent of the total in the first map. In all three maps, counties in Southern California are highlighted, as are urban counties across the country.

The next six maps show where ambient air pollutants are most concentrated. National ambient air quality standards have been established under the Clean Air Act for six pollutants: carbon monoxide, lead, nitrogen dioxide, ozone, particulates, and sulfur dioxide. These maps differ among themselves more than the first three maps do, because local industries as well as other urban sources contribute to the ambient concentrations of such pollutants.

CHAPTER 6

ENVIRONMENTAL JUSTICE

In the autumn of 1982, civil rights leaders from around the country joined local activists in Warren County, North Carolina, to protest the governor's proposal to dump polychlorinated biphenyls (PCBs), which have been shown to cause cancer and birth defects in laboratory animals, near the town of Afton. Warren County has less-than-ideal geophysical features for a toxic waste landfill, with a water table just five feet below the ground at some points and most local residents drinking well water. It also has the highest percentage of African Americans and among the poorest residents of any county in the state.

The National Association for the Advancement of Colored People (NAACP) requested an injunction to stop the PCB shipments on the basis of racial discrimination. Over 500 people were thrown into jail during the protests, including the Reverend Benjamin F. Chavis, Jr., director of the United Church of Christ Commission for Racial Justice (CRJ), the Reverend Joseph Lowery of the Southern Christian Leadership Conference, and Walter Fauntroy, the Washington, D.C., congressional delegate.[1]

The demonstrations failed to turn back the truckloads of PCB, but they marked the beginning of a new grass-roots movement aimed at combating environmental injustice. Soon after the arrests in Warren County, Congressman Fauntroy requested a report from the U.S. General Accounting Office (GAO) on the demographics of southern communities with toxic waste sites. Three of the four landfills the GAO investigated were located in predominantly poor, black communities.[2]

The Commission for Racial Justice followed up on the GAO findings by hiring Public Data Access, Inc., to prepare the first national study of toxic wastes and race. The results were staggering: communities with commercial hazardous waste facilities were found to have twice the percentage of racial minorities as communities without such facilities. Communities with more than one facility or with the largest toxic waste dumps have three times as many people of color. Three of the five largest landfills in the country are in black and Latino communities. Race proved to be the single most significant predictor of where commercial toxic waste treatment, storage, and disposal occur nationwide.[3]

By the end of the 1980s, neighborhoods across the country had successfully mobilized to implement more equitable solutions to local environmental problems. In 1989, for example, the EPA wanted to ship a huge quantity of PCBs from a Houston Superfund site to the predominantly African American community of Emelle, Alabama, in the heart of the southern Black Belt, where the nation's largest toxic waste landfill is located. Emelle's economy is so dependent on the dump site's tax revenues that John Zippert of the Federation of Southern Cooperatives likens the relationship to a drug addiction; Wendell Paris, chair of the Minority People's Council on the Tennessee-Tombigee Waterway (just a few miles east of Emelle), calls the tax dollars "blood money," increasing environmental risks instead of fostering the kind of safe, well-planned economic development that is most urgently needed in poor communities.[4]

Linda Wallace Campbell of Alabamians for a Clean Environment (ACE), which headed up the fight to keep the PCBs out of Emelle, summed up the local viewpoint as follows: "It's unacceptable that a shipment of poison can leave a white suburban community with the political clout of Houston, to be dumped in a black rural town in Alabama, especially without a public hearing to air community concerns about health and safety." This time, Campbell and the other ACE activists won the support of the attorney general and the governor, and stopped the PCB shipment.[5]

No one is safe from the many sources of toxic pollution that threaten our planet; however, we are not all endangered equally. Experts often try to tell us which environmental risks are serious enough to worry about and which ones are not.[6] Some argue that society cannot advance unless it takes such risks.[7] The reality, however, is that the benefits and costs of technological advances are rarely distributed equitably. The maps provide overwhelming evidence that certain parts of the country are disproportionately threatened by toxins and mortality. Many risks that are of little concern to national policy makers may be destroying the health of particular communities. The data in this atlas suggest that the racial and socioeconomic disparities Public Data Access uncovered for the CRJ study of toxic wastes and race hold true for most other pollution and mortality factors as well.

Based on the evidence in the maps, poor, black, Latino, and native American communities are consistently hit more severely by pollution and death. In the counties that rank the worst across all of the industrial toxins measures, minorities comprise more than twice the percentage of the population than the average for the rest of the country. The demographics are nearly the same for counties with the worst mortality from all diseases. In addition, poverty is nearly 50 percent higher and educational levels are 23 percent lower in counties with the highest mortality rates compared with the rest of the country. In the CRJ study, we found that the toxic dumps were located in neighborhoods with significantly lower incomes than their surrounding counties. We would also expect other sources of toxic pollution to be concentrated within lower-income neighborhoods of urban counties, but this analysis requires more geographic detail than is available in the county maps.

Air pollution, for example, is usually highest in disadvantaged neighborhoods within urban counties. A 1975 Ford Foundation study observed: "One need not be poor, or black, or live in a low-rent apartment, or be low on the occupational ladder to call a polluted area home; however, if a person falls into one or more of these categories, the chance of living in such an area increases."[8] Los Angeles's infamous automobile pollution is worst in the working class neighborhoods along freeway exits and crowded streets; the Latino and black communities of East Los Angeles, Huntington Park, and Watts are also home to metal plating and furniture manufacturers that handle and emit toxic chemicals.[9] The predominantly black and Latino Southside of Chicago boasts the largest concentrations of municipal and hazardous waste dumps in the country.[10] In Washington, D.C., carbon monoxide from traffic and sulfur dioxide from factories and power plants tend to reach their highest levels in the air of African American and lower-income neighborhoods.[11]

Children and the elderly often suffer the most from inner-city pollution. For example, African American children living below the poverty line are exposed to lead levels dangerous enough to cause severe learning disabilities and other neurological disorders at about nine times the national rate for more advantaged children.[12] Asthma deaths are also extremely high among black inner-city children, and are increasing at such an alarming rate that they are pushing up the national asthma mortality rate for all children.[13]

The disproportionate impact of toxic hazards on minority and low-income people extends well beyond the inner city and the home environments. In the workplace, according to the National Institute for Occupational Safety and Health (NIOSH), "minority workers tend to encounter a disproportionately greater number of [serious health and safety hazards] because they have often been employed in especially dirty and dangerous jobs."[14] In fact, mortality from acutely hazardous exposures among minority men is 50 percent higher than among white men. On the farm, most pesticide exposures occur among Latino and

African American migrant workers.[15] On the reservations, native Americans are grappling with some of the worst pollution problems in the country: uranium mill tailings, water contamination, chemical lagoons, and illegal dumps.[16] Navajo teenagers living in uranium districts suffer from reproductive organ cancer at 17 times the national rate.[17] Puerto Ricans have seen large U.S. pharmaceutical, electronics, and petrochemical industries inundate their island since the late 1950s, contaminating underground drinking water sources for 22 municipalities.[18] The native people of the Marshall Islands in the Pacific Ocean have witnessed the irradiation of their entire homeland from U.S. nuclear testing, and suffer long-term health effects decades later.[19]

Many of the advances in the health status of racial and ethnic minorities that accompanied the civil rights struggles of the 1960s and 1970s reversed themselves during the 1980s.[20] For the first time this century, black life expectancy began to decline in the 1980s.[21] Minorities suffer significantly higher mortality rates than whites for eight of the ten causes of death portrayed in the maps, and for half of these causes, minority rates diverge even further from those for whites: birth defects, all cancers, lung cancers, and acutely hazardous exposures. In some cases the differences between rich and poor counties are as stark as between nations. Take Fisher County, Texas, for example, where minorities suffer from infant mortality rates that are as high as the national rate for Haiti, the poorest nation in the Americas; higher than every Latin American country; higher than 80 percent of Asian countries; higher than half of African nations; and almost nine times higher than the national rate for whites.[22] (Chapter 3 and the methods appendix provide further details on the racial disparities in mortality.)

Part of the problem is deteriorating health care. Some 37 million Americans with no health insurance and another 53 million who are underinsured have limited access to medical services—many of them are children and young adults.[23] Physician visits for prenatal care and other reasons by low-income and minority people declined throughout the 1980s.[24] This trend is compounded by the poorer preventive care that physicians have traditionally delivered to black and Latino patients, such as significantly fewer mammographies and influenza vaccinations.[25] Lower income groups receive far fewer preventive services than more affluent people, yet they end up receiving more medical treatment because of significantly greater rates of illness.[26] Rural Americans receive the poorest care of all, because of a combination of inequitable Medicare reimbursements, higher percentages of uninsured residents, and the lack of hospitals and other health care facilities.[27]

Even more important than declining medical care, however, is the impact of increasing disparities in economic, social, and environmental conditions on American health. The gap increased throughout the 1980s, with income levels across the South falling farther behind the national rate, and with all regions of the United States growing apart economically for the first time in 50 years (regional gross domestic production and per capita incomes were converging up until then).[28] The Sunbelt's economic gains during the 1970s benefited the major metropolitan areas throughout the South, but completely missed the southern Black Belt, which is made up of counties that remain among the poorest in the country (the map of African Americans on page 294 shows where these counties are located).[29]

Rural white communities in the Southeast also remain among the poorest and, along with the Black Belt communities, account for the highest rates of heart disease in the country. Identifying specific causes of death in these locations is often difficult, however, as one health official noted: "In some of these counties, there is no physician, and the coroner has no medical training; when someone dies who the coroner does not know, the cause of death is listed either as heart stopped or senility."[30] In metropolitan areas, the income gap between central cities and suburbs also widened dramatically during the past two decades.[31] As geographic disparities in income become more severe, inequalities in health and environmental quality quickly follow, as is clearly evident from the epidemic proportions of inner-city health problems throughout the country, with skyrocketing rates of tuberculosis, hepatitis A, syphilis, gonorrhea, measles, mumps, whooping cough, complicated ear infections, and AIDS.[32]

These blatant disparities in living conditions across the nation are often ignored or simply blamed on the people most affected. When entire communities are affected by unhealthful conditions, such as smoking, alcoholism, and obesity—as is the case among many lower-income and minority populations—then there are clearly broader social causes at the root of the problem. As experts point out, for example, "Cigarette smoking is a symptom of a society at odds with itself."[33] Unemployment and job insecurity, racism, marital instability and family tensions, thwarted career aspirations, financial difficulties, and inadequate housing are all significantly associated with elevated levels of stress, dysfunctional coping responses, and illness.[34]

Indicative of the utter lack of attention given to Americans with the poorest health is the fact that public health experts continue to call the rural Southeast the "enigma area," because that is where America's number-one killer, heart disease, reaches its highest rates in the nation (see chapter 3 for more on this). Many of the counties with the highest heart disease rates are in Georgia, the home state of the Centers for Disease Control (in Atlanta), and the nation's highest rate of uncontrolled hypertension can be found in the neighboring state of Alabama.[35]

People with lower incomes have higher rates of illness, and once sick they have significantly lower rates of survival. This includes higher case fatality rates for cancer and many chronic diseases.[36] The incidence of heart conditions is three times higher, and that of arthritis—the second leading cause of disability after heart disease—two times higher among people with lower incomes. Cases of hypertension, high blood pressure, diabetes, infectious and parasitic diseases are all significantly more prevalent among lower-income groups. And the disparities increase with age, indicating the cumulative effects of lifetime impoverishment.[37]

In some respects the very ways in which health statistics are collected obscure the root causes of current disparities in the state of Americans' health. The vital statistics of the United States, for example, are recorded solely by race, sex, and age, and not by socioeconomic class, as is done in England and many other countries. The National Center for Health Statistics (NCHS) mortality database divides people into two groups: white and nonwhite, based on categories the Census Bureau defined prior to the Civil War. African Americans comprise the bulk of the nonwhite population in most states. Yet less than 0.3 percent of the significant excess deaths among African Americans are due to clear-cut genetic causes related to race (such as sickle cell anemia); the rest—over 99.7 percent—are due to environmental and social factors.[38] Asian and Pacific islanders represent large shares of the nonwhite population in Hawaii, California, Washington, and Colorado, and native Americans comprise much of the minority population in Arizona, Oklahoma, and Washington. The differences in diet, social and cultural practices, and other aspects of living conditions among these racial groups are as great as any between them and whites. Yet the government lumps all of these diverse groups into the negatively defined nonwhite race group for the purpose of recording vital statistics.[39]

For that matter, the official, "white" group includes people with European backgrounds as diverse as Italian, Irish, Spanish, etc. As with racial minorities, white people of various foreign stock have settled all across the country. German and Scandinavian decendents, for example, are most concentrated in the northern Midwest and Mountain regions of the United States, people of Southern European extraction are most concentrated in the mid-Atlantic and New England states, and Latin Americans have settled mostly in the Southwest.[40] Differing cultural origins can affect health status as much as any racial distinctions. For example, high rates of stomach cancer have been correlated with people of Polish origin living in the New Jersey–New York–Philadelphia metropolitan region, and with people from Austria, the Soviet Union, and Scandinavia living in the North Central states (North and South Dakota, Minnesota, Wisconsin, and northern Michigan).[41] In these countries, stomach cancer rates are also relatively high. Significant differences between immigrant mortality rates and rates in their homeland, on the other hand, often indicate the influence of environmental agents.[42]

Latino Americans are the second largest minority group in the United States, and their share of the population continues to grow, including people with origins in Mexico (60 percent), Puerto Rico (14 percent), Cuba (6 percent), and other Spanish-speaking countries. Despite their significance in American demographics and history, the 1980 census was the first to ask about Spanish origins on every questionnaire, and Hispanic mortality statistics were published for the first time in 1984. Less than half of the states collected the information even at that late date.[43] Moreover, federal statistics subsume people with Spanish origins within the much larger white category. When a doctor writes on a death certificate that a deceased's race is Mexican, for example, state health departments are supposed to enter the person's race as white. The data on Latino Americans are lost within the statistics for the white population as a whole by the time they get into the official NCHS mortality database. Thus deaths of Latino Americans have no impact on county mortality rates for minorities; they may, however, affect white mortality rates, especially in the Southwest.

The technique of classifying mortality rates along such arbitrary racial categories has a subtle, but pervasive, impact on public perceptions of health disparities. A good example was the media reporting on a 1988 study of toxins and mortality along the Mississippi River that Public Data Access, Inc., conducted for Greenpeace USA. Counties bordering the lower reaches of the Mississippi (below the Ohio River confluence) suffer from among the highest rates of pollution, poverty, and mortality anywhere in the country, as is plainly evident in the maps. The Missouri Department of Health responded to these results with its own report, which concentrated on the demographics of the area, and did not examine the environmental situation. Their report received a front-page headline in the *St. Louis Post-Dispatch* that read: DEATH RATE, RACE TIED, STATE SAYS.[44] The director of the health department said, "Race, education, and income account for eighty-four percent of the excess deaths."

The effect of this response was to understate the severe health and environmental problems along the lower Mississippi River, by telling white, middle-class people, Don't worry, you're safe. But this is far from true. All races in this area are suffering from higher mortality and pollution. Measures of toxic releases to the air and water, pesticide use, and toxic waste production ranged from 50 percent to 5,400 percent higher along the river than the rest of the nation. Of 37 measures examined in the Greenpeace report, 34 were higher along the Mississippi than in the rest of the country, and most were higher in counties along the river than in their surrounding states. Cancer rates along the lower Mississippi River are 4 percent higher for all women and 14 percent higher for all men, and are rising twice as fast as the national rates for both sexes. Adult and infant mortality from all diseases are also significantly higher along the lower Mississippi, and are falling significantly behind the trend for the rest of the country.[45]

The health department's treatment of these disturbing facts not only confuses correlation with causation (the so-called ecological fallacy discussed in chapter 2), hiding this error within the false pretense of accuracy to "84 percent," but it also fails to suggest causal factors in the first place. The color of your skin does not kill you, nor does the lack of dollar bills in your pocket, nor the number of books on your shelves. The correlations indicate something is happening, but the causal factors lie elsewhere.

The maps clearly illustrate how geographic disparities in mortality and pollution disproportionately affect low-income and minority communities. Before World War II, blacks had lower rates of heart disease and cancer than whites. Now African Americans have the highest risk of death from these diseases and from many others. We know that depressed economic conditions increase stress and hypertension, and that inadequate nutritional education and access to medical care accelerate local rates of sickness and death. Toxic exposures from neighborhood dumps and on-the-job hazards can also play a role. The maps force us to ask: which factors are responsible for elevated rates in the hardest-hit communities, and what can be done to correct these local problems?

The following maps indicate concentrations of different racial, ethnic, and socioeconomic groups. Comparing these maps with those in the other chapters that locate clusters of mortality and elevated pollution with help you identify where different ethnic and socioeconomic groups are most affected. Educational levels also show a correlation with health status; the maps of high school and college graduates indicate where lack of education may be contributing to poor health. The maps of health services suggest where access to and quality of medical care may be contributing to elevated mortality rates.

Emerging grass-roots coalitions for environmental quality are raising the issue of equity. In the past, mainstream organizations have often overlooked questions of inequality, as they fought for the passage of laws intended to mitigate the most obvious national and global environmental problems. Yet the most serious abuses often ravage the neighborhoods and communities where fewer economic resources are available to improve the environment, and where people of color more frequently reside. The new grass-roots coalitions want jobs and development, but through ecologically sustainable investments. Workers want a voice in the technological decisions that potentially endanger their lives. Neighbors want the right to inspect and negotiate with local businesses in order to improve the quality of the air and water in their communities and to protect their health and their children's. These ongoing struggles are changing environments at home and at work throughout the country.

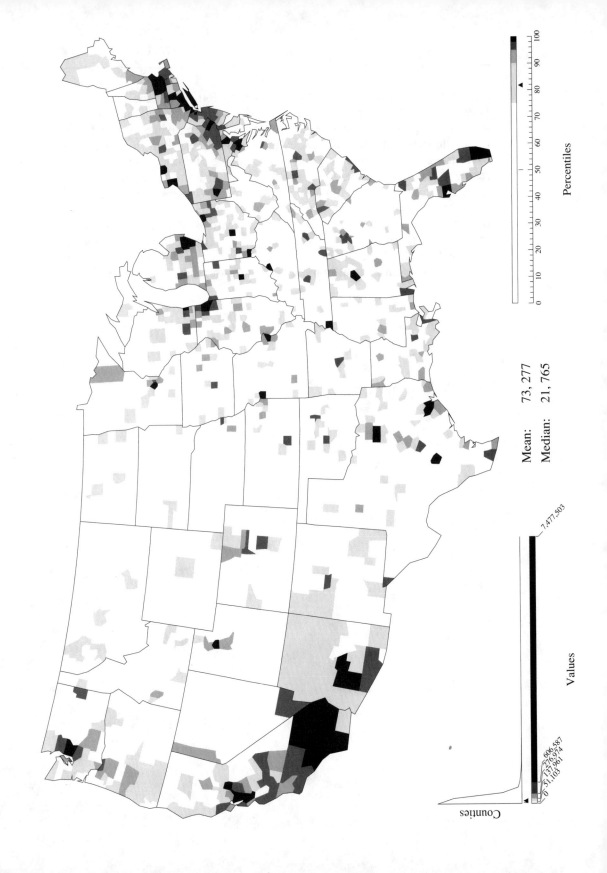

Mean: 73, 277

Median: 21, 765

Percentiles

Values

Counties

7,477,503

606,587
276,974
137,961
51,103
0

0 10 20 30 40 50 60 70 80 90 100

TOP COUNTIES SHADED BLACK

RANK	COUNTY	STATE	VALUE
1	LOS ANGELES	CA	7,477,503
2	NEW YORK CITY	NY	7,071,639
3	COOK	IL	5,253,655
4	HARRIS	TX	2,409,547
5	WAYNE	MI	2,337,891
6	ORANGE	CA	1,932,709
7	SAN DIEGO	CA	1,861,846
8	PHILADELPHIA	PA	1,688,210
9	DADE	FL	1,625,781
10	DALLAS	TX	1,556,390
11	MARICOPA	AZ	1,509,052
12	CUYAHOGA	OH	1,498,400
13	ALLEGHENY	PA	1,450,085
14	MIDDLESEX	MA	1,367,034
15	NASSAU	NY	1,321,582
16	SANTA CLARA	CA	1,295,071
17	SUFFOLK	NY	1,284,231
18	KING	WA	1,269,749
19	ALAMEDA	CA	1,105,379
20	BROWARD	FL	1,018,200
21	ERIE	NY	1,015,472
22	OAKLAND	MI	1,011,793
23	BEXAR	TX	988,800
24	ST LOUIS	MO	973,896
25	MILWAUKEE	WI	964,988
26	HENNEPIN	MN	941,411
27	SAN BERNARDINO	CA	895,016
28	HAMILTON	OH	873,224
29	FRANKLIN	OH	869,132
30	WESTCHESTER	NY	866,599
31	TARRANT	TX	860,880
32	ESSEX	NJ	851,116
33	BERGEN	NJ	845,385
34	HARTFORD	CT	807,766
35	FAIRFIELD	CT	807,143
36	BALTIMORE CITY	MD	786,775
37	SACRAMENTO	CA	783,381
38	SHELBY	TN	777,113
39	MARION	IN	765,233
40	NEW HAVEN	CT	761,337
41	FAIRFAX	VA	729,023
42	PINELLAS	FL	728,531
43	MONROE	NY	702,238
44	MACOMB	MI	694,600
45	JEFFERSON	KY	685,004
46	SAN FRANCISCO	CA	678,974
47	JEFFERSON	AL	671,324
48	PRINCE GEORGES	MD	665,071
49	RIVERSIDE	CA	663,166
50	DU PAGE	IL	658,835
51	CONTRA COSTA	CA	656,380
52	BALTIMORE	MD	655,615
53	SUFFOLK	MA	650,142
54	HILLSBOROUGH	FL	646,960
55	WORCESTER	MA	646,352
56	MONTGOMERY	PA	643,621
57	DISTRICT OF COLUMBIA	DC	638,333
58	ESSEX	MA	633,632
59	JACKSON	MO	629,266
60	SALT LAKE	UT	619,066
61	NORFOLK	MA	606,587

BOTTOM COUNTIES SHADED WHITE

RANK	COUNTY	STATE	VALUE
1	LOVING	TX	91
2	YELLOWSTONE NAT. PARK	MT	275
3	HINSDALE	CO	408
4	KING	TX	425
5	ARTHUR	NE	513
6	KENEDY	TX	543
7	MC PHERSON	NE	593
8	PETROLEUM	MT	655
9	DAGGETT	UT	769
10	ESMERALDA	NV	777
11	MC MULLEN	TX	789
12	CLARK	ID	798
13	MINERAL	CO	804
14	CAMAS	ID	818
15	SAN JUAN	CO	833
16	LOUP	NE	859
17	BORDEN	TX	859
18	BLAINE	NE	867
19	GRANT	NE	877
20	BANNER	NE	918
21	THOMAS	NE	973
22	TREASURE	MT	981
23	LOGAN	NE	983
24	HOOKER	NE	990
25	GOLDEN VALLEY	MT	1,026
26	WHEELER	NE	1,060
27	HARDING	NM	1,090
28	ALPINE	CA	1,097
29	BILLINGS	ND	1,138
30	KENT	TX	1,145
31	SLOPE	ND	1,157
32	ROBERTS	TX	1,187
33	EUREKA	NV	1,198
34	STERLING	TX	1,206
35	KEYA PAHA	NE	1,301
36	GLASSCOCK	TX	1,304
37	PIUTE	UT	1,329
38	HAYES	NE	1,356
39	IRION	TX	1,386
40	JONES	SD	1,463
41	WIBAUX	MT	1,476
42	STOREY	NV	1,503
43	WHEELER	OR	1,513
44	CUSTER	CO	1,528
45	TERRELL	TX	1,595
46	JEFF DAVIS	TX	1,647
47	GARFIELD	MT	1,656
48	DOLORES	CO	1,658
49	HARDING	SD	1,700
50	JACKSON	SD	1,719
51	BUFFALO	SD	1,795
52	CARTER	MT	1,799
53	PRAIRIE	MT	1,836
54	GREELEY	KS	1,845
55	SIOUX	NE	1,845
56	JACKSON	CO	1,863
57	WAYNE	UT	1,911
58	OURAY	CO	1,925
59	KIOWA	CO	1,936
60	MOTLEY	TX	1,950
61	KEWEENAW	MI	1,963
62	SULLY	SD	1,990

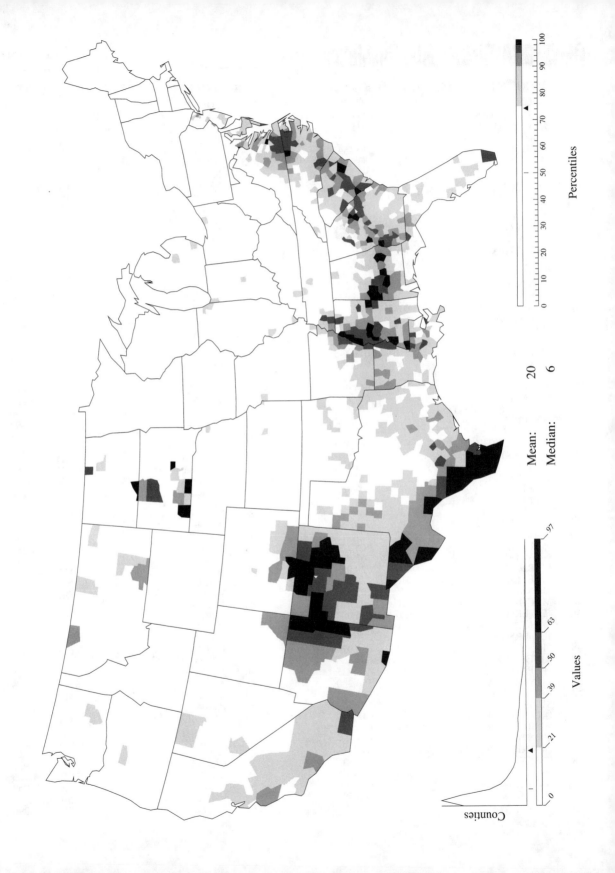

Mean: 20

Median: 6

Percentiles

Values

Counties

0   21   39   50   63   97

(PERCENT OF TOTAL POPULATION)

TOP COUNTIES SHADED BLACK

RANK	COUNTY	STATE	VALUE
1	STARR	TX	97
2	SHANNON	SD	94
3	MAVERICK	TX	93
4	WEBB	TX	92
5	JIM HOGG	TX	91
6	ZAVALA	TX	89
7	MORA	NM	87
8	BROOKS	TX	86
9	DUVAL	TX	86
10	RIO ARRIBA	NM	85
11	MACON	AL	85
12	GUADALUPE	NM	84
13	SAN MIGUEL	NM	83
14	KENEDY	TX	83
15	JEFFERSON	MS	82
16	HIDALGO	TX	82
17	WILLACY	TX	81
18	COSTILLA	CO	80
19	MC KINLEY	NM	80
20	DIMMIT	TX	79
21	APACHE	AZ	79
22	CHARLES CITY	VA	79
23	GREENE	AL	78
24	HANCOCK	GA	78
25	CAMERON	TX	78
26	TODD	SD	78
27	PRESIDIO	TX	77
28	ZAPATA	TX	76
29	TAOS	NM	76
30	CLAIBORNE	MS	75
31	SANTA CRUZ	AZ	75
32	LOWNDES	AL	75
33	DISTRICT OF COLUMBIA	DC	74
34	LA SALLE	TX	74
35	TUNICA	MS	73
36	HOLMES	MS	72
37	BUFFALO	SD	71
38	SUMTER	AL	70
39	WILCOX	AL	69
40	FRIO	TX	69
41	BULLOCK	AL	68
42	JIM WELLS	TX	68
43	WILKINSON	MS	67
44	EL PASO	TX	67
45	HUMPHREYS	MS	66
46	REEVES	TX	66
47	SHARKEY	MS	66
48	TALIAFERRO	GA	65
49	VAL VERDE	TX	65
50	SIOUX	ND	65
51	NOXUBEE	MS	65
52	STEWART	GA	65
53	TALBOT	GA	65
54	COAHOMA	MS	65
55	CULBERSON	TX	64
56	WARREN	NC	64
57	ALLENDALE	SC	63
58	BOLIVAR	MS	63
59	HALE	AL	63
60	CONEJOS	CO	63
61	WILLIAMSBURG	SC	63

BOTTOM COUNTIES SHADED WHITE

NOTE: TOO MANY COUNTIES TO LIST
HAD ZERO VALUES FOR THIS MEASURE

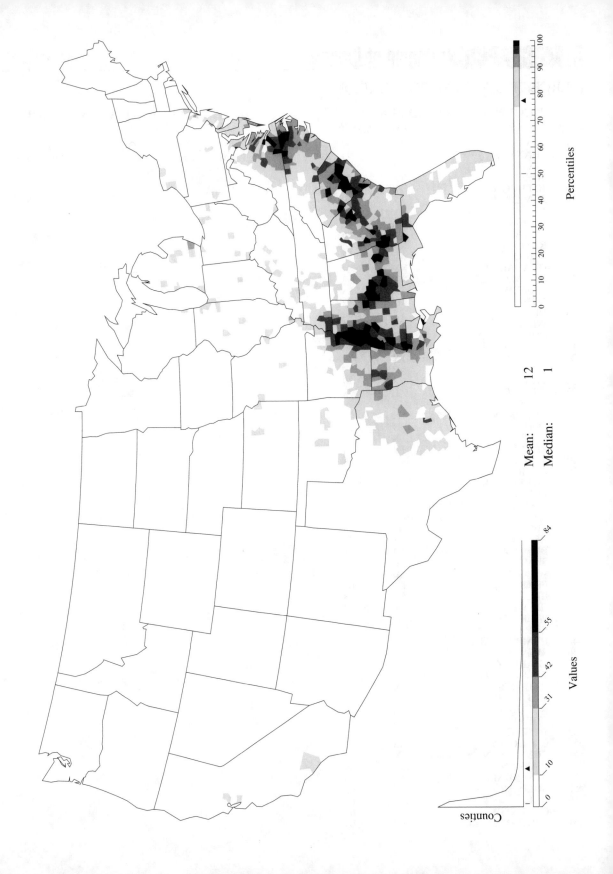

Percentiles

Mean: 12

Median: 1

Values

Counties

(PERCENT OF TOTAL POPULATION)

TOP COUNTIES SHADED BLACK

RANK	COUNTY	STATE	VALUE
1	MACON	AL	84
2	JEFFERSON	MS	82
3	HANCOCK	GA	78
4	GREENE	AL	78
5	LOWNDES	AL	75
6	CLAIBORNE	MS	75
7	TUNICA	MS	73
8	HOLMES	MS	71
9	CHARLES CITY	VA	71
10	DISTRICT OF COLUMBIA	DC	70
11	SUMTER	AL	69
12	WILCOX	AL	69
13	BULLOCK	AL	68
14	WILKINSON	MS	67
15	SHARKEY	MS	66
16	HUMPHREYS	MS	66
17	TALIAFERRO	GA	65
18	NOXUBEE	MS	65
19	TALBOT	GA	65
20	STEWART	GA	64
21	COAHOMA	MS	64
22	HALE	AL	63
23	ALLENDALE	SC	63
24	SURRY	VA	63
25	WILLIAMSBURG	SC	62
26	BOLIVAR	MS	62
27	CLAY	GA	62
28	SUNFLOWER	MS	62
29	LEE	SC	61
30	EAST CARROLL	LA	61
31	SUSSEX	VA	61
32	TERRELL	GA	61
33	NORTHAMPTON	NC	61
34	MC CORMICK	SC	61
35	PERRY	AL	60
36	GADSDEN	FL	60
37	WARREN	GA	60
38	WARREN	NC	59
39	BERTIE	NC	59
40	LEFLORE	MS	59
41	MADISON	LA	59
42	FAIRFIELD	SC	58
43	WEST FELICIANA	LA	58
44	CALHOUN	GA	57
45	CLARENDON	SC	57
46	BRUNSWICK	VA	57
47	TALLAHATCHIE	MS	57
48	BAMBERG	SC	57
49	JASPER	SC	57
50	QUITMAN	GA	57
51	MACON	GA	56
52	RANDOLPH	GA	56
53	QUITMAN	MS	56
54	ORANGEBURG	SC	56
55	MADISON	MS	56
56	WASHINGTON	MS	56
57	ISSAQUENA	MS	56
58	ORLEANS	LA	55
59	CALHOUN	SC	55
60	LEE	AR	55
61	HERTFORD	NC	55

BOTTOM COUNTIES SHADED WHITE

NOTE: TOO MANY COUNTIES TO LIST
HAD ZERO VALUES FOR THIS MEASURE

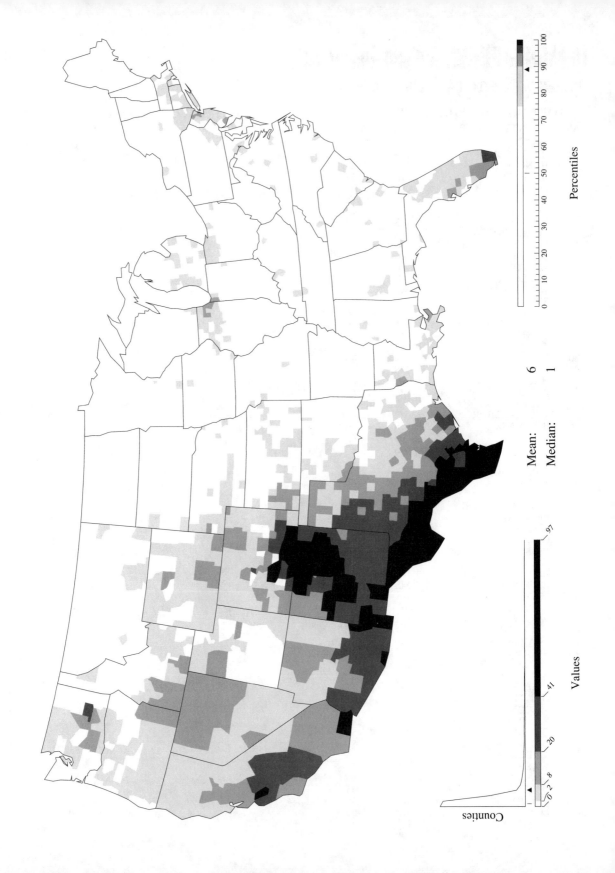

Mean: 6

Median: 1

Percentiles

Values

Counties

(PERCENT OF TOTAL POPULATION)

TOP COUNTIES SHADED BLACK

RANK	COUNTY	STATE	VALUE
1	STARR	TX	97
2	WEBB	TX	92
3	JIM HOGG	TX	91
4	MAVERICK	TX	90
5	ZAVALA	TX	89
6	MORA	NM	87
7	BROOKS	TX	86
8	DUVAL	TX	85
9	GUADALUPE	NM	83
10	KENEDY	TX	83
11	SAN MIGUEL	NM	81
12	HIDALGO	TX	81
13	WILLACY	TX	80
14	DIMMIT	TX	78
15	COSTILLA	CO	77
16	CAMERON	TX	77
17	PRESIDIO	TX	77
18	ZAPATA	TX	76
19	RIO ARRIBA	NM	75
20	SANTA CRUZ	AZ	74
21	LA SALLE	TX	74
22	TAOS	NM	69
23	FRIO	TX	68
24	JIM WELLS	TX	67
25	CULBERSON	TX	63
26	VAL VERDE	TX	63
27	EL PASO	TX	62
28	REEVES	TX	62
29	CONEJOS	CO	61
30	HUDSPETH	TX	58
31	KINNEY	TX	57
32	IMPERIAL	CA	56
33	SANTA FE	NM	56
34	UVALDE	TX	55
35	KLEBERG	TX	52
36	DONA ANA	NM	52
37	GRANT	NM	51
38	NUECES	TX	49
39	PECOS	TX	49
40	ATASCOSA	TX	48
41	GREENLEE	AZ	48
42	EDWARDS	TX	48
43	COLFAX	NM	47
44	JEFF DAVIS	TX	47
45	HIDALGO	NM	47
46	SOCORRO	NM	47
47	BEXAR	TX	47
48	SAN PATRICIO	TX	46
49	BEE	TX	46
50	SAN BENITO	CA	46
51	CROCKETT	TX	45
52	HARDING	NM	44
53	HUERFANO	CO	44
54	VALENCIA	NM	44
55	LAS ANIMAS	CO	44
56	MEDINA	TX	43
57	TERRELL	TX	43
58	KARNES	TX	43
59	BREWSTER	TX	43
60	SAGUACHE	CO	41
61	TORRANCE	NM	41

BOTTOM COUNTIES SHADED WHITE

NOTE: TOO MANY COUNTIES TO LIST
HAD ZERO VALUES FOR THIS MEASURE

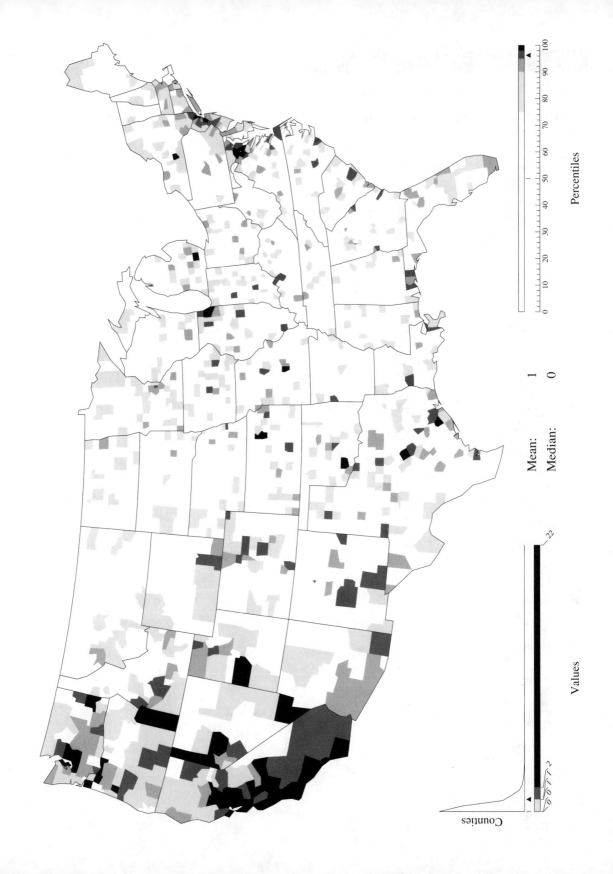

Percentiles

Mean: 1
Median: 0

Values

Counties

(PERCENT OF TOTAL POPULATION)

TOP COUNTIES SHADED BLACK

RANK	COUNTY	STATE	VALUE
1	SAN FRANCISCO	CA	22
2	SAN MATEO	CA	10
3	ALAMEDA	CA	8
4	SANTA CLARA	CA	8
5	SOLANO	CA	8
6	SUTTER	CA	7
7	MONTEREY	CA	7
8	SAN JOAQUIN	CA	6
9	LOS ANGELES	CA	6
10	SACRAMENTO	CA	5
11	SAN DIEGO	CA	5
12	ARLINGTON	VA	5
13	KING	WA	5
14	ORANGE	CA	5
15	CONTRA COSTA	CA	5
16	YOLO	CA	4
17	MONTGOMERY	MD	4
18	GEARY	KS	4
19	FAIRFAX	VA	4
20	NEW YORK CITY	NY	3
21	PIERCE	WA	3
22	YUBA	CA	3
23	ISLAND	WA	3
24	COLUSA	CA	3
25	KITSAP	WA	3
26	SANTA BARBARA	CA	3
27	DU PAGE	IL	3
28	FORT BEND	TX	3
29	KINGS	CA	3
30	WHITMAN	WA	3
31	FRESNO	CA	3
32	VENTURA	CA	3
33	MALHEUR	OR	3
34	BENTON	OR	3
35	MULTNOMAH	OR	3
36	MARIN	CA	3
37	HUDSON	NJ	3
38	SANTA CRUZ	CA	3
39	COMANCHE	OK	3
40	PRINCE GEORGES	MD	3
41	SUFFOLK	MA	3
42	TOMPKINS	NY	2
43	MERCED	CA	2
44	BERGEN	NJ	2
45	HOOD RIVER	OR	2
46	CHURCHILL	NV	2
47	THURSTON	WA	2
48	CORYELL	TX	2
49	NAPA	CA	2
50	PULASKI	MO	2
51	COOK	IL	2
52	WASHINGTON	OR	2
53	SAN LUIS OBISPO	CA	2
54	RILEY	KS	2
55	CLATSOP	OR	2
56	MILLARD	UT	2
57	HOWARD	MD	2
58	WASHTENAW	MI	2
59	CLARK	NV	2
60	WASHOE	NV	2
61	MIDDLESEX	NJ	2

BOTTOM COUNTIES SHADED WHITE

NOTE: TOO MANY COUNTIES TO LIST
HAD ZERO VALUES FOR THIS MEASURE

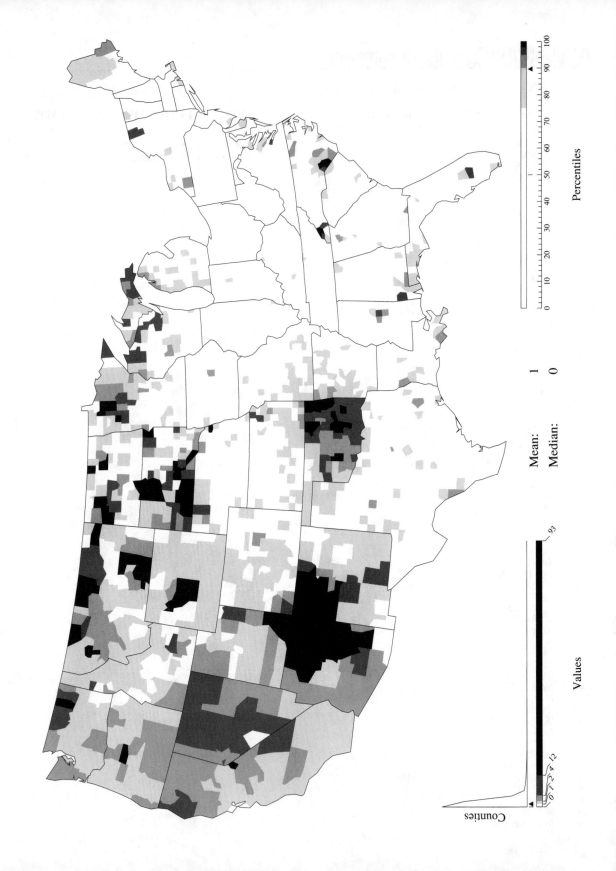

Percentiles

Mean: 1
Median: 0

Values

Counties

(PERCENT OF TOTAL POPULATION)

TOP COUNTIES SHADED BLACK

RANK	COUNTY	STATE	VALUE
1	SHANNON	SD	93
2	TODD	SD	78
3	APACHE	AZ	75
4	BUFFALO	SD	71
5	MC KINLEY	NM	66
6	SIOUX	ND	65
7	ZIEBACH	SD	58
8	DEWEY	SD	58
9	ROLETTE	ND	58
10	NAVAJO	AZ	48
11	CORSON	SD	47
12	BIG HORN	MT	46
13	GLACIER	MT	46
14	SAN JUAN	UT	46
15	JACKSON	SD	43
16	MELLETTE	SD	39
17	BENNETT	SD	39
18	ROOSEVELT	MT	37
19	ROBESON	NC	35
20	THURSTON	NE	34
21	ADAIR	OK	33
22	SAN JUAN	NM	33
23	BLAINE	MT	32
24	BENSON	ND	29
25	COCONINO	AZ	28
26	SANDOVAL	NM	27
27	CHEROKEE	OK	26
28	ROSEBUD	MT	24
29	SWAIN	NC	24
30	LYMAN	SD	23
31	DELAWARE	OK	21
32	ROBERTS	SD	19
33	MAHNOMEN	MN	18
34	CADDO	OK	18
35	CHARLES MIX	SD	18
36	JEFFERSON	OR	17
37	FERRY	WA	17
38	LAKE	MT	17
39	ALPINE	CA	15
40	OKFUSKEE	OK	15
41	SEQUOYAH	OK	15
42	VALENCIA	NM	14
43	LATIMER	OK	14
44	GILA	AZ	14
45	MAYES	OK	14
46	HUGHES	OK	14
47	SEMINOLE	OK	14
48	MC KENZIE	ND	13
49	HILL	MT	13
50	OTTAWA	OK	13
51	BELTRAMI	MN	13
52	HOKE	NC	13
53	CRAIG	OK	12
54	MC INTOSH	OK	12
55	OSAGE	OK	12
56	MOUNTRAIL	ND	12
57	COAL	OK	12
58	GRAHAM	AZ	12
59	FREMONT	WY	12
60	RIO ARRIBA	NM	12

BOTTOM COUNTIES SHADED WHITE

NOTE: TOO MANY COUNTIES TO LIST
HAD ZERO VALUES FOR THIS MEASURE

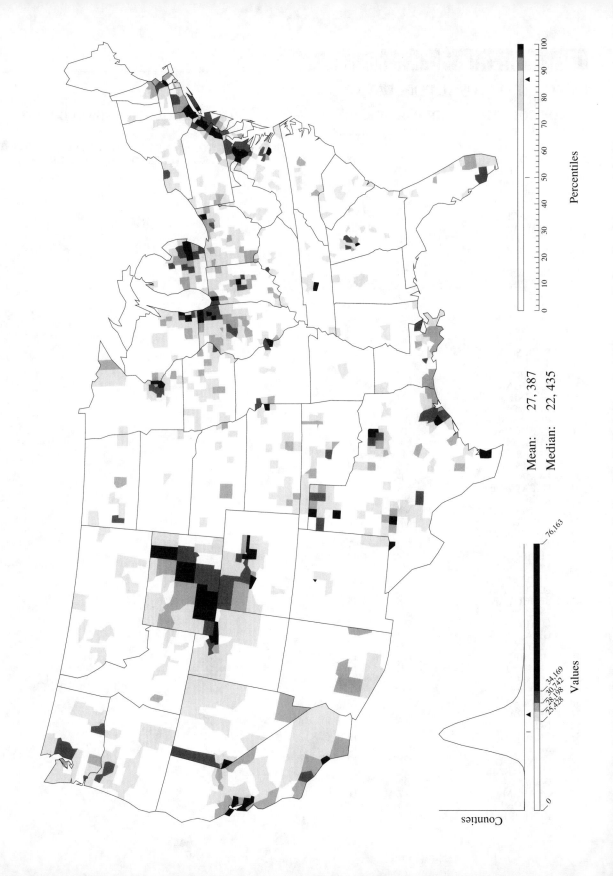

Mean: 27, 387

Median: 22, 435

Percentiles

Values

Counties

76,163

34,169
30,742
28,098
25,428

TOP COUNTIES SHADED BLACK

RANK	COUNTY	STATE	VALUE
1	LOVING	TX	76,163
2	MONTGOMERY	MD	46,282
3	DOUGLAS	CO	45,757
4	KENEDY	TX	44,495
5	FAIRFAX	VA	42,595
6	LAKE	IL	41,860
7	DU PAGE	IL	41,831
8	NASSAU	NY	41,779
9	MARIN	CA	41,522
10	MORRIS	NJ	41,048
11	SOMERSET	NJ	40,875
12	OAKLAND	MI	40,795
13	HOWARD	MD	40,136
14	JOHNSON	KS	40,104
15	FAIRFIELD	CT	40,078
16	WESTCHESTER	NY	39,986
17	OZAUKEE	WI	39,653
18	SHERMAN	TX	39,523
19	ROCKWALL	TX	39,445
20	LOS ALAMOS	NM	39,414
21	FORT BEND	TX	39,165
22	WAUKESHA	WI	39,151
23	BERGEN	NJ	38,592
24	ROCKLAND	NY	38,413
25	GEAUGA	OH	38,396
26	HAMILTON	IN	38,316
27	DOUGLAS	NV	38,267
28	ARAPAHOE	CO	37,997
29	MIDLAND	TX	37,917
30	HUNTERDON	NJ	37,772
31	FAYETTE	GA	37,645
32	CAMPBELL	WY	37,636
33	MONTGOMERY	PA	37,329
34	SAN MATEO	CA	37,315
35	LOUDOUN	VA	37,111
36	PITKIN	CO	36,995
37	JEFFERSON	CO	36,378
38	ORANGE	CA	36,063
39	SANTA CLARA	CA	35,895
40	LIVINGSTON	MI	35,843
41	CONTRA COSTA	CA	35,827
42	PRINCE WILLIAM	VA	35,790
43	ARLINGTON	VA	35,585
44	COLLIN	TX	35,448
45	WASHINGTON	MN	35,411
46	PUTNAM	NY	35,280
47	CHESTER	PA	35,225
48	WILLIAMSON	TN	35,206
49	MACOMB	MI	35,206
50	DAKOTA	MN	34,987
51	ST LOUIS	MO	34,964
52	MC HENRY	IL	34,943
53	KENDALL	IL	34,928
54	NATRONA	WY	34,875
55	SWEETWATER	WY	34,720
56	PORTER	IN	34,629
57	NORFOLK	MA	34,468
58	CHESTERFIELD	VA	34,435
59	RANDALL	TX	34,284
60	UNION	NJ	34,282
61	SUMMIT	UT	34,169

BOTTOM COUNTIES SHADED WHITE

RANK	COUNTY	STATE	VALUE
1	HANCOCK	TN	12,033
2	OWSLEY	KY	12,106
3	CLINTON	KY	12,956
4	MORA	NM	13,589
5	NEWTON	AR	13,653
6	SEARCY	AR	13,938
7	MC CREARY	KY	14,032
8	SIERRA	NM	14,107
9	FENTRESS	TN	14,142
10	JACKSON	KY	14,183
11	BUFFALO	SD	14,328
12	RIPLEY	MO	14,332
13	JEFFERSON	MS	14,343
14	LEE	AR	14,347
15	PICKETT	TN	14,348
16	STARR	TX	14,357
17	SANBORN	SD	14,463
18	WAYNE	KY	14,493
19	CONEJOS	CO	14,519
20	OREGON	MO	14,572
21	DOUGLAS	SD	14,695
22	STEWART	GA	14,710
23	TALIAFERRO	GA	14,724
24	CASEY	KY	14,729
25	WOLFE	KY	14,731
26	COSTILLA	CO	14,771
27	HOLMES	MS	14,820
28	CAMPBELL	SD	14,825
29	QUITMAN	GA	14,953
30	MENIFEE	KY	14,982
31	FULTON	AR	15,044
32	STONE	AR	15,050
33	TUNICA	MS	15,076
34	MINER	SD	15,116
35	HICKORY	MO	15,121
36	WHEELER	GA	15,181
37	JOHNSTON	OK	15,183
38	KEWEENAW	MI	15,233
39	MC PHERSON	SD	15,278
40	PERRY	AL	15,303
41	GREENE	AL	15,311
42	SHANNON	MO	15,366
43	WILKINSON	MS	15,401
44	ROCKCASTLE	KY	15,402
45	ZIEBACH	SD	15,438
46	GUADALUPE	NM	15,442
47	CUMBERLAND	KY	15,482
48	JOHNSON	TN	15,495
49	CLAY	KY	15,529
50	PRESIDIO	TX	15,531
51	CLAY	TN	15,656
52	SWAIN	NC	15,745
53	BOYD	NE	15,748
54	WAYNE	MO	15,765
55	LEAKE	MS	15,806
56	LEE	KY	15,824
57	FAULK	SD	15,851
58	KEMPER	MS	15,858
59	ZAVALA	TX	15,859
60	MORGAN	KY	15,883
61	GREGORY	SD	15,889
62	LAKE	MI	15,917

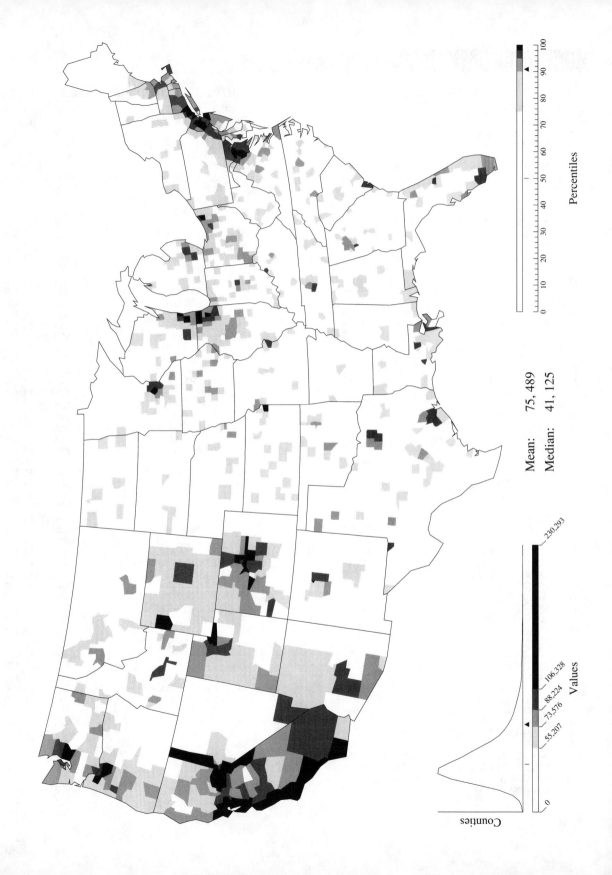

Mean: 75, 489
Median: 41, 125

Percentiles

Values

Counties

230,293

106,328
88,224
73,576
55,207

0

TOP COUNTIES SHADED BLACK

RANK	COUNTY	STATE	VALUE
1	MARIN	CA	230,293
2	SAN MATEO	CA	204,744
3	PITKIN	CO	179,356
4	SANTA CLARA	CA	175,123
5	SAN FRANCISCO	CA	162,684
6	MONTGOMERY	MD	161,312
7	SANTA BARBARA	CA	159,787
8	ORANGE	CA	158,616
9	CONTRA COSTA	CA	157,215
10	FAIRFIELD	CT	156,239
11	LOS ANGELES	CA	153,081
12	FAIRFAX	VA	152,266
13	VENTURA	CA	145,329
14	SANTA CRUZ	CA	144,804
15	ARLINGTON	VA	143,862
16	MONTEREY	CA	143,720
17	MORRIS	NJ	143,419
18	DOUGLAS	CO	141,616
19	SAN DIEGO	CA	141,532
20	DOUGLAS	NV	140,104
21	ALAMEDA	CA	138,710
22	NANTUCKET	MA	135,508
23	SOMERSET	NJ	135,253
24	LAKE	IL	132,382
25	DU PAGE	IL	131,083
26	SONOMA	CA	130,899
27	HOWARD	MD	129,492
28	ARAPAHOE	CO	127,543
29	WAUKESHA	WI	127,168
30	SUMMIT	CO	126,985
31	JEFFERSON	CO	126,806
32	WESTCHESTER	NY	126,713
33	BERGEN	NJ	126,066
34	OZAUKEE	WI	126,024
35	MONO	CA	124,634
36	BOULDER	CO	121,901
37	NAPA	CA	121,292
38	PLACER	CA	121,107
39	LOS ALAMOS	NM	121,011
40	TETON	WY	119,939
41	EL DORADO	CA	119,722
42	KING	WA	119,662
43	HUNTERDON	NJ	118,797
44	JOHNSON	KS	114,826
45	WASHOE	NV	114,809
46	SAN JUAN	WA	114,490
47	DISTRICT OF COLUMBIA	DC	113,831
48	WASHINGTON	OR	113,596
49	GEAUGA	OH	113,391
50	ALPINE	CA	113,254
51	CLEAR CREEK	CO	112,216
52	MC HENRY	IL	111,116
53	SUMMIT	UT	110,464
54	NEVADA	CA	110,133
55	HENNEPIN	MN	108,938
56	MONMOUTH	NJ	108,136
57	SOLANO	CA	107,042
58	PRINCE WILLIAM	VA	106,830
59	CLACKAMAS	OR	106,697
60	SAN LUIS OBISPO	CA	106,605
61	UNION	NJ	106,328

BOTTOM COUNTIES SHADED WHITE

RANK	COUNTY	STATE	VALUE
1	BANNER	NE	3,226
2	SLOPE	ND	5,947
3	BILLINGS	ND	6,021
4	BLAINE	NE	7,813
5	MC PHERSON	NE	8,213
6	ZIEBACH	SD	8,342
7	BUFFALO	SD	8,739
8	SHANNON	SD	8,924
9	BORDEN	TX	10,685
10	SIOUX	NE	10,759
11	SANBORN	SD	11,152
12	PETROLEUM	MT	11,578
13	ESMERALDA	NV	11,667
14	CARTER	MT	11,816
15	LOUP	NE	12,111
16	GARFIELD	MT	12,152
17	ARTHUR	NE	12,190
18	WHEELER	NE	12,402
19	SIOUX	ND	12,535
20	HARDING	SD	12,695
21	MELLETTE	SD	12,735
22	CORSON	SD	12,815
23	HAYES	NE	12,926
24	KING	TX	13,084
25	NEWTON	AR	13,703
26	MORA	NM	13,795
27	SHERIDAN	ND	14,357
28	AURORA	SD	14,553
29	DEWEY	SD	14,616
30	OWSLEY	KY	14,717
31	HARDING	NM	14,803
32	TODD	SD	14,814
33	ELLIOTT	KY	15,117
34	MC MULLEN	TX	15,152
35	CAMPBELL	SD	15,153
36	GRANT	NE	15,419
37	MADISON	AR	15,440
38	DOUGLAS	MO	15,463
39	OZARK	MO	15,552
40	WOLFE	KY	15,685
41	GLASSCOCK	TX	15,729
42	KEYA PAHA	NE	15,772
43	POWDER RIVER	MT	15,895
44	KIOWA	CO	15,957
45	MINER	SD	16,156
46	HANCOCK	TN	16,164
47	SEARCY	AR	16,175
48	CLARK	SD	16,313
49	WORTH	MO	16,325
50	DALLAS	MO	16,442
51	KEMPER	MS	16,558
52	JACKSON	SD	16,599
53	JACKSON	KY	16,678
54	LESLIE	KY	16,724
55	SHANNON	MO	16,726
56	PAWNEE	NE	16,759
57	KENEDY	TX	16,909
58	MARIES	MO	17,047
59	GOLDEN VALLEY	MT	17,233
60	TALIAFERRO	GA	17,386
61	ROBERTSON	KY	17,415
62	CLEARWATER	MN	17,459

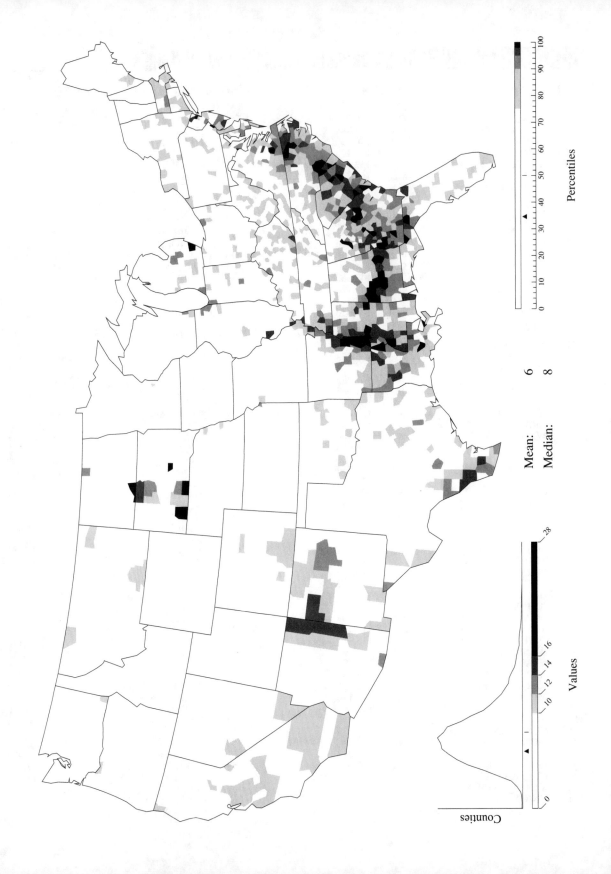

Mean: 6

Median: 8

Percentiles

Values

Counties

(PERCENT OF TOTAL FAMILIES)

TOP COUNTIES SHADED BLACK				BOTTOM COUNTIES SHADED WHITE			
RANK	COUNTY	STATE	VALUE	RANK	COUNTY	STATE	VALUE
1	SHANNON	SD	28	1	MC PHERSON	NE	0
2	HANCOCK	GA	23	2	LOVING	TX	0
3	TODD	SD	22	3	BANNER	NE	1
4	BUFFALO	SD	22	4	DAGGETT	UT	1
5	BALTIMORE CITY	MD	22	5	PIUTE	UT	2
6	MACON	AL	21	6	BILLINGS	ND	2
7	EAST CARROLL	LA	21	7	OLIVER	ND	2
8	BULLOCK	AL	21	8	DUNDY	NE	2
9	HOLMES	MS	21	9	CAMAS	ID	2
10	GADSDEN	FL	20	10	GLASSCOCK	TX	2
11	LOWNDES	AL	20	11	RICH	UT	2
12	GREENE	AL	20	12	CAMPBELL	SD	2
13	BOLIVAR	MS	20	13	WAYNE	UT	2
14	STEWART	GA	19	14	MC INTOSH	ND	2
15	ORLEANS	LA	19	15	LOGAN	NE	2
16	SIOUX	ND	19	16	BORDEN	TX	2
17	MACON	GA	19	17	JERAULD	SD	2
18	HUMPHREYS	MS	19	18	KEYA PAHA	NE	2
19	DISTRICT OF COLUMBIA	DC	19	19	TREASURE	MT	3
20	JEFFERSON	MS	19	20	ARMSTRONG	TX	3
21	ESSEX	NJ	19	21	KIDDER	ND	3
22	DALLAS	AL	19	22	KING	TX	3
23	ALLENDALE	SC	18	23	ESMERALDA	NV	3
24	SUMTER	AL	18	24	MARTIN	TX	3
25	ST LOUIS CITY	MO	18	25	STEVENS	KS	3
26	PHILADELPHIA	PA	18	26	SHERMAN	TX	3
27	FULTON	GA	18	27	SHERMAN	OR	3
28	CLAIBORNE	MS	18	28	MEADE	KS	3
29	MARION	SC	18	29	SMITH	KS	3
30	NOXUBEE	MS	18	30	CUMING	NE	3
31	CLARENDON	SC	18	31	MERCER	ND	3
32	RANDOLPH	GA	18	32	SLOPE	ND	3
33	PEACH	GA	18	33	FURNAS	NE	3
34	JEFFERSON	GA	18	34	LOGAN	ND	3
35	HALE	AL	18	35	STEELE	ND	3
36	LEE	SC	18	36	LIPSCOMB	TX	3
37	WASHINGTON	GA	18	37	MORGAN	UT	3
38	MADISON	LA	18	38	HITCHCOCK	NE	3
39	HOKE	NC	18	39	MINER	SD	3
40	WASHINGTON	MS	18	40	HAMILTON	NE	3
41	JASPER	SC	18	41	PERKINS	NE	3
42	PERRY	AL	17	42	LA MOURE	ND	3
43	COAHOMA	MS	17	43	ANTELOPE	NE	3
44	MARLBORO	SC	17	44	EDDY	ND	3
45	WILCOX	AL	17	45	PLATTE	WY	3
46	HALIFAX	NC	17	46	MINERAL	CO	3
47	ROBESON	NC	17	47	RIO BLANCO	CO	3
48	EDGECOMBE	NC	17	48	HETTINGER	ND	3
49	SUNFLOWER	MS	17	49	GOLDEN VALLEY	MT	3
50	PHILLIPS	AR	17	50	CAVALIER	ND	3
51	MADISON	FL	17	51	WAYNE	NE	3
52	TERRELL	GA	17	52	PHILLIPS	KS	3
53	DINWIDDIE	VA	17	53	PAWNEE	NE	3
54	SCOTLAND	NC	17	54	ROUTT	CO	3
55	MITCHELL	GA	17	55	DECATUR	KS	3
56	WAYNE	MI	16	56	BLAINE	NE	3
57	IBERVILLE	LA	16	57	GARFIELD	WA	3
58	QUITMAN	GA	16	58	CLAY	KS	3
59	BIBB	GA	16	59	REPUBLIC	KS	3
60	WARREN	NC	16	60	POWDER RIVER	MT	3
61	NEW YORK CITY	NY	16	61	MOTLEY	TX	3
				62	CROCKETT	TX	3

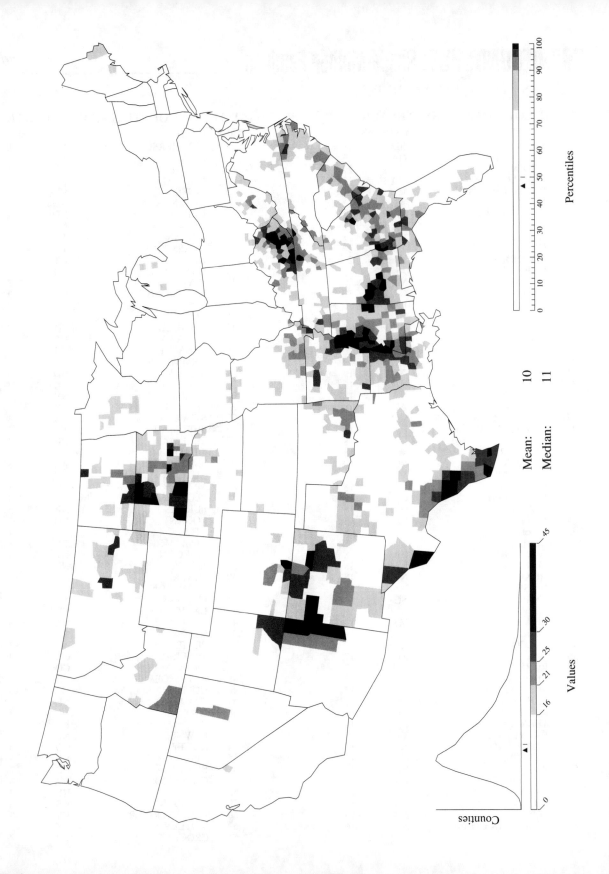

Percentiles

Mean: 10

Median: 11

Values

Counties

(PERCENT OF TOTAL FAMILIES)

TOP COUNTIES SHADED BLACK				BOTTOM COUNTIES SHADED WHITE			
RANK	COUNTY	STATE	VALUE	RANK	COUNTY	STATE	VALUE
1	STARR	TX	45	1	LOVING	TX	0
2	TUNICA	MS	45	2	DU PAGE	IL	2
3	SHANNON	SD	43	3	OZAUKEE	WI	2
4	OWSLEY	KY	41	4	WAUKESHA	WI	2
5	HANCOCK	TN	40	5	ESMERALDA	NV	2
6	HOLMES	MS	39	6	UINTA	WY	3
7	TODD	SD	39	7	JOHNSON	KS	3
8	BUFFALO	SD	38	8	SOMERSET	NJ	3
9	ZIEBACH	SD	37	9	MORRIS	NJ	3
10	CLAY	KY	37	10	HOWARD	MD	3
11	SHARKEY	MS	37	11	MONTGOMERY	MD	3
12	MORA	NM	37	12	LAKE	OH	3
13	LOWNDES	AL	37	13	BERGEN	NJ	3
14	LEE	AR	37	14	CLEAR CREEK	CO	3
15	WILCOX	AL	36	15	CAMPBELL	WY	3
16	JEFFERSON	MS	36	16	LAKE	CO	3
17	GREENE	AL	36	17	DOUGLAS	CO	3
18	JACKSON	KY	36	18	PUTNAM	NY	3
19	LA SALLE	TX	36	19	HAMILTON	IN	3
20	APACHE	AZ	35	20	ARAPAHOE	CO	3
21	HUMPHREYS	MS	35	21	MC HENRY	IL	3
22	CLINTON	KY	35	22	HUNTERDON	NJ	3
23	ZAVALA	TX	35	23	MONTGOMERY	PA	3
24	PRESIDIO	TX	35	24	JEFFERSON	CO	3
25	EAST CARROLL	LA	35	25	SUMMIT	CO	3
26	TALLAHATCHIE	MS	34	26	KENDALL	IL	3
27	MAVERICK	TX	34	27	HENDRICKS	IN	3
28	MC CREARY	KY	34	28	RANDALL	TX	3
29	CORSON	SD	34	29	WASHINGTON	MN	3
30	TENSAS	LA	34	30	ST CHARLES	MO	3
31	STEWART	GA	34	31	ST LOUIS	MO	3
32	MC KINLEY	NM	33	32	DOUGLAS	NV	3
33	CHICOT	AR	33	33	MOFFAT	CO	3
34	HALE	AL	33	34	FAIRFAX	VA	4
35	MADISON	LA	33	35	LOS ALAMOS	NM	4
36	CLAY	GA	33	36	CALUMET	WI	4
37	PERRY	AL	33	37	NANTUCKET	MA	4
38	MELLETTE	SD	33	38	CUMBERLAND	PA	4
39	DIMMIT	TX	33	39	GEAUGA	OH	4
40	SANBORN	SD	33	40	MEDINA	OH	4
41	COSTILLA	CO	32	41	DAKOTA	MN	4
42	HANCOCK	GA	32	42	NASSAU	NY	4
43	QUITMAN	GA	32	43	SHEBOYGAN	WI	4
44	MORGAN	KY	32	44	WASHINGTON	WI	4
45	BOLIVAR	MS	32	45	LAKE	MN	4
46	CASEY	KY	31	46	SHERIDAN	WY	4
47	KNOX	KY	31	47	ANOKA	MN	4
48	BREATHITT	KY	31	48	CLAY	MO	4
49	PHILLIPS	AR	31	49	CHESTERFIELD	VA	4
50	WAYNE	KY	31	50	PORTER	IN	4
51	LESLIE	KY	31	51	ROUTT	CO	4
52	QUITMAN	MS	31	52	WELLS	IN	4
53	NOXUBEE	MS	31	53	MACOMB	MI	4
54	COAHOMA	MS	31	54	LAKE	IL	4
55	KEMPER	MS	30	55	NATRONA	WY	4
56	WOLFE	KY	30	56	CARROLL	MD	4
57	SUNFLOWER	MS	30	57	LITCHFIELD	CT	4
58	LEE	KY	30	58	WHITLEY	IN	4
59	MAGOFFIN	KY	30	59	RIO BLANCO	CO	4
60	FENTRESS	TN	30	60	TOLLAND	CT	4
61	WILLACY	TX	30	61	OAKLAND	MI	4
				62	BALTIMORE	MD	4

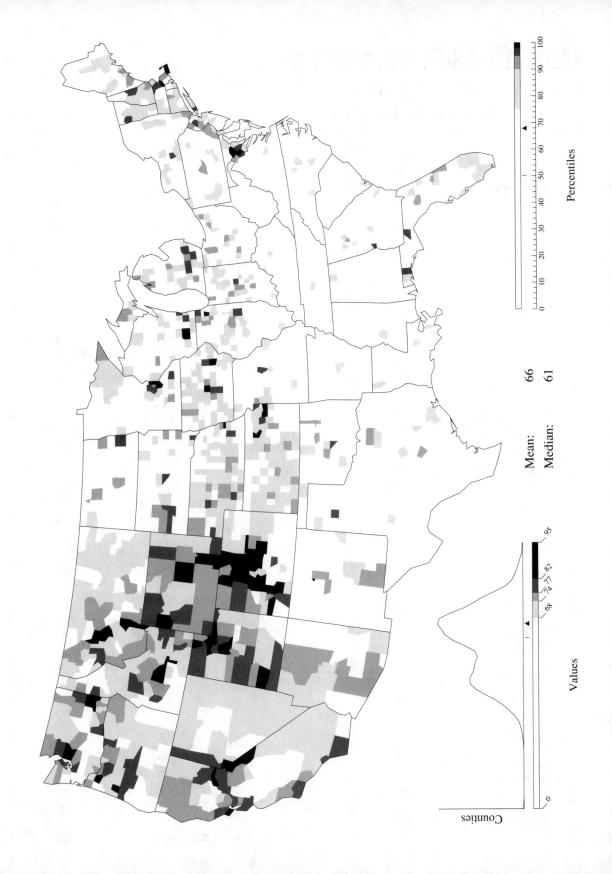

Percentiles

Mean: 66
Median: 61

Values

Counties

(PERCENT OF PEOPLE 25 AND OVER)

	TOP COUNTIES SHADED BLACK				BOTTOM COUNTIES SHADED WHITE		
RANK	COUNTY	STATE	VALUE	RANK	COUNTY	STATE	VALUE
1	SUMMIT	CO	95	1	TALIAFERRO	GA	25
2	PITKIN	CO	95	2	JACKSON	KY	25
3	LOS ALAMOS	NM	94	3	ZAVALA	TX	26
4	TETON	WY	90	4	STARR	TX	27
5	GUNNISON	CO	90	5	WOLFE	KY	27
6	MARIN	CA	90	6	CLAY	KY	28
7	EAGLE	CO	90	7	HANCOCK	TN	29
8	JOHNSON	KS	89	8	MC CREARY	KY	29
9	ARAPAHOE	CO	89	9	BAKER	GA	29
10	DOUGLAS	CO	89	10	CUMBERLAND	KY	29
11	MONO	CA	88	11	OWSLEY	KY	29
12	ROUTT	CO	88	12	WAYNE	KY	30
13	BLAINE	ID	88	13	LA SALLE	TX	30
14	SAN JUAN	WA	88	14	MAGOFFIN	KY	30
15	CLEAR CREEK	CO	88	15	MORGAN	KY	30
16	FAIRFAX	VA	88	16	CLINTON	KY	30
17	BOULDER	CO	87	17	LESLIE	KY	31
18	MONTGOMERY	MD	87	18	TUNICA	MS	31
19	GILPIN	CO	87	19	WARREN	GA	31
20	HINSDALE	CO	87	20	ELLIOTT	KY	31
21	ARLINGTON	VA	87	21	MENIFEE	KY	32
22	JEFFERSON	CO	86	22	GLASCOCK	GA	32
23	BENTON	OR	86	23	LEE	AR	32
24	ALPINE	CA	86	24	MAVERICK	TX	32
25	SARPY	NE	86	25	MONROE	KY	32
26	BARNSTABLE	MA	86	26	JACKSON	TN	33
27	DAVIS	UT	86	27	GRUNDY	TN	33
28	WHITMAN	WA	86	28	TREUTLEN	GA	33
29	JOHNSON	IA	86	29	LEWIS	KY	33
30	STORY	IA	86	30	METCALFE	KY	33
31	RILEY	KS	86	31	LAKE	TN	33
32	DUKES	MA	85	32	CASEY	KY	33
33	SAN MIGUEL	CO	85	33	BUCHANAN	VA	33
34	DOUGLAS	NV	85	34	DICKENSON	VA	33
35	WASHINGTON	OR	85	35	HANCOCK	GA	34
36	ALBANY	WY	85	36	TWIGGS	GA	34
37	CACHE	UT	84	37	FENTRESS	TN	34
38	GALLATIN	MT	84	38	WILLACY	TX	34
39	SUMMIT	UT	84	39	GREENSVILLE	VA	34
40	CAMAS	ID	84	40	KENEDY	TX	34
41	DANE	WI	84	41	DOOLY	GA	34
42	GRAND	CO	84	42	POWELL	KY	34
43	DAKOTA	MN	84	43	CLAY	TN	34
44	MINERAL	CO	83	44	LEE	VA	34
45	MORGAN	UT	83	45	CHATTOOGA	GA	34
46	TELLER	CO	83	46	CLINCH	GA	34
47	IRON	UT	83	47	ROCKCASTLE	KY	34
48	DU PAGE	IL	83	48	GRAINGER	TN	34
49	HOWARD	MD	83	49	MARTIN	KY	34
50	WASHINGTON	MN	83	50	LEE	KY	35
51	UTAH	UT	83	51	BUTLER	KY	35
52	EL PASO	CO	83	52	ADAIR	KY	35
53	LARIMER	CO	83	53	CALHOUN	GA	35
54	KING	WA	83	54	MACON	TN	35
55	NATRONA	WY	83	55	JIM HOGG	TX	35
56	LEWIS AND CLARK	MT	82	56	GREENE	GA	35
57	PARK	CO	82	57	WEBSTER	WV	35
58	DOUGLAS	KS	82	58	JOHNSON	GA	35
59	ISLAND	WA	82	59	ATKINSON	GA	35
60	NEVADA	CA	82	60	OVERTON	TN	35
61	NORFOLK	MA	82	61	JENKINS	GA	35
				62	MACON	GA	35

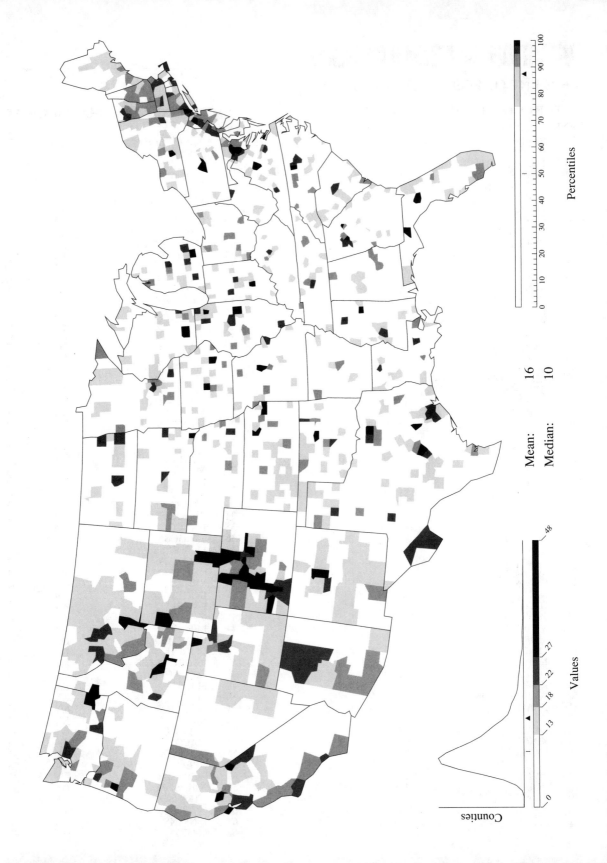

Mean: 16

Median: 10

Percentiles

0 10 20 30 40 50 60 70 80 90 100

Values

Counties

0 13 18 22 27 48

(PERCENT OF PEOPLE 25 AND OVER)

TOP COUNTIES SHADED BLACK

RANK	COUNTY	STATE	VALUE
1	LOS ALAMOS	NM	48
2	PITKIN	CO	46
3	MONTGOMERY	MD	43
4	ARLINGTON	VA	43
5	FAIRFAX	VA	41
6	ORANGE	NC	41
7	GUNNISON	CO	40
8	SUMMIT	CO	39
9	JOHNSON	IA	39
10	HOWARD	MD	39
11	MARIN	CA	38
12	WHITMAN	WA	37
13	BENTON	OR	37
14	BOULDER	CO	36
15	TOMPKINS	NY	36
16	WASHTENAW	MI	36
17	SAN MIGUEL	CO	36
18	ALBANY	WY	36
19	DOUGLAS	KS	35
20	CLARKE	GA	35
21	BOONE	MO	35
22	EAGLE	CO	35
23	STORY	IA	34
24	JOHNSON	KS	33
25	TETON	WY	33
26	YELLOWSTONE NAT. PARK	MT	33
27	ALPINE	CA	32
28	LEON	FL	32
29	ALBEMARLE	VA	32
30	ARAPAHOE	CO	32
31	BRAZOS	TX	32
32	ROUTT	CO	32
33	RILEY	KS	32
34	MONROE	IN	31
35	SAN JUAN	WA	31
36	DANE	WI	31
37	HINSDALE	CO	31
38	CLAY	SD	31
39	GALLATIN	MT	30
40	BLAINE	ID	30
41	TRAVIS	TX	30
42	CHAMPAIGN	IL	30
43	CLEAR CREEK	CO	30
44	LATAH	ID	30
45	ALACHUA	FL	29
46	DU PAGE	IL	29
47	LARIMER	CO	29
48	MORRIS	NJ	29
49	OKTIBBEHA	MS	28
50	SAN FRANCISCO	CA	28
51	WESTCHESTER	NY	28
52	DE KALB	GA	28
53	DISTRICT OF COLUMBIA	DC	27
54	CENTRE	PA	27
55	PAYNE	OK	27
56	DOUGLAS	CO	27
57	JAMES CITY	VA	27
58	SANTA FE	NM	27
59	CACHE	UT	27
60	YOLO	CA	27
61	COLLIN	TX	27

BOTTOM COUNTIES SHADED WHITE

RANK	COUNTY	STATE	VALUE
1	UNION	TN	3
2	BUTLER	KY	3
3	COOSA	AL	4
4	SCOTT	AR	4
5	PERRY	TN	4
6	MORGAN	TN	4
7	ECHOLS	GA	4
8	GREEN	KY	4
9	NEWTON	TX	4
10	LAWRENCE	AL	4
11	WAYNE	MO	4
12	GRAINGER	TN	4
13	CALHOUN	AR	4
14	JOHNSON	TN	4
15	MENIFEE	KY	4
16	HANCOCK	TN	4
17	WASHINGTON	MO	4
18	JACKSON	KY	4
19	PAULDING	GA	4
20	LOVING	TX	4
21	HEARD	GA	4
22	BRYAN	GA	4
23	BOONE	WV	4
24	DAWSON	GA	4
25	MACON	TN	4
26	DICKENSON	VA	5
27	CARLISLE	KY	5
28	CLINTON	KY	5
29	LINCOLN	KY	5
30	CLAY	AR	5
31	GLASCOCK	GA	5
32	RIPLEY	MO	5
33	BRANTLEY	GA	5
34	REYNOLDS	MO	5
35	GALLATIN	IL	5
36	GRUNDY	TN	5
37	LINCOLN	WV	5
38	CURRITUCK	NC	5
39	DECATUR	TN	5
40	BOLLINGER	MO	5
41	BAKER	GA	5
42	BIBB	AL	5
43	DIXIE	FL	5
44	CAMDEN	NC	5
45	SCOTT	VA	5
46	LOGAN	ND	5
47	MC NAIRY	TN	5
48	VAN BUREN	TN	5
49	RAINS	TX	5
50	BANKS	GA	5
51	ATKINSON	GA	5
52	WAYNE	TN	5
53	YELL	AR	5
54	YADKIN	NC	5
55	ALLEN	KY	5
56	LARUE	KY	5
57	HARDIN	TN	5
58	SCOTT	TN	5
59	BUCHANAN	VA	5
60	WYOMING	WV	5
61	TWIGGS	GA	5
62	ALLEGHANY	NC	5

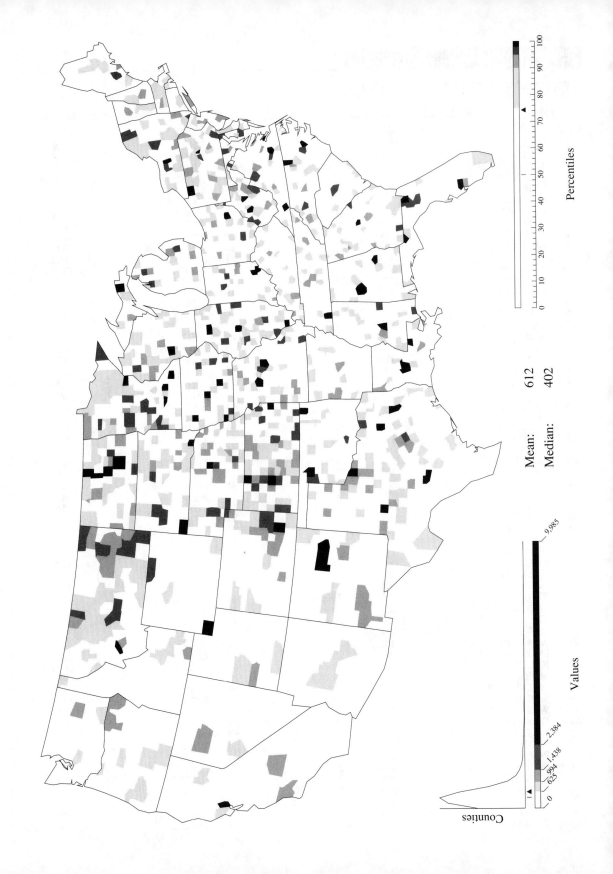

Mean: 612
Median: 402

Percentiles

Values

Counties

9,985

2,384
1,438
994
625
0

(PER 100,000 PEOPLE)

TOP COUNTIES SHADED BLACK

RANK	COUNTY	STATE	VALUE
1	MONTOUR	PA	9,985
2	LUCE	MI	8,395
3	BALDWIN	GA	8,176
4	BAKER	FL	8,019
5	EAST FELICIANA	LA	7,736
6	BENT	CO	7,637
7	DE SOTO	FL	6,439
8	MILLS	IA	6,348
9	CRAIG	OK	6,088
10	GADSDEN	FL	5,584
11	LEWIS	WV	5,183
12	LEE	IL	4,999
13	JAMES CITY	VA	4,924
14	JENNINGS	IN	4,594
15	KERR	TX	4,503
16	WILBARGER	TX	4,482
17	MACON	AL	4,249
18	STUTSMAN	ND	4,028
19	DEER LODGE	MT	4,010
20	ROLETTE	ND	3,958
21	YANKTON	SD	3,831
22	CALLAWAY	MO	3,804
23	NORTON	KS	3,782
24	PIERCE	ND	3,730
25	GARFIELD	NE	3,724
26	HARDEMAN	TN	3,695
27	ROANE	WV	3,648
28	CHEROKEE	TX	3,391
29	LOGAN	IL	3,321
30	SALINE	MO	3,303
31	GRANVILLE	NC	3,240
32	CARLTON	MN	3,200
33	KAUFMAN	TX	3,065
34	SENECA	NY	3,059
35	FALL RIVER	SD	3,057
36	WARREN	PA	3,005
37	MONROE	WI	2,999
38	BOONE	IA	2,960
39	UINTA	WY	2,934
40	RANKIN	MS	2,915
41	TUSCALOOSA	AL	2,912
42	NAPA	CA	2,841
43	NICOLLET	MN	2,822
44	HOWARD	TX	2,776
45	RAPIDES	LA	2,737
46	WOODWARD	OK	2,735
47	MARION	IA	2,713
48	DINWIDDIE	VA	2,688
49	JEFFERSON	IN	2,679
50	SMYTH	VA	2,661
51	OLMSTED	MN	2,644
52	LENOIR	NC	2,596
53	ST LOUIS CITY	MO	2,592
54	CHEROKEE	IA	2,587
55	NESS	KS	2,557
56	UNION	IL	2,556
57	SAN MIGUEL	NM	2,554
58	MIAMI	KS	2,424
59	RICE	MN	2,424
60	WELLS	ND	2,393
61	GUERNSEY	OH	2,384

BOTTOM COUNTIES SHADED WHITE

NOTE: TOO MANY COUNTIES TO LIST
HAD ZERO VALUES FOR THIS MEASURE

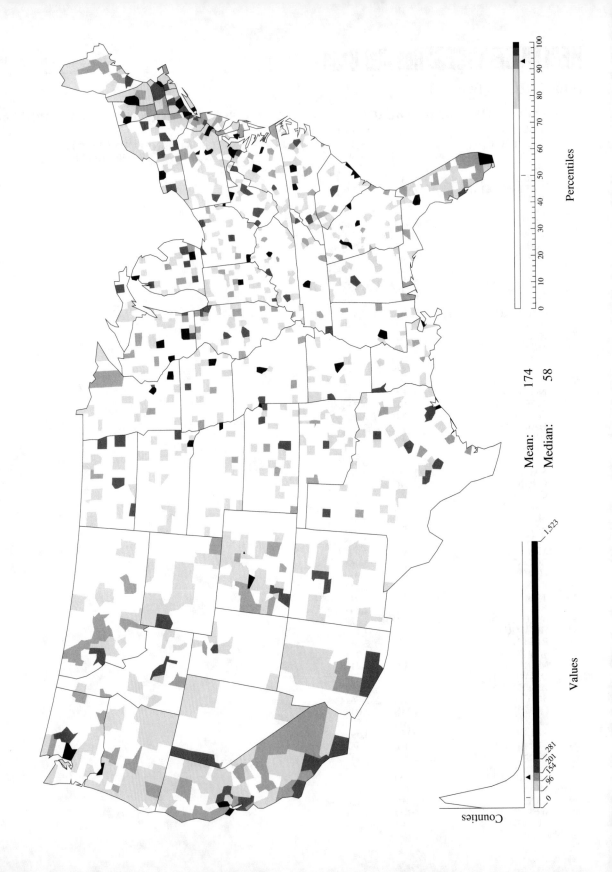

Mean: 174

Median: 58

Percentiles

Values

Counties

0 96 154 201 281 1,523

(PER 100,000 PEOPLE)

TOP COUNTIES SHADED BLACK

RANK	COUNTY	STATE	VALUE
1	MONTOUR	PA	1,523
2	OLMSTED	MN	1,516
3	ORANGE	NC	1,207
4	JOHNSON	IA	1,137
5	DURHAM	NC	872
6	ALBEMARLE	VA	764
7	SUFFOLK	MA	703
8	ST LOUIS CITY	MO	657
9	BOONE	MO	651
10	WASHTENAW	MI	633
11	SAN FRANCISCO	CA	612
12	GRAFTON	NH	565
13	MONONGALIA	WV	548
14	DENVER	CO	541
15	BALTIMORE CITY	MD	537
16	ALACHUA	FL	533
17	DISTRICT OF COLUMBIA	DC	511
18	MONTGOMERY	MD	473
19	FAYETTE	KY	454
20	CHITTENDEN	VT	447
21	DANE	WI	418
22	RICHMOND	GA	417
23	ORLEANS	LA	415
24	GALVESTON	TX	412
25	FULTON	GA	408
26	ALBANY	NY	374
27	MULTNOMAH	OR	371
28	WESTCHESTER	NY	366
29	FORSYTH	NC	366
30	HENRICO	VA	363
31	MARIN	CA	360
32	HINDS	MS	352
33	MONTGOMERY	PA	351
34	EMMET	MI	348
35	DAVIDSON	TN	348
36	YANKTON	SD	332
37	TALBOT	MD	328
38	CHARLESTON	SC	325
39	DUKES	MA	324
40	PHILADELPHIA	PA	324
41	DOUGLAS	NE	323
42	PULASKI	AR	322
43	HENNEPIN	MN	318
44	NEW HAVEN	CT	318
45	OHIO	WV	318
46	NEW YORK CITY	NY	312
47	NORFOLK	MA	306
48	NASSAU	NY	305
49	PITKIN	CO	300
50	HOWARD	MD	299
51	WOOD	WI	294
52	WYANDOTTE	KS	292
53	NAPA	CA	291
54	BALDWIN	GA	291
55	MONROE	NY	290
56	HAMILTON	OH	287
57	LA CROSSE	WI	286
58	KING	WA	285
59	DADE	FL	284
60	DAUPHIN	PA	282
61	MARION	IN	281

BOTTOM COUNTIES SHADED WHITE

NOTE: TOO MANY COUNTIES TO LIST
HAD ZERO VALUES FOR THIS MEASURE

METHODS

MAP DESIGN

More on the Legend

As discussed briefly in chapter 1, the legend beneath the maps provides much more information than a typical map legend. Understanding its various parts will tell you much more about the variable being mapped.

To the left is a value scale and a distribution curve. The length of each shaded segment of the left-hand scale indicates the magnitude of the data variation within that class (without reference to the number of counties involved). To the right is a percentile scale, which remains identical in all of the maps, except that the positions of the small black triangle and vertical line (indicating the mean and median) vary. The lengths of the shaded segments of the right-hand scale lengths indicate the number of counties that fall within each class, which is identical for every map. The national means are straightforward averages (the sum of all county values divided by the number of counties—3,073), except for the following variables, which were weighted by county populations: mortality rates, health services, education, socioeconomics, and demographics (except total population). National medians indicate the 50th percentile for each measure.

In addition to the mean and median statistics, the distribution curve indicates the value of the measure's mode. The highest point (or points) on the curve is a mode, that is, a value that counties most frequently share. There is a simple way to determine the modal value using the legend that is better than just eyeballing it:

- Using a pencil, measure the distance from the highest point on the distribution curve to the vertical axis on the left.
- See how many percentiles the same distance covers on the right-hand percentile scale.
- Consider the number of percentiles a percentage (for example, 30 percentiles equals 30 percent) and multiply this percentage by the maximum value on the left-hand scale.

The result is the value of the mode, calculated as a percentage of the maximum value.

The shape of a distribution curve, and the values of the mode, mean, and median tell a lot about the variable being mapped. A normal distribution is bell shaped and symmetrical. With a normally distributed variable, the mode, mean, and median would all be equal. In many cases, the variables are not normally distributed. If the mode is closer to the lower end (or tail) of the scale, for example, then the distribution is positively skewed, meaning that most counties are below the mean. This can happen when a few counties have extremely high values. In this case, the value scale's black segment will be very long—the top 2 percent of the counties will account for a larger portion of the data variation. An extreme example is the map of toxic waste generators, which are highly concentrated geographically: the mean is about seven times greater than the median, and the top 2 percent of the counties account for over 93 percent of the data variation. Again, this can be determined by translating the length of the black segment into percentages, using the right-hand scale.

An earlier version of this legend was developed by the U.S. Environmental Protection Agency (EPA), in order to highlight those counties most in need of attention, follow-up, and control.[1] This is why the shaded groups contain fewer and fewer counties at the upper tail of the variable distributions, focusing on the top 10, 5, and 2 percentiles.

County Boundaries

Data for every continental U.S. county is included in the maps. In order to maintain consistency, however, data for certain counties have been incorporated into adjacent or encompassing counties when appropriate data values variables are unavailable or when changes have taken place over time. Table A-1 provides the details on every transformation that was necessary for preparing the maps. Most changes are made to Virginia's independent cities, which would not be visible without the alterations anyway. The county boundary maps are from the Census Bureau.

MORTALITY MEASURES

Statistical Interpretations

Seven additional bar charts are presented below that summarize the geographic and race-sex disparities among the causes of death, and the correlations of each cause with the pollution and social structure measures.

Figure A-1 portrays each mortality rate's geographic inequality and how these inequalities are changing.[2] The chart measures the degree to which counties vary from each other relative to the national average. The geographic inequality from all diseases, for example, is roughly double that for all cancers (ten versus five). Causes with more deaths generally have greater levels of inequality, but this is not always the case. Of the ten causes, young-adult infectious disease, for example, was responsible for the fewest deaths during 1968–83, but its level of geographic inequality was greater than three other causes.

I. Arizona
   a. Yuma County includes the new La Paz County
II. New Mexico
   a. Valencia County includes the new Cibola County
III. New York
   a. New York City includes Bronx, Kings, New York, Richmond, and Queens counties
IV. South Dakota
   a. Jackson County includes the former Washabaugh county
V. Virginia
   a. Surrounding counties contain Virginia independent cities as follows:
      1. Albemarle County includes Charlottesville
      2. Alleghany County includes Clifton Forge and Covington
      3. Augusta County includes Staunton and Waynesboro
      4. Bedford County includes Bedford
      5. Campbell County includes Lynchburg
      6. Chesterfield County includes Colonial Heights
      7. Dinwiddie County includes Petersburg
      8. Fairfax County includes Alexandria, Fairfax, and Falls Church
      9. Frederick County includes Winchester
     10. Grayson County includes Galax
     11. Greensville County includes Emporia
     12. Halifax County includes South Boston
     13. Henrico County includes Richmond
     14. Henry County includes Martinsville
     15. James City County includes Williamsburg
     16. Montgomery County includes Radford
     17. Pittsylvania County includes Danville
     18. Prince George County includes Hopewell
     19. Prince William County includes Manassas and Manassas Park
     20. Roanoke County includes Roanoke and Salem
     21. Rockbridge County includes Buena Vista and Lexington
     22. Rockingham County includes Harisonburg
     23. Southhampton County includes Franklin
     24. Spottsylvania County includes Fredricksburg
     25. Washington County includes Bristol
     26. Wise County includes Norton
     27. York County includes Poquoson
   b. The following seven adjacent independent cities are combined (and called Tidewater):
      1. Chesapeake
      2. Hampton
      3. Newport News
      4. Norfolk
      5. Portsmouth
      6. Suffolk
      7. Virginia Beach
VI. Wisconsin
   a. Oconto County and Shawano County contain parts of the new Menominee County

TABLE A-1. Transformations Needed to Map Counties

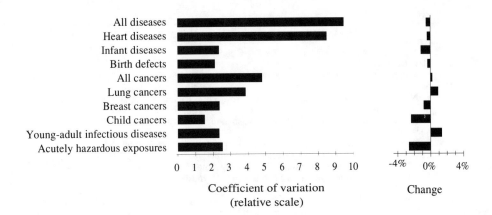

FIGURE A-1.   Geographic Inequalities and Average Annual Changes

Figures A-2 and A-3 contrast mortality rates and geographic inequalities for whites versus minorities, and for males versus females (ratios greater than one mean higher rates for minorities or males, ratios less than one mean lower rates for these groups relative to whites or females). These two figures also indicate that the differences between these population groups are diverging for many causes of death (positive numbers indicate divergences, negative numbers indicate convergences). Differences between the sexes are greater than between races for all but three of the causes; the exceptions are infant diseases, birth defects, and young adult infectious diseases. Part of the gender gap in mortality is biological; however, men suffer mortality from acutely hazardous exposures at a rate almost four times higher than women, suggesting occupational exposures are significantly higher.

Figure A-2 shows that the most striking differences in mortality between these groups are for lung cancers, young-adult infectious diseases, and acutely hazardous exposures. The biggest gap is for young-adult infectious diseases. Minorities suffer from this cause of death at a rate that is over four times greater than whites. The picture changed rapidly as white male mortality from AIDS skyrocketed, resulting in a convergence between whites and minorities of almost 3 percent a year, and a divergence between men and women of almost 4 percent a year. Males suffer from lung cancer mortality at a rate more than four times higher than females, but unlike AIDS, the rates between the sexes are converging by almost 4 percent a year, possibly due to the fact that large numbers of women began smoking later than men, and the toll for women is finally beginning to register.

Figure A-3 shows the race-sex disparities in geographic inequality are not as great as those for mortality rates. Even though minorities die at higher rates for most causes, whites have greater geographic inequalities, because whites in some communities are dying at much higher rates than in others. Even so,

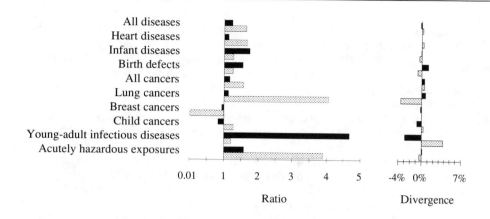

FIGURE A-2. Comparison of Age-Adjusted Mortality Rates by Race and Sex

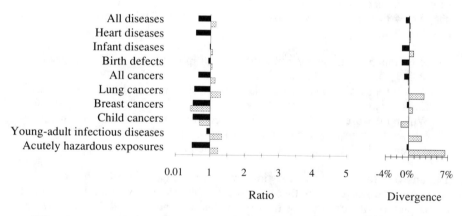

FIGURE A-3. Comparison of Geographic Inequalities by Race and Sex

inequalities among minorities are increasing relative to whites for seven of the ten causes. For males, geographic inequalities are worse than for females for seven causes of death, and all are diverging further. Unlike the disparities in mortality rates, the differences between races are greater than between sexes in all causes except infant diseases, breast cancers, and young-adult infectious diseases.

Figures A-4 and A-5 provide details on mortality rates and geographic inequalities for the four race-sex cohorts (a cohort is a population group with race, sex, and/or age in common). Minority males and white females represent the top and bottom extremes (respectively) for eight of the ten causes of death. The greatest difference is for mortality from acutely hazardous exposures, from which minority males die at a rate six times higher than the white female rate. Minority males also endure mortality rates nearly six times higher than the white female rate for young-adult infectious diseases, almost five times higher for lung cancers, and double the white female rates for infant diseases, all diseases, birth defects, all cancers, and heart diseases. Figure A-5 again shows greater geographic variations among the white cohorts, despite the higher mortality rates among minorities.

These five bar charts (plus the two bar charts in chapter 3) illustrate formidable disparities in mortality not only between race and sex groups but also between communities after adjusting for age, race, and sex. We conducted a series of statistical tests to appraise the degree to which 75 measures of industrial toxins, nonindustrial pollution, and social structure are associated with the geographic inequalities in mortality. Most of these measures are mapped in chapters 4 through 6. The statistical tests ask three basic questions for each cause of death:

- How much of the geographic variation in mortality can the 75 factors explain?
- Which types of measures correlate most frequently with geographic variations in mortality?
- Which measures best differentiate the counties with the most extreme mortality rates from the rest of the country? (Counties with extremely high and extremely low rates are listed opposite each map.)

The answers to these three questions offer a reasonable context for assessing the maps, and suggest hypotheses and leads for further research. They paint a broad picture of contributing factors to the ten causes of death but do not provide definitive answers to cause and effect because of the uncertainties associated with statistical testing and the ecological fallacy (as explained in chapter 2).

Figure A-6 summarizes how much of the geographic variation in mortality the 75 measures can explain. The measures included in the atlas can account for close to half of the geographic variation in mortality from all diseases, a significant degree of association.[3] In decreasing order, they can explain slightly less of the variation in heart diseases, followed by lung cancers, all cancers, breast

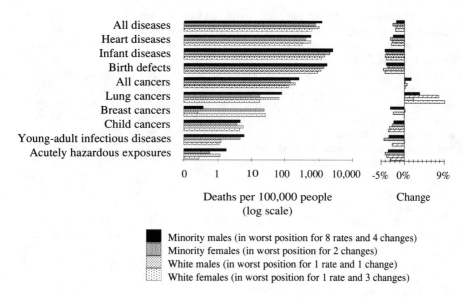

FIGURE A-4. Age-Adjusted Mortality Rates Among Race-Sex Groups

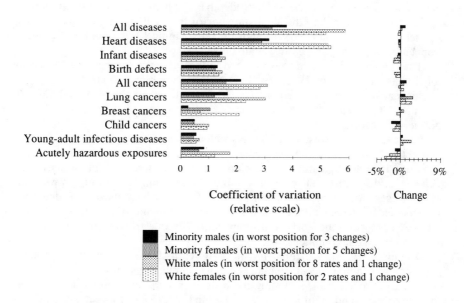

FIGURE A-5. Geographic Inequalities Among Race-Sex Groups

cancers, infant diseases, and acutely hazardous exposures. The measures were least able to explain the geographic inequalities in child cancers.

Figure A-7 summarizes which types of measures most frequently correlate with geographic variations in mortality.[4] Societal factors—including demographics, socioeconomics, education, and health services—are most frequently cited. On average, over two-thirds of the social structure factors are significantly associated with the mortality variations, ranging from a third of them for child cancers, to over 90 percent for all cancers and lung cancers. Nonindustrial pollution measures come next, with an average of almost 40 percent of such measures being significantly associated with the geographic inequalities in mortality. Seventeen percent of the industrial toxins measures, on average, are also associated with geographic inequalities in mortality. Three of the four cancer mortality rates—all, lung, and breast cancers—are associated with the most measures. Industrial toxins comprise a larger share of the measures associated with all four cancer rates than with the other causes of death. More than a third of the industrial toxins measures are significantly associated with the geographic inequalities of mortality from all cancers.

Answers to the third question are discussed in chapter 3 along with the maps on each cause of death, and are summarized in Table A-2.

Causes of Death

All mortality data are from the National Center for Health Statistics (NCHS) Mortality Surveillance System (MSS) database, which houses all death certificate data used to tabulate the vital statistics of the United States. All mortality data refer to the 15 years 1968 through 1983, excluding 1972. Data for 1972 were dropped because they were only available as a 50 percent sample.

The ten mortality categories mapped in this atlas are aggregates of International Classifications of Diseases (ICDs). ICDs are the official definitions of specific causes of death used by NCHS as well as by the National Cancer Institute (NCI).[5] Table A-3 provides the exact ICDs included in each of the ten mortality categories.

The category "all diseases" includes all causes of death other than external causes (such as automobile accidents, violent acts, etc.) The category "heart diseases" includes all cardiovascular diseases.[6] The category "infant diseases" includes all deaths from disease among infants less than 1 year old. As with the "all diseases" category, the definition of infant mortality used here does not include deaths from external causes such as accidents. The category "birth defects" comprises the portion of infant mortality due to congenital malformations and perinatal complications.

The category "all cancers" includes all deaths from malignant neoplasms. The category "lung cancers" includes deaths from malignant neoplasms located in any respiratory organ, including the nose, nasal cavity, sinuses, larynx, trachea, bronchus, and pleura, as well as the lung. All respiratory sites are important when considering air pollution effects, but lung cancers are by far the

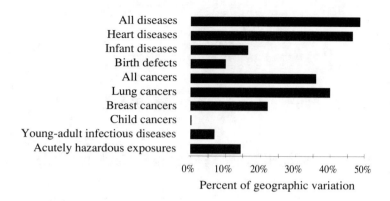

FIGURE A-6.   Geographic Variation in Mortality That 75 Factors Can Explain

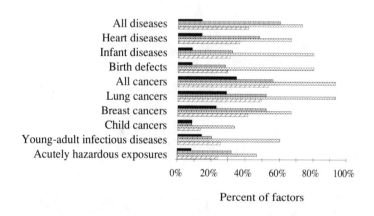

FIGURE A-7.   Percent of 75 Factors Correlated Significantly with Mortality

TABLE A-2. Summary of Statistical Tests[t]

Measure				—— MORTALITY ——					
	All Diseases	Heart Diseases	Infant Diseases	Birth Defects	All Cancers	Lung Cancers	Breast Cancers	Child Cancers	Acutely Hazardous Exposures	Young-Adult Infectious Diseases
INDUSTRIAL TOXINS										
INDUSTRIAL AIR EMISSIONS:										
SMOKE STACKS	0.74	0.25	0.24	0.19 θθ	3.22 25	1.93 +	0.92	0.15	0.41	0.17
HAZARDOUS CHEMICALS (TONS/YEAR)	0.39	0.36	0.19 θ	0.30 +	2.46 27	1.20 +	0.80	0.11	0.09 *	0.15
SUSPECTED CARCINOGENS (TONS/YEAR)	0.13	0.10	0.10 *	0.11 *	4.68 +	2.16 +	0.32	0.12	0.15	0.05
ACUTELY HAZARDOUS CHEMICALS (TONS/YEAR)	0.43	0.43	0.42 θθ	0.21 θθ	5.78 18	2.99 +	0.36	0.23	0.12	0.34
HAZARDOUS WASTE INCINERATORS	1.61 +	0.56	0.00	0.00	7.53 18	1.91 +	2.50 +	0.27	0.00	0.28
RADIATION FROM COMMERCIAL REACTORS (CURIES)	0.00	0.01	0.00	0.00	1.32 +	0.00	0.09	0.00	0.00	0.00
POTENTIAL TOTAL HAZARD INDEX[tt]	0.42	0.31	0.53	0.25	4.37 22	3.51 9	0.70	0.19	0.45	0.09
POTENTIAL CANCER HAZARD INDEX[tt]	0.37	0.26 *	0.16	0.20	4.51 +	1.81 +	0.87	0.17	0.17	0.07
POTENTIAL ACUTE HAZARD INDEX[tt]	0.85 θ	0.86 θθ	0.75	0.31	3.76 +	3.14 +	0.35	0.31	0.15	0.24 θ
PERMIT VIOLATORS[tt]	0.65 θ	0.24 θθ	0.60	0.62	5.00 +**	1.97 +	3.05	0.19	0.14 θ	0.54
INDUSTRIAL WATER DISCHARGES:										
FACILITIES	1.43 19***	1.01 +	0.38	0.32	2.93 2***	1.91 6***	1.48 +	0.27 ***	0.34	0.45
HAZARDOUS CHEMICALS (TONS/YEAR)	0.64	0.02	0.05	0.03	1.05 +	0.77	0.25	0.01	0.00	0.01
SUSPECTED CARCINOGENS (TONS/YEAR)	0.67	0.75	0.07	0.03	3.91 +	1.30 22*	0.90	0.10	0.00	0.00
ACUTELY HAZARDOUS CHEMICALS (TONS/YEAR)	0.73	0.00	0.05	0.02	0.94	0.83	0.28	0.01	0.00	0.01
POTENTIAL TOTAL HAZARD INDEX[tt]	2.14 +	0.04	0.03	0.06	2.79 +	2.47 +	0.79	0.01	0.01	0.01
POTENTIAL CANCER HAZARD INDEX[tt]	0.41	0.68	0.09	0.04	3.93 +θθ	1.76 +θθ	0.65	0.13	0.00	0.00
POTENTIAL ACUTE HAZARD INDEX[tt]	1.83 +	0.00	0.03	0.05	2.33 +	2.07 +	0.69	0.01	0.01	0.01
HAZARDOUS WASTES:										
GENERATORS	0.82	0.25	0.08	0.06	4.54	1.23 +	3.21 +	0.06	0.14	0.08
ESTIMATED GENERATION (TONS/YEAR)	0.98	0.26	0.19	0.07	5.23	1.91 +	2.55 +	0.09	0.45	0.04
TREATMENT, STORAGE, AND DISPOSAL FACILITIES	0.81	0.30	0.12	0.09	4.23 4	1.52 +	2.04 +	0.09	0.28	0.12 *
LAND DISPOSAL FACILITIES	0.55	0.39	0.25	0.24	2.99	2.30 +	0.67	0.17	0.24	0.14
UNDERGROUND INJECTION FACILITIES	0.00	0.00	0.00	0.00	4.84 +	4.92 +	0.00 +	0.00	1.67	0.00 +
COMMERCIAL TREATMENT STORAGE DISPOSAL FACILITIES	0.58	0.24	0.12	0.00	4.26 16	1.87 +	1.67 +*	0.23	0.60	0.23
COMMERCIAL LANDFILL CAPACITY (ACRE-FEET)	0.00	0.00	0.00	0.00	2.22 +θθθ	8.85 11	0.00	0.21	0.32	0.00 *
UNCONTROLLED CLOSED SITES	1.09 +***	0.53 θθ	0.32	0.26	3.50 +θθθ	1.49 +**	1.33 11	0.19	0.37	0.25
SUPERFUND NATIONAL PRIORITIES LIST SITES	0.31	0.14	0.09	0.13	3.90	0.96 +	2.69 12	0.00	0.00	0.05
TREATMENT AND STORAGE FACILITIES[tt]	0.59	0.34	0.06	0.07	5.73 13	1.34 16	3.79 3	0.10	0.21	0.03
GROUNDWATER MONITORING VIOLATORS[tt]	0.63	0.24	0.28	0.24	2.48 13	2.28 +	0.33 4	0.16	0.37	0.28 θθ
WORKPLACE TOXINS:										
PETROCHEMICALS EMPLOYMENT (PERSONS/YEAR)	1.08 +	0.24	0.17	0.12	5.96 8	2.67 +	3.52 8	0.03	0.47	0.00
INSPECTIONS WITH ILLEGAL EXPOSURES (% OF TOTAL)	1.29 +*	1.13 9*	0.77	0.71	1.05 12*	1.12 +*	0.93 +	0.66 **	0.48	0.82 8θθθ
ILLEGAL OCCUPATIONAL EXPOSURES	1.21 +θθ	0.44 +*	0.17	0.14	3.91 +	1.64 +θθθ	1.83 +	0.19 θ	0.13	0.19
INSPECTIONS	1.08 +	0.40	0.16	0.12	4.29 +	1.68 +***	2.04 +	0.17	0.10	0.15
SAMPLES WITH ILLEGAL EXPOSURES (% OF TOTAL)[tt]	1.46 +	1.15 +	0.91	0.86	1.07 +	1.31 +	0.88	0.70	0.50 8	1.06
TEST SAMPLES[tt]	1.03 +	0.38	0.11	0.10	3.76 +	1.23 +	1.67 6	0.17	0.14	0.14
SAMPLES EXCEEDING PERMISSIBLE EXPOSURE LIMITS[tt]	1.33 +	0.51	0.17	0.17	4.02 +	1.63 +	1.64 +	0.23	0.16	0.19

NONINDUSTRIAL POLLUTION

	(1)	(2)	(3)	(4)	(5)	(6)	(7)	(8)	(9)
PESTICIDES:									
TOTAL USAGE (POUNDS/YEAR)	0.61 **6*****	0.74 **13*****	0.59 θθ	0.59	0.62 **20**	0.61	0.71 **	0.69	0.53
POTENTIAL TOTAL HAZARD INDEX	0.90	1.16 **7**	1.13 +	0.99	0.33	0.64	0.50 **	0.91	0.88 +**
POTENTIAL CANCER HAZARD INDEX	0.62 **4**	0.77 **12**	0.32 ***	0.39	0.69 **	0.50 **14*****	0.72 θθθ	0.61	0.39
POTENTIAL ACUTE HAZARD INDEX	0.73	0.98	0.55 ***	0.62 +	0.59	0.74 **15*****	0.74 θθθ	0.67	0.48
AVERAGE APPLICATION RATE (POUNDS/TREATED ACRE)	1.06 +**	1.22 **5*****	0.77 **4**θθθ	0.76 **4****	1.09 **11*****	1.02 **5**	0.96 θθθ	0.79	0.77 **9**
AVERAGE COVERAGE (% OF CROP LAND)	1.33 **16*****	1.39 **16*****	0.84	0.81 *	0.96	1.22 +***	0.77 **2**	0.80 **5***	0.76 **3**
WATER QUALITY:									
HOUSES SERVED BY PRIVATE WELLS (% OF TOTAL)	1.09 **8**θθθ	1.25 **6**θθθ	1.02 **6***	1.05 +θ	0.63 **19*****	1.09 **8**θθθ	0.89 **5**	1.09 +θ	1.06 +
GROUNDWATER USAGE (MILLION GALLONS/DAY)	0.14	0.05	0.78	0.75	0.49	0.79	0.57	0.61	0.17
MILES OF IMPAIRED RIVERS AND STREAMS (% OF TOTAL)	1.30 +	1.16 +	0.74	0.50	1.91 +	1.41 +	1.04 +	0.31	0.43
PUBLIC SUPPLY VIOLATIONS	2.20 **7**	2.20 **10**	1.06 +	0.61	0.95 **21**	0.99	0.93	0.29	1.33 +*
SEWAGE OUTFLOW (MILLION GALLONS/DAY)	1.69 **18**	0.16	0.03	0.02	6.02 **26**	1.68 +	2.57 +	0.03	0.01
PUBLIC SUPPLY RISK[ττ]	6.80 **14**	1.31 +	0.27	0.13	1.99 +	0.51	1.48 +	0.03	0.47
AIR QUALITY:									
URBAN HAZARDOUS CHEMICAL EMISSIONS (TONS/YEAR)	0.97	0.45	0.20	0.15	3.30 **24**θθ	1.33 +θ	1.82	0.14	0.16
URBAN SUSPECTED CARCINOGEN EMISSIONS (TONS/YEAR)	0.98	0.42	0.18	0.15	3.52	1.37 +	1.95	0.13	0.15
URBAN ACUTELY HAZARDOUS CHEMICAL EMISSIONS (TPY)	0.92 **	0.60	0.36	0.29	2.78 +	1.16 +θ	1.40 **9**	0.20	0.26
CARBON MONOXIDE CONCENTRATIONS (PARTS/MILLION)	1.12 +θθ	0.00 **	0.00	0.00	4.67 +θ	1.43 +	2.79	0.21	0.00
LEAD CONCENTRATIONS (MICROGRAMS/CUBIC METER)	0.96 **12**	0.20	0.07	0.00	3.62 +	1.83 +	2.72 **10**	0.00	0.22
NITROGEN DIOXIDE CONCENTRATIONS (PARTS/MILLION)	1.43 +	1.03 +***	0.00	0.00	4.93	1.86 +	2.95	0.20	0.16
OZONE CONCENTRATIONS (PARTS/MILLION)	0.54 θθθ	0.16 **17**θθθ	0.07 **	0.08 θθθ	3.00 **10**θθθ	1.52 **12**θθθ	1.31 +***	0.19	0.18
PARTICULATE CONCENTRATIONS (MICROGR./CUB. METER)	0.87 θθθ	0.67 θθθ	0.29 θθθ	0.49 θθθ	1.97 +***	1.04 **23**θθθ	1.40 **16***	0.34	0.29 **6**θ
SULFUR DIOXIDE CONCENTRATIONS (PARTS/MILLION)	0.59 θθθ	0.93 θθθ	0.00	0.01 θθ	4.44 **14*****	1.28 +***	2.42 **17**	0.15	0.20
URBAN EMISSION POTENTIAL TOTAL HAZARD INDEX[ττ]	0.99	0.40	0.15	0.12	3.64 +	1.41 +	2.19 +	0.11	0.12
URBAN EMISSION POTENTIAL CANCER HAZARD INDEX[ττ]	1.02 θθ	0.49	0.25	0.20	3.17 **23**	1.71 +	1.36 **18****	0.17	0.21
URBAN EMISSION POTENTIAL ACUTE HAZARD INDEX[ττ]	0.88 **6**	0.57	0.35	0.28	2.64 +*	1.11 θθ	1.33 **10**θ	0.20	0.25
STANDARDS NOT ATTAINED[ττ]	0.35 ***	0.00 ***	0.24 **	0.46 **	3.69 +θθθ	1.17 +	2.14 +	0.47	0.12

SOCIAL STRUCTURE

	(1)	(2)	(3)	(4)	(5)	(6)	(7)	(8)	(9)
DEMOGRAPHICS:									
TOTAL POPULATION	0.87 **17**	0.40	0.18	0.14	3.54 **3**	1.20 **19**	1.82 θ	0.12	0.16
PEOPLE OF COLOR (% OF TOTAL POPULATION)	1.98 +	1.69 +	1.63 +θθ	1.23 +***	1.21 +**	1.78 +**	0.87 θ	1.34 **3**	1.36 **10****
AFRICAN AMERICANS (% OF TOTAL POPULATION)	2.94 +	2.62 +	1.29 +θ	0.95 ***	1.53 +θθ	2.57 θθθ	0.69 **13**θθ	1.35 +	0.70
LATINO AMERICANS (% OF TOTAL POPULATION)	0.24 **5**	0.21 **1**	2.40 **5**θ	1.26 **6**θθθ	0.73 **9*****	0.62 **9*****	1.15 +θ	1.33 **4**	2.39 **1**
ASIAN AMERICANS (% OF TOTAL POPULATION)	0.60	0.35 **14**	0.63 **	0.53 ***	1.45 **8**	0.75 **21**	1.12 +θ	0.53	0.51 **
NATIVE AMERICANS (% OF TOTAL POPULATION)	1.16 +	0.21 **11**	1.88 +θ	1.17 +θθθ	0.36 θθθ	0.18 θθθ	1.21 +θ	1.56 +	3.04 +θθ
POPULATION DENSITY (PEOPLE/SQUARE MILE)[ττ]	2.60 **15****	0.38	0.14	0.12	8.91 **1**	2.81 **20**	4.17 +**	0.14	0.14
SOCIOECONOMICS:									
MEAN HOUSEHOLD INCOME	0.87 **13**θθ	0.87 **15**θθ	0.87 θ	0.91 θθ	1.09 **28**	0.95 θθθ	1.07 +	0.94 **6**	0.90 **4**
MEAN VALUE OF OWNER-OCCUPIED HOMES	0.82 **11****	0.77	0.67 **8*****	0.68 ***	1.24 +θθθ	0.95 **24**	1.16 +	0.73 **1**	0.70 **2**θθ
SINGLE-MOTHER FAMILIES (% OF TOTAL FAMILIES)	0.84 **1**θθθ	0.73 **4**θθθ	0.54 **1**θθθ	0.47 **1**	0.75 θθθ	0.79 **1**θθθ	0.52 θ	0.45 **2***	0.48
FAMILIES IN POVERTY (% OF TOTAL FAMILIES)	1.49 **3**θθθ	1.49 **3**θθθ	1.41 **2**	1.26 **2**	0.91 **5*****	1.35 **3**θθθ	0.87 **1*****	1.19 +	1.27 **7**θθ
EDUCATION:									
HIGH SCHOOL GRADUATES (% OF PEOPLE 25 AND OVER)	0.77 **2*****	0.76 **2*****	0.84 **3*****	0.91 **5*****	1.01 θθθ	0.85 **4*****	1.10 **15*****	0.95	0.92 **
COLLEGE GRADUATES (% OF PEOPLE 25 AND OVER)	0.70 **9*****	0.67 **8*****	0.77 *	0.83	1.06 **17**θθθ	0.81 **17**θθθ	1.21 +	0.91	0.83 **5**
HEALTH SERVICES:									
HOSPITAL BEDS (PER 100,000 PEOPLE)	0.93 ***	0.82 ***	1.07 **7**	1.45 **3**	1.24 θθθ	0.97	1.10 +*	0.67	1.00
PHYSICIANS (PER 100,000 PEOPLE)	1.08 **10*****	0.71	0.64	0.91	2.00 **15*****	1.21 **13**	1.43 +***	0.47	0.65
VARIATION EXPLAINED (NON-PARAMETRIC)[τττ]	48.7%	46.5%	16.4%	9.9%	35.9%	39.9%	22.0%	14.3%	6.9%

τ Values to left are ratios of means comparing counties in top two percentiles for mortality (by cause of death) with U.S. average. For example, the first number in the upper left-hand corner reveals the average number of smokestacks in counties with the highest mortality from all diseases is 74% of the U.S. average.

Bold underlined values to left identify the five highest ratios of means.

+ Plus signs to right highlight ratios greater than 1.

Bold values to right are discriminant analysis rankings, which rank each measures according to their significance in differentiating between three groups of counties: (1) counties in top 2 percent for mortality by cause of death (shaded black in maps); (2) counties in bottom 3 percent (shaded white); and (3) rest of U.S. A rank of 1 indicates the most significant discriminator; other significant discriminators follow in rank order. For example, in the first column, the percent of single mother families is most significant in differentiating between the groups of counties. Insignificant measures (p < .15) have no discriminant rank.

* Asterisks indicate a value's significance in non-parametric multivariate regression tests: one asterisk means significance at p < .10; two asterisks at p < .05; and three asterisks at p < .01.

θ Thetas mean the same as asterisks, only the sign of the association is the opposite of that indicated by the ratio of means.

ττ Measures are not mapped in the atlas.

τττ These percentages indicate the portion of the variation in county percentile rankings by cause of death that can be explained through multiple regression using these 75 variables (the "adjusted R-squared").

TABLE A-2 (Continued)

CAUSE OF DEATH	AGE GROUPS	REVISION OF THE INTERNATIONAL CLASSIFICATION OF DISEASES	
		9TH (1979–83)	8TH (1968–78)
All diseases	All ages	<E800	<E800
Heart diseases	All ages	390–448	390–448
Young-adult infectious diseases	25–34 years	000–136	000–139
Infant diseases	Under 1 year	<E800	<E800
Birth defects	Under 1 year	740–778	740–779
All cancers....................................	All ages	140–208 ex 202.2	140–207
Lung cancers	All ages	160–163,163.0	160–162
Breast cancers	All ages	174–175	174
Child cancers	1–14 years	140–208 ex 202.2	140–207
Acutely hazardous exposures	All ages	E862–E864 E866–E867 E868.0,E868.1 E868.8,E868.9 E869,E891 E894,E921 E923,E926 E929.2	E864–E867 E870–E872 E875–E877 E891,E894 E921,E923 E926,E942

TABLE A-3. Definition of Causes of Death by ICD

predominant form of respiratory cancer. This category, therefore, is called "lung cancers" for simplification. The category "breast cancers" includes female deaths from malignant neoplasms located in the breast. Breast cancers do occur among males; however, male breast cancer is extremely rare and thus is not included in the maps. The category "child cancers" includes all deaths from all cancers, including leukemia, among children ages 1 to 14.

The category "acutely hazardous exposures" includes external causes of death that approximate mortality from lethal exposures to chemicals with acute toxicity, corrosivity, ignitability, reactivity, or other hazardous property. This mortality category is distinct from diseases such as cancer that may be caused by chronic exposures to toxic chemicals. The category primarily includes exposures associated with industrial or agricultural activities. Acute exposures to hazardous chemicals used in the home, such as paints and cleansers, or resulting from personal activities, such as carbon monoxide from automobile exhaust, are excluded. More specifically, the acutely hazardous exposures category includes the following causes of death (with the number of 1987 deaths and percent of the total of such deaths in parentheses):

- accidental poisoning by *(a)* petroleum products and other solvents not elsewhere classified, *(b)* agricultural and horticultural chemicals, *(c)* corrosives and caustics not elsewhere classified, *(d)* heavy metals and their fumes, *(e)* gas distributed by pipeline, *(f)* liquefied petroleum gas distributed in mobile containers, *(g)* other utility gases, *(h)* carbon monoxide from sources other than motor vehicle exhaust and domestic fuels, *(i)* other gases and vapors (558 deaths, 57 percent)
- accident caused by explosive material (216 deaths, 22 percent)
- conflagration in building or structure other than private dwelling (103 deaths, 10 percent)
- ignition of highly inflammable material—not clothing (55 deaths, 6 percent)
- accident caused by explosion of pressure vessel (39 deaths, 4 percent)
- late effects of accidental poisoning (17 deaths, 2 percent)
- exposure to radiation (0 deaths, 0 percent)

The category "young-adult infectious diseases" includes all mortality among persons 25 to 34 years old from infectious diseases. During the 1980s, Acquired Immune Deficiency Syndrome (AIDS) became a major cause of death among persons in this age group.

Age-Race-Sex-Adjusted Mortality Rates

All mortality data in the atlas are adjusted for the effects of differences in age, race, and sex distributions. A hypothetical example should help to clarify the importance of age adjustment. Say that county A has 10 times the number of deaths observed in county B. If county A also has twice the population of county B, however, its crude mortality rate is only 5 times higher than that of county B. A crude mortality rate divides the number of deaths by the number of people in a place so that areas with different population sizes can be compared. Yet if county A's elderly population is 20 times larger than county B's, one would still expect county A to have a higher mortality rate, because more older people die than younger people. By adjusting for population size but not for age, one might think county A's mortality is 5 times worse than county B's when, in fact, they are similar.

Twelve age groups are used in the age-adjustment procedure:

1. under 1 year	7. 35–44 years
2. 1–4 years	8. 45–54 years
3. 5–9 years	9. 55–64 years
4. 10–14 years	10. 65–74 years
5. 15–24 years	11. 75–84 years
6. 25–34 years	12. 85+ years

Mortality rates for infant diseases and birth defects need no adjustment, since they only include the youngest age group. Similarly, the mortality rates for child cancer and young adult infectious diseases are only adjusted for the appropriate age groups. Values for total mortality rates and excess deaths are adjusted for race and sex distributions as well as age.

The total 1970 U.S. population is used as the standard population for age adjusting. Mortality rates are expressed, as is the convention, in the number of deaths per 100,000 people in the population. Although infant mortality is more commonly expressed as deaths per 1,000 live births, here mortality from infant diseases is expressed as deaths per 100,000 to remain consistent with the other mortality measures.

The mathematical formulas used for age adjustment are as follows:

$$ADJ_{kyc} = \sum_i [R_{ikyc} * (P_{i70c} / P_{70c})]$$

where

ADJ_{kyc} = age-adjusted death rate in county k, time y, race-sex cohort c

R_{ikyc} = age-specific death rate for age group i, county k, time y, race-sex cohort c

P_{i70c} = national population in age group i, race-sex cohort c in 1970

P_{70c} = national population in race-sex cohort c in 1970

$$ADJ_k = \sum_y (ADJ_{kyc}) / \text{Number of time periods}$$

where

ADJ_k = age-adjusted death rate in county k
(the average of the time-specific, age-race-sex adjusted rates)

ADJ_{kyc} = age-adjusted death rate in county k, time y, race-sex cohort c

Some county mortality rates are further adjusted to avoid spurious percentile classification. A large variability in mortality rates can be due to very few deaths for a rare disease or to very few people in a small county. As the U.S. Environmental Protection Agency (EPA) and NCI point out, "Such statistical instability makes the identification of 'extreme' rates difficult and tends to conceal patterns by breaking up clusters of counties . . . with similar rates."[7]

The top 10 percentiles, or top three classes, include only counties for which the probability is greater than 90 percent that their rates are not the result of chance variations. We use a standard poisson test for statistical significance based on the county's observed and expected deaths (see below).[8] Poisson refers to the statistical distribution of rare events such as deaths. Counties with high mortality rates that fail this statistical test are placed in the class shaded light gray. By using this stabilization technique, the probability is less than 10 percent that a county is spuriously included among those shaded medium gray, dark gray, and black. Counties shaded light gray, on the other hand, include those with mortality rates in percentiles above that class, but which failed the statistical test. The top and bottom counties listed under the maps include only those that pass this test of significant deviation from the mean. The 90 percent probability level was selected to minimize the number of times a county is reclassified into a lower percentile group, while maintaining a degree of statistical confidence about the stability of the higher mortality rates.

Annual Excess Deaths

The measure of annual excess deaths estimates the population at risk from high mortality rates. The purpose of this measure is to help target the allocation of scarce resources to locations where the greatest number of people suffer from excessive mortality. The excess death count can function as a screening device for making policy decisions.

Total excess deaths are the difference between the observed and expected number of deaths in a county. Expected deaths are the number that would have occurred if a county had the same mortality rate as the United States as a whole, adjusted for age, race, and sex. Larger estimates of excess death are a function of both the number of people in a county and how much higher the county's mortality rate is than the national norm. Negative figures indicate how many fewer people died than expected and occur when a county has a lower rate of mortality than the U.S. norm.

The mathematical formulas used to calculate total excess deaths are as follows:[9]

$$EXPECT_{kyc} = \sum_{i} (N_{iyc} * P_{ikyc})$$

where

$EXPECT_{kyc}$ = expected death count in county k, time y, race-sex cohort c

N_{iyc} = age-specific national death rate for age group i, time y, race-sex cohort c

P_{ikyc} = population in age group i, county k, time y, race-sex cohort c

$$EXPECT_k = \sum_{y} (EXPECT_{kyc})$$

where

$EXPECT_k$ = expected deaths in county k

$EXPECT_{kyc}$ = expected deaths in county k, time y, race-sex cohort c

$$OBSERV_k = \sum_{y} (OBSERV_{kyc})$$

where

$OBSERV_k$ = observed deaths in county k

$OBSERV_{kyc}$ = observed deaths in county k, time y, race-sex cohort c

$$\text{EXCESS(OBSERV, EXPECT)} = \text{OBSERV} - \text{EXPECT}$$

where
EXCESS	= total excess death count
OBSERV	= observed death count
EXPECT	= expected death count

INDUSTRIAL TOXINS MEASURES

There are some significant differences between the data in the atlas and those in the EPA's Toxic Chemical Release Inventory (TRI). The TRI covers only manufacturing industries. Many other sectors of the economy also generate toxic pollution, such as utilities, oil and gas extraction, national security activities, mining, sewage treatment, and others. Nonmanufacturing industries covered by our data, but not in TRI, comprise about half of all facilities with emissions regulated under the Clear Air Act, and 70 percent of facilities with discharges regulated under the Clean Water Act.[10] Moreover, TRI covers only around 300 chemicals, less than a third of the number regulated under the Emergency Planning and Community Right-to-Know Act of 1986 (EPCRA). Our estimates of air and water toxins include a number of hazardous chemicals that are regulated under EPCRA but not included in TRI. Though the overall pictures end up with many similarities, our county maps of industrial toxins highlight some counties that TRI might not.[11]

Industrial Air Emissions

The counts of industrial emission sources include all facilities with emission permits issued under the Clean Air Act (CAA) and listed in the EPA's National Emissions Data System (NEDS) as of 1985.

The county estimates of the annual tons of industrial emissions of hazardous chemicals are derived from data submitted by these permitted facilities pursuant to CAA regulations and catalogued in NEDS as of 1985 for 145,229 smokestacks and other identifiable emission points nationwide. Hazardous chemicals represent a sample of the chemicals subject to reporting under EPCRA. The estimates are based on reported emissions of volatile organic compounds (VOC) and total suspended particulates (TSP), disaggregated into 651 compounds using EPA-developed apportionment or speciation factors for each industrial process.[12] Of these 651 chemicals, 136 are regulated under EPCRA. As indicated in Table A-4, this sample includes 13 percent of the chemicals subject to reporting under EPCRA. While some inaccuracy is associated with any estimation procedure, the value of these emission estimates is that they provide a consistent method for comparing counties. Table A-5 provides a detailed listing of the chemicals included in all of the industrial emissions maps.

The county estimates of the annual tons of industrial emissions of suspected carcinogens are calculated with the method just described, but they include only

CHEMICAL CATEGORY	TOTAL IN SOURCE DATA	HAZARDOUS CHEMICALS	SUSPECTED CARCINOGENS	ACUTELY HAZARDOUS CHEMICALS	TOXIC RELEASE INVENTORY
		Number of Chemicals			
Subject to EPCRA reporting	1,106	1,106 (100%)	191 (100%)	402 (100%)	322 (100%)
In the maps	276	233[a] (21%)	56 (29%)	40 (10%)	149 (46%)
Industrial air emissions	651	136[a] (13%)	27 (14%)	20 (5%)	96 (30%)
Industrial water discharges	1,611	158[a] (14%)	45 (24%)	32 (8%)	101 (31%)
Urban air emissions	78	76 (7%)	22 (12%)	9 (2%)	56 (17%)
Pesticides	25	25 (na)	5 (na)	6 (na)	
	Facilities	**Estimated or Reported Tons**			
Subject to EPCRA Reporting			235,818[b]		3,120,515[b]
In the maps					
Industrial air emissions	145,229	1,287,635	146,102	90,332	1,213,785[b]
Industrial water discharges	113,047	39,797	582	34,003	180,797[b]
Hazardous wastes	88,839	97,770,532			
Urban air emissions		2,700,650	714,783	124,823	
Pesticides		207,812			
		Selection Criteria			
In the Maps		CERCLA Reportable Quantity[c]	CERCLA Cancer Hazard Ranking[d]	Section 302 Threshold Planning Quantity[c]	

Percentages are of the number of chemicals at the top of each column.

[a] The Emergency Planning and Community Right-to-Know Act (EPCRA) regulates chemical categories as well as individual chemicals. Because these categories include more than one chemical, the maps include 43 more chemicals than are specifically listed under EPCRA: 3 in the industrial air emissions estimates (for 139 total), and 40 in the industrial water discharges estimates (for 198 total). In all, the maps include 276 chemicals grouped into 233 EPCRA entries.

[b] These are reported 1988 TRI amounts for reference purposes only; they are not the amounts reflected in the maps.

[c] Source: Office of Toxic Substances, *Title III List of Lists: Consolidated List of Chemicals Subject to Reporting Under Title III of the Superfund Amendments and Reauthorization Act (SARA) of 1986* (Washington, DC: U.S. EPA, 1988). Other factors are used for selecting pesticides, as explained later in the methods appendix.

[d] Source: Environmental Monitoring & Services, Inc., *Technical Background Document to Support Rulemaking Pursuant to CERCLA Section 102*, Volume 3 (Washington, DC: U.S. EPA, 1986), Appendix A.

TABLE A-4. Summary of Chemicals Included in the Maps

TABLE A-5. Chemicals Included in the Maps of Industrial and Urban Toxins

CHEMICAL NAME	INDUSTRIAL AIR EMISSIONS	INDUSTRIAL WATER DISCHARGES	URBAN AIR EMISSIONS	TOTAL HAZARD INDICATOR	CANCER HAZARD INDICATOR	ACUTE HAZARD INDICATOR	TOXIC RELEASE INVENTORY
(1,1'-BIPHENYL)-4,4'DIAMINE,3,3'DICHLORO-		X		1	MEDIUM		X
1,1-DICHLOROETHANE		X		1,000			
1,1-DICHLOROETHYLENE		X		5,000	LOW		X
1,2,4-TRICHLOROBENZENE		X		100			X
1,2-BENZANTHRACENE, 7,12-DIMETHYL-			X	1	HIGH		
1,2-BENZENEDICARBOXYLIC ACID ANHYDRIDE	X			5,000			X
1,2-BENZENEDICARBOXYLIC ACID, DIETHYL ESTER		X		1,000			X
1,2-BENZENEDICARBOXYLIC ACID,[BIS(2-ETHYLHEXYL)		X		1	LOW		X
1,2-BENZPHENANTHRENE	X		X	1	MEDIUM		
1,2-DICHLOROETHANE	X	X	X	5,000	LOW		X
1,2-DICHLOROPROPANE		X		1,000			X
1,2-DIPHENYLHYDRAZINE		X		1	MEDIUM		X
1,2-TRANS-DICHLOROETHYLENE		X		1,000			
1,3-DICHLOROPROPENE		X		100			X
1-BUTANOL	X		X	5,000			X
1-METHYLBUTADIENE	X			100			
2,4,5-T		X		1,000			
2,4-DICHLOROPHENOL		X		100			X
2,4-DIMETHYLPHENOL		X		100			X
2,4-DINITROPHENOL		X		10			X
2,5-FURANDIONE	X			5,000			X
2-BUTANONE	X		X	5,000			X
2-ETHOXYETHANOL	X			1			X
2-FURANCARBOXALDEHYDE	X			5,000			
2-METHOXYETHANOL	X						X
4,4'-METHYLENE DIANILINE	X						X
ACENAPHTHENE	X	X	X	100			
ACENAPHTHYLENE	X	X	X	5,000			
ACETALDEHYDE	X		X	1,000			X
ACETIC ACID	X	X		5,000			
ACETIC ACID, ETHYL ESTER	X		X	5,000			
ACETIC ANHYDRIDE	X			5,000			
ACETONE	X	X	X	5,000			X
ACETOPHENONE		X		5,000			
ACROLEIN	X	X	X	1		500	X
ACRYLIC ACID	X			5,000			X
ACRYLONITRILE	X	X	X	100	MEDIUM	10,000	X
ADIPIC ACID	X			5,000			
ALDRIN		X		1	HIGH	500	X
ALUMINUM (FUME OR DUST)	X	X	X				X
AMMONIA	X	X		100		500	X
ANILINE	X	X		5,000		1,000	X
ANTHRACENE	X	X	X	5,000			X
ANTIMONY	X	X		5,000			X
ARSENIC	X	X	X	1	HIGH		X
ASBESTOS		X		1	HIGH		X
BARIUM AND COMPOUNDS	X	X	X				X
BENZENE	X	X	X	1,000	MEDIUM		X
BENZENE, 1,2-DICHLORO-	X	X		100			X
BENZENE, 1,3-DICHLORO-	X			100			X
BENZENE, 1,4-DICHLORO-	X	X	X	100			X
BENZENE, 1-METHYL-2,4-DINITRO-		X		1,000	MEDIUM		X
BENZENE, 1-METHYL-2,6-DINITRO-		X		1,000	LOW		X
BENZENE, 1-METHYLETHYL-	X			5,000			X
BENZENE, 2,4-DIISOCYANATOMETHYL-	X			100			
BENZENE, CHLORO-	X		X	100			X
BENZENE, DIMETHYL-			X	1,000			X
BENZENE, HEXACHLORO		X		1	MEDIUM		X
BENZENE, HEXAHYDRO-	X			1,000			X
BENZENE, M-DIMETHYL-	X	X	X	1,000			X
BENZENE, METHYL-	X	X	X	1,000			X
BENZENE, O-DIMETHYL-	X	X	X	1,000			X
BENZENE, P-DIMETHYL-	X		X	1,000			X
BENZIDINE		X		1	HIGH		X
BENZOIC ACID	X	X		5,000			
BENZOL[B]FLUORANTHENE	X	X		1	HIGH		
BENZO[A]PYRENE	X	X	X	1	HIGH		
BENZO[GHI]PERYLENE	X	X	X	5,000			
BENZO[J,K]FLUORENE	X		X	100			
BENZO[K]FLUORANTHENE	X	X		1			
BENZYL CHLORIDE	X			100	LOW	500	X
BENZ[A]ANTHRACENE	X		X	1	MEDIUM		
BENZ[J]ACEANTHRYLENE,1,2-DIHYDRO-3-METHYL-			X	1	MEDIUM		
BERYLLIUM	X	X	X	1	MEDIUM		X
BIPHENYL	X		X				X
BIS(2-CHLOROETHOXY) METHANE		X		1,000			
BIS(2-CHLOROISOPROPYL) ETHER		X		1,000			X
BROMINE	X	X				500	
BROMOFORM		X		100			X
BUTADIENE	X		X	5,000			X
BUTYL ACETATE			X	5,000			
BUTYL ACRYLATE	X						X
BUTYL BENZYL PHTHALATE	X	X		100			X
BUTYRALDEHYDE	X		X				X
CADMIUM	X	X	X	1	MEDIUM		X
CAPTAN		X		10			X
CARBARYL		X		100			X
CARBOFURAN		X		10		10	
CARBON DISULFIDE		X		100		10,000	X
CARBON TETRACHLORIDE	X	X	X	5,000	MEDIUM		X
CARBONYL SULFIDE			X				X

TABLE A-5. Chemicals Included in the Maps of Industrial and Urban Toxins (*Continued*)

CHEMICAL NAME	INDUSTRIAL AIR EMISSIONS	INDUSTRIAL WATER DISCHARGES	URBAN AIR EMISSIONS	TOTAL HAZARD INDICATOR	CANCER HAZARD INDICATOR	ACUTE HAZARD INDICATOR	TOXIC RELEASE INVENTORY
CATECHOL			X				X
CHLORDANE (TECHNICAL MIXTURE AND METABOLITES)		X					
CHLORINATED FLUOROCARBON (FREON 113)	X						X
CHLORINATED PHENOLS		X					X
CHLORINE	X	X		10		100	X
CHLORODIBROMOMETHANE		X		100			
CHLOROETHANE	X	X		100			X
CHLOROFORM	X	X	X	5,000	MEDIUM	10,000	X
CHLOROPRENE	X	X					X
CHROMIUM	X	X	X	1	HIGH		X
COBALT	X	X	X				X
COPPER	X	X	X	5,000			X
CREOSOTE	X			1	HIGH		
CRESOL(S)	X		X	1,000			X
CROTONALDEHYDE			X	100		1,000	
CROTONALDEHYDE, (E)-	X			100		1,000	
CYANIDES (SOLUBLE CYANIDE SALTS)		X	X	10			X
CYCLOHEXANONE	X		X	5,000			
DDD		X		1	MEDIUM		
DDE		X		1	MEDIUM		
DDT		X		1	MEDIUM		
DIAZINON		X		1			
DIBENZ[A,H]ANTHRACENE	X		X	1	HIGH		
DIBUTYL PHTHALATE	X	X		10			X
DICHLOROBENZENE (MIXED)		X		100			X
DICHLOROBROMOMETHANE		X		5,000			X
DICHLORODIFLUOROMETHANE	X	X		5,000			
DICHLOROETHYL ETHER		X		1	MEDIUM	10,000	X
DICHLOROPROPANE	X			1,000			
DIELDRIN		X		1	HIGH		
DIMETHYL PHTHALATE	X	X		5,000			X
DINITROCRESOL		X		10		10	X
DIOCTYL PHTHALATE		X		5,000			X
ENDOSULFAN AND METABOLITES		X					
ENDRIN		X		1		500	
ENDRIN ALDEHYDE		X		1			
EPICHLOROHYDRIN	X			1,000	LOW	1,000	X
ETHANE, 1,1'-OXYBIS-	X			100			
ETHANE, 1,1,1-TRICHLORO-2,2-BIS(P-METHOXYPHENYL)		X		1			X
ETHANE, 1,1,2-TRICHLORO-	X	X		1	LOW		X
ETHANE, 1,2-DIBROMO-	X		X	1,000	HIGH		X
ETHENE, 1,1,2,2-TETRACHLORO-	X	X	X	1	LOW		X
ETHENE, CHLORO-	X		X	1	MEDIUM		X
ETHYL ACRYLATE	X			1,000			X
ETHYLBENZENE	X	X	X	1,000			X
ETHYLENE	X						X
ETHYLENE GLYCOL	X						X
ETHYLENE OXIDE	X			1	MEDIUM	1,000	X
FERROUS SULFATE		X		1,000			
FLUORENE	X	X	X	5,000			
FLUORINE	X	X		10		500	
FORMALDEHYDE	X	X	X	1,000	MEDIUM	500	X
FORMIC ACID	X			5,000			
FURAN, TETRAHYDRO-		X		1,000			
GLYCOL ETHERS			X				X
GUANIDINE, N-NITROSO-N-METHYL-N'-NITRO-		X		1	MEDIUM		
HEPTACHLOR		X		1	HIGH		X
HEPTACHLOR EPOXIDE		X		1	HIGH		
HEXACHLORO-1,3-BUTADIENE		X		1	LOW		X
HEXACHLOROCYCLOPENTADIENE		X		1		100	X
HYDRAZINE		X		1	HIGH	1,000	X
HYDROCYANIC ACID		X		10		100	X
HYDROGEN SULFIDE			X	100		500	
INDENO(1,2,3-CD)PYRENE	X	X	X	1	LOW		
ISO-BUTYL ACETATE	X			5,000			
ISOBUTYL ALCOHOL	X			5,000			
ISOBUTYRALDEHYDE	X						X
ISOPHORONE		X		5,000			
ISOPRENE	X	X		100			
ISOPROPYL ALCOHOL (MFG.-STRONG ACID PROCESSES)	X						X
KEPONE		X		1	MEDIUM		
LEAD	X	X	X	1			X
LINDANE		X		1	MEDIUM	1,000	X
MANGANESE AND COMPOUNDS	X	X	X				X
MERCURY	X	X	X				X
METHANE, CHLORO-	X	X		1	LOW		X
METHANE, DIBROMO-	X			1,000			X
METHANE, DICHLORO-	X	X	X	1,000			X
METHANE, TRICHLOROFLUORO-	X			5,000			
METHANOL	X		X	5,000			X
METHYL ACRYLATE	X						X
METHYL BROMIDE		X		1,000		1,000	X
METHYL CHLOROFORM	X		X	1,000			X
METHYL DISULFIDE			X			100	
METHYL ISOBUTYL KETONE	X	X	X	5,000			X
METHYL ISOTHIOCYANATE		X				500	
METHYL METHACRYLATE	X			1,000			X
METHYLENE BIS(PHENYLISOCYANATE) (MBI)	X						X
N-NITROSODIPHENYLAMINE		X		100			X
NAPHTHALENE	X	X	X	100			X
NAPHTHENIC ACID		X		100			

TABLE A-5. Chemicals Included in the Maps of Industrial and Urban Toxins *(Continued)*

CHEMICAL NAME	INDUSTRIAL AIR EMISSIONS	INDUSTRIAL WATER DISCHARGES	URBAN AIR EMISSIONS	TOTAL HAZARD INDICATOR	CANCER HAZARD INDICATOR	ACUTE HAZARD INDICATOR	TOXIC RELEASE INVENTORY
NICKEL	X	X	X	1	HIGH		X
NITROBENZENE	X	X		1,000		10,000	X
NITROGLYCERINE		X		10			X
NITROSODIMETHYLAMINE		X		1	MEDIUM	1,000	X
O-NITROPHENOL		X		100			X
OZONE		X				100	
P-NITROPHENOL		X		100			X
PARAQUAT		X				10	
PENTACHLOROPHENOL		X	X	10			X
PHENANTHRENE	X	X	X	5,000			
PHENOL	X	X	X	1,000		500	X
PHENOL,2,4,6-TRICHLORO		X		10	LOW		X
PHOSPHORUS	X	X		1		100	X
PHTHALATE ESTERS		X					
POLYBROMINATED BIPHENYLS (PBBS)		X					X
POLYCHLORINATED BIPHENYLS (PCBS)		X		10	MEDIUM		X
PROPIONALDEHYDE	X		X				X
PROPIONIC ACID	X			5,000			
PROPYLENE (PROPENE)			X				
PROPYLENE OXIDE	X			100		10,000	X
PSEUDOCUMENE	X		X				X
PYRENE	X	X	X	5,000		1,000	
SEC-BUTYL ALCOHOL	X						X
SELENIUM	X	X	X	100			X
SILVER	X	X		1,000			X
SODIUM	X	X		10			
SODIUM NITRITE		X		100			
STYRENE	X	X		1,000			X
SULFUR TRIOXIDE	X	X				100	
TELLURIUM		X				500	
TEREPHTHALIC ACID	X						X
TERT-BUTYL ALCOHOL	X						X
THALLIUM	X	X		1,000			X
TOXAPHENE (CAMPHECHLOR)		X		1	MEDIUM	500	X
TRICHLOROETHYLENE	X	X	X	1,000	LOW		X
TRICHLOROPHENOL		X		10	LOW		
TRIMETHYLAMINE	X			100			
VANADIUM (FUME OR DUST)	X		X				X
VINYL ACETATE MONOMER	X	X		5,000		1,000	X
ZINC	X	X		1,000			X
CHEMICAL GROUPS							
CHLORINATED BENZENES	X	X					
CHLORINATED ETHANES		X					
CHLORINATED NAPHTHALENE		X					
CHLORINATED PHENOLS		X					X
CHLOROALKYL ETHERS		X					
CYANIDE AND COMPOUNDS	X	X					X
ENDOSULFAN AND METABOLITES		X					
HALOETHERS		X					
HALOMETHANES		X					
NITROSAMINES		X					
RADIONUCLIDES		X		1			

INDUSTRIAL AIR EMISSIONS: The maps of industrial air emissions include chemicals with an X in this column.

INDUSTRIAL WATER DISCHARGES: The maps of industrial water discharges include chemicals with an X in this column.

URBAN AIR EMISSIONS: The maps of urban air emissions include chemicals with an X in this column.

TOTAL HAZARD INDICATOR: This column lists the CERCLA reportable quantity (RQ in pounds) for each chemical. Smaller RQs indicate more hazardous chemicals. All listed chemicals are included in the maps of hazardous chemicals. These chemicals are subject to reporting under either section 302, 304 or 313 of EPCRA, even if there is a blank in this column (indicating that EPA has not assigned a final RQ to the chemical). Source: Office of Toxic Substances, *Title III List of Lists: Consolidated List of Chemicals Subject to Reporting Under Title III of the Superfund Amendments and Reauthorization Act (SARA) of 1986* (Washington, DC: U.S. EPA, 1988).

CANCER HAZARD INDICATOR: This column lists the CERCLA cancer hazard ranking for each chemical. The maps of suspected carcinogens include chemicals with values in this column. EPA suspects these chemicals of posing either high, medium, or low cancer risks. Source: Environmental Monitoring & Services, Inc., *Technical Background Document to Support Rulemaking Pursuant to CERCLA Section 102*, Volume 3 (Washington, DC: U.S. EPA, 1986), Appendix A.

ACUTE HAZARD INDICATOR: This column lists the EPCRA Section 302 threshold planning quantity (TPQ in pounds) for each chemical. The maps of acutely hazardous chemicals include substances with values in this column. These chemicals are subject to the reporting provisions of EPCRA's emergency planning section 302. Smaller TPQs indicate more acutely hazardous chemicals. Source: *Title III List of Lists*, op. cit.

TOXIC RELEASE INVENTORY: Chemicals with an X in this column are subject to reporting under section 313 of EPCRA and are thus included in EPA's Toxic Chemical Release Inventory (TRI).

those hazardous chemicals that the EPA suspects cause cancer (and for which EPA has developed speciation factors).[13] As Table A-4 indicates, this sample includes 14 percent of all suspected carcinogens subject to reporting under EPCRA.

The county estimates of the annual tons of industrial emissions of acutely hazardous chemicals are also calculated with this method, but they include only those chemicals the EPA considers extremely hazardous (and for which EPA has developed speciation factors). As Table A-4 indicates, this sample includes 5 percent of all such chemicals subject to reporting under section 302 of EPCRA.

The counts of operating hazardous waste incinerators include all facilities used for thermal treatment of hazardous wastes during 1987.

The industrial emissions of low-level radiation from commercial power reactors include the total reported curies emitted during the years 1970 through 1981. These emissions data were submitted during the years 1970 through 1981. These emissions data were submitted to the U.S. Department of Energy (DOE) by commercial U.S. nuclear power plants. The DOE's Brookhaven National Laboratory in Upton, New York, compiles these data for the U.S. Nuclear Regulatory Commission.[14]

For the industrial emissions total hazard index, which is included in the statistical tests but not in the maps, the estimated industrial emission of the sample hazardous chemicals are multiplied by weights indicating relative hazards, and the resultant products are aggregated. The weights used for the total hazard index are based on the quantities EPA considers sufficient to require reporting under the Comprehensive Emergency Response Compensation and Liability Act (CERCLA) and under EPCRA, or the so-called CERCLA reportable quantities (RQs). The inverses of RQs are used as the hazard weights for the total hazard index. Hazard indices are used to correct distortions that arise from comparisons of aggregate quantities.

Quantities may not reflect the relative hazard of emissions when individual chemical potencies vary significantly. Consider, for example, a case where chemical A and chemical B are emitted in the same amounts. If the RQ for chemical is 10 pounds and the RQ for chemical B is 100 pounds, then chemical A's total hazard index is 10 times greater than chemical B's, since chemical A must be reported even if it is present in only one-tenth of the amount of chemical B. A wide range of potential health and environmental hazards is considered in the EPA's determination of RQs. Table A-5 provides the RQ values for all of the chemicals used in this atlas.

The industrial emissions cancer hazard index (used only in the statistical tests) serves the same function, but for the sample of suspected carcinogens. The EPA developed a rating of chemicals based on both their cancer-causing potency and the weight of evidence of the potency estimates. These cancer hazard ratings are one of the factors the EPA considers in the development of RQs. The EPA rated 191 chemicals as having high, medium, or low cancer hazard. The cancer hazard weights are the inverses of what the RQs for the suspected carcinogens would be if they were set solely on the basis of the EPA's cancer hazard ratings.[15]

The industrial emissions acute hazard index (used only in the statistical tests) serves the same function as the other two industrial emissions indices, but for the sample of extremely hazardous chemicals. The hazard weights used for this index are the inverses of EPCRA section 302 threshold planning quantities (TPQs). To develop TPQs, the EPA considers a variety of acute hazards, such as acute toxicity and chemical reactivity, reflected by measures such as immediately dangerous to life and health (IDLH) levels and others.

The counts of permit violators (used only in the statistical tests) include all facilities that failed to comply with the requirements of their CAA emission permit during 1985 according to the EPA's Compliance Data System (CDS).

Industrial Water Discharges

The counts of industrial dischargers include all facilities with National Pollution Discharge Elimination System (NPDES) permits issued under the Clean Water Act that were catalogued in the EPA's Permit Compliance System (PCS) as of 1985.

The county estimates of annual tons of industrial discharges of hazardous chemicals are of discharges from some 40,000 facilities nationwide of a sample of the chemicals subject to reporting under EPCRA. These data are aggregated directly from Discharge Monitoring Reports (DMRs) catalogued in PCS during 1984 and 1985. The data are annual averages for the 2-year period. Data on 1,611 measurement parameters are reported in PCS, of which 158 chemicals are regulated under EPCRA. As indicated in Table A-4, this sample includes 14 percent of the chemicals subject to reporting under EPCRA. Unfortunately, there is great variation in the reporting of these chemicals and the quality of the source data, so all the maps of industrial discharges are useful only in identifying reported amounts. Table A-5 provides a detailed listing of the chemicals included in the maps of industrial discharges.

The county estimates of the annual tons of industrial discharges of suspected carcinogens are calculated with the method just described, but they include only those hazardous chemicals that the EPA suspects cause cancer. This sample includes all such suspected carcinogens that are reported in PCS. As Table A-4 indicates, this sample includes 24 percent of all such chemicals subject to reporting under EPCRA.

The county estimates of the annual tons of industrial discharges of acutely hazardous chemicals are also calculated with the method just described, but they include only those chemicals the EPA considers extremely hazardous. This sample includes all such acutely hazardous chemicals that are reported in PCS. As Table A-4 indicates, this sample includes 8 percent of all chemicals subject to reporting under section 302 of EPCRA.

The industrial discharges total hazard index, cancer hazard index, and acute hazard index (used only in the statistical tests) serve the same functions and are calculated with the same methods and weights used for the emissions indices, but use discharge quantities instead of estimated emissions.

Hazardous Wastes

The counts of hazardous waste generators include all facilities that correctly notified the EPA pursuant to reporting requirements of the Resource Conservation and Recovery Act (RCRA) that they generated large quantities of hazardous waste. The counts are calculated from data in the EPA's Hazardous Waste Data Management System (HWDMS) as of 1987.

Estimates of annual hazardous waste generation were developed using an empirical method of economic analysis called input-output analysis. No government data on hazardous waste generation are available on a county basis nationwide.[16] The estimates used here are derived from the number of employees in every major plant of more than 200 manufacturing and nonmanufacturing industries, based on the Trinet, Inc., Database of U.S. Business Information, and from per-employee rates of hazardous waste generation derived from various technical government documents. The generation estimates are scaled to a U.S. total of 100 million tons so that the disaggregated figures can be interpreted as a percent of the U.S. total. Fifty percent of the total is attributed to the petrochemicals industries, in general accord with government estimates.[17] The EPA now estimates that the actual amount of hazardous wastes managed each year could be as high as 500 million tons.[18]

The counts of operating hazardous waste treatment, storage, and disposal facilities (TSDFs) are calculated from data in HWDMS as of 1987. The counts of operating hazardous waste storage and treatment facilities include all containers, tanks, waste piles, or surface impoundments used for hazardous waste treatment or storage during 1987 according to HWDMS. The counts of operating hazardous waste land disposal facilities include all landfills, surface impoundments, and land applications used for hazardous waste disposal during 1987. The counts of operating hazardous waste underground injection facilities include all facilities with injection wells used for the disposal of hazardous wastes during 1987.

The counts of operating commercial hazardous waste TSDF facilities are also calculated from HWDMS as of 1987. The EPA defines a commercial facility as a "facility [public or private] that accepts hazardous waste from a third party for a fee or other remuneration, for the specific purpose of treating, storing, or disposing of that waste, except captive facilities."[19]

Estimates of landfill capacities at operating commercial hazardous waste landfill facilities during 1986 are derived from HWDMS, EPA documents, commercial directories, and interviews with plant managers. Telephone interviews were conducted in August and September 1986 with plant managers or other responsible personnel at all landfill facilities listed in HWDMS, other EPA documents, or the commercial directory called *Industrial and Hazardous Waste Management Firms* (Environmental Information Ltd., 1986). Twenty-seven commercial facilities were found to have operating landfills, of which current capacity amounts were unavailable for two. The standard unit of measurement for landfill capacity is acre-feet. One acre-foot is defined as the volume of water that will cover an area of one acre to a depth of one foot, and equals 43,560 cubic feet or 1,613 cubic yards. Facility estimates of current landfill capacity may differ from the amounts designed to be handled during interim status and from the amount applied for in a permit.

The counts of groundwater violators (used only in the statistical tests) include all hazardous waste facilities that had one or more violations of RCRA groundwater monitoring requirements during 1987 according to HWDMS.

The counts of uncontrolled or closed toxic waste sites are aggregated from the EPA's CERCLA Information System (CERCLIS) as of 1987. The sites in the file include the closed TSDFs that the EPA has catalogued in its ongoing survey of sites that require cleanup. Superfund sites, or those toxic waste sites that EPA selects for priority cleanup, are among the sites included in the count. Closed units of certain operating facilities are also included, as are serious spills.

The counts of Superfund National Priorities List (NPL) sites are aggregated from CERCLIS as of 1987. NPL sites are those uncontrolled TSDFs that the EPA considers the most dangerous in the country, requiring priority cleanup because of their serious hazards.

Workplace Toxins

The average annual employment figures for petrochemicals industries are derived from Census Bureau County Business Patterns (CBPs). An annual average for the five years 1980–84 is calculated for all counties with an annual average of 100 or more employees at any time from 1950 through 1984. The numbers represent the average number of person-years employed in the Standard Industrial Classification (SIC) industries 28 (chemical products) and 29 (oil and gas products).

Measures of the level of workplace exposures to hazardous chemicals are derived from data in the U.S. Occupational Safety and Health Administration's (OSHA) Integrated Management Information System (IMIS) for the years 1980 through 1985. The frequency of federal OSHA inspections varies significantly across the country, with some states having no federal inspections, because a state agency has authority for OSHA regulation. Therefore, inspection frequencies as well as illegal exposures are considered in the workplace toxins maps.

The workplace toxins measure of inspections with illegal exposures is the percentage of total federal OSHA inspections with chemical sampling during 1980–85 that found worker exposures to hazardous chemicals exceeding Permissible Exposure Limits (PELs). The measure of illegal occupational exposures is the total number of worker exposures to hazardous chemicals exceeding PELs that federal OSHA inspectors found during 1980–85. The inspections measure is the total number of federal OSHA inspections with chemical sampling conducted during 1980–85.

NONINDUSTRIAL POLLUTION MEASURES

Pesticides

The measures of pesticide usage are derived from a database developed for the EPA Office of Pesticides and Toxic Substances by Resources for the Future (RFF). The RFF database contains 1982–83 data from the U.S. Department of Agriculture Economic Research Service, the EPA's Office of Pesticide Programs, and California's Department of Food and Agriculture.

The county pesticide annual usage estimates include the pounds of 25 active ingredients applied to the following 77 different crops:

Alfalfa	Citrus	Nectarines	Safflower
Almonds	Collards	Oats	Seed crops
Apples	Corn	Okra	Sod
Apricots	Cotton	Olives	Sorghum
Artichokes	Cranberries	Onoins	Soybeans
Asparagus	Cucumbers	Other hay	Spinach
Avocados	Dates	Pasture	Squash
Barley	Egplant	Peaches	Strawberries
Beans	Figs	Peanuts	Sugarbeets
Beets	Filberts	Pears	Sugarcane
Blackberries	Flax	Peas	Sunflowers
Blueberries	Garlic	Pecans	Sweet corn
Broccoli	Grapes	Pistachios	Sweet pepper
Brussels sprouts	Guar	Plums	Sweet potatoes
Cabbage	Hops	Potatoes	Tobacco
Cantaloupes	Hot peppers	Pumpkins	Tomatoes
Carrots	Lettuce	Radishes	Walnuts
Cauliflower	Melons	Rice	Watermelons
Celery	Mint	Rye	Wheat
Cherries			

The pesticide total hazard index, cancer hazard index, and acute hazard index serve the same functions as the emissions and discharge hazard indices (which are not mapped), but use estimated pesticide usage instead of emissions or discharge quantities. The pesticide total hazard index and acute hazard index are calculated with the same weights used for the emissions and discharge indices; however, the cancer hazard index uses as weights the inverse of oncogenic potency factors developed by the EPA.[20] Table A-6 lists the 25 pesticide active ingredients and their corresponding hazard weights.

The estimates of annual county pesticide application rates include the average pounds used per acres treated of 25 active ingredients applied to the 77 different crops as reported in the RFF database. The county pesticide annual coverage estimate includes the average percent of crop acreage covered by 25 active ingredients in each county.

TABLE A-6. Active Ingredients Included in the Pesticide Maps

PESTICIDE ACTIVE INGREDIENT	TOTAL HAZARD WEIGHT	CANCER HAZARD WEIGHT	ACUTE HAZARD WEIGHT
Acifluorfen			
Alachlor		0.0595	
Atrazine			
Bensulide			
Carbaryl	0.01		
Carbofuran	0.1		0.1
Chlorothalonil		0.024	
Cyanazine			
Diazinon	1		
Disulfoton	1		0.002
Ethoprop			
Fluometuron			
Malathion	0.01		
Methamidophos			0.01
Methyl Parathion	0.01		0.01
Metiram		0.0176	
Metolachlor		0.0021	
Parathion	1	0.0018	0.01
PCNB	1		
Phorate	0.1		0.1
Propanil			
Thiobencarb			
Trifluralin			
Vernolate			
2,4-D	0.01		

Water Quality

The measure of houses served by private wells is the number of housing units that obtained their water from private wells as a percent of all housing units during 1980. The remaining percentage of housing units obtained their water from public and private utilities. These data are from the Census Bureau's Summary Tape File 3A (STF 3A).

The groundwater usage map shows the volume of groundwater removed in millions of gallons per day, using 1984 U.S. Geological Survey data.[21]

Public water supply risk (used only in the statistical tests) indicates the number of exposures to unhealthful levels of priority pollutants in drinking water. The number of times a water supply exceeded maximum contamination limits (MCLs) for any priority pollutant is multiplied by the number of people who drink from the supply. When MCLs are exceeded, drinking water no longer passes federal standards to protect public health. The data are from the EPA

Public Water Supply Program's Federal Reporting Data System (FRDS) as of 1985. The public water supply violations measure is the number of MCLs that were exceeded during 1985 as reported in FRDS. During that year, violations were reported for the following pollutants:

Arsenic	Fluoride	Selenium
Barium	Gross alpha	Silver
Cadmium	Lead	THM
Chromium	Lindane	Toxaphene
Coliform	Mercury	Turbidity
Combined radium	Methoxychlor	2,4-D
Endrin	Nitrate	2,4,5-TP silvex

The river impairment map uses data from a 1982 survey conducted by the Association of State and Interstate Water Pollution Control Administrators (AS-IWPCA) in cooperation with the EPA and converted to county form based on the EPA's REACH file in its Storage and Retrieval of Water Quality Information (STORET) database.[22] The values identify the percentages of river mileage that did not fully support their designated uses.

The sewage outflow map uses data from the EPA's Industrial Facilities Discharge (IFD) file as of 1985 that measure the flows from publicly owned treatment works (POTWs) in millions of gallons per day (MGD).

Air Quality

The county estimates of annual tons of area-source emissions of hazardous chemicals include a sample of the chemicals subject to reporting under EPCRA. These estimates are derived from the EPA's Hazardous Emissions Model and Integrated System (HEMIS), which calculates emissions of 78 air pollutants from the following 27 area sources as of 1985.

- air-conditioning towers
- commercial fuel combustion—coal, oil, natural gas, wood stoves, and fireplaces
- industrial fuel combustion—coal, oil, natural gas, wood stoves, and fireplaces
- residential fuel combustion—coal, oil, natural gas, wood stoves, and fireplaces
- heavy-duty road vehicles—diesel and gasoline
- light-duty road vehicles—diesel and gasoline
- solvent usage—degreasers, dry cleaners, nonindustrial, painting and graphics, plastics manufacturing, surface coating (paving), and other industrial uses
- volatilization from sewage treatment plants
- waste oil burning
- wood treatment (waterproofing)

Of these 78 chemicals, 76 are regulated under EPCRA. As indicated in Table A-4, this sample includes 7 percent of all chemicals subject to reporting under EPCRA. While some inaccuracy is associated with any estimation procedure, the value of these emission estimates is that they provide a consistent method for comparing counties. Table A-5 provides a detailed listing of the chemicals included in all of the area-source emissions maps.

The county estimates of annual tons of area-source emissions of suspected carcinogens are calculated with the method just described, but they include only those hazardous chemicals that the EPA suspects cause cancer. As Table A-4 indicates, this sample includes 12 percent of the suspected carcinogens subject to reporting under EPCRA.

The county estimates of annual tons of area-source emissions of acutely hazardous chemicals are also calculated with the method just described. As Table A-4 indicates, this sample includes 2 percent of the extremely hazardous chemicals subject to reporting under section 302 of EPCRA.

The area-source emissions total hazard index, cancer hazard index, and acute hazard index (used only in the statistical tests) serve the same functions and are calculated with the same methods and weights used for the industrial emissions indices but using the estimates of sample area-source emissions instead of the industrial emissions quantities.

The six maps of ambient air pollution concentrations show the average values for each pollutant during the years 1981 to 1985. These are the pollutants for which National Ambient Air Quality Standards (NAAQS) have been established under the Clean Air Act. These data are derived from the EPA's National Aerometric Data Bank (NADB) as of 1985.[23] The six primary, health-related standards include:

Pollutant	*Measure*	*Primary NAAQS*[24]
Carbon monoxide	2nd-highest 8-hour average	9 ppm
Lead	maximum quarterly average	1.5 $\mu g/m^3$
Nitrogen dioxide	annual arithmetic mean	0.053 ppm
Ozone	2nd-highest daily maximum 1-hr. avg.	0.12 ppm
Particulates	annual geometric mean	75 $\mu g/m^3$
Sulfur dioxide	2nd-highest 24-hour average	0.14 ppm

SOCIAL STRUCTURE MEASURES

Demographics

Total population includes all county residents counted by the 1980 census according to the Census Bureau's STF 3A. The measure of minority residents as a percent of all 1980 county residents is derived from the Census Bureau's STF 3A. Minority population, as defined by the Commission for Racial Justice, includes all African Americans, Latino Americans, Asian Americans, Pacific islanders, native Americans, and Aleutians, and all other people the Census Bureau classifies as nonwhite.[25]

Socioeconomics

The measure of mean household income is derived from the Census Bureau's STF 3A. Adjustments are made to reflect inflationary increases of 35 percent during the five-year period from 1979 to 1984 (data collected for the 1980 census relate to the year 1979). These increases are based on Bureau of Labor Statistics consumer price indices for rent and all consumer goods during the five-year period. The resulting values reflect more easily understood and updated 1984 dollars. This variable is included to measure standard of living, as reflected by income.

Mean values of owner-occupied homes are also derived from the Census Bureau's STF 3A. Adjustments are made to reflect inflationary increases of 35 percent during the five-year period from 1979 to 1984. In addition, home values are adjusted upward by 25 percent to help compensate for the estimated understatement of such values by respondents who were fearful that their answers would be used for tax assessment purposes. The 25 percent adjustment is based on discussions with realtors in Los Angeles and New York, where understatement is reported to be even greater. (The Census Bureau would not offer an official estimate of the admitted degree of understatement.) This variable is included to indicate areas of affluence, as reflected by such assets.

The measure of single-mother families is the numbers of families with a child, a female head of household, and no spouse of the householder present as a percentage of total households in each county during 1980. This variable is derived from the Census Bureau's STF 3A.

The counts of families in poverty are the numbers of families that earned income below the poverty level as a percentage of all county families in 1979. The definition of poverty level varied according to family size as follows:

2-person family	=	$ 4,725
3-person family	=	$ 5,784
4-person family	=	$ 7,412
5-person family	=	$ 8,775
6-person family	=	$ 9,914
7-or-more-person family	=	$12,280

This variable is derived from the Census Bureau's City and County Data Book (CCDB) database.

Education

The measures of high school and college graduates as percentages of all 1980 county residents 25 years and older are from the Census Bureau's CCDB.

Health Services

The measure of the number of hospital beds for every 100,000 persons (or fraction thereof) in a county during 1980 is from the Census Bureau's CCDB. The Census Bureau obtained these data from the American Hospital Association.

The measure of the number of physicians for every 100,000 persons (or fraction thereof) in a county during 1980 is from the Census Bureau's CCDB. The Census Bureau obtained these data from the American Medical Association.

DATA SOURCES

Bureau of the Census, U.S. Department of Commerce. "Census of Population and Housing, 1980: Summary Tape File 3A" (STF 3A). Washington, DC: Bureau of the Census, 1982.

——. "City and County Data Book" (CCDB) Database. Washington, DC: Bureau of the Census, 1983.

——. "County Business Patterns" (CBP). Washington, DC: U.S. GPO, 1950–1985.

Environmental Information, Ltd. *Industrial and Hazardous Waste Management Firms.* Minneapolis, MN: Environmental Information, Ltd., 1986.

Environmental Monitoring & Services, Inc. *Technical Background Document to Support Rulemaking Pursuant to CERCLA Section 102,* Volume 3 (Washington, DC: U.S. EPA, 1986), Appendix A.

National Center for Health Statistics. "Mortality Surveillance System" (MSS). Washington, DC: NCHS, 1987.

Occupational Safety and Health Administration, U.S. Department of Labor. "Integrated Management Information System" (IMIS). Washington, DC: U.S. OSHA, 1985.

Public Data Access, Inc. "County Mortality Data System" (PDAMORT). New York, NY: PDA, 1990.

——. "County Quality of Life Database" (CQOL). New York, NY: PDA, 1987.

——. "Radioactive Emissions and Health Database" (RADEM). New York, NY: PDA, 1987.

Resources for the Future. "Pesticide Usage Database." Washington, DC: U.S. EPA, 1987.

Tichler, J., and Benkovitz, C. *Radioactive Materials Released from Nuclear Power Plants—1981.* NUREG/CR-2907, Volume 2, BNL-NUREG-51581. Washington, DC: U.S. Nuclear Regulatory Commission, June 1984.

Trinet, Inc. "Database of U.S. Business Information." New York: Control Data Corporation, 1985.

U.S. Environmental Protection Agency. "Compliance Data System" (CDS). Washington, DC: U.S. EPA, 1985.

———. "Comprehensive Environmental Response, Compensation and Liability Act Information System" (CERCLIS). Washington, DC: U.S. EPA, 1988.

———. "Federal Reporting Data System" (FRDS). Washington, DC: U.S. EPA, 1985.

———. "Hazardous Emissions Model and Integrated System" (HEMIS). Washington, DC: U.S. EPA, 1988.

———. "Hazardous Waste Data Management System" (HWDMS). Washington, DC: U.S. EPA, 1987.

———. "Industrial Facilities Discharges" (IFD). Washington, DC: U.S. EPA, 1985.

———. "National Aerometric Data Bank" (NADB). Washington, DC: U.S. EPA, 1985.

———. "National Emissions Data System" (NEDS). Washington, DC: U.S. EPA, 1985.

———. "Permit Compliance System" (PCS). Washington, DC: U.S. EPA, 1984–85.

———. "Storage and Retrieval of Water Quality Information" (STORET). Washington, DC: U.S. EPA, 1986.

———. "Title III Lists of Lists" (LOL). Washington, DC: U.S. EPA, 1988.

RESOURCES

This appendix is a guide to where to go for further information and help. It lists many national and local organizations, their addresses, phone numbers, and major issue areas. The issues are identified according to the chapters (and sections) of this book. Many of these organizations cover multiple issues, so our categorizations may seem somewhat arbitrary; they are merely intended to help you get started.

A few codes are used to identify issue areas and certain organizations, including:

> M = Mortality (AE = acutely hazardous exposures; BD = birth defects; CA = all cancers; CL = lung cancers; HD = Heart Diseases; YI = Young adult infectious diseases)
> T = Industrial toxics (AP = industrial air emissions; HW = hazardous wastes; WD = industrial water discharges; WK = workplace toxics)
> R = Nonindustrial toxics (AQ = air quality; PE = pesticides; WQ = water quality)
> S = Social structure.

CCHW = Citizens Clearinghouse for Hazardous Waste
COSH = Committee on Occupational Safety and Health
PIRG = Public Interest Research Group

NATIONAL GOVERNMENT AND INDUSTRY ORGANIZATIONS

ORGANIZATION	CITY	ST	PHONE NUMBER		ISSUES		

Mortality

ORGANIZATION	CITY	ST	PHONE NUMBER				
Agency for Toxic Substances & Disease Registry	Atlanta	GA	(404)452-4100	M	T		
Association of State & Territorial Health Officials	McLean	VA	(703)556-9222	M			
Centers for Disease Control	Atlanta	GA	(404)639-3311	M			
EPA National Toxicology Program	Res Triangle Pk	NC	(919)541-4532	M	T		
NCI Cancer Information Service	Bethesda	MD	(800)422-6237	M			CA
National AIDS Information Clearinghouse	Rockville	MD	(800)458-5231	M			YI
National Health Information Clearinghouse	Washington	DC	(800)336-4797	M			
National Heart, Lung & Blood Institute	Bethesda	MD	(301)951-3260	M			
U.S. Conference of Local Health Officials	Washington	DC	(202)293-7330	M			
U.S. General Accounting Office	Gaithersburg	MD	(301)275-6241	M	T	R	
U.S. Government Printing Office	Washington	DC	(202)783-3238	M	T	R	S
U.S. Public Health Service	Rockville	MD	(301)443-2403	M			

Industrial Toxics

ORGANIZATION	CITY	ST	PHONE NUMBER				
Association of State & Interstate Water Pollution Control Admin	Washington	DC	(202)624-7782		T		WD
Association of State & Territorial Waste Management Officials	Washington	DC	(202)624-5828		T		HW
Chemical Manufacturers Association	Washington	DC	(800)262-8200		T		
Chemical Referral Center	Washington	DC	(800)262-8200`		T		
Chemical Transportation Emergency Center (CHEMTREC)	Washington	DC	(800)424-9300		T		AE
Council for Solid Waste Solutions	Washington	DC	(202)371-5319		T		.HW
EPA Air Control Technology Center	Res Triangle Pk	NC	(919)541-0800		T		AP
EPA Air Risk Information Support Center	Res Triangle Pk	NC	(919)541-0888		T		AP
EPA Asbestos Hotline	Washington	DC	(800)835-6700		T		
EPA Best Available Control Technology	Res Triangle Pk	NC	(919)541-5432		T		AP
EPA Hazardous Waste/Superfund Hotline	Washington	DC	(800)424-9346		T		
EPA National Air Toxics Information Clearinghouse	Res Triangle Pk	NC	(919)541-0850		T		AP
EPA Right-to-Know Hotline	Washington	DC	(800)535-0202		T		
EPA Toxic Substances Control Act Hotline	Washington	DC	(202)554-1404		T		
Federal Emergency Management Agency	Washington	DC	(202)646-2400		T		
Hazardous Waste Treatment Counci	Washington	DC	(202)783-0870		T		HW
Mine Safety & Health Administration	Arlington	VA	(703)235-1452		T		WK
National Academy of Sciences Environmental Studies & Toxicology	Washington	DC	(202)334-2216		T		
National Conference of State Legislatures	Denver	CO	(303)623-7800		T	R	
National Institute for Environmental Health Sciences	Res Triangle Pk	NC	(919)541-7634		T	R	
National Institute for Occupational Safety & Health (NIOSH)	Atlanta	GA	(404)639-3691		T		WK
National Response Center Hotline	Washington	DC	(800)424-8802		T		AE
National Solid Waste Management Association	Washington	DC	(202)659-4613		T		HW
National Transportation Safety Board	Washington	DC	(202)382-6600		T		AE
Nuclear Regulatory Commission	Washington	MD	(301)951-0550		T		
Occupational Safety & Health Administration (OSHA)	Washington	DC	(202)523-8148	M	T		WK
Office of Technology Assessment, U.S. Congress	Washington	DC	(202)228-6150	M	T		

Nonindustrial Pollution

ORGANIZATION	CITY	ST	PHONE NUMBER				
Association of State Drinking Water Administrators	Arlington	VA	(703)524-2428			R	WQ
EPA Headquarters	Washington	DC	(202)382-2090		T	R	
EPA National Pesticide Hazard Assessment Program	Corvallis	OR	(503)757-5086			R	PE
EPA Office of Community Liaison	Washington	DC	(202)382-4454		T	R	
EPA Region I (ME, NH, VT, MA, CT, RI)	Boston	MA	(617)565-3424		T	R	
EPA Region II (NJ, NY, PR)	New York	NY	(212)264-2515		T	R	
EPA Region III (DC, DE, MD, PA, VA, WV)	Philadelphia	PA	(215)579-9370		T	R	
EPA Region IV (AL, FL, GA, KY, MS, NC, SC, TN)	Atlanta	GA	(404)347-3004		T	R	
EPA Region V (IL, IN, MI, MN, OH, WI)	Chicago	IL	(312)353-2072		T	R	
EPA Region VI (AR, LA, NM, OK, TX)	Dallas	TX	(214)655-2200		T	R	
EPA Region VII (IA, KS, MO, NE)	Kansas City	MO	(913)551-7003		T	R	
EPA Region VIII (CO, MT, ND, SD, UT, WY)	Denver	CO	(303)293-1692		T	R	
EPA Region IX (AZ,CA,HI,NV)	San Francisco	CA	(415)556-5145		T	R	
EPA Region X (AK,ID,OR,WA)	Seattle	WA	(206)442-1465		T	R	
EPA Safe Drinking Water Hotline	Washington	DC	(800)426-4791		T	R	WQ
National Association of State Departments of Agriculture	Washington	DC	(202)628-1566			R	PE
National Pesticide Information Clearinghouse	Lubbock	TX	(800)858-7378			R	PE
National Water Well Association	Dublin	OH	(614)761-1711			R	

Social Structure

ORGANIZATION	CITY	ST	PHONE NUMBER				
Bureau of Labor Statistics	Washington	DC	(202)523-1222				S
Bureau of the Census	Suitland	MD	(301)763-4100				S

352

NATIONAL ENVIRONMENTAL AND PUBLIC INTEREST ORGANIZATIONS

ORGANIZATION	CITY	ST	PHONE NUMBER					ISSUES

Mortality

ORGANIZATION	CITY	ST	PHONE NUMBER					
ACT-UP	New York	NY	(212)564-2437	M				YI
American Cancer Society	Atlanta	GA	(404)320-3333	M				CA
American Heart Association	Dallas	TX	(214)373-6300	M				HD
American Lung Association	New York	NY	(212)315-8700	M				CL
American Public Health Assoc.	Washington	DC	(202)789-5600	M				
Center for Atomic Radiation Studies	Marlborough	NH	(603)847-9649	M	T			
Center for Science in the Public Interest	Washington	DC	(202)332-9110	M				
Center for the Biology of Natural Systems	Flushing	NY	(718)670-4182	M	T	R		
Child Trends, Inc.	Washington	DC	(202)223-6288	M				CC
Children's Defense Fund	Washington	DC	(202)628-8787	M			S	
Citizen Action	Washington	DC	(202)775-0370	M		R	S	
Environmental Health Network	Harvey	LA	(504)362-6574	M				
Environmental Research Foundation	Washington	DC	(202)328-1119	M	T	R	S	
Gay Men's Health Crisis (GMHC)	New York	NY	(212)807-6655	M				YI
March of Dimes	White Plains	NY	(914)428-7100	M				BD
National Association of Radiation Survivors	Berkeley	CA	(415)654-0100	M	T			
National Center for Environmental Health Strategies	Vorhees	NJ	(609)429-6843	M	T			
National Committee of Radiation Victims	Takoma Park	MD	(301)891-3990	M	T			
National Environmental Health Association	Denver	CO	(303)756-9090	M	T	R	S	
National Network to Prevent Birth Defects	Washington	DC	(202)543-5450	M	T	R		BD
National Rural Health Care Assoc.	Kansas City	MO	(816)421-3075	M				
National Safety Council	Chicago	IL	(312)527-4800	M				AE
National Women's Health Network	Washington	DC	(202)347-1140	M				
People With AIDS Coalition	New York	NY	(212)627-7037	M				YI
Physicians for Social Responsibility	Washington	DC	(202)785-3777	M	T			
Public Citizen	Washington	DC	(202)785-3704	M	T	R	S	
Public Data Access, Inc.	New York	NY	(212)529-0890	M	T	R	S	
Radiation and Public Health Project	New York	NY	(212)529-0890	M	T	R		
U.S. Public Interest Research Group (U.S.PIRG)	Washington	DC	(202)546-9707	M	T	R	S	
White Lung Association	Baltimore	MD	(301)727-6029	M				CL

Industrial Toxics

ORGANIZATION	CITY	ST	PHONE NUMBER					
AFL-CIO, Department of Occupational Safety & Health	Washington	DC	(202)637-5366		T			WK
American Trial Lawyers Assoc.	Washington	DC	(202)965-3500		T			
Center for Environment, Commerce & Energy	Washington	DC	(202)543-3939		T	R	S	
Center for Environmental Education, Inc.	Washington	DC	(202)429-5609		T	R	S	
Center for Safety in the Arts	New York	NY	(212)227-6220		T			WK
Citizens Clearinghouse for Hazardous Wastes, Inc. (CCHW)	Arlington	VA	(703)276-7070		T		S	
Citizens for a Better Environmen	Chicago	IL	(312)939-1530		T	R		
Clean Sites, Inc.	Alexandria	VA	(703)683-8522		T			
Coalition on Superfund	Washington	DC	(202)393-4760		T			
Concern, Inc.	Washington	DC	(202)328-8160		T	R		PE
Council on Economic Priorities	New York	NY	(212)420-1133		T	R		
Council on Environmental Quality	Washington	DC	(202)395-5750		T	R		
Earth Island Institute	San Francisco	CA	(415)788-3666		T	R		
Environment and Policy Institute East-West Center	Honolulu	HI	(808)944-7265		T	R		
Environmental Action, Inc.	Washington	DC	(202)745-4870		T	R		
Environmental Defense Fund, Inc.	New York	NY	(212)505-2100		T	R		
Environmental Hazards Management Institute	Durham	NH	(603)868-1496		T			
Environmental Law Institute	Washington	DC	(202)328-5150		T	R		
Environmental Policy Institute	Washington	DC	(202)544-2600		T	R		
Federation of American Scientists	Washington	DC	(202)546-3300		T	R		
Friends of the Earth	Washington	DC	(202)544-2600		T	R		
Global Tomorrow Coalition	Washington	DC	(202)628-4016		T	R`	S	
Greenpeace USA	Washington	DC	(202)462-1177		T	R		
Human Environment Center	Washington	DC	(202)331-8387		T	R	S	
Inform	New York	NY	(212)689-4040		T	R		
Institute for Local Self Reliance	Washington	DC	(202)232-4108		T	R	S	
League of Conservation Voters	Washington	DC	(202)785-8683		T	R		
League of Women Voters	Washington	DC	(202)429-1965		T	R		
National Association for Environmental Education	Troy	OH	(513)698-6493		T	R	S	
National Campaign for Radioactive Waste Safety	Albuquerque	NM	(505)262-1862		T			
National Center for Policy Alternatives	Washington	DC	(202)387-6030		T	R		
National Clean Air Coalition	Washington	DC	(202)543-8200		T	R		AQ
National Lawyers Guild Toxics Committee	Portland	OR	(503)228-5222		T			

ORGANIZATION	CITY	ST	PHONE NUMBER	ISSUES			
National Toxics Campaign	Boston	MA	(617)232-0327	T			
Natural Resources Defense Council	New York	NY	(212)727-2700	T	R		
Nature Conservancy	Arlington	VA	(703)841-5300	T	R		
Nuclear Information & Resource Service	Washington	DC	(202)328-0002	T			
Oil, Chemical & Atomic Workers Union	Denver	CO	(303)987-2229	T			WK
PIRG Toxics Action	Berkeley	CA	(415)644-3591	T			
Public Citizen Critical Mass Energy Project	Washington	DC	(202)546-4996	T			
Radioactive Waste Campaign	New York	NY	(212)473-7390	T			
Relocation Assistance & Information Network (RAIN)	Camp Hill	PA	(717)737-4324	T			
Sierra Club	San Francisco	CA	(415)567-6100	T	R		
Sierra Club Legal Defense Fund, Inc.	San Francisco	CA	(415)567-6100	T	R		
Trial Lawyers for Public Justice	Washington	DC	(202)463-8600	T		S	
Union of Concerned Scientists (UCS)	Cambridge	MA	(617)547-5552	T	R		
Work on Waste	Canton	NY	(315)379-9200	T			
Working Group on Community Right-to-Know	Washington	DC	(202)546-9707	T			

Nonindustrial Pollution

ORGANIZATION	CITY	ST	PHONE NUMBER	ISSUES			
Acid Rain Foundation, Inc	St. Paul	MN	(612)454-2621		R		
Acid Rain Information Clearinghouse	Rochester	NY	(716)546-3796		R		
Agricultural Resources Center	Carrboro	NC	(919)967-1886		R		PE
Air Pollution Control Association	Pittsburgh	PA	(412)232-3444		R		AQ
American Rivers Conservation Council	Washington	DC	(202)547-6900		R		WQ
American Water Resources Association	Bethesda	MD	(301)493-8600		R		
Association for Commuter Transportation (ACT)	Washington	DC	(202)659-0600		R		
Bio-Integral Resource Center	Berkeley	CA	(415)524-2567		R		PE
CATA- Farmworker Support Committee	Glassboro	NJ	(609)881-2507		R	S	PE
Center for Clean Air Policy	Washington	DC	(202)624-7709		R		AQ
Citizen/Labor/Energy Coalition	Washington	DC	(202)857-5153		R	S	
Citizens for Ocean Law	Washington	DC	(202)462-3737		R		WQ
Clean Water Action Project	Washington	DC	(202)457-1286		R		WQ
Conservation Foundation / World Wildlife Fund	Washington	DC	(202)293-4800		R		
Cousteau Society, Inc.	Norfolk	VA	(804)627-1144		R		WQ
Defenders of Wildlife	Washington	DC	(202)659-9510		R		
Energy Conservation Coalition	Washington	DC	(202)745-4874		R		
Environmental Coalition for North America	Washington	DC	(202)289-5009		R		
Farmworker Justice Fund	Washington	DC	(202)462-8192	T	R	S	PE
Global Greenhouse Network	Washington	DC	(202)466-2823		R	S	
Green Seal	Washington	DC	(202)328-8095	T	R		
Izaak Walton League of America, Inc.	Arlington	VA	(703)528-1818		R		
National Association for Plastic Container Recovery	Charlotte	NC	(704)357-3250		R		
National Audubon Society	New York	NY	(212)832-3200		R		
National Coalition Against the Misuse of Pesticides	Washington	DC	(202)543-5450		R		PE
National Pesticide Telecommunication Network	Lubbock	TX	(800)858-7378		R		PE
National Recycling Association	Washington	DC	(202)625-6406		R		
National Wildlife Federation	Washington	DC	(202)637-3700	T	R		
Oceanic Society	Washington	DC	(202)328-0098		R		
Rachel Carson Council, Inc.	Chevy Chase	MD	(301)652-1877		R		PE
Renew America	Washington	DC	(202)232-2252		R		
Resources for the Future	Washington	DC	(202)328-5000		R		
United Farm Workers (UFW)	Keene	CA	(805)822-5571		R	S	PE
Water Pollution Control Federation	Alexandria	VA	(703)684-2400		R		WQ
Wilderness Society	Washington	DC	(202)833-2300		R		
Worldwatch Institute	Washington	DC	(202)452-1999		R		

Social Structure

ORGANIZATION	CITY	ST	PHONE NUMBER	ISSUES			
Americans for the Environment	Washington	DC	(202)797-6665			S	
Assoc. of Community Organizations for Reform Now (ACORN)	Chicago	IL	(312)939-7488			S	
Black Women's Health Network	Atlanta	GA	(404)753-0916			S	
CEIP Fund, Inc.	Boston	MA	(617)426-4375			S	
Commission for Racial Justice, United Church of Christ	New York	NY	(212)870-2077	T		S	
Eco-Justice Project, CRESP	Ithaca	NY	(607)255-4225			S	
Economic Justice Task Force, United Methodist Church	Washington	DC	(202)488-5649		R	S	
Economic Justice Working Group, National Council of Churches	New York	NY	(212)870-2483			S	
Environmental Consortium for Minority Outreach	Washington	DC	(202)331-8387			S	
Environmental Racism Project, Center for Constitutional Rights	New York	NY	(212)614-6464			S	

NATIONAL ENVIRONMENTAL AND PUBLIC INTEREST ORGANIZATIONS *(Continued)*

ORGANIZATION	CITY	ST	PHONE NUMBER	ISSUES			
Government Accountability Project	Washington	DC	(202)347-0460			S	
Grassroots Leadership	Charlotte	NC	(704)332-3090			S	
Highlander Education and Research Center	New Market	TN	(615)933-3443			S	
Labor Institute	New York	NY	(212)674-3322			S	
Migrant Legal Action Center	Washington	DC	(202)462-7744		R	S	PE
National Congress of American Indians	Washington	DC	(202)546-9404	T	R	S	
National Women's Health Network	Washington	DC	(202)347-1140			S	
North Carolina A. Philip Randolph Institute	Winston-Salem	NC	(919)924-8588			S	
Panos Institute	Washington	DC	(202)483-0044			S	
Partners for Livable Places	Washington	DC	(202)887-5990			S	
Planned Parenthood Federation of America	New York	NY	(212)541-7800			S	
Scenic America	Washington	DC	(202)546-1100			S	
Zero Population Growth, Inc.	Washington	DC	(202)332-2200			S	

STATE AGENCIES

STATE	POSTAL CODE	HEALTH	TOXIC RELEASES	OSHA
Alabama	AL	(205)261-5052	(205)271-7700	(205)822-7100
Alaska	AK	(907)561-4406	(907)465-2600	(907)271-5152
Arizona	AZ	(602)542-1024	(602)244-0504	(602)542-5795
Arkansas	AR	(501)661-2111	(501)682-4534	(501)324-6291
California	CA	(916)445-1248	(916)324-8124	(213)432-3434*
Colorado	CO	(303)331-4600	(303)331-4858	(303)234-4471
Connecticut	CT	(203)566-2038	(203)566-4856	(203)244-2294
Delaware	DE	(302)736-4700	(302)736-4764	(302)573-6115
District of Columbia	DC	(202)673-7700	(202)727-6161	(202)523-5224
Florida	FL	(904)488-4115	(904)487-1472	(904)791-2895
Georgia	GA	(404)894-7501	(404)656-6905	(404)221-4767
Hawaii	HI	(808)548-6505	(808)548-6505	(808)546-3157
Idaho	ID	(208)334-5945	(208)334-5898	(208)384-1867
Illinois	IL	(217)782-4977	(217)782-3637	(312)631-8200
Indiana	IN	(317)633-8400	(317)243-5176	(317)269-7290
Iowa	IA	(515)281-5605	(515)281-6175	(515)284-4794
Kansas	KS	(913)296-1343	(913)296-1690	(316)267-6311
Kentucky	KY	(502)564-3970	(502)564-2150	(502)582-6111
Louisiana	LA	(504)568-5048	(504)342-6363	(504)923-0718
Maine	ME	(207)289-3201	(207)289-4080	(617)223-6710
Maryland	MD	(301)225-6500	(301)631-3800	(301)962-2840
Massachusetts	MA	(617)727-0201	(617)292-5810	(617)890-1289
Michigan	MI	(517)335-8024	(517)373-8481	(313)226-6720
Minnesota	MN	(612)623-5460	(612)296-2233	(612)725-2571
Mississippi	MS	(601)960-7634	(601)960-9973	(601)969-4606
Missouri	MO	(314)751-6010	(314)751-7929	(314)425-5461
Montana	MT	(406)444-2544	(406)444-3948	(406)657-6649
Nebraska	NE	(402)471-2133	(402)471-4230	(402)221-9341
Nevada	NV	(702)885-4740	(702)885-4240	(702)883-1226
New Hampshire	NH	(603)271-4501	(603)271-2231	(603)224-1995
New Jersey	NJ	(609)292-7837	(609)292-6714	(201)645-5930
New Mexico	NM	(505)827-2613	(505)827-9222	(505)766-3411
New York	NY	(518)474-2011	(518)457-4107	(518)472-6085
North Carolina	NC	(919)733-3446	(919)733-3867	(919)755-4770
North Dakota	ND	(701)224-2372	(701)224-2374	(701)250-4521
Ohio	OH	(614)466-2253	(614)644-2270	(614)469-5582
Oklahoma	OK	(405)271-4200	(405)521-2481	(918)581-7676
Oregon	OR	(503)229-5032	(503)378-2885	(503)221-2251
Pennsylvania	PA	(717)787-6436	(717)783-8150	(215)597-4955
Puerto Rico	PR	(809)766-2200	(809)722-0077	(809)753-4457
Rhode Island	RI	(401)277-2231	(401)277-2808	(401)528-4466
South Carolina	SC	(803)734-4880	(803)734-5200	(803)765-5904
South Dakota	SD	(605)773-3361	(605)773-3153	(605)336-2980
Tennessee	TN	(615)741-3111	(800)262-3300	(615)251-5313
Texas	TX	(512)458-7375	(512)463-8527	(512)397-5783
Utah	UT	(801)538-6111	(801)538-6121	(801)524-5080
Vermont	VT	(802)863-7260	(802)863-7281	(802)828-2765
Virgin Islands	VI	(809)774-0117	(809)774-3320	(809)773-1994
Virginia	VA	(804)786-3561	(804)225-2513	(804)782-2864
Washington	WA	(206)753-5871	(800)633-7585	(206)753-6307
West Virginia	WV	(304)348-2971	(304)348-2967	(304)343-6181
Wisconsin	WI	(608)266-1511	(608)255-9255	(414)291-3315
Wyoming	WY	(307)777-7656	(307)777-7566	(307)777-7786

* The Los Angeles number for CalOSHA is given above; the number for San Francisco is (415)556-7260.

ORGANIZATION	CITY	ST	PHONE NUMBER	ISSUES				
Alabama Conservancy	Birmingham	AL	(205)322-3126		T	R		
Alabamians for a Clean Environment	York	AL	(205)392-7443		T			
Center for Labor Education & Research, Univ. of AL	Birmingham	AL	(205)934-2101		T			WK
National Toxics Campaign, Southern Office	Livingston	AL	(205)652-9854		T			
Alaska Center for the Environment	Anchorage	AK	(907)274-3621		T	R		
Alaska Health Project	Anchorage	AK	(907)276-2864		T			WK
Alaska PIRG (AKPIRG)	Anchorage	AK	(907)278-3661	M	T	R	S	
Greenpeace Alaska	Anchorage	AK	(907)277-8234		T	R		
Arizona Citizen Action	Glendale	AZ	(602)274-5622	M	T	R	S	
Earth First!	Tucson	AZ	(602)622-1371		T	R		
Environmental Action	Sedona	AZ	(602)282-4775		T	R		
Maricopa County Organizing Project	Phoenix	AZ	(602)268-6099		T	R		
Toxic Waste Investigative Group	Phoenix	AZ	(602)272-6997		T			
Environmental Congress of Arkansas	Benton	AR	(501)794-0102		T	R		
Environmental Congress of Arkansas	Eureka Springs	AR	(501)253-8440		T	R		
Abalone Alliance Clearinghouse	San Francisco	CA	(415)861-0592		T	R		
CCHW/West	Riverside	CA	(714)681-9913		T		S	
California Clean Growers	Kingsburg	CA	(209)896-6107			R		PE
California Institute for Rural Studies	Davis	CA	(916)756-6555			R		PE
California PIRG (CalPIRG)	Los Angeles	CA	(213)278-9244	M	T	R	S	
California Rural Legal Assistance Foundation	San Francisco	CA	(415)863-3520			R	S	PE
Campaign California	San Jose	CA	(408)286-6113		T	R	S	
Center for Labor Research and Education, Univ. of CA	Los Angeles	CA	(213)825-3537		T			WK
Citizens for a Better Environment	San Francisco	CA	(415)243-8373		T	R		
Clean Water Action	San Francisco	CA	(415)362-3040			R		WQ
Consumer Pesticide Project	San Francisco	CA	(415)826-6314			R		PE
Ecology Center of Southern Califonia	Los Angeles	CA	(213)559-9160		T	R		
Environmental Health Coalition	San Diego	CA	(619)235-0281		T			
Greenpeace Pacific Southwest	San Francisco	CA	(415)474-6767		T	R		
Labor Occupational Health Progam, Univ. of CA	Berkeley	CA	(415)642-5507		T			WK
Labor-Community Strategy Center	Van Nuys	CA	(818)781-9922	M	T	R	S	WK
Los Angeles COSH (LACOSH)	Los Angeles	CA	(213)749-6161		T			WK
National Toxics Campaign, California	Richmond	CA	(415)232-3427		T			
National Toxics Campaign, West Coast	Sacramento	CA	(916)446-3350		T			
Pesticide Action Network	San Francisco	CA	(415)771-2763			R		PE
Sacramento COSH (SACOSH)	Sacramento	CA	(916)444-8134		T			WK
San Diego Citizen Action	San Diego	CA	(619)583-4183	M	T	R	S	
San Francisco Bay Area COSH (BACOSH)	Berkeley	CA	(415)642-5507		T			WK
Santa Clara COSH (SCCOSH)	San Jose	CA	(408)998-4050		T			WK
Silicon Valley Toxics Coalition	San Jose	CA	(408)287-6707		T			
Tools for Change	San Francisco	CA	(415)861-6838				S	
Toxics Coordinating Project	San Francisco	CA	(415)781-2745		T			
West County Toxics Coalition	Richmond	CA	(415)237-4996		T			
Clean Water Action	Denver	CO	(303)839-9866			R		WQ
Colorado Citizen Action	Denver	CO	(303)421-0960	M	T	R	S	
Colorado PIRG (CoPIRG)	Denver	CO	(303)355-1861	M	T	R	S	
National Toxics Campaign, Western Office	Denver	CO	(303)333-9714		T			
Citizen Action Group for Environmental Protection	East Haven	CT	(203)469-2302	M	T	R		
Connecticut Fund for the Environment	New Haven	CT	(203)787-0646		T	R		
Connecticut COSH (ConnectiCOSH)	Hartford	CT	(203)549-1877		T			WK
Connecticut Citizen Action Group	Hartford	CT	(203)523-9232	M	T	R	S	
Connecticut PIRG (ConnPIRG)	Storrs	CT	(203)486-5002	M	T	R	S	
Labor Education Center, Univ. of CT	Storrs	CT	(203)486-3417		T			WK
People Against Pollution	Bristol	CT	(203)582-6544		T	R		
Alice Hamilton Occupational Health Center	Washington	DC	(202)543-0005		T			WK
Greenpeace Northeast	Washington	DC	(202)462-1177		T	R		
National Toxics Campaign, Washington D.C.	Washington	DC	(202)291-0863		T			
CCHW/South	Crestview	FL	(904)892-2831		T		S	
Concerned Citizens of North Florida	Micanopy	FL	(904)466-4215		T	R		
Conchshell Alliance	Miami	FL	(305)253-2635		T	R		
Farmworker Association of Central Florida	Apopka	FL	(305)886-5151			R	S	PE
Florida Consumer Federation	West Palm Beach	FL	(407)832-6077		T	R	S	
Florida Defenders of the Environment	Gainesville	FL	(904)372-6965		T	R		
Florida PIRG (FPIRG)	Tallahassee	FL	(904)224-5304	M	T	R	S	
Greenpeace Southeast	Jacksonville	FL	(904)241-4310		T	R		
Legal Environmental Assistance Foundation (LEAF)	Tallahassee	FL	(904)681-2591				S	

ORGANIZATION	CITY	ST	PHONE NUMBER			ISSUES		
Citizens for Safe Progress	Fortson	GA	(404)568-0299		T	R		
ECO Project	Atlanta	GA	(404)577-5071		T	R		
Georgia Citizen Action	Atlanta	GA	(404)240-0376	M	T	R	S	
Georgia Environmental Project	Atlanta	GA	(404)479-1708		T	R		
Toxic Communications & Assistance Project (T-CAP)	Albany	GA	(912)430-4811		T		S	
Center for Labor Education & Research, Univ. of HI	Honolulu	HI	(808)948-7145		T			WK
World Council of Indigenous People	Honolulu	HI	(808)531-1182				S	
Idaho Citizens Network	Boise	ID	(208)385-9146		T	R	S	
Idaho Conservation League	Boise	ID	(208)345-6933		T	R		
Palouse-Clearwater Environmental Institute	Moscow	ID	(208)882-1444		T	R		
Snake River Alliance	Boise	D	(208)344-9161		T	R		
Chicago COSH (CACOSH)	Chicago	IL	(312)666-1611		T			WK
Chicago Labor Education Program	Chicago	IL	(312)996-2623		T			WK
Citizen Action	Chicago	IL	(312)645-6013	M	T	R	S	
Greenpeace Great Lakes	Chicago	IL	(312)666-3305		T	R		
Illinois Environmental Council	Springfield	IL	(217)544-5954		T	R		
Illinois PIRG	Chicago	IL	(312)498-9828	M	T	R	S	
Illinois Public Action	Chicago	Il`	(312)431-1600		T	R	S	
Illinois Public Action Council	Chicago	IL	(312)427-6262		T	R	S	
Institute of Labor & Industrial Relations, Univ. of IL	Champaign	IL	(217)333-0980		T			WK
Midwest Academy	Chicago	IL	(312)645-6010				S	
Citizens Action Coalition	Indianapolis	IN	(317)921-1120	M	T	R	S	
Division of Labor Studies, Indiana Univ.	Bloomington	IN	(812)337-9082		T			WK
Indiana Citizen Action Coalition	Indianapolis	IN	(317)921-1120	M	T	R		
Indiana PIRG (INPIRG)	Bloomington	IN	(812)335-7575	M	T	R	S	
Mothers Against Toxic Hazards	Terre Haute	IN	(812)299-2672		T	R		
People Against Hazardous Landfill Sites	Wheeler	IN	219)465-7466		T			HW
Clean Water Action	Cedar Rapids	IA	(319)365-4700			R		WQ
Iowa Citizen Action Network	Iowa City	IA	(319)354-8116	M	T	R	S	
Iowa Citizens Action Network	Des Moines	IA	(515)244-9311		T	R		
Iowa PIRG	Ames	IA	(515)294-8094	M	T	R	S	
Soil & Water Conservation Society	Ankeny	IA	(515)289-2331			R		WQ
Kansas Save the Earth Campaign	Rose Hill	KS	(316)776-0921		T	R		
Center for Labor Education & Research, Univ. of KY	Lexington	KY	(606)258-4811		T			WK
Coalition for Health Concern	Benton	KY	(502)527-1217		T	R		
Kentuckians for the Commonwealth	Murry	KY	(502)585-3279		T	R		
Kentucky Citizen Action	Louisville	KY	(502)589-6691	M	T	R	S	
Kentucky Resources Council	Frankfort	KY	(502)875-2428		T	R		
Ecology Center of Louisiana	New Orleans	LA	(504)891-2447		T	R		
Gulf Coast Tenants Leadership Development Project	New Orleans	LA	(504)949-4919		T	R	S	
Louisiana Citizen Action	Baton Rouge	LA	(504)925-1331	M	T	R	S	
Louisiana Consumers League	Baton Rouge	LA	(504)344-7416		T		S	
Louisiana Environment Action Network	Baton Rouge	LA	(504)928-1315		T	R		
South Louisiana Against Pollution (SLAP)	Morgan City	LA	(504)385-2547		T	R		
Southern Environmental Network	New Orleans	LA	(504)861-1421		T	R		
Southern Environmental Network	Plaquemine	LA	(504)687-6270		T	R		
Bureau of Labor Education, Univ. of ME	Orono	ME	(207)581-7032		T			WK
Maine Labor Group on Health	Augusta	ME	(207)622-7823		T			WK
Maine PIRG	Portland	ME	(207)780-4044	M	T	R	S	
Maine Peoples Alliance	Portland	ME	(207)761-4400		T	R	S	
National Toxics Campaign, Northeast Office	Poland Spring	ME	(207)926-3424		T			
Natural Resources Council of Maine	Augusta	ME	(204)622-3101		T	R		
AFL-CIO Labor Studies Center, Antioch	Silver Spring	MD	(301)431-6400		T			WK
Alliance for the Chesapeake Bay	Baltimore	MD	(301)377-6270		T	R		
Baltimore Environmental Center	Baltimore	MD	(301)366-2070		T	R		
Chesapeake Bay Foundation	Annapolis	MD	(301)268-8816		T	R		
Institute for Alternative Agriculture	Greenbelt	MD	(301)441-8777			R		PE
Maryland Citizen Action Coalition	Baltimore	MD	(301)235-5588	M	T	R	S	
Maryland Citizens Action	Baltimore	MD	(301)235-5588		T	R	S	
Maryland PIRG (MaryPIRG)	College Park	MD	(301)454-5601	M	T	R	S	
Save the Bay	Annapolis	MD	(301)269-0481		T	R		WQ
Center for Environmental Management, Tufts Univ.	Medford	MA	(617)381-3486		T	R		
Clamshell Alliance	Winchester	MA	(617)729-6420		T			
Clean Water Action	Boston	MA	(617)423-4661			R		WQ
Clean Water Action	Northampton	MA	(413)584-9830			R		WQ

ORGANIZATION	CITY	ST	PHONE NUMBER				ISSUES	
Community Environmental Health Technical Resource Ctr	Boston	MA	(617)482-9485	M	T	R		
Conservation Law Foundation of New England, Inc.	Boston	MA	(617)742-2540			R		
Coolidge Center for Environmental Leadership	Cambridge	MA	(617)864-5085				S	
Department of Urban & Environmental Policy, Tufts Univ.	Medford	MA	(617)381-3451		T	R		
Greenpeace New England	Cambridge	MA	(617)576-1650		T	R		
Massachusetts Audubon Society	Lincoln	MA	(617)259-9500		T	R		
Massachusetts COSH (MassCOSH)	Boston	MA	(617)247-3456		T			WK
Massachusetts Citizen Action	Cambridge	MA	(617)864-2277	M	T	R	S	
Massachusetts Fair Share	Boston	MA	(617)482-7186		T	R		
Massachusetts PIRG (MassPIRG)	Boston	MA	(617)292-4800	M	T	R	S	
Western MassCOSH	Springfield	MA	(413)247-9413		T			WK
Augusta Environmental Strategy Committee	Milan	MI	(313)461-9132		T	R		
Citizens for Alternatives to Chemical Contamination	Lake	MI	(517)544-3318		T	R		
Evergreen Alliance	Detroit	MI	(313)832-1738		T	R		
Institute of Labor & Industrial Relations, Univ. of MI	Ann Arbor	MI	(313)763-1187		T			WK
Labor Program Service, MI State Univ.	East Lansing	MI	(517)355-5070		T			WK
Michigan Citizens Lobby	Lansing	MI	(517)372-7111		T	R	S	
Michigan Ecology Center (MEC)	Ann Arbor	MI	(313)662-3744		T	R		
Michigan Environmental Council	Lansing	MI	(517)487-9539		T	R		
Michigan United Conservation Clubs (MUCC)	Lansing	MI	(517)371-1041		T	R		
PIRG in Michigan (PIRGIM)	Ann Arbor	MI	(313)662-6597	M	T	R	S	
South East Michigan COSH (SEMCOSH)	Detroit	MI	(313)961-3345		T			WK
UAW Toxic Waste Squad	Ypsilanti	MI	(313)482-8320		T			WK
Citizens for a Better Environment	Minneapolis	MN	(612)824-8637		T	R		
Clean Water Action	Rochester	MN	(507)281-1390		T	R		WQ
Clean Water Action	Duluth	MN	(218)628-1191		T	R		WQ
Clean Water Action Project	Minneapolis	MN	(612)623-3666		T	R		WQ
Freshwater Foundation	Navarre	MN	(612)471-8407			R		WQ
Labor Education Service, IRC, Univ. of MN	Minneapolis	MN	(612)373-3662		T			WK
Minnesota COACT	Minneapolis	MN	(612)379-7811		T	R	S	
Minnesota PIRG (MPIRG)	Minneapolis	MN	(612)627-4035	M	T	R	S	
Wright County People for a Clean Environment	Buffalo	MN	(612)963-3781		T	R		
Mississippi Environmental Management Organization	Jackson	MS	(601)366-1205		T	R		
Coalition for the Environment	St. Louis	MO	(314)727-0600		T	R		
Crawdad Alliance	St. Louis	MO	(314)644-3014		T	R		
Missouri Against Hazardous Waste	Wright City	MO	(314)745-3980		T	R		
Missouri Citizen Action	Kansas City	MO	(816)531-2443	M	T	R	S	
Missouri PIRG (MoPIRG)	St. Louis	MO	(314)534-7474	M	T	R	S	
Environmental Information Center	Helena	MT	(406)443-2520		T	R		
Montana PIRG (MontPIRG)	Missoula	MT	(406)721-6040	M	T	R	S	
Center for Rural Affairs	Walthill	NE	(402)846-5428		T	R		
Nebraska Citizen Action	Lincoln	NE	(402)477-8658	M	T	R	S	
Citizen Alert	Reno	NV	(702)827-4200		T	R		
Clamshll Alliance	Concord	NH	(603)224-4163		T			
Grassroots Network Press	Hillsboro	NH	(603)464-3225		T	R	S	
National Toxics Campaign, New Hampshire	Salem	NH	(603)894-6447		T			
New Hampshire Citizen Action	Concord	NH	(603)225-2097	M	T	R	S	
New Hampshire Toxic Hazards Campaign	Newton Junction	NH	(603)382-6963		T	R		
Association of New Jersey Environmental Commissions	Mendham	NJ	(201)539-7547		T	R		
Environmental Response Network	Ocean View	NJ	(609)398-4030		T	R		
Labor Education Center, Rutgers Univ.	New Brunswick	NJ	(908)932-9502		T			WK
New Jersey Citizen Action	Hackensack	NJ	(201)488-2804	M	T	R	S	
New Jersey Environmental Federation	New Brunswick	NJ	(908)846-4224		T	R		WQ
New Jersey Environmental Federation	Trenton	NJ	(609)396-4871		T	R		WQ
New Jersey Environmental Federation	Montclair	NJ	(201)783-5112		T	R		WQ
New Jersey Environmental Federation	Belmar	NJ	(908)280-8988		T	R		WQ
New Jersey Grassroots Environmental Organization	Newark	NJ	(201)429-8965		T	R		
New Jersey PIRG (NJPIRG)	New Brunswick	NJ	(908)247-4606	M	T	R	S	
State Coalition against Incineration	Maplewood	NJ	(201)762-4912		T	R		
New Mexico PIRG (NMPIRG)	Albuquerque	NM	(505)277-2757	M	T	R	S	
South West Organizing Project (SWOP)	Albuquerque	NM	(505)247-8832		T	R	S	
Southwest Research & Information Center	Albuquerque	NM	(505)262-1862		T	R	S	
Alleghany COSH (ALCOSH)	Jamestown	NY	(716)488-0720		T			WK
Atlantic States Legal Founadation, Inc.	Syracuse	NY	(315)475-1170		T	R		WQ
Buffalo Greens	Buffalo	NY	(716)837-6104		T	R		

ORGANIZATION	CITY	ST	PHONE NUMBER					ISSUES
Citizen Action of New York	Albany	NY	(518)465-4600	M	T	R	S	
Community Environmental Health Center, Hunter College	New York	NY	(212)481-4355		T	R		
Eastern New York COSH (ENYCOSH)	Schenectady	NY	(518)393-1386		T			WK
Ecumenical Task Force	Niagara Falls	NY	(716)884-4800		T	R		
New York COSH (CNYCOSH)	Syracuse	NY	(315)471-6187		T			WK
New York COSH (NYCOSH)	New York	NY	(212)627-3900		T			WK
New York Environmental Institute	Albany	NY	(518)462-5527		T	R		
New York PIRG (NYPIRG)	New York	NY	(212)349-6460	M	T	R	S	
New York PIRG (NYPIRG)	Albany	NY	(518)436-0876	M	T	R	S	
New York PIRG (NYPIRG)	Syracuse	NY	(315)476-8381	M	T	R	S	
Rochester COSH (ROCOSH)	Rochester	NY	(716)458-8553		T			WK
School of Industrial & Labor Relations, CUNY	New York	NY	(212)697-2247		T			WK
School of Industrial & Labor Relations, Cornell Univ.	Ithaca	NY	(607)256-3281		T			WK
School of Industrial & Labor Relations, SUNY	Buffalo	NY	(716)842-4270		T			WK
Shad Alliance	New York	NY	(212)249-6689		T	R		
Shad Alliance	Brooklyn	NY	(718)857-1330		T	R		
West Harlem Environmental Action	New York	NY	(212)234-5096		T	R		
Western New York COSH (WNYCOSH)	Buffalo	NY	(716)897-2110		T			WK
Center for Community Action	Lumberton	NC	(919)739-7851		T	R	S	
Clean Water Fund	Raleigh	NC	(704)251-0518		T	R		
Conservation Council of North Carolina	Chapel Hill	NC	(919)851-5870		T	R		
Granville Residents Opposing Waste	Oxford	NC	(919)690-4769		T	R		
Institute for Environmental Studies, UNC	Chapel Hill	NC	(919)966-1171		T	R		
Institute for Southern Studies	Durham	NC	(919)688-8167		T	R	S	
National Toxics Campaign, North Carolina	Raleigh	NC	(919)828-5539		T			
North Carolina COSH (NCOSH)	Durham	NC	(919)286-9249		T			WK
North Carolina Fair Share	Raleigh	NC	(919)832-7130		T	R		
Clean Water Action	Fargo	ND	(701)235-5431			R		WQ
Dakota Resource Council	Dickinson	ND	(701)227-1851		T	R		
Access to Justice	Columbus	OH	(614)464-2964		T	R	S	
CCHW/Midwest	Spencerville	OH	(419)647-6824		T		S	
FLOC	Toledo	OH	(419)243-3456			R	S	PE
Labor Education & Research Center, OH State Univ.	Columbus	OH	(614)422-8157		T			WK
Ohio Citizen Action	Cleveland	OH	(216)861-5200	M	T	R	S	
Ohio Citizens Action	Columbus	OH	(614)224-4111		T	R		
Ohio Environmental Council	Columbus	OH	(614)224-2900		T			
Ohio PIRG (OPIRG)	Columbus	OH	(614)299-7474	M	T	R	S	
Ohio Public Interest Campaign (OPIC)	Cleveland	OH	(216)861-5200		T	R	S	
Ohio Valley Environmental Coalition	Proctorville	OH	(614)886-5796		T	R		
Sunflower Alliance	Ashtabula	OH	(216)964-3536		T	R		
Sunflower Alliance	Jefferson	OH	(216)576-5515		T	R		
Workers Against Toxic Chemical Hazards (WATCH)	Girard	OH	(216)545-0234		T			WK
Environmental Action	Snow	OK	(405)298-2803		T	R		
National Toxics Campaign, Oklahoma	Oklahoma City	OK	(405)843-3249		T			
Native Americans for a Clean Environment (NACE)	Tahlequah	OK	(918)458-4322		T	R		
Ponca City Concerned Citizens	Ponca City	OK	(405)765-9891		T	R		HW
Environmental Education Association Of Oregon	Portland	OR	(800)322-3326		T	R		
Labor Education & Research Center, Univ. of OR	Eugene	OR	(503)686-5054		T			WK
Northwest Coalition for Alternatives to Pesticides	Eugene	OR	(503)344-5044			R		PE
Oregon Environmental Council	Portland	OR	(503)222-1963		T	R		
Oregon Fair Share	Porltland	OR	(503)239-7611		T	R	S	
Oregon PIRG (OSPIRG)	Portland	OR	(503)222-9641	M	T	R	S	
Pacific Northwest Labor College	Maryhurst	OR	(503)245-1315		T			WK
Toxic Victims Assoc.	Portland	OR	(503)283-2598		T			WK
CCHW/Appalachia	Wendel	PA	(412)864-0845		T		S	
Citizens for Environmental Rights	Philadelphia	PA	(215)241-7214		T	R	S	
Clean Air Council	Philadelphia	PA	(215)545-1832		T	R		AQ
Clean Water Action	Allentown	PA	(215)434-9223			R		WQ
Clean Water Action	Philadelphia	PA	(215)735-8409			R		WQ
Clean Water Action	Pittsburgh	PA	(412)765-3053			R		WQ
Delaware Valley Toxics Coalition	Philadelphia	PA	(215)627-5300		T	R		
Pennsylvania Citizen Action	Harrisburg	PA	(717)232-5053	M	T	R	S	
Pennsylvania Environmental Council	Philadelphia	PA	(215)563-0250		T	R		
Pennsylvania PIRG (Penn PIRG)	Philadelphia	PA	(215)574-0852	M	T	R	S	
Pennsylvania Public Interest Coalition	Philadelphia	PA	(215)568-8145		T	R	S	
Philadelphia Project OSH (PHILAPOSH)	Philadelphia	PA	(215)386-7000		T			WK

ORGANIZATION	CITY	ST	PHONE NUMBER	ISSUES			
Clean Water Action	Providence	RI	(401)331-6972		R		WQ
Clean Water Action	Newport	RI	(401)846-1673		R		WQ
Rhode Island COSH (RICOSH)	Providence	RI	(401)751-2015	T			WK
Citizens Asking for Safe Energy (CASE)	Sumter	SC	(803)494-9178	T	R		
Citizens Local Environmental Action Network (CLEAN)	Columbia	SC	(803)252-9837	T	R		
Energy Research Foundation	Columbia	SC	(803)256-7298	T	R		
Environmentalist Inc.	Columbia	SC	(803)782-3000	T	R		
Grass Roots Organizing Workshop	Columbia	SC	(803)254-4565	T	R	S	
Greenpeace	Columbia	SC	(803)252-1265	T	R		
South Dakota Resources Coalition	Garretson	SD	(605)594-3558	T	R		
Americans for a Clean Environment	Lenoir City	TN	(615)986-6899	T	R		
Commission on Religion in Appalachia (CORA)	Knoxville	TN	(615)584-6133			S	
Concerned Citizens of Tennessee	Dixon Springs	TN	(615)832-0392	T	R	S	
Service Training for Environmental Programs	Nashville	TN	(615)322-6278	T		S	
Southern Empowerment Project	Maryville	TN	(615)984-6500			S	
Tennessee COSH (TNCOSH)	Knoxville	TN	(615)525-3147	T			WK
Tennessee Citizen Action	Nashville	TN	(615)367-1094	M	T	R	S
Tennessee Environmental Council	Nashville	TN	(615)321-5075	T	R		
The Natural Rights Center	Summertown	TN	(615)964-2334	T	R	S	
CCHW/South Central	Grand Prairie	TX	(817)795-7552	T		S	
National Toxics Campaign, Texas	Houston	TX	(713)529-8038	T		S	
Texans United	Houston	TX	(713)529-0049	T	R		
Texas COSH (TexCOSH)	Beaumont	TX	(409)898-1427	T			WK
Texas Center for Policy Studies	Austin	TX	(512)474-0811	T	R	S	
Texas Citizen Action	Austin	TX	(512)478-7887	M	T	R	S
Downwinders Inc.	Salt Lake City	UT	(801)467-8215	T	R		
Salt Lake Citizens' Congress	Salt Lake City	UT	(801)364-7765	T	R		
Utah Environment Center	Salt Lake City	UT	(801)322-0220	T	R		
Environmental Opportunities	Stowe	VT	(802)253-9336		R		
Vermonters Organized for Clean-Up	Barre	VT	(802)476-7757	T	R		
CCHW/Appalachia	Christiansburg	VA	(703)789-4700	T		S	
Citizens for a Better America	Halifax	VA	(804)476-7757	T	R		
Clean Water Action	Norfolk	VA	(804)355-2891		R		WQ
Clean Water Action	Richmond	VA	(804)355-2891		R		WQ
College of Architecture & Urban Studies, VA Polytechnic Inst.	Blacksburg	VA	(703)231-6415		R		
Health & Environment Action League	Dungannon	VA	(703)467-2388	T	R		
Centro Campesino	Granger	WA	(509)854-2052		R	S	PE
Greenpeace Northwest	Seattle	WA	(206)632-4326	T	R		
Washington Environmental Council	Chimacum	WA	(206)732-4334	T	R		
Washington Fair Share	Seattle	WA	(206)329-9764	T	R	S	
Washington PIRG (Wash PIRG)	Seattle	WA	(206)322-9064	M	T	R	S
Washington Toxics Coalition	Seattle	WA	(206)632-1545	T	R		
West Virginia Citizen Action Group	Charleston	WV	(304)346-5891	M	T	R	S
West Virginia Environmental Council	Charleston	WV	(304)346-5891	T	R		
West Virginia PIRG	Morgantown	WV	(304)293-2108	M	T	R	S
Citizens for a Better Environment	Milwaukee	WI	(414)271-7280	T	R		
Citizens for a Better Environment	Green Bay	WI	(414)432-1909	T	R		
Citizens for a Better Environment	Madison	WI	(608)251-2804	T	R		
Extension School for Workers, Univ. of WI	Madison	WI	(608)262-2111	T			WK
Wisconsin Action	Madison	WI	(608)256-1250	T	R	S	
Wisconsin Action Coalition	Milwaukee	WI	414)272-2562	T	R		
Wisconsin Environmental Decade	Madison	WI	(608)251-7020	T	R		
Wyoming Pollution Posse	Evansville	WY	(307)266-1978	T	R		

PERIODICALS

	CITY	ST	PHONE NUMBER	ISSUES
The Amicus Journal	New York	NY	(212)727-2700	Quarterly
Audubon	New York	NY	(212)546-9100	Bimonthly
BioCycle	Emmaus	PA	(215)967-4135	Monthly
Buzzworm	Boulder	CO	(303)442-1969	Bimonthly
CBE Environmental Review	Milwaukee	WI	(414)271-7280	Quarterly
Citizen Action	Cleveland	OH	(216)861-5200	Quarterly
Community Plume	Washington	DC	(202)544-2600	Quarterly
Cycle (formerly Waste Paper)	New York	NY	(212)677-1601	Quarterly
The Delicate Balance	Voorhees	NJ	(609)429-5358	Quarterly
E: The Environmental Magazine	Norwalk	CT	(203)854-5559	Bimonthly
Earth First!	Tucson	AZ	(602)622-1371	8/year
Earth Island Journal	San Francisco	CA	(415)788-3666	Quarterly
EcoSource	Guelph	ON	(519)763-8888	Bimonthly
Environment	Washington	DC	(202)362-6445	Monthly
Environment Watch (BNA)	Washington	DC	(202)452-4200	Weekly
Environmental Action	Washington	DC	(202)745-4875	Bimonthly
Environmental Forum	Washington	DC	(202)328-5150	Monthly
Everyone's Backyard	Arlington	VA	(703)276-7070	Bimonthly
Friends of the Earth	Washington	DC	(202)544-2600	Bimonthly
Garbage	Brooklyn	NY	(718)788-1700	Bimonthly
Global Pesticide Campaigner	San Francisco	CA	(415)541-9140	Quarterly
Green Consumer Letter	Washington	DC	800-955-GREEN	Monthly
Greenpeace	Washington	DC	(202)462-1177	Bimonthly
Harrowsmith	Charlotte	VT	(802)425-3961	Bimonthly
High Country News	Paonia	CO	(303)527-4898	Biweekly
In These Times	Mt. Morris	IL	(800)435-0715	Weekly
Issues in Science & Technology	Washington	DC	(202)334-3318	Quarterly
Journal of Pesticide Reform	Eugene	OR	(503)344-5044	Quarterly
Mother Earth News	New York	NY	(212)242-2460	Bimonthly
Multinational Monitor	Washington	DC	(202)387-8034	Monthly
National Environment Enforcement Journal	Washington	DC	(202)628-0435	Monthly
Nutrition Action Health Letter	Washington	DC	(202)332-9110	Monthly
The People's Doctor Newsletter	Evanston	IL	(708)328-1550	Monthly
Pesticides & You	Washington	DC	(202)543-5450	Bimonthly
Public Citizen	Washington	DC	(202)293-9142	Bimonthly
Public Citizen Health Letter	Washington	DC	(202)293-9142	Monthly
Race, Poverty & the Environment	San Francisco	CA	(415)649-7877	Quarterly
RACHEL's Hazardous Waste News	Washington	DC	(202)328-1119	Weekly
Recycling Times	Washington	DC	(202)861-0708	Biweekly
Rocky Mountain Institute Newsletter	Snowmass	CO	(303)927-3128	Quarterly
Sierra	San Francisco	CA	(415)776-2211	Bimonthly
Silicon Valley Toxic News	San Jose	CA	(408)287-6707	Quarterly
Technology Review	Boston	MA	(617)253-8250	8/year
Toxic Times	Boston	MA	(617)232-0327	Quarterly
Toxics Watchdog	San Francisco	CA	(415)781-2745	Monthly
UNEP North America News	New York	NY	(212)963-8093	Bimonthly
Upstate Environment	Rochester	NY	(716)546-3796	Bimonthly
Waste Age	Washington	DC	(202)659-4613	Monthly
Waste Not	Canton	NY	(315)379-9200	Weekly
Wastelines	Albany	NY	(518)457-2344	Quarterly
Workbook	Albuquerque	NM	(505)262-1862	Quarterly
Working Notes on Community Right-To-Know	Washington	DC	(202)546-9707	Monthly
Workplace Safety & Health	Chicago	IL	(312)939-0690	Monthly
World Rainforest Report	San Francisco	CA	(415)398-4404	Quarterly
WorldWatch	Washington	DC	(202)452-1999	Bimonthly

NOTES

CHAPTER 1: OVERVIEW

1 U.S. Congress, Senate Committee on Environment and Public Works (1985), *The Ability to Respond to Toxic Chemical Emergencies,* 99th Cong., 1st Sess., 99–12, pp. 18–21.

CHAPTER 2: AN ATLAS FOR ACTION

1 John Snow, "On the mode of communication of cholera, 2nd edition 1854," in *Snow on Cholera* (New York, NY: The Commonwealth Fund, 1936) reprinted in E. Gurney Clark, Anna Gelman, and Milton Terris, "Epidemiology exercise: Snow on cholera" (New York, NY: New York Medical College, 1967), pp. 9–11.

2 See Abraham M. Lilienfeld and David E. Lilienfeld, *Foundations of Epidemiology,* 2nd Edition (New York, NY: Oxford University Press, 1980), pp. 36–37.

3 World Commission on Environment and Development, *Our Common Future* (New York, NY: Oxford University Press, 1987).

4 Mostafa K. Tolba, "1982 Annual Report of the Executive Director" (New York, NY: United Nations Environment Program, 1982).

5 World Health Organization, *Sixth Report on the World Health Situation* (Geneva: WHO, 1980).

6 These ecological interactions have been called a web of causation by B. MacMahon and T. F. Pugh, *Epidemiologic Principles and Methods* (Boston, MA: Little, Brown & Co., 1970).

7 Donald W. Large and Preston Michie, "Proving that the strength of the British Navy depends on the number of old maids in England: a comparison of scientific proof with legal proof," *Environmental Law,* vol. 11, no. 557, 1980–81, p. 555.

8 Cited in Lilienfeld and Lilienfeld, op. cit., p. 84.

9 Some county data have been assembled by nongovernmental sources, for example, Dr. Bernard Cohen, formerly at the University of Pittsburgh and now with The Radon Project, has measured average county and ZIP code radon levels. See Bernard L. Cohen, *Radon: A Homeowner's Guide to Detection and Control* (New York, NY: Avon Books, 1989). See also U.S. Environmental Protection Agency, *Unfinished Business: A Comparative Assessment of Environmental Problems, Overview Report* (Washington, DC: EPA, February 1987).

10 See U.S. Department of Health and Human Services, *The Health Consequences of Smoking: Cancer—A Report of the Surgeon General* (Washington, DC: U.S. Government Printing Office, 1982), and U.S. Department of Health and Human Services, *The Health Consequences of Smoking: Cardiovascular Disease—A Report of the Surgeon General* (Washington, DC: U.S. Government Printing Office, 1984).

11 U.S. Department of Health and Human Services, "Smoking-attributable mortality and years of potential life lost—United States, 1984," *Morbidity and Mortality Weekly Report,* vol. 36, no. 42, 1987.

12 See U.S. Department of Health and Human Services, *Reducing the Health Consequences of Smoking: 25 Years of Progress—A Report of the Surgeon General* (Washington, DC: U.S. Government Printing Office, 1989), pp. 282–83.

13 The state with the highest percentage of male smokers is Alaska, followed by North Carolina, Mississippi, and West Virginia. The state with the highest percentage of female smokers is Nevada, followed by Michigan, Kentucky, and Rhode Island. See ibid., and U.S. Department of Health and Human Services, *Health United States, 1988* (Washington, DC: U.S. Government Printing Office, 1989) pp. 8–9.

14 Richard Doll and Richard Peto, *The Causes of Cancer: Quantitative Estimates of Avoidable Risks of Cancer in the United States Today* (New York, NY: Oxford University Press, 1981), p.1244, Table 19.

15, See Judith M. Aronchick, "Lung cancer: epidemiology and risk factors," *Seminars in Roentgenology,* vol. 25, no. 1., 1990, pp. 5–11, and Irving J. Selikoff, Edward C. Hammond, and J. Churg, "Asbestos exposure, smoking and neoplasia," *Journal of the American Medical Association,* vol. 204, 1968, pp. 106–12.

16 Doll and Peto, op. cit., p. 1256, Table 20.

17 See Samuel S. Epstein, "Losing the war against cancer: who's to blame and what to do about it," *International Journal of Health Services,* vol. 20, no. 1, 1990, pp. 53–71.

18 Thomas J. Mason, F. W. McKay, Robert Hoover, William J. Blot, and Joseph F. Fraumeni, Jr., *Atlas of Cancer Mortality for U.S. Counties: 1950–69* (Washington, DC: U.S. Government Printing Office, 1975).

19 William J. Blot and Joseph F. Fraumeni, Jr., "Geographic patterns of lung cancer: Industrial correlations," *American Journal of Epidemiology,* vol. 103, 1976, pp. 539–50.

20 William J. Blot, Joseph M. Harrington, A. Toledo, Robert Hoover, C. W. Heath, and Joseph F. Fraumeni, Jr., "Lung cancer after employment in shipyards during World War II," *New England Journal of Medicine,* vol. 299, 1978, pp. 620–24.

21 Robert Hoover and Joseph F. Fraumeni, Jr., "Cancer mortality in U.S. counties with chemical industries," *Environmental Research,* vol. 9, 1975, pp. 196–207 and William J. Blot and Joseph F. Fraumeni, Jr., "Arsenical air pollution and lung cancer," *Lancet,* July 26, 1975, pp. 142–45.

22 Thomas J. Mason, F. W. McKay, Robert Hoover, William J. Blot, and Joseph F. Fraumeni, Jr., *Atlas of Cancer Mortality Among U.S. Nonwhites: 1950–69* (Washington, DC: U.S. Government Printing Office, 1976); Thomas J. Mason,

Joseph F. Fraumeni, Jr., Robert Hoover, William J. Blot, *An Atlas of Mortality from Selected Diseases* (Washington, DC: U.S. Government Printing Office, 1981); and Linda J. Pickle, Thomas J. Mason, N. Howard, Robert Hoover, and Joseph F. Fraumeni, Jr., *Atlas of U.S. Cancer Mortality Among Whites: 1950–1980* (Washington, DC: U.S. Government Printing Office, 1987).

23 Wilson B. Riggan et al., *U.S. Cancer Mortality Rates and Trends 1950–1979,* vol. IV (Washington, DC: U.S. Environmental Protection Agency, 1987), and Jack Griffith, Robert C. Duncan, Wilson B. Riggan, and Alvin C. Pellom, "Cancer mortality in U.S. counties with hazardous waste sites and ground water pollution," *Archives of Enivronmental Health,* vol. 44, no. 2, 1989, pp. 69–74.

24 Lois Gibbs, who alerted the nation to the toxic wastes at Love Canal and now heads the Citizens Clearinghouse for Hazardous Waste, warns local residents against conducting their own health surveys in expectation of such results. If you do decide to conduct such a survey, a good reference book to start with is: Marvin S. Legator, Barbara L. Harper, and Michael J. Scott, eds., *The Health Detective's Handbook: A Guide to the Investigation of Environmental Hazards by Nonprofessionals* (Baltimore, MD: Johns Hopkins University Press, 1985).

25 For more on this, see Public Data Access, Inc., *Mortality and Toxics Along the Mississippi River* (Washington, DC: Greenpeace USA, 1988).

26 Telephone interview with Hobson Woodward, *The Inquirer and Mirror,* March 13, 1991.

27 Note that while diseases differ in their lethality and in the efficacy of existing treatments, this has no bearing on a map of the geographic variation from a single disease.

28 See Jay M. Gould and Nancy McFadden, "Toxic waste in Chesapeake Bay: bad for people as well as fish," *Council on Economic Priorities Newsletter,* November 1985, for evidence of the correlation of mortality with hospital beds.

29 National morbidity maps are infeasible at present anyway, because there is no national database of county morbidity (though some states do maintain cancer registries).

30 Last, op cit., pp. 112–13.

31 See J.C. Bailar, III, and E. M. Smith, "Progress against cancer?" *New England Journal of Medicine,* vol. 314, 1986, pp. 1226–32.

32 See Office of Technology Assessment, *Assessment of Technologies for Determining Cancer Risks from the Environment* (Springfield, VA: National Technical Information Service, 1981); David S. Schottenfeld and Joseph F. Fraumeni, Jr., *Cancer Epidemiology and Prevention* (Philadelphia, PA: Saunders, 1982); and U.S. Department of Health and Human Services, *Disease Prevention/ Health Promotion: The Facts* (Palo Alto, CA: Bull Publishing Co., 1988).

33 John J. Cohrssen and Vincent T. Covello, *Risk Analysis: A Guide to Principles and Methods for Analyzing Health and Environmental Risks* (Washington, DC: Council on Environmental Quality, 1989), p. 45.

34 See Samuel S. Epstein, *The Politics of Cancer* (New York, NY: Anchor Press, 1979).

35 National Research Council, *Toxicity Testing: Strategies to Determine Needs and Priorities* (Washington, DC: National Academy Press, 1984).

36 Bruce N. Ames, Renae Magaw, and Lois Swirsky Gold, "Ranking possible carcinogenic hazards," *Science,* vol. 236, 1987, pp. 271–80. For a rebuttal of these views see Samuel S. Epstein and Joel B. Swartz, "Carcinogenic risk estimation," *Science,* vol. 240, 1988, pp. 1043–45.

37 Doll and Peto, op. cit.

38 See Gina Kolata, "Scientists question methods used in animal cancer tests," *The New York Times,* August 31, 1990, p. 1; Bruce N. Ames and Lois Swirsky Gold, "Too many rodent carcinogens: mitogenesis increases mutagenesis," *Science,* vol. 249, 1990, pp. 970–71; and Samuel M. Cohen and Leon B. Ellwein, "Cell proliferation in carcinogenesis," *Science,* vol. 249, 1990, pp. 1007–11.

39 Because the intent is to indicate where potential hazards are most severe and not to link specific exposures to individual cases of disease, the precise date of a given measure is relatively insignificant. In many cases, for example, the mortality data reflect a period prior to the measure of the toxic release. Maps of changes in the measures of industrial and other toxins indicate that in most cases, places that rank among the highest percentiles for potential hazards have done so a number of decades. In most cases the same can be said for mortality.

40 Centers for Disease Control, "Increase in national hospital discharge survey rates for septicemia," *Morbidity and Mortality Weekly Report,* vol. 39, no. 2, 1990, p. 31.

41 See National Center for Health Statistics, *Monthly Vital Statistics Report,* vol. 37, no. 13, 1989, p. 8.

42 Much of the evidence of the linkage between immune systems and cancer has come from transplant patients who as a group suffer from extremely high rates of cancer. See Elizabeth Rosenthal, "Transplant patients illuminate link between cancer and immunity," *The New York Times,* December 5, 1989.

43 In the late 1970s, Congress passed a spate of laws and amendments to control hazardous pollutants, including the 1976 Resource Conservation and Recovery Act (RCRA, which covers hazardous waste management), the Toxic Substances Control Act of 1976 (TSCA, which requires premarket testing of chemicals), the Clean Water Amendments of 1977 (CWA, which regulates priority pollutants), and others. The Superfund law for cleaning up toxic waste sites passed in 1980. Many of these laws' major provisions began to take effect in the early 1980s, just when the Reagan administration took office with its pledge to "get government off our backs." See Joan Claybrook and the Staff of Public Citizen, *Retreat from Safety: Reagan's Attack on America's Health* (New York, NY: Pantheon Books, 1984), and Norman J. Vig, "Presidential leadership: from the Reagan to Bush administration," in *Environmental Policy in the 1990s,* eds. Norman J. Vig and Michael E. Kraft (Washington, DC: Congressional Quarterly Press, 1990).

44 In constant 1982 dollars, the EPA'S fiscal year 1990 budget was $1.5 million and its fiscal 1975 budget was $1.4 million. Throughout the 1980s, Congress continued expanding the EPA's statutory requirements, passing a host of new laws: TSCA amendments of 1982, Hazardous and Solid Waste Amendments of 1984, Safe Drinking Water Act Amendments of 1986, Superfund Amendments and

Reauthorization Act of 1986 (SARA), CWA Amendments of 1987, and the Open Dumping Act of 1988, among others. See Michael E. Kraft and Norman J. Vig, "Environmental policy from the seventies to the nineties: continuity and change," in *Environmental Policy in the 1990s*, eds. Norman J. Vig and Michael E. Kraft (Washington, DC: Congressional Quarterly Press, 1990), p. 19. Other regulatory agencies fared even worse. See Leonard W. Weiss and Micael W. Klass, eds., *Regulatory Reform: What Actually Happened* (Boston, MA: Little, Brown & Company, 1986), pp. 3–6.

45 For a variety of perspectives on how government has fared in protecting the environment, see: Peter Borrelli, ed., *Crossroads: Environmental Priorities for the Future* (Washington, DC: Island Press, 1988); Barry Commoner, "A reporter at large: the environment," *The New Yorker*, June 15, 1987, pp. 46–70; The Conservation Foundation, *State of the Environment: A View Toward the Nineties* (Washington, DC: The Conservation Foundation, 1987); "EPA: the first twenty years," *EPA Journal*, vol. 16, no. 5, 1990; Peter Montague, ed., "Celebrating EPA's birthday," *RACHEL'S Hazardous Waste News*, nos. 209 and 210, 1990; and Paul R. Portney, ed., *Public Policies for Environmental Protection* (Washington, DC: Resources for the Future, 1990).

46 The Conservation Foundation, *State of the Environment: A View Toward the Nineties* (Washington, DC: The Conservation Foundation, 1987), p. 138.

47 TRI is a product of The Emergency Planning and Community Right-to-Know Act of 1986, which Congress passed as part of the amendments to Superfund (EPCRA is Title III of the Superfund Amendments and Reauthorization Act, Public Law 99–499). EPCRA has a number of other important provisions relating to public information about toxic hazards. EPCRA's four major provisions include: emergency planning (Sections 301–303), emergency release notification (Section 304), community right-to-know reporting requirements (Section 311–312), and toxic chemical release reporting-emissions inventory (Section 313). Under the law every governor establishes a state emergency response commission (SERC), which in turn designates local emergency planning committees (LEPCs). The LEPCs (of which there are about 4,500) develop emergency response plans for potential chemical accidents, using data from industry that had not been previously disclosed. Industrial facilities must submit Occupational Safety and Health Administration (OSHA) material safety data sheets (MSDSs) that describe the dangers of and emergency treatments for all hazardous chemicals used on-site, as well as a two-tiered inventory of all such chemicals, to appropriate SERCs, LEPCs, and fire departments. The SERCs and LEPCs must make all of this information available to the public on request. In addition, the U.S. Environmental Protection Agency (EPA) is required to maintain and provide public access to a computerized information system of toxic chemical releases. For an overall discussion of EPCRA, see Benjamin A. Goldman, "The environment and community right to know: information for participation," in *Computers for Social Change and Community Organizing*, John Downing et al., eds. (Binghamton, NY: The Haworth Press, 1991), and Susan G. Hadden, *A Citizen's Right to Know: Risk Communication and Public Policy* (Boulder, CO: Westview Press, 1989).

48 See Benjamin A. Goldman, "Community right to know: environmental information for citizen participation," *Environmental Impact Assessment Review,* 1991.

49 Philip Shabecoff, "Industry to give vast new data on toxic perils," *The New York Times,* February 14, 1988, p. 1.

50 To find out how to get on-line access, call the National Library of Medicine at (800) 638-8480. To find out about other ways to get TRI data, call the EPA's right-to-know hotline at (800) 535-0202, or call the nonprofit Working Group on Community Right to Know at (202) 546-9707. An especially good source for TRI data, including maps, is Citizens Fund, *Poisons in Our Neighborhoods: Toxic Pollution in the United States* (Washington, DC: Citizens Fund, 1990). Also see U.S. Environmental Protection Agency, *Toxics in the Community: National and Local Perspectives* (Washington, DC: Government Printing Office, 1990), and U.S. Environmental Protection Agency, *The Toxic Release Inventory: A National Perspective* (Washington, DC: U.S. Government Printing Office, 1989).

51 The Census Bureau's data files were the easiest to use, as one might suspect given the bureau's two centuries of experience in disseminating information. But we had problems even with their data: 6 million white people were missing in the file they sent us. (This discrepancy was reported in: Commission for Racial Justice, *Toxic Waste and Race in the United States: A National Report on the Racial and Socio-Economic Characteristics of Communities with Hazardous Waste Sites* [New York, NY: United Church of Christ, 1987], p. 64.) The mortality data were the most difficult to use, because of the tremendously complex computer processing techniques needed to derive meaningful measures (adjusting for age, statistical tests, and so forth). Moreover, the 13 million records in the massive 300-megabyte mortality file are randomly sorted, so even the simplest calculations require enormous computer resources.

52 See Roger I. Glass, "New prospects for epidemiologic investigations," *Science,* vol. 234, 1986, pp. 951–55.

53 Telephone interview with Deborah Ingram, National Center for Health Statistics, September 1990.

54 Jay M. Gould and the Council of Economic Priorities, *Quality of Life in American Neighborhoods: Levels of Affluence, Toxic Waste, and Cancer Mortality in Residential Zip Code Areas* (Boulder, CO: Westview Press, 1986).

55 See Jeremy Brecher and Tim Costello, *Building Bridges: The Emerging Grassroots Coalition of Labor and Community* (New York, NY: Monthly Review Press, 1990); Mary Douglas and Aaron Wildavsky, *Risk and Culture: An Essay on the Selection of Technical and Environmental Dangers* (Berkeley, CA: University of California Press, 1982); Ira Katznelson, *City Trenches: Urban Politics and the Patterning of Class in the United States* (Chicago, IL: University of Chicago Press, 1981); and Alan Wolfe, "Why is there no green party in the United States?" *World Policy Journal,* vol. 1, 1983, pp. 159–80.

56 Letter from Thomas Jefferson to Charles Jarvis, September 28, 1820.

57 Richard Kazis and Richard L. Grossman, *Fear at Work: Job Blackmail, Labor and the Environment* (New York, NY: The Pilgrim Press, 1982).

58 Gloria Tierney, "Toxic chemicals bond old foes [labor unions and environmentalists back right-to-know laws]," *Sierra,* vol. 71, no. 6, 1986, pp. 21–24.

59 David Tikulsker, Statement at From the Right to Know to the Power to Act Conference. North Brunswick, NJ, May 23, 1988.

60 Caron Chess, "Looking behind the factory gates," *Technology Review,* August/September 1986, pp. 43–53.

61 Caron Chess, *Winning the Right to Know: A Handbook for Toxics Activists* (Washington, DC: The Conference on Alternative State and Local Policies, 1984), p. 37.

62 *The Wall Street Journal,* April 7, 1981.

63 *The Philadelphia Inquirer,* cited in Chess, op. cit., 1984, pp. 37–38.

64 Tierney, op. cit.

65 Chess, op. cit., 1986, p. 44.

66 Charles E. Ellison, "What you don't know can hurt you: the politics of right-to-know in Cincinnati," *Social Policy,* vol. 14, no. 3, 1984, pp. 18–23.

67 Barry Meier, "Use of right to know rules is increasing public's scrutiny of chemical companies," *The Wall Street Journal,* May 23, 1985, p. 10.

68 See David Allen, "Preventing pollution" in *Fighting Toxics,* Gary Cohen and John O'Connor, eds. (Washington, DC: Island Press, 1990), and Barry Commoner, *Making Peace with the Planet* (New York, NY: Pantheon, 1990).

69 See Public Data Access, Inc., *The Phildelphia Toxics Story* (Boston, MA: National Toxics Campaign, 1987).

70 See Vincent T. Covello, Peter M. Sandman, and Paul Slovic, *Risk Communication, Risk Statistics, and Risk Comparisons: A Manual for Plant Managers* (Washington, DC: Chemical Manufacturers Association, 1988); J. Clarence Davies, Vincent T. Covello, and Frederick W. Allen, *Risk Communication* (Washington, DC: The Conservation Foundation, 1987); National Research Council, *Improving Risk Communication* (Washington, DC: National Academy Press, 1989); and Emilie Roth et al., "What do we know about making risk comparisons?" *Risk Analysis,* vol. 10, no. 3, 1990, pp. 375–87.

71 Steven Ebbin and Raphael Kasper, *Citizen Groups and the Nuclear Power Controversy* (Cambridge, MA: MIT Press, 1974). See also Sherry Arnstein, "A ladder of citizen participation," *Journal of American Institute of Planners,* vol. 35, July 1969, pp. 215–24; Jerome Price, *The Antinuclear Movement: Revised Edition* (Boston, MA: Twayne Publishers, 1990); and Walter A. Rosenbaum, "The politics of public participation in hazardous waste management," in James P. Lester and Ann O'M. Bowman, eds., *The Politics of Hazardous Waste Management* (Durham, NC: Duke University Press, 1983) pp. 176–95.

72 Jost Halfmann, "Risk avoidance and sovereignty: new social movements in the United States and West Germany," *Praxis International,* vol. 8, no. 1, 1988, pp. 14–25.

73 See Ken Geiser, "Toxic times and class politics," *Radical America,* vol. 17, No. 2–3, 1983, pp. 39–50; Peter Montague, "What we must do—a grass-root offensive against toxics in the 90s," *The Workbook,* vol. 14, no. 3, 1989, pp. 90–113; and Jim O'Brien, "Environmentalism as a mass movement: historical notes," *Radical America,* vol. 17, no. 2–3, 1983, pp. 7–27.

74 See Philip Shabecoff, "Environmental groups told they are racists in hiring," *The New York Times,* February 1, 1990, p. A20.

75 See Carla Atkinson, "A white, 'green' movement: where do minorities fit into the environmental picture?" *Public Citizen,* September/October, 1990, pp. 16–20; "Beyond white environmentalism: minorities and the environment," *Environmental Action,* January/February, 1990 pp. 19–30; "Is environmentalism white, middle class, and 40?" *EcoSource,* August 1990, pp. 51–52; Celene Krauss, "The elusive process of citizen activism," *Social Policy,* Fall 1983, pp. 50–55; Charles Lee, "The integrity of justice: evidence of environmental racism," *Sojourners,* February/March 1990, pp. 22–25; and Celeste Wesson, ed., " 'It does affect you': women at Love Canal and Three Mile Island," *Radical America,* vol. 17, no. 2–3, 1983, pp. 29–36.

76 Dick Russell, "The rise of the grass-roots toxics movement," *The Amicus Journal,* Winter 1990, pp. 18–21.

77 To find out about some important new computer bulletin boards on environmental issues, call: ECONET at (415) 923-0900, ENVIRONET at (415) 474-6767, RACHEL at (202) 328-1119, RTK-NET at (202) 234-8494, and TOXNET (where TRI is housed) at (800) 638-8480.

78 *Working Notes on Community Right-to-Know,* February 1990.

79 Jeffrey Tryens and Richard Schrader, *Making the Difference: Using the Right-to-Know in the Fight Against Toxics* (Washington, DC: The National Center for Policy Alternatives, 1990).

80 Russell, op. cit., p. 19; John Holusha, "McDonald's expected to drop plastic burger box," *The New York Times,* November 1, 1990, p. 1; and John Holusha, "Packaging and public image: McDonald's fills a big order," *The New York Times,* November 2, 1990, p. 1.

81 Poje and Horowitz, op. cit., p. 83.

82 Philip Shabecoff, "Du Pont to halt chemicals that peril ozone," *The New York Times,* March 25, 1988, p. 1.

83 Richard C. Paddock, "New bounty hunters will target polluters," *The Los Angeles Times,* February 14, 1988.

84 Paul Jacobs, "Anti-toxics conflict seen by supporters Proposition 65," *The Los Angeles Times,* October 15, 1986; Paul Jacobs, "Foes of toxics measure outspend backers 4 to 1 Proposition 65," *The Los Angeles Times,* October 8, 1986; Robert Lindsey, "Many states move to curb disposal of chemicals," *The New York Times,* December 21, 1986; and Dick Russell, "Product-warning law: Prop 65 goes to the market," *The Nation,* June 4, 1988, pp. 786–89.

85 Marc Osten of MASSPIRG, cited in Tryens and Schrader, op. cit., p. ii.

86 Christopher B. Daly, "New laws to reduce industrial poisons: Massachusetts, Oregon imposing stricter standards on use," *The Washington Post,* July 25, 1989.

87 From the Right to Know to the Power to Act Conference in North Brunswick, NJ, May 23, 1988, was organized by the Industrial Union Council of the AFL-CIO, the New Jersey Environmental Federation, and dozens of other union and environmental organizations. These efforts are unprecedented in this country, but not elsewhere. Work-site health and safety committees established under

Canadian provincial law, and especially in Quebec, were used as models for those proposed in the New Jersey law.

88 Scott Tobey, "Taking control: workers and communities demand the right to act," *Multinational Monitor,* June 1990, pp. 29–31.

89 See Goldman, 1990, op. cit.

90 See Meredeth Turshen, "The political ecology of disease," *Review of Radical Political Economics,* vol. 9, no. 1, 1977, pp. 45–60.

91 Edwin Chadwick, *Report on the Sanitary Condition of the Labouring Population of Great Britain, 1842,* edited by M. W. Flinn (Chicago, IL: Aldine Press, 1965).

92 Sidney and Beatrice Webb, *English Poor Law History: Part II, the Last Hundred Years,* Vol. 1 (London: Longmans, Green & Co., 1929), p. 32.

CHAPTER 3: MORTALITY

1 Mortality statistics are not published for social or economic groups in the United States. See Steve Wing, Michele Casper, Wayne Davis, Carl Hayes, Wilson Riggan, and H. A. Tyroler, "Trends in the geographic inequality of cardiovascular disease mortality in the United States, 1962–1982," *Social Science Medicine,* vol. 30, no. 3, 1990, pp. 261–66.

2 The fifteen-year period excludes 1972 because NCHS had incomplete data for that year.

3 These changes are current to 1987, the most recent year for which detailed national statistics were available at the time of this writing. See National Center for Health Statistics, *Vital Statistics of the United States, 1987, Vol. II, Mortality, Part A* (Washington, DC: Public Health Service, 1990).

4 David Schottenfeld, Ann Zauber, Jon Kerner, and M. Ellen Warshauer, "Recent trends in cancer survival," *Trans. Association of Life Insur. Medical Dir. Am.,* vol. 69, 1986, pp. 66–86.

5 The change is calculated from the average for the first five years of the time period, 1968–73, to the average for the last five years, 1979–83. The remaining figures refer to changes during these years.

6 Four mortality rates in Fig. 3-5 (young adult infectious diseases, infant diseases, birth defects, and child cancer) appear greater than other causes compared with Fig. 3-4, because the populations used in their denominators are limited by age.

7 See the methods appendix for details about how geographic inequality is measured.

8 See Wing et al., 1990, op. cit.

9 Michael R. Greenberg, *Urbanization and Cancer Mortality: The United States Experience, 1950–1975* (New York, NY: Oxford University Press, 1983).

10 See, for example, Herbert I. Sauer and Darrel W. Parke, "Counties with extreme death rates and associated factors," *American Journal of Epidemiology,* vol. 99, no. 4, 1974, pp. 258–64, and Herbert I. Sauer and H. Denny Donnell, Jr., "Age and geographic differences in death rates," *Journal of Gerontology,* vol. 25, no. 2, 1970, pp. 83–86.

11 See Dick Russell, "You are my river: the small-town fight to save the Great Mississippi," *Greenpeace,* September/October 1988, pp. 12–18.

12 Pat Costner and Joe Thornton, *We All Live Downstream: The Mississippi River and the National Toxics Crisis* (Washington, DC: Greenpeace USA, 1989).

13 Public Data Access, Inc., *Mortality and Toxics Along the Mississippi River* (Washington, DC: Greenpeace USA, 1988), p. 17. See also Lower Mississippi Delta Development Commission, *Body of the Nation* (Memphis, TN: Lower Mississippi Delta Development Commission, 1989).

14 Michael R. Greenberg, "The changing geography of major causes of death among middle-age white Americans, 1939–1981," *Socio-Economic Planning Sciences,* vol. 21, no. 4, 1987, pp. 223–28.

15 Michael R. Greenberg, "Sunbelt, frostbelt and public health," *Society,* vol. 21, July-August 1984, pp. 68–75.

16 Elliot D. Sclar, "Community economic structure and individual well-being: a look behind the statistics," *International Journal of Health Services,* vol. 10, no. 4, 1980, pp. 563–79.

17 Greenberg, 1987, op. cit.

18 See, for example, Fund for Renewable Energy and the Environment, *The State of the States, 1989* (Washington, DC: Renew America, 1990).

19 See Thomas J. Mason, Joseph F. Fraumeni, Jr., Robert Hoover, and William J. Blot, *An Atlas of Mortality from Selected Diseases* (Washington, DC: U.S. Government Printing Office, 1981), pp. xii and 44.

20 This statistic refers to the age-adjusted rate for white males ages 45–64 during 1983–85. The states include (from the highest rate down): West Virginia, Kentucky, North Carolina, Mississippi, South Carolina, Georgia, Arkansas, Tennessee, Louisiana, and New York. U.S. Department of Health and Human Services, *Health United States, 1988* (Washington, DC: U.S. Government Printing Office, 1989), p. 11.

21 Melinda S. Meade, "Cardiovascular disease in Savannah, Georgia," in *Geographical Aspects of Health,* ed. Neil D. McGlashan (New York, NY: Academic Press, 1983), pp. 175–96.

22 See, for example, George W. Comstock, "The Epidemiologic perspective: water hardness and cardiovascular disease," *Journal of Environmental Pathology and Toxicology,* vol. 4, nos. 2–3, 1980, pp. 9–25; R. Fabsitz and M. Feinleib, "Geographic patterns in county mortality rates from cardiovascular diseases," *American Journal of Epidemiology,* vol. 111, no. 3, 1980, pp. 315–28; and Jacob Freedman, *Trace Element Geochemistry in Health and Disease* (Boulder, CO: The Geological Society of America, 1975).

23 See American Heart Association, "Impact of environment on cardiovascular disease: a report of the American Heart Association task force on cardiovascular disease," *AHA Task Force Report Circulation,* vol. 63, no. 1, 1981, pp. 242A–271A.

24 See Meade, op. cit., pp. 176–78.

25 Steve Wing, Carl Hayes, Gerardo Heiss, Esther John, Marylin Knowles, Wilson Riggan, and H. A. Tyroler, "Geographic variation in the onset of decline of

ischemic heart disease mortality in the United States,'' *American Journal of Public Health,* vol. 76, no. 12, 1986, pp. 1404–8.

26 Steve Wing, Michelle Casper, Wilson Riggan, Carl Hayes, and H. Tyroler, ''Socioenvironmental characteristics associated with the onset of decline of ischemic heart disease mortality in the United States,'' *American Journal of Public Health,* vol. 78, no. 8, August 1988, p. 925.

27 Steve Wing, Michele Casper, Wayne B. Davis, Alvin Pellom, Wilson Riggan, H. A. Tyroler, ''Stroke mortality maps. United States whites aged 35–74 years, 1962–1982,'' *Stroke,* vol. 19, no. 12, 1988, pp. 1507–13.

28 Wing, 1988, op. cit., p. 924.

29 See Meade, op. cit., p. 195.

30 U.S. Department of Health and Human Services, *Health Status of Minorities and Low-income Groups* (Washington, DC: U.S. Government Printing Office, 1979), cited in, p. 36.

31 Wing, 1988, op. cit., p. 925.

32 See Lisa F. Berkman and Lori Breslow, *Health and Ways of Living: The Alameda County Study* (New York, NY: Oxford University Press, 1983), Chapter 4.

33 Greenberg, 1984, op. cit., p. 71.

34 See Alfred Kahn, R. B. Rutledge, G. L. Davis, J. A. Atlas, G. A. Gantner, C. A. Thornton, and N. D. Wallace, ''Carboxyhemoglobin sources in the metropolitan St. Louis population,'' *Archives of Environmental Health,* vol. 29, 1974, pp. 127–35, and U.S. Department of Health and Human Services, *Disease Prevention/Health Promotion: The Facts* (Palo Alto, CA: Bull Publishing Co., 1988), p. 51.

35 National Safe Workplace Institute, *Safer Work: Job Safety and Health Challenges for the Next President and Congress* (Chicago, IL: The National Safe Workplace Institute, 1988), p. 31.

36 The percentage of the fats and oils that are polyunsaturated (which can decrease cholesterol levels) is not provided. For more on heart disease and diet, see Myron Winick, Brian L. G. Morgan, Jaime Rozovski, and Robin Marks-Kaufman, *The Columbia Encyclopedia of Nutrition* (Mount Vernon, NY: Consumers Union, 1988), pp. 99–107. For regional diets, see U.S. Department of Agriculture, *Food Consumption: Households in the United States, Seasons and Year 1977–78* (Washington, DC: U.S. Government Printing Office, 1983); U.S. Department of Agriculture, *Food Consumption: Households in the Northeast, Seasons and Year 1977–78* (Washington, DC: U.S. Government Printing Office, 1983); U.S. Department of Agriculture, *Food Consumption: Households in the North Central Region, Seasons and Year 1977–78* (Washington, DC: U.S. Government Printing Office, 1983); U.S. Department of Agriculture, *Food Consumption: Households in the South, Seasons and Year 1977–78* (Washington DC: U.S. Government Printing Office, 1983); and U.S. Department of Agriculture, *Food Consumption: Households in the West, Seasons and Year 1977–78* (Washington DC: U.S. Government Printing Office, 1983).

37 C. Sempos, R. Cooper, M. G. Kovar, and M. McMiller, ''Divergence of recent

trends in coronary mortality in the four major race-sex groups in the United States," *American Journal of Public Health,* vol. 78, no. 11, 1988, pp. 1422–27.

38 U.S. Department of Health and Human Services, *Reducing the Health Consequences of Smoking: 25 Years of Progress. A Report of the Surgeon General* (Washington, DC: U.S. Government Printing Office, 1989).

39 Lawrence Garfinkel, "Cigarette smoking and coronary heart disease in blacks: comparison to whites in a prospective study," *American Heart Journal,* vol. 108, no. 3, 1984, pp. 802–7.

40 *Health United States, 1988,* op. cit., p. 11.

41 Richard Cooper and Brian E. Simmons, "Cigarette smoking and ill health among black Americans," *New York State Journal of Medicine,* July 1985, pp. 344–49.

42 Mac W. Otten, Jr., Seven M. Teutsch, David F. Williamson, and James S. Marks, "The effects of known risk factors on the excess mortality of black adults in the United States," *Journal of the American Medical Association,* vol. 263, no. 6, 1990, p. 845.

43 E. J. Roccella and C. Lenfant, "Regional and racial differences among stroke victims in the United States," *Clinical Cardiology,* vol. 12, no. 4, 1980, pp. 18–22.

44 See R. M. Davis, "Current trends in cigarette advertising and marketing," *New England Journal of Medicine,* vol. 316, 1987, pp. 725–32.

45 See Wing et al., 1990, op. cit., p. 264.

46 Steve Wing, "Social inequalities in the decline of coronary mortality," *American Journal of Public Health,* vol. 78, no. 11, 1988, pp. 1415–16.

47 Telephone interview with Pat Brown, August 10, 1990, and Michael H. Brown, "Love Canal revisited: Ten years later there are still more questions than answers," *The Amicus Journal,* Summer 1988, pp. 37–44.

48 Samuel Epstein, Lester Brown, and Carl Pope, *Hazardous Waste in America,* (San Francisco, CA: Sierra Club Books, 1982), p. 93.

49 Michael H. Brown, "Love Canal revisited," *The Amicus Journal,* Summer 1988, p. 41.

50 Sam Howe Verhovek, "At Love Canal, land rush on a burial ground," *The New York Times,* July 26, 1990, p. 1.

51 "Landfill Linked to Cases of Leukemia and Low Birth Weight," *The New York Times,* February 5, 1989, p. 33.

52 California Department of Health Services, "State health department releases Fairchild studies," *Department of Health Services News,* January 16, 1985.

53 See Mitchel Benson, "More wells fouled: toxic leaks taint 46 in Santa Clara County," *San Jose Mercury News,* September 27, 1987, and David E. Sanger, "Pregnancy transfers by AT&T: miscarriages feared after study on chips," *The New York Times,* January 14, 1987.

54 Centers for Disease Control, "Low birthweight—United States, 1975–87," *Morbidity and Mortality Weekly Report,* vol. 39, no. 9, 1990, pp. 148–51.

55 Centers for Disease Control, "Contribution of birth defects to infant mortality

—United States, 1986,'' *Morbidity and Mortality Weekly Report,* vol. 38, 1989, pp. 633–35.

56 Robert Pear, "Study says U.S. needs to attack infant mortality," *The New York Times,* August 6, 1990, p. 1.

57 Kolata, op. cit.

58 Marlene Cimons, "Key infant mortality factor rises after 10-year decline," *Los Angeles Times,* March 9, 1990.

59 Casey J. Jason, Michael E. Samuhel, Barry J. Glick, and Anne K. Welsh, "Geographic distribution of unexplained low birth weight," *Journal of Occupational Medicine,* vol. 28, no. 8, 1986, pp. 728–40.

60 See Gina Kolata, "Defects top cause of infant deaths," *The New York Times,* September 22, 1989, and Robert L. Brent and David A. Beckman, "Environmental teratogens," *Bulletin of the New York Academy of Medicine,* vol. 66, no. 2, 1990, pp. 123–63.

61 Jason et al., op. cit.

62 "Harlem reflects concerns at children's summit," *The New York Times,* September 30, 1990, p. 17.

63 Keith Schneider, "Birth defects and pollution: issue raised in Texas town," *The New York Times,* April 15, 1990, p. 14.

64 Ibid.

65 See Centers for Disease Control, *Congenital Malformations Surveillance* (Atlanta, GA), which publishes the results of the CDC's ongoing Birth Defects Monitoring Program. Also see "Contribution of birth defects to infant mortality —United States, 1986," *Morbidity and Mortality Weekly Report,* vol. 38, 1989, pp. 633–35; Frank Greenberg, Levy M. James, and Godfrey P. Oakley, Jr., "Estimates of birth prevalence rates of spina bifida in the United States from computer-generated maps," *American Journal of Obstetrics and Gynecology,* vol. 145, no. 5, 1983, pp. 570–73; Peter F. Infante, "Oncogenic and mutagenic risks in communities with polyvinyl chloride production facilities," *Annals of the New York Academy of Sciences,* vol. 271, 1976, pp. 49–57; and Roberta H. Raven, Bruce S. Schoenberg, Nadir E. Bharucha, and Thomas J. Mason, "Geographic distribution of anencephaly in the United States," *Neurology,* vol. 33, 1983, pp. 1243–46.

66 See Lisa F. Berkman, "Assessing the physical health effects of social networks and social support," *Annual Review of Public Health,* vol. 5, 1985, pp. 413–32.

67 See John Elkington, *The Poisoned Womb: Human Reproduction in a Polluted World* (New York, NY: Viking Penguin, Inc., 1985), and Ian C. T. Nisbet and Nathan J. Karch, *Chemical Hazards to Human Reproduction* (Washington, DC: Council on Environmental Quality, 1981).

68 See Sandra Blakeslee, "Research on birth defects shifts to flaws in sperm," *The New York Times,* January 1, 1991, p. 1.

69 See U.S. Department of Health and Human Services, *Report of the Secretary's Task Force on Black and Minority Health, Volume I: Executive Summary* (Washington, DC: U.S. Government Printing Office, 1985), pp. 175–79.

70 See Ronald Anderson, Aida Giachello, and Lu Ann Aday, "Access of Hispan-

ics to health care and cuts in services: a state-of-the-art overview," *Public Health Reports,* vol. 101, no. 3, 1986, p. 240, and National Center for Health Statistics, *Health United States, 1989 and Prevention Profile* (Hyattsville, MD: Public Health Service, 1990), pp. 12–13.

71 The probability is less than 1 percent that these results were due to chance.

72 The list of counties with the highest teratogenic pollution was computed from the EPA's Toxic Chemical Release Inventory by Citizens Fund, *Poisons in Our Neighborhoods: Toxic Pollution in the United States* (Washington, DC: Citizens Fund, 1990). Los Angeles has below-average birth-defect mortality despite its high rate of teratogenic pollution, but the rate is not good enough to sway the picture for the ten counties as a whole (and is deteriorating significantly).

73 Stephanie Abarbanel, "Toxic nightmare on main street," *Family Circle,* August 14, 1990, pp. 77–128.

74 Dick Russell, Gary Cohen, Henry S. Cole, and Adrienne Anderson, *Destroying Our Nation's Defenses: A Citizen Indictment of the Environmental Protection Agency and the Reagan-Bush Administration* (Boston, MA: The National Toxics Campaign, 1988), pp. 19–20.

75 Dick Russell, "The Jacksonville scandal: burning the people," *Toxic Times,* Fall 1989, pp. 16–18.

76 Abarbanel, op. cit., p. 87.

77 Eleven of the CDC investigations were in Connecticut, eight in California, Illinois, and New York, seven in Georgia, six in Pennsylvania, and five in Iowa. See Glyn G. Caldwell, "Twenty-two years of cancer cluster investigations at the Centers for Disease Control," *American Journal of Epidemiology,* vol. 132, suppl., no. 1, 1990, pp. S43–S47.

78 Michael deCourcy Hinds, "Plan to burn dioxin stirs fear in Arkansas," *The New York Times,* August 7, 1990, p. 1.

79 Bobbi Ridlehover and Don Johnson, "No burning, 600 tell officials: Jacksonville gathering warned dioxin in fumes too risky," *Arkansas Democrat,* August 10, 1990, p. 1.

80 Abarbanel, op. cit., p. 127.

81 *Health United States, 1988,* p. 10.

82 G. Reza Najem, Donald B. Louria, Marvin A. Lavenhar, and Martin Feuerman, "Clusters of cancer mortality in New Jersey municipalities; with special reference to chemical toxic waste disposal site and per capita income," *International Journal of Epidemiology,* vol. 14, no. 4, 1985, pp. 528–37, and Michael R. Greenberg, "A note on the changing geography of cancer mortality within metropolitan regions of the United States," *Demography,* vol. 18, no. 3, 1981, pp. 411–20.

83 Richard Doll and Richard Peto, *The Causes of Cancer: Quantitative Estimates of Avoidable Risks of Cancer in the United States Today* (New York, NY: Oxford University Press, 1981), p. 1256.

84 G. Marie Swanson, "Cancer prevention in the workplace and natural environment: a review of etiology, research design, and methods of risk reduction," *Cancer,* vol. 62, 1988, pp. 1725–46.

85 *Disease Prevention/Health Promotion,* op. cit., p. 51.

86 International Agency for Research in Cancer, "Chemicals, industrial processes and industries associated with cancer in humans," *IARC Monographs, Supplement 4,* 1982.

87 Conger Beasley, Jr., "Of pollution and poverty: keeping watch in cancer alley," *Buzzworm,* July-August 1990, p. 41.

88 See Pelayo Correa, Linda W. Pickle, Elizabeth Fontham, Nancy Dalager, Youpling Lin, William Haenszel, and William D. Johnson, "The causes of lung cancer in Louisiana," in *Lung Cancer: Causes and Prevention,* M. Mizell and P. Correa, eds. (Deerfield Beach, FL: Verlag Chemie International, 1984), pp. 73–82.

89 Beasley, Jr., op. cit., p. 39.

90 Sierra Club Delta Chapter, A preliminary report to the Louisiana House Natural Resources Subcommittee on Oversight concerning the annual dumping of almost 200 million pounds of toxic chemicals into the air in the Geismar and Saint Gabriel communities by 18 petrochemical plants and numerous accidental toxic chemical releases during the first 9 months of 1986 (New Orleans, LA: Sierra Club, 1986).

91 U.S. Environmental Protection Agency, *Toxics in the Community: National and Local Perspectives* (Washington, DC: U.S. Government Printing Office, 1988) p. 61.

92 Citizens Fund, *Poisons in our Neighborhoods: Toxic Pollution in the United States* (Washington, DC: Citizens Fund, 1990), pp. 12, 16.

93 Telephone interview with Amos Favorite, November 15, 1990.

94 Telephone interview with Amos Favorite, August 17, 1990.

95 We use the phrase lung cancer to mean cancer of any organ of the respiratory system, as discussed in the methods appendix.

96 Linda W. Pickle, Pelayo Correa, and Elizabeth Fontham, "Recent case-control studies of lung cancer in the United States," in Mizell and Correa, op. cit., pp. 101–15.

97 Judith M. Aronchick, "Lung cancer: epidemiology and risk factors," *Seminars in Roentgenology,* vol. 25, no. 1., 1990, pp. 5–11.

98 Michael R. Greenberg, "Sunbelt, frostbelt and public health," *Society,* vol. 21, July-August 1984, pp. 68–75.

99 Kentucky, West Virginia, and Oklahoma are the three southern states with the highest rates of lung cancer and smoking. See U.S. Department of Health and Human Services, *Reducing the Health Consequences of Smoking: 25 Years of Progress—A Report of the Surgeon General* (Washington, DC: U.S. Government Printing Office, 1989), pp. 282–83.

100 Ibid., and Correa et al., op. cit.

101 Doll and Peto, op. cit., p. 1244, Table 19.

102 Exposure to asbestos is estimated to increase the risk of contracting lung cancer by as much as fourfold for nonsmokers, and by as much as tenfold for smokers. See Judith M. Aronchick, "Lung cancer: epidemiology and risk factors," *Seminars in Roentgenology,* vol. 25, no. 1., 1990, pp. 5–11; L. A. Fingerhut, R. W. Wilson, and J. J. Feldman, "Health and disease in the United States," *Annual Review of Public Health,* vol. 1, 1980, p. 31; and Irving J. Selikoff, Edward C.

Hammond, and J. Churg, "Asbestos exposure, smoking and neoplasia," *Journal of the American Medical Association,* vol. 204, 1968, pp. 106–12.

103 William J. Blot, Joseph M. Harrington, A. Toledo, Robert Hoover, C. W. Heath, and Joseph F. Fraumeni, Jr., "Lung cancer after employment in shipyards during World War II," *New England Journal of Medicine,* vol. 299, 1978, pp. 620–24; William J. Blot, J. E. Davies, L. M. Brown, C. W. Nordwall, E. Buiatti, A. Ng, and J. F. Fraumeni, Jr., "Occupation and the high risk of lung cancer in northeast Florida," *Cancer,* vol. 50, 1982, pp. 364–71; William J. Blot, L. E. Morris, R. Strouge, I. Tagnon, and J. F. Fraumeni, Jr., "Lung and laryngeal cancers in relation to shipyard employment in coastal Virginia," *Journal of the National Cancer Institute,* vol. 65, 1980, pp. 571–75.

104 Pickle, Correa, and Fontham, op. cit., p. 107.

105 See William J. Blot and Joseph F. Fraumeni, Jr. "Geographic patterns of lung cancer: Industrial correlations, *American Journal of Epidemiology,* vol. 103, 1976, pp. 539–50, and Robert Hoover and Joseph F. Fraumeni, Jr., "Cancer mortality in U.S. counties with chemical industries," *Environmental Research,* vol. 9, 1975, pp. 196–207.

106 Correa et al., op. cit.

107 William J. Blot, Linda M. Brown, Linda M. Pottern, B. J. Stone, and Joseph F. Fraumeni, Jr., "Lung cancer among long-term steel workers," *American Journal of Epidemiology,* vol. 117, 1983, pp. 706–16.

108 Linda M. Brown, Linda M. Pottern, and William J. Blot, "Lung cancer in relation to environmental pollutants emitted from industrial sources," *Environmental Research,* vol. 34, 1984, pp. 250–61.

109 William J. Blot and Joseph F. Fraumeni, Jr., "Arsenical air pollution and lung cancer," *Lancet,* July 26, 1975, pp. 142–44.

110 Janet B. Schoenberg, Annette Stemhagen, Thomas J. Mason, Joan Patterson, Joan Bill, and Ronald Altman, "Occupation and lung cancer risk among New Jersey white males," *Journal of the National Cancer Institute,* vol. 79, 1987, pp. 13–22.

111 B. J. Stone, William J. Blot, and Joseph F. Fraumeni, Jr., "Geographic patterns of industry in the United States: an aid to the study of occupational disease," *Journal of Occupational Medicine,* vol. 20, no. 7, 1978, pp. 472–77.

112 Aronchick, op. cit., p. 7, and Keith Schneider, "Uranium miners inherit dispute's sad legacy," *The New York Times,* January 9, 1990. p. 1.

113 The U.S. Department of Energy found Rocky Flats to be the most environmentally hazardous in the nuclear weapons industry, and a criminal investigation has begun over pollution violations. See David Johnston, "Energy dept. accused of concealing violations at site near Denver," *The New York Times,* June 10, 1989, p. 1.

114 See Carl J. Johnson, "Cancer incidence in an area contaminated with radionuclides near a nuclear installation," *Ambio,* vol. 10, 1981, pp. 176–82; "Weapons plant workers contract a lung disease," *The New York Times,* January 15, 1990, p. A14; and D. J. Zeigler, J. H. Johnson, and S. D. Brunn, *Technological Hazards* (Washington, DC: Association of American Geographers, 1983), p. 48.

115 See Matthew L. Wald, "Energy dept. to pay $73 million to settle uranium case

in Ohio: accord involves thousands near nuclear plant," *The New York Times,* July 1, 1989, p. 1.

116 See Jay M. Gould and Benjamin A. Goldman, *Deadly Deceit: Low-Level Radiation, High-Level Cover-up* (New York, NY: Four Walls Eight Windows, 1990), pp. 46–47, and Keith Schneider, "Severe accidents at nuclear plant were kept secret up to 31 years," *The New York Times,* October 1, 1988, p. 1.

117 Jay H. Lubin and John D. Boice, Jr., "Estimating Rn-induced lung cancer in the United States," *Health Physics,* vol. 57, no. 3, 1989, pp. 417–27.

118 Michael R. Greenberg, *Urbanization and Cancer Mortality: The United States Experience, 1950–1975* (New York, NY: Oxford University Press, 1983).

119 Thomas Mancuso and Theodore Sterling, "Lung cancer among black and white migrants in the U.S.: etiological considerations," *Journal of the National Medical Association,* vol. 67, no. 2, 1975, p. 102.

120 Paolo Vineis, Terry Thomas, Richard B. Hayes, William J. Blot, Thomas J. Mason, Linda W. Pickle, Pelayo Correa, Elizabeth T. H. Fontham, and Janet Schoenber, "Proportion of lung cancers in males, due to occupation, in different areas of the USA," *International Journal of Cancer,* vol. 42, 1988, pp. 851–56.

121 William J. Miller, Jr., and Richard Cooper, "Rising lung cancer death rates among black men: the importance of occupation and social class," *Journal of the National Medical Association,* vol. 74, no. 3, 1982, pp. 253–58.

122 Richard Cooper and Brian E. Simmons, "Cigarette smoking and ill health among black Americans," *New York State Journal of Medicine,* July 1985, pp. 344–49.

123 Centers for Disease Control, "Cigarette smoking among blacks and other minority populations," *Morbidity and Mortality Weekly Report,* vol. 36, no. 25, 1987, pp. 404–7, and Lawrence Garfinkel, "Cigarette smoking and coronary heart disease in blacks: comparison to whites in a prospective study, *American Heart Journal,* vol. 108, no. 3, 1984, pp. 802–7.

124 Miller and Cooper, op. cit., p. 256.

125 Telephone interview with Ellyn Troisi, Nassau County Board of Health, October 29, 1990.

126 Telephone interview with Bert Nelson, superintendent of Hewlett-Woodmere School District, October 29, 1990.

127 See Irvin Molotsky, "Study finds ground water periled by toxic chemicals," *The New York Times,* January 19, 1981, and Frances Cerra, "Contamination of L.I. wells a constant worry to many," *The New York Times,* January 19, 1981.

128 New York State Department of Health, "Small area analysis of breast cancer incidence rates in Nassau and Suffolk counties, New York, 1978–1987."

129 G. Reza Najem, and Teresa W. Greer, "Female reproductive organs and breast cancer mortality in New Jersey counties and the relationship with certain environmental variables," *Preventive Medicine,* vol. 14, 1985, pp. 620–35.

130 *Health United States, 1988,* op. cit., p. 20.

131 Linda J. Pickle, Thomas J. Mason, N. Howard, Robert Hoover, and Joseph F. Fraumeni, Jr., *Atlas of U.S. Cancer Mortality Among Whites: 1950–1980* (Washington, DC: U.S. Government Printing Office, 1987), p. 15.

132 Susan P. Helmrich, Samuel Shapiro, Lynn Rosenberg, David W. Kaufman, Dennis Slone, Christopher Bain, Olli S. Miettinen, Paul D. Stolley, Neil B. Rosenshein, Rober C. Knapp, Thomas Leavitt, Jr., David Schottenfeld, Ralph L. Engle, Jr., and Micha Levy, "Risk factors for breast cancer," *American Journal of Epidemiology,* vol. 117, no. 1, 1983, pp. 35–45.

133 Sakari Karjalainen and Eero Pukkala, "Social class as a prognostic factor in breast cancer survival," *Cancer,* vol. 66, no. 4, 1990, pp. 819–25.

134 William J. Blot, Joseph F. Fraumeni, Jr., and B. J. Stone, "Geographic patterns of breast cancer in the United States," *Journal of the National Cancer Institute,* vol. 59, no. 5, 1977, pp. 1407–11.

135 Nancy Krieger, "Social class and the black/white crossover in the age-specific incidence of breast cancer: a study linking census-derived data to population-based registry records," *American Journal Epidemiology,* vol. 131, 1990, pp. 804–14.

136 See Helmrich et al., op. cit.; Curtis Mettlin, "Diet and the epidemiology of human breast cancer," *Cancer,* vol. 53, no. 3, supplement, 1984, pp. 605–11; and "Study discounts pill-cancer link," *The New York Times,* September 6, 1989.

137 Anna E. Waller, Susan P. Baker, and Andrew Szocka, "Childhood injury deaths: a national analysis and geographic variations," *American Journal of Public Health,* vol. 79, no. 3, 1989, pp. 310–15.

138 In 1987, 16,216 children between the ages of 1 and 14 died in the United States. External causes (injuries, etc.) resulted in 8,250 of these deaths (51 percent). Cancer caused 1,686 childhood deaths (10 percent), 665 of which were from leukemia (40 percent of childhood cancer deaths). Congenital anomalies, the second leading natural cause of death among children, accounted for 1,372 deaths (9 percent). See *Vital Statistics of the United States, 1987,* op. cit., and Lois A. Fingerhut and Joel C. Klienman, "Mortality among children and youth," *American Journal of Public Health,* vol. 79, no. 7, 1989, pp. 899–901.

139 J. L. Young, Jr., L. G. Ries, E. Silverger, J. W. Horm, and R. W. Miller, "Cancer incidence, survival, and mortality for children younger than age 15 years," *Cancer,* vol. 58, suppl. 2, 1986, pp. 598–602.

140 See Adrienne Anderson, "Colorado," *Toxic Times,* Summer 1990, p. 9; T. R. Reid and Cass Peterson, "Twelve children dead in 'cancer cluster' community," *The Washington Post,* October 4, 1984, p. 2; and Philip Shabecoff, "Uncertainties of a chemical filled world bring fear to a suburb of Denver," *The New York Times,* April 19, 1987, p. 19.

141 Telephone interview with Helen Solar, August 1990.

142 Carol Strickland, "Something stinks in Morgan City," *The Nation,* October 23, 1989, pp. 448–51.

143 See N. E. Breslow and B. Langholz, "Childhood cancer incidence: geographical and temporal variations," *International Journal of Cancer,* vol. 32, 1983, pp. 703–16 and R. S. Greenberg and J. L. Shuster, Jr., "Epidemiology of cancer in children," *Epidemiology Review,* vol. 7, 1985, pp. 22–48.

144 See American Cancer Society, *Cancer Facts and Figures—1990* (Atlanta, GA: 1990, American Cancer Society, Inc.), p. 14.

145 See Environmental Defense Fund and Robert H. Boyle, *Malignant Neglect* (New York, NY: Vintage Books, 1980), p. 209.

146 Aaron Blair, Joseph F. Fraumeni, Jr., and Thomas Mason, "Geographic patterns of leukemia in the United States," *Journal of Chronic Diseases,* vol. 33, 1980, pp. 251–60.

147 Breslow and Longholz, op. cit., p. 708; Michael R. Greenberg, P. Preuss, and R. Anderson, "Clues for case control studies of cancer in the northeast urban corridor," *Social Science and Medicine,* vol. 14D, 1980, pp. 37–43; and Michael R. Greenberg, "Environmental toxicology in the United States," in *Geographical Aspects of Health,* Neil D. McGlashan, ed. (New York, NY: Academic Press, 1983), p. 165.

148 See T. B. Haddy, "Cancer in black children," *American Journal of Pediatric Hematology and Oncology,* vol. 4, no. 3, 1982, pp. 285–92; J. A. Pratt, R. Velez, J. D. Bender, and K. G. Manton, "Racial differences in acute lymphocytic leukemia mortality and incidence trends," *Journal of Clinical Epidemiology,* vol. 41, no. 4, 1988, pp. 367–71; and Young et al., op. cit.

149 Blair et al., op. cit.

150 Pickle et al., 1987, op. cit., p. 17.

151 J. D. Buckley, L. L. Robinson, R. Swotinsky, D. H. Garabrant, M. LeBeau, P. Manchester, M. E. Nesbit, L. Odom, J. M. Peters, and W. G. Woods, "Occupational exposures of parents of children with acute nonlymphocytic leukemia: a report from the Children's Cancer Study Group," *Cancer Research,* vol. 49, no. 14, 1989, pp. 4030–37; and Ruth A. Lowengart, J. M. Peters, C. Cicioni, J. Buckley, L. Bernstein, S. Preston-Martin, and E. Rappaport, "Childhood leukemia and parents' occupational and home exposures," *Journal of the National Cancer Institute,* vol. 79, no. 1, 1987, pp. 39–46.

152 *Health United States, 1988,* op. cit., pp. 26–27.

153 Strickland, op. cit., p. 450.

154 Buckley et al., op. cit., and Lowengart et al., op. cit.

155 Cited in Environmental Defense Fund and Boyle, op. cit., p. 208.

156 E. G. Knox, Alice M. Stewart, and George W. Kneale, "Background radiation and childhood cancer," *Journal of Radiology Protection,* vol. 8, no. 1, 1988, pp. 9–18.

157 Martin J. Gardner, Michael P. Snee, Andrew J. Hall, Caroline A. Powell, Susan Downes, and John D. Terrell, "Results of case-control study of leukaemia and lymphoma among people near Sellafield nuclear plant in West Cumbria," *British Medical Journal,* vol. 300, 1990, pp. 423–29.

158 D. G. Baker, "Radiology, is there an occupational hazard?" *American Industrial Hygiene Association Journal,* vol. 49, no. 1, 1988, pp. 17–20.

159 James L. Franklin, "Leukemia link to Pilgrim plant found for '72–79," *Boston Globe,* October 10, 1990, p. 1; Richard W. Clapp, Sidney Cobb, C. K. Chan, and Bailus Walker, Jr., "Leukaemia near Massachusetts nuclear power plant," *Lancet,* December 5, 1987, pp. 1324–25; and Gould and Goldman, op. cit., p. 68.

160 Paul Brodeur, "Annals of radiation: calamity on Meadown Street," *The New Yorker,* July 9, 1990, pp. 38–72; Samuel Milham, Jr., "Mortality leukemia in

workers exposed to electrical and magnetic fields,'' *New England Journal of Medicine,* vol. 307, 1982, p. 249; David A. Savitz, Howard Wachtel, Frank A. Barnes, Esther M. John, and Jiri G. Tvrdik, ''Case-control study of childhood cancer and exposure to 60-Hz magnetic fields,'' *American Journal of Epidemiology,* vol. 128, no. 1, 1988, pp. 21–38; Nancy Wertheimer and Ed Leeper, ''Electrical wiring configurations and childhood cancer,'' *American Journal of Epidemiology,* vol. 109, no. 3, 1979, pp. 273–84; and William E. Wright, John M. Peters, and Thomas M. Mack, ''Leukaemia in workers exposed to electrical and magnetic fields,'' *Lancet,* November 20, 1982, pp. 1160–61.

161 Keith Schneider, ''Radiation danger found in oilfields across the nation,'' *The New York Times,* December 3, 1990, p. 1.

162 Ronald E. Roel, ''Hazardous duty,'' *Newsday,* June 10, 1988, pp. 1, 3, 31.

163 Richard Seltzer, ''Impact widening from explosion of Nevada rocket oxidizer plant,'' *Chemical and Engineering News,* August 8, 1988, cited in Lenny Siegel, ''No free launch: the untold polluting power of the 'new' space program,'' *Mother Jones,* vol. 15, September/October 1990, p. 24.

164 Kathy Sawyer, ''Nevada rocket plant destroyed by explosions,'' *The Washington Post,* May 5, 1988, p. A1.

165 ''Accident tolls demand action,'' *The Community Plume,* May-June 1989, p. 1.

166 Sawyer, op. cit., p. A18.

167 ''Special commission under way,'' *Working Notes on Community Right to Know,* October 1990, p. 1, and *The Community Plume,* op. cit., pp. 1, 4.

168 For more on poisoning, see Centers for Disease Control, ''Unintentional poisoning mortality—United States, 1980–1986,'' *Morbidity and Mortality Weekly Report,* vol. 38, 1989, pp. 153–57.

169 See Paul Slovic, ''Perception of risk,'' *Science,* vol. 236, 1987, pp. 280–85.

170 With the exception of breast cancers, of course, which are extremely rare among all men.

171 According to the CDC, accidental deaths cause 2,319,400 years of potential life lost (YPLL) before age 65 each year. One percent of these deaths, or 231,940 YPLL, are due to acutely hazardous exposures. Average per capita income is around $15,000, so this cause of death eliminates $3.5 billion in personal income each year. See Centers for Disease Control, ''Years of potential life lost before ages 65 and 85—United States, 1987 and 1988,'' *Morbidity and Mortality Weekly Report,* vol. 39, no. 2, 1990, p. 21.

172 See Susan P. Baker, R. A. Whitfield, and Brian O'Neill, ''County mapping of injury mortality,'' *The Journal of Trauma,* vol. 28, no. 6, 1988, pp. 741–45.

173 Occupational fatalities in agriculture, forestry, fishing, and mining was 30.6 per 100,000 full-time employees in 1984 compared with 3.7 fatalities per 100,000 in manufacturing, wholesale and retail trade, finance, insurance, real estate, and services. Derived from Bureau of Labor Statistics data cited in *Disease Prevention/Health Promotion,* op. cit., pp. 65, 70. See also National Safety Council, *Accident Facts 1990* (Chicago, IL: National Safety Council, 1990).

174 Michael R. Greenberg, George W. Carey, and Frank J. Popper, ''Violent death, violent states and American youth,'' *Public Interest,* Spring 1987, pp. 38–48.

175 National Center for Health Statistics, *Monthly Vital Statistics Report,* vol. 38, no. 13, 1990, pp. 6–7.

176 Centers for Disease Control, "Update: acquired immunodeficiency syndrome —United States, 1989," *Morbidity and Mortality Weekly Report,* vol. 39, no. 5, 1990, pp. 81–86, and Frank D. Cox, *The AIDS Booklet* (Dubuque, IA: Wm. C. Brown Publishers, 1990).

177 Lytt I. Gardner, John F. Brundage, Donald S. Burke, John G. McNeil, Robert Visintine, and Richard N. Miller, "Evidence for the spread of the human immunodeficiency virus epidemic into low prevalence areas of the United States," *Journal of Acquired Immune Deficiency Syndromes,* vol. 2, no. 6, 1989, pp. 521–32.

178 Centers for Disease Control, "Update: acquired immunodeficiency syndrome —United States, 1989,"op. cit.

179 Last, op. cit., pp. 112–13.

180 See Gerald F. Pyle, *The Diffusion of Influenza: Patterns and Paradigms* (Totowa, NJ: Rowman & Littlefield, 1986).

181 Centers for Disease Control, "Estimates of HIV prevalence and projected AIDS cases: summary of workshop, October 31–November 1, 1989," *Morbidity and Mortality Weekly Report,* vol. 39, no. 7, 1990, pp. 110–19.

182 Homicide among black teenagers ages 15 to 24 increased during the latter half of the 1980s (following a decline), but the same cannot be said for young adults ages 25 to 34, which is the cohort considered in this section. See U.S. Department of Health and Human Services, *Health United States, 1989* (Washington, DC: U.S. Government Printing Office, 1990) pp. 137–42.

183 James W. Buehler, Owen J. Devine, Ruth L. Berkelman, and Frances M. Chevarley, "Impact of the human immunodeficiency virus epidemic on mortality trends in young men, United States," *American Journal of Public Health,* vol. 80, no. 9, 1990, pp. 1080–86.

184 Diane B. Dutton, "Social class, health and illness," in *Applications of Social Science to Clinical Medicine and Health Policy,* eds. L. Aiken and D. Mechanic (New Brunswick, NJ: Rutgers University Press, 1986), pp. 31–62.

185 Everett R. Rhoades, John Hammond, Thomas K. Welty, Aaron O. Handler, and Robert W. Amler, "The Indian burden of illness and future health interventions," *Public Health Reports,* vol. 102, no. 4, 1987, pp. 361–68.

186 Walter R. Gove, "Sex, marital status, and mortality," *American Journal of Sociology,* vol. 79, no. 1, 1973, pp. 45–67.

187 Steve Wing, Michele Casper, Wayne Davis, Carl Hays, Wilson Riggan, and H. A. Tyroler, "Trends in the geographic inequality of cardiovascular disease mortality in the United States, 1962–82," *Social Science Medicine,* vol. 30., no. 3, 1990, pp. 261–66.

188 From 1970 to 1980 mortality declined by 1.3 percent each year among young adults ages 24 to 34 years. If this trend continued through the 1980s, there would have been approximately 10,000 fewer young adult deaths in 1989, 2,000 (or 21 percent) more than the number of young adult AIDS deaths that year. Looking just at the change from 1988 to 1989, there were nearly 3,000 more deaths in the

second year, or about 1,000 (33 percent) more than could be accounted for by the increased number of AIDS deaths or any increases in the young adult population. See National Center for Health Statistics, *Monthly Vital Statistics Report,* vol. 38, no. 13, 1990, pp. 16–17, 24.

189 See Linda Lee Davidoff, "Multiple chemical sensitivities," *The Amicus Journal,* Winter 1989, pp. 13–23; Robert Reinhold, "When life is toxic," *The New York Times Magazine,* September 16, 1990, pp. 50–70; George P. Schmid, "The global distribution of Lyme disease," *Reviews of Infectious Diseases,* vol. 7, no. 1, 1985, pp. 41–50; and Jesse A. Stoffe and Charles R. Pelligrino, *Chronic Fatigue Syndrome: The Hidden Epidemic* (New York, NY: Harper & Row, Publishers, 1990).

190 Centers for Disease Control, "Years of potential life lost before 65 and 85— United States, 1987 and 1988," *Morbidity and Mortality Weekly Report,* vol. 39, no. 2, 1990, pp. 20–22.

191 Much of the evidence of the linkage between immune systems and cancer has come from transplant patients who as a group suffer from extremely high rates of cancer. See Elizabeth Rosenthal, "Transplant patients illuminate link between cancer and immunity," *The New York Times,* December 5, 1989.

192 See National Center for Health Statistics, *Monthly Vital Statistics Report,* vol. 37, no. 13, 1989, p. 8.

193 Many studies have linked this increase to greater outdoor and indoor air pollution, which can be exacerbated even further by lifestyle factors such as poor household ventilation and high room temperatures. See Brunello Wüthrich, "Epidemiology of the allergic diseases: are they really on the increase?" *International Archives of Allergy and Applied Immunology,* vol. 90, 1989, pp. 3–10.

194 See "Asthma deaths of black children found to push up U.S. rate," *The New York Times,* October 3, 1990, p. A24; A. Sonia Buist and William M. Vollmer, "Reflections on the rise in asthma morbidity and mortality," *Journal of the American Medical Association,* vol. 264, no. 13, 1990, pp. 1719–20; and Kevin B. Weiss and Diane K. Wagener, "Geographic variations in U.S. asthma mortality: small-area analyses of excess mortality, 1981–1985," *American Journal of Epidemiology,* vol. 132, suppl., no. 1, 1990, pp. S107–15.

195 Centers for Disease Control, "Asthma—United States, 1980–1987," *Morbidity and Mortality Weekly Report,* vol. 39, no. 29, 1990, pp. 493–97.

196 See John Eyles and Kevin J. Woods, *The Social Geography of Medicine and Health* (New York, NY: St. Martin's Press, 1983), p. 16.

197 See Melinda Meade, John Florin, and Wilbert Gesler, *Medical Geography* (New York, NY: The Guilford Press, 1988), p. 15.

198 Robert S. Root-Bernstein, "Do we know the cause(s) of AIDS?" *Perspectives in Biology and Medicine,* vol. 33, no. 4, 1990, pp. 480–500.

199 John W. Ward et al., "The natural history of transfusion-associated infection with human immunodeficiency virus: factors influencing the rate of progression to disease," *New England Journal of Medicine,* vol. 321, no. 14, 1989, pp. 947–52.

200 Root-Bernstein, op. cit.

201 See Peter H. Duesberg, "Human immunodeficiency virus and acquired immu-

nodeficiency syndrome: correlation but not causation," *Proceedings of the National Academy of Sciences,* vol. 86, 1989, pp. 755–64, and Malcolm Gladwell and Michael Specter, "Researcher sees second possible cause of AIDS," *The Washington Post,* June 22, 1990, p. A3.

202 See Philip J. Hilts, "Researchers find an AIDS-like virus," *The New York Times,* November 23, 1990, p. A29.

203 Mirko D. Grmek, *History of AIDS: Emergence and Origin of a Modern Pandemic* (Princeton, NJ: Princeton University Press, 1990), p. 82.

204 For occupational exposures, see National Institute of Occupational Safety and Health, *Occupational Safety and Health Status FY 1986* (Cincinnati, OH: NIOSH, 1986). A NIOSH estimate of 10 million workers exposed to 11 high-volume carcinogens is cited in Samuel S. Epstein, "Losing the war against cancer: who's to blame and what to do about it," *International Journal of Health Services,* vol. 20. no. 1, 1990, p. 55. For electromagnetic radiation see Paul Brodeur, "Annals of radiation," *The New Yorker,* June 12–26, 1989, and Kazim Shiekh, "Exposure to electromagnetic fields and the risk of leukemia," *Archives of Environmental Health,* vol. 41, no. 1, 1986, pp. 56–63. For military and civilian radioactive waste Gould and Goldman, op. cit.; and Public Citizen, *Nuclear Legacy: An Overview of the Places, Problems, and Politics of Radioactive Waste in the United States* (Washington, DC: Public Citizen, 1989). For pesticide residues see National Research Council, *Regulating Pesticides in Food: The Delaney Paradox* (Washington, DC: National Academy Press, 1987), and Lawrie Mott and Karen Snyder, *Pesticide Alert: A Guide to Pesticides in Fruits and Vegetables* (San Francisco, CA: Sierra Club Books, 1987). For toxic releases see Citizens Fund, *Poisons in Our Neighborhoods: Toxic Pollution in the United States* (Washington, DC: Citizens Fund, 1990).

205 See Richard S. Norris, Thomas Cochran, and William Arkin, *Known U.S. Nuclear Tests, July 1945 to December 1987* (Washington, DC: Natural Resources Defense Council, 1988), and Gould and Goldman, op. cit.

206 See Michael Callen, *Surviving AIDS* (New York, NY: HarperCollins Publishers, 1990).

CHAPTER 4: INDUSTRIAL TOXICS

1 U.S. Environmental Protection Agency, *Toxics Substances Control Act Chemical Substance Inventory* (Washington, DC: U.S. Government Printing Office, 1985).

2 Fred Hoerger, William H. Beamer, and James S. Hanson, "The cumulative impact of health, environmental, and safety concerns on the chemical industry during the seventies," *Law and Contemporary Problems,* vol. 46, no. 3, Summer 1983, p. 77.

3 Andrew C. Kimbrell, "Environmental House Cleaning," in *The Green Lifestyle Handbook,* ed. Jeremy Rifkin (New York, NY: Henry Holt & Co., 1990), p. 11.

4 National Research Council, *Toxicity Testing: Strategies to Determine Needs and Priorities* (Washington, DC: National Academy Press, 1984), p. 12.

5 See Benjamin A. Goldman, James A. Hulme, and Cameron Johnson, *Hazard-*

ous Waste Management: Reducing the Risk (Washington, DC: Island Press, 1986), Chapter 3.

6 Center for Environmental Research, *1986 National Screening Survey of Hazardous Waste Treatment, Storage, Disposal, and Recycling Facilities* (Washington, DC: U.S. Environmental Protection Agency, September 1988).

7 Citizens Fund, *Poisons in Our Neighborhoods: Toxic Pollution in the United States* (Washington, DC: Citizens Fund, 1990).

8 Ibid.

9 Bob Hall, "The green scorecard," *Southern Exposure*, Spring 1990.

10 Ruth Caplan and Environmental Action, *Our Earth, Ourselves: The Action-Oriented Guide to Help You Protect and Preserve the Environment* (New York, NY: Bantam Books, 1990), p. 141.

11 For more on this community's struggles see Michael H. Brown, *The Toxic Cloud: The Poisoning of America's Air* (New York, NY: Harper & Row, 1987), chapter 17, and Robert D. Bullard, *Dumping in Dixie: Race, Class, and Environmental Quality* (Boulder, CO: Westview Press, 1990), chapter 3.

12 "Mary McCastle et al. v. Rollins Environmental Services of Louisiana, Inc. et al., no. 83-C-2621," in 456 *Southern Report*, 2nd series (Louisiana, 1984), pp. 612–15.

13 Interview with Mary McCastle and Steve Irving, August 6, 1984.

14 Citizens Fund, op. cit.

15 Ben A. Franklin, "In the shadow of the valley," *Sierra*, May/June 1986, p. 39.

16 William R. Greer, "Union Carbide reports 33 more leaks at U.S. site," *The New York Times*, January 31, 1985, p. 9.

17 U.S. Environmental Protection Agency, *Acute Hazardous Events Database* (Springfield, VA: National Technical Information Service, December 1985).

18 Barry Meier, "Carbide changing procedures at site in Institute, W. Va.," *The Wall Street Journal*, March 6, 1985.

19 "Carbide to resume making methyl isocyanate in U.S.," *The Wall Street Journal*, May 2, 1985.

20 U.S. Environmental Protection Agency, *Toxics in the Community: National and Local Perspectives* (Washington, DC: U.S. Government Printing Office, 1990), p. D-3.

21 "Air: 78% unregulated!" *Working Notes on Community Right to Know*, May 1990, p. 4.

22 Citizens Fund, op. cit.

23 "Air bill passes," *Working Notes on Community Right to Know*, November 1990, p. 4.

24 U.S. Environmental Protection Agency, *Unfinished Business: A Comparative Assessment of Environmental Problems, Overview Report* (Washington, DC: EPA, February 1987), p. 29.

25 See Jay M. Gould and Benjamin A. Goldman, *Deadly Deceit: Low-Level Radiation, High-Level Cover-up* (New York, NY: Four Walls Eight Windows, 1990), Chapter 5.

26 Jean True, "Toxics corner," *Balancing the Scales*, November 19, 1987, p. 9.

27 Dick Russell, "You are my river," *Greenpeace Magazine,* September-October 1988, p. 15.

28 Jim Sibbison, "Keeper of the bluegrass state," *Environmental Action,* July-August 1989, p. 13.

29 Russell, op. cit.

30 Sibbison, op. cit.

31 According to U.S. EPA's Permit Compliance System, 1989 discharges of half a dozen high-volume toxins (phosphorus, chlorine, lead, copper, chromium, and carbon tetrachloride) totaled approximately 155 million tons. Four other major waste streams (sewage, nitrogen, nitrogen ammonia, and phosphate) total to nearly 7 billion tons a year.

32 Center for Environmental Research. op. cit.

33 *Toxics in the Community,* op. cit., p. 158, and Citizens Fund, op. cit., p. 8.

34 See "Citizens push discharge reductions," *Working Notes on Community Right-to-Know,* December 1989, p. 1, and Donald T. Hammer and Henry S. Cole, *The Houston Ship Channel and Galveston Bay: Texas Water Commission and EPA Turn Their Backs* (Washington, DC: Clean Water Action and Clean Water Fund, 1989).

35 See Pat Costner and Joe Thornton, *We All Live Downstream: The Mississippi River and the National Toxics Crisis* (Washington, DC: Greenpeace USA, 1989); Jay M. Gould and Nancy McFadden, "Toxic waste in Chesapeake Bay: bad for people as well as fish," *Council on Economic Priorities Newsletter,* November 1985; Marco Kaltofen and Irene Kessel, *Boston Harbor Toxic Project: Third Annual Report on Toxic Discharges into Boston Harbor* (Boston, MA: National Toxics Campaign, 1989); and Steven O. Rohmann, Roger L. Miller, Elizabeth A. Scott, and Warren R. Muir, *Tracing a River's Toxic Pollution: Case Study of the Hudson* (New York, NY: Inform, 1985).

36 See Walter H. Corson, ed., *The Global Ecology Handbook: What You Can Do About the Environmental Crisis* (Boston, MA: Beacon Press, 1990), p. 163.

37 To compare these maps with one generated from TRI, see U.S. Environmental Protection Agency, *The Toxics Release Inventory: A National Perspective, 1987* (Washington, DC: U.S. Government Printing Office, 1989), p. 132.

38 Adrienne Anderson "Toxic Ponca City," *Toxic Times,* Summer 1988, p. 143.

39 Ibid. and Dick Russell, Gary Cohen, Henry S. Cole, and Adrienne Anderson, *Destroying Our Nation's Defenses: A Citizen Indictment of the Environmental Protection Agency and the Reagan-Bush Administration* (Boston, MA: The National Toxics Campaign, 1988), pp. 18–19.

40 Marilyn Garcia, "Oklahoma grassroots united against toxics," *Toxic Times,* Spring 1989, p. 10.

41 Bureau of National Affairs, *National Environment Watch,* July 30, 1990, p. 6, and Marilyn Parris-Garcia, "Oklahoma," *Toxic Times,* Summer 1990, p. 15.

42 Keith Schneider, "Chemical plants buy out neighbors as safety zone," *The New York Times,* November 28, 1990, p. 1.

43 Joe W. Grisham, ed., *Health Aspects of the Disposal of Waste Chemicals* (New York, NY: Pergamon Press, 1986).

44 See Samuel Epstein, Lester Brown, and Carl Pope, *Hazardous Waste in America* (San Francisco, CA: Sierra Club Books, 1982).

45 See Jack Griffith, Robert C. Duncan, Wilson B. Riggan, and Alvin C. Pellom, "Cancer mortality in U.S. counties with hazardous waste sites and ground water pollution," *Archives of Environmental Health,* vol. 44, no. 2, 1989, pp. 69–74; G. Reza Najem and Teresa W. Greer, "Female reproductive organs and breast cancer mortality in New Jersey counties and the relationship with certain environmental variables," *Preventive Medicine,* vol. 14, 1985, pp. 620–35; G. Reza Najem, Donald B. Louria, Marvin A. Lavenhar, and Martin Feuerman, "Clusters of cancer mortality in New Jersey municipalities; with special reference to chemical toxic waste disposal sites and per capita income," *International Journal of Epidemiology,* vol. 14, no. 4, 1985, pp. 528–37; and G. Reza Najem, Inderjit Thind, Marvin A. Lavenhar, and Donald B. Louria, "Gastrointestinal cancer mortality in New Jersey counties, and the relationship with environmental variables," *International Journal of Epidemiology,* vol. 12, no. 3, 1983, pp. 276–88.

46 See Westat, Inc., *National Survey of Hazardous Waste Generators and Treatment, Storage, and Disposal Facilities Regulated Under RCRA in 1981* (Washington, DC: U.S. Environmental Protection Agency, 1984).

47 See Ibid. and U.S. Congressional Budget Office, *Hazardous Waste Management: Recent Changes and Policy Alternatives* (Washington, DC: U.S. Government Printing Office, 1985).

48 See Goldman et al., op. cit.

49 See "Banning the burn in North Carolina," *Toxic Times,* Spring 1990, p. 10; "Connecticut citizens defeat incinerator proposal," *Toxic Times,* Fall 1989, p. 20; "Hazardous waste incineration—part 3: citizens slow growth of incineration," *RACHEL's Hazardous Waste News,* no. #206, November 7, 1990; and "Incinerator proposal generates heat in Green River," *High County News,* July 1990, p. 5.

50 Telephone interview with Frank Carsner, August 22, 1990.

51 David Weyeneth, "Description of activity," (Portland, OR: Toxic Victims Association, 1986).

52 This is part of a general trend of increased community-labor activism. See Jeremy Brecher and Tim Costello, eds., *Building Bridges: The Emerging Grassroots Coalition of Labor and Community* (New York, NY: Monthly Review Press, 1990).

53 Alexandra Allen "Confronting GM toxics," *Multinational Monitor,* May 1990, pp. 7–8.

54 Christopher Jensen, "OSHA cites GM Lordstown plant," Cleveland *Plain Dealer,* December 19, 1989, p. D1, and Jennifer Feehan, "GM Lordstown plants fined," *The Tribune Chronicle,* December 19, 1989, p. A1.

55 "Standing with workers at General Motors," *Toxic Times,* Spring 1990, p. 21.

56 Jane Nogaki, "Citizens negotiate a good neighbor agreement in New Jersey," *Toxic Times,* Spring 1989, p. 11.

57 Richard Youngstrom, "The neighborhood inspection," in *Fighting Toxics: A Manual for Protecting Your Family, Community, and Workplace,* edited

by Gary Cohen and John O'Connor (Washington, D.C.: Island Press, 1990), p. 127.

58 Jeffrey Tryens and Richard Schrader, *Making the Difference: Using the Right-to Know in the Fight Against Toxics* (Washington, DC: National Center for Policy Alternatives, 1989), p. 15.

59 Scott Tobey, "Taking control: workers and communities demand the right to act," *Multinational Monitor,* June 1990, pp. 29–31.

60 Christopher B. Daly, "New laws to reduce industrial poisons: Massachusetts, Oregon imposing stricter standards on use," *The Washington Post,* July 25, 1989.

61 Indoor radon tied for first place for cancer risks, but was not among the top group for noncancer risks. See *Unfinished Business,* op. cit.

62 Richard Doll and Richard Peto, *The Causes of Cancer: Quantitative Estimates of Avoidable Risks of Cancer in the United States Today* (New York, NY: Oxford University Press, 1981), p. 1256, Table 20.

63 See ibid., p. 67, and Philip J. Landrigan, "Prevention of toxic environmental illness in the twenty-first century," *Environmental Health Perspectives,* vol. 86, 1990, pp. 197–99.

64 These are data from the Bureau of Labor Statistics, Centers for Disease Control, National Institute of Occupational Safety and Health, and National Safety Council, cited in U.S. Department of Health and Human Services, *Disease Prevention/Health Promotion: The Facts* (Palo Alto, CA: Bull Publishing Co., 1988), p. 65.

65 See National Safe Workplace Institute, *Safer Work: Job Safety and Health Challenges for the Next President and Congress* (Chicago, IL: NSWI, 1988), p. 9.

66 See David S. Sundin, David H. Pedersen, and Todd M. Frazier, "Occupational hazard and health surveillance," *American Journal of Public Health,* vol. 76, no. 9, 1986, pp. 1083–84.

67 See D. H. Wegman and J.R. Froines, "Surveillance needs for occupational health," *American Journal of Public Health,* vol. 75, no. 11, 1985, pp. 1259–61.

68 The literature on occupational diseases is massive. The numbers cited are from the following: *Disease Prevention/Health Promotion,* op. cit., pp. 67–70; Landrigan, op. cit.; Pierre Decouflé, William A. Blattner, and Aaron Blair, "Mortality among chemical workers exposed to benzene and other agents," *Environmental Research,* vol. 30, 1983, pp. 16–25; and L. A. Fingerhut, R. W. Wilson, and J. J. Feldman, "Health and disease in the United States," *Annual Review of Public Health,* vol. 1, 1980, pp. 1–36. For other leads, see Office of Technology Assessment, *Reproductive Health Hazards in the Workplace* (Washington, DC: OTA, 1985), and Jeanne M. Stellman and Susan M. Daum, *Work Is Dangerous to Your Health: A Handbook of Health Hazards in the Workplace and What You Can Do About Them* (New York, NY: Vintage Books, 1973). For the geographic distribution of some of the major occupational diseases, see U.S. Department of Health and Human Services, *Health United States, 1988* (Washington, DC: U.S. Government Printing Office, 1989).

69 See Wendy Chavkin, ed., *Double Exposure: Women's Health Hazards on the Job and at Home* (New York, NY: Monthly Review Press, 1984).

70 "Repetitive motion disorders lead increases in job illnesses," *The New York Times,* November 16, 1990.

71 See Linda L. Davidoff, "Multiple chemical sensitivities," *The Amicus Journal,* Winter 1989, pp. 13–23.

72 U.S. EPA, op. cit.

73 Robert Hoover and Joseph F. Fraumeni, Jr., "Cancer mortality in U.S. counties with chemical industries," *Environmental Research,* vol. 9, 1975, pp. 196–207.

74 See Joan Claybrook and the Staff of Public Citizen, *Retreat from Safety: Reagan's Attack on America's Health* (New York, NY: Pantheon Books, 1984), and Public Citizen, *Risking America's Health and Safety: George Bush and the Task Force on Regulatory Relief* (Washington, DC: Public Citizen, 1988).

75 See *Disease Prevention/Health Promotion,* op. cit., p. 73.

76 See Joseph A. Kinney, *Failed Opportunities: The Decline in U.S. Job Safety in the 1980s* (Chicago, IL: National Safe Workplace Institute, 1988), p. 3.

CHAPTER 5: NONINDUSTRIAL POLLUTION

1 See National Academy of Public Administration, *A Strategy for Implementing Federal Regulation of Underground Storage Tanks* (Washington, DC: NAPA, 1986), and Seymour I. Schwartz and Wendy B. Pratt, *Hazardous Waste from Small Quantity Generators: Strategies and Solutions for Business and Government* (Washington, DC: Island Press, 1990).

2 See U.S. Environmental Protection Agency, *Final Report on the Federal/State/ Local Nonpoint Source Task Force and Recommended National Nonpoint Source Policy* (Washington, DC: U.S. EPA, 1985).

3 See U.S. Environmental Protection Agency, *An Update on the Air Toxics Problem in the United States: An Analysis of Cancer Risk for Selected Pollutants* (Research Triangle Park, NC: U.S. EPA, 1987).

4 See, for example, U.S. Environmental Protection Agency, *Comparing Risks and Setting Environmental Priorities: Overview of Three Regional Projects* (Washington, DC: U.S. EPA, 1989).

5 See Allan R. Gold, "Two Brooklyn areas ask what factories are doing to them," *The New York Times,* April 21, 1990, pp. 25–26; Community Environmental Health Center, *Hazardous Neighbors? Living Next Door to Industry in Greenpoint-Williamsburg* (New York, NY: Hunter College, 1989); and "Waste not wanted in neighborhood," *New York Newsday,* April 19, 1987.

6 Jim Stiak, "The pesticide wars: a grass-roots coalition takes on the industry," *The Amicus Journal,* Summer 1988, pp. 8–9.

7 Conger Beasley, Jr., "Of pollution and poverty: reaping America's unseemly harvest," *Buzzworm,* vol. 2, no. 3, 1990, pp. 41–47.

8 Justin Castillo, "Breaking the pesticide habit," *Multinational Monitor,* March 1989, pp. 32–34.

9 George DeVault and Andrew Roblin, "Just say no," *Environmental Action,* January/February, 1990, pp. 13–14.

10 Lawrie Mott and Karen Snyder, *Pesticide Alert: A Guide to Pesticides in Fruits and Vegetables* (San Francisco, CA: Sierra Club Books, 1987), p. 6.

11 Kevin Roderick, "Cancer cluster claimed in farm town of Earlimart," *Los Angeles Times,* September 15, 1989, p. 30.

12 Ron Harris, "Jackson to put campaign focus on cancer cluster town," *Los Angeles Times,* May 28, 1990, p. 30.

13 Ronald B. Taylor, "Cancer cluster probe focuses on dozen pesticides," *Los Angeles Times,* December 31, 1987, pp. 3, 20.

14 Janny Scott, "Child cancer cluster poses puzzle," *Los Angeles Times,* September 21, 1990, p. 2.

15 Beasley, Jr., op. cit., p. 44.

16 Scott, op. cit., p. 3.

17 Devault and Roblin, op. cit., p. 14, and telephone interview with Paul Buxman, January 11, 1991.

18 Beasley, Jr., op. cit., p. 45.

19 See "California's green vote," *Environmental Action,* September/October 1990, p. 7; Robert Pear, "Voters spurn array of plans for protecting the environment," *The New York Times,* November 8, 1990, p. B1; James Ridgeway, "Turning green: how the cream of wheat got skimmed, and why it doesn't matter," *The Village Voice,* November 20, 1990, pp. 19–20; Jim Schwab, "Farmers and environmentalists: the attraction is chemical," *The Nation,* October 16, 1989, pp. 416–21; and Vanessa Tait, "Republican victory, 'Big Green' defeat in California," *The Guardian,* November 21, 1990, p. 5.

20 See John T. O'Connor and Sanford Lewis, *Shadow on the Land: A Special Report on America's Hazardous Harvest* (Boston, MA: National Toxics Campaign, 1988), and National Toxics Campaign, "Organizing kit: a practical strategy to reduce dangerous pesticides in our food and the environment" (Boston, MA: NTC, n.d.).

21 U.S. Environmental Protection Agency, *National Pesticide Survey: Project Summary* (Washington, DC: EPA, 1990).

22 Elizabeth B. Nielsen and Linda K. Lee, *The Magnitude and Costs of Groundwater Contamination from Agricultural Chemicals: A National Perspective* (Washington, DC: National Technical Information Service, 1987).

23 See National Research Council, *Regulating Pesticides in Food: The Delaney Paradox* (Washington, DC: National Academy Press, 1987), and U.S. Environmental Protection Agency, *Unfinished Business: A Comparative Assessment of Environmental Problems, Overview Report* (Washington, DC: EPA, February 1987), Table 2-2. The number of cancer deaths from pesticide residues are based on the EPA's estimate of 6,000 deaths per year extended over an average lifetime of more than 70 years.

24 Walter J. Rogan et al., "Pollutants in breast milk," *New England Journal of Medicine,* vol. 302, 1980, p. 1451 cited in "Human breast milk is contaminated," *RACHEL's Hazardous Waste News,* no. 193, August 8, 1990.

25 See David Weir and Mark Schapiro, *Circle of Poison: Pesticides and People in a Hungry World* (San Francisco, CA: Institute for Food and Development Policy, 1981).

26 U.S. Environmental Protection Agency, "Pesticide industry sales and usage 1985 market estimates," September 1986, cited in Mott and Snyder, op. cit., p. 5, and Stiak, op. cit., p. 9.

27 See Justin R. Ward, F. Kaid Benfield, and Anne E. Kinsinger, *Reaping the Revenue Code: Why We Need Sensible Tax Reform for Sustainable Agriculture* (New York, NY: Natural Resources Defense Council, 1989), p. 48, and Rachel Carson, *Silent Spring* (Boston, MA: Houghton Mifflin Co., 1962), pp. 15–16.

28 Schwab, op. cit.

29 Marion Moses, "Diseases associated with exposure to chemical substances—pesticides," in *Maxy-Rosenau Public Health and Preventive Medicine,* edited by John M. Last (East Norwalk, CT: Appleton-Century-Crofts, 1986).

30 Mott and Snyder, op. cit., p. 7.

31 *The New York Times Health Magazine,* October 8, 1989, p. 57.

32 Joseph A. Kinney, *Failed Opportunities: The Decline in U.S. Job Safety in the 1980s* (Chicago, IL: National Safe Workplace Institute, 1988).

33 Valerie A. Wilk, *The Occupational Health of Migrant and Seasonal Farmworkers in the United States* (Washington, DC: Farmworker Justice Fund, Inc., 1986), p. 105.

34 See K. P. Cantor, "Farming and mortality from non-Hodgkin's lymphoma: a case-control study," *International Journal of Cancer,* vol. 29, 1982, pp. 239–47; K. P. Cantor and Aaron Blair, "Farming and mortality from multiple myeloma: a case-control study with the use of death certificates," *Journal of the National Cancer Institute,* vol. 72, 1984, pp. 251–55; Aaron Blair and T. L. Thomas, "Leukemia among Nebraska farmers: a death certificate study," *American Journal of Epidemiology,* vol. 110, 1979, pp. 264–73; Aaron Blair and D. W. White, "Leukemia cell types and agricultural practices in Nebraska," *Archives of Environmental Health,* vol. 40, 1985, pp. 211–14; Aaron Blair and D. W. White, "Death certificate study of leukemia among farmers from Wisconsin," *Journal of the National Cancer Institute,* vol. 66, 1981, pp. 1027–30; Leon Burmeister et al., "Selected cancer mortality and farm practices in Iowa," *American Journal of Epidemiology,* vol. 118, 1983, pp. 72–77; and Sheila Hoar et al., "Agricultural herbicide use and risk of lymphoma and soft-tissue sarcoma," *Journal of the American Medical Association,* vol. 256, 1986, pp.1141–47.

35 See chapter 3 for a presentation of the evidence linking pesticide exposure with leukemia and child cancer.

36 Office of Technology Assessment, *Neurotoxicity: Identifying and Controlling Poisons of the Nervous System* (Washington, DC: OTA, 1990).

37 Nadir E. Bharucha, Bruce S. Schoenberg, Roberta H. Raven, Linda W. Pickle, David P. Byar, Thomas J. Mason, "Geographic distribution of motor neuron disease and correlation with possible etiologic factors," *Neurology,* vol. 33, no. 7, 1983, pp. 911–15.

38 See Kenneth Bacon, "U.S. fails to adequately monitor risks of many toxic chemicals, study finds," *The Wall Street Journal,* May 17, 1990, p. 22.

39 Leon Olson, "The immune system and pesticides," *Journal of Pesticide Reform,* Summer 1986.

40 See Keith Schneider, "Migrant worker group is subject of wide study," *The New York Times,* August 19, 1990, p. 16.

41 See Leonard P. Gianessi, *Patterns of Pesticide Use in the United States: Results from the RFF National Pesticide Use Inventory* (Washington, DC: Resources for the Future, 1987).

42 Ward et al., op. cit., p. 47.

43 See Phil Brown and Edwin J. Mikkelsen, *No Safe Place: Toxic Waste, Leukemia, and Community Action,* (Berkeley, CA: University of California Press, 1990).

44 See Laraine Hofstetter, "Poison on tap," *Everybody's Backyard,* June 1990, p. 21.

45 See Nicholas Freudenberg, *Not in Our Backyards! Community Action for Health and the Environment* (New York, NY: Monthly Review Press, 1984), pp. 15–17; Samuel S. Epstein, Lester O. Brown, and Carl Pope, *Hazardous Waste in America* (San Francisco, CA: Sierra Club Books, 1982), pp. 47–68; and C. S. Clark et al., "An environmental health survey of drinking water contamination by leachate from a pesticide waste dump in Hardeman County, Tennessee," *Archives of Environmental Health,* vol. 37, no. 1, 1982, pp. 9–18.

46 See Eric P. Jorgensen, *The Poisoned Well: New Strategies for Groundwater Protection* (Washington, DC: Island Press, 1989), chapter 3.

47 See Philip Shenon, "Despite laws, water in schools may contain lead, study finds," *The New York Times,* November 1, 1990, p. 1.

48 Jorgensen, op. cit., p. 7.

49 Samuel Epstein et al., op. cit., pp. 300–301.

50 Elizabeth B. Nielsen and Linda K. Lee, *The Magnitude and Costs of Groundwater Contamination from Agricultural Chemicals: A National Perspective* (Washington, DC: National Technical Information Service, 1987), p. 1.

51 U.S. Environmental Protection Agency, *National Pesticide Survey: Project Summary* (Washington, DC: EPA, 1990), p. 1.

52 See the National Toxics Campaign Fund, *A Consumer's Guide to Protecting Your Drinking Water* (Boston, MA: NTCF, n.d.).

53 See U.S. Environmental Protection Agency, *Toxics in the Community: National and Local Perspectives* (Washington, DC: Government Printing Office, 1990), p. 56, and Benjamin A. Goldman, James A. Hulme, and Cameron Johnson, *Hazardous Waste Management: Reducing the Risk* (Washington, DC: Island Press, 1986), p. 44.

54 See Patrick W. Holden, *Pesticides and Groundwater Quality: Issues and Problems in Four States* (Washington, DC: National Academy Press, 1986).

55 Nielsen and Lee, op. cit., p. 20. Also see John T. O'Conner and Sanford Lewis, *Shadow on the Land: A Special Report on America's Hazardous Harvest* (Boston, MA: National Toxics Campaign, 1988).

56 See Public Data Access, Inc., *Mortality and Toxics Along the Mississippi River* (Washington, DC: Greenpeace USA, 1988), p. 27.

57 See "U.S. is faulted for role in water quality," *The New York Times,* October 8, 1990, p. 9.

58 Eric Mann, "Lighting a spark: L.A.'s smogbusters," *The Nation,* September 17, 1990, p. 257.

59 Alice Bredin, "On ill health and air pollution," *The New York Times Magazine,* October 7, 1990, p. 19.

60 Dick Russell, "L.A. air: the smog capital of the U.S. will soon begin cracking down on automobiles," *The Amicus Journal,* Summer 1988, pp. 10–20.

61 See Richard W. Stevenson, "California to get tougher air rules," *The New York Times,* September 27, 1990, p. 1, and Robert Reinhold, "Southern California takes steps to curb its urban air pollution," *The New York Times,* March 18, 1989, p. 1.

62 Mann, op. cit.

63 See U.S. Environmental Protection Agency, *National Air Pollution Emission Estimates 1940–1988* (Research Triangle Park, NC: EPA, 1990), p. 22; Maura Dolan and Rudy Abramson, "Lead levels put 25% of Southland children at risk," *Los Angeles Times,* March 6, 1990, p. 1; and John Rosen, "Metabolic abnormalities in lead-toxic children: public health implications," *Bulletin of the New York Academy of Medicine,* vol. 65, no. 10, 1989, pp. 1067–83.

64 U.S. Environmental Protection Agency, *National Air Quality and Emissions Trends Report, 1988* (Research Triangle Park, NC: EPA, 1990), p. 15.

65 Bredin, op. cit., p. 16.

66 See Alice S. Whittemore, "Air pollution and respiratory disease," *Annual Review of Public Health,* vol. 2, 1981, pp. 397–429.

67 EPA estimates indicate area sources release as much as 2.7 million tons of hazardous chemicals into the air compared with 1.2 million tons of toxic air emissions reported in the Toxic Release Inventory. See the methods appendix, Table A-4.

68 See U.S. Environmental Protection Agency, *Final Report of the Philadelphia Integrated Environmental Management Project* (Washington, DC: EPA, 1986), and Public Data Access, Inc., *The Philadelphia Toxics Story* (Boston, MA: The National Toxics Campaign, 1987).

CHAPTER 6: ENVIRONMENTAL JUSTICE

1 See Robert D. Bullard, *Dumping in Dixie: Race, Class, and Environmental Quality* (Boulder, CO: Westview Press, 1990), pp. 35–38; Charles Lee, "The integrity of justice: evidence of environmental racism," *Sojourners,* February/March 1990, pp. 22–25; and Hawley Traux, "Minorities at risk," *Environmental Action,* January/February 1990, pp. 19–21.

2 U.S. General Accounting Office, *Siting of Hazardous Waste Landfills and their Correlation with Racial and Economic Status of Surrounding Communities* (Washington, DC: U.S. General Accounting Office, 1983).

3 Commission for Racial Justice and Public Data Access, Inc., *Toxic Wastes and*

Race in the United States: A National Report on the Racial and Socio-Economic Characteristics of Communities with Hazardous Waste Sites (New York, NY: United Church of Christ Commission for Racial Justice, 1987).

4 Charles Lee, "From Montgomery to Emelle: the continuing struggle over disposal of toxic wastes," *elsa,* October 1984, pp. 29–33.

5 "Victory! Alabamians halt PCBs at Emelle landfill," *Toxic Times,* Winter 1989, p. 18.

6 See, for example, H. W. Lewis, *Technological Risk* (New York, NY: W. W. Norton and Co., 1990), and John Allen Paulos's review in *The New York Times Book Review,* November 25, 1990, p. 11.

7 See Aaron Wildavsky, *Searching for Safety* (New Brunswick, NJ: Transaction Publishers, 1988).

8 William J. Kruvant, "People, energy, and pollution," in *The American Energy Consumer,* Dorothy K. Newman and Dawn Day, eds. (Cambridge, MA: Ballinger, 1975), pp. 125–67, cited in Julian McCaull, "Discriminatory air pollution: if poor, don't breath," *Environment,* March 1976, p. 27.

9 See Eric Mann, "Lighting a spark: L.A.'s smogbusters," *The Nation,* September 17, 1990, p. 268. Also see Michael Belliveau, Michael Kent, and Grant Rosenblum, *Richmond at Risk: Community Demographics and Toxic Hazards from Industrial Polluters* (San Francisco, CA: Citizens for a Better Environment, 1989).

10 See Benjamin A. Goldman, James A. Hulme, and Cameron Johnson, *Hazardous Waste Management: Reducing the Risk* (Washington, DC: Island Press, 1986), p. 206.

11 See McCaull, op. cit., pp. 26–31.

12 John F. Rosen, "Metabolic abnormalities in lead toxic children: public health implications," *Bulletin of the New York Academy of Medicine,* vol. 65, no. 10, 1989, pp. 1067–83.

13 "Asthma deaths of black children found to push up U.S. rate," *The New York Times,* October 3, 1990, p. 24.

14 Nora Lapin and Karen Hoffman, *Occupational Disease Among Minority Workers: An Annotated Bibliography* (Hyattsville, MD: National Institute for Occupational Safety and Health, June 1981).

15 See Valerie A. Wilk, *The Occupational Health of Migrant and Seasonal Farmworkers in the United States* (Washington, DC: Farmworker Justice Fund, Inc., 1986).

16 See Marjane Ambler, "Native lands: the lands the Feds forgot," *Sierra,* May/June 1989, pp. 44–48; Robert Tomsho, "Dumping grounds: Indian tribes contend with some of worst of America's pollution," *The Wall Street Journal,* vol. 216, no. 106, 1990, p. 1; and Warner K. Reeser, *Inventory of Hazardous Waste Generators and Sites on Selected Indian Reservations* (Denver, CO: Council of Energy Resource Tribes, 1985).

17 Alternative Policy Institute, *Toxics & Minority Communities* (Oakland, CA: Center for Third World Organizing, 1986).

18 See Jimmy Emerman, "The environmental struggle in Puerto Rico: poisoned paradise," *Earth Island Journal,* Spring 1989, pp. 17–19.

19 See Catherine Caufield, *Multiple Exposures: Chronicles of the Radiation Age* (Chicago, IL: University of Chicago Press, 1989), pp. 112–15.

20 See Ronald M. Anderson, Aida L. Giachello, and Lu Ann Aday, "Access 'of Hispanics to health care and cuts in services: a state-of-the-art overview," *Public Health Reports,* vol. 101, no. 3, 1986, pp. 238–52, and Richard Cooper, Michael Steinhauer, Arthur Schatzkin, and William Miller, "Improved mortality among U.S. blacks, 1968–1978: the role of the antiracist struggle," *International Journal of Health Services,* vol. 11, no. 4, 1981, pp. 511–22.

21 Philip J. Hilts, "Life expectancy for blacks in U.S. shows sharp drop," *The New York Times,* November 19, 1990, p. 1.

22 For global figures, see The International Institute for Environment and Development and The World Resources Institute, *World Resources 1987* (New York, NY: Basic Books, 1987), pp. 252–53.

23 Gail R. Wilensky, "Filling the gaps in health insurance: impact on competition," *Health Affairs,* Summer 1988, pp. 133–49.

24 Howard E. Freeman, Robert J. Blendon, Linda H. Aiken, Seymour Sudman, Connie F. Mullinix, and Christopher R. Corey, "Americans report on their access to health care," *Health Affairs,* Spring 1987, pp. 6–17.

25 Donald H. Gemson, Jack Elinson, and Peter Messeri, "Differences in physician prevention practice patterns for white and minority patients," *Journal of Community Health,* vol. 13, no. 1, 1988, pp. 53–64.

26 Diane B. Dutton, "Social class, health and illness," in *Applications of Social Science to Clinical Medicine and Health Policy,* eds. L. Aiken and D. Mechanic (New Brunswick, NJ: Rutgers University Press, 1986), p. 43.

27 Wendy Zentz, "Rural health care: a losing battle?" *Public Citizen,* January/ February 1990, pp. 17–20.

28 "50-year trend reversed as U.S. regions grow apart economically," *The New York Times,* August 23, 1987.

29 William W. Falk and Thomas A. Lyson, *High Tech, Low Tech, No Tech: Recent Industrial and Occupational Change in the South* (Albany, NY: State University of New York Press, 1988).

30 Michael R. Greenberg, "Disease competition as a factor in ecological studies of mortality: the case of urban centers," *Social Science and Medicine,* vol. 23, no. 10, p. 930.

31 Frank Levy, *Dollars and Dreams: The Changing American Income Distribution* (New York, NY: W. W. Norton and Co., 1988), p. 111.

32 Elisabeth Rosenthal, "Health problems of inner city poor reach crisis point," *The New York Times,* December 24, 1990, p. 1.

33 Richard Cooper and Brian E. Simmons, "Cigarette smoking and ill health among black Americans," *New York State Journal of Medicine,* July 1985, p. 344.

34 See Lisa F. Berkman and Lori Breslow, *Health and Ways of Living: The Alameda County Study* (New York, NY: Oxford University Press, 1983), chapter 4, and James S. House, Karl R. Landis, and Debra Umberson, "Social relationships and health," *Science,* vol. 241, 1988, p. 540–45.

35 James S. Marks, Gary C. Hogelin, Eileen M. Gentry, Jack T. Jones, Karen L.

Gaines, Michele R. Forman, and Frederick L. Trowbridge, "The behavioral risk factor surveys: I. state-specific prevalence estimates of behavioral risk factors," *American Journal of Prevention Medicine,* vol. 1, no. 6, pp. 1–8.

36 S. Leonard Symes and Lisa F. Berkman "Social class, susceptibility, and sickness," *The American Journal of Epidemiology,* vol. 104, no. 1–8, 1976, p. 5.

37 See Dutton, op. cit.

38 See Cooper and Simmons, op. cit., p. 344, and Mac W. Otten, Steven M. Teutsch, David F. Williamson, and James S. Marks, "The effect of known risk factors on the excess mortality of black adults in the United States," *Journal of the American Medical Association,* vol. 263, 1990, pp. 845–50.

39 NCHS's latest internal data system now differentiates between black and other "nonwhite," but these data are, as yet, not available to the public.

40 Michele M. Morin, Linda W. Pickle, and Thomas J. Mason, "Geographic patterns of ethnic groups in the United States," *American Journal of Public Health,* vol. 74, no. 2, February 1984, pp. 133–38.

41 See Robert Hoover, Thomas J. Mason, F. W. McKay, and Joseph F. Fraumeni, Jr., "Cancer by county: new resource for etiological clues," *Science,* vol. 189, 1975, pp. 1005–7; Michael R. Greenberg, P. Preuss, and R. Anderson, "Clues for case control studies of cancer in the Northeast Urban Corridor," *Social Science and Medicine,* vol. 14D, 1980, pp. 37–43; and Michael R. Greenberg, "Environmental toxicology in the United States," in *Geographical Aspects of Health,* Neil D. McGlashan, ed. (New York, NY: Academic Press, 1983), p. 165.

42 See Environmental Defense Fund and Robert H. Boyle, *Malignant Neglect* (New York, NY: Vintage Books, 1980), pp. 10–14.

43 U.S. Bureau of the Census, *1980 Census of Population and Housing: User's Guide* (Washington, DC: Government Printing Office, 1982), p. 11, and National Center for Health Statistics, *Vital Statistics of the United States, 1987, Vol. II, Mortality, Part A* (Washington, DC: Public Health Service, 1990), section 7, p. 6.

44 Robert Manor and Christine Bertelson, "Death rate, race tied, state says," *St. Louis Post-Dispatch,* November 3, 1988, p. 1.

45 Public Data Access, Inc., *Mortality and Toxics Along the Mississippi River* (Washington, DC: Greenpeace USA, 1988), p. 20.

METHODS

1 See Wilson B. Riggan, John R. Creason, William C. Nelson, Kenneth G. Manton, Max A. Woodbury, Eric Stallard, Alvin C. Pellom, and Jefferson Beaubier, *U.S. Cancer Mortality Rates and Trends 1950–1979, Volume IV: Maps* (Washington, DC: U.S. Government Printing Office, 1987).

2 The charts of geographic inequality use a statistic called the "coefficient of variation." The coefficient of variation for each cause of death is the standard deviation of county mortality rates divided by the national mean. The mortality rates are age-race-sex adjusted and weighted by population when calculating the coefficients, so the effects on the coefficients of high rates due to unusual

distributions or small populations are minimized. See Steve Wing, Michele Casper, Wayne Davis, Carl Hayes, Wilson Riggan, and H. A. Tyroler, "Trends in the geographic inequality of cardiovascular disease mortality in the United States, 1962–1982," *Social Science Medicine,* vol. 30, no. 3, 1990, pp. 261–66.

3 In statistical terms, these percentages represent the adjusted R-squares of non-parametric multivariate regression tests against the percentiles for total age-race-sex-adjusted mortality from each cause of death. All but one of these regression tests are significant at a probability level of 1 in 10,000 (F-test p < .0001). The exception is mortality from child cancers, for which the probability that the regression results are due to chance is less than 15 percent p < .15).

4 Two types of statistical tests were performed to appraise the significance of the correlations between the 75 variables and each cause of death: a nonparametric regression (using the mortality rate percentiles, which are already adjusted for significance, as the dependent variables); and a discriminant analysis (dividing the counties into three groups: those in the top 2 percentiles, the bottom 2 percentiles, and the rest).

5 See U.S. Department for Health and Human Services, *Vital Statistics of the United States* (Washington, DC: U.S. Government Printing Office, any year); National Center for Health Statistics, "Documentation for Mortality and Population Surveillance Tapes, 1968–83" (Washington, DC: National Technical Information Service, 1986); and Linda W. Pickle et al., *Atlas of U.S. Cancer Mortality Among Whites 1950–80* (Bethesda, MD: National Cancer Institute, 1987).

6 See NCHS, op. cit., pp. 51–52.

7 Riggan, op. cit., volume IV, p. xv.

8 This is the same test used by EPA and NCI in Wilson B. Riggan et al., *U.S. Cancer Mortality Rates and Trends 1950–1979,* volume I (Washington, DC: U.S. Government Printing Office, 1983), p. xii. The EPA and NCI have since developed a two-stage empirical Bayes procedure for statistically adjusting mortality rates to avoid this problem (used in volume IV). The EPA/NCI stabilization technique, however, is very complicated and very expensive to use, so the simpler method is employed here. Also see The SAS Institute, *SAS User's Guide: Basics, Version 5 Edition* (Cary, NC: SAS Institute, 1985), p. 260.

9 See Riggan et al., op. cit., volume I (1983), p. xii.

10 According to data for 1989 from the EPA's air and water program databases, AIRS and PCS.

11 For other issues regarding TRI's information, see Gerald V. Poje and Daniel M. Horowitz, *Phantom Reductions: Tracking Toxic Trends* (Washington, DC: National Wildlife Federation, 1990); National Academy of Sciences, *Tracking Toxic Substances at Industrial Facilities: Engineering Mass Balance Versus Materials Accounting* (Washington, DC: National Academy Press, 1990); and U.S. Environmental Protection Agency, *Toxics in the Community: National and Local Perspectives* (Washington, DC: Government Printing Office, 1990). Also see the newsletter put out by U.S. Public Interest Research Group Education Fund called *Working Notes on Community Right-to-Know,* especially the February 1990, July 1989, and May 1989 issues.

12 The industrial processes include about 2,000 Source Classification Codes (SCCs) for about 500 Standard Industrial Classification (SIC) industries. These speciation factors were developed for the Pollutant Assessment Branch of the EPA's Office of Air Quality Planning, and Standards (OAQPS) by Radian Corporation as of November 1987.

13 See Environmental Monitoring & Services, Inc., *Technical Background Document to Support Rulemaking Pursuant to CERCLA Section 102*, volume 3 (Washington, DC: U.S. EPA, 1986), Appendix A.

14 See J. Tichler and C. Benkovitz, *Radioactive Materials Released from Nuclear Power Plants—1981*, NUREG/CR-2907, volume 2, BNL-NUREG-51581 (Washington, DC: U.S. Nuclear Regulatory Commission, June 1984). See also Jay M. Gould et al., *Nuclear Emissions Take Their Toll*, (New York, NY: Council on Economic Priorities, December 1986).

15 See ibid.

16 See U.S. General Accounting Office, *Hazardous Waste: Uncertainties of Existing Data* (Washington, DC: GAO, 1987), and Jay M. Gould, *Quality of Life in American Neighborhoods: Levels of Affluence, Toxic Waste, and Cancer Mortality in Residential ZIP Code Areas* (Boulder, CO: Westview Press, 1986).

17 See U.S. Congressional Budget Office, *Hazardous Waste Management: Recent Changes and Policy Alternatives* (Washington, DC: CBO, 1985); Westat, Inc., *National Survey of Hazardous Waste Generators and Treatment, Storage, and Disposal Facilities Regulated Under RCRA in 1981* (Washington, DC: U.S. EPA, 1984); and Benjamin A. Goldman et al., *Hazardous Waste Management: Reducing the Risk* (Washington, DC: Island Press, 1986).

18 Center for Environmental Research, *1986 National Screening Survey of Hazardous Waste Treatment, Storage, Disposal, and Recycling Facilities* (Washington, DC: U.S. Environmental Protection Agency, September 1988).

19 EPA, "HWDMS data dictionary" (Washington, DC: U.S. EPA, 1987), p. 48.

20 National Research Council, *Regulating Pesticides in Foods: The Delaney Paradox* (Washington, DC: National Academy Press, 1987), p. 55.

21 See U.S. Geological Survey, "National water survey 1984: USGS water supply paper 2275" (Washington, DC: U.S. GPO, 1985).

22 See Association of State and Interstate Water Pollution Control Administrators, *America's Clean Water: The State's Evaluation of Progress, 1972–1982* (Washington, DC: ASIWPCA, 1984).

23 See U.S. Environmental Protection Agency, *National Air Quality and Emissions Trends Report, 1985* (Washington, DC: U.S. EPA, 1987).

24 Sulfur dioxide also has an annual arithmetic mean NAAQS, carbon monoxide also has a 1-hour NAAQS, and there are secondary (welfare-related) NAAQSs for particulates and sulfur dioxide; however, these measures are not included in the maps. PPM = parts per million; $\mu g/m^3$ = micrograms per cubic meter.

25 See Commission for Racial Justice and Public Data Access, Inc., *Toxic Wastes and Race in the United States: A National Report on the Racial and Socio-Economic Characteristics of Communities with Hazardous Waste Sites* (New York, NY: United Church of Christ Commission for Racial Justice, 1987).

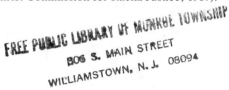

INDEX OF COUNTIES
BY STATE